# Secularism and Its Critics

## Themes in Politics Series

PARTHA CHATTERJEE
**State and Politics in India**

NIVEDITA MENON
**Gender and Politics in India**

NIRAJA GOPAL JAYAL
**Democracy in India**

ZOYA HASAN
**Parties and Party Politics in India**

CAROLYN ELLIOTT
**Civil Society and Democracy**

# Secularism and Its Critics

*Edited by*
Rajeev Bhargava

OXFORD
UNIVERSITY PRESS

# OXFORD
UNIVERSITY PRESS

YMCA Library Building, Jai Singh Road, New Delhi 110 001

Oxford University Press is a department of the University of Oxford. It furthers the
University's objective of excellence in research, scholarship, and education
by publishing worldwide in

Oxford   New York

Auckland   Cape Town   Dar es Salaam   Hong Kong   Karachi   Kuala Lumpur
Madrid   Melbourne   Mexico City   Nairobi   New Delhi   Shanghai   Taipei   Toronto

With offices in

Argentina   Austria   Brazil   Chile   Czech Republic   France   Greece   Guatemala
Hungary   Italy   Japan   Poland   Portugal   Singapore   South Korea   Switzerland
Thailand   Turkey   Ukraine   Vietnam

Oxford is a registered trademark of Oxford University Press
in the UK and in certain other countries

Published in India
by Oxford University Press, New Delhi

First published 1998
Oxford India Paperbacks 1999
Fifth impression 2006

ISBN 13: 978-0-19-565027-3
ISBN 10: 0-19-565027-1

Typeset by Excellent Laser Typesetters, Pitampura, Delhi 110 034
Printed by Pauls Press, New Delhi 110 020
Published by Oxford University Press
YMCA Library Building, Jai Singh Road, New Delhi 110 001

# Acknowledgements

Like many other things that require time and thought but always get done in a scramble, this hastily prepared list runs the risk of omitting the name of someone who has contributed in an important way in putting this volume together. I thank all those who discussed issues related to secularism or gave me the opportunity to present my views to a wider audience—Alok Rai, Charles Taylor, Rustam Bharucha, Jerry Cohen, Sudipta Kaviraj, Achin Vanaik, Neeladri Bhattacharya, Bhikhu Parekh, Partha Chatterjee, Javeed Alam, Brian Barry, Sumit Sarkar, Peter D'Souza, Yael Tamir, Kumar Shahani, Dennis Thompson, Romila Thapar, Imtiaz Ahmed, Akeel Bilgrami, Andrew Graham, Christophe Jaffrelot, Alan Montefiore, Gyan Prakash, D. L. Sheth, Dilip Gaonkar, K. N. Panikkar, Fred Dallmayr, Tanika Sarkar, Thomas Pantham, Zoya Hasan, Valerian Rodriguez, and Gita Kapur. Without Violette Graff's invaluable help I would have been unable to include Professor Jean Bauberot's article.

Thanks are also due to Amritha Menon, Rinku Lamba Aranyani, and Prakash Sarangi for help with the proofs, to Prakash Sarangi for the preparation of the bibliography and to Nitasha Devasar and Nagraj Adve for exemplary fortitude at the astounding pace at which the project moved.

Friends who continue to provide support and insight, I can hardly thank enough—Shalini Advani, Andrew Graham, Anuradha Chenoy, Chitra Joshi, Shamshad, Sheila Sandhu, Pankaj Butalia, Kamal Chenoy, Shikha, Sanjeev, Sehba, Rukun Advani, Shabana, Pam, Peggotty Graham, and Praful. As always, Tani has worked far beyond the call of duty natural among friends. Over the years my debt to her seems to multiply at an alarming speed.

This book is dedicated to foot soldier and comrade, S.P.

# Acknowledgements to Publishers

The publishers wish to thank the following for permission to include the following articles/extracts in this volume:

Princeton University Press for T.M. Scanlon, 'The Difficulty of Tolerance'.

Harvard University Press for Michael J. Sandel, 'Religious Liberty: Freedom of Choice or Freedom of Conscience'. Reprinted by permission of the publisher from *Democracy's Discontent* by Michael Sandel, Cambridge, Mass.: Harvard University Press, Copyright (c) 1996 by Michael J. Sandel.

Averbury Press for Joseph H. Carens and Melissa S. Williams (1996) 'Muslim Minorities in Liberal Democracies: The Politics of Misrecognition', in R. Baubock, A. Heller, and A. Zolberg (eds), *The Challenge of Diversity: Integration and Pluralism in Societies of Immigration*, Public Policy and Social Welfare Volume 22, Aldershot, UK: Averbury.

Cambridge University Press for Marc Galanter, 'Secularism, East and West', *Comparative Studies in Society and History*, Volume VII, No. 2, January 1965, pp 133–59.

*Economic and Political Weekly* for Partha Chatterjee, 'Secularism and Tolerance', *EPW*, Volume XXIX, No. 28, 9 July 1994, pp 1768–77.

Penguin Books for Amartya Sen, 'Secularism and Its Discontents', in Kaushik Basu and Sanjay Subrahmanyam (eds), *Unravelling the Nation: Sectarian Conflict in India*, 1996.

# Contents

*Contributors*                                                    xi

Introduction                                                       1
*Rajeev Bhargava*

I  THE SECULAR IMPERATIVE

  1. Modes of Secularism                                          31
     *Charles Taylor*
  2. The Difficulty of Tolerance                                  54
     *T.M. Scanlon*

II  SECULARISM IN THE WEST

  3. Religious Liberty: Freedom of Choice
     or Freedom of Conscience                                     73
     *Michael J. Sandel*
  4. The Two Thresholds of Laïcization                            94
     *Jean Bauberot*
  5. Muslim Minorities in Liberal Democracies:
     The Politics of Misrecognition                              137
     *Joseph H. Carens and Melissa S. Williams*

III  SECULARISM IN INDIA: THE EARLY DEBATE

  6. India as a Secular State                                    177
     *D.E. Smith*
  7. Secularism, East and West                                   234
     *Marc Galanter*
  8. Hinduism, Secularism, and the Indian Judiciary              268
     *Marc Galanter*

## IV SECULARISM IN INDIA: THE RECENT DEBATE

9. Secularism in Its Place   297
   *T.N. Madan*
10. The Politics of Secularism and the Recovery
    of Religious Toleration   321
    *Ashis Nandy*
11. Secularism and Tolerance   345
    *Partha Chatterjee*
12. Secularism, Nationalism, and Modernity   380
    *Akeel Bilgrami*
13. The Crisis of Secularism in India   418
    *Stanley J. Tambiah*
14. Secularism and Its Discontents   454
    *Amartya Sen*
15. What is Secularism For?   486
    *Rajeev Bhargava*

*Bibliography*   543

# Contributors

CHARLES TAYLOR is Professor of Philosophy, McGill University. From 1976–81 he was the Chichele Professor of Social and Political Theory at Oxford. His books include *Hegel* (1975) and *Sources of the Self: The Making of Modern Identity* (1989).

THOMAS M. SCANLON is Alford Professor of Natural Religion, Moral Philosophy and Civil Polity at Harvard University. He has published in *Ethics, Nomos and Philosophy* and *Public Affairs* and co-edited, among other works, *War and Moral Responsibility; Equality and Preferential Treatment;* and *Medicine and Moral Philosophy.*

MICHAEL J. SANDEL is Professor of Government at Harvard University. His publications include *Liberalism and the Limits of Justice* (1982) and *Democracy's Discontent: America in Search of a Public Philosophy* (1996).

JEAN BAUBEROT is former Chairman of the EPHE and holds the first ever chair of the study of Laïcité at the Sorbonne. He had for years held the chair on Protestant Studies at the same university and has written extensively on religion and Laïcité.

JOSEPH H. CARENS is Professor, Department of Political Science, University of Toronto and has written extensively on problems of cultural difference and the status of immigrants.

MELISSA S. WILLIAMS teaches at the Department of Political Science, University of Toronto. Her publications include *Voice, Trust and Memory: Marginalized Groups and the Failings of Liberal Representation* (forthcoming).

DONALD SMITH is Professor, Department of Politics, University of Pennsylvania. His books include *India as a Secular State* (1963) and *South Asian Politics and Religion* (1966).

MARC GALANTER is Evjue-Bascom Professor of Law and South Asian Studies and Director of the Institute for Legal Studies, University of Wisconsin-Madison Law School. His publications include *Competing Equalities: Law and the Backward Classes in India* (1984) and *Law and Society in Modern India* (1989).

T.N. MADAN is Hon. Professor (Sociology) at the Institute of Economic Growth, Delhi. His publications include *Family and Kinship: A Study of Pandits of Rural Kashmir* (1965) and *Non-Renunciation: Themes and Interpretation of Hindu Culture* (1987).

ASHIS NANDY is Senior Fellow at the Centre for the Study of Developing Societies, Delhi. His publications include *At the Edge of Psychology: Essays in Politics and Culture* (1980); *The Intimate Enemy* (1983); and *The Illegitimacy of Nationalism* (1996).

PARTHA CHATTERJEE is Director of the Centre for Studies in Social Sciences, Calcutta. His publications include *Nationalist Thought and the Colonial World: A Derivative Discourse* (1986), *The Nation and its Fragments* (1993), and *A Possible India: Essays in Political Criticism* (1997).

AKEEL BILGRAMI is Professor of Philosophy, Columbia University. His publications include *Belief and Meaning* (1992).

STANLEY J. TAMBIAH is Professor at the Department of Anthropology, Harvard University. His publications include *Culture, Thought and Social Action: An Anthropological Perspective* (1985) and *Levelling Crowds: Ethnonationalist Conflict and Collective Violence* (1996).

AMARTYA SEN is Master, Trinity College, Cambridge. Formerly, he was Lamont University Professor of Economics and Philosophy, Harvard University. His publications include *Collective Choice and Social Welfare* (1970); *Poverty and Famines: An Essay on Entitlement and Deprivation* (1981); and *Inequality Reexamined* (1992).

RAJEEV BHARGAVA teaches at the Centre for Political Studies, Jawaharlal Nehru University, New Delhi. His publications include *Individualism in Social Science* (1992) and *Multiculturalism, Liberalism and Democracy* (co-edited) (1999).

# Introduction

## I

What is secularism? What problems does it address and what aspirations does it embody? Can it be understood independently of the values it is meant to promote? What, anyway, is it for? Initial motivations of Western secularism were complex and variegated: to check absolutism, religious bigotry, and fanaticism, to ensure that the values enshrined in particular religions did not trump other values, to manage religious conflicts reasonably. These general functions apart, secularism was intended to play a significant role in attaining objectives that needed particular emphasis in India. In a society where numerical supremacy of one religious group may predispose it to disfavour smaller religious groups, secularism was to deter the persecution of religious minorities. More than anything else, it was meant to impose limits on the political expression of cultural or religious conflicts between Hindus and Muslims, limits that were tragically transgressed immediately before and in the aftermath of the declaration of Independence in August 1947. The Nehru–Gandhi consensus on the secular state was grounded in the acceptance of the necessity of these limits and of the values they made possible.

Has secularism performed these functions? On the face of it, rather poorly. There is perhaps as much, if not greater, religious bigotry today than before. Religious minorities continue to feel disadvantaged and often face discrimination. The scale and intensity of religious conflict does not seem to have declined: if anything it has proliferated, touching people who have never known it before. The verdict against secularism appears unequivocal: it has failed to realize the objectives for which it was devised.

However, critics, not content with showing that secularism lacks the potential for solving these problems or has exhausted its possibilities, go so far as to claim a direct causal link between the conceptual structure of the doctrine and the re-emergence of problems concerning religious and intercommunal relations. For example, for Madan 'it is not religious zealots alone who contribute to fundamentalism or fanaticism but also secularists who deny temporary legitimacy of religions in human life and society and provoke a reaction'. Secularism, the argument goes, has not only failed to deliver the goods, but exacerbated the very problems that, in the first place, it was devised to overcome. As a result, some social and political thinkers have called for an abandonment of the secular project altogether. Ashis Nandy openly put forward his flamboyant anti-secular manifesto. Similarly, T.N. Madan looks to reopen avenues of a spiritually justified limitation of religion in areas of contemporary life. Likewise, for Partha Chatterjee the defence of secularism is an inappropriate ground where the Hindu Right can be challenged. The aggressive cultural nationalism of Hindutva forces is unlikely, he believes, to pit itself against the idea of a secular state.

Against these views are pitted others who argue, one way or another, that secularism in India, as elsewhere, is indispensable, and therefore that the critical need of the hour is to work out an alternative conception of secularism, not to seek an alternative. The question for them is: Given a commitment to a minimal set of political and moral values, and given the desirability of one or another version, what form must secularism take to improve its performance in India today?

This debate, between those who defend secularism and those deeply critical of it, constitutes the principal substance of this volume. My primary aim in putting together this collection is to provide the reader with recent writing on the debate over secularism in India. However, I must mention several other objectives underlying this anthology. To begin with, a widespread misconception exists in India that a unique, uncomplicated separation of religion from the state is a feature of all modern Western societies, that this separation is conceived in the same manner everywhere, and because consensus on the precise relation between religion and state practice is an incontrovertible fact, the secularity of the state is a settled, stable feature in all Western politics. Barring a few, who in the West questions the value of tolerating religious diversity? Or, that religion is a private matter, an issue not to be contested in the public domain? One of my objectives in including a small sample of writing from the West is to show that Western secularism too, is essentially contested, with no agreement on what it entails, the values it seeks to promote, or how best to pursue it. Nor is radical disagreement among religious groups confined to people in India. Deep diversity is a prominent feature of the internal life of Western societies—something many in the West painfully realized over the Salman Rushdie affair in Britain or the head scarf issue in France. It is a lesson that many in India learnt after the mercurial rise of communalism in Indian politics. I must confess I was surprised by the discovery of different forms of the secular state in the West. As Tim Scanlon puts it, non-establishment represents a mixed strategy everywhere; each country in the West has worked out a particular political compromise rather than implementing a solution uniquely required by the configuration of values embodied in secularism. The separation thesis means different things in the US, in France, Germany, and Britain, and, is interpreted differently at different times in each place, a point to which Michael Sandel's contribution in this volume draws our attention.

It is of course true that this mix of ignorance and motivated, self-benefiting bias is not unique to India. It is particularly striking in the case of Western countries. For all the talk of the fact of pluralism and multiculturalism, the mention of how such issues arise or are tackled in India is astoundingly infrequent. Worse, there is scarcely any curiosity on the part of political philosophers about the precise inflection of such issues in places such as India. I, for one, believe that aspiring political philosophers must take a crash course in Indian politics and society, and philosophers already well established should consider a one-year mandatory sabbatical in India to really come to terms with the deep diversity and with incommensurable but coexisting world-views values! Debates around the world on issues such as group rights, secession, differentiated citizenship, affirmative action, and gender equality are bound to be considerably enriched by the Indian experience. So will reflection on secularism. Really, a genuine search for transcultural ideals cannot do without such cross-references.

In assembling these articles my second objective is to bring sociologists, anthropologists, and political scientists face to face with political philosophers. I do so with a pronounced vested interest for I feel severely handicapped by the dearth of normative social and political philosophy in India. I do not wish to flog this point but it cannot be denied that academic interest in deep conceptual or normative matters is practically non-existent in India. This is no doubt partly due to the ethnocentrism of political philosophy mentioned above and, at least till recently, because of its abstract character, but it has to do also with the domination of a certain model of social science that takes the description of events and processes as unproblematic and is obsessed with explanations appropriate to the natural sciences. This model hardly encourages public deliberation over values, because like coarse logical positivists, it assumes the impossibility of a reasoned discourse over values or else, like vulgar Marxists, assumes its dispensability—normative values are seen to be sedimented so firmly that further discussion on them is otiose. Whatever the cause, the outcome has been singularly detrimental to the development of political philosophy. Towards this end, the articles by Taylor, Scanlon, Sen, Sandel, and Carens and Williams will, I believe, be particularly helpful.

My third objective is to remind ourselves that the writing of secularism in India has a history; that between the debate of the 1950s and the 1980s there exist continuities and discontinuities from which there is much to learn. This is particularly desirable for those who studied politics during and after the 1970s, or who wrote on secularism, if not in ignorance, at least in partial disregard of some of the early writings on the subject.[1]

I end this section with a note of caution to the reader: the objective of this volume is neither to be a comprehensive anthology of secularism—although in my judgement all the articles it contains are significant, it does not follow that the volume includes every good piece on the subject—nor provides an adequate comparative perspective on secularism. Such a perspective necessarily requires the inclusion of the experience of secularism, say in Turkey or countries of the formerly communist bloc as well as the experience of other South Asian countries. A victim of its own multifarious ambitions, this volume has had to regrettably leave out much excellent writing on the subject.[2]

[1] I must here speak for myself because I would not have known of, say, Galanter's review of Smith's book had he not sent it to me along with the permission to reprint the other article included in the volume.
[2] I particularly have in mind selections from V.P. Luthera's book *The Concept of Secular State and India* (OUP: Calcutta, 1964), Sudipta Kaviraj's, 'Religion,

# II

Three distinct issues are raised in the volume: conceptual, normative, and explanatory. Conceptual issues divide into three kinds. First, about how we are to broadly understand the concepts of secular and secularism. Second, whether or not a distinction can be drawn between political and more comprehensive varieties of secularism. Finally, if such a distinction is possible, what if any are the different forms of political secularism.

The normative issue has at least three dimensions too. The first involves the evaluation of the very concept of secularism. For instance, some writers feel that the ideal itself is deeply flawed, at least in the Indian context (Madan, Nandy, Chatterjee). The second pertains to the evaluation of different conceptions of secularism with the implicit assumption that the concept is valuable, even indispensable in India. The third normative dimension concerns the evaluation of the means by which the concept or any of its conceptions is implemented, the manner in which consensus around it is forged, the particular institutional framework in which it is embedded. Bilgrami's criticism of Nehruvian secularism as Archimedean falls within this category. The two issues, conceptual and normative, are related because secularism in part is what justifies it. The point of this complex doctrine is integral to what we understand it to be.

Finally, the articles in this volume deal with explanatory issues. These roughly divide into two groups. One examines conditions under which secularism becomes more or less mandatory, or asks how, under which standing conditions, or with the help of which factors it emerged in India or elsewhere. The second explores causes of its current crisis by either constructing an empirical account of factors that generate its difficulty or by a broader conceptual account of why, given the absence of certain cultural conditions, secularism is bound to fail in a place like India. Alternatively, we can categorize its crisis, its alleged failure as due to external or

---

Politics and Modernity', in B. Parekh and U. Baxi (eds), *Crisis and Change in Contemporary India* (Sage: New Delhi, 1996), Bhikhu Parekh's pieces on the Salman Rushdie affair, Achin Vanaik's *Communalism Contested: Religion, Modernity and Secularization* (Vistaar Publications: New Delhi, 1997), and Rustam Bharucha's *The Question of Faith* (Orient Longman: New Delhi, 1993).

internal causes. For example, some scholars (Smith, Tambiah) believe that secularism has run into difficulties with the breakdown of the Congress party, the increased power of a centralized state, the consequent movement for secession in Kashmir and Punjab, and the implementation of the Mandal Commission recommendations. Such explanations refer to causes external to the ideal, or else, the crisis is explained by internal factors. The cause for its failure may be (a) a totalizing world-view of which secularism is an integral component (Madan and Nandy) or (b) the flawed demand of equidistance that can be met by no state (Chatterjee). Other articles fall somewhere in between: for Tambiah, at least part of the crisis arises because of ambiguities in the very formulation of secularism in the Indian Constitution. For Bilgrami, problems inhere in its Archimedean character.

Most contributions combine several of these concerns quite naturally and unselfconsciously. Taylor explains why secularism is a functional requirement of the modern, democratic state and then argues that a particular form of secularism is more appropriate under conditions obtaining almost everywhere in the world. Similarly, Madan and Nandy not only explain why secularism is in crisis but also, more implicitly, why it lacks legitimacy or adequate justification.

Several hidden questions lie in the articles. For example, how far can a distinction between religious and cultural practice be drawn in societies dominated by religions that emphasize practice rather than belief. Where religious and cultural practice is more or less indistinguishable, does the politics of multiculturalism assume the form of the politics of secularism? In such societies, is secularism directly linked to a defence of minority rights? How can we identify models of secularism that actually govern politics in India, America, or France? How do we disentangle them from false stereotypes? More generally, is there a difference between Western and Eastern secularism? Is the Indian version a mere specification of an idea with Western origin and imprint? Or is it a genuine alternative to its Western counterpart, one from which everyone, including the West, may benefit? What is the relationship between secularism and science and, more generally, between secularism and Western rationalism? Does secularism always entail giving public reasons formulated in non-religious terms, backed by scientific evidence and argument? If so, what in the last instance, is its relation with religions seen from the inside, from the believer's point of view? Must secularism trivialize their faith? Is hostility between the two inevitable?

## III

A threefold distinction helps to not only clarify many issues in the debate over secularism but also to individuate its different variants. We need to first distinguish the policy and practice of the state from the values that underlie it and which may be seen to provide first-order justification for state policy. In turn, these values may be justified by other higher-order values which consequently lend second-order justification to state policy.

Disputes over secularism occur at each of these levels. At the first, there may be differences over whether or not the state should be secular at all, and if the secularity of the state is not in question, then over what is required of a secular state. If political secularism means at least minimally a form of independence of the political from the religious domain, then clear battle lines are drawn between defenders and opponents of this separation. The form of this independence too, is a matter of sharp contention. For some, independence or separation means mutual exclusion of two domains, whereafter the state adopts a policy of either interventionist control or of strict non-interference. For others, independence entails neutrality understood as equidistance, that is a policy to help or hinder different religions to an equal degree. For still others like myself, it means principled distance, a flexible but value-based relation that accommodates intervention as well as abstention.

Judgement on whether or not state policies are secular depends on an understanding of what independence or separation means. For some, the secularity of the state requires that no support in any form be given to religion. It entails, for others, support to the same degree to all religions. There are still others who find a mixed strategy morally admissible, not in any way diluting the secularity of the state. Consider, for example, special taxes for the promotion of any religion or state-aid for educational institutions run by religious bodies. For some, the secularity of the state requires that neither be permitted. No financial support is to be extended to schools that impart religious instruction; conversely, religious instruction cannot be imparted in a school maintained wholly by state funds, and no one can be compelled to pay taxes to promote a particular religious denomination. Others believe that the secularism of the state necessitates financial support of the same degree to all schools irrespective of the religious instruction they impart. Even compulsory taxation specifically meant for the maintenance of religion is permissible, provided no discrimination against any particular religion exists. Others find some forms of support compatible with secularism. For example compulsory taxation may be impermissible in the case of every religion but state-aid be given to a school that imparts religious instruction. Indeed, no violation of secular principles may occur if support is permitted in the case of one religion but prohibited in the case of another. The variability in decision is a function of the nature or current state of both religions. One religion may require state-funds merely in order to survive, while the other need not. Thus, equidistance is not the best available secular strategy.

At the second, intermediate level, differences surface over values promoted by separation. For some scholars the distance between religious institutions and the state is necessary to prevent sectarian warfare, to ensure that disagreements between religious groups do not turn violent. Civic peace provides strong sufficient motivation for separation. The justification of separation is found in toleration by others. Full religious liberty is cited by some scholars as the principal reason behind the separation of state and religion. Others justify it by the requirements of a life lived within the bounds of human reason, by a full-blooded notion of autonomy. Ordinary life lived with dignity is the *raison d'être* of secularism for some, while still others find the value of citizenship embodied in democracy the principal justification for separation of the religious from the political.

A third level exists where disagreements abound. These centre around deeper grounds for the separation of state from religion. At least five strategies are available here. The first two demand not only some agreement on first-order justification but a deeper consensus on second-order justification. Taylor's independent mode and common-ground strategy fall within this category. However, the two modes differ, in that the first requires a foundational ethic abstracted from all religions in a society and the other leans on all existing religions. The other three strategies abandon the possibility or need for agreement on second-order justification. One of these, a constrained modus vivendi, requires 'partial agreement on grounds that neither implies nor automatically produces an agreement on political principles'.[3] It involves 'practical accommodation constrained by an agreement on some general normative premises'. The second, a bare modus vivendi, requires 'mere practical accommodation expressed in terms of ad hoc maxims regarded neither as true nor as reasonable, for reasons that are not shared'.[4] Last but not the least, is the Rawlsian model of overlapping consensus that involves a bonafide normative agreement on first-order justifications but not on the deeper, second-order grounds that justify them.

How then is secularism individuated? Secularism is defined extremely narrowly by some as the separation of religion from the policy and practice of state, without reference to values justifying separation. Others believe that secularism is a normative, purposive concept because of which the values advanced by separation in part constitute its meaning. For a third group, deeper second-order justifications are also integral to the definition of secularism. The first two distinguish political from comprehensive secularism but the third group finds such a distinction untenable. Political secularism, in this view, inevitably carries the heavy baggage of a larger, comprehensive, hyper-substantive, secular world-view. In the Indian debate, Madan and Nandy stand right here. For Nandy, secularism is part of a larger modernist project. Madan sees it as an outcome of a dialectic between Protestantism and Science. Likewise, Michael Sandel claims that at least some versions of the wall of separation thesis rely on an autonomy-based liberalism that presupposes an individualist conception of the person. Of the three distinct modes of secularism discussed by Charles Taylor, the independent-ethic mode is a variety of comprehensive secularism. It not only separates religion from the practices of the state but justifies it, all the way down, by reasons entirely independent of particular religious world-views.

[3] Henry S. Richardson, 'The Problem of Liberalism and the Good', in R. Bruce Douglass, Gerld M. Mara, and Henry S. Richardson (eds), *Liberalism and the Good* (Routledge: London, 1990), p. 10.
[4] Ibid.

# IV

What is secularism for? One answer in the literature emphasizes its value for and its constitutive link with modern democracy and equal citizenship. Two routes exist for the identification of this relation. The first begins by exploring the minimum conditions of democracy.[5] At least three such conditions exist. First, the supervenience of democracy on the state: no democracy can exist without a state. This claim needs to be unpacked. Every democracy presupposes the state, but from this it does not follow that the mere existence of a state entails democracy. It is trivially true that undemocratic states exist. All that is being stated here is that the reproduction of democracy is not automatic but depends upon the presence of the state. Second, the pacification of politics, by which is meant that individuals compete for power peacefully, not by physically eliminating one another. Democracy is incompatible with violent settlement of disputes over power. Third, the state must be relatively independent of classes and ethnic groups in a society. No class or ethnic group must be in complete control of state power. If this is so, state power cannot be used to push any one agenda in its entirety. Therefore each class and ethnic group must learn to live with the fact that its objectives cannot be met in entirety. This happens in two ways, because of the presence of two kinds of situations. It happens when a perfect balance of forces exists or else when each class or ethnic group happens to have just about as much power as every other one. People may then realize the necessity of a consensus for which no compelling reason exists from within. A democracy produced in such tremulous situations is a modus vivendi. Quite another situation arises when out of enlightened self-interest, or for a broader moral vision of granting one another respect, people are prepared from within their own set of internal reasons to forsake in part their objectives to arrive at a principled compromise. This is a necessary condition for stable democracies. To sum up, every democracy presupposes a state with power relatively independent of classes and ethnic groups, for which individuals and groups compete peacefully and which is never used to undermine the fundamental interests of any class or ethnic group.

5 On conditions of democracy, see David Held (ed.), *Prospects for Democracy* (Stanford University Press: California, 1993).

What then links secularism to democracy? There are two routes to the answer of this question. On the first route, we must return to the section of the conditions of democracy. Examine once again the condition that stipulates that the state must be relatively autonomous of classes or ethnic groups. For a moment let us leave out class and consider religious groups as the only ethnic groups. A particular specification of that condition now obtains, namely that the relative autonomy of the state is virtually a precondition for democracy. Since secularism is the very idea that the state be relatively autonomous of religious groups (normally captured by the idea of separation or distance), the link between secularism and democracy is brought into sharp relief. Secularism is a condition of democracy. If democracy is to exist or survive, different religious groups, no matter what their numerical strength, must renounce the idea that they can use the political process to implement an agenda in toto, to create a society congruent only with their particular values and interests.

A second approach that inextricably links secularism with democracy is delineated by Charles Taylor. Taylor argues in favour of this connection by outlining certain features of a modern democratic polity. He draws our attention to how 'the modern social imaginary' involves a shift from hierarchical, mediated-access societies to horizontal, direct-access societies. A vertically stratified society, say, with a traditional caste structure, is hierarchical in the sense that different communities have different rankings on a fixed scale of values so that a community with a higher rank is presumed superior to others. More importantly, no individual can be a member of this society without access to one or the other mediating lower-level communities. Membership in society is conditional upon belonging to any one of its components. The phrase mediated-access means this. In modern social imaginary, all this is changed. Hierarchical relations begin to disappear and membership of the polity is independent of these mediating communities. We access our polity directly, unmediated by any other person or by membership of subsociety. Taylor tells us that modern societies are suffused with images of direct access, for example we discuss our politics directly in the newspaper as concerned citizens and not necessarily as members of intermediate groups. The second feature of the modern social imaginary is that 'trans-local entities', such as the nation or state, are seen to rest upon and result from interconnected social action occurring in purely secular time. A key idea has now taken hold of people's imagination: that together, by our action here and now, we can create and sustain large solidarities. Taylor explains how the idea that societies are built by collective action in secular time and the understanding that individuals have direct and equal access to them are linked. So long as events are placed within a higher time, they are not immediately available to ordinary people. To partake in these higher events, people must first relate to privileged persons or agencies such as kings or priests. Once secular time is detached from higher time the importance of privileged access is also eroded. Hence the link between the idea of simultaneity—events occurring in different places at the same time completely unrelated to higher time—and the understanding of a large, interconnected social whole to which everyone has direct access.

For Taylor, democratic legitimacy, the legitimacy of the government flowing from the will of the people, presupposes a horizontal, direct-access society. Only such a society can be given a political form by the common action of everyone here and now. This has other functional requirements, among which a relatively high level of public involvement is particularly important. This is impossible without change in the self-understandings of people who must see themselves as active and committed citizens for whom political relationship matters more than other relations. Hence the strong premium on building solidarity among citizens, relative to which every other divisive relation must be subordinate, be it family, class, gender, even religion. This also explains the necessity of political secularism: religion is irrelevant to citizenship. Being a fellow-citizen is more important than being the religious other.

If Taylor's essay illuminates political secularism as a functional requirement of modern citizenship, Scanlon's fully fleshes out its implications and what it requires of us when the value of equal citizenship is taken seriously. Taylor asserts the moral significance of secularism in comparison with ethnic cleansing. Scanlon illuminates it further and tells us why this should be so. How must we relate to all those who are born and live in the same political society as us but whose views and behaviour differ radically? The minimalist moral requirement of course is that we not kill each other but live peacefully. However such peace is compatible with much that is morally obnoxious. Others may be denigrated, stigmatized or exploited without being eliminated. To improve upon this simple moral requirement, people may be allowed to do as they please within the precincts of their private space. This too falls short of what is morally acceptable, for such people can still be denied citizenship. With all sorts of public restrictions, they receive only wafer-thin benefits from the state. Secularism demands more than this and carries a weightier morality. If political secularism requires the state to be independent of existing religious groups, and if this has implications of equal citizenship, then it clearly entails that— in some as yet unspecified sense—one's religious affiliation or confessional allegiance cannot be a condition of citizenship. Often this is taken to mean that every member of society will receive benefits from the state, not merely the protection of the legal system but education, health care, and access to public office. In minimally democratic societies, it also means that every member, no matter what his religion, has the right to vote and to hold political office. Such a political system embodies a fair degree of toleration.

To see citizens as recipients of benefits is however to view them purely one dimensionally, as passive figures whose life is marked by private concerns and only marginally, very formally with politics.[6] This view is deficient on many counts but principally inadequate because it fails to grasp that people have a vital interest not only in their own well-being but in the well-being of others, an interest in society as a whole, and a wish to define and determine its course in the future. They do this not only by participating more actively in formal political institutions of their society, but also by taking part in what Scanlon calls the informal politics of social life, and of which the activity of religious groups and competition amongst them provides as good an example as any. People's lives are marked by public concerns, and this dimension of their life is captured by the more politically sensitive models of the active citizen. Equality in active citizenship entails therefore an acceptance of the idea that citizens are equally entitled to try and shape their political community in the manner they best see it. In a deeply diverse society this implies competition among

6 See Michael Walzer, *Obligations* (Harvard University Press: Cambridge, Mass., 1970), p. 210.

citizens over the future direction of society. However, at this point the sceptic may ask: why must this equality be accepted? What is the case for it? What is its value? To answer this a clearer difference between passive and active citizenship is necessary. In the passive model, each citizen has a relationship with the state but no relation invests with one another. The active citizenship model captures this political relation and invests it with a value. On this account, the passive citizen is fundamentally alienated from fellow citizens.

How is this alienation to be overcome? One way is to collectively determine the nature and direction of society, possible when agreement over substantive values exists. However, under conditions of deep difference in substantive values or conceptions of the good, people are likely to pursue competing goals rather than participate strongly in common projects. How then must active citizens relate to one another under these conditions? For Scanlon, the requirement of toleration steps in just at this point. Toleration requires that people who fall on the wrong side of differences should still be treated as equals and must be equally entitled to determine society in ways they see best. To my mind, this is a refined restatement of political secularism where radical disagreements in religious beliefs and practices are irrelevant to membership of the same political community. The denial of political secularism betrays a moral failure of nerve required for fellow citizenship. Thus, Scanlon defends political secularism on the ground that 'our common membership of a political society goes deeper than religious disagreements and serious conflicts over the nature and directions of out society, or else', he claims, 'we are just rival groups contending over the same territory'.

Scanlon carefully points out that his argument holds only for the political community: only here can religion not be a ground for exclusion. In other associations, it may be legitimately deployed to include or exclude. What is so special about a political community? Why only here is exclusion on religious grounds unacceptable? Rawls provides an answer that I endorse:

We enter a political community only by birth and exit only by death (or so we may appropriately assume). To us, it seems that we have simply materialized, as it were, from nowhere at this position in the social world with all its advantages and disadvantages, according to our good or bad fortune. I say from nowhere, because we have no prior public or non-public identity: we have not come from somewhere else into this social world. Political society is closed: we come to be within it and we do not, and indeed cannot, enter or leave it voluntarily.[7]

If this is so, our relationship with fellow members of a political community is non-contractual. In contractual relations, obligations are defeasible by a voluntary act but in non-contractual relations we can neither sign on nor easily withdraw from obligations. It does not follow from this that we cannot renounce them ever but such obligations have features that make abandoning them unattractive. Our obligations to fellow citizens are morally binding non-contractual obligations. This is the reason why arbitrary exclusion is morally wrong. Active citizenship entails that this obligation be fulfilled. Toleration makes it possible for us to do so.

## V

Three articles on secularism in the West make up a distinct section in this anthology. Michael Sandel draws attention to the changes in the meaning of secularism in the US, and to different interpretations of the wall of separation thesis. To begin with, government neutrality on religious matters is not a long-standing principle of constitutional law in the US. Sandel reminds us that it was only in 1947 that the Supreme Court upheld the neutralist version of political secularism and implemented the non-establishment clause of the Constitution with any seriousness. More importantly, the neutralist justification of the separation of church and state lends itself to distinct interpretations. The first interpretation justifies neutrality by protecting the interests of both religion and the state. The neutral state serves the interests of religion by checking corruption that frequently follows excessive dependence on civil authority, and advances the interests of the state by preventing civil strife caused by church–state entanglements. The second view, Sandel tells us, justifies neutrality in the name of the individual's freedom to choose. If neutrality in part depends on what justifies it, then state neutrality in this second sense presupposes a conception of a person defined independently

[7] John Rawls, *Political Liberalism* (Columbia University Press: New York, 1993), pp 135–6.

of values and commitments sustained only within the community. It assimilates demands of conscience that flow from the way we are and obligations imposed by the substantive content of our beliefs to obligations that stem solely from the fact that our beliefs and preferences are voluntarily chosen. This conflation has the effect of misrecognizing religious persons as well as misunderstanding the way persons relate to their beliefs and to the community in which these are sustained. It follows that for religious persons a secular state justified on liberal-individualist grounds is morally unacceptable. Sandel's intervention shows that by treating our highest ideals on par with mundane desires and preferences, and confusing the pursuit of preference with the exercise of duty, the liberal justification of neutrality fails to bolster religious liberty. Such a neutral state, claims Sandel, forbids religious practices, such as donning Yarmulkes in the military, that it should allow and permits practices, such as nativity scenes in public squares, that it should probably restrict. Either way, a neutral state justified on the grounds of individual choice fails to take religion seriously and therefore is unlikely to be supported by committed believers.

The article by Carens and Williams raises issues connected with secularism in Western liberal democracies. It shows how, given the political culture and the nature of states in the West, the problem of religious and cultural minorities can be usefully addressed. The authors claim that Muslim minorities are subject to at least three kinds of misrecognition. First, by the prejudice of viewing some distinctly objectionable practices as being essentially Islamic, as having the sanction of Islam when in fact it is not so. Second, by the incorrect perception that Islamic practice conflicts with values fundamental to a liberal democracy. Third, by a remarkable inconsistency that, in the name of religious freedom, forsakes important values such as equality in the case of some religions but refuses such tolerance when it comes to Islam. Most liberal-democratic states valorize religious liberty over other values. This priority is often reversed when dealing with Islam. Two conclusions follow from this contribution, only one of which is more explicitly registered. First, that the conceptual structure underpinning liberal democracies is not fully equipped to realize important values such as gender equality or minority rights. To realize these values fully we must move beyond liberal democracy. Second, even so, the condition of Muslim migrants could improve considerably if only principles of liberal democracy were consistently implemented. Were liberal democrats to treat Muslim minorities the way other religious groups such as Catholics, Protestants, or Jews are treated, there would be remarkable improvement in the quality of their lives.

Bauberot's article on French secularism makes much the same point when he warns that it would be disastrous if 'instead of working out the tension between republicanism and democracy for all religions, one were to apply the republican model, effectively only to Islam, while Christianity and Judaism were to benefit from the democratic demand'. The French model of secularism is widely believed to exemplify the strict separation of religion from state practice. Moreover, the justification for separation is widely believed not to rely upon religion. It appears that French Republican secularism is the clearest expression of what Taylor calls the independent ethic mode of secularism. Bauberot's masterly historical survey brings out crucial dimensions in the understanding of the French case. First, that the republican model of secularism did not drop fully formed from the sky but was developed out of conflict and compromise with religion. The republican model of the secular state won out in the end but not in a zero-sum game. Second, the laicization that occurred in France involved two distinct stages. It had to, as he says, cross two thresholds. The first was characterized by three features: (a) The differentiation of spheres by virtue of which Roman Catholicism stopped being an inclusive institution coextensive with the whole society; (b) The continuation of the view that religion provides the foundation of morality and performs a useful public service for which the state must give financial support; (c) The official recognition that this public service can be performed by all existing religions, and that therefore the state must guarantee freedom of different religions, including of course the freedom of views that do without 'the succour of religion'.

The second threshold too is marked by three features: (a) The non-inclusivity of religion is given a particular interpretation, namely its privatization and optionalization; (b) Religion is no longer seen to provide a public service; (c) The subsumption of religious liberty under wider public liberties. The state guarantees religious freedom with a legal, private rather than a public status. Bauberot concludes however that the logic of neither threshold has evolved a static, rigidly established situation. 'History induces movement and no reality escapes a possible reorientation, nor indeed new attempts at breaking it up.'

# VI

The *locus classicus* on the secular state in India remains Donald Smith's *India as a Secular State*. Smith begins with a theoretical outline of a secular state, surveys factors enabling or inhibiting secularism in Asia, provides an analysis of the relations between the state and religion in India, evaluates the Indian achievement, and diagnoses its malaise.

Smith's working definition of the secular state involves three distinct, interrelated sets of relationships concerning the state, religion, and the individual. First, a relationship between the individual and religion from which the state is excluded. Second, a relationship between the individual and the state from which religion is excluded. A secular state must view the individual as a citizen independent of membership of any particular religious group. Finally the institutional arrangement for these relationships separates religion from the state. This effectively rejects state religions. However, he emphasizes that the conception of the secular state must not be identified with separation of religion from the state. A mere separation does not guarantee religious liberty; when this happens, a secular state, as he conceives it, does not exist. Likewise, religious liberty and non-discrimination in the political arena may exist without strict separation. The church–state separation is, for Smith, the institutional embodiment of the principle of religious liberty and of the neutrality of the state in religious matters.

For Smith, India's prospects for strengthening her secular state were good. Hinduism had many characteristics conducive to secularism. The presence of large, well-articulated minorities provided powerful deterrents to the violation of secular principles. The British left behind a legacy of religious neutrality and, under the leadership of Gandhi and Nehru, Indian nationalism knit an inclusivist character. Nevertheless, the consolidation of the secular state in India was never smooth. Smith foresaw several problems. The chief contributor is blind loyalty to caste and religious community which can easily slide into communal rivalry and more dangerously into communal conflict. Aid to groups based on communal classification threatens the consolidation of the secular state too by undermining 'the emotional integration of the nation by which the individual's consciousness of caste or community will be subordinated to his Indian citizenship'. For Smith, extensive interference by the state in Hindu religious institutions that bolstered its image as the principle agent of Hindu reform and separate personal laws for each religious community constitute the second problem as these are diametrically opposed to the principles of secularism. The protection of a religious group, a suspect classification for the basis of welfare, privilege or immunity undermines the secularity of the state. The protection of minorities, Smith believes, must be made possible not by neurotic over-protection of religious groups but only within the framework of 'equal citizenship'. For these reasons, the existence of separate personal laws is inconsistent with secularism. The final problem revolves around the definition of the secular state: India has yet to resolve whether non-sectarianism or non-religiosity is the true meaning of secularism appropriate in its context. Smith warned of external factors that may weaken a secular state in the recently independent India; a war with Pakistan, the fissures and the possible break-up of the Congress and subsequent consolidation of Hindu communal parties may well lead to the decline of the secular state. Smith saw secularism as part of a larger project of develop-ment so that a crisis in that project would invariably precipitate an accompanying crisis in secularism. Despite these problems, Smith's answer to the question whether India was a secular state or not was in the affirmative and his prognosis was that it had more than an even chance of survival in India.

Galanter shows that Smith's critique of the Indian practice of secularism is unconvincing due to inadequacies in his theory of the secular state. Galanter takes up the charge that the Indian state interferes with and promotes Hinduism, thereby compromising its secular credentials. Similarly, he examines Smith's contention that the Indian state departs from principles of the secular state by subsidizing schools conducted by religious bodies. He begins by the critique that Smith unwittingly shifts from a descriptive to a normative view of religion. At times, religious liberty implies the freedom to do whatever people believe their religion to be and at other times to do only what is essentially there. 'Essential' has a clear normative import. For Galanter, a secular state cannot function without presupposing a normative conception of religion; it must judge and evaluate religion. Thus, some degree of interference by a secular state in religious matters is unavoidable. To pretend otherwise or criticize it for not being strictly neutral is to misunderstand the analytical and normative strands within secularism. If so, then transformation, a certain clipping, and trimming of religion is inevitable. This is bad news not for secularism but for the particular formulation of it which is highly idealized and not thought through.

Galanter claims that Smith's ideal of a completely secular state is transposed from the American experience, laced with an extra dose of separation. For Galanter, Smith works with two conceptions of secularism, with the strict wall of the separation doctrine and with the no-preference doctrine. He then slots Indian secularism into the second, poor cousin of the first. Galanter's understanding of Indian secularism conforms to neither. Fashioned by an ingenious set of balances between progress and religious liberty, Indian secularism cannot be judged with reference to an idealized American pattern. Smith's principal flaw is to see the uniqueness of Indian secularism as its principal deficiency. Galanter urges us not to be encumbered by a single notion of secularism serving as a descriptive and transcultural ideal. What is required is a reformulation of secularism delinked from its Western moorings.

Galanter's second article asks us to consider the mode in which Indian law must contribute to the transformation of religion in India. Here too, Galanter begins by asking us not to equate secularism with 'a formal standard of religious neutrality'. Consider the Constitution of the US. It involves a normative view of religions, favouring those that do not require official support and which tolerate internal dissenters as well as other religions. Every secular state recognizes and encourages, is indifferent to, and curtails or proscribes religion and elements thereof. Secular states cannot leave religion entirely untouched. The state, and in particular its law, exercises an overall arbitral role. If this is the starting point of our understanding of secularism, then we need to ask the mode of transformation of religion best suited to India. Here Galanter distinguishes two, the first he calls the mode of limitation and the other the mode of intervention. In the mode of limitation, public standards are promulgated, their field of operation specified, and thereafter religion is shaped in accordance with these standards. In the mode of intervention, religious authority is directly challenged and a change is attempted from within the religious tradition. Both modes accept the external superiority of legal norms and, by virtue of this, distance themselves from the strict separation-of-powers variant of secularism. However, unlike the intervention mode that requires legal specialists to be skilled at the authoritative exposition of religious norms, the limitation mode of secularism makes no such demands. According to Galanter, secularism embodied in the Indian Constitution exemplifies the limitation mode. It follows that taking refuge in the separation-of-powers mode or indulging in the interventionist mode marks a departure from principles that undergrid the Indian Constitution. Galanter notes that the judges of Indian Supreme Court often depart from the secularism of the Indian Constitution. He explains this as a tendency in the Westernized ruling élite to actively reformulate Hinduism. He gives the example of the Supreme Court handling in 1966 of a puritanical Vaishnavite sect called Satsangis that claimed exemption from the Temple Entry Act on the plea that they were not Hindus. Galanter argues that the Supreme Court, adopting the mode of intervention, rejected the claims of the Satsangis by an appeal to the true tenets of Hinduism as defined by it. Two decades later the same attitude of the court landed Indian secularism in deep trouble when the court granted alimony to Shah Bano, once again on the plea that this was not in keeping with the true teaching of Islam.

## VII

Isaiah Berlin is known to have once remarked that the history of ideas is replete with instances of great liberating ideas turning into straitjackets. Quite rightly, he did not claim that in undergoing this change they necessarily, irrevocably lose emancipatory potential or moral force. What he must have meant though is that something akin to permanent revolution is necessary for the growth of such ideas; they must be subjected to detailed scrutiny and criticism, appear for a time ineluctably bedridden before they are rehabilitated publicly. Professors T.N. Madan and Ashis Nandy are among the few scholars who first caught secularism in such a moment of crisis. Their articles in this volume articulate this crisis, offer suggestive, plausible explanations, and set many scholars down a path on how best to respond to its challenge.

For Madan, secularism is a late Christian idea, 'a gift of Christianity' to India. Not indigenous to the religious cultures of India, imported from the West, it continues to sit uneasily with home-grown world-views. What does secularism mean for Madan? Secularism constitutes an entire world-view that establishes a hierarchical relation between the secular and the religious, and which in its political form expels religion from public life. Secularism is culturally inappropriate in India because the established hierarchy in Indian culture encompasses the secular within the religious, and because it is too much of a public matter to be privatized.

Madan believes that the demand for the removal of religion from public life is predicated within the secular framework upon the mainstream Enlightenment view of religion as irrational. This makes scientific management and rationalism natural allies of secularism. Indeed, he delineated it as the view that seeks to eject religion from public life in order to replace it by modern, scientific principles. This triggers off an irreconcilable conflict between scientific secularism and religion. Religion in India becomes a source of resistance to this alien world-view and sometimes curdles into bigotry and violence. This eruption of religious fanaticism and communal violence naturally worries Madan. To counter it, Madan offers two prescriptions at odds with one another. First, to keep religion in public life and use its resources of toleration to prevent fanaticism and interreligious conflict. There is no place for modern secularism in this solution. However, a veiled suggestion for an alternative solution exists that rejects available versions of secularism but admits to the need for some form of modern secularism appropriate in the Indian cultural context.

Ashis Nandy begins by drawing a distinction between religion-as-faith and religion-as-ideology: a faith when it is 'a way of life, a tradition which is definitionally non-monolithic and operationally plural', an ideology, when it is a 'sub-national, national or cross-national identifier of populations contesting for or protecting non-religious, usually political or socio-economic, interest'. Modernization first produces religion-as-ideology and then generates secularism to meet its challenge to the 'ideology of modern statecraft'. As is clear from the context, by modern statecraft Nandy means the scientific management of state institutions. The public realm, he claims, is a contested arena between religion and science. By excluding religion from public life, secularism facilitates its takeover by science. The fraternal link between secularism and scientific politics is self-evident as are its ties with the nation-state, another monstrous product of modernity.

Nandy reiterates the thesis of the cultural inappropriateness of secularism on the grounds that to the faithful the public/private distinction lying at the heart of modern secularism makes no sense. To ask believers to expunge their faith from the public realm is at best insensitive to what gives their life worth and often displays outright hostility. Religion is not merely a matter of private preference where religion is of 'immense importance'. When the public–private distinction fails to hold, religion inevitably enters public life through the back door. This explains the communalization of politics: the resurgence of communal political parties, mobilization on the basis of religious symbols, demand for reservations on the basis of religious classification, and the dispute over Babri Masjid. Over time, Nandy claims, secularism mutates into an intolerant ideology excessively concerned with economic growth, national security, modernization, and scientific development as its natural concomitant. Apart from deepening the alienation of believers, this secularism breeds old and new forms of violence against which there is little protection; old, because the backlash of marginalized believers reinvigorates fanaticism and bigotry, and new because it generates communal violence as well as a conflict between the nation-state and religious communities. Nandy's solution, less ambivalent than Madan's, polemically demands a rejection of secularism and emphasizes the need to cement notions of tolerance by using the symbolism and theology of the various faiths in India.

Nandy and Madan's views do not go unchallenged in the volume. For Bilgrami, Nandy's critique of secularism is marred by uncritical anti-nationalism, a skewed historiography, and traditionalist nostalgia. Indeed, Bilgrami's strategy is not so much an attempt to counter Nandy's hostility towards modernity as to disconnect—as far as is possible—the explanation of the crisis of secularism from the debate about modernity and its good or evil. For him, Nandy and Madan do not get to even the terms of a meaningful debate about secularism but also dangerously derail it. For Amartya Sen, too, the characterization of 'secularism as modernism is not particularly cogent, nor does it provide an especially persuasive basis for rejecting secularism'. For Sen, the principle of secularism basically demands symmetric treatment of different religious communities in politics, and it is not obvious why symmetric treatment must somehow involve the use of violence as Nandy claims all modernist projects do.

Tambiah raises a more pointed objection to Nandy. He offers two principal criticisms of the Madan–Nandy view. First, he is troubled by Nandy's unsubstantiated collation of state secularists and the planners and instigators of collective political violence as arch representatives of bureaucratic, instrumental rationality. He is equally bothered by Nandy's simple-minded contrast between those who plan collective political violence and those in the rank and file who participate in that violence. For Tambiah, Nandy's argument cannot proceed unless he provides a coherent account of the motivations that underlie the commitment to religious cultural revivalism characteristic of people who he claims exemplify instrumental rationality. Second, if the distinction between faith and ideology holds, how do masses steeped in traditional faiths, get easily drawn into modernist, nationalist campaigns and how do ordinary people, customarily peaceful and tolerant, suddenly become violent and intolerant for the cause of religion-as-ideology? Nandy's explanation of ethnocentric politics, fueled by a sense of defeat and feeling of impotence, leaves Tambiah unconvinced. He is compelled to demand that the power and performative efficacy of Hindu nationalism be sketched in motivational and experimental terms, and related better to the politics of preferential collective entitlements and to mass participatory electoral strategies through which this politics is conducted.

In my article I claim that the Madan–Nandy thesis misrecognizes the complex motivations underlying even the vulnerable forms of the secularism it justifiably attacks. The source of the rational management of politics does not lie only in a comprehensive world-view but also in the minimally moral resolution of deep conflicts; similarly, behind the surface obsession with rules lies the more accommodative spirit of pluralism. The Madan–Nandy thesis cannot see resources of toleration in any version of secularism because it focuses only on a version that does not possess such a resource.

At least one person in this volume sympathizes with Madan and Nandy but draws different conclusions from it. Partha Chatterjee responds directly to the threat posed by the Hindu Right to religious and cultural minorities and with an array of arguments attempts to show that secularism is an inappropriate ground for meeting the challenge of Hindu majoritarianism. Chatterjee's argument may be read in the following way: either secularism means the strict separation between the modern state and traditional religion or it means strict neutrality and non-preferentialism. In the former interpretation, secularism is unsuitable for the defence of minorities because the Hindu Right easily accepts this separation and, indeed, can use the vast machinery of the state to persecute minorities. This appears plausible because the mere separation of religion from politics is compatible with the absence of religious liberty and the presence of religious discrimination. If the second interpretation is adopted, Chatterjee argues, we must face up to the historical reality of the Indian situation where neutrality (which he understands as equidistance) has hardly ever been the norm. After all, the Indian state has intervened selectively in the personal laws of religious communities. Chatterjee therefore accepts that the Indian state has never been and is hardly ever likely to be secular in this sense. So, either the secular state (in the first sense) is unlikely to be of help to religious minorities or the state simply cannot be secular (in the second sense). Further, he claims that an attempt to reinterpret liberal secularism is doomed by its ultimate refusal to give up a universalist but untenable framework of reason. He then proposes his own view according to which religious minorities can be best protected by a democratized state that ensures religious toleration. For Chatterjee, toleration is acceptance of a group that insists on its right not to give reasons for doing things differently *provided it explains itself adequately in its own chosen forum*. I italicize this to underscore the importance Chatterjee places on internal democratic norms, a strong condition because a number of possibilities open up if the group is not internally democratic. Should the state intervene to insist on internal democratic norms? Should other groups insist upon reasons if leaders of the group do not conform to widely shared democratic standards? Chatterjee does not answer these questions; instead he proposes that such toleration be given a proper institutional form by allowing religious groups their own parliament, that is a deliberative body to decide on matters of the entire community to which members are elected. Chatterjee's writing points to the extent to which rethinking on secularism is being undertaken within the 'left and democratic forces' in India.

The critique of Nehruvian secularism comes also from those who wish to defend it in some other form. For Akeel Bilgrami, the principal fault line in secularism is the assumption that secularism stands outside the arena of substantive political commitments. The refusal of the Congress party, of Nehru in particular, to let secular policy emerge through negotiation between different communitarian voices provides a clue into the integral flaw in Nehruvian secularism, that is its Archimedean character. This ultra-proceduralism, to use a phrase from my own article, made it impossible for secularism to emerge out of a creative dialogue between different communities. The usurpation by the Congress of the arena in which different communities could express their own voices, and its presumption that it alone represents all these communities quashed any chances of an emergent secularism with greater moral legitimacy and stability. For Bilgrami, had secularism emerged from below, from negotiations on procedure and substance with religious communities and codified into law, the present controversy surrounding Muslim personal law would be redundant.

Stanley Tambiah in his article notes many connotations of secularism in the West. First, as an orientation to the world linked to Protestantism and enlightenment rationalism. The second is associated with the separation of society and culture from the domain of religion. The third narrower meaning pertains to the political sphere and specifies a charter for state policy. In India, both Nehru and Gandhi, who made religion irrelevant to the definition of citizenship or nationality, converged on this third sense. Tambiah explains the necessity in India of political secularism on the basis of two factors. One, its religious diversity and two, the trauma of Partition which made generosity towards Muslims mandatory on the Hindu majority. This coincides roughly with my own views expressed in the article included in this volume. He identifies many external reasons for the crisis of secularism but an important, internal one refers to ambiguities in the Indian Constitution and in the Nehruvian view. Both fail to give clear directives on how secularism is to implement differential claims on state support advanced by different religious groups. Tambiah notes that Art. 25 does not provide unambiguous criteria for the evaluation of a demand for legislative intervention in the name of welfare and justice by a Hindu majority, where intervention may be detrimental to the distinctive practices and norms of a minority like the Muslims. It remains silent on how to separate secular from religious matters. Much of the crisis of secularism stems from the failure of the Congress party to have a consistent or uniform understanding of the relationship between politics and religion. The Shah Bano case is as good an illustration of this point as any. The contradiction between fundamental and minority rights on the one hand, and between minority rights and directive principles of state policy, on the other, surfaced dramatically with this issue.

Amartya Sen's is perhaps the most unambiguous, unrelenting defence of Nehruvian secularism. The stated objective of Sen's article is to meet various forms of scepticism concerning secularism and to enable fellow secularists to shed a traditional reluctance to explicitly delineate reasons behind their habitually accepted positions. Sen's article is important not only because it seeks to meet the challenge of scepticism within India (a task undertaken by several others in the volume), but also scepticism outside India which has scarcely received any attention in much recent debate on the subject. Its distinctiveness lies in taking seriously, more seriously than do most other articles, what might be called a common-sense critique of secularism. Criticism of secularism is fast becoming part of the common-sense of the Indian middle class as distinct from the scholarly forays of intellectuals. For example, it is widely believed that Muslims are a favoured community, that much of the Hindutva reaction is forced upon Hindus by the failure of Muslims to see themselves as Indians, and that by treating Hinduism merely as one of the many religions in India, secularism does injustice to its own historical heritage and turns 'epistemic error into a political blunder'. Sen concludes that the discontent with secularism and the interesting lines of argument it throws up, though worth scrutinizing, do not undermine the basic case for secularism in India.

In my article, I reiterate the desirability and inescapability of secularism. In my view, the real challenge before us continues to be one of working out an alternative conception of secularism rather than simply an alternative to it. To those who reject secularism, I offer reasons for its desirability and ineradicability. To uncritical proponents of secularism, I show valuable elements in the anti-secularist critique and explain why my version of secularism is better than other vulnerable variants.


New Delhi
June 1997

# I

# The Secular Imperative

# 1

# Modes of Secularism

*Charles Taylor*

## I

It is not entirely clear what is meant by secularism. There are indeed quite different formulae that go under the name. The first thing I would like to attempt is to sort these out.

Perhaps the best way to undertake this is historically, trying to say something about how this kind of formula arises, whereby in some way or another, the state distances itself from established religions or in some way can be considered neutral between them. This takes us back to the use of the term 'secular' in Christendom, because it is there that the story starts.

Coming to the question from this angle enables us also to raise another issue, which can sometimes inflame the discussion. It is frequently claimed by or on behalf of societies outside the European cultural zone, that secularism is an invention of this civilization and, by implication, that it does not travel well and should not be imposed on other cultures. For many Muslims, for instance, it is seen as a creation of Christendom, and the attempt to apply its formulae in Muslim countries is perceived as an attempt to impose on them an alien form, most dramatically put, as a continuation of the crusades by other means.

Now, in fact, there is truth in the claim that secularism has Christian roots, but it is wrong to think that this limits the application of its formulae to post-Christian societies. Why this is so will emerge, I hope, in the ensuing discussion.

'Secular' itself is a Christian term, that is, a word that finds its original meaning in a Christian context. *Saeculum*, the ordinary Latin word for century, or age, took on a special meaning as applied to profane time, the time of ordinary historical succession, which the human race lives through between the Fall and the Parousia. This time was interwoven with higher times, different modes of what is sometimes called 'eternity', the time of the Ideas, or of the Origin, or of God. Human beings were seen as living in all these times, but certain acts, or lives, or institutions, or social forms could be seen as more thoroughly directed towards one or another. Government was more 'in the *saeculum*' by contrast with the Church, for instance. The state was the 'secular arm'. A similar point could be expressed by contrasting the 'temporal' and the 'spiritual'. Or, in another context, ordinary parish clergy, ministering to people who were very much embedded in the world and history, were called 'secular' to distinguish them from the religious orders or 'regular clergy'.

The existence of these oppositions reflected something fundamental about Christendom, a requirement of distance, of non-coincidence between the Church and the world. There were, through the medieval centuries, great overlap and great conflict between Church and state, but in all versions, and on all sides, it was axiomatic that there had to be a separation of spheres. From one side, the standpoint of one party, this might appear as an attempt to maintain the integrity of the political function; but more fundamentally, the need for distance, for a less than full embedding in the secular, was understood as essential to the vocation of the Church. One of the motivations for defining a space of the secular has always been theological in Christendom, and continues to be so today.

The secularisms of today build on this original distinction, but of course also involves a transformation in it. The origin point of modern Western secularism was the Wars of Religion; or rather, the search in battle-fatigue and horror for a way out of them. The need was felt for a ground of coexistence for Christians of different confessional persuasions. This meant in practice that the public domain had to be regulated by certain norms or agreements which were independent of confessional allegiance, and could in some way be ensured against overturn in the name of such allegiances. Rules of peace, even with heretics, and of obedience to legitimate authority, even where schismatic, had to be put beyond revocation in the name of one or other version of orthodoxy. There were, in fact, two ways in which this could be done, and although there was not a great deal of political significance in this distinction at the time, these two approaches turn out to be ancestral to rather different understandings of secularism today.

The first could be described as the common ground strategy. The aim was to establish a certain ethic of peaceful coexistence and political order, a set of grounds for obedience, which while still theistic, even Christian, was based on those doctrines which were common to all Christian sects, or even to all theists. This could be grounded on a version of Natural Law, which like Aquinas' was indeed conceived as being independent of revelation, but still connected to theism, because the same reasoning which brings us to the law brings us to God. The crucial step that needed to be taken was to hold that the political injunctions that flowed from this common core trumped the demands of a particular confessional allegiance. So while the proponents of struggle could feel justified in tearing up treaties as soon as it was advantageous to do so, on the grounds that you do not need to keep faith with heretics, the defenders of the common ground argued that our obligation to God required that we keep our word to fellow human beings (or perhaps theists), and that this trumped any demands stemming for confessional allegiance. Arguably, Pufendorf and Locke offered versions of Natural Law of this kind. Leibniz's search for grounds of agreement between the great confessional blocks was an attempt to push this logic a little further. Carried through to the end, this could lead to a downplaying of confessional dogma in favour of common beliefs; and pushed further, beyond the bounds of Christianity, this could end in Deism.

There was, however, a second strategy, which consisted in trying to define an independent political ethic. Grotius is the most celebrated early explorer of this avenue. This allows us to abstract from our religious beliefs altogether. We look for certain features of the human condition which allow us to deduce certain exceptionless norms, including those of peace and political obedience. Grotius would appear at times to be arguing almost more geometrico. Humans are rational creatures, who are also sociable. If we take these as axioms, we can derive theorems about how we ought to treat one another. For instance, the violation of our solemnly given word can be argued to be at odds with the nature of a sociable being who is also rational, that is to say proceeds by rules or precepts. Grotius is led to pronounce the words: *etsi Deus non daretur...*, even if God didn't exist, these norms would be binding on us.[1] We have the basis of an independent ethic.

This difference in strategy has proved to be important for us because it is the basis of two rather different ways of understanding the grounds of peaceful and equitable coexistence between people of different faiths, or different fundamental commitments. One way involves appealing to these different commitments, and arguing to a convergence between them on certain fundamentals. The other asks us to abstract from these deeper or higher beliefs altogether for purposes of a political morality. It looks for an independent ground. Somewhere, in a protected area, immune from all these warring beliefs, lies a common basis for living together, which on its own can be shown to be so compelling that it will command our political allegiance.

Sometimes, of course, we have to do a job on these beliefs, to ensure they do not overstep their bounds, and start challenging the independent ethic. A good example is what Hobbes does to Christian revelation, in the second part of the Leviathan. The first part of the book presents one of the most (in)famous independent ethics of early modernity, based supposedly on undeniable facts of the human conditions, and the unchallengeable meaning our key terms—like 'liberty', 'law', 'justice'—must take on in the light of these facts. But the second enters the theologians' own terrain, to show that the supposedly religious obligation to withhold obedience to sovereigns cannot stand up in Scripture. The Christian demands have to be shrunk, in order to leave the independent ethic unchallenged.

What Hobbes does is to make the demands of Christian faith, as confessionally defined, irrelevant to the public sphere. There the independent ethic reigns supreme. In the private realm, the believer can and must do what conscience demands, but he commits no sin in respecting publicly established forms and ceremonies. Defining these is the sovereign's God-given right. Implicitly, this means that the wise sovereign will allow his subjects full leeway of private practice. Religion, where it really counts in people's lives and

---

1 See Richard Tuck, *Natural Rights Theories: Their Origin and Development* (Cambridge University Press, 1979). His version of Grotius' argument is somewhat different from mine, but it has the same ultimate thrust, that is, it gives us reasons to accept certain norms whatever else we believe about human life and God's demands on us.

commitments, essentially will exist only in the private sphere. That is the logic of Hobbes' arguments. Pushed further, this logic can lead to the extrusion of religion altogether from the public domain. The state upholds no religion, pursues no religious goals, and religiously-defined goods have no place in the catalogue of ends it promotes. This is one of the meanings of the principle widely accepted in the West today of the separation of church and state.

But it is not the only meaning. It is the one which seems to flow most naturally from the independent ethic approach, but not from that of the common ground. Here the goal is not to make religion less relevant to public life and policy, in the name of an independent ethic, but rather to prevent the state from backing one confession rather than another. The goal is a state which is even-handed between religious communities, equidistant from them, as it were, rather than one where religious reasons play no overt role.

This appears in fact to have been the basis of the original American separation. Indeed, the original pre-ratification amendment reads 'Congress shall make no law....' The aim seems to have been to keep the federal government neutral, but in a union where many states still had established churches. The goal was significantly narrower than it has since been interpreted, where separation is deemed binding on all levels of government. But even with this extension, the separation can still be conceived on the logic of the common ground. In this context, there is not necessarily a problem of the polity conceiving itself as 'one people under God', even though established churches are prohibited. Indeed, a strong motive for this prohibition can be the sense among believers that an established church is already a corrupted one, open to secular manipulation. In the actual, chequered history of the American separation, both models have been in play, with the common ground justification being paramount in the early days, and the independent ethic outlook gaining ground in more recent times. But in ideal–typical terms there are two rather different ways of conceiving this separation, even as there are of understanding the secularism of which it is an expression.

Each model has its weaknesses. A clear problem with the common ground approach is that with the widening band of religious and metaphysical commitments in society, the ground originally defined as common becomes that of one party among others. The Founders seemed to concur in some kind of Christian outlook, verging on a New Testament-inspired Deism in some cases. This could be pushed laterally into a vaguer biblical theism to accommodate Jews. But the US now contains substantial numbers of non-believers, as well as Muslims, Hindus, Buddhists, and adherents of many other views. The common ground shifts, or becomes rapidly etiolated. This seems to lend plausibility to the other approach.

But this too has severe difficulties. The very diversification that has undercut the common ground approach also challenges the independent ethic. As long as everyone is Christian, the definition of an ethic as independent, while alarming some theologians, does not necessarily appear as a threat. Such an independent ethic may be rather 'Christian' in spirit, and besides, the proposition is seen in the counter factual form presented by Grotius: *etsi Deus non daretur*. We are not actually asked to set aside our Christian beliefs, just to recognize that some of the things we hold do not depend on them.

But the situation is very different if there are real live atheists in society. They will live the independent ethic not as some thought experiment, but as the basis of their moral lives. Moreover, they will tend to think that this is the proper way of living this ethic. They will often be suspicious of religious believers who profess it, and consider them at best as lukewarm supporters, perhaps even as potential traitors to it. They will also tend to want to police the boundary between independent and religious ethic more closely, and to want to push farther the process of making religion irrelevant in the public sphere. All this easily provokes reactions from believers, and the society now can find itself sliding down the road of a *Kulturkampf*, in which 'secularists' slug it out with believers on issues about the fundamentals of their society.

The dissensus takes this form: what the unbelieving 'secularist' sees as a necessary policing of the boundary of a common independent public sphere, will often be perceived by the religious as a gratuitous extrusion of religion in the name of a rival metaphysical belief. What to one side is a more strict and consistent application of the principles of neutrality is seen by the other side as partisanship. What this other side sees as legitimate public expressions of religious belonging will often be castigated by the first as the exaltation of some peoples' beliefs over others. This problem is compounded when society diversifies to contain substantial numbers of adherents of non-Judaeo–Christian religions. If even some Christians find the 'post-Christian' independent ethic partisan, how much harder will Muslims find it to swallow it.

We come back to the charge levelled by many non-European societies against 'secularism', that it is an import from ex-Christendom. The Christian origins of the idea are undeniable, but this does not have to mean that it has no application elsewhere. What does, however, give colour to this story of imposition is precisely the independent ethic model. Defined and pursued out of the context of Western unbelief, it understandably comes across as the imposition of one metaphysical view over others, and an alien one at that. In this form, indeed, Western secularism may not 'travel' very well outside its heartland; or only in the form of an authoritarian programme designed to diminish the hold of religion on the masses, as in Turkey under Atatürk or China under Mao.

The charge, however, is not at all true of the other model, which whatever its Christian origins, can be readapted to ever-new contexts. But not in its original form. Perhaps in the light of the above discussion, we might rather define the mode which can travel as a third one, equidistant from—or perhaps a hybrid between—the two others. We saw above in fact that the common ground model runs into more and more trouble as society diversifies. The difficulties of both the historical approaches is what pushes us to define this third one.

This is the one best described by the term 'overlapping consensus' made famous by Rawls. I want to use this term, even while I have some difficulties with its detailed working out in Rawls' theory. I will come to these below. For the moment, I just want to describe this approach in general terms. The problem with the historical common ground approach is that it assumes that everyone shares some religious grounds for the norms regulating the public sphere, even if these are rather general: non-denominational Christianity, or only Biblical theism, or perhaps only some mode of post-Enlightenment Deism. But even this latter is asking too much of today's diversified societies. The only thing we can hope to share is a purely political ethic, not its embedding in some religious view. Here the independent ethic seems to fill the bill, because it offers as common ground just such a political ethic, for example a doctrine of human rights, of popular sovereignty, of freedom and equality. But its problem is that it too demands not only the sharing of the ethic but also of its foundation—in this case, one supposedly independent of religion.

The property of overlapping consensus view is just that it lifts the requirement of a commonly held foundation. It aims only at universal acceptance of certain political principles (this is hard enough to attain). But it recognizes from the outset that there cannot be a universally agreed basis for these, independent or religious. It renounces this from the outset, acknowledging that making this a requirement of a well-ordered democratic society can only lead to the tyrannical attempt to impose some people's philosophies on others (their 'comprehensive theories of the good', in Rawls' terms).

The overlapping consensus approach recognizes that this common political ethic will not suffice by itself; that everyone who adheres to it will have some broader and deeper understanding of the good in which it is embedded. It aims to respect the diversity of such understandings, while building consensus on the ethic. Now I believe that this model, unlike the independent ethic, and unlike the earlier, specifically Christian versions of the common ground approach, can be usefully followed—we should better say, re-invented—almost anywhere. It will, moreover, have to be adopted more and more in the historical heartland of secularism, as these societies diversify. But before going on to discuss this model a little further, I want to set out reasons why I think it not only can but must be followed; why, in other terms, the pretext that it is Western and thus alien will not wash anywhere in the world today.

## II

I stress today, because the inescapability of secularism flows from the nature of the modern state. More particularly, from the nature of the democratic state. In order to make this clearer, I want to draw out certain features of this kind of polity.

Modern nation-states are 'imagined communities' in Benedict Anderson's celebrated phrase.[2] We might say that they have a particular kind of social imaginary, that is, socially shared ways in

2 Benedict Anderson, *Imagined Communities: Reflections on the Origin and Spread of Nationalism* (Verso: London, 1983; 2nd edn, 1991).

which social spaces are imagined. There are two important features of the modern imaginary, which I can best bring out by contrasting them in each case with what went before in European history.

First, there is the shift from hierarchical, mediated-access societies to horizontal, direct-access societies. In the earlier form, hierarchy and what I am calling mediacy of access went together. A society of ranks—'society of orders', to use Tocqueville's phrase—like seventeenth-century France, for instance, was hierarchical in an obvious sense. But this also meant that one belonged to this society via belonging to some component of it. As a peasant one was linked to a lord who in turn held from the king. One was a member of a municipal corporation which has a standing in the kingdom, or exercised some function in a parliament with its recognized status, and so on. By contrast, the modern notion of citizenship is direct. In whatever many ways I am related to the rest of society through intermediary organizations, I think of my citizenship as separate from all these. My fundamental way of belonging to the state is not dependent on or mediated by any of these other belongings. I stand, alongside all my fellow citizens, in direct relationship to the state, which is the object of our common allegiance.

This does not of course necessarily change the way things get done. I know someone whose brother-in-law is a judge, or an MP, and so I phone her up when I am in a jam. We might say that what has changed is the normative picture. But underlying this, without which the new norm could not exist for us, is a change in the way people imagine belonging. There were certainly people in seventeenth-century France, and before, for whom the very idea of direct access would have been foreign; impossible to grasp clearly. The educated had the model of the Ancient Republic. But for many others, the only way they could understand belonging to a larger whole, like a kingdom, or a universal church, was through the imbrication of more immediate, understandable units of belonging—parish, manor, town, cloister—into the greater entity. Modernity has involved, among other things, a revolution in our social imaginary, the relegation of these forms of mediacy to the margins, and the diffusion of images of direct-access.

This has come about in a number of forms: the rise of a public sphere, in which people conceive themselves as participating directly in a nationwide (sometimes even international) discussion;

the development of market economies, in which all economic agents are seen as entering into contractual relations with others on an equal footing; and, of course, the rise of the modern citizenship state. But we can think of other ways as well in which immediacy of access takes hold of our imaginations. We see ourselves as in spaces of fashion, for instance, taking up and handing on styles. We see ourselves as part of the worldwide audience of media stars. And while these spaces are in their own sense hierarchical—they centre on quasi-legendary figures—they offer all participants an access unmediated by any of their other allegiances or belongings. Something of the same kind, along with a more substantial mode of participation, is available in the various movements, social, political, religious, which are a crucial feature of modern life, and which link people translocally and internationally into a single collective agency.

These modes of imagined direct-access are linked to, indeed are just different facets of modern equality and individualism. Directness of access abolishes the heterogeneity of hierarchical belonging. It makes us uniform, and that is one way of becoming equal. (Whether it is the only way is the fateful issue at stake in much of today's struggles over multiculturalism.) At the same time, the relegation of various mediations reduces their importance in our lives; the individual stands more and more free of them, and hence has a growing self-consciousness as an individual. Modern individualism, as a moral idea, does not mean ceasing to belong at all—that is the individualism of anomie and breakdown—but imagining oneself as belonging to ever wider and more impersonal entities: the state, the movement, the community of humankind.

The second important feature of the modern social imaginary is that it no longer sees the greater translocal entities as grounded in something other, something higher, than common action in secular time. This was not true of the pre-modern state. The hierarchical order of the kingdom was seen as based in the Great Chain of Being. The tribal unit was seen as constituted as such by its law, which went back 'since time out of mind', or perhaps to some founding moment which had the status of a 'time of origins' in Eliade's sense. The importance in pre-modern revolutions, up to and including the English Civil War, of the backward look, of establishing an original law, comes from the understanding that the political entity is in this sense action-transcendent. It cannot simply create itself by its own action. On the contrary, it can act as an entity because it is already constituted as such; and that is why such legitimacy attaches to returning to the original constitution.

Seventeenth-century social contact theory, which sees a people as coming together out of a state of nature, obviously belongs to another order of thought. But it was not until the late eighteenth century that this new way of conceiving things entered the social imaginary. The American Revolution is in a sense the watershed. It was undertaken in a backward-looking spirit, in the sense that the colonists were fighting for their established rights as Englishmen. Moreover, they were fighting under their established colonial legislatures, associated in a congress. But out of the whole process emerges the crucial fiction of 'we, the people', into whose mouth the declaration of the new Constitution is placed.

Here the idea is invoked that a people, or as it was also called at the time, a 'nation', can exist prior to and independently of its political constitution, so that this people can give itself its own constitution by its own free action in secular time. Of course the epoch-making action comes rapidly to be invested with images drawn from older notions of higher time. The 'Novus Ordo Seclorum', just like the new French revolutionary calendar, draws heavily on Judaeo–Christian apocalyptic. The constitution-founding comes to be invested with something of the force of a 'time of origins', a higher time, filled with agents of a superior kind, which we should ceaselessly try to reapproach. But nevertheless, a new way of conceiving things is abroad. Nations, people, can have a personality, can act together outside of any prior political ordering. One of the key premises of modern nationalism is in place, because without this the demand for self-determination of nations would make no sense. This just is the right for peoples to make their own constitution, unfettered by their historical political organization.

What is immensely suggestive about Anderson's account is that it links these two features. It shows how the rise of direct-access societies was linked to changing understandings of time, and consequently of the possible ways of imaging social wholes. Anderson stresses how the new sense of belonging to a nation was prepared by a new way of grasping society under the category of simultaneity:[3] society as the whole consisting of the simultaneous happening of all the myriad events that mark the lives of its members at that moment. These events are the fillers of this segment of a kind of homogeneous time. This very clear, unambiguous concept of simultaneity belongs to an understanding of time as exclusively secular. As long as secular time is interwoven with various kinds of higher time, there is no guarantee that all events can be placed in unambiguous relations of simultaneity and succession. The high feast is in one way contemporaneous with my life and that of my fellow pilgrims, but in another way it is close to eternity, or the time of origins, or the events it prefigures.

A purely secular time-understanding allows us to imagine society 'horizontally', unrelated to any 'high points', where the ordinary sequence of events touches higher time, and therefore without recognizing any privileged persons or agencies—such as kings or priests—who stand and mediate at such alleged points. This radical horizontality is precisely what is implied in the direct-access society, where each member is 'immediate to the whole'. Anderson is undoubtedly right to argue that this new understanding could not have arisen without social developments, like that of print capitalism, but he does not want to imply by this that the transformations of the social imaginary are sufficiently explained by these developments. Modern society also required transformations in the way we figure ourselves as societies. Crucial among these has been this ability to grasp society from a decentred view which is no one's. That is, the search for a truer and more authoritative perspective than my own does not lead me to centre society on a king or sacred assembly, or whatever, but allows for this lateral, horizontal view, which an unsituated observer might have—society as it might be laid out in a tableau without privileged nodal points. There is a close inner link between modern direct-access societies, their self-understandings, their refraction in categorical identities, and modern synoptic modes of representation in the 'Age of the World Picture':[4] society as simultaneous happenings, social interchange as impersonal 'system', the social

---

3  Anderson, op. cit., p. 37.
4  Martin Heidegger, 'Die Zeit des Wtlbildes', in *Holzwege* (Niemeyer: Frankfurt).

terrain as what is mapped, historical culture as what shows up in museums, etc.[5]

The horizontal, direct-access society, given political form by an act of the people, forms the background to the contemporary sources of legitimate government in the will of the people. This principle is getting harder and harder to gainsay in the modern world. It comes close to being the only acceptable basis for any regime that does not declare itself as merely temporary or transitional, with the partial exception of so-called 'Islamic' regimes—although this does not prevent it from being used to justify the most terrible tyrannies. Communist regimes were also supposedly based on popular sovereignty, and Fascism was supposed to emanate from the united will of a conquering people.

Now this has certain functional requirements. Let us first of all take the case where the attempt is made to live out the principle of popular sovereignty through a representative democracy. Now the nature of this kind of society, as with any other free society, is that it requires a certain degree of commitment on the part of its citizens. Traditional despotisms could ask of people only that they remain passive and obey the laws. A democracy, ancient or modern, has to ask more. It requires that its members be motivated to make the necessary contributions: of treasure (in taxes), sometimes blood (in war), and always of some degree of participation in the process of governance. A free society has to substitute for despotic enforcement with a certain degree of self-enforcement. Where this fails, the system is in danger. For instance, democratic societies where the level of participation falls below a certain threshold cease to be legitimate in the eyes of their members. A government elected in a turnout of twenty per cent cannot claim to have the mandate of the people. It can only claim to have got there by the rules, which is a much weaker defence if ever it affronts a crisis.

Democracies require a relatively strong commitment on the part of their citizens. In terms of identity, being citizens has to rate as an important component of who they are. I am speaking in general, of course; in any society, there will be a wide gamut of cases,

[5] Craig Calhoun, 'Nationalism and Civil Society: Democracy, Diversity and Self-Determination', in *Social Theory and the Politics of Identity* (Blackwell: Oxford, 1994), ch. 11, pp 234–5. I want to reiterate how much the discussion in this section owes to Calhoun's recent work.

stretching from the most gung-ho and motivated to the most turned-off internal exiles. But the median point of this gamut has to fall closer to the upper than the lower limit. This membership has got to be one that matters. In particular, it has to matter more than the things that can divide the citizens.

In other words, the modern democratic state needs a healthy degree of what used to be called patriotism, a strong sense of identification with the polity, and a willingness to give of oneself for its sake. That is why these states try to inculcate patriotism, and to create a strong sense of common identity even where it did not previously exist. And that is why one thrust of modern democracy has been to try to shift the balance within the identity of the modern citizen, so that being a citizen will take precedence over a host of other poles of identity, such as family, class, gender, even (perhaps especially) religion. This may be promoted in a deliberate way, on the basis of an express ideology, as in the case of French Republicanism. Or it may be fostered in more indirect ways, as a consequence of the injunction to render other modes of description—gender, race, religion, etc.—irrelevant in the operation of public life.[6]

This has been one of the motivations for secularism of the independent ethic mode. State-builders reached for it as a potential common point of allegiance for citizens, above and beyond their other differences, in the recognition that the democratic state requires such a strong common allegiance. This attempt is likely to fail, as I argued above. The supposedly binding identity around an independent ethic itself can become a source of division. But this excursus into the nature of modern democracies can serve to

---

[6] I have not discussed the case of non-democratic regimes based on popular will, but these plainly push in the same direction, indeed, even farther and faster. Just because emanating from the common will is essential to their legitimacy, they cannot leave their citizens alone in a condition of obedient passivity, as earlier despotic regimes were content to do. They must always mobilize them into repeated expressions of unshakable, unanimous will: phony elections, demonstrations, May Day parades, and the like. This is the essence of modern 'totalitarianism' in its distinction from earlier despotism.

Calhoun stresses, however, how easily the search for national identity, even in democratic contexts, leads to an attempt to induce people to suppress their other (gender, religious, minority-cultural) identities in favour of a 'national' one. The modern quest for patriotism is full of dangers.

show how some form of secularism becomes indispensable, even while the temptation to depart from it may be very strong.

Both the need and the temptation come from the same source. Modern democracies require a 'people', that is, a citizen body which is supposedly sovereign, and that therefore must see itself (a) as made up of roughly equal and autonomous members, while being (b) bonded together in this common enterprise of self-rule. Their sense of legitimacy depends on meeting these requirements. Democratic legitimacy requires that the laws we live under in some sense result from our collective decisions. The people for these purposes is thought to form a collective unit of decision. But we do more than decide on issues that are already clear-cut. If that were the case, the best way to do things would be to put everything to a referendum. We also have to deliberate, clarify things, make up our minds, so that the people also has to be conceived as a collective unit of deliberation. Now in the meaning of the act, the people is also seen as made up of equal and autonomous members. Because to the extent that this is not the case, and that some are dependent on others, the decision would be held to emanate from the influential part, and not from the whole people. If we put these two together, we have the idea of a process of deliberation and decision in which everybody can be heard. Of course, if we were very exigent, this would always turn out to be utopian. Indeed, democratic societies are usually satisfied with some approximation in principle to this norm. But if it appears that in some systematic way, there are obstacles to certain sections of the population being heard, then the legitimacy of democratic rule in that society is under challenge.

Now, there are a number of ways in which a case can be made out that a certain segment of the population is being systematically unheard. A case of this kind was made on behalf of the working class in earlier times; it could be made today with great plausibility on behalf of the non-working, marginalized poor, and is often vigorously made on behalf of women. What concerns me here is the way that a case of this kind can be made in relation to an ethnic, linguistic, or religious group. A minority group can come to feel (a) that their way of seeing things is different from that of the majority, (b) that this is generally not understood or recognized by the majority, (c) that consequently the majority is not willing to alter the terms of the debate to accommodate this difference, and therefore (d) that the minority is being systematically unheard. Their voice cannot really penetrate the public debate. They are not really part of the deliberative unit. When this is so, the political society will cease to be fully legitimate in their eyes; and in drawing this conclusion, they will be following the logic of popular sovereignty itself.

This is why secularism in some form is a necessity for the democratic life of religiously diverse societies. Both the sense of mutual bonding and the crucial reference points of the political debate that flow from it have to be accessible to citizens of different confessional allegiances, or of none. If the people in this sense were to be confessionally defined, then non-members would be excluded in fact from full participation in self-rule. Not only would they be defined outside the bonded group, but their alternative outlook and perspectives would be by definition accorded a lesser legitimacy. They would not be full members of the sovereign. But this kind of exclusion can also be a temptation. Just because a successful democracy requires bonding in the way I have been describing, there can be an all-but-irresistible pull to build the common identity around the things that strongly unite people, and these are frequently ethnic or religious identities. The very functional requirement of a democratic 'people' that seems to make secularism indispensable can be turned around and used to reject it.

The history of the Indian republic is a case in point. The Nehru–Gandhi secularism was of the common ground variety (although Nehru himself, unlike Gandhi, had some sympathy for the independent ethic of Western Enlightenment). Religiously inspired ethics, like non-violence, had a strong presence. Even though not 'established', they helped set the terms of the debate. The state was not averse to having recourse to historical religious symbols and figures, like King Ashoka. But what was supposed to draw people together was a sense of India as an historically continuing civilization, which had been able to contain and partly absorb so many different religions and languages. But there was always a strand for which India meant or ought to mean the society of the Hindus. On this understanding, democracy had to mean Hindu Raj. This movement has now become powerful in the form of the Bharatiya Janata Party (BJP). This kind of 'nationalism' is a quintessentially modern phenomenon. It draws on popular sovereignty as a legitimating ideal. The claim it is trying to make is that the people of India, the group bonded into a unit of self-rule, is essentially defined by its Hindu origin. Because it has not yet gone all the way in exclusion, if feels a need to find some way of incorporating minorities. They have only to accept the historic predominance of Hinduism. But in fact this mode of national identity gravitates ineluctably towards a point where the non-Hindu is a total non-member. And when this point arises, a democratic anomaly exists. There are residents who have been residents for centuries and who have no part in democratic self-rule. The obvious shift at this point is to claim that they really belong somewhere else—Pakistan, for instance.

I do not want to dwell further on the case of Hindu chauvinist movements. I use it only to illustrate how the modern democratic age makes secular regimes necessary, just in virtue of the require-ments of democratic legitimacy itself. It is not that there are no alternatives. Indeed, they can look more tempting. Instead of building an inclusive people around a sense of identity to which all have access, it can seem more expedient, even historically right, to take a communal identity to nationhood. The problem is that the requirements of democratic legitimacy then place the minori-ties in an anomalous position, which can only in the end be 'finally' resolved by removal, emigration, or worse. Things were very different in the good old days of hierarchical mediated-access societies. Here each community had its own niche which, while not on a footing of equality with others, was nevertheless recog-nized and safe. But democracy no longer recognizes such niches. One can only be a member of the sovereign or a resident alien. And that is not a status which a community can have over generations.[7]

Consequently, the logic of non-secular or exclusionary regimes in the democratic age is frightening. The anomaly of the minority is hard to tolerate. They are a perpetual source of objection to our legitimacy. And, moreover, if they were to increase in numbers, they might even take over and alter the regime. The temptation to expel can become very powerful. In the absence of inclusionary

---

[7] Hence the unease experienced around the situation of *Gastarbeiter* in certain European countries, like Germany, who appear to be settling into residence over many generations, but still are not being given citizenship. Hence also the anomalous position of Israel and South Africa before the recent political changes in both these countries.

definitions of the people, of modes of coexistence around commonly accessible identities—which secularism among other contemporary forms tries to facilitate—the logic of democracy can become that of ethnic cleansing. The end of hierarchy is not of itself the dawn of liberalism. Rather it ups the ante: either the civilized coexistence of diverse groups, or new forms of savagery. It is in this sense that secularism is not optional in the modern age.

## III

After this excursus, I want to return briefly to discuss the mode of secularism which I called after Rawls' 'overlapping consensus'. I think political philosophy is greatly in Rawls' debt for the definition of this term. It provides a way beyond the two previously existing models of secular regimes which increasing diversity was bringing, each in its own way, under steadily greater strain. Existing common grounds were no longer really accessible to people whose moral and spiritual backgrounds were in non-Western civilizations. While at the same time, the post-Enlightenment independent ethic risked being understood as just one spiritual family among many striving for 'establishment' at the expense of others.

The development of secularism probably lies in a third direction. As with the independent ethic, the ground of convergence will be a set of politico-ethical principles and goods. These will typically include a charter of rights, attributed first to individuals, but also in certain cases to communities. These rights attach to citizenship, and are therefore to be enjoyed equally. The political ethic will also typically be a democratic one, entrenching popular sovereignty as the basis of legitimacy, and valuing political freedom, in Tocqueville's sense. In addition, liberal regimes also give a positive value to individual negative freedom, both as a negative injunction against interference by the state or other powerful agencies, and sometimes also positively enjoining society to help provide some of the conditions for full individual self-development and self-expression.

This political ethic will typically not exhaust the common identity by which the people are bound together. This will also include some particularistic elements—of history, language, culture, even in come cases religion. But it does give expression to something like the ethical core of modern democratic patriotism. If not every society is bonded by a *Verfassungspatriotismus* in the pure sense (indeed, is any society purely so bonded?), at least liberal democracies have a substantial ethical component in their definition of national identity. The previous paragraph is an attempt to gesture at some of the essential features of this component.

But unlike the earlier independent ethic, it will be understood that this ground of convergence does not stand on its own. It is essential to the overlapping consensus that it be generally understood that there is more than one set of valid reasons for signing on to it. For instance, the right to life—which will be further defined legally in terms of a set of rights guaranteeing against arbitrary arrest or punishment, and connected to various rights of free exercise. This can be grounded in an Enlightenment-inspired doctrine of the dignity of human beings as rational agents. But it can also be underpinned by a religious perspective in which humans are seen as made in the image and likeness of God. Or instead of this typically Jewish or Christian perspective, a Buddhist may draw strong reasons to uphold rights of this kind from a certain reading of the ethical demand of non-violence.[8] We could continue the list indefinitely. What the convergence is around is the moral imperative to respect the integrity and freedom of human beings, however the underlying reasons for this may vary.

But put this way, it sounds a lot simpler than it is (even though, put just this way, it is far from easy to attain). The formula involves distinguishing the ethic converged on from the underlying reasons. In Rawls' language, we distinguish justice as fairness from the comprehensive notions of the good in which it is embedded. But these two do not always come apart that easily. In particular, what looks like the same schedule of rights may easily be understood somewhat differently when set against the background of these different views. The basic fact underlying this diversity is that a political ethic does not interpret itself, any more than a charter of rights does. As it extends to further cases, it will be interpreted in the light of the entire background of justification from which it

---

8 Vitit Muntabhorn and Charles Taylor, *Report on Human Rights and Democratic Development in Thailand* (Montreal Centre for Human Rights and Democratic Development: Montreal, 1994).

springs. When there are several such backgrounds, the interpretations are going to diverge, often seriously.

We already see this with our abortion debates in some Western societies, where the generally accepted 'right to life' is given a very different meaning by people with a different basic understanding of human agency and its place in the universe or in God's plan. In a society conceived as an overlapping consensus, this kind of dissensus will ineluctably become more common.

How are these differences to be adjudicated? The answer is that there is no canonical body of thought, or corpus of doctrine against which to make the decision. Or, rather, there are too many of them. This was the advantage of the older models, common ground or independent ethic. They could offer such an agreed matrix. Of course, we still ended up disagreeing, but at least we had the comforting assurance that we agree where the answer is to be found. Authoritative adjudication by experts in the certain body of law provides this kind of assurance. This facilitates acquiescence even by those who lose out in any given decision, because at least they accept and respect that in the name of which the decision is taken.

Under overlapping consensus, we have to get used to cases where this kind of justification from the background corpus can no longer be the basis for authoritative political decisions. At certain points, where the shape and limits of the ethic converge or come into dispute, we will have to proceed by persuasion indeed, but also by a certain degree of negotiated compromise. Not all of us will be able to enshrine just the catalogue of rights that we can justify out of our background philosophy. Of course, most of us cannot even today. But we take this as an invitation to go on arguing with our compatriots out of our supposedly shared premises; in genuinely diverse societies under overlapping consensus, this may no longer be the appropriate move.

Not that debate and intellectual confrontation should ever cease. It is open to me to try to convince a Buddhist, a Muslim, or an unbeliever, that they could see their Buddhism, Islam, humanism differently, and thus accept different consequences. They should be ready to return the favour. This kind of debate is even essential to a healthy society under diversity and is both sign and support of real mutual respect among people of different fundamental commitments. The kind of pale 'ecumenicism' where each feels constrained from speaking about the other's views is actually a way of preserving, under the mothballs of respectful silence, all the old misconceptions and contempt. But nevertheless, in the political arena, we have to operate on the assumption that disagreement will continue, that there will be no agreement on the authoritative canon for adjudication. And this means that we will have to live with compromises between two or more such views. That is, this will have to be understood as not an abnormal, scandalous, and hopefully temporary shift, but as the normal state of affairs for the indefinite future.

(One might indeed argue that the abortion debate will have to come to be seen in the light of, and not as a battle against those who have perverted some manifestly evident commonly endorsed principle, before we can learn to live with one another in spite of our disagreements. Some Western societies seem to have come closer to this, and hence to a liveable compromise on abortion than others. But where the very notion of compromise seems unconscionable, then it is possible for some unbalanced souls to be excited even to the point of murder. This is not a formula for liberal democracy.)

This is where I would like to suggest certain modifications in Rawls' conception of the overlapping consensus. The way I am putting it, the formula means that we converge on some political principles, but not on our background reasons for endorsing these. Rawls rightly distinguishes the overlapping consensus from a mere 'modus vivendi'. The latter implies that we can agree to act together on some basis, but do not necessarily see this as morally binding. Maybe we can agree to respect one another just because the balance of forces will make any attempt to deviate from this terribly destructive. But if we ever get stronger, well then....

But the overlapping consensus holds when we feel ourselves morally bound to the convergent principles. What makes it overlapping is that the underlying reasons are different. Here I would argue that Rawls still tries to hold on to too much of the older independent ethic. He sees a liberal society as converging on justice as fairness. But he defines this, not just in terms of the principles of justice as guides for action, but also in terms of the rationale for these, in a doctrine of political constructivism, reasonable mutual expectations, and just terms of cooperation. This seems to me to be asking for too much. The whole point of the overlapping consensus—better put, its superiority as a basis for society over the old post-Enlightenment independent ethic—was just that it does not prescribe any underlying justification. These are left to the different spiritual families whose members make up society. The slogan should rather be: Let people subscribe for whatever reasons they find compelling, only let them subscribe.

This enshrining of the background reasoning in the overlap allows Rawls to draw rather fine interpretations out of his principles. Thus in a footnote to *Political Liberalism*, Rawls offers a view of the appropriate abortion legislation which allegedly flows from the principles.[9] But it is clear that this could not be concurred as such by a great many of the spiritual outlooks whose adherents one would nevertheless hope to see subscribing to the convergent ethic. That is, it could not be agreed to as what justice demands simpliciter—although one could imagine people coming to this kind of position as a reasonable compromise.

(Another area in which it will no longer be possible to apply a single background justification rigidly is that centrepiece of secularism, the separation of church and state. Some kind of distancing is obviously required by the very principle of equidistance and inclusion which is of the essence of secularism. But there is more than one formula that can satisfy this. Complete disentanglement of government from any religious institutions is one such, but far from the only one. One may decide that separation forbids the funding of confessional schools out of taxes; but it may also be that the best solution is to fund many such schools on a fair basis. To insist on one formula, as the only one consistent with 'liberal' principles is precisely to erect one background justification as supreme and binding on all, thus violating the essential point of the overlapping consensus. The US provides an unfortunate example of this.)

The secularism of overlapping consensus will thus be susceptible to conflicts of a new kind—or perhaps to a multiplication of these conflicts which up to now have seemed rare and abnormal (like the abortion debate). It will be hard to manage. It will require a change of our mindset, away from the highly charged moralism which will only settle for the single right answer generated from

9 John Rawls, *Political Liberalism* (Columbia University Press: New York, 1993), p. 243, n32.

unchallenged foundational principles—a mindset which has been all too common among liberals nourished on a post-Enlightenment independent ethic.

But what emerges from the above discussion—at least, this is my view—is that this is the only form of secularism available to us in the diverse societies of today. The two earlier forms, which emerge out of the evolution of secular societies in Western history, are for different reasons no longer viable. But since, as I argued in the second section, secularism is not an optional extra for a modern democracy, we have no choice but to make a go of its only available mode. Whether we like it or not, the overlapping consensus has got to be made to work.

# 2

# The Difficulty of Tolerance*

*T.M. Scanlon*

## What is Tolerance?

Tolerance requires us to accept people and permit their practices even when we strongly disapprove of them. Tolerance thus involves an attitude that is intermediate between wholehearted acceptance and unrestrained opposition.[1] This intermediate status makes tolerance a puzzling attitude. There are certain things, such as murder, that ought not to be tolerated. There are limits to what we are able to do to prevent these things from happening, but we need not restrain ourselves out of tolerance for these actions as expressions of the perpetrators' values. In other cases, where our feelings of opposition or disapproval should properly be reined in, it would be better if we were to rid ourselves of these feelings altogether. If we are moved by racial or ethnic prejudice, for example, the preferred remedy is not merely to tolerate those whom we abhor, but to stop abhorring people just because they look different or come from a different background.

Perhaps everything would, ideally, fall into one or the other of these two classes. Except where wholehearted disapproval and opposition are appropriate, as in the case of murder, it would be best if the feelings that generate conflict and disagreement could be eliminated altogether. Tolerance, as an attitude that requires us

* I am grateful to Joshua Cohen and Will Kymlicka for their helpful comments on earlier drafts of this article.
1 As John Horton points out in his contribution in David Heyd (ed.), *Tolerance: An Exclusive Virtue*, (Princeton University Press: Princeton, New Jersey, 1997).

to hold in check certain feelings of opposition and disapproval, would then be just a second best—a way of dealing with attitudes that we would be better off without but that are, unfortunately, ineliminable. To say this would not be to condemn tolerance. Even if it is, in this sense, a second best, the widespread adoption of tolerant attitudes would be a vast improvement over the sectarian bloodshed that we hear of every day in many parts of the globe. Stemming this violence would be no mean feat.

Still, it seems to me that there are pure cases of tolerance, in which it is not merely an expedient for dealing with the imperfections of human nature. These would be cases in which persisting conflict and disagreement are to be expected and are, unlike racial prejudice, quite compatible with full respect for those with whom we disagree. But while respect for one another does not require us to abandon our disagreement, it does place limits on how this conflict can be pursued. In this article, I want to investigate the possibility of pure tolerance of this kind, with the aim of better understanding our idea of tolerance and the difficulty of achieving it. Because I particularly want to see more clearly why it is a difficult attitude and practice to sustain, I will try to concentrate on cases in which I myself find tolerance difficult. I begin with the familiar example of religious toleration, which provides the model for most of our thinking about toleration of other kinds.

Widespread acceptance of the idea of religious toleration is, at least in North America and Europe, a historical legacy of the European Wars of Religion. Today, religious toleration is widely acknowledged as an ideal, even though there are many places in the world where, even as we speak, blood is being spilled over what are, at least, partly religious divisions.

As a person for whom religion is a matter of no personal importance whatever, it seems easy for me, at least at the outset, to endorse religious toleration. At least this is so when toleration is understood in terms of the twin principles of the First Amendment to the Constitution of the US: 'Congress shall make no law respecting an establishment of religion, or prohibiting the free exercise thereof.' Accepting these principles seems to be all benefit and no cost from my point of view. Why should I want to interfere with other people's religious practice, provided that they are not able to impose that practice on me? If religious toleration has costs, I am inclined to say, they are borne by others, not by me.

So it seems at first (although I will later argue that this is a mistake) that for me religious toleration lacks the tension I just described: I do not feel the opposition it tells me to hold in check. Why should I want to tell others what religion to practice, or to have one established as our official creed? On the other hand, for those who do want these things, religious toleration seems to demand a great deal: if I thought it terribly important that everyone worship in the correct way, how could I accept toleration except as an uneasy truce, acceptable as an alternative to perpetual bloodshed, but even so a necessity that is to be regretted? Pure toleration seems to have escaped us.

I want to argue that this view of things is mistaken.[Tolerance involves costs and dangers for all of us, but it is nonetheless an attitude that we all have reason to value.]

## What Does Toleration Require?

This is a difficult question to answer, in part because there is more than one equally good answer, in part because any good answer will be vague in important respects. Part of any answer is legal and political. Tolerance requires that people who fall on the 'wrong' side of the differences I have mentioned, should not for that reason be denied legal and political rights: the right to vote, to hold office, to benefit from the central public goods that are otherwise open to all, such as education, public safety, the protections of the legal system, health care, and access to 'public accommodation'. In addition, it requires that the state not give preference to one group over another in the distribution of privileges and benefits.

It is this part of the answer that seems to me to admit of more than one version. For example, in the US the requirement that each religious group is equally entitled to the protections and benefits conferred by the state is interpreted to mean that the state may not support, financially or otherwise, any religious organization. The main exception, not an insignificant one, is that any religious organization can qualify for tax-exempt status. So even our idea of 'non-establishment' represents a mixed strategy: some forms of support are prohibited for *any* religion, others are allowed provided they are available for *all* religions. This mixture strikes me more as a particular political compromise than as a solution uniquely required by the idea of religious toleration. A society in which there was a religious qualification for holding public office could not be accounted tolerant or just. But I would not say the same about just any form of state support for religious practice. In Great Britain, for example, there is an established church, and the state supports denominational as well as non-denominational schools. In my view, the range of these schools is too narrow to reflect the religious diversity of contemporary Britain, but I do not see that just any system of this kind is to be faulted as lacking in toleration. Even if it would be intolerant to give one religion certain special forms of support, there are many different acceptable mixtures of what is denied to every religion and what is available to all. The particular mixture that is now accepted in the US is not the only just solution.

This indeterminacy extends even to the area of freedom of expression, which will be particularly important in what follows. Any just and tolerant society must protect freedom of expression. This does not mean merely that censorship is ruled out, but requires as well that individuals and groups have some effective means of bringing their views before the public. There are, however, many ways of doing this.[2] There are, for example, many ways of defining and regulating a 'public forum', and no one of these is specifically required. Permitted and protected modes of expression need not be the same everywhere.

Let me now move from the most clearly institutional aspects of toleration to the less institutional and more attitudinal, thereby moving from the indeterminate to the vague. I have said that toleration involves 'accepting as equals' those who differ from us. In what I have said so far, this equality has meant equal possession of fundamental legal and political rights, but the ideal of equality that toleration involves goes beyond these particular rights. It

[2] More exactly, there are many ways of trying to do it. I believe that our ideas of freedom of expression must be understood in terms of a commitment both to certain goals and to the idea of certain institutional arrangements as crucial means to those goals. But the means are never fully adequate to the goals, which drive their constant evolution. I discuss this 'creative instability' in 'Content Regulation Reconsidered', in J. Lichtenberg (ed.), *Democracy and the Mass Media* (Cambridge University Press: New York, 1991).

might be stated as follows: all members of society are equally entitled to be taken into account in defining what our society is and equally entitled to participate in determining what it will become in the future. This idea is unavoidably vague and difficult to accept. It is difficult to accept in so far as it applies to those who differ from us or disagree with us, and who would make our society something other than what we want it to be. It is vague because of the difficulty of saying exactly what this 'equal entitlement' involves. One mode of participation is, of course, through the formal politics of voting, running for office, and trying to enlist votes for the laws and policies that one favours. But what I now want to stress is the way in which the requirements of toleration go beyond this realm of formal politics into what might be called the informal politics of social life.

The competition among religious groups is a clear example of this informal politics, but it is only one example. Other groups and individuals engage in the same political struggle all the time: we set and follow examples, seek to be recognized or have our standard-bearers recognized in every aspect of cultural and popular life. A tolerant society, I want to say, is one that is democratic in its informal politics. This democracy is a matter of law and institutions (a matter, for example, of the regulation of expression). But it is also, importantly and irreducibly, a matter of attitude. Toleration of this kind is not easy to accept—it is risky and frightening—and it is not easy to achieve, even in one's own attitudes, let alone in society as a whole.

To explain what I have in mind, it is easiest to begin with some familiar controversies over freedom of expression and over 'the enforcement of morals'. The desire to prevent those with whom one disagrees from influencing the evolution of one's society has been a principal motive for restricting expression—for example, for restricting religious proselytizing and restricting the sale of publications dealing with sex, even when these are not sold or used in a way that forces others to see them. This motive supports not only censorship but also the kind of regulation of private conduct that raises the issue of 'the enforcement of morals'. Sexual relations between consenting adults in the privacy of their bedrooms are not 'expression', but it is no mistake to see attempts to regulate such conduct and attempts to regulate expression as closely related. In both cases, what the enforcers want is to prevent the spread of certain forms of behaviour and attitude both by deterring it and, at least as important, by using the criminal law to make an authoritative statement of social disapproval.

One form of liberal response has been to deny the legitimacy of any interest in 'protecting society' from certain forms of change. (The analogue of declaring religion to be purely a private matter.) This response seems to me to be mistaken.[3] We all have a profound interest in how prevailing customs and practices evolve. Certainly, I myself have such an interest, and I do not regard it as illegitimate. I do not care whether other people, individually, go swimming in the nude or not, but I do not want my society to become one in which nude bathing becomes so much the norm that I cannot wear a swimsuit without attracting stares and feeling embarrassed. I have no desire to dictate what others, individually, in couples, or in groups, do in their bedrooms, but I would much prefer to live in a society in which sexuality and sexual attractiveness, of whatever kind, was given less importance than it is in our society today. I do not care what others read and listen to, but I would like my society to be one in which there are at least a significant number of people who know and admire the same literature and music that I do, so that that music will be generally available, and so that there will be others to share my sense of its value.

Considered in this light, religious toleration has much greater risks for me than I suggested at the beginning of this article: I am content to leave others to the religious practices of their choice provided that they leave me free to enjoy none. But I will be very unhappy if this leads in time to my society becoming one in which almost everyone is, in one way or another, deeply religious, and in which religion plays a central part in all public discourse. Moreover, I would feel this way even if I were to continue to enjoy the firm protection of the First Amendment. What I fear is not merely the legal enforcement of religion but its social predominance.

So I see nothing mistaken or illegitimate about at least some of the *concerns* that have moved those who advocate the legal enforcement of morals or who seek to restrict expression in order to prevent what they see as the deterioration of their society. I might disagree with them in substance, but I would not say that concerns of this kind are ones that anyone should or could avoid

---

[3] Here I draw on points made in section 5 of my article, 'Freedom of Expression and Categories of Expression', *University of Pittsburgh Law Review* 40 (1979), pp 479–520.

having. What is objectionable about the 'legal enforcement of morals' is the attempt to restrict individuals' personal lives as a way of controlling the evolution of mores. Legal moralism is an example of intolerance, for example when it uses the criminal law to deny that homosexuals are legitimate participants in the informal politics of society.

I have not tried to say how this informal politics might be regulated. My aims have been, rather, to illustrate what I mean by informal politics, to point out what I take to be its great importance to all of us, and to suggest that for this reason toleration is, for all of us, a risky matter, a practice with high stakes.

## The Value of Tolerance

Why, then, value tolerance? The answer lies, I believe, in the relation with one's fellow citizens that tolerance makes possible. It is easy to see that a tolerant person and an intolerant one have different attitudes toward those in society with whom they disagree. The tolerant person's attitude is this:

Even though we disagree, they are as fully members of society as I am. They are as entitled as I am to the protections of the law, as entitled as I am to live as they choose to live. In addition (and this is the hard part) neither their way of living nor mine is uniquely *the* way of our society. These are merely two among the potentially many different outlooks that our society can include, each of which is equally entitled to be expressed in living as one mode of life that others can adopt. If one view is at any moment numerically or culturally predominant, this should be determined by, and dependent on, the accumulated choices of individual members of the society at large.

Intolerant individuals deny this. They claim a special place for their own values and way of life. Those who live in a different way—Turks in Germany, for example Muslims in India, and homosexuals in some parts of the US—are, in their view, not full members of their society, and the intolerant claim the right to suppress these other ways of living in the name of protecting their society and 'its' values. They seek to do this either by the force of criminal law or by denying forms of public support that other groups enjoy, such as public subsidies for the arts.

What I have just provided is description, not argument. But the first way of making the case for tolerance is simply to point out, on the basis of this description, that tolerance involves a more attractive and appealing relation between opposing groups within a society. Any society, no matter how homogeneous, will include people who disagree about how to live and about what they want their society to be like. (And the disagreements within a relatively homogeneous culture can be more intense than those within a society founded on diversity, like the US.) Given that there must be disagreements, and that those who disagree must somehow live together, is it not better, if possible, to have these disagreements contained within a framework of mutual respect? The alternative, it seems, is to be always in conflict, even at the deepest level, with a large number of one's fellow citizens. The qualification 'even at the deepest level' is crucial here. I am assuming that in any society there will over time be conflicts, serious ones, about the nature and direction of the society. What tolerance expresses is a recognition of common membership that is deeper than these conflicts, a recognition of others as being just as entitled as we are to contribute to the definition of our society. Without this, we are just rival groups contending over the same territory. The fact that each of us, for good historical and personal reasons, regards it as *our* territory and *our* tradition just deepens the conflict.

Whether or not one accepts it as sufficient justification for tolerance, the difference that tolerance makes in one's relation to those who are 'different' is easy to see. What is less obvious, but at least as important, is the difference tolerance makes in one's relation with those to whom one is closest. One's children provide the clearest case. As my children, they are as fully members of our society as I am. It is their society just as much as it is mine. What one learns as a parent, however, is that there is no guarantee that the society they will want is the same one that I want. Intolerance implies that their right to live as they choose and to influence others to do so is conditional on their agreement with me about what the right way to live is. If I believe that others, in so far as they disagree with me, are not as entitled as I am to shape the mores of our common society, then I must think this of my children as well, should they join this opposition. Perhaps I hold that simply being *my children* gives them special political standing. But this seems to me unlikely. More likely, I think, is that this example brings out the fact that intolerance involves a denial of full membership to 'others'. What is special about one's children is, in this case, just that their membership is impossible to deny. But intolerance forces one to deny it, by making it conditional on substantive agreement with one's own values.

My argument so far is that the case for tolerance lies in the fact that rejecting it involves a form of alienation from one's fellow citizens. It is important to recognize, however, that the strength of this argument depends on the fact that we are talking about membership in 'society' as a political unit. This can be brought out by considering how the argument for tolerance would apply within a private association, such as a church or political move-ment.[4] Disagreements are bound to arise within any such group about how their shared values are to be understood. Is it then intolerant to want to exclude from the group those with divergent views, to deny them the right to participate in meetings and run for office under the party label, to deny them the sacraments, or to stop inviting them to meetings? It might be said that this also involves the kind of alienation I have described, by making others' standing as members conditional on agreement with our values. But surely groups of this kind have good reason to exclude those who disagree. Religious groups and political movements would lose their point if they had to include just anyone.

In at least one sense, the ideas of tolerance and intolerance that I have been describing do apply to private associations. As I have said, disagreements are bound to arise within such groups, and when they do it is intolerant to attempt to deny those with whom one disagrees the opportunity to persuade others to adopt their interpretation of the group's values and mission. Tolerance of this kind is required by the very idea of an association founded on a commitment to 'shared values'. In what sense would these values be 'shared' unless there were some process—like the formal and informal politics to which I have referred—through which they evolve and agreement on them is sustained?[5] But there are limits. The very meaning of the goods in question—the sacraments, the

---

[4] Here I am indebted to very helpful questions raised by Will Kymlicka. I do not know whether he would agree with my way of answering them.

[5] As Michael Walzer has written, addressing a similar question, ' When people disagree about the meaning of social goods, when understandings are contro-versial, then justice requires that the society be faithful to the disagreements, providing institutional channels for their expression, adjudicative mechanisms, and alternative distributions.' *Spheres of Justice* (Basic Books: New York, 1984), p. 313.

party label—requires that they be conditional on certain beliefs. So it is not intolerant for the group as a whole, after due deliberation, to deny these goods to those who clearly lack these beliefs.

Tolerance at the level of political society is a different matter. The goods at stake here, such as the right to vote, to hold office, and to participate in the public forum, do not lose their meaning if they are extended to people with whom we disagree about the kind of society we would like to have, or even to those who reject its most basic tenets. One can become a member of society, hence one is entitled to these goods just by being born into it (as well as in other ways), and one is required to obey its laws and institutions as long as one remains within its territory. The argument for tolerance that I have been describing is based on this idea of society and on the idea that the relation of 'fellow citizen' that it involves is one we have reason to value. The form of alienation I have mentioned occurs when the terms of this relation are violated: when we deny others, who are just as much members of our society as we are, the right to their part in defining and shaping it.[6]

As I have said, something similar can occur when we deny fellow members of a private association their rightful share in shaping it. But the relation of 'fellow member' that is violated is different from the relation of 'fellow citizen', and it is to be valued for different reasons. In particular, the reasons for valuing such a relation often entail limits on the range of its application. It would be absurd, for example, for Presbyterians to consider everyone born within the fifty states of the US a member of their church, and it would therefore not be intolerant to deny some of them the right to participate in the evolution of this institution. But the relation of 'fellow citizen' is supposed to link at least everyone born into a society and remaining within its borders. So it does not entail and is in fact incompatible with any narrower limits.

## The Difficulty of Tolerance

Examples of intolerance are all around us. To cite a few recent examples from the US: there are the referenda against gay rights

---

6 Intolerance can also be manifested when we deny others the opportunity to *become* members on racial or cultural grounds. But it would take me too far a field to discuss here the limits on just immigration and naturalization policies.

in Oregon and Coloardo, attempts by Senator Jesse Helms and others to prevent the National Endowment for the Arts and the National Endowment for the Humanities from supporting projects of which they (Helms et al.) disapprove, recent statements by the governor of Mississippi that 'America is a Christian nation', and similar statements in the speeches at the 1992 Republican National Convention by representatives of the Christian right.

But it is easy to see intolerance in one's opponents and harder to avoid it oneself. I am thinking here, for example, of my reactions to recurrent controversies in the US over the teaching of evolution and 'creation science' in public schools, and to the proposal to amend the Constitution if necessary in order to allow organized prayer in public schools. I firmly believe that 'creation science' is bogus and that science classes should not present scientific theory and religious doctrine as alternatives with similar and equal claim to the same kind of assent. I therefore do not think that it is intolerant *per se* to oppose the creationists. But I confess to feeling a certain sense of partisan zeal in such cases; a sense of superiority over the people who propose such things and a desire not to let them win a point even if it did not cost anyone very much. In the case of science teaching, there is a cost, as there is in the case of school prayer. But I am also inclined to support removing 'In God We Trust' from our coinage and to favour discontinuing the practice of prayer at public events.

These changes appeal to me because they would make the official symbolism of our country more thoroughly secular, hence more in line with my own outlook, and I can also claim that they represent a more consistent adherence to the constitutional principle of 'non-establishment' of religion. Others see these two reasons as inconsistent. In their view, I am not simply removing a partisan statement from our official symbolism, but also at the same time replacing it with another; I am not making our public practice neutral as between secularism and religiosity but asking for an official step that would further enthrone secularism (which is already 'officially endorsed' in many other ways, they would say) as our national outlook. I have to admit that, whatever the right answer to the constitutional question might be (and it might be indeterminate), this response has more than a little truth to it when taken as an account of my motives, which are strongly partisan.

But why should they not be partisan? It might seem that here I am going too far, bending over backwards in the characteristically liberal way. After all, the argument that in asking to have this slogan removed from our money I am asking for the official endorsement of *ir*religiosity is at best indirect and not really very persuasive. Whereas the slogan itself does have that aggressively inclusive, hence potentially exclusive 'we': 'In God *We* Trust' (Who do you mean by 'we'?).

Does this mean that in a truly tolerant society there could be no public declarations of this kind, no advocacy or enforcement by the state of any particular doctrine? Not even tolerance itself? This seems absurd. Let me consider the matter in stages.

First, is it intolerant to enforce tolerance in behaviour and prevent the intolerant from acting on their beliefs? Surely not. The rights of the persecuted demand this protection, and the demand to be tolerated cannot amount to a demand to do whatever one believes one must.

Second, is it intolerant to espouse tolerance as an official doctrine? We could put it on our coins: 'In Tolerance We Trust'. (Not a bad slogan, I think, although it would have to be pronounced carefully.) Is it intolerant to have tolerance taught in state schools and supported in state-sponsored advertising campaigns? Surely not, and again for the same reasons. The advocacy of tolerance denies no one their rightful place in society. It grants to each person and group as much standing as they can claim while granting the same to others.

Finally, is it contrary to tolerance to deny the intolerant the opportunities that others have to state their views? This would seem to deny them a standing that others have. Yet to demand that we tolerate the intolerant in even this way seems to demand an attitude that is almost unattainable. If a group maintains that I and the people who like me simply have no place in our society, that we must leave or be eliminated, how can I regard this as a point of view among others that is equally entitled to be heard and considered in our informal (or even formal) politics? To demand this attitude seems to be to demand too much.

If toleration is to make sense, then we must distinguish between one's attitude toward what is advocated by one's opponents and one's attitude toward those opponents themselves: it is not that their *point of view* is entitled to be represented but that *they* (as fellow citizens, not as holders of that point of view) are entitled to be heard. So I have fought my way to the ringing statement attributed to Voltaire, that is, to a platitude.[7] But in the context of our discussion, I believe that this is not only a platitude but also the location of a difficulty, or several difficulties.

What Voltaire's statement reminds us is that the attitude towards others that tolerance requires must be understood in terms of specific rights and protections. He mentions the right to speak, but this is only one example. The vague recognition of others as equally entitled to contribute to informal politics, as well as to the more formal kind, can be made more definite by listing specific rights to speak, to set an example through one's conduct, to have one's way of life recognized through specific forms of official support. To this we need to add the specification of kinds of support that *no* way of life can demand, such as prohibiting conduct by others simply because one disapproves of it. These specifications give the attitude of tolerance more definite content and make it more tenable. One *can* be asked (or so I believe) to recognize that others have these specific rights no matter how strongly one takes exception to what they say. This move reduces what I earlier called the vagueness of the attitude of tolerance, but leaves us with what I called the indeterminacy of more formal rights. This residual indeterminacy involves two problems.

The first is conceptual. Although some specification of rights and limits of exemplification and advocacy is required in order to give content to the idea of tolerance and make it tenable, the idea of tolerance can never be fully identified with any particular system of such rights and limits, such as the system of rights of free speech and association, rights of privacy, and rights to free exercise (but non-establishment) of religion that are currently accepted in the US. Many different systems of rights are acceptable; none is ideal. Each is therefore constantly open to challenge and revision. What I will call the spirit of tolerance is part of what leads us to accept such a system and guides us in revising it. It is difficult to say more exactly what this spirit is, but I would describe it in part as a spirit of accommodation; a desire to find a system of rights that others

---

[7] He is said to have said, 'I disapprove of what you say, but I will defend to the death your right to say it.'

(all those within the broad reach of the relation 'fellow citizen') could also be asked to accept. It is this spirit that I suspect might be lacking in my own attitudes regarding public prayer and the imprint on our coins. I need to ask myself the question of accommodation: is strict avoidance of any reference to religion indeed the only policy I could find acceptable, or is there some other compromise between secularism and the many varieties of religious conviction that I should be willing to consider?

The second, closely related problem is political. There is little incentive to ask this question of accommodation in actual politics, and there are usually much stronger reasons, both good and bad, not to do so. Because the boundaries of tolerance are indeterminate, and accepted ways of drawing them can be portrayed as conferring legitimacy on one's opponents, the charge of intolerance is a powerful political coin.

When anyone makes a claim that I see as a threat to the standing of my group, I am likely to feel a strong desire, perhaps even an obligation, not to let it go unanswered. As I have said, I feel such a desire even in relatively trivial cases. But often, especially in non-trivial cases, one particularly effective form of response (of 'counter-speech') is to challenge the limits of the system of informal politics by claiming that one cannot be asked to accept a system that permits what others have done, and therefore demanding that the system be changed, in the name of toleration itself, so that it forbids such actions.

The pattern is a familiar one. For example, in the early 1970s, universities in the US were disrupted by protesters demanding that speeches by IQ researchers, such as Richard Herrnstein and William Schockley, be cancelled. The reason given was that allowing them to speak aided the spread of their ideas and thereby promoted the adoption of educational policies harmful to minority children. Taken at face value, this seemed irrational, because the protests themselves brought the speakers a much wider audience than they otherwise could have hoped for. But the controversy generated by these protests also gained a wider hearing for the opponents. Because 'freedom of speech' was being challenged, civil libertarians, some of them otherwise friendly to the protesters' cause, others not so friendly, rushed into the fray. The result, played out on many campuses, was a dramatic and emotional event, provoking media coverage and anguished or indignant editorials in many newspapers. Whether the challenge to the prevailing rules of tolerance made any theoretical sense or not, it made a great deal of sense as a political strategy.

Much the same analysis seems to me to apply to more recent controversies, such as those generated by campus 'hate-speech' rules and by the Indianapolis and Minneapolis anti-pornography statutes. I find it difficult to believe that adopting these regulations would do much to protect the groups in question. But *proposing them*, just because it challenges accepted and valued principles of free expression, has been a very effective way of bringing issues of racism and sexism before the minds of the larger community (even if it has also had its costs, by giving its opponents a weapon in the form of complaints about 'political correctness').

Challenging the accepted rules of tolerance is also an effective way of mobilizing support within the affected groups. As I have already said, victims of racist or anti-Semitic attacks cannot be expected to regard these as expressing 'just another point of view' that deserves to be considered in the court of public opinion. Even in more trivial cases, in which one is in no way threatened, one often fails (as I have said of myself) to distinguish between opposition to a message and the belief that allowing it to be uttered is a form of partisanship on the part of the state. It is therefore natural for the victims of hate-speech to take a willingness to ban such speech as a litmus test for the respect that they are due.[8] Even if this is an unreasonable demand, as I believe it often is, the indeterminacy and political sensitivity of standards of tolerance make it politically irresistible.

Because of the indeterminacy of such standards—because it is always to some degree an open question just what our system of toleration should be—it will not seem out of the question, even to many supporters of toleration, to demand that one specific form of conduct be prohibited in order to protect a victimized group. This can be so even when the proposed modification is in fact unfeasible because a workable system of toleration cannot offer this form of support to every group. On the other hand, because of

[8] See, for example, Mari Matsuda, 'Public Response to Racist Speech: Considering the Victim's Story', *Michigan Law Review* 87 (1989). Matsuda emphasizes that legal prohibition is sought because it represents public denunciation of the racists' position.

this same indeterminacy, a system of toleration will not work unless it is highly valued and carefully protected against erosion. This means that any proposed modification will be politically sensitive and will elicit strong opposition, hence valuable publicity for the group in question.

Moreover, once this protection has been demanded by those speaking for the group—once it has been made a litmus test of respect—it is very difficult for individual members of the group not to support that demand.[9] The result is a form of political gridlock in which the idea of tolerance is a powerful motivating force on both sides: on one side, in the form of a desire to protect potentially excluded groups; on the other, in the form of a desire to protect a workable system of tolerance. I do not have a solution to such problems. Indeed, part of my point is that the nature of tolerance makes them unavoidable. The strategy suggested by what I have said is to try, as far as possible, to prevent measures inimical to the system of tolerance from becoming 'litmus tests' of respect. Civil libertarians like me, who rush to the defence of that system, should not merely shout 'You can't do that!', but should also ask the question of accommodation: 'Are there other ways, not damaging to the system of tolerance, in which respect for the threatened group could be demonstrated?'[10]

## Conclusion

I began by considering the paradigm case of religious toleration, a doctrine that seemed at first to have little cost or risk when

[9] I am thinking here particularly of the Salman Rushdie case. Ayatollah Khomeini's demand that *The Satanic Verses* be banned was unreasonable. On the other hand, many Muslims living in Britain felt they were treated with a lack of respect by their fellow citizens. Even if they could see that the Ayatollah's demand was unreasonable, it was difficult for them not to support it once it had been issued. Here the situation was further complicated (and the appeal to 'unfeasibility' clouded) by the existence of a British blasphemy law that protected Christianity but not Islam. The result was gridlock of the kind described in the text.

[10] I do not mean to suggest that this is always called for. It depends on the case, and the group. But the difficult cases will be those in which tolerance speaks in favour of protecting the group as well as against the measure they have demanded.

viewed from the perspective of a secular liberal with secure constitutional protection against the 'establishment' of a religion. I went on to explain why toleration in general, and religious toleration in particular, is a risky policy with high stakes, even within the framework of a stable constitutional democracy. The risks involved lie not so much in the formal politics of laws and Constitutions (though there may be risks there too) but rather in the informal politics through which the nature of a society is constantly redefined. I believe in tolerance despite its risks, because it seems to me that any alternative would put me in an antagonistic and alienated relation to my fellow citizens, friends as well as foes. The attitude of tolerance is nonetheless difficult to sustain. It can be given content only through some specification of the rights of citizens as participants in formal and informal politics. But any such system of rights will be conventional and indeterminate and is bound to be under frequent attack. To sustain and interpret such a system, we need a larger attitude of tolerance and accommodation, an attitude that is itself difficult to maintain.

# II

# Secularism in the West

# 3

# Religious Liberty: Freedom of Choice or Freedom of Conscience

*Michael J. Sandel*

After the Second World War, the Supreme Court assumed as its primary role the protection of individual rights against government infringement. Increasingly, it defined these rights according to the requirement that government be neutral on the question of good life, and defended neutrality as essential to respecting persons as free and independent selves, unencumbered by moral ties antecedent to choice. The modern Supreme Court thus gives clear expression to the public philosophy of the procedural republic. In its hands, American constitutional law has come to embody the priority of the right over the good. The areas of religion and speech illustrate the influence of this liberalism in our constitutional practice; they also display the difficulties it confronts.

## Seeking Neutrality Toward Religion

The principle of government neutrality found its first sustained application in cases involving religion. Time and again the Supreme Court has held that 'in the relationship between man and religion, the State is firmly committed to a position of neutrality'.[1] 'Government in our democracy, state and national, must be neutral

---

[1] *Abington Township School District* v. *Schempp*, 374 US 203, 226 (1963).

in matters of religious theory, doctrine, and practice....' The First
Amendment mandates governmental neutrality between religion
and religion, and between religion and non-religion.[2] Whether
described as 'a strict and lofty neutrality',[3] a 'wholesome neutrality',[4] or a 'benevolent neutrality',[5] the principle 'that the Government must pursue a course of complete neutrality toward religion'[6]
is well established in American constitutional law.

In liberal political thought, religion offers the paradigmatic
case for bracketing controversial conceptions of the good.[7] The
Supreme Court has conveyed its insistence on bracketing religion
by invoking Jefferson's metaphor of a 'wall of separation between
church and state'.[8] While some have complained that 'a rule of law
should not be drawn from a figure of speech',[9] most see the wall
as a symbol of resolve to keep religion from bursting the constitutional brackets that contain it. Since 'the breach of neutrality that
is today a trickling stream may all too soon become a raging
torrent',[10] the 'wall between Church and State... must be kept high
and impregnable'.[11]

For all its familiarity, the requirement that government be
neutral on matters of religion is not a long-standing principle of
constitutional law, but a development of the last fifty years. Not
until 1947 did the Supreme Court hold that government must be
neutral toward religion.[12] The American tradition of religious
liberty goes back further, of course. The Constitution forbids

2 *Epperson* v. *Arkansas*, 393 US 97, 103–4 (1968).
3 *Everson* v. *Board of Education of Ewing Township*, 330 US 1, 24 (1947), Justice
Jackson dissenting.
4 *Abington*, 374 US at 221.
5 *Walz* v. *Tax Commission of the City of New York*, 397 US 664, 669 (1970).
6 *Wallace* v. *Jaffree*, 472 US 38, 60 (1985).
7 See, for example, John Locke, *A Letter Concerning Toleration* (1689) (ed.),
James H. Tully Hackett (Indianapolis, 1983); and John Rawls, 'Justice as
Fairness: Political not Metaphysical', *Philosophy and Public Affairs*, 14 (Summer
1985), p. 249.
8 *Everson*, 330 US at 16. The quotation is from Jefferson's letter to the Baptists
of Danbury, Connecticut, Jan. 1802, in D. Merrill (ed.), *Jefferson Writings*
(Peterson Library of America: New York, 1984), p. 510.
9 *McCollum* v. *Board of Education*, 333 US 203, 247 (1948), Justice Reed
dissenting.
10 *Abington*, 374 US at 203.
11 *McCollum*, 333 US at 203.
12 In *Everson*, 330 US.

religious tests for federal office (Art. VI), and the first words of the First Amendment declare that 'Congress shall make no law respecting an establishment of religion, or prohibiting the free exercise thereof.' But the Bill of Rights did not apply to the states, and at the time of its adoption, six of the thirteen states maintained religious establishments.[13] Far from prohibiting these arrangements, the First Amendment was enacted in part to protect state religious establishments from federal interference.[14]

Within the states, the most eventful struggle for the separation of church and state occurred in Virginia, where it was waged by Jefferson and Madison. In 1776 the legislature disestablished the Anglican church but left open the possibility of a 'general assessment', or tax for the support of religion. Jefferson argued for complete separation of church and state, and in 'A Bill for Establishing Religious Freedom' (1779) he proposed that 'no man shall be compelled to frequent or support any religious worship, place, or ministry whatsoever'.[15]

After several years of inconclusive debate, Patrick Henry introduced a general assessment bill to support 'teachers of the Christian Religion'. Under Henry's proposal, each taxpayer could designate which Christian church would receive his tax. Henry defended his plan on the non-sectarian grounds that the diffusion of Christian knowledge would help 'correct the morals of men, restrain their vices, and preserve the peace of society'. Madison led the opposition and wrote a pamphlet, *Memorial and Remonstrance against Religious Assessments* (1785), that helped turn opinion against the bill. After defeating the general assessment, Madison won passage of Jefferson's bill guaranteeing separation of church and state.[16]

---

13 Unlike European religious establishments, the American versions, at least after the Revolution, were multiple rather than exclusive establishments, allowing support for more than a single denomination. Some states established Protestantism, others Christianity, as the religion eligible for tax support. See Leonard W. Levy, *The Establishment Clause* (Macmillan: New York, 1986), ch. 2.

14 See Mark DeWolfe Howe, *The Garden and the Wilderness* (University of Chicago Press: Chicago, 1965), ch. 1; and Wilbur G. Katz, *Religion and American Constitutions* (Northwestern University Press: Evanston, Ill., 1964), p. 9.

15 *Jefferson Writings*, p. 347.

16 See Leo Pfeffer, *Church, State, and Freedom*, rev. edn (Beacon Press: Boston, 1967), pp 108–11; and Levy, *The Establishment Clause*, pp 51–61.

Some states did not disestablish religion until well into the nineteenth century. Connecticut continued tax support for religion until 1818, and Massachusetts until 1833. New Jersey restricted full civil rights to Protestants until 1844, and Maryland required belief in God as a condition of public office until the US Supreme Court struck it down in 1961.[17] Even in states without establishments, some nineteenth-century courts held Christianity to be part of the common law. In a New York case in 1811, Chancellor James Kent upheld a conviction for blasphemy on the grounds that 'we are a Christian people, and the morality of the country is deeply ingrafted upon Christianity'.[18]

In 1845 the US Supreme Court confirmed that the Bill of Rights did not prevent the states from infringing religious freedom: 'The Constitution makes no provision for protecting the citizens of the respective states in their religious liberties; this is left to the state constitutions and laws.'[19] As far as the US Constitution was concerned, the states were free to establish a church or even 'to recreate the Inquisition', at least until the adoption of the Fourteenth Amendment.[20]

Even after the adoption of the Fourteenth Amendment, attempts to assert government neutrality toward religion confronted difficulty. In 1876 President Grant spoke out against public support for sectarian schools, and fellow Republican James G. Blaine introduced in Congress a constitutional amendment to that end: 'No State shall make any law respecting an establishment of religion or prohibiting the free exercise thereof; and no money raised by taxation in any state for the support of public schools ... shall ever be under the control of any religious sect or denomination.' The amendment was passed in the House but was defeated in the Senate, partly because of Catholic opposition, partly because of a belief that existing constitutional protections were adequate.[21]

---

[17] See Richard E. Morgan, *The Supreme Court and Religion* (Free Press: New York, 1972), pp 30–1. The Maryland case was *Torcaso* v. *Watkins*, 367 US, 488 (1961).

[18] Kent quoted in Pfeffer, *Church, State, and Freedom*, p. 665.

[19] *Permoliv* v. *New Orleans*, 44 US 589, 609 (1845).

[20] Levy, *The Establishment Clause*, p. 122.

[21] Anson Phelps Stokes and Leo Pfeffer, *Church and State in the United States*, rev. edn (Harper and Row: New York, 1964), pp 433–4; Pfeffer, *Church, State, and Freedom*, pp 146–7; Morgan, *The Supreme Court and Religion*, pp 50–1.

Two years later the Supreme Court upheld a federal law banning polygamy, a practice the Mormons regarded a religious duty. In *Reynolds* v. *United States* (1878), a Mormon convicted under the statute complained it denied him the free exercise of religion guaranteed in the First Amendment. After citing Madison's *Memorial and Remonstrance* and Jefferson's 'wall of separation', the Court nonetheless upheld the conviction, arguing that the First Amendment protected religious belief but not practice. 'Polygamy has always been odious' among Western nations, the Court declared, adding that polygamy was less conducive than monogamy to democratic government.[22]

Not until the 1940s did the Court apply the First Amendment's religion clauses to the states and declare the separation of church and state a principle of constitutional law. In *Cantwell* v. *Connecticut* (1940), the Court held that the Fourteenth Amendment incorporated both the establishment and free exercise clauses of the Bill of Rights and 'rendered the legislatures of the states as incompetent as Congress to enact such laws'.[23] In *Everson* v. *Board of Education of Ewing Township* (1947), the Court gave the establishment clause a broad interpretation and enforced, for the first time, Jefferson's 'wall of separation between church and state'.[24]

Writing for the Court, Justice Black gave forceful expression to the principle of government neutrality. 'Neither a state nor the Federal Government can set up a church. Neither can pass laws which aid one religion, aid all religions, or prefer one religion over another.... No tax in any amount, large or small, can be levied to support any religious activities or institutions.' The First Amendment 'requires the state to be a neutral in its relations with groups of religious believers and non-believers'.[25]

Since *Everson*, religion has generated much constitutional controversy, but the principle that government must be neutral toward religion has rarely been questioned.[26] For the most part, the justices have cast their disagreements as arguments about the proper application of neutrality, not about the principle itself.

22 *Reynold* v. *United States*, 98 US 145, 164 (1878).
23 *Cantwell* v. *Connecticut*, 310 US 296, 303 (1940).
24 *Everson*, 330 US at 16.
25 Ibid., pp 15–16.
26 A recent exception is Justice Rehnquist's dissent in *Wallace*, 472 US at 91.

Indeed, Black's landmark opinion in *Everson* came in the course of upholding a state subsidy for bus transportation of parochial school students. The dissenters applauded the Court's insistence on 'complete and uncompromising separation' but found it 'utterly discordant' with the result in the case.[27]

In 1963 the Court ruled that Bible reading in public schools was a religious exercise at odds with the requirement 'that the Government maintain strict neutrality, neither aiding nor opposing religion'. Justice Potter Stewart dissented, but in the name of neutrality. Permission of religious exercises is necessary, he argued, 'if the schools are truly to be neutral in the matter of religion. A refusal to permit religious exercises thus is seen, not as the realization of state neutrality, but rather as the establishment of a religion of secularism or, at the least, as government support of the beliefs of those who think that religious exercises should be conducted only in private'.[28]

In 1968 the Court struck down an Arkansas law that banned the teaching of evolution. 'Government must be neutral in matters of religious theory, doctrine, and practice', wrote Justice Abe Fortas. 'It may not be hostile to any religion.' In a concurring opinion, Justice Black agreed with the result but doubted that the principle of neutrality supported it. If Darwinism contradicts some people's religious convictions, then it is hardly neutral to teach it in public schools: 'If the theory is considered anti-religious, how can the State be bound by the Federal Constitution to permit its teachers to advocate such an anti-religious doctrine to school-children?'[29]

Black pointed out that the Court might simply take the view that fundamentalists who regard evolution as anti-religious are wrong. But that would be taking sides in the controversy the Court purports to bracket. 'Unless this Court is prepared simply to write off as pure nonsense the views of those who consider evolution an anti-religious doctrine', Black argued, the issue was more

[27] *Everson,* 330 US at 19.
[28] *Abington,* 374 US at 225, 313. In *Engel* v. *Vitale,* 370 US 421 (1962), by contrast, Stewart had defended school prayer by appealing not to neutrality but to 'the history of the religious traditions of our people', and 'the deeply entrenched and highly cherished spiritual traditions of our Nation'.
[29] *Epperson,* 393 US at 113.

difficult than the Court acknowledged. A better way to bracket, he suggested, might be to remove the controversial subject from schools altogether, as Arkansas arguably did. So long as the biblical account of creation was not taught instead, 'does not the removal of the subject of evolution leave the state in the neutral position toward these supposedly competing religious and anti-religious doctrines?'[30]

The contest for the mantle of neutrality continued in 1985, when the Court struck down a moment-of-silence statute permitting voluntary prayer in Alabama schools. The Court held that since the purpose of the law was to restore prayer to schools, it violated 'the established principle that the Government must pursue a course of complete neutrality toward religion'. Chief Justice Warren Burger dissented, arguing that the prohibition 'manifests not neutrality but hostility toward religion'.[31]

Even in cases in which the Supreme Court has upheld government involvement in arguably religious practices, it has taken pains to maintain that the religious aspect is only incidental, that the involvement does not endorse or advance or prefer religion. In *McGowan* v. *Maryland* (1961), the Court upheld Sunday closing laws on the grounds that they no longer retained their religious character. Notwithstanding their religious origins, wrote Chief Justice Warren, laws prohibiting business and commercial activity on Sundays now served the secular purpose of 'providing a Sunday atmosphere of recreation, cheerfulness, repose and enjoyment.... The air of the day is one of relaxation rather than one of religion'.[32]

In 1984 the Burger Court upheld on similar grounds a city-sponsored Christmas display, including a crèche or nativity scene. The purpose of the display was to celebrate the holiday and to depict its origins, the Court held. 'These are legitimate secular purposes.' Any benefit it brought to religion was 'indirect, remote

30 Ibid. The dispute over the proper interpretation of neutrality also arose in *Edwards* v. *Aguillard*, 482 US 578 (1987), a case involving a Louisiana law mandating 'balanced treatment' of creationism and evolution in public schools.

31 *Wallace*, 472 US at 60, 85. In a separate dissent, Justice Rehnquist challenged the assumption, accepted since *Everson*, that the establishment clause requires government to be neutral between religion and irreligion; ibid., p. 99.

32 *McGowan* v. *Maryland*, 366 US 420, 448 (1961).

and incidental'. Display of the crèche was no more an advancement or endorsement of religion than the exhibition of religious paintings in governmentally supported museums.[33]

In both cases, dissenters criticized the Court for failing to take seriously the religious character of the practices they upheld. 'No matter what is said, the parentage of [the Sunday closing] laws is the Fourth Commandment,' wrote Justice William O. Douglas. 'They serve and satisfy the religious predispositions of our Christian communities.'[34] Dissenting in the crèche case, Justice Harry A. Blackmun complained that the majority had done 'an injustice to the crèche and the message it manifests'. In the hands of the Court, 'The crèche has been relegated to the role of a neutral harbinger of the holiday season, useful for commercial purposes, but devoid of any inherent meaning and incapable of enhancing the religious tenor of a display of which it is an integral part.... Surely, this is a misuse of a sacred symbol.'[35]

## Justifying Neutrality Toward Religion

In order to assess the Court's conflicting applications of neutrality, it is necessary to consider the reasons for neutrality. What counts as neutrality depends partly on what justifies neutrality, and the Court has offered two different sorts of justification for insisting that government be neutral toward religion.

The first has to do with protecting the interests of religion, on the one hand, and those of the state on the other. 'The First Amendment rests on the premise that both religion and government can best work to achieve their lofty aims if each is left free from the other within its respective sphere.'[36] 'We have staked the very existence of our country on the fact that complete separation between the state and religion is best for the state and best for

[33] *Lynch* v. *Donnelly*, 465 US 668, 681, 683 (1984). In *Marsh* v. *Chambers*, 463 US 783 (1983), the Court upheld the Nebraska legislature's practice of opening each day with a prayer by a chaplain paid by the state, citing the long history of the practice. Writing in dissent, Justice Brennan construed the decision as carving out a narrow exception to the establishment clause doctrine.

[34] *McGowan*, 366 US at 572-3.

[35] *Lynch*, 465 US at 727.

[36] *McCollum*, 333 US at 212.

religion.'[37] 'In the long view the independence of both church and state in their respective spheres will be better served by close adherence to the neutrality principle.'[38]

The religious interest served by separation is in avoiding the corruption that comes with dependence on civil authority. A century and a half before Jefferson stated the secular case for a 'wall of separation' between church and state, Roger Williams gave the metaphor a theological meaning. 'When they have opened a gap in the hedge or wall of separation between the garden of the church and the wilderness of the world,' he wrote, 'God hath ever broke down the wall itself, removed the candlestick, and made His garden a wilderness, as at this day.'[39]

The Court has invoked the theological argument for separation only occasionally, and usually in combination with other arguments. In striking down school prayer, for example, Justice Black argued that the establishment clause 'rested on the belief that a union of government and religion tends to destroy government and to degrade religion'. The history of established religion 'showed that many people lost their respect for any religion that had relied upon the support of government to spread its faith'. The Founders sought by the Establishment clause to avoid the 'unhallowed perversion' of religion by a civil magistrate.[40] And Justice William J. Brennan emphasized that separation is important not only for the sake of the non-believer but also for 'the devout believer who fears the secularization of a creed which becomes too deeply involved with and dependent upon the government'.[41]

The political interest served by separation is in avoiding the civil strife that has historically attended church–state entanglements. Providing public funds for religion brings 'the struggle of sect against sect…. It is only by observing the prohibition rigidly that the state can maintain its neutrality and avoid partisanship in the dissensions inevitable when sect opposes sect over demands for public moneys'.[42] Opposing public school involvement in a

---

[37] *Everson*, 330 US at 59, Justice Rutledge dissenting.

[38] *Abington*, 374 US at 245, Justice Brennan concurring.

[39] Roger Williams quoted in Howe, *The Garden and the Wilderness*, pp 6–7.

[40] *Engel*, 370 US at 432.

[41] Concurring opinion in *Abington*, 374 US at 259.

'released time' programme for religious instruction, Justice Frankfurter wrote that 'the public school must be kept scrupulously free from entanglement in the strife of sects'.[43] In a similar case, Justice Black vividly recalled the danger of sectarian strife that separation was meant to prevent. 'Colonial history had already shown that here as elsewhere zealous sectarians entrusted with governmental power to further their causes would sometimes torture, maim and kill those they branded "heretics", atheists or agnostics.'[44]

Existing alongside the argument that neutrality is best for both religion and the state is an argument in the name of individual freedom. On this justification, the state must be neutral not only to avoid compromising religion and provoking sectarian strife, but also to avoid the danger of coercion. This argument goes back to the eighteenth century concern for freedom of conscience, and in its modern form emphasizes respect for persons' freedom to choose their religious convictions for themselves. It thus connects the case for neutrality with the liberal conception of the person.

In its modern, or voluntarist version, this argument for religious liberty first appears in *Cantwell*, the case that announced the incorporation of the religion clauses. 'Freedom of conscience and freedom to adhere to such religious organization or form of worship as the individual may choose cannot be restricted by law.' The First Amendment 'safeguards the free exercise of the chosen form of religion'.[45] In banning Bible reading in the public schools, the Court found justification for neutrality in 'the right of every person to freely choose his own course' with reference to religion, 'free of any compulsion from the state'. Justice Stewart dissented from the result but endorsed the view that neutrality is required for the sake of respect for individual choice, 'a refusal on the part of the state to weight the scales of private choice'.[46]

Contemporary commentators have identified the voluntarist argument for neutrality as the primary justification for the separation of church and state. '[T]he fundamental principle

---

[42] *Everson*, 330 US at 53, 59, Justice Rutledge dissenting.
[43] *McCollum*, 333 US at 216–17.
[44] *Zorach* v. *Clauson*, 343 US 306, 319 (1952), Justice Black dissenting.
[45] *Cantwell*, 310 US at 303.
[46] *Abington*, 374 US at 222, 317, Justice Clark for the Court, Justice Stewart in dissent.

underlying both religion clauses is the protection of individual choice in matters of religion—whether pro or con'.[47] '[S]ince freedom of religious choice, not neutrality per se, is the fundamental establishment value, the neutrality tool is useful only insofar as it promotes that choice'.[48] '[T]he moral basis of the anti-establishment clause is...equal respect', not for religious beliefs themselves, but 'for the processes of forming and changing such conceptions'.[49]

By the 1980s and 1990s, the freedom of choice assumed to be at stake in religion cases was not only the right to choose a form of worship that expresses one's religious beliefs but also the right to choose the beliefs themselves. In a case involving a city-sponsored display of a menorah alongside a Christmas tree, Justice Sandra Day O'Connor approved the arrangement on the grounds that it did not endorse religion but conveyed 'a message of pluralism and freedom to choose one's own beliefs'.[50] Concurring in a case that banned prayers led by clergy at public school graduation ceremonies, Justice Blackmun wrote: 'Even subtle pressure diminishes the right of each individual to choose voluntarily what to believe.'[51]

Perhaps the most explicit statement of the voluntarist conception of religious liberty is the one that appears in Justice John Paul Stevens' opinion for the Court in a 1985 case striking down Alabama's moment of silence for voluntary prayer in public schools. '[T]he individual's freedom to choose his own creed is the counterpart of his right to refrain from accepting the creed established by the majority', Stevens wrote; 'the Court has unambiguously concluded that the individual freedom of conscience protected by the First Amendment embraces the right to select any religious faith or none at all. This conclusion derives support not only from the interest in respecting the individual's

[47] Gail Merel, 'The Protection of Individual Choice: A Consistent Understanding of Religion under the First Amendment', *University of Chicago Law Review* 45 (1978), 806.

[48] Alan Schwarz, 'No Imposition of Religion: The Establishment Clause Value', *Yale Law Journal* 77 (1968), 728.

[49] David A. J. Richards, *Toleration and the Constitution* (Oxford University Press: New York, 1986), p. 140.

[50] *Allegheny County* v. *ACLU*, 492 US 573, 634 (1989).

[51] *Lee* v. *Weisman*, 112 S. Ct. 2649, 2665 (1992).

freedom of conscience, but also from the conviction that *religious beliefs worthy of respect are the product of free and voluntary choice by the faithful*'.[52]

Stevens' opinion illustrates the connection between the voluntarist justification of neutrality and the liberal conception of the person. It holds that government should be neutral toward religion in order to respect persons as free and independent selves, capable of choosing their religious convictions for themselves. The respect this neutrality commands is not, strictly speaking, respect for religion, but respect for the self whose religion it is, or respect for the dignity that consists in the capacity to choose one's religion freely. Religious beliefs are 'worthy of respect', not in virtue of what they are beliefs *in*, but rather in virtue of being 'the product of free and voluntary choice', in virtue of being beliefs of a self unencumbered by convictions antecedent to choice.

By invoking the voluntarist conception of neutrality, the Court gives constitutional expression to the version of liberalism that conceives the right as prior to the good and the self as prior to its ends, at least where religion is concerned. We are now in a position to see how both the promise and the problems of the theory make themselves felt in the practice the theory informs.

The voluntarist case for neutrality, insisting as it does on respect for persons, seems to secure a firm foundation for religious liberty. Unlike Roger Williams' case for separation of church and state, it does not depend on any particular religious doctrine. And unlike the political case for separation, it does not leave religious liberty hostage to uncertain calculations about how best to avoid civil strife. Under present conditions, such calculations may or may not support the separation of church and state. As Justice Lewis Powell has observed, the risk 'of deep political division along religious lines' is by now 'remote'.[53] We do not live on the brink of the Wars of Religion that made the case for separation so pressing. Even granting the importance of avoiding sectarian strife, a strict separation of church and state may at times provoke more strife than it prevents. The school prayer decisions of the early 1960s,

---

52 *Wallace*, 472 US at 52–3, emphasis added.
53 *Wolman* v. *Walter*, 433 US 229, 263 (1977), Justice Powell concurring and dissenting. See also Chief Justice Burger's dissent in *Meek* v. *Pittenger*, 421 US 349 (1975).

for example, set off a storm of political controversy that has persisted over three decades.[54] A Court concerned above all to avoid social discord might reasonably have decided those cases the other way.

The voluntarist case of neutrality, by contrast, does not tie religious liberty to such contingencies. In affirming a notion of respect for persons, it recalls the ideal of freedom of conscience. By emphasizing the individual's right to choose his or her beliefs, it points beyond religion to 'the broader perspective' of autonomy rights in general, including 'the rights of privacy and personhood'.[55] It thus casts religious liberty as a particular case of the liberal claim for the priority of the right over the good and the self-image that attends it. Respecting persons as selves defined prior to the religious convictions they affirm becomes a particular case of the general principle of respect for selves defined prior to their aims and attachments.

But as we have seen, the image of the unencumbered self, despite its appeal, is inadequate to the liberty it promises. In the case of religion, the liberal conception of the person ill-equips the Court to secure religious liberty for those who regard themselves as claimed by religious commitments they have not chosen. Not all religious beliefs can be redescribed without loss as 'the product of free and voluntary choice by the faithful'.

# Freedom of Conscience versus Freedom of Choice

This difficulty can be seen by contrasting the voluntarist account of religious liberty with freedom of conscience as traditionally conceived. For Madison and Jefferson, freedom of conscience meant the freedom to exercise religious liberty—to worship or not, to support a church or not, to profess belief or disbelief—without

---

[54] See President Ronald Reagan's 'State of the Union Address', 27 Jan. 1987, in *Public Papers of the Presidents of the United States: Ronald Reagan, 1987* (US Government Printing Office: Washington, D.C., 1989), vol. 1, p. 59; and, generally, Richard E. Morgan, *The Politics of Religious Conflict* (University Press of America: Washington, D.C., 1980).

[55] Laurence Tribe, *American Constitutional Law* (Foundation Press: Mineola, NY, 1978), p. 885.

suffering civil penalties or incapacities. It had nothing to do with a right to choose one's beliefs. Madison's 'Memorial and Remonstrance' consists of fifteen arguments for the separation of church and state, and not one makes any mention of 'autonomy' or 'choice'.[56] The only choice referred to in Jefferson's 'Bill for Establishing Religious Freedom' is attributed to God, not man.[57]

Madison and Jefferson understood religious liberty as the right to exercise religious duties according to the dictates of conscience, not the right to choose religious beliefs. Indeed, their argument for religious liberty relies heavily on the assumption that beliefs are not a matter of choice. The first sentence of Jefferson's Bill states this assumption clearly: 'The opinions and beliefs of men depend not on their own will, but follow involuntarily the evidence proposed to their own minds.'[58] Since I can believe only what I am persuaded is true, belief is not the sort of thing that coercion can compel. Coercion can produce hypocrisy but not conviction. In this assumption Jefferson echoed the view of John Locke, who wrote in *A Letter Concerning Toleration* (1689), 'it is absurd that things should be enjoined by laws which are not in men's power to perform. And to believe this or that to be true, does not depend upon our will'.[59]

It is precisely because belief is not governed by the will, that freedom of conscience is inalienable. Even if he would, a person could not give it up. This was Madison's argument in 'Memorial and Remonstrance':

The Religion then of every man must be left to the conviction and conscience of every man; and it is the right of every man to exercise it as these may dictate. This right is in its nature an unalienable right. It is

56 James Madison, 'Memorial and Remonstrance against Religious Assessments' (1785), in Marvin Meyers (ed.), *The Mind of the Founder*, rev. edn (University Press of New England: Hanover, NH, 1981), pp 6–13.

57 In 1779 Jefferson asserted that God 'chose not to propagate' religion by coercion, 'as was in his Almighty power to do, but to extend it by its influence on reason alone'; *Jefferson Writings*, p. 346.

58 Ibid.

59 Locke, *A Letter Concerning Toleration*, p. 46. Jefferson's argument may also have reflected the influence of the eighteenth century philosopher Thomas Hutcheson, whose account of belief is discussed in Morton White, *The Philosophy of American Revolution* (Oxford University Press: New York, 1978), pp 195–202.

unalienable, because the opinions of men, depending only on the evidence contemplated by their own minds cannot follow the dictates of other men: it is unalienable also, because what is here a right towards men, is a duty towards the Creator.[60]

Oddly enough, Justice Stevens cited this passage from Madison in support of the voluntarist view. But freedom of conscience and freedom of choice are not the same; where conscience dictates, choice decides. Where freedom of conscience is at stake, the relevant right is to perform a duty, not to make a choice. This was the issue for Madison and Jefferson. Religious liberty addressed the problem of encumbered selves, claimed by duties they cannot renounce, even in the face of civil obligations that may conflict.

To question the voluntarist justification of religious liberty is not necessarily to agree with Locke that people never choose their religious beliefs. It is simply to dispute what the voluntarist view asserts, that religious beliefs worthy of respect are the products of free and voluntary choice. What makes a religious belief worthy of respect is not its mode of acquisition—whether by choice, revelation, persuasion, or habituation—but its place in a good life or, from a political point of view, its tendency to promote the habits and dispositions that make good citizens.[61] In so far as the case for religious liberty rests on respect for religion, it must assume that, generally speaking, religious beliefs and practices are of sufficient moral or civic importance to warrant special constitutional protection.

For procedural liberalism, however, the case for religious liberty derives not from the moral importance of religion but from the need to protect individual autonomy; government should be neutral toward religion for the same reason, that it should be neutral toward competing conceptions of the good life generally—to respect people's capacity to choose their own values and ends. But despite its liberating promise, or perhaps because of it, this broader mission depreciates the claims of those for whom religion

---

[60] Madison, 'Memorial and Remonstrance', p. 7.
[61] The civic consequences of religion vary widely, of course, according to political circumstance and the particular religion. For a favourable account of the civic consequences of religion in nineteenth-century America, see Alexis de Tocqueville, *Democracy in America* (1835), trans. Henry Reeve, ed. Phillips Bradley (Alfred A. Knopf: New York, 1945), vol. 1, pp 299–314.

is not an expression of autonomy but a matter of conviction unrelated to choice. Protecting religion as a 'life-style', as one among the values that an independent self may have, may miss the role that religion plays in lives of those for whom the observance of religious duties is a constitutive end, essential to their good and indispensable to their identity. Treating persons as 'self-originating sources of valid claims'[62] may thus fail to respect persons bound by duties derived from sources other than themselves.

The case of *Thornton* v. *Caldor, Inc.* (1985) shows how voluntarist assumptions can crowd out religious liberty for encumbered selves. In an eight-to-one decision, the Supreme Court struck down a Connecticut statute guaranteeing sabbath observers a right not to work on their sabbath.[63] Although the law gave all workers the right to one day off each week, it gave to sabbath observers alone the right to designate their day. In this lack of neutrality the Court found constitutional infirmity.

Chief Justice Burger, writing for the Court, noted that sabbath observers would typically take a weekend day, 'widely prized as a day off'. But 'other employees who have strong and legitimate, but non-religious reasons for wanting a weekend day off have no rights under the statute'. They 'must take a back seat to the Sabbath observers'. Justice O'Connor echoed this worry in a concurring opinion: 'All employees, regardless of their religious orientation, would value the benefit which the statute bestows on Sabbath observers—the right to select the day of the week in which to refrain from labour.'[64]

But this objection confuses the right to perform a duty with the right to make a choice. Sabbath observers, by definition, do not *select* the day of the week they rest; they rest on the day their religion enjoins. The benefit the statute confers is not the right to choose a day of rest, but the right to perform the duty of sabbath observance on the only day it can be carried out.

Considered together with earlier decisions upholding Sunday closing Laws, *Thornton* v. *Caldor* yields a curious constitutional conclusion: A state may require everyone to rest on Sunday, the

---

62 The phrase is from John Rawls, 'Kantian Constructivism in Moral Theory', *Journal of Philosophy*, 77 (Sept. 1980), p. 543.

63 *Thornton* v. *Caldor, Inc.*, 474 US 703 (1985).

64 Ibid., Burger at 710, O'Connor at 711.

day of the Christian sabbath, so long as the aim is not to accommodate observance of the sabbath. But it may not give sabbath
observers the right to rest on the day of the week their religion
requires. Perverse though this result may seem from the standpoint
of respecting religious liberty, it aptly reflects the constitutional
consequences of seeing ourselves as unencumbered selves.

The Court has on occasion accorded greater respect to the claims
of encumbered selves. When a Seventh-Day Adventist was fired
from her job for refusing to work on Saturday, her sabbath,
she was denied unemployment compensation under a rule requiring applicants to accept available work. The Supreme Court
decided in her favour, holding that the state could not force a
worker to choose between her religious convictions and means
of support. According to the Court, requiring the state to take
account of sabbath observance in the administration of its unemployment programme did not prefer religion in violation of
neutrality. Rather, it enforced 'the governmental obligation of
neutrality in the face of religious differences'. In this case at least,
the Constitution was not blind to religion but alive to its
imperatives.[65]
   In cases involving conscientious objection to military service, the
Court has interpreted the federal law broadly and refused to restrict
exemptions to those with theistic beliefs. The relevant test is 'whether
a given belief that is sincere and meaningful occupies a place in the
life of its possessor parallel to that filled by the orthodox belief in
God'.[66] What matters is not 'conventional piety' but an imperative
of conscience rising above the level of a policy preference.[67] The
point of the exemption, according to the Court, is to prevent

65 *Sherbert* v. *Verner*, 374 US 398, 409 (1963). Three justices argued that the
decision was inconsistent with *Braunfeld* v. *Brown*, 336 US 599 (1961), where
the Court had refused to exempt Orthodox Jewish store owners from Sunday
blue laws, even though this meant they had to forego business two days each
week instead of one. Other employment compensation cases decided in line
with *Sherbert* are *Thomas* v. *Review Board of Indiana Employment Security Div.*,
450 US 707 (1981); and *Hobbie* v. *Unemployment Appeals Comm'n of Florida*,
480 US 136 (1987).
66 *United States* v. *Seeger*, 380 US 163, 166 (1965).
67 *Gillette* v. *United States*, 401 US 437, 454 (1971). See also *Welsh* v. *United
States*, 398 US 333 (1970).

persons bound by moral duties they cannot renounce from having to violate either those duties or the law. This aim is consistent with Madison's and Jefferson's concern for the predicament of persons claimed by dictates of conscience they are not at liberty to choose. As the Court wrote, 'the painful dilemma of the sincere conscientious objector arises precisely because he feels himself bound in conscience not to compromise his beliefs or affiliations'.[68]

In *Wisconsin* v. *Yoder* (1972), the Court upheld the right of the Old Order Amish not to send their children to school beyond the eighth grade, despite a state law requiring school attendance until the age of sixteen. Higher education would expose Amish children to worldly and competitive values contrary to the insular, agrarian way of life that sustains the Amish community and religious practice. The Court emphasized that the Amish claim was 'not merely a matter of personal preference, but one of deep religious conviction' that pervades their way of life. Though 'neutral on its face', Wisconsin's school attendance law unduly burdened the free exercise of religion, and so offended 'the constitutional requirement for governmental neutrality'.[69]

The Court's occasional hospitality to the claims of encumbered selves did not extend to Captain Simcha Godman, an Orthodox Jew whom the Air Force prohibited from wearing a yarmulke while on duty in the health clinic where he served. Justice William H. Rehnquist, writing for the Court, held for the Air Force on grounds of judicial deference to the 'professional judgment of military authorities' on the importance of uniform dress. Of the precedents he cited in support of deference to the military, all involved interests other than religious duties or conscientious imperatives. 'The essence of military service "is the subordination of the desires and interests of the individual to the needs of the service".' Standardized uniforms encourage 'the subordination of personal preferences and identities in favour of the overall mission'. Having compared the wearing of a yarmulke to 'desires', 'interests', and 'personal preferences' unrelated to religion, Rehnquist did not require the Air Force to show that an exception for yarmulkes would impair its disciplinary objectives. Nor even did he acknowledge that a religious duty was at stake, allowing only that, given

---

[68] *Gillette*, 401 US at 454.
[69] *Wisconsin* v. *Yoder*, 406 US 205, 220 (1972).

the dress code, 'military life may be more objectionable for petitioner'.[70]

The Court's lack of concern for persons encumbered by religious convictions found its most decisive expression in a 1990 case that involved the sacramental use of the drug peyote by members of the Native American Church. Two members of the church were fired from their jobs at a private drug rehabilitation centre because they ingested peyote, a drug prohibited by state law, as part of a religious ceremony. The workers were denied unemployment compensation on the grounds that they had been dismissed for violating a law. The Supreme Court upheld the denial. Writing for the Court, Justice Antonin Scalia maintained that the right of free exercise protects persons only from laws directed against their religion, not from neutral laws of general applicability that happen to burden their religious practice. Provided it did not target a particular religion, a state could pass laws that burdened certain religious practices even without having to show a 'compelling state interest', or special justification.[71]

It might seem that Court rulings refusing special protection for sacramental peyote, the wearing of yarmulkes, or the accommodation of sabbath observance are decisions that depart from liberal principles. Since they fail to vindicate the rights of individuals against the prerogatives of the majority, such decisions might seem at odds with the liberalism that asserts the priority of the right over the good. But these cases illustrate two features of procedural liberalism that ironically lead to illiberal consequences where religion is concerned. First, the conception of persons as freely choosing selves, unencumbered by antecedent moral ties, supports the notion that religious beliefs should be regarded, for constitutional purposes at least, as products of 'free and voluntary choice'. If all religious beliefs are matters of choice, however, it is difficult to distinguish between claims of conscience, on the one hand, and personal preferences and desires, on the other. Once this distinction is lost, the right to demand of the state a special justification for laws that burden religious beliefs is bound to appear as nothing more than 'a private right to ignore generally applicable laws'. So

70 *Goldman* v. *Weinberger*, 475 US 503, 507–9 (1986).
71 *Employment Division* v. *Smith*, 494 US 872, 879, 885 (1990).

indiscriminate a right would allow each person 'to become a law unto himself' and create a society 'courting anarchy'.[72]

Second, the procedural liberal's insistence on neutrality fits uneasily with the notion that the Constitution singles out religion for special protection. If religious beliefs must be accorded constitutional protection that other interests do not enjoy, then judges must discriminate, at least to the extent of assessing the moral weight of the governmental interest at stake and the nature of the burden that interest may impose on certain religious practices. The attempt to avoid substantive moral judgments of this kind leads some to insist on neutrality even at the cost of leaving religious liberty subject to the vagaries of democratic politics. For example, Scalia concedes that leaving religious accommodation to the political process will place religious minorities at a disadvantage, but he maintains that this 'unavoidable consequence of democratic government must be preferred to a system in which each conscience is a law unto itself or in which judges weigh the social importance of all laws against the centrality of all religious beliefs'.[73]

Outrage from religious organizations and civil liberties groups at the weakening of religious liberty in the peyote case prompted the Congress to enact the Religious Freedom Restoration Act (1993), a statute barring government from substantially burdening the exercise of religion without demonstrating a compelling governmental interest.[74] But the way the constitutional law of religion has unfolded over the past half century sheds light on the liberal political theory it came to express. The Court's tendency to assimilate religious liberty into liberty in general reflects the aspiration to neutrality: people should be free to pursue their own interests and ends, whatever they are, consistent with a similar liberty for others. But this generalizing tendency does not always serve religious liberty well. It confuses the pursuit of preferences with the exercise of duties, and so forgets the special concern of religious liberty with the claims of conscientiously encumbered selves.

[72] Ibid., at 885, 886, 888.
[73] Ibid., at 890.
[74] *Congressional Quarterly Weekly Report* 51 (30 Oct. 1993), p. 2984; ibid., (6 Nov. 1993), p. 3057. See also Angela C. Carmella, 'The Religious Freedom Restoration Act', *Religion and Values in Public Life* 3 (Winter 1995), pp 5–7.

This confusion has led the Court to restrict religious practices it should permit, such as yarmulkes in the military, and also to permit practices it should probably restrict, such as nativity scenes in the public square. In different ways, both decisions fail to take religion seriously. Permitting Pawtucket's crèche might seem to be a ruling sympathetic to religion, but as Justice Blackmun rightly protested, the Court's permission came at the price of denying the sacred meaning of the symbol it protected.

# 4

# Two Thresholds of Laïcization***

*Jean Bauberot*

## I

## The First Threshold

*A Society in 'Christendom'*

Religion pervaded French society as a whole in 1789. The liturgical calendar punctuated daily life. Since the Revocation of the Edict of Nantes (1685), the monolithic Roman Catholic faith had become compulsory for all. Communion at Easter mass and confession to a priest were required of everyone. The clergy was the foremost of the three orders of the kingdom.

The monarchy rested upon a religious justification (the theory of the divine right of kings), notably expressed in the coronation ceremony at Reims Cathedral. As God's lieutenant on earth, the king possessed a politico-religious power. The defence of Roman Catholicism was counted among his basic duties.

The Roman Catholic Church was a comprehensive institution, exercising in various ways influence or power over other institutions. As a consequence, the latter, which often existed only in embryonic states, were within its sphere of influence when not under its direct rule. Registration of births, deaths and marriages, medical and social welfare, and education were in the hands of clerics, or closely controlled by them. Thus, a physician could have been imprisoned for having concealed from his patient that the

* This chapter includes excerpts from Jean Bauberot's 'La Laicité quel heritage? De 1789 à nos jours', Genève, Editions Labour, Fides, 1990. The French excerpts have been translated into English by James Walker (Auroville) and revised by Pasteur Jean Pierre Monsarrat (Paris).

hour of death drew near. One had to be able to prepare oneself for the passage beyond and, above all, arrive there already provided with the last rites.

This does not mean that the society of that time should be viewed too schematically. Gradually, the monarchy had established a largely autonomous political and administrative structure. Since the Concordat of 1516, the power was shared between the King and the Pope for the appointments in the upper clergy. A Gallican movement, in favour of an autonomous French Catholic Church free of the direct rule of the Pope, subsequently developed. Without advocating a break with Rome, it favoured a national conception of Catholicism. The spirit of the *Lumières*, the French word for the Enlightenment, had permeated sections of the nobility and bourgeoisie. In certain respects, this spirit differed from that of the English Enlightenment or the German *Aufkldrung*. In northern Europe, it had appeared as a confrontation within an already diversified Protestantism; in France, the philosophers directly attacked the Roman Catholic Church. *Écrasons l'infâme*, 'let us crush the infamous', wrote Voltaire.

This confrontation, of course, opposed individual people. Although few non-religious spirits (Voltaire himself was a deist and had a chapel built at Ferney) existed at that time, one can see that religion had become a far more inner and individual affair. In certain provinces, the custom of putting in one's will in religious concerns disappeared. Notwithstanding the fact that they were prohibited by the Roman Catholic Church, contraceptive practices, known for a long time, became more widespread.

Continued persecution of Reformed Protestants had become increasingly irrelevant given the spirit of the time. In November 1787, the edict 'of toleration' recognized the existence of 'non-Catholics' in France. It granted them the right of having a registrar, for birth, marriage and death, other than the parish priest. However, Louis XVI specified in Article I: 'The Roman Catholic religion...alone will continue to enjoy public worship in our realm.' As shown by the Registers of Grievances, this bias was shared by almost all his subjects. With the exception of a few places, namely where they were drawn up by Protestants, the Registers of Grievances of the Third Estate—that is everybody except the nobility and the Roman Catholic clergy—showed, at best, only a *de facto* toleration restricted and under control. The possibility of a society in which the State and the Church were not at one was entirely foreign to them, as was the idea of an eventual equality of the different faiths before the law.

## The Declaration of Rights and Religious Freedom

Article 10 of the 'Declaration of the Rights of the Man and the Citizen' proclaimed, nevertheless, the principle of religious freedom. It brought about the first rift between the Revolution and the Roman Catholic Church. The latter was not entirely opposed to the Declaration of Rights. Of course, for two centuries, the way in which this matter had been considered had evolved mainly from the works of authors within the Protestant sphere of influence, Hugo de Groot, called Grotius, and from John Milton to Jean-Jacques Rousseau, by way of Samuel Pufendorf, Christian Wolff, Pierre Bayle, and John Locke. Likewise, it were the Protestant Americans who had first been involved in the elaboration of the Declaration of Rights. All of which might have given the Declaration of Rights of Man and Citizens a heretical flavour. But, one quarter of the deputies of the Constituent Assembly were members of the Roman Catholic clergy and a fair number among them showed themselves to be 'patriots'. It was a committee representative of the whole of the Constituent Assembly, and presided over by a bishop, that was the author of the draft put to the debate. And, when the Pope repudiated the Declaration in March 1791, the French bishops replied: 'We have wished to establish a true empire of public liberty and we have willingly recognised the natural equality which excludes no citizen from such station to which he is called by Providence through his talents and virtues.'

Can liberty filter into the realm of religion? In 1789, the Roman Catholic clergy was not alone in answering that it could not. Various drafts of the Declaration of Rights admitted toleration, not freedom, and only in as much as it was respectful of the 'national religion'. Such was the predominant leaning of the following Articles which were debated on 22 August.

'Article 16. As the law is unable to apprehend secret offences, religion and ethics are to supplement it. It is thus essential for the good order of society that both law and religion be respected.

Article 17. The maintenance of religion requires public worship. Respect for public worship is, therefore, indispensable.

Article 18. A citizen who does not disturb the established religion shall not be troubled.'

All this was drafted from the perspective of a fundamental social usefulness of religion. Such a conception belonged to the speech of the French Enlightenment, 'never was a State founded without religion serving as its basis' wrote Rousseau at the end of the *Contrat Social* (The Social Contract); so did it to that of Roman Catholic apologetics ('Truth is the basis of what is useful'). Those two ways of thinking did certainly quarrel with each other but on the basis of a common idea: religion is a constitutive element of the social bond.

Concretely, those paragraphs were intended to repudiate intolerance. However, they continued to assert the necessity of not disrupting the established religion (in the singular). That is to say, they decided not to re-establish a rival form of public worship, to retain censorship of literary works concerning religious matters, etc.

Without denying the social usefulness of religion, the advocates of religious freedom were grounded in another logic: that of individual rights. For them, religion is first a source of personal conviction before being an aspect of social ethics, and among the prescriptions of religion was included the obligation to publicly celebrate one's faith. Those were the ideas of members of nobility who proposed a draft of one sentence: 'No man may be troubled because of his religious opinions, nor disturbed in the practice of his religion.'

## Religious Freedom Leads to New Measures

The logic of religious freedom was progressively applied to minorities; not, however, without problems. On 24 December 1789, the Assembly decreed that 'non-Catholics may vote and are eligible [to the Assembly], and...are qualified for all civil and military types of employment, just as all other citizens', but added 'without prejudging anything concerning the Jews'. Therefore, only Protestants were admitted to all types of employment. Antisemitism was strong in eastern France. It was feared the population would react strongly should the Jews be emancipated.

The Constitution was adopted on 3 September 1791 guaranteeing, as a 'natural and civil right', each citizen's 'freedom to practise the form of religion to which he is committed'. This time, total religious freedom was unequivocally recognized. That rendered the decree against the Jews formulated in December 1789 all the more incongruous: 'Jews cannot be excluded from the enjoyment of these rights, while pagans, Turks, Muslims, even Chinese, in a word men of all sects, are entitled to them,' Adrien Duport, a member of parliament, said at that time.

On 27 and 28 September, equality and full citizenship were granted to those Jews who took a civic oath (a condition not restricted to them) and renounced 'all privileges and exceptions formerly introduced in their favour'.

Individual freedom, an oath actively incorporating each one in the social bond and the Nation understood as the result of the unanimous and voluntary allegiance of all, constituted the ideal pattern for the Revolution. In that perspective, the choice of religion (including its collective manifestations) was one of the dimensions of individual freedom. That is, in embryo, the principle of the Law of Separation of Church[1] and State passed in 1905. We have seen how it applied to religious minorities. It also entailed a certain number of other measures touching the relationship between the State and religion which I will now briefly review.

The Declaration of Rights was proclaimed in the 'presence' and under the 'auspices of the Supreme Being', a religious formula but one with which all could agree (at least those ranging from the Deists to the Roman Catholics). The Constitution of 1791 divested the monarchy of its religious character, which was considered henceforth to stem from a contract entered into with the Nation. The fact that this contract was not respected by the King led to the establishment of the Republic (August–September 1792). The State had no longer any religious foundation.

Legal aspects of life in society were changed. The registers of births, marriages, and deaths, maintained until then by the Roman Catholic clergy, were transferred to the town and village political authorities. From a legal point of view, marriage became simply a civil contract, bringing an end to ecclesiastical prohibitions and providing the possibility of divorce (September 1792). Similar measures were contemplated to establish a social welfare and an educational system under the auspices of the State rather than the Roman Catholic Church, but the bills worked upon did not lead

---

[1] Without further explication, this term designates any religious organization, whether Christian or not.

to comprehensive legislation and the acts passed by vote, particularly regarding schools, were barely implemented.

Finally, in October 1793, the creation of a new calendar stripped time itself of its religious dimension. Included in the whole process of promoting the decimal system, it substituted a period of ten days for the week, and the tenth day replaced Sunday as a day of rest. This rationalization was, however, ambiguous. The founding of the Republic became year I of the new era, playing the same role as the birth of Christ in the Christian calendar. That could mean the transfer to the Republic of a religious dimension, and worship on every tenth day would tend to confirm that.

## Revolutionary Cults

As early as 1789, the Revolution sought to celebrate the changes it had brought about and the new order that it had instituted. Roman Catholicism lent a religious foundation to these celebrations (traditional hymns of thanksgiving, patriotic sermons, the blessing of new flags, acceptance of oaths, etc.). This was still the case at Bastille Day on 14 July 1790. But a year later in Paris, the church of St Geneviève was converted into a pantheon. Voltaire's body was transferred there, the first significant ceremony in which Roman Catholicism played no part.

After the break induced by the Civil Constitution of the clergy, it was no longer self-evident that the 'religion of the fathers' would be capable of celebrating the new society. Moreover, had it not been closely associated with the old order and had it not guaranteed its legitimacy? Immediately following 14 July 1789, anti-revolutionary propaganda had begun to liken the suffering figure of Louis XVI to that of Christ on the Cross. Henceforth, revolutionary feasts led to the creation of a new religion.

By year II, that is to say, the autumn of 1793, the institution of revolutionary cults went hand in hand with a violent struggle (it was the period of the Terror) directed against revealed religions. Roman Catholicism was the principal target, but Protestantism and Judaism were also affected. It is true that the constitutional Catholic clergy as well as Protestant and Jewish bourgeoisies were often linked with the opposition party in the Convention; but that does not fully explain the persecution of revealed religions that the government had not really wanted and which it scarcely mastered. Basically, it was due to the fact that the Revolution (and its ideals) tended to be considered as sacred. The 'regeneration' thus implied the purification of the old religious forms and the establishment of new cults. The violent means used—closure of religious buildings, arrests and executions of Roman Catholic priests—were viewed as a means of emancipation from 'fanaticism' and 'superstition' accused of having 'made streams of blood flow'.

'The cult of eternal Reason is the only one worthy of a free and enlightened nation.' 'We shall revere only Reason; Equality and Liberty are our only gods.' 'Let us erase superstition's yoke to the last trace. Let Reason take its place, Reason which is heaven-sent.' 'Henceforth, Saint Reason will be our religion.' Hundreds of messages of this nature were sent to the Convention. In Paris, a celebration of the Goddess Reason was held at Notre Dame on 20 Brumaire of year II (10 November 1793). Cities, towns, and villages followed suit.

Revolutionary cults, which were later to fascinate Durkheim, were syncretic. In addition to the interchangeable female deities—Reason, Liberty, Motherland—there was the cult of the Sacred Heart of Marat, a hero of the Revolution who had been stabbed to death, as well as of other martyrs and pilgrimages to the tombs of 'patriot saints' who were victims of the counter-revolutionaries, the Whites, in the West. The significance of these different forms of religion is the same: a ritualized gathering of the community around common values that were socially fundamental and regarded as sacred.

Robespierre would subsequently accuse these cults of propagating 'atheism'. On 18 Floreal of year II (7 May 1794), he decreed that 'the French people recognize the existence of the Supreme Being and the immortality of the soul', officially establishing a new cult, less removed from the revealed religions. However, quite often Reason was already the voice of the Supreme Being, and the cult of the latter would utilize the setting, rituals, and indeed the actors of the cult of Reason.

## From the First Separation to the Concordat

A certain breathlessness manifested itself at Robespierre's downfall. The law of 3 Ventôse of year III (21 February 1795) proclaimed once again the freedom of worship (although it was very strictly regulated) and implemented the first separation of Church and

State in France; in the US it had existed since 1791. No longer were religions funded (officially, if not always in practice, the Roman Catholic Church had still been so). Reporting on the bill, the Protestant Boissy d'Anglas asserted the necessity of the State's religious neutrality: 'Man's heart is a sacred refuge on which the eyes of government may not fall.' He also made use of more pragmatic arguments: 'Keep watch over what you cannot prevent, regulate what you cannot forbid.'

Boissy d'Anglas was supported by an atheist, Cambon, who had earlier obtained the cancellation of the budget for religions. He wanted the state to retain its distance from all religions, including the revolutionary cults. The First Republic resumed the 1792 policy of restraining the part played by religion in public life. It should be emphasized that fluctuations of revolutionary religious policy were inspired in part by the conviction that the unity of the nation must be founded on a national religion, and in part by the opposite and growing idea that religion must be set aside as a purely personal matter.

Despite its limitations (outward expressions of religion were prohibited outside the premises chosen for worship), the separation allowed for a gradual reorganization of the Jewish and Protestant religious minorities. The Constitutional Catholic Church, led by Bishop Gregory, stopped being persecuted and could worship openly again. It held a Council from August to November 1797. Organically linked to the State when it was set up, it now found itself in a difficult situation. In some places, it had to share the ecclesiastical premises with the existing revolutionary cults, which added to the confusion. The refractory Roman Catholicism, sometimes given freedom, sometimes persecuted anew, held the Constitutional Church to be 'heretic' and 'schismatic', and by the end of the Revolution it found itself pushed to the margins by the Directory who wanted to maintain the Republican cult, and subsequently by Bonaparte whose policy was to come to a direct understanding with Rome.

Before breaking up, the Convention decreed, in October 1795, a number of national holidays. They were to celebrate the Republic, agriculture, youth, etc. The Directory added commemorations (the death of Louis XVI, 14 July). In 1798, the Minister for Home Affairs established the tenth-day worship, linked to the organization of the week decided in year II. The law of 13 Fructidor

of year VI (30 August 1798) codified the ceremonies of those
secularized rites (civic acts, reading of laws, singing, recitations,
gymnastics), but the tenth day scarcely succeeded in supplanting
Sunday. The Consulate reduced the number of national holidays
to two and eliminated the tenth-day worship.

Bonaparte dealt as a politician with the problem of the social
status of religion. The chaotic situation that he had inherited was
detrimental to the maintenance of order; the influence and vitality
of refractory Roman Catholicism in some regions served the
advocates of monarchy. He thought it was possible to restore to
a reunified Roman Catholic Church an official position, on
condition, however, that he was able to control it and maintain
a certain number of the great achievements of the Revolution:
religious freedom and state autonomy with regard to religion.

Delicate negotiations were entered into with the Pope. Narrow
was the path between pontifical requirements, those of the Consul,
and the existing opposition in France to the very idea of a
Concordat. Signed on 10 Messidor of year IX (15 July 1801), the
Concordat re-established a unified Roman Catholic Church in
France, putting an end to the Constitutional Church. Some of its
personnel were of course reintegrated as parish priests or bishops
of the new church, but it was, in fact, rebuilt primarily on the basis
of the refractory Church. The Roman Catholic Church was
proclaimed the 'religion of the great majority of the French'
without, however, being given the status of State religion. Its
activities could take place freely and in public and had to be 'in
accordance with such police regulations as deemed necessary by the
government for the public peace'.

In fact, the Organic Articles that Bonaparte unilaterally added
to the Concordat went far beyond the simple policing of religion.
They clearly showed that henceforth, 'the Church is in the State',
whereas 'the State is not in the Church'. Other Organic Articles
concerned Protestantism and the reorganization of the Lutheran
and Reformed Churches. The plurality of religions was, therefore,
official. The law of 18 Germinal of year X (8 April 1802)
promulgated, at the same time, the Concordat and the Organic
Articles of the Roman Catholic and Protestant religions. This
pluralism was completed in 1807 by the meeting of two Jewish
assemblies, one of the rabbis, the other of the representatives of
the most prominent Jewish families. In March 1808, a decree
reorganized the 'Jewish religion'. That which is commonly, but

rather inaccurately, termed the 'Concordat system' was thus established. It would, in fact, be truer to speak of a 'system of recognized religions', but the expression 'Concordat system' clearly indicates the dominant character of the Roman Catholic Church.

## A New Logic: The First Threshold of Laïcization

Stemming from a draft dating from the Constituent Assembly, the Civil Code was elaborated between 1800 and 1804. It completed and made more lasting the break with the authority of the Roman Catholic Church over French legislation which had been initiated by the Revolution: 'There exists a universal and immutable Law,' one reads in the Preliminary Book of the Code, the source of all positive laws; 'it is nothing else than natural reason, insofar as it governs all men'. Moreover, the Civil Code was mute as regards religion, clearly showing that the state was, from the moment, non-religious in its foundation. For some legal experts, 1804, the date of the Civil Code, is more fundamental as it pertains to the establishment of a neutrally religious state than is 1905, the year of the Law of Separation of Church and State.

Significantly, it was one of the authors of the Civil Code, Jean-Étienne Portalis, who was to justify and apply the Concordat system. He used three arguments that fit into one another, rather like Russian dolls:

- Religion is necessary. It is socially useful because it constitutes a moral force and an element of sociability.
- This religion must be a 'positive religion', that is to say, a religion based on the reference to a revelation, a tradition and associated with a Church. Only accessible to a small number, 'natural religion' could never be the social vehicle of morality. The turmoil of revolutionary religiosity showed how dangerous is an unstructured religious sphere.
- In France, 'positive religion' necessarily implied 'Roman Catholicism'. There was no other realistic choice. Thus, it must be reinstated. Portalis described to the legislative body an enlightened Catholicism, theologically close to Gallican and Jansenist thought and brought closer to certain elements of Protestantism (some saw in the latter a possible reconciliation between a rationalized Christianity and a spiritualized Revolution). Portalis specified, moreover, that Roman Catholicism was no longer 'either the exclusive religion or the dominant

religion'. Religious pluralism and the consistency ascribed to the State and civil society without any religious reference, entailed, in effect, a situation structurally different from that existing prior to 1789.

To name that situation, the French use the world *laïcité*, for which there is no real English equivalent. The evolution, the policy that leads to such a situation, is the meaning of the French word *laïcization*. Hereafter both these words, with the adjective *laïque*, used to qualify what belongs to *laïcité*, its supporters, shall appear in French as technical terms.

It is possible to evaluate this situation by means of a method of appraisal that leads to the profile we shall call the first threshold of *laïcization*.[2] Schematically, it is marked by three characteristics in relationship with the general framework of a state that no longer ensures the salvation of the French people, involves itself only with their common earthly interest, and, therefore, considers itself not to be in a position to impose specific religious doctrines. Those characteristics are as follows:

## (1) INSTITUTIONAL FRAGMENTATION OR DISSOCIATION

Roman Catholicism was no longer an inclusive institution, coextensive with the whole of society. Divested of its role as registrar, the clergy, in addition, had to confine itself in its religious activities which were henceforth clearly distinguished from 'profane' activities. Thus, 'educational needs and health needs' assumed a gradual autonomy in relation to 'religious needs', and were provided for by specific institutions. Nonetheless, there existed instances of overlapping between the various institutions (the religious institution being one among others).

## (2) RECOGNITION OF LEGITIMACY

Socially objective 'religious needs' continue to exist. Religion, the foundation of morality, is useful for society; an idea that implies that there is a basic agreement between religious morality and common social morals. The service provided by religion was a public service, and thus the State ensured a stipend to ministers of recognized religions.

2 Constructed on the basis of Weber's ideal type, each threshold of secularization is an abstract notion enabling the comparison and measurement of diverse elements of concrete reality.

## (3) RELIGIOUS PLURALISM

The State officially recognized several religions which could, in their way, satisfy the 'religious needs' of their followers and work towards the moral well-being of the country. Within the framework defined by law, the State therefore guaranteed freedom to various religions. While generally upholding religion, the State liked to see itself as an impartial arbiter. Freedom was even given to those who decided to do without the 'succour of religion'.

This profile delineates a logic that was dominant for roughly a century. The situation that it describes was not static or rigid, but quite contrary. This was because, at the beginning of the nineteenth century, a number of aspects of the Concordat system were far from entirely realized. Not only was this system questioned *per se* by certain religious or political forces, it also became the object of struggle as attempts were frequently made to bend one or the other of its features to take advantage.

### A Few Aspects of the First Threshold

The situation created was new. Thus, the Roman Catholic Church received subsidies paid by the State. It looked as if things had gone back to the time of the Constituent Assembly when, following the decision to sell ecclesiastical properties, it was decided that the nation would provide for, 'in an appropriate manner, the expenses of the Church and the maintenance of its ministers'. Here was a totally new element. It was no longer one religion, the Roman Catholic Church; the State's responsibility was merely one of providing 'religions': as of 1804, the Protestant, Lutheran, and Reformed clergymen were also paid by the State. In 1830, rabbis received stipends. The symbolic aspect of this financial arrangement is important: it shows concretely the legal equality of recognized religions, nothwithstanding huge differences in their membership.

Besides, the process by which the State took over from the Church the registration of births, deaths, and marriages was complete in 1792. However, with the advent of revolutionary cults no one had really been released from the obligation of religious practice. Now, each individual had the legal right to abstain from religious observances. This would gradually become something anyone could quite normally choose to do, with more or less difficulty, depending upon the religious acts in question. At the beginning of the nineteenth century, when the head of the village learned that someone was dying, he was likely without second thought, to send for a priest to provide the 'succours of religion' and the last rites. In his understanding, this appeared to be one of his duties rather in the way that today, should a near acquaintance be manifestly ill, one would call a physician without being overly concerned about the person's opinion and without feeling that a fundamental individual freedom had been violated.

Although religious practice was no longer mandatory, access to religious 'goods' was still a right and, when the Concordat system was implemented, the State attempted to protect the citizen—one could almost say the user—against being deprived of this right. The authors of the Concordat asserted, in fact, that 'by the authorization granted to religion, the state undertakes to protect the doctrine, discipline, and the ministers, and also undertakes, as a necessary consequence, to enable those who profess a religion to enjoy the spiritual benefits which it may offer'.

The problem lay with only those who professed a religion. Yet the State acknowledged the right of the clergy to determine the rules for obtaining the 'spiritual benefits' which their Church offered. This is a typical example of the delicate tension between the right of the State to ensure that a public service was provided by a large institution which it supports and at the same time a recognition by the same State of the autonomy of the institution and its competence in a field in which the State should not interfere. When the Concordat system was enforced, the Ministry for Religious Affairs, it appears, ensured that the necessities of public service prevailed over the clergy's refusal to grant certain religious burials. On the other hand, a different attitude was shown in the case of marriage: the religious marriage contract being distinct from that of civil marriage, it was necessary that those who asked for it accept the regulations specific to each ecclesiastical organization (thus, for example a Roman Catholic could not divorce). This was an ambivalent situation arising out of the logic of the first threshold of *laïcization*.

The Revolution had fought against the Roman Catholic religious orders and congregations and abolished monastic vows. However, it had to take into account the socially useful aspect of certain congregations. Thus, the decree of 18 August 1792 suppressed the religious congregations that ran hospitals but took measures to enable the more or less secularized sisters to continue to care for the sick.

Unresolved by the Concordat, the problem of Catholic religious orders and congregations would be raised throughout the nineteenth century. Portalis shared with the Enlightenment the dislike for lifetime vows, which 'deprived society of useful subjects'. However, the demand for social services—hospital workers, teachers—was greater than the available non-clerical personnel, which enabled the religious orders to justify their authorization on grounds of social utility.

The solution had a circumstantial aspect: it was not a question of giving the Roman Catholic Church authority in non-religious fields—on the contrary, the university was set up, a body of medical practitioners organized, quite apart from the church—but on recognition that the church could serve a useful purpose so long as other institutions were not in a position to satisfy the needs that arose in their field. The question was whether Roman Catholicism would accept this secular, institutional fragmentation which, from its point of view, could be seen as an institutional stricture, a negation of its 'mission'.

## The Great Education Laws

The Revolution had formulated a design, Quinet a programme, and the teacher Jean Macé provided a practice. He was convinced in 1848 that the education of the people was an indispensable corollary of universal suffrage. In 1863, he founded the Society of Communal Libraries of Alsace. Three years later, he founded the League of Education, with its headquarter in Paris, where an active group was at work when the war broke out in 1870. The League presented a charter containing nearly 850,000 signatures in support of compulsory education at the session of the National Assembly in June 1872. Local societies proliferated, blending militant support of the Republic and struggle in favour of education. The League was the indispensable counterpart as a voluntary society to the State's initiatives in developing an educational system on a religiously neutral basis, that is in accordance with the principles of *laïcité*.

Still in force, the Falloux law was made worse—from the Republican point of view—by a law of 12 July 1875 bringing freedom to higher education, ending the State monopoly in conferring degrees. Jules Ferry, the minister for public education from 1879 to 1883, introduced a new educational system which subsequently became fully operational. Significantly, the first law to be voted (August 1879) obliged every territorial department to have a women teachers' training college. For Ferry and his friends, the Roman Catholic Church upheld its influence in the country through women. It was thus a matter of life or death for democracy: 'Women must belong to Science (and not) to the (Roman Catholic) Church.'

Regarding higher education, the State again was the only authority to confer degrees (18 March 1880). But Ferry was unable to prohibit teaching by unauthorized religious congregations (Art. 7). Two decrees were substituted for this article, one expelling the Jesuits and the other obliging other unauthorized congregations to be registered. Soon thereafter, Ferry became the head of government (September 1880).

Free education in primary schools was adopted without any great deal of difficulty (June 1881). Such was not the case with regard to religious neutrality, the principle of *laïcité*. Bishop Charles Freppel criticized the very idea of a possible 'neutrality' in education:

Not to speak to the child about God for seven years while one teaches it six hours a day, is to make it positively believe that God does not exist, or that one has no need to be concerned with him. The teacher is to withdraw into a complete abstention regarding religious matters! But, abstention is impossible; for, according to whether or not one believes in the existence of God and the immortality of the soul, human thought and life take an entirely different course.

Some Republicans were not very far removed from the concerns of the bishop. The philosopher Jules Simon, author in 1856 of the work *La religion naturelle*, 'Natural Religion', also protested against the possible removal of the mention of God in education. In his opinion, a kind of non-denominational religious instruction appeared to be possible: one could speak to the children of God 'without mixing therewith the theories which trouble the philosophers'. For Ferry, on the contrary, only neutrality went hand in hand with the respect for every individual conscience. In such times of politico-religious strife, it guaranteed the absence of 'irreligious or anti-religious education'. The teacher who gave himself over to that 'would be as severely reprimanded as he had committed that other misdeed of beating his students or indulging in reprehensible ill-treatment of them'.

Another sensitive point was the possibility of permitting ministers of recognized religions to use school buildings outside class hours for religious instruction. Ferry accepted this, but the Radical Party was firmly opposed to it. The proposal, made in the Assembly to authorize this when the school and the religious premises were more than two kilometres apart, came up against the twofold opposition of Roman Catholic deputies and some Republicans.

The law of 28 March 1882 made primary school education compulsory and *laïque*. 'Moral and civic instruction' took the place of 'moral and religious instruction', and children were given a weekly off day other than Sunday 'so as to enable parents to have religious instruction given outside the school structure, should they want to do so'.

Following Ferry's departure, two other laws completed the whole system: that of 30 October 1886, which gave the teaching personnel a purely secular status, and of 19 July 1889, determining expenditure on primary education and payment of teachers by the State.

## *The Foundation of Morality According to the Principles of* Laïcité

A morality with no religious connection or *laïqué*, to use the French word, would henceforth be taught. Its creation is at the centre of the conflict of the two Frances. Both camps were convinced about the necessity of an underlying moral unity for French society, and each held itself alone to be in a position to bring this essential unification into being.

The logic of the first threshold of *laïcization* entailed the conception of religion as a moral force vital to the sound functioning of society. In principle, it was a question of a society that could be either conservative or progressive. Bonaparte and Portalis, however, considered religion to be a safeguard against 'subversion' and the dominant religion had increasingly become synonymous with an order hostile to the values of 1789.

Which religion could become a moral leaven for a post-revolutionary society? This question runs through the entire nineteenth century. Protestantism attracted a number of intellectuals who compared the progress made by the countries of northern Europe, mainly Protestant, to the decline of the Latin countries, all Roman Catholic (Spain, etc.). Other less-structured religious forms also had followers: numerous varieties of Deism, spiritualism, religion of Humanity, etc. One also spoke of 'natural morality' in connection with 'natural religion'. During the Second Empire, a journal, *La Morale Indépendate*, 'Independent Morality', made so bold as to assert that moral law was sufficient unto itself. One of its collaborators, a follower of Kant, Charles Renouvier, published *Science de las Morale*, 'The Science of Morality', in 1869. These different reflections, in particular the latter, prepared the ground for a moral doctrine severed from any religious foundation. It had five characteristics:

- The first is the opposition between the universality of ethics and the particularity of religions. Ferry defended the idea that, far from being a fruit of religions, morality was the substantial core that enabled their ascendancy. He thus wanted to extract from religion the 'eternal morality' shrouded beneath metaphysical speculation.
- The second was the idea that science now provides morality with much sounder foundations than those that religion could provide. The times were becoming those in which the scientist was to be considered to be a moral paradigm and medical doctors would extend their sphere of influence. Indeed, some practitioners wrote, for example, works on marriage.
- Third, even the structure of the secular school appeared to engender morality. As a place for learning tolerance, it enabled all French children, irrespective of social class or religion, to come to know and accept one another. Boys and girls too would receive the same education, thus promoting unity, from the unity of the couple to that of the country. Through the school, the Republic itself was the bearer of values.
- Fourth, ethics became a subject in moral and civic education. Ferry explicitly promised religious neutrality, not 'philosophic or political neutrality'. Republican values, deriving from 1789, had to be taught. To love France was also to love liberty, justice, and tolerance. Patriotism and universalism merged in Republican civic-mindedness.

• Finally, as the fifth and last aspect, Ferry allowed the National Curriculum Council to introduce 'duties towards God' in the ethics course. Although religion was no longer taught *per se*, transcendence as a moral inspiration and a way of surpassing the finitude of human existence remained one of the foundations of secular morality.

# II

# Separation of Church and State and the Second Threshold of *Laïcization*

## *The Morality in* Laïcité: *A Reorientation of the First Threshold*

The creation of a State educational system in accordance with the principles of *laïcité* took place within the context of the Concordat. Did it develop within the logic of the first threshold of *laïcization*, or in defiance of it? The answer will be a qualified one. To a certain extent, the end of the link between the academic world and the Roman Catholic Church was, in a key area, a result of the first threshold. In the nineteenth century, the teacher was controlled by the priest and was in part under his authority. He could, for instance, be made to interrupt his class to assist the priest at a burial. The new laws freed him of all clerical supervision. This was an achievement of institutional fragmentation.

However, the fact that academic and religious fields were now distinct did not mean that clashes in relation to education did not exist between Church and State. The banning of all catechetical teaching in school buildings not only put an end to the temporary alliance between Church and State that had made it possible, but meant that the social value of that teaching was no longer recognized. Religion was pushed to the margin. Ferry knew, nevertheless, that banning religious teaching in school buildings had seemed 'even to the least clerical of our peasants inexplicable and hurtful'. The setting aside of religion forecast the advent of another logic.

Generally speaking, the creation of a non-religious morality raised the question of the moral usefulness of religion. Ferry could state that morality 'holds together by itself' and that any contribution to the moral education of the individual-cum-citizen as well, even that made by positive religions, was welcome. Did that include Roman Catholicism? This would presuppose a degree of compatibility between Catholic morality and morals taught by *laïcité*. On 15 December 1882, Rome put four moral handbooks on the Index. Among the incriminated passages, one finds an account of the non-religious principles of morality in *laïcité*. For instance, these remarks: the school should first 'educate men and women so that their resolute souls do not subordinate the idea of morality to religious beliefs and are capable of remaining moral without having been or after having ceased to be believers'.

Other condemned passages set forth the principles of democracy ('Governments should only consider themselves instruments of the will of the people'), compared the guillotine with the dragonnades, contrasted the Inquisition with freedom of thought and belief, hinted at the completeness of civil marriage ('The religious marriage is only the consecration in church of the marriage which is definitive when it has been civically solemnized'), and asserted that 'motherhood has raised woman above the low level to which man has relegated her'.

The Pope's decision initiated a clash. A number of ecclesiastics read the Roman Catholic condemnation from the pulpit; indeed threatened to withhold the sacraments from those using the impugned handbooks. The government stopped payment of the stipends of two thousand priests. But soon, Pope Leo XIII and Ferry calmed the situation. In November 1883, Ferry wrote his oft-quoted 'Letter to Teachers.' It stressed that they must keep their teaching within the bounds of a basic morality that could not offend 'a single honest man.... You are in no way the apostles of a new Gospel', wrote the minister to the schoolteachers.

What was made of this? From a reading of the indexed passages, he was led to consider that Catholic morality and the morality of *laïcité* were totally opposed. From a reading of Ferry's letter he learnt that *laïcité* implied neutrality; that nothing should be said in school that might shock even a single Catholic father. In brief, the teacher had to find a few basic rules of common morality and confine himself to them. Of course, not all teachers adopted this attitude, although many did.

In creating a school system independent of the Churches, Ferry sought to act as an innovator and peacemaker, but was there not an intrinsic contradiction in such an undertaking? To promote or teach morality grounded in *laïcité* presupposes as much instruction in any other system of values; a committed, critical, indeed polemical attitude. But, so as to avoid building a state ideology, rule applied to schools involved neutrality in relation to the different beliefs that were 'personal, free, and varied'. Ideally, to be a *laïque*, that is to say, an active supporter of *laïcité*, meant combining these two attitudes. Hardly an easy task.

## Other Measures for Promotion of Laïcité

The measures taken by the 'Republic of Republicans' involved not only the academic field. A law from November 1814 had prohibited 'ordinary work' on Sundays and religious feast days. It was repealed in July 1880, and had never been seriously enforced. Already during the Second Empire it had appeared difficult for the government to impose external precepts of the religions professed in France without violating religious freedom as well as the freedom of commerce.

In 1884, other measures were taken. Best known of which is the restoration of divorce (27 July), primarily due to the action of a medical doctor—a significant example of the role played by men of science in the service of *laïcité*. A mention must also be made of the law passed in April prohibiting 'the making of any distinctions or special regulations in burial grounds' because of the beliefs of the deceased or the circumstances of their death. This put an end to the burial on 'an accursed ground' of the bodies of Protestants as well as of those who committed suicide. On the other hand, the constitutional revision of 14 August abrogated public prayers in Churches at the reopening of the legislative assemblies.

To these specific measures were added more general provisions concerning various liberties. Thus, the necessity of prior authorization for public meetings was abolished in 1881. Protestants praised this 'truly liberal law' which, according to them, put an end to the harassments to which their endeavours to evangelize had been subject at various times during the century.

The movement towards *laïcization* in the medico-social field was less conspicuous than in the case of education. Medical practitioners, quite frequently anti-clerical, had gained some political weight and comprised at least ten per cent of the members of parliament. However, in the hospitals, nuns remained an essential part of the staff. Bourneville, editor of *Progrès Médical* and a member of Parliament, was instrumental in the *laïcization* of the Parisian hospitals and in the creation of the nursing profession. 'Servants devoted to the poor,' the nurses were required to competently assist male medical doctors; schools were established for their training. In 1893, a law set up free medical assistance: thus the nation took upon itself the care of the poor, until then principally the concern of the church. And, more generally, the design for the promotion of health care was linked to the whole social question.

On the ideological level, the establishment of a republican *laïcité* put the Roman Catholic camp in opposition to the supporters of *laïcité*, which ranged from resolute atheists to members of religious minorities and different types of spiritualists. But, only militants—in a broad sense of the term—confronted one another on a permanent basis. The majority of the French people held themselves aloof from organized ideologies, adding a pinch of salt to them. Not only were a number of convinced Roman Catholics (critics of 'intransigent' Roman Catholicism) to be found among the architects of *laïcité*, but a large part of those that constituted the Republicans' electoral support continued to relate to Roman Catholicism. Those Roman Catholics who agreed with universal suffrage found in religion a setting for belief and a symbolic reference, and in the Republic, hope for progress and social advancement. They contributed towards shaping a French *laïcité* and drawing the boundaries between Church and State which they could not overstep without risking a backlash. A further question arises: if women at that time had had the right to vote, would *laïcité* have been shaped in the same way?

## Towards the Disestablishment of the Churches

In 1892, Pope Leo XIII called upon French Roman Catholics to accept the Republic as the 'representative of a power come from

God'. This call was conditional: an attempt to change the legislation without violating the constitution, an endeavour which moreover was part of the democratic game. The appeal was not fruitless, but did not avoid a new crisis at the turn of the century.

This crisis arose out of the Dreyfus case in which a Jewish military officer was wrongly accused of, and condemned for, high treason; it was marked by the rise of nationalist and 'intransigent' Roman Catholic anti-Semitism, but also by bashfulness and ambiguity on the part of the Republican and *laïque* camp. Nevertheless, once again the impression prevailed that the Republic was threatened by the 'clerical peril'. The governments of 'Republican Defence' (1899) and the Left Block (1902) followed a policy hostile to the religious Roman Catholic congregations and led France towards the separation of Church and State.

Subsequent to the decrees of 1880, several thousand members of religious orders were expelled, which caused the resignation of many magistrates and army officers by way of protest. The important law of July 1901 on voluntary societies excluded religious congregations from the right to free association. They alone had to apply for legislative authorization, because only they presupposed commitment for life. Members of unauthorized congregations did not have the right to teach. One might ask whether it was not a question of suppressing all public services rendered by clerics so as to prove to them their lack of social worth.

In 1902 and 1903 schools and other institutions run by religious orders were closed down, sparking off serious incidents. For its part, the Parliament refused recognition to almost all the congregations that had sought it. A law passed in July 1904 prohibited members of religious orders from teaching. In Brittany, priests were forbidden to preach and teach catechism in Breton, the local language. This great tension was combined with a struggle between France and the Holy See which led to a severance of diplomatic relations (30 July 1904).

Thus disestablishment, the so-called separation of Church and State, appeared to be inevitable. It had been on the Republican agenda for thirty-five years; but public opinion had been unable to accept it. The Concordat gave the government considerable leeway in intervening with the life of the Churches. Conversely,

Pope Leo XIII had finally accepted *laïc* education, largely because the Concordat was not questioned, even though funds had been trimmed. Due to the support provided by the Republic to overseas missions, France had become a Roman Catholic colonial power. Would that support last if the Concordat was repealed?

Delayed, the separation thus took place in a climate of confrontation. The situation ruled out the suggestion from a Protestant legal expert to have religious organizations benefit from the law of 1901 on the freedom to associate. The promulgation of a specific law was necessary and several models of separation were possible, three of which are found schematically in the elaborated proposals.

One model was anti-religious and combative. Such was the bill of the so-called 'Little Father Combes' in October 1904, who was then head of the government (and a spiritualist by personal conviction). Each existing ecclesiastical organization would be broken up into as many religious associations as there were territorial administrative departments. Other drafts, according to the socialist Aristide Briand who criticized them, would lead to a law 'pointed at the Church like a gun'. It was indeed Roman Catholicism that it was aimed at, but because of their frailty, the minority religions would have been even more seriously affected than the Roman Catholic Church.

A second model was democratic and competitive. It left to the churches the task of organizing themselves at the national level. Religious buildings, that had been public property since the Revolution, were to be turned over to specific religious bodies set up locally. Priests, chosen by their congregation, would be able to disagree with their bishop without the intervention of the State. After the separation, 'dissident' Churches would be free to establish themselves and be granted ecclesiastical buildings. In the Roman Catholic Church itself, legal authority would come from the grass roots. The Roman Catholic newspaper *La Croix*, 'The Cross', denounced this as an 'attempt to change in a Protestant way Roman Catholicism' (14 June 1905). Indeed, a number of Protestants supported this model hoping to attract new Churches into the orbit of their religious denomination.

A third model was liberal and respected the self-organization of each Church. Jean Jaurès, the celebrated socialist leader, hopeful of achieving a law that would bring peace and eventually make it possible to combat social problems, insisted upon the model. For him, the Republican State must hope for an internal evolution of Roman Catholicism and not allow the growth of Churches competing with it. 'Believers', because they were to be the people funding their Churches, would be able to further that evolution. A radical and anti-clerical newspaper accused Jaurès of practising 'popish socialism' and of 'fabricating a law of preservation, that is of retreat'. Jaurès answered: 'The great reform of separation must be accomplished smoothly, without turmoil, and must be acceptable to the entire country.'

## The Logic of the Second Threshold

Presented by Aristide Briand, a socialist, prepared by Méjan, a Protestant, and Grunebaum-Ballin, a Jew, the law of separation was promulgated on 11 December 1905. 'The Republic ensures the freedom of conscience. It guarantees the free exercise of religions' with some reservations owing to the safeguard of 'public order' (Art. 1). It 'neither recognizes nor pays nor subsidizes any religion' (Art. 2). Art. 4 stipulated that associations which conformed to the general 'rules of organization of the religion whose practice they intended to maintain, would have at their disposal the state-owned ecclesiastical buildings. *De facto*, that left room for the Roman Catholic hierarchy and Briand insisted upon that when the bill was discussed: 'Churches are institutions which we cannot ignore; this is a basic fact and our first duty as legislators is to do nothing detrimental to the free constitution of [already existing] Churches.'

Thus, the last model prevailed, although with traces of the other two. The three models had common points. A certain reversal from the logic of the first threshold of *laïcization* towards another logic had already been evident with the setting up of a state-run religiously neutral educational system. This new logic found its overall structure in the achievement of the separation of church and state. Here again, we can evaluate this new logic on the basis of a method that provides a sort of profile of this second threshold of *laïcization*. It has three characteristics.

## (1) INSTITUTIONAL DISSOCIATION

Religion was no longer officially considered to be something that structured the whole of society. It had been institutionally marginalized and privatized. Whereas going to school and, to a certain extent, looking after one's health, became institutionally compulsory, religion was in this respect entirely optional.

## (2) THE ABSENCE OF LEGITIMACY

Having become a 'private matter', 'religious needs' no longer possessed a socially recognized objectivity. The question as to the usefulness of religion for society was no longer publicly relevant. Other institutions tended more or less to replace it on a functional level.

## (3) FREEDOM OF RELIGION

It belonged to the sphere of public liberties. The State guaranteed each citizen freedom of conscience, and allowed each one to assemble with others in various religious societies or associations, with a legal private, not public, status.

The separation of Church and State need not necessarily entail a similar logic in every instance. In other countries, the disestablishment of the Churches had already been accomplished in other ways. Without entering into a debate on the advantages of the different types of separation (as regards which was the most 'authentic'), a few remarks may be made.

The French separation, like that of other countries, was a historic and social product. The outcome of a set of actions and reactions due to the actual groups opposing one another in French society. By its general attitude, the Catholic camp brought about the separation just as much (though in a different way!) as the *laïque*.

The separation of 1905 was marked by the victory of the *laïque* camp and the concern of some of its members that a compromise be reached. Things moved when the Combes government fell in January 1905, in the same direction as Ferry's policy: to play for peace in the long term rather than complete victory in the short term.

The logic of the second threshold now introduced a more static, rigidly established situation than the logic of the first. History induces movement and no reality escapes a possible reorientation, nor indeed new attempts at breaking it up.

## Laïcité *Reduced to the Defence of State Education*

The Resistance, the underground movement that fought the German occupation of France, had united unbelievers and believers in a common struggle. In 1945, the bishops held that there could be a positive meaning of the term *laïcité*, alongside its negative connotation. At the very time when a militant Roman Catholicism was reintroduced into French political life by the creation of a Christian Democratic Party, the Republican Popular Movement, *laïcité*, was officially proclaimed by the Constitution of the Fourth Republic, 1946.

Tensions were thenceforth principally apparent in the field of education. The position of the supporters of *laïcité* was clear: 'public funds for public schools, private funds for private schools'. This viewpoint was increasingly demolished for two reasons. First, public opinion was less mobilized than at the turn of the century: the Roman Catholic Church no longer appeared to be a menacing counter-society, but rather one among numerous pressure groups in a democratic society. Then, in other areas (the medico-social sector, youth movements, etc.), private initiatives (whether denominational or not) were subsidized, as they were seen to offer a public service.

In 1951, the Barangé and Marie laws granted subsidies for all schoolchildren in public and private schools and provided scholarships to students in private schools. Negotiations were held between France and the Holy See, from 1952 to 1957, seeking to resolve the problems relating to the departments in the east as well as those pertaining to education. An intermediary system between public and private schooling was to be created. Educational establishments were to negotiate agreements with the State, and the degree of integration was to vary in accordance with the financial commitment of the latter.

At the outset of the Fifth Republic, the Debré law (1959) once again took up this plan, reorienting it in a way that was more favourable to private education. In compensation for substantial financial aid by way of teachers' wages and day-school expenses, the programmes and methods of public education were to be adapted to respect freedom of conscience. The State, however, also recognized the 'specific character' (a rather vague notion) of private schools linked by a specific contract to the State.

Demonstrations in favour of *laïcité* and a petition with eleven million signatures failed to bring about modifications in the law. On the contrary, it was strengthened by the Guermeur law in 1977 which, among other things, increased the powers of headmasters and extended the exercise of the 'specific character' of private schools.

The Right wing was in power from 1958 to 1981 when the left took over. Sixteen per cent of the children attended private schools; ninety per cent of them were Roman Catholic, although religion was only one of the reasons cited by the parents for the choice. Advocates of private schools were anxious to preserve acquired advantages, whereas the National Committee for Action in favour of *laïcité* was against the laws that had been enacted since 1945.

The minister, Alain Savary, entered into quite difficult negotiations with all opposing parties. He proposed a general reform of national education through some degree of decentralization and greater autonomy for schools. The private schools under contract were to be introduced into the new framework. Complex means of implementation were foreseen. The plan did not really satisfy the supporters of *laïcité* and worried defenders of private education. It was voted by the Assembly with amendments that reinforced the integrating logic (May 1984). In June, a large, hostile demonstration of nearly 1.5 million people was held in Paris. On 12 July, Francois Mitterand announced the rescission of the Savary law.

The failure was due to several causes. Certainly the right had found in the defence of 'the denominational school' a fine way of embarrassing the government. However, a large number of the supporters of *laïcité* appeared to lag behind the majority of public opinion. Public opinion had become pragmatic: genuinely satisfied with no school, they wanted at least to be able to choose. The complexity of the Savary bill contributed to its losing the media battle against the simple phrase 'freedom of education'. *Laïcité* appeared to be in a crisis.

## The Crisis of Laïcité

The failure of a unified organization for education under the banner of *laïcité*, promised by the left in 1981, took place at the time of the centenary celebration of the laws establishing *laïcité* in education. In a hundred years time, *laïcité* seemed to have lost its dimension as a social movement, while the very principle under-lying it—which the Fifth Republic had written down in its Constitution—no longer seemed subject to frontal attack.

Culturally, the dynamic element in *laïcité* had been the devel-opment of a morality independent of any religious foundation and authority. Better than a particular religion, *laïcité*, it was thought, should be able to ensure the moral unity and 'moral health' of the country. From 1880 to 1920, the values of *laïcité* were at the centre of the intellectual debate. Philosophers such as Alain and Bouglé, sociologists like Durkheim, as well as societies such as 'The Union of Freethinkers and Free Believers for a Moral Culture' influenced this debate.

But the supporters of *laïcité*, having generally won its battles, disbanded, particularly after the 'Great War'. Its militant members remained among the teachers. Could they adapt, renew a morality historically linked with the political takeover by the Republicans? To take an example, despite Jaurès, the morality taught in *laïcité* appeared to be primarily social, that is to say teaching solidarity rather than socialism. Teachers found themselves influenced by the theme of class struggle and then by the question of colonialism. Briefly, without forgetting concrete professional concerns, new battles were to be fought and a new intellectual climate was born: the 'immoralism' of André Gide, the 'non-conformism' of the 1930s, Sartre's combination of existentialism and Marxism after the Second World War.

In this context, the notion of neutrality as extolled by the Republican school of *laïcité*, became increasingly incomprehen-sible. This is doubtlessly connected with the successive failures of the supporters of *laïcité* regarding education, for the notion of *laïcité* appears to have been gradually reduced to that field alone. Nevertheless, other battles, those fought in the 1950s and 1960s for the legalization of contraception, bore an undeniable dimension of *laïcité*—the teaching of the Roman Catholic Church being the principal obstacle to that legalization—but that was not really comprehended by public opinion.

Generally speaking, over a period of a hundred years, five basic aspects of the morality of *laïcité* were undone. We shall consider them in reverse order to the one adopted earlier.

• The question of transcendence, a delicate matter since the turn of the century, had been proposed to eliminate 'duties towards

God' from the curriculum in State schools. Undertaken in many places, it was officially resolved by the 'National Bloc' government in 1923 at the time of separation to extend it to the country at large. Generally speaking, the whole question of transcendence was left to the religions.

- Republican civic-mindedness continued for a longer time. The underground Resistance to the German occupation during the Second World War was able to infuse it with new impetus, but subsequently the colonial wars, in Indo-China and Algeria, undermined it. History no longer followed a moral pattern and patriotism and universalism could no longer be harmoniously or clearly combined.

- The form of the State school grounded in *laïcité* was itself questioned. It was criticized as being a 'police school', a disciplinary instrument to make children conform to a capitalist society, that reproduces social inequalities. Criticisms, voiced since the beginning of the century, were very much present in the upheavals of May 1968. Other issues such as the lack of efficiency of the educational institution were later raised.

- Science and morality were dissociated. Science was increasingly understood as a 'techno-science', the functional efficiency of which was undeniable, but which, far from helping to resolve moral questions, created new ones, harder to resolve because of their intrinsic power. The development of genetics is significant, and in committees on bioethics, representatives with a 'religious outlook' are often asked to give their point of view.

- The 'good old morality' of Ferry, universal and eternal morals, stable moral evidence were all considered somewhat dated ideas. Changes had taken place in various fields, for instance sexuality (prior to 1965 a ban on complete nudity in magazines and films; in 1975, permission for the representation of non-simulated sexual acts or the representation of violence in films or television was given. The privatization of morality was followed by the privatization of religion.

## A Renewal of Laïcité

Are the culture and ethics of *laïcité* still possible in this context? Is *laïcité* simply an institutional rule; an outcome of history no longer relevant and open to numerous interpretations? At the very time when *laïcité* may have been viewed by some as anachronic, there was a renewal.

In the 1980s, moral terms reappeared with new relevance; some journalists spoke of a 'moral generation'. To the slogan 'The only solution, Revolution' raised by the militants of May 1968, their sons and daughters replied by asserting the need to 'respect differences'. There were many questions, notably concerning persons of non-European origin recently settled in France. Initially, very few references were made to *laïcité* as a possible answer to this type of concern, in all probability this being perceived as a stereotyped vision of French society.

However, a twofold evolution took place after 1984. Questions raised about the idea of 'the right to differ', even if magnanimous, were alone capable of resolving problems linked with the arrival of new communities. Carrying with them their history and civilization, the behaviour of such communities has not been without social impact and possibly questions French culture and its symbolic identity.

Many, of course, hesitate to publicly broach such questions for fear of nurturing racism. They do, however, perceive that elements of civilization—in which they lose interest in as much as they think they have become established—are the historical result of struggles and efforts that must be adapted to our times without allowing them to disappear. There is a wish to reconcile life in common, a form of unity, with pluralism and diversity. That is precisely the problem that *laïcité* faces on a long-term basis.

## *Laïcité* Today in France

In 1982, when the debate about schools was suddenly revived, Alain Savary, the minister, delivered a programmatic speech commemorating the laws of the 1880s that first established *laïcité*; he sought 'to enlighten the memory and to broaden the vision of *laïcité*'.

An analysis of his speech shows basic elements of issues that came to life after 1984. The historical section describes *laïcité* as a process of which the French Revolution represented a decisive stage and made it possible a century later to 'resolve the conflict between the old and the new France'. *Laïcité* endeavoured to be tolerant, reconciliatory, and respectful to the rights of minorities. It was given to conflict only in so far as a 'Roman Catholic Party' declared its 'incompatibility with the democratic spirit and modern society' and mobilized 'its own system of education against the Republic'. Without having said as much, this position takes up, to a considerable degree, the view held at the end of the nineteenth century by Fredinand Buisson, the right-hand man of Jules Ferry, and his successors in organizing schools in tune with *laïcité*.

Alain Savary proposed that *laïcité* 'be adapted to the contemporary situation'. For him, 'tolerance is only contested today by extremists and not by political parties or by the churches'. On the other hand, 'the division of our youth, that nightmare of the Republicans in 1880, alarms us perhaps less than the risk of uniformity through the possibilities offered by mass culture'. Schools based on *laïcité*, as conceived by the minister, should 'accommodate, so many signs of wealth, the cultural diversities, beginning with those of linguistic minorities with which our national community nurtures itself day after day'. Thanks to the 'ethical civilization' that *laïcité* builds, the 'one and indivisible Republic also provides each of its citizens with the possibility of being faithful to his or her particular membership'.

Between 1985 and 1990 the League of Education became the principal architect of the renewal of reflection on *laïcité*, to the extent of being accused by its partners in the National Centre of Action for Laïcité, *Centre National d'Action Laïque*, (CNAL) of acting on its own.

The League of Education is a confederation of societies of both teaching and non-teaching adults. Its educational and cultural activities cover a wide extra-curricular area, which makes it more attentive than the unions to developments in society, as well as a natural advocate of a concept of *laïcité* less isolated from the school debate.

In 1985 and 1986, the League undertook a series of initiatives intended to restore a dynamic vision to *laïcité*, making it an instrument of dialogue between different intellectual and spiritual trends; a method by which to approach the major problems of society. The situation was favourable: firmly in power, notwithstanding the interlude of the first cohabitation of a socialist president of the Republic with a Right-wing government in 1986–8, the government of the left was completely taken up with the necessity of managing the country. Marxism in the midst of intellectual rout freed a space for reflection, indeed, for utopia. In

1984 the 'defeat'of the supporters of *laïcité* in education was too recent for resistance to this renewal to be voiced.

It was firstly a matter of 'reactivating' a more complete memory of what *laïcité* meant. The foundation texts were republished. Without neglecting the school question, emphasis was placed on *laïcité* as the 'conscience of democracy', a 'creative ethics of solidarity', an effort 'to prevent the ossification of scientific thought in dogma', and 'to contain religion within its limits without denying its immense cultural significance', historical and social.

This reactivated memory then enabled an outline of the future of *laïcité*. The League started discussions with intellectual circles and religious figures in order to link *laïcité* with the major problems of society and to questions pertaining to the meaning of life. After a series of discussions had led to the confrontation of diverse versions of *laïcité*, meetings and a colloquium on the theme '*Laïcité* 2000' proposed a multidimensional approach: 'managing the legacy', 'powers and limits of science', '*laïcité*, religion, culture', 'citizenship and cultural identity', and 'to which extent the state?' were among some of the very meaningful topics considered.

Thus, numerous problems were deemed relevant for an active *laïcité*. For example emphasis was placed on the conflict which, among 'children of immigrants', opposes the culture taught at school and that handed down by the family, which is 'often from a rural milieu and more rooted in tradition'. In this situation, to ensure 'rights to the languages of emigration is a duty of *laïcité*', and a 'bilingual education' must be promoted in which 'the thorough knowledge of the mother language as the basis of the identity of an historic community' is added to the 'knowledge of a language of world communication which enables full participation in universal dialogue'. Moreover, it is necessary to abandon a concept of the universal centred on Western values and to recognize 'the universal aspect contained in various particular cultures'. French messianism, which considers this country to be the bearer of universal values, as 'the native country of the rights of man' (reference to the Declaration of 1789), is certainly a precious heritage: but to be progressively rejuvenated it must become a French contribution towards the elaboration of a new universality, the outcome of an encounter of cultures and values.

Another aspect advanced by the League of Education was to promote a process that aimed at introducing *laïcité* to industrial life, that is to say, 'opening up wide, firms and companies to the critical mind', to prevent them from being confined to 'the dual monarchy of employer power and a trade unionism at the mercy of a corporate propensity'. The school and its 'constituent bodies', on condition that they do not become isolated, could contribute towards introducing greater reflection, criticism, experimentation, and democracy into the everyday life of the industrial firm. This perspective, therefore, proposes a development of the relationship between the two institutions (which have the common tendency to want to deal with 'their affairs as family affairs', without outside interference) in the form of a critical contribution by the school to the industrial life and not, as is more generally the case, in the subordination of the educational institution to the needs of the market.

A last example is the reinterpretation of the idea of clericalism. The most threatening danger today for a '*laïcité* democracy' is seen to lie in 'civil clerics': abusive experts, a large state corps imbued with privileges, bosses by divine right, arrogant senior officials. The *laïcité* of the year 2000 must ensure that the citizens are not deprived of public debates on essential questions relating to medical ethics, information, education, etc.

## New Issues

A new meaning was given to *laïcité* by this intellectual effervescence. Even though it risked changing *laïcité* into a catch-all idea without much substance because of its very extensiveness. Without giving up a broad vision of *laïcité*, the League of Education decided to examine major contemporary questions in themselves and to redefine it in the context of a dialogue with religions.

Since the nineteenth century, protestantism has been a minority party participating in *laïcité*. This was once more the case through a statement drafted jointly by the League of Education and the Protestant Federation of France. Roman Catholicism gradually adapted itself. The role of the Christian Democratic Popular Republican Movement in 1946 made possible in the preceding year by a declaration of the French cardinals and archbishops in which a non-totalitarian *laïcité* was positively viewed. The second Vatican Council profoundly changed the hierarchic relations and the mentality of Roman Catholicism in France, without making evident the consequences of *laïcité*.

Nevertheless, even before the conflict over education could abate, the President of the Republic, Francois Mitterand, in February 1983 instituted the National Advisory Committee for Ethics in which, along with medical and scientific persons, five representatives of the major spiritual and philosophical groupings (Catholicism, Protestantism, Judaism, Islam, and non-religious Humanism) appointed by him were invited to participate. The creation of this committee appeared to be justified by the necessity to 'find references likely to lend meaning, and not only utilitarian efficiency, to the techno-scientific means' generated by biomedical research. It would enable the committee to constitute 'an instant representative of the existing plurality of currents of thought, among which there is no prevailing agreement as to the ultimate foundations of the individual' and to be able to base an ethical argumentation in reason which, within given metaphysical options and without harm to anyone, explains the foundations and ensures the coherence of the adopted principles.

This initiative, although it would have been little perceived at the time, marked a cultural turning point in French *laïcité*. In the nineteenth century, the refusal of the Roman Catholic Church to approve birth control by means other than continence had been (notwithstanding the prudence of confessors) one of the reasons for the rift between the Roman Catholic system of authority and a significant section of the population. From 1884 (re-establishment of divorce) to 1975 (authorization of abortion under certain conditions), the evolution of problems related to birth, sexuality, family, and death moved in the direction of an emancipation of society from religious norms. At the same time, medical interventionism was increasing, but it was presented as being solely functional and not interfering with freedom of choice, directed rather towards the possibility of well-being. This perspective implied that all scientific and technical progress in this regard was morally desirable.

The creation of the National Advisory Committee for Ethics shows that new problems such as *in vitro* fertilization, the development of antenatal genetic diagnosis, organ transplants, prolongation of life by medical means, and euthanasia give rise to a morally ambivalent perception of biomedical progress. At the same time it intervenes, in the form of increased efficiency, above all with that which lies innermost in every living system as well as in any social system; indeed, in the intellectual and emotional structuring of every human being.

In these circumstances, two typical positions could be defended. The first held it impossible to limit scientific and technical progress, viewing the freedom of the researcher to be absolute; or (a more moderate version), that it was for scientists and only for them, to establish the ethical guidelines in these matters. The second position asserted that, as non-scientific factors played an essential role—ranging from economic to ethical issues—one could neither passively submit to progress nor accept that the examination of problems raised could be restricted to an internal debate in the scientific community.

Just as Anglo-Saxon bioethics moved from enthusiasm for biomedical progress to the fear of biocrats, the creation of the National Advisory Committee for Ethics concluded in favour of the second solution. It admitted again that in this field moral reflection is socially relevant. Political power of course guards against too great an influence by religious institutions. Adopting a neo-Gallican view, it is the highest representative (the head of State) who appoints persons responsible for expressing various spiritual and philosophical views. But the turn-about remains no less evident. Instead of considering that religious and social norms be kept apart from one another, it is now admitted that religious traditions can contribute, within a pluralistic debate, to the building of meaning in society. The paradox to be noted here is that whereas anti-clericalism in the nineteenth century aimed unambiguously at religious clericalism, with the physician often appearing as a new moral authority for *laïcité* and ensuring freedom from clerical influence, in the National Advisory Committee for Ethics, the representatives of spiritual and philosophic views are 'lay people'. Because they more or less represent public opinion, their presence should make it possible to preclude a new clericalism, and prevent the debate from being exclusively that of biomedical experts.

Bioethics did not constitute, in the 1980s, the sole area in which new approaches of *laïcité* appeared. On 1 June 1988, the daily *Le Figaro* printed an article, 'History of Religions, a Surprising

Consensus'. It explained that there existed an 'agreement as to the necessity of a course in the history of religions, unconnected with catechism', between leaders of the *laïcite* movement and Roman Catholic authorities. However, as the journalist added, 'an understanding on how to move things forward is still to come'.

What are the reasons for such an agreement? Having been raised already at the beginning of the century, the question of a course in the history of religions in public education was brought up again in 1986 by teachers who were troubled by the lack of education their students received in religion. This issue was soon taken up by responsible authorities. On the side of *laïcité*, not only the League of Education, but also a powerful society, the Federation of National Education, declared itself to be in favour of such a course. The latter justified its position on the grounds that in order to enable students to understand present reality an information regarding religions was necessary. The Federation's national secretary noted that for several decades 'the existence of the Shiites and Sunnites has been known, the Irish problem or that of the Sikhs or Tamils has existed, the issues of the state of Israel have been considered. And, practically all of these conflicts have, if not a religious basis, at least a religious presentation.' On the side of the Roman Catholic Church, the perception of an increasing distance between the common culture and a basic knowledge of religious matters led them to believe that neutral teaching of this knowledge would be preferable to ignorance, even if, from a 'perspective of faith' the approach would be different.

Public opinion appeared to be ready for such an innovation. In September 1988, an opinion poll indicated that two out of three Frenchmen favoured the development of a course in the history of religions. Only 14 per cent felt that it would run counter to the principle of *laïcité*, and 19 per cent feared the risk of 'indoctrination'. A ministerial committee worked on the matter within the general framework of replanning the school syllabus. Nuances remained: while some propounded the idea of a specific course taught by teachers trained in the history of religions, others emphasized the necessity of conveying religious culture in various disciplines: literature, history, philosophy, etc.

Generally speaking, one notes in the late 1980s an important development of reflection, confrontation and of attempted self-understanding in civic and ethical as well as the political and religious spheres on the basis of *laïcité*. In effect, *laïcité* was a common reference that made it possible for groups of an educational or civic nature professing social or religious ethics to enter into a dialogue with one another despite their differences. The most significant encounter was perhaps the colloquium on '*Laïcité* and Current Issues', organized in April 1989 by *La Croix*, a Catholic daily, which, a century earlier had been one of the most adamant opponents of *laïcité*. Leaders of organizations supporting *laïcité*, Freemasons, academic, and political representatives of all persuasions exchanged viewpoints with members of religious orders and bishops. This was tantamount to explicitly recognizing the new reality that a Roman Catholic organization can offer a legitimate platform for reflection on and discussion of *laïcité*.

## *Laïcité* and Islam: The Confrontation of Two Models

Thus, the situation seems to have completely transformed over a few years. The extent of the changes should not, conceal the continued tensions that re-emerged at the end of 1988. The weekly magazine *L'Express*, of 4 November 1988, saw the condemnation of the Martin Scorsese film, '*The Last Temptation of Christ*' by the episcopate as 'vengeance of the Christian state'. Shortly afterwards, the Roman Catholic hierarchy took its position against the contraceptive RU 486 and against publicity promoting the use of condoms within the context of the fight against AIDS. The difficulties encountered by Muslims in finding mosques and the effect of Ayatollah Khomeini's fatwa against Salman Rushdie, the author of *The Satanic Verses*, raised problems—linked with *laïcité*— of religious freedom and the right to criticize religion.

The climate became heavy and grew impassioned once Islam was involved. If populations originating in the Maghreb had been largely considered 'migrant workers' until the beginning of 1980, their religious membership or origin became subsequently more important. Structural modifications (the end of temporary immigration, the policy regarding family reunion), international events, and a relative revival of religious fervour contributed to this change in social perception.

It was in this context that in the autumn of 1989 a problem arose at a secondary school in Creil. The principal, a dark-skinned

Frenchman from the Caribbean, forbade three Muslim students access to classrooms because they refused to remove the head-scarves concealing their hair. Taxed with 'racism', he claimed *laïcité*. The Minister for National Education, Lionel Jospin, decided that students ought to be talked out of displaying religious insignia at school; however, should they persist, they could not be forbidden from attending classes.

On 2 November 1989, *Le Nouvel Observateur* published a manifesto polemically written by five philosophers that denounced the instructions of the Minister as the 'Munich of the Republican School' (Munich, a reference to the pre-Second World War appeasement of the Nazis, that is to say giving in to fundamentalism). 'The only institution consecrated to the universal,' the school must be a 'place of emancipation' that refuses 'communal, religious, and economic pressures'. *Laïcité* is a constant 'battle' that demands 'discipline' and 'courage'. This met with a certain echo: for a number of teachers in particular, the head-scarf symbolized the subservience of women, and the refusal to remove it in class represented a loss of authority of the teacher over the students. Also brought into question was the strategy of Islamist groups seeking a special status for the Muslim community. The affair aroused fears amongst the public which had already been manifested in hostile reactions to the construction of mosques.

Some intellectuals denounced a 'Vichy of immigrant integration'. They drew attention to feelings of exclusion that permeated the Maghreb community and bolstered fundamentalism as well as the extreme right. They proposed the construction of a *laïcité ouverte*, an open *laïcité*, capable of offering to each person 'the objective conditions for individual choice in his or her own time' (*Politis*, 9 November 1989). This point of view did not defend the wearing of the head-scarf but held its immediate and authoritarian prohibition to be counter-productive because it obstructed a process in which intermediary stages and compromises were necessary: 'One does not transplant a tree by cutting its roots'. Supporters of this position advocated another way of understanding school. For them it was a fallible institution which should constitute a critical element in society, but without isolating itself. Rather than ignoring television, for example, the school should teach youth to watch it with a critical mind.

Several problems intermingled (the conception of school; a better 'strategy' to be adopted in the face of fundamentalism and to prevent exclusion, the extent to which plurality is compatible with national unity, the relationship to temporality, etc.), and this debate has become a central symbol of French passions. It will not come to an end: when removed in one place, the head-scarf appeared elsewhere on two separate occasions. The Council of State on 27 November 1989 and 2 November 1992 attempted to create a space for tolerance, between permissiveness and prohibition, by recommending that each case be dealt with on its merit and the wearing of religious insignia was not incompatible with *laïcité*. It becomes so if it is ostentatious, proselytizing or causes disorder, a pretext for refusing regular school attendance. In the autumn of 1994, the minister, Francois Bayrou, asked that the prohibition for 'ostentatious insignia' be included in the internal regulations of schools. Indeed, without being specifically named, the head-scarf was what was meant by ostentatious insignia, as the wearing of the Christian cross or the Jewish *kipa* were not considered to be ostentatious. Local conflicts revived the affair without really bringing new elements to bear on it. The disquiet of teachers, divided between the refusal to yield to pressure groups, manifest more in 1994 than in 1989, and the realization that the problem could not be resolved through exclusion, had become more acute over a period of five years.

This is hardly surprising. A comparison enables us to understand to *what* extent the quarrel over the head-scarf is indicative of the usually concealed socio-cultural crisis of French society. Another significant affair surfaced in the autumn of 1993: a draft for the revision of the Falloux law that would have allowed parity in public subsidies for investments in public and private schools. On 16 January 1994, a large demonstration protested in the name of *laïcité*. It was as large as the one held in June 1984 by the supporters of independent schools, and for many represented a form of 'symbolic revenge'. Furthermore, prior to the demonstration, the Constitutional Council had rescinded the contested measure, while conceding the very principle of subsidy.

This balanced position resolved the conflict as quickly as it had developed and did not affect the public image of the heirarchy of the Roman Catholic Church, which had shown prudence on this occasion. It can be said that tensions that brought the Roman Catholic Church into question—principally the policy of Pope John Paul II opposing population control inspired by the UNO (World Conference on Population and Development in Cairo,

September 1994) and his opposition to abortion and even to contraception—scarcely affected the positive view that the French have always had of Roman Catholicism. An opinion poll in December 1994 showed that this religion was favoured by 68 per cent of the French people. On the other hand, a poll conducted in September 1994 indicated that, for the majority of the French, fanaticism, submission, and the rejection of Western values were characteristic of Islam. For their part, Muslims who were questioned felt an increase in racism and violence on television. They thought that the three key-words of their religion were 'justice', 'liberty', 'democracy', and were convinced that life in France was compatible with regard to 'all the prescriptions of Islam'. The divergence in cultural perception between the Muslims living in France and the rest of the population is clear.

This divergence indicates the growing difficulty in the integration of immigrant populations of Muslim belief or origin who are often settled on the outskirts of a city; areas prone to break up and directly subject to increased unemployment and the crisis of the Welfare State. The supporters of *laïcité* are divided on this constellation of problems. The 'Conference of *Laïcité*' organized in October 1990 by Freemasons and the conference on 'Pluralistic *Laïcité*' held in December that year under the aegis of the League of Education illustrate this divergence.

The first position favours a return to, and the development of, 'Republican principles', which are considered as a precious historical acquisition, specifically French as well as expressing universal values still fully relevant. Free and equal individuals are, by contrast, integrated in a society that ensures freedom of conscience by clearly separating religious adherence from citizenship and implementing that separation. The use of reason of which the school is the vigilant guardian ensures, to a necessary and adequate degree, the cohesion of public space. This French 'republican model' is contrasted with the Anglo-Saxon 'democratic model' in which religion intervenes in the public space. According to the philosopher Régis Debray, this difference is, in its origin, the result of the socio-cultural break brought about by the Protestant Reformation which asserted itself in Anglo-Saxon countries but was thwarted in France:

In countries with Protestant roots, lands by choice of democracy, the right of dissidence was included in belief, the spirit of religion was one with the spirit of freedom. On Roman Catholic territory, the right of dissidence had to be wrested by the state from the church because the latter declared itself the eternal owner of truth and goodness.

For R. Debray this rift gave rise to different types of cultures, leading to different views regarding politics and social issues:

The universal idea governs the republic, the local idea governs democracy, [...]. The former proclaims to the world the rights of a universal man no one has ever seen. The second defends the rights of Americans, Englishmen or Germans, rights which have already been acquired by clearly limited but real communities. [...] The state, when a republic, is unitary and by nature centralized. It unifies, in spirit of customs and corporate bodies, weights and measures, dialects, local administrations, educational programmes. On the other hand, democracy, which blossoms out in the multicultural, is federal by calling and decentralized by scepticism.

The 'universal' in this conception differs from that supported by the League of Education, and is embodied by French republican values, whereas the 'particular', that which belongs to a particular community, would be a rule in democracies of the Anglo–Saxon kind. But why would the specific history of France have given birth to the universal? Because, not having a religion that accepted pluralism (the Roman Catholic Church views itself as one and hierarchical in its structure, whereas the Protestant churches are plural and understand unity on a federal basis), France at the time of the French Revolution and in the course of the nineteenth century when *laïcité* came into being and matured, had to gain liberty at the expense of the social influence of religion. Liberty was a conquest of Reason which was considered as universal. In the French republican school, one does not learn to believe, 'but to reason'.

The second position, which seems to me to be both more in keeping with historical reality and more open to dialogue of civilizations and cultures does not deny the salience of the 'republican model' in the development of *laïcité* in France. It has a more qualified and evolutionary vision of things.

First, this position considers that the republican model has never worked historically without entering into a certain number of compromises with religions. Thus, when the school of *laïcité* was set up, the institution of a school-free day in the middle of the week, to enable children to follow catechism, whose parents so wished, was a conciliatory measure which displeased some very strict Republicans. Likewise, the separation of Church and State in 1905 was the most liberal arrangement and one that best respected the specific characteristics of each religion that eventually prevailed. That has a certain logic, for the French Republic also wants, in its manner, democracy. There thus exists in the French system itself an internal tension between a specific republican model—such as Régis Debray describes in broad outline—and the general requirements of democracy—the possibility of collective and public manifestations of the freedom of conscience and religion—that bring the French situation closer to that of other democracies.

Now, this second position holds that the republican model, in its historic specificity, finds itself in a new situation today. We have already considered the loss of a strong reference to the ethics of *laïcité* and the reason for that crisis. One must also emphasize the integration of France in a global exchange of not only material, but cultural and symbolic goods. This leads to a confrontation of the different models rather than considering them to be immutable. Finally, one might ask how to distinguish a dynamic process of immigrant integration from a policy of pure and simple assimilation.

The same individual can give a certain value to one or other of these two models and hesitate on what ought to be done. The first position today receives manifold political support. References to the 'republican pact' are numerous in the France of 1995, on both the Right and on the Left. They sometimes risk changing the renewal of republican *laïcité* into a primarily defensive attitude conveying diverse fears in the face of Islam; fears that challenge the European construction. It would be disastrous if, instead of working out the tension between republicanism and democracy for all religions, we were to apply the republican model effectively only to Islam while Christianity and Judaism benefit from democratic demands. It is also for this reason that the second position appears to me to be better than the first but it also proceeds more by trial and error. It raises essential questions without having (yet?) found the answers that contribute to unity and dynamism. It is also easier to find Roman Catholic partners for the second position rather than Muslim. I believe that it constitutes an opportunity for a future in which socio-cultural and socio-religious conflicts have been relatively mastered and contribute to the construction of the future.

Any reflection on *laïcité* implies a consideration of the elements of democracy. What is its encompassing institution? Certainly no longer religion and definitely not education or medicine, linked as they are with ideologies of progress currently in a state of crisis. On the other hand, communication can perhaps be seen as an inclusive institution. The Church is no longer at the centre of the village but TV screens are found at the heart of each home.

# 5

# Muslim Minorities in Liberal Democracies: The Politics of Misrecognition[*]

*Joseph H. Carens and Melissa S. Williams*

## Muslim Migrants and the 'Clash of Civilizations'

O ver the past three decades, immigrants from Asia, Africa, and Latin America have settled in Europe and North America in much larger numbers than in previous eras. Their arrival has brought to the fore questions about cultural difference and liberal democracy. In what ways may receiving states expect immigrants to adapt to the dominant culture and way of life in their new home? In what ways should the receiving states recognize the cultural commitments and group identities of the immigrants?

These questions are often seen as particularly urgent with regard to the social and political integration of immigrants of Islamic faith. Muslims have featured prominently in a number of recent political

[*] Versions of this article were presented at the 1994 meeting of the International Political Science Association in Berlin, the 1994 meeting of the American Political Science Association in New York, and a November 1995 conference organized by the European Task Force on Canadian Studies in cooperation with the Association for Canadian Studies in the Netherlands on 'Organizing Diversity: Migration Policy and Practice in Canada and Europe' in Berg en Dal, the Netherlands. We thank the participants at these meetings for their responses. We would particularly like to acknowledge the able research assistance of Pak-cheong Choo and Katherine Bullock and the helpful comments of Katherine Bullock, Shelley Burtt, and Amy Gutmann.

conflicts. In Britain, there was the Salman Rushdie affair; in France, *L'affaire des foulards*; in Germany, the debate over the status of the descendants of the Turkish guest workers. In all these cases and others, questions about the relation of Muslim immigrants to the states where they have settled have provoked public debates about the meaning of citizenship and the requirements of liberal-democratic principles. Some people speak almost apocalyptically about a 'clash of civilizations' between Islam and the West.[1] Much of this alleged clash involves relations between states, but immigrants of Islamic faith are often constructed as a kind of fifth column in this struggle, because they live in the West yet (supposedly) carry with them these threatening values and alien ways of life. Thus, some people argue, it is particularly important to identify the conflicts between Islamic beliefs and practices and those that undergird the liberal-democratic institutions of the West and to limit the capacity of Muslim immigrants to pass on their norms and values to others, including their children.

We think that this stance is wrong, both in the way it portrays Muslim migrants as a threat and in the way it fails to respect their legitimate concerns. While it is reasonable to ask questions about the kinds of cultural adaptation receiving states can expect of immigrants, any serious commitment to liberal-democratic principles requires a much greater openness to Islam and to Muslim migrants than those allegedly concerned with defending Western civilization seem prepared to acknowledge. The article develops our view in three stages. First, we consider whether the centrality of Islam in the lives of Muslims conflicts with the requirements of democratic citizenship. In the second section, we critically examine common critiques of Islamic practice and doctrine among would-be defenders of liberal democracy and gender equality; and we attempt to show the ways in which these views tend to mischaracterize the normative issues that particular practices raise, wrongly attribute objectionable practices to Islam as such, or indulge a double standard by ignoring parallel issues within religious traditions that liberal-democratic cultures already accept. Finally, we step back from particular practices in Islam to assess

1 Samuel Huntington, 'The Clash of Civilizations?', *Foreign Affairs* 72, 3 (Summer 1993), pp 22–49. For a review and critique of this view of Islam, also see Esposito, 1992.

the strength of Muslim claims to special forms of group recognition in the light of their status as immigrants.

## Islam as a Communal Identity in Liberal Society

One question that one frequently encounters, either implicitly or explicitly, is whether Muslims, given the strength of their communal identity, can be full members of liberal-democratic societies. In the view of some democratic theorists, membership in the democratic process requires a capacity to distance oneself from one's identity in order to put oneself in the position of another. On this view, this capacity for reflective distance from one's commitments is a prerequisite for genuine dialogue. But both Muslims and non-Muslims have argued that Islam constitutes, for many of its members, a communal identity which is, to borrow Sandel's term, thoroughly constitutive of their identity as individuals, something from which they cannot and do not wish to distance themselves.[2] As Anne Phillips has articulated this concern.

Democracy surely does imply tolerance of difference,...[yet] it is none-theless hard to conceptualize without some means of distancing ourselves from those qualities we used to think of as most intrinsic. Somehow or other, we have to be able to stand back from the things that are peculiar to us...and try to think ourselves into another person's place. Part of the anxiety generated by fundamentalism—whether it is of a religious or political variety—is that it makes it impossible for its adherents to engage in the process, for even in principle they cannot treat their beliefs as detached.[3]

Does this pose a problem for the position of Muslims in liberal democracies? In considering this question, we should first draw attention to the variability among Muslims. Muslims do not all fit a single mould. We should not suppose that they all have exactly the same understanding of Islamic doctrine and its implications for social life, the same unqualified and unambivalent commitment to Islam, and so on. Indeed, there is enormous variability among

[2] See Michael Sandel, *Liberalism and the Limits of Justice* (Cambridge University Press: Cambridge, 1982).
[3] See Anne Phillips, *Engendering Democracy* (Pennsylvania State University Press: University Park, PA, 1991), p. 57.

Muslims as there is among Christians, Jews, and other religious groups, with regard to doctrine, practice, and ways of life. For some immigrants, Islam may be primarily a cultural marker, a symbolic locus of identity that has little bearing on the norms that guide their actions in public and private life. For others, the commitment to Islam is at the centre, guiding every activity and choice. For many, it is something in between.

Second, if we focus only on those Muslims who do have a powerful sense of communal identity as described, we have to consider whether the same questions would be raised about Christians or Jews with comparably strong senses of religious identification. Anyone who reads the anti-immigrant literature from the nineteenth and early twentieth century is bound to be struck by the similarity between the doubts and fears expressed with respect to Catholics and Jews then and the doubts and fears expressed with regard to Muslims now. One finds the same rhetoric about alien invasions, with Catholics and Jews portrayed as threatening and unassimilable because of their illiberal and un-democratic values.[4] Nobody today would defend those earlier views (or at least nobody should). Nobody today would question whether Christians or Jews could be full members of a liberal-democratic society, whatever their religious beliefs, although many committed Jews and Christians would reject the idea that they are obliged to distance themselves from their own religious identities to engage in the democratic process. One of the recurring and largely justifiable complaints of Muslims is that the standards used to evaluate their behaviour and beliefs are different from those used with respect to other members of society.

Finally, we might ask whether the problem here lies not with the Muslims but with an understanding of democracy that would

---

[4] For original sources, see William Henry Wilkins, *The Alien Invasion* (Methuen: London, 1982), 30 entries in John Bueaker and Nicholas Burckel, *Immigration and Ethnicity: A Guide to Information Sources* (Gale Research Company: Detroit, 1977), pp 208–10. For a scholarly discussion, see Robert Dwine, *American Immigration Policy* (Yale University Press: New Haven, 1957), John Garrard, 'Parallels of Protest: English Reaction to Jewish and Commonwealth Immigration', *Race* 9, 1 (1967); John Higham, *Strangers in the Land: Patterns of American Nativism* (Atheneum: New York, 1963), and *Send These to Me: Jews and Other Immigrants in Urban America* (Athenum: New York, 1975).

exclude or require fundamental changes from not only many Muslims but many other people, at least if as well applied consistently. This model of deliberative democracy requires that people abstract themselves from their identities. But there is an alternative model of democracy that simply requires that people listen and interact with each other. To treat other people with respect—which is a requirement of deliberative democracy—does not necessarily require that one suspend one's own commitments or distance oneself from one's own identity. Indeed, conversations are often most fruitful when people speak from their deepest selves.

Someone might object that religious beliefs can have no standing in a pluralist society that must be committed to respect for all religions. But consider the case of Martin Luther King, Jr. whose effective leadership of the civil rights struggle in the US, a struggle for democratic justice, was inextricably linked to his religious rhetoric. King's understanding of justice was rooted in his Christian convictions, and he could not have articulated it adequately without reference to them. Other Christians were of course staunch defenders of segregation, while many of those who supported the civil rights struggle were not Christian. But that does not make King's method of communication inappropriate. To be sure, religious rhetoric can often be abused and manipulated, but so too can a purely secular rhetoric. Muslims should therefore themselves be free to bring their religious views to the democratic dialogue—recognizing, of course, that to be effective in persuading others they will have to find a way (as King did) to communicate their convictions in ways that resonate with people who do not share their religion.

Assuredly, there may be a point at which the claims of religious community become incommensurable with the claims of democratic citizenship. This seems especially likely at the point where religious communities seek to reshape the public sphere in their own image and at the expense of other religious or moral conceptions. An inquiry into the deeper question of what liberal democracies may in general claim of religious communities would take us far beyond the scope of this article.[5] Our point here is

---

[5] Other theorists, however, have taken this question up directly. For illuminating recent discussions, see Shelley Burtt, 'Religious Parents, Secular Schools: A Liberal Defense of an Illiberal Education', *The Review of Politics*

simply that it is wrong to make allowances for Christian and Jewish communities and to refuse to make them for Muslim communities.

## Islam and Gender Equality

To acknowledge the right of Muslims to participate in the democratic dialogue without abandoning their fundamental convictions is not to say how non-Muslims should respond to them. In the next section of this article, we will focus on one particular area where the beliefs and practices of Muslims are often alleged to be in fundamental conflict with the values and practices of liberal-democratic societies: the issue of gender equality.

We begin by articulating views critical of Islam that we wish to challenge. According to the critics, Islamic practices and conceptions of women's role in society are incompatible with the liberal-democratic commitment to equal citizenship. The critics say that Islam authorizes the genital mutilation of young girls, that it legitimates patriarchal authority and even wife-beating, that it permits polygamy, and that it requires women to dress in restrictive ways that limit their capacity to act in the public sphere. From the critics' perspective, rather than accommodating these practices as a way of respecting the cultural commitments of Muslim immigrants, liberal-democratic states should challenge and constrain these practices as much as possible, prohibiting some of them and insisting on a legal regime and an educational system based on principles of gender equality.

In our view, the critics' account is inaccurate both with regard to Islam and to the requirement of liberal democracy. Some of the practices mentioned above are deeply objectionable and should be prohibited, but it is wrong, or at least deeply misleading, to describe them as Islamic practices. Some of the practices are Islamic but are less in conflict with gender equality than the critics suppose.

56 (Winter 1994), pp 51–70; Sanford Levinson, 'The Confrontation of Religious Faith and Civil Religion: Catholics Becoming Justices', *De Paul Law Review* 39 (Summer 1990), pp 1047–81, and 'Religious Language and Public Square', *Harvard Law Review* 105 (June 1992), pp 2061–79; and Stephen Macedo, 'Liberal Civic Education and Religious Fundamentalism: The Case of God v. John Rawls?', *Ethics* 105 (April 1995), pp 468–96.

Finally, liberal democracies do and must tolerate some departures from gender equality in the name of respect for religious freedom.

Let us begin with the last point. As we noted above in discussing the issue of communal identification, it is unreasonable to make demands of Muslims that are not made of adherents of other religions with comparable views and practices. The overall claim that women are subordinated within Islam is a claim that can also be made about Christianity and Judaism. Both Christianity and Judaism have deeply patriarchal elements in their religious traditions. Some versions of both religions, as they are understood and practised today, have very negative views of female sexuality, teach that women's primary responsibilities are in the home, assert the authority of the husband within the household, and so on. Yet no reasonable person suggests that traditional Catholics or fundamentalist Protestants or orthodox Jews should be required to modify these religious beliefs and practices as a condition of full membership in liberal-democratic societies.

Some might object that there is a tremendous range of theological views within Christianity and Judaism, and that this deep patriarchalism is characteristic of only a small part of each. But there is great variability within Islam as well, both in practice and in theological interpretation. Muslim feminists argue that there is nothing in Islam properly understood that requires the subordination of women.[6] The question here, however, is how to respond to those elements in a religious tradition—whether Islam or Christianity or Judaism—that see patriarchalism (in some form) as religiously mandated.

Why are patriarchal versions of Christianity and Judaism tolerated? Perhaps because the commitment to gender equality in liberal-democratic states is not as deep in practice as is alleged when ideological contrasts are drawn between Islam and the West, but

---

[6] See Leila Ahmed, *Women and Gender in Islam: Historical Roots of a Modern Debate* (Yale University Press: New Haven, 1992); Fatima Mernissi, *Beyond the Veil: Male–Female Dynamics in Modern Muslim Society* (Indiana University Press: Bloomingtory 1987), and *The Veil and the Male Elite: A Feminist Interpretation of Women's Rights in Islam* (trans.), Mary Jo Lakeland (Addison-Wesley Pub. Co.: Reading, Mass., 1991); Nawal Sa'dwaj, *The Hidden Face of Eve: Women in the Arab World*, (trans. and ed.), Sherif Hetata (Zed Press: London, 1980); Amina Wadud-Muhsin, *Qur'an and Woman* (Penerbit Fajar Bakti Sdn. Bld.: Kuala Lumpur, 1992).

also because, even at the level of principle, the commitment to gender equality stands in some tension with other liberal-democratic commitments. Liberal-democratic principles entail a deep commitment to freedom of religion, of conscience, of thought, and of opinion. For that reason, a liberal-democratic state cannot require intellectual or moral conformity, not even to its own ideals, although the state may legitimately try to inculcate key elements of the public democratic culture through the educational system and may establish a legal order that reflects its basic principles. Furthermore, a commitment to individual autonomy entails the recognition of some sort of private or personal sphere that the state may not regulate, including much of the activity within the family sphere. At a minimum then, any liberal-democratic state will have to leave untouched some beliefs and practices that conflict with gender equality, and it is unreasonable to demand more of Muslims in this respect than of the adherents of other faiths.

## Female Circumcision

How then should we respond to the specific practices that critics claim are characteristic of Islam and in conflict with gender equality? Consider first the charge that Islam authorizes the genital mutilation of young girls. We will argue that the most prevalent forms of the practice to which the critics object should indeed be prohibited, but that modified forms might be permissible and that it is misleading and harmful to claim that Islam authorizes the practice. We consider first the question of how to respond to the practice, assuming that some immigrants want to continue it for cultural and religious reasons. Then we turn to questions about the relation of this practice to Islam.

In a number of countries in Africa, Asia, and South America—mainly in 20 countries in the middle belt of Africa—girls commonly undergo some form of circumcision. The procedure ranges from what is sometimes called 'circumcision proper' (incision or removal of the prepuce of the clitoris), to clitoridectomy or excision (removing part or all of the clitoris and often part or all of the labia minora as well), to infibulation (removing the clitoris, the labia minora, and part of the labia majora, and sewing together the two sides of the vulva, leaving only a small opening for menstrual blood and urine).[7] The most common version appears to be some form of excision. In the mid-1980s, it was estimated that 75–80 million females in Africa were affected. This is an ancient practice whose origins are unclear. The (overlapping) reasons offered for continuing the practice of female circumcision are that it is traditional, that it is connected to cultural norms regarding sexuality and reproduction, that it is religiously required or at least encouraged, and that girls will not be accepted as eligible

[7] For information on this topic, we have drawn upon Dorkenoo and Elworthy, *Female Genital Mutilation: Proposals for Change*, 3rd edn (London and Minority Rights Group, 1992); Fran Hosken, *The Hosken Report: Genital and Sexual Mutilation of Females*, 3rd edn (Women's International Network News: Lexington, MA, 1983); United Nations Commission on Human Rights (UNCHR), *Report of the Working Group on Traditional Practices Affecting the Health of Women and Children* (UNCHR: New York, 1986); Olayinka Koso-Thomas, *The Circumcision of Women: A Strategy for Eradication* (Zed: London, 1987); Nahid Toubia, *Female Genital Mutilation: A Call for Global Action*, 2nd edn (Rainbow/Women Ink: New York, 1995); Sami Aldeeb Abu-Salieh, 'To Mutilate in the Name of Jehovah or Allah: Legitimization of Male and Female Circumcision', unpublished paper available from the author at Ochettaz 17, 1025 St. Salpice, Switzerland (1994); Janice Boddy, *Wombs and Alien Spirits: Women, Men, and the Zar Cult in Northern Sudan* (University of Wisconsin Press: Madison, 1996).

There is some variation in terminology in the literature, with some people restricting the use of the term 'circumcision' to the less radical procedures, though the broader usage (which we follow here) seems more common. The use of the term 'circumcision proper' for the mildest form of the procedure clearly takes male circumcision as the standard of reference. Some people refer to (removal of the prepuce) as 'Sunna circumcision', an Islamic term whose significance in this context we discuss below in the text. Toubia says that, in her medical practice in Sudan, she has 'not found a single case of female circumcision in which only the skin surrounding the clitoris is removed, without damage to the clitoris itself'. (Toubia [1995], p. 712, cited in Boddy [1996], p. 7 [see above]).

Some people object to the use of the term 'female circumcision' precisely because it suggests a procedure analogous to male circumcision and thus conceals the much more drastic character of infibulation or even of clitoridectomy. They insist on the term 'genital mutilation' (see, for example, Bronwy Winter, 'Women, the Law, and Sexual Relativism in France: The Case of Excision', *Signs* 19, 4, pp 939–74). In our view, it is indeed important not to permit the physical reality to be obscured, though it is also important

marriage partners and full members of the community unless they have been circumcised. These reasons continue to have weight for some immigrants who have their daughters circumcised either in the West (usually covertly) or in their countries of origin while visiting on vacation—although most immigrants from countries where female circumcision is common do not continue the practice after they have arrived in the West, and some people leave their countries of origin (even seeking refugee status) precisely to avoid having their daughters subjected to circumcision.

Suppose someone argued that female circumcision should be permitted in liberal-democratic states because it is clearly an important social practice for some people and immigrants cannot reasonably be expected simply to abandon their pre-existing cultural and religious commitments.[8] That sort of argument would have considerable weight with regard to some issues, as we shall see later. How does it work here?

Our basic answer is this: the respect due to particular cultural and religious commitments must be assessed in the context of their implications for other fundamental human interests. Female circumcision as normally practised has horrific physical and psychological consequences that have been well documented. Even the mildest form of clitoridectomy is painful, permanent, debilitating, and devoid of health benefits. One crucial responsibility of any

---

to recognize that every description, including medical and scientific ones, is culturally laden (Boddy [1996] [see above]). We have chosen to use the term 'female circumcision' because that is the term used by the people who practise it and we want to consider the argument that the practice is defensible, or at least ought to be tolerated in Western states on the grounds of cultural and religious freedom. 'Mutilation' is a highly evaluative term. If we define as genital mutilation a practice that the people who engage in it call female circumcision, we face the reasonable objection that we have simply begged the question about its moral status.

[8] This sort of argument has actually been advanced in public debates and in legal trials in France. See Winter (1994), fn. 7, for a review and discussion. The question of what is appropriate to permit within the legal framework of a Western liberal-democratic state is different from the question of whether it is appropriate for Westerners to intervene in some way against female circumcision in the states where it is traditionally practised. The latter question raises a host of complications that we do not attempt to address here. For a sensitive discussion of some aspects of the issue, see Boddy (1996), fn. 7.

liberal-democratic state is to protect the physical safety and bodily integrity of its inhabitants, including children. This responsibility obliges the state to set strict limits to the authority of parents over their children, regardless of the parents' motives (that is even if they believe themselves to be acting in the best interests of the child). Thus, it is proper for the state to restrict or prohibit cultural and religious practices that cause serious harm to children. Given the consequences of female circumcision, any liberal-democratic state not only may but should regard the practice as genital mutilation and prohibit it from being performed upon young girls.[9]

This general line of argument is subject to two important qualifications, the first focusing on the involuntary nature of the procedure, the second on the degree of harm it causes. So far we have described female circumcision as it is most widely practised: that is, upon girls who are usually not consulted and who are too young to consent even if they were. But suppose it were a question of an adult woman voluntarily undergoing circumcision? This is not a purely hypothetical or unimaginable example. Bhikhu Parekh has told one of us in conversation that, after giving a lecture in which he criticized the practice of female circumcision, he was challenged by a Nigerian woman who said that she had voluntarily undergone excision as an adult just before the birth of her first child as a way of reducing her sexual desires. She described this adult, pre-childbearing circumcision as the normal practice of her community.[10]

Would it still be obligatory or even permissible for a liberal-democratic state to ban the practice for adults? Every liberal regime must grant considerable latitude to individuals to lead their lives and even to treat their bodies however they choose. Liberal states permit women to undergo a wide variety of cosmetic surgeries (breast enlargement and reduction, liposuction, facelifts, etc.) and bodily alterations (tattooing, body-piercing) in order to meet

[9] To say that genital mutilation should be legally prohibited is not necessarily to say that an aggressive criminal prosecution of those who continue the practice is the best strategy for eliminating it. In France, for example, the opponents of genital mutilation are divided among themselves about the best approach to the problem (see Winter [1994], fn. 7).

[10] For a general account of the practice in Nigeria, see Robert A. Myers et al., 'Circumcision: Its Nature and Practice Among Some Ethnic Groups in Southern Nigeria', *Social Science and Medicine* 21, 5 (1985), pp 581–8.

cultural norms regarding beauty and sexuality. On the one hand, feminists rightly criticize many of these practices for the ways in which they reflect, serve, and reinforce problematic ideals of the female body.[11] These practices, too, could be described as forms of bodily mutilation. But feminists also insist on the rights of women to control their own bodies and are wary of granting state authorities the power to restrict women's choices. Criticism is one thing, prohibition and control another. Why should female circumcision be treated differently from these other forms of bodily mutilation?

One possible answer to this question would be that female circumcision has much more harmful consequences than the other forms of mutilation, both in terms of health risks and in terms of normal bodily functioning even if it is performed under sound medical conditions.[12] This answer carries some weight, although it may underestimate the health risks of the other procedures which have become apparent with the public controversy over the consequences of breast implants. In any event, it points to what we think is the right principle here. There are some limits even to control over one's own body. People are not permitted to sell their organs, for example. Some forms of bodily alteration are so harmful that they should not be permitted even if the person consents.

Does female circumcision fall into this category? In our view, infibulation probably does, but as one moves in the direction of less radical forms of circumcision, the answer is much less clear.

[11] Kathryn Pauly Morgan, 'Women and the Knife: Cosmetic Surgery and the Colonization of Women's Bodies', *Hypatia* 6, 3 (1991), pp 25–53.

[12] Many of these worst consequences of female circumcision stem from the fact that it is normally performed without anaesthesia and in unhygienic conditions. In recent years, people committed to having their daughters circumcised for cultural and religious reasons but concerned about the health consequences have sought to have the procedures performed in modern medical facilities when they could afford to do so. While this would doubtlessly reduce some of the negative health consequences of circumcision, the WHO and other agencies concerned with the practice have consistently opposed this sort of effort and have urged professional medical personnel not to be involved in performing female circumcisions. [See World Health Organization (WHO), 'A Traditional Practice that Threatens Health—Female Circumcision', *WHO Chronicle* 40, 1 (1986).] We think this is the right course.

We find the practice of clitoridectomy abhorrent, and we would want to challenge anyone who would defend it. But should an adult woman like the one who confronted Parekh be legally prohibited from undergoing such a procedure in a licensed medical facility? We think not. Our tentative view is that such a ban interferes too much with the right people ought to have to conduct their lives in accordance with their own convictions and cultural commitments.

What should we think of what has been called 'circumcision proper' (that is, removal only of the prepuce of the clitoris)? Some discussions of female circumcision seem to dismiss altogether the cultural and religious dimensions of the practice, as though these should carry no weight at all—at least in deciding whether infants and children may be subjected to circumcision. But on such a view, it seems hard to understand why the practice of male circumcision should be tolerated either, at least in the absence of evidence about its health benefits. Medical views of male circumcision have varied over the years, and we are not in a position to assess them. At a minimum, it seems safe to say that there have been times when the prevailing view was that there was no medical justification for circumcising all males. Nevertheless, so far as we know, no liberal-democratic state in recent times has tried to prevent people from having their male children circumcised for cultural and religious reasons. (Male circumcision is traditionally practised by Muslims, Jews, and some Africans who are neither Muslim nor Jewish.) Some people have argued for the prohibition of male circumcision on the grounds that male circumcision involves cutting healthy tissue without medical reason, causes some pain, and occasionally leads to serious complications.[13] These arguments have never prevailed politically, even though in most jurisdictions male circumcision has religious or cultural significance only for a minority of the population. The conventional view seems to be that the minor pain and small risk associated with the practice are outweighed by the meaning attached to it by the child's parents and the cultural and religious community to which they belong and which the child will therefore join. We think that is a reasonable view. Physical well-being is essential, but it is not the

[13] See Sami Aldeeb Abu-Salieh (1994), fn. 8 and Gérard Zwang, *La fonction érotique*, 3rd edn (Robert Laffort: Paris, 1978).

only human interest. It is entirely appropriate to give weight to the concerns people may have to maintain rituals and practices that have deep importance in a community.

If female circumcision were culturally important and caused no more harm than male circumcision, we think that it would be appropriate to permit it, too, even for children. Would 'circumcision proper' fall into this category? That requires information about its health consequences that we do not have. At the least, though, we can say that it seems possible to imagine a form of female circumcision in which the health risks were small enough that it should be permitted for cultural or religious reasons. This is not merely a hypothetical possibility. On one account that we have read, a woman who wanted her daughter to maintain the cultural ties and communal standing that come with passage through this rite of initiation into womanhood, but did not want her to suffer the physical consequences of mutilation, persuaded the relevant actors (themselves female) in her community to accept a pinprick of blood from the clitoris as a satisfactory performance of the ritual.[14] It may be objected that this is not the traditional practice, but traditions can evolve without disintegrating. If a particular community were to find that this sort of ritual played an important cultural role, it is hard to see why it should be prohibited.

Let us turn now to the question of the relation between Islam and female circumcision.[15] Female circumcision is practised by Muslims in some countries, but not by those in others—including Saudi Arabia, Algeria, Iran, Iraq, Libya, Morocco, and Tunisia, all of which have predominantly Islamic populations. We have not been able to find any estimates of the overall percentage of Muslims who practise female circumcision; but judging from the relative populations of countries in which it is and is not practised, it would appear to be a minority practice within Islam. Furthermore, in those countries in Africa where female circumcision is most common, it is practised by Christians, animists, and others besides

---

[14] See Christine Hodge, 'Throwing Away the Circumcision Knife', *the Globe & Mail Toronto*, 15 Jan. 1994, p. D2.

[15] Our discussion of circumcision and Islam draws upon Dorkenoo and Elworthy (1992), pp 13–14, UNCHR (1986), pp 12–13, Boddy (1989), p. 53, and Aldeeb Abu-Salieh (1994). (See fn. 7.)

Muslims and clearly pre-dates Islam. Interviews with women who have been circumcised or have had their daughters circumcised cite a variety of reasons for continuing the practice, as noted above, with religious motivations playing some role but generally a less important one than tradition and social acceptance.

From a doctrinal perspective, the status of female circumcision within Islam appears to be contested, in contrast with the status of male circumcision which all Muslims agree is mandatory. The debate focuses primarily around the interpretation of Prophet Muhammad's injunction to a traditional practitioner of circumcision not to go to extremes. Most Muslims take this as a criticism of the most severe forms of female circumcision such as infibulation, and in countries where Islamic revitalization movements have had success (as in Sudan) there have been religious pressures to modify traditional practices. What seems more in dispute is whether the statement by the Prophet implies some endorsement of the practice in a less severe form. Some argue that it does not, and further claim that other Koranic injunctions against bodily harm provide an Islamic basis for opposing the practice of female circumcision altogether. Others claim that the statement implies that female circumcision is '*sunna*', which is sometimes presented as meaning permissible and other times as recommended for those aspiring to be good Muslims. And among those who take the view that female circumcision is *sunna*, there seems to be disagreement about whether this applies only to 'circumcision proper' or also to some form of clitoridectomy or excision.

In sum, many Muslims do not practice female circumcision or see it as part of Islam; but some do. This makes it descriptively misleading, though not entirely inaccurate, to describe female circumcision as an Islamic practice. But how is this relevant to the question of how liberal-democratic states should respond to Muslim immigrants? After all, it is not the business of political authorities in a liberal-democratic state to pass judgements on what is authentically Islamic.

In one sense, this objection is certainly correct. For the most part, it is appropriate for political authorities to take religious claims at face value. If some Muslim immigrants say that they feel they have a religious obligation to practice female circumcision, it is not the responsibility of state officials to challenge their interpretation of Islam, in the absence of evidence of deliberate deception. Some immigrants will undoubtedly defend the practice in this way, emphasizing their religious motivations (and downplaying such other factors as tradition) because of the privileged status normally granted to religious practice in liberal states.[16]

The problem with characterizing female circumcision as an Islamic practice is not located primarily in the sphere of interactions between officials enforcing laws and immigrants advancing religious claims, but rather in the sphere of public discourse in which this characterization contributes to the construction of a negative image of Islam and of Muslim immigrants. Popular discussions of Islam frequently identify female circumcision as an Islamic practice and use it to illustrate and define the nature of the presumed conflict of values between Islam and the West. For example, one recent article in the popular press bore the headline 'Women Are being Abused, Even Mutilated...All in the Name of Islam'.[17] The message is typical. The effect of such articles is implicitly to create an identification of the West with civilization and Islam with barbarism, and the next step, sometimes quite explicit, is to define immigrants from Islamic countries as threats because they are bearers of this barbaric culture. Thus, female circumcision often plays a crucial symbolic and political role in attempts to discredit Islam.

Imagine a comparable attempt to discredit Christianity. The people who engage in violent opposition to abortion (bombing abortion clinics, murdering doctors who perform abortions, and so on) frequently describe themselves as acting out of a sense of Christian religious duty. In most cases, there is no reason to doubt the sincerity of these claims and, in any event, state officials (such as judges in a criminal trial) should not try to assess the doctrinal merits of their beliefs, at least under normal circumstances. They need only conclude that such actions are not legally permissible, regardless of their religious foundations. But most Christians (even among those opposed to abortion) would object strenuously if such activities were described as Christian practices, because they do not

---

16 As we argued above, we think such an attempt to defend female circumcision on grounds of religious freedom should fail and that liberal states can and should prohibit the practice of most forms of female circumcision, even if sincerely motivated by religious beliefs.

17 See Ann Louise Bardach, 'Women are Being Abused, Even Mutilated... All in the Name of Islam', *Reader's Digest* (Jan. 1994), pp 78–82.

engage in these activities themselves and do not wish to be associated with them. Similarly, most Muslim immigrants do not practise female circumcision and do not wish to be identified with the practice. Of course, the construction of public discourse is multifaceted and Muslims can contribute to a dissociation between Islam and female circumcision by criticizing the practice publicly as un-Islamic—just as, for example some Catholic bishops in the US recently criticized violence against abortion clinics as unchristian.

## Wife-beating

Consider now, much more briefly, the claim that Islam legitimates patriarchal authority within the household, including the right of the husband to beat his wife under certain circumstances. Interpretations of religious traditions are always subject to contestation. Muslims disagree among themselves to some extent about the correct understanding of Islamic teaching on the family and relations between spouses. For example, one author develops a highly egalitarian reading of Islamic teaching and insists, among other things, that 'The Qur'an never orders a woman to obey her husband.'[18] Another, perhaps more common view, asserts at least some duty on the part of a wife to obey her husband:

Because of his natural ability and his responsibility for providing for his family, the man is the head of the house and of the family. He is entitled to the obedience and cooperation of his wife and, accordingly, it is not permissible for her to rebel against his authority, causing disruption.[19]

The same range of views can be found within other religious traditions such as Christianity and Judaism. Apart of course from physical violence, in addressing the issue of Islamic legitimation of patriarchal authority, we encounter the problem, discussed above, that liberal-democratic commitments to religious freedom and personal autonomy preclude any attempt to directly regulate the character of relationships between spouses or between parents and children, even where some cultural tradition prescribes patterns of

18 See Wadud-Muhsin (1992), p. 77, fn. 6.
19 See Yusuf al-Qaradawi, *The Lawful and the Prohibited in Islam*, (trans.) Kamal el Helbawys and M. Mo Syed Shukry (International Islamic Federationist Student Organization: Kuwait, 1993), p. 205.

authority and deference within the household that are quite at odds with equality of the sexes.

Physical violence is, however, another matter. As we noted above, protection of physical security is a core task of any liberal-democratic government. Cultural and religious commitments cannot provide a ground for exemptions from the general prohibitions on violence, including domestic violence. But is there any reason to believe that it is appropriate to identify Muslim immigrants as a special focus of concern in this regard? The actual record of Western states with regard to domestic violence provides no grounds for self-congratulation or complacent comparisons with non-Western cultures. The use of violence by men against their partners and children has deep cultural roots in the West and, until quite recently, has been largely supported by the legal system. Even now when public norms have apparently begun to change, the amount of domestic violence is staggering.[20] It might be instructive to compare the actual use of force by Muslim men within their own households (in Western societies) with the use of force by non-Muslims. What if the Muslim rate proved to be lower than that of other groups? Would that have any bearing on the question of what sorts of cultural adaptation were required to meet the requirements of the Western commitment to gender equality?

We have not been able to find any empirical studies on the relation between culture or religion and domestic violence that would help us to address the questions we just posed. In the absence of such data, is there any reason to suppose that Islam legitimates wife-beating? Critics of Islam point to a passage in the Qur'an that permits a husband to strike his wife under certain circumstances. But Muslims insist, with good reason, that it is unfair to take the passage out of context. Some argue that the passage should be read as severely restricting the practices prevalent at the time rather than as granting ongoing permission for this sort of behaviour.[21] Even conservative Islamic scholars emphasize the steps that must be taken before the husband may use physical force and the drastic limits on the kind of physical force that may be employed.[22] We

[20] See Janice Brakieh and Connie Guberman, 'Violence in the Family', in Karen Anderson et al. (eds), *Family Matters* (Methuen: Agincourt, Ont., 1987).
[21] See Wadud-Muhsin (1992), pp 74–8, fn. 6.
[22] See al Qaradawi (1993), p. 225, fn. 19.

would want to challenge even this highly circumscribed legitimation of physical force in relations between spouses, but clearly this
cannot be taken as a general legitimation of domestic violence.
Spousal abuse is undoubtedly a problem among Muslims as among
every group in Western societies, and it may be that some Muslim
men seek to justify their actions by appealing to the Qur'an; but
both their behaviour and their appeals are contrary to Islam as
understood by most Muslims.[23]

In sum, our response to the issue of spousal abuse parallels the
one given to female circumcision. The state can and should
prohibit domestic violence, but it is deeply misleading and harmful
to say that Islam legitimates wife-beating.

## Polygamy

What about Islam's endorsement of polygamy? First, it should be
noted that many authors have argued that there are resources
within Islam for prohibiting polygamy, based on the Qur'anic
injunction that a husband must treat each of his wives justly and,
if unable to treat more than one justly, should marry only one.[24]
Furthermore, a legal prohibition of polygamy does not prevent a
Muslim man from doing anything required by his religion (provided that he has not yet taken more than one wife) but only limits
something that is permitted by Islam.

Polygamy is significantly different from female circumcision
and wife-beating in one important respect. It is not obvious why
it should be legally prohibited. Every liberal-democratic state does
forbid it, of course, but it is not clear how that fits with the general
principle that adults should normally be able to enter into
whatever contracts or personal relationships they choose. If the
defence of the prohibition rests on a concern for the well-being of
women and children in such relationships, it would appear
appropriate to also consider the effects of easy divorce. Muslim
commentators rightly point out that the relative ease of divorce
and remarriage in Western states creates a kind of *de facto* serial

[23] See Kamran Memom, 'Family: Wife Abuse in the Muslim Community',
*Islamic Horizons* 23, 4 (1993).
[24] See John L. Esposito, *Islam: The Straight* Path, expanded edn (Oxford
University Press: New York, 1991), p. 96.

polygamy; and recent studies show that the economic position of women and children after the breakup of a marriage is usually greatly reduced for a significant period, while that of men often improves quite rapidly.[25] If the issue is asymmetry between men and women, that would appear to be remedied by a legal regime that permitted women as well as men to have multiple spouses, even if, among Muslims, only men availed themselves of this opportunity.[26]

## Hijab

Consider finally the issue of Islamic dress. This is a particularly puzzling issue. The right to dress as one chooses—subject only to standards of public decency (themselves highly contestable and often gender-biased)—would seem the quintessential liberal right. Indeed, one of the objections against Islamic regimes is that they require all women to conform to a narrow, publicly-determined dress code, thus unduly restricting their personal liberty. So, why would anyone object if Muslim women choose to wear the *hijab* as a way of expressing their cultural identity or religious convictions?[27]

In some contexts, however, there are norms of dress, so that wearing the *hijab* would require an exemption from the norms that others are expected to follow. For example, in Montreal a judge recently expelled a Muslim woman for refusing to remove her *hijab* on the grounds that there was prohibition against wearing anything on one's head in court. The judge's action was widely condemned in the press on the grounds that it was insensitive to the cultural

[25] See Lenore Weitzman, *The Divorce Revolution* (The Free Press: New York, 1985).

[26] See Amy Gutmann, 'The Challenge of Multiculturalism in Political Ethics', *Philosophy and Public Affairs* 22, 3 (1993), pp 171–206.

[27] It is striking what positions this form of dress can arouse. A graduate student in our department whose strong feminist views were well known recently converted to Islam after years of study and reflection and, after her conversion, began to wear the *hijab* out of conviction that this was the proper thing for her to do as a good Muslim. It is hard to imagine a more apt case for the Millian injunction about respecting the right of a mature adult to live her life in the way she sees fit and avoiding the tyrannical intrusions of public opinion, yet she has been subject to disapproval and even hostility from many of her peers.

and religious significance of the *hijab*.[28] One Muslim critic wondered rhetorically whether the judge would have required a Catholic nun in a traditional habit to remove her head covering. In the Canadian context, with its institutionalized commitment to multiculturalism, it seems obvious that the judge was wrong. A Muslim woman shows no disrespect to the legal system by keeping her *hijab* on in court. If the right to do so is considered a special right, it is precisely the sort of special right required by the deeper commitment to equal treatment. It does not privilege Muslim women over other people, merely ensuring that their cultural and religious differences from the majority do not become unfair sources of disadvantage.

In France, the expulsion of three girls for wearing the *hijab* to a public school became the focal point for a national debate on special rights, the integration of immigrants, women's equality, and the principle of secularity in French public life.[29] We cannot recapitulate all of the elements of that debate here, but we can perhaps use it to draw attention to one of the important complicating considerations in thinking about gender equality and Islam in liberal-democratic states, namely the range of legitimate variability among liberal-democratic regimes.

If every liberal-democratic state must recognize certain principles, such as freedom of speech, freedom of religion, majority rule, and so on, there are many different ways of interpreting these principles and many different forms of practice among liberal-democratic states. Now the mere fact that a practice exists in a state that we call liberal-democratic does not make it morally legitimate. We need only mention the example of legally-supported segregation in the US prior to 1954 to make that clear. Yet it would be astonishing if someone argued that there was only one correct way

[28] See *Montreal Gazette* (1993).
[29] See Miriam Feldblum, 'Paradoxes of Ethnic Politics: The Case of Franco-Maghrebis in France', *Ethnic and Racial Studies* 16, 1 (1993), pp 52–74; Maxim Silverman, *Deconstructing the Nation: Immigration, Racism and Citizenship in Modern France* (Routledge: London, 1992); Ana Elisabetta Galeotti, 'Citizenship and Equality: The Place for Toleration', *Political Theory* 21, 4 (1993), pp 585–605; Norma Claire Moruzzi, 'A Problem with Head Scarves: Contemporary Complexities of Political and Social Identity', *Political Theory* 22, 4 (1194), pp 653–72; Bruno Cooren, 'Head Scarves in France', unpublished paper, (1995).

of institutionalizing liberal-democratic principles. For example, the First Amendment of the US Bill of Rights (as it has been interpreted by the courts in modern times) permits fewer restrictions on speech than arrangements like those in Canada and Great Britain. Are all approaches besides that of the US undemocratic and morally illegitimate? That would be a surprising claim. It seems far more plausible to suppose that there is a range of reasonable disagreement about what the principles of democratic justice require, and that within that range different states are free to adopt different institutional arrangements. But how wide is that range with regard to gender equality and the toleration of difference?

One central element of the argument for prohibiting the wearing of the *hijab* in the French public schools emphasized the distinctiveness of the French political tradition, especially as compared with Anglo-Saxon traditions. France has a tradition of a strong state and expansive public sphere. One French author writing about the challenge posed to the French by Muslim immigrants wrote that in the 1980s, 'the state got the impression that it no longer had complete control over the norms of society'.[30] No American author could have written such a line about the US, for it would never occur to an American that the state could or should have complete control over the norms of society. But does that mean that the French model is undemocratic and illegitimate?

The French political system has a history of strictly limiting the role of intermediate groups in public life, of confining religious matters to the private sphere, and of insisting on the strict secularity of the state. Again, all these fundamental principles of the modern French state differ in various ways from the practices of Anglo-Saxon states. (For example, marriages in France must be performed before a civil authority to be legally binding, whereas other states delegate to religious officials the authorization to perform legally binding marriages.) The French tradition of dealing with immigrants had strongly resisted the sort of ethnic group formation that developed in North America and had pursued a strategy of assimilating immigrants as individuals, relying heavily

---

[30] Remy Leveau, 'Maghrebi Immigration to Europe: Double Insertion or Double Exclusion?', *Annals of the American Academy of Political and Social Science* 524 (1990), p. 173.

upon public schools (and the army and the unions) to bring about the necessary cultural transformations.

One may object that these generalizations say more about the myths of French political traditions than about the realities of French political life.[31] The objection has merit, but it would be an exaggeration to claim that there were no significant differences along these lines between, say, France and the US. In any event, many prominent intellectuals and public figures in France feared that what they regarded as deep and distinctive principles of the French state would be threatened by the wearing of the *hijab* in public schools. This is, at the least a more plausible claim in the French context than it would be in a North American context. Whether it is sufficient to warrant the requirement that girls not wear the *hijab* to school seems more doubtful, however.

The claim that the *hijab* as a religious symbol was incompatible with the secularism of the public sphere was weakened in the actual case by the fact that no such restrictions had been placed on wearing Christian religious symbols as for instance the cross. Even if that inconsistency were tidied up, however, the question remains whether the French state could legitimately ban all religious symbols from such compulsory institutions as public schools, as some of the defenders of secularism advocated. In our view, the answer is no. It should certainly count as a powerful argument against such a prohibition that, in some religious traditions (including some forms of Islam), the wearing of certain items is seen not merely as an admirable expression of faith but as obligatory. In such a context, the prohibition interferes with religious practice in a way that calls for a stronger justification than appeal to a political tradition of secularism.

The French Conseil d'Etat took a somewhat similar view, ruling that the mere wearing of religious signs could not be prohibited. The Conseil went on to assert that it was permissible to prohibit students from wearing religious signs in such an ostentatious way as to pressure other students or amount to a form of proselytization or provocation, and left it up to local administrators to decide when that was the case. Drawing upon this opening, some people

---

31 See Martin Schain, 'French Jacobianism: The Challenge of American Multiculturalism', paper presented at the annual meeting of the American Political Science Association, 1995.

have argued that, in the current context in France, wearing the *hijab* is not so much an expression of faith as it is a political challenge to French liberal democracy. They note that most of France's Muslim population is of North African origin or ancestry. They draw attention to the list of Islamic fundamentalism in North Africa and the use of terror in some states there against females who do not wear the *hijab*. They note the experience in France itself of terrorist attacks in the name of these fundamentalist movements. They say that the fundamentalists see female separation from and subordination to males as an essential element in their project, thus viewing Muslim girls as a particularly important target for their efforts and public indicator of their success or failure. In all these circumstances, they argue that it is appropriate to construe wearing the *hijab* in school as both a political provocation and a threat or at least a form of undue pressure against Muslim girls who do not wear it. For all these reasons, they claim, it is legitimate to ban the *hijab* from French public schools.[32]

In our view, the kinds of considerations adduced on behalf of a restrictive policy in France are relevant, and, in that regard it appears clear that a stronger case can be made for banning the *hijab* in French schools than could be made in most other liberal-democratic states. Still, we do not think the case is strong enough. We would agree that what people wear often carries symbolic meaning and that the meaning depends in part on the social context. We would even stipulate, though some civil libertarians would disagree, that it might be permissible to restrict certain forms of dress in school because of their symbolic associations. For example, wearing Nazi insignia is banned in schools in a number of states. Some schools in Los Angeles have banned wearing colours associated with gangs. The *hijab* cannot however reasonably be equated with Nazi insignia or gang colours, even allowing for the differences in circumstances.

The *hijab* has long played a central role in the Western imagination, standing particularly as a symbol of the subordination

[32] See Badinter et al., 'Profs, ne capitulons pas', *Le Nouvel Observateur* 2, 8 (1989), pp 58–9; Camille Lacoste-Dujardin, 'Les fichus islamistes: approche ethnologique d'une straégie d'anti-intégration', *Hérodote* (Jan. 1990); Jean-Claude William: 'Le Conseil d'Etat et la Laicité', *Revue Francaise de Science Politique* 41, 1 (1991), pp 28–58; Michéle Aulagnon, 'Enlever le voile, c'est être libre', *Le Monde* (2 Oct 1994), p. 10; Cooren (1995). (See fn. 29.)

of women within Islam and hence as a proof of the moral superiority of the West. Precisely for that reason many women in the anti-colonial movement who had never worn the *hijab* began to put it on, using it as a symbol of their rejection of Western values. Doubtless, the contemporary wearers of the *hijab* in France sometimes mean to evoke this rejection of French colonialism and to assert an alternative set of norms. Yet part of what they deny in doing so is that the *hijab* does stand for the subordination of women. Indeed, one could make a plausible case that French *haute couture*, by constructing female identity in terms of women's ability to dress in ways that are attractive to men, has contributed more to the subordination of women—think of short skirts and high heels—than the *hijab* ever did. But even if the *hijab* does stand for the subordination of women within Islam, why should Muslim girls not be permitted to wear it should they choose to do so?

Some allege that the girls who first wore the *hijab* were pressurized into doing so by their parents and were not acting out of religious conviction, but rather were being used by others as tools for purposes of political mobilization.[33] It is remarkable how this sort of construction treats all the pressures within French society *not* to wear the *hijab* (including perhaps pressures for Muslim parents who want their daughters to conform more to the dominant French norms) as background conditions of free choice, and only those pressures from parents or others to wear the *hijab* as coercive. Of course, there are some sorts of pressures that the state must intervene to prevent, notably the threat of bodily harm, and there are states such as Algeria and Iran where girls and women face physical threats for failing to conform to what some people regard as the norms of Islamic dress. But that is not the case in France today. If anything, the pressures for most Muslim girls are overwhelmingly in the other direction.

There may well be a good deal of truth to the claim that non-religious motives play a role for some of the girls who wear the *hijab*; but it can scarcely be denied that the *hijab* has a deep and long-standing religious significance within Islam, or that devout Muslims living in the West frequently wear the *hijab* without any political goals in view. In the end, we do not see why the potential

[33] Jean-Francois Monnet, 'A Creil, L'origine de L'affaire des foulards', *Herodote* 56 (Jan. 1990), pp 45–54.

of the *hijab* to serve multiple purposes, including political ones, should have any bearing on the right of the girls to wear this religiously important form of dress.

These various examples of alleged conflicts between liberal commitments and the place of women in Islam suggest that in fact, liberal critiques of Islam often demand more of Muslims than of members of other religious communities. For the most part, a commitment to equality would seem more strongly to support a modification of Western attitudes towards Muslim immigrants than a demand that Muslims modify their practices.

## Islam as an Immigrant Culture: Implications for Equality and Difference

If liberal democracies share the aspiration to treat their citizens with, in Dworkin's phrase, 'equal concern and respect', the content of that aspiration is undergoing profound change. The principle of non-discrimination, of securing individual basic rights and liberties without reference to differences of race, ethnicity, religion, sex, etc.—while still an indispensable component of liberal equality— is no longer seen as adequate, for precisely these social differences can often mean that treating all citizens alike functions to disadvantage some and advantage others. Equality is increasingly understood to require that we recognize social difference and allow some departures from uniform or 'universal' citizenship. These departures, which comprise what Iris Young has named 'differentiated citizenship',[34] take a multiplicity of forms, including degrees of self-government (as in the case of minority aboriginal cultures), exemptions from or special emendations to the obligations of citizenship that members of the majority regularly meet, and special political representation in legislative bodies.[35]

The place of Islam in liberal democracies poses a number of problems to the categories of analysis that are typically brought to bear on discussions of group claims for special recognition. In

[34] Iris Marion Young, 'Polity and Group Difference: A Critique of the Ideal of Universal Citizenship', *Ethics* 99 (1989), pp 250–74.

[35] For a taxonomy of the form of group-differentiated citizenship, see Will Kymlicka, *Multicultural Citizenship: A Liberal Theory of Minority Rights* (Oxford University Press: Oxford, 1995), pp 26–33.

this section, we will focus on the fact that, with the exception of the Nation of Islam in the US and scattered converts to Islam from the majority cultures, Muslims in liberal-democratic societies are immigrants or the children of immigrants. Although the principle of religious toleration—which has come to mean the freedom to practice one's religion in the 'private sphere' without penalty— would not seem to be affected by a religious group's immigrant status, debates over forms of special group recognition often focus on the nature of the groups whose claims to recognition should be met. Because the benefits conferred in arrangements of differentiated citizenship often do impose costs on other groups, and because group claims to recognition may conflict, we need some criterion by which to distinguish the groups that merit recognition from those who do not. Different criteria have emerged in the literature; on the face of it, many would seem to exclude immigrant communities from at least some forms of differentiated citizenship.

Will Kymlicka, for example, has offered a defence of special rights of self-government for minority cultural communities to enable them to protect themselves from gradual dissolution under pressures from the surrounding majority culture. In particular, Kymlicka is concerned with protecting the claims of aboriginal peoples to self-government. His argument rests on the view that collective or community rights can best be understood and defended as extensions of the rights that we have as individuals. Because our cultures provide the 'context of choice' in which we, as individuals, can make meaningful choices about the course our lives will take, the security and stability of our culture is a primary good, a condition for the exercise of our capacity for autonomy. Members of the majority culture may take the security of this cultural context of choice for granted. Cultural change certainly occurs as a product of changing dynamics *within* the culture, but those dynamics are themselves subject to some degree of control or shaping by members of the culture. In contrast, for members of minority cultures, the *external* sources of cultural changes are generally more powerful than the internal powers of cultural maintenance and self-direction. In the interests of the moral agency of members of minority cultures, therefore, Kymlicka defends the creation of special collective rights—including rights of self-government—to enable minority cultures to protect themselves from the encroachments of the majority culture.

But Kymlicka offers strong reasons why immigrant communities neither do nor should receive the same recognition that national minorities[36] should and do receive. 'The answer here, I believe, lies in the fact that the original immigrants chose to come to Canada and thereby relinquished some of the rights to cultural protection that they may have had in their homeland.' He does acknowledge, however, that 'it is not clear which rights they can be said to have relinquished and which they retain'.[37] Elsewhere, Kymlicka explains:

If I and others decide to emigrate to China, we have no right that the Chinese government provide us with public services in our mother-tongue..., for in choosing to leave Canada, we relinquish the rights that go with membership in our cultural community. *Public subsidization of the ethnic activities of voluntary immigrant groups is best seen as a matter of policy, which no one has a right to, or a right against.*[38] [emphasis added]

Kymlicka's argument has much to recommend it. Part of it, relating to the claims of aboriginal communities turned on the fact that they did not willingly acquiesce in the absorption of their communities into the majority community, but had no means of preventing it. Absorption was something imposed upon them involuntarily. But immigrants choose voluntarily to enter their host societies; and in so doing, we may presume—following Locke—that they consent to the fact that they may not be able to sustain their cultural distinctiveness, at least not on the terms they would prefer. It is true that they have lost the secure culture that provides a meaningful context of choice, but that sacrifice was itself something that they must have (or should have) weighed against the benefits they gained from immigrating.

However, as is suggested by Kymlicka's acknowledgement that it is hard to know which cultural rights immigrants relinquish and

[36] Kymlicka distinguishes between two forms of cultural pluralism within modern societies: 'multi-nation' states contain a plurality of cultural communities defined by a shared history, territory, and language, and are more or less institutionally complete; 'polyethnic' states contain a plurality of cultural groups as a consequence of immigration from diverse cultures. See Kymlicka (1995), pp 10–26. (See fn. 35.)
[37] See Will Kymlicka, 'Individuals and Community Rights', in Judith Baker (ed.), *Group Rights* (University of Toronto Press: Toronto, 1994), pp 17–34.
[38] See Will Kymlicka, 'Liberalism and the Politicization of Ethnicity', *Canadian Journal of Law and Jurisprudence* 4 (1991), pp 239–56.

which they retain, it seems overly harsh to say that immigrant communities have *no* justice-based claims to special recognition. Not that there are not many members of the majority culture who are willing to reach that harsh conclusion. On the various occasions of tension between Muslims and non-Muslims, there have been those who have been willing to say, 'If you don't like the way we do things here, you can go back where you came from.' In the heat of the Rushdie affair, the *Sunday Sport* put it only slightly more delicately, in response to Muslim demands for the banning of *The Satanic Verses* in demonstrations that were perfectly legal: 'Those who say their deep religious convictions prevent them from obeying the law of this land should quit Britain immediately and go to live in a country where the conflict does not exist.'[39]

Why does it seem unduly harsh to conclude that Muslims, as an immigrant community, have absolutely no claims to special recognition? Well, first, because it too easily justifies host countries' abdication of responsibility for the social consequences of their immigration policies. It is irrational to expect that a substantial influx of a culturally distinct group will place no transformative pressure upon the majority's ways of doing things. We also question whether it is reasonable to ask immigrant groups to give up central features of their religious beliefs and commitments upon entering Western societies, given liberal-democratic commitments to individuals' freedom of conscience and of religion.[40] Even if one concludes that it is, there is the further problem of intergenerational transmission of culture. When the numbers of an immigrant community are large enough, it seems reasonable to predict that they will, as a matter of fact, be able to sustain some of their distinctive cultural beliefs and practices and to pass on their cultural identity to their children. But what of the children of immigrants? No one can tell them that they consented to relinquish their cultural identity upon entering the country; they did not consent

[39] Lisa Appignanesi and Sara Maitland, *The Rushdie File* (Fourth Estate: London, 1989), p. 126.

[40] For further discussion of what it is reasonable for host countries to ask of immigrants, see Joseph H. Carens, 'Immigration, Political Community, and the Transformation of Identity: Quebec's Immigration Politics in Critical Perspective', in Joseph H. Carens (ed.), *Is Quebec's Nationalism Just? Perspectives from Anglophone Canada* (McGill-Queen's University Press: Montreal & Kingston, 1995), pp 20–81.

to be born there. They are now, and should be regarded as full members of the society—and yet remain, like their parents, distinct from the cultural majority.

The issues are further complicated by the fact that immigrant groups are sometimes near the bottom of the pile in terms of socio-economic status, which is in fact very much the case for Pakistani immigrants to Britain, Algerians in France, and Turks in Germany. In fact, it was often to fill employment categories that native citizens were unwilling to fill that immigrants were admitted in the first place. To the extent that members of the majority are already inclined to bigotry and resentment against immigrants, they are encouraged by the fact that immigrants are often doing the work that they disdain. Such resentment becomes all the more intense during hard economic times, when the members of the majority hit bottom and resent immigrants for competing for scarce jobs. Both dynamics tend to create relations of hostility between majority and minority communities, leading the immigrant community to turn inward rather than fighting a losing battle for inclusion and respect. Such dynamics can also radicalize immigrant communities, encouraging them to define themselves in opposition to the majority rather than attempting to fit in as quietly and peacefully as possible. Thus, it does not take long for racism or other forms of bigotry to produce the dialectic of inclusion/ separation that also tends to characterize the relationship between the dominant majority and groups that have been oppressed over a long history, such as African-Americans. These dynamics pro-duce relations of mutual distrust that severely undermine the prospects for shared citizenship and leave the minority community vulnerable to the majority's neglect or violation of their interests.

When we reconstruct the position of Muslim communities in this way, the picture looks somewhat different from a group that consents to relinquish its claims to cultural distinctiveness upon entering the country. The group's distinct identity within the host society is something that has been maintained by a number of forces: not only by the voluntary choices of parents who inculcate their religious beliefs and cultural practices in their children, but also by the insularity that is a natural response to a hostile reception from the majority.

Finally, there are some aspects of the minority culture that have distinct social advantages for the majority, and so are encouraged by them. In the case of Muslim immigrants in Britain, their law-abidingness, 'devotion to family values, hard work and personal integrity are rightly admired'.[41] Given, then, that a distinct group identity does exist for Muslims in the present, and seems likely to persist for at least a generation longer, does a commitment to equality require that the majority go beyond the principle of non-discrimination to affirmatively accommodate group difference through the kinds of special or group-specific measures described above?

In another context, one of the authors of this article has presented an argument for special political recognition of histori-cally marginalized groups.[42] There, she identifies three character-istics of marginalized groups that constitute strong egalitarian grounds for special recognition. First, marginalized groups possess a distinctive political 'voice', a distinctive perspective on social and political issues that arises out of the fact that their social and political experience is markedly different from that of relatively dominant groups. Whether or not there is on the part of dominant groups an actual intention to exclude a marginalized group's perspectives from political debate, the simple fact that the expe-rience of the groups is so different means that, without some means of assuring that the minority or marginalized group's perspective is represented in public discourse, it is very likely to be overlooked, and hence the group's interests unlikely to be met. Second, whether or not the dominant group possesses a clear understanding of the interests of the marginalized group, relations of *trust* between the groups are weak: that is, the marginalized group tends to be the subject of prejudicial or bigoted attitudes on the part of the

[41] This newspaper editorial continues: 'It is important that their spiritual values should be respected, and that they should be spared from racial discrimination in all its forms. They in turn, however, must not seek to impose their values either on their fellow Britons of other faiths or on the majority who acknowledge no faith at all.' See Appignanesi and Maitland (1989), p. 68. (See fn. 39.)

[42] In that work, she is arguing for recognition in the form of enhanced political representation for historically marginalized groups; but the dimen-sions of group experience discussed below are relevant to other forms of special recognition as well, including forms of multiculturalism and self-government. See Melissa S. Williams, *Voice, Trust and Memory: Marginalized Groups and the Failings of Liberal Representation* (1997).

dominant group, and there is often active hostility between the groups. In such circumstances, the marginalized group's capacity to trust the dominant group to look after its interests is minimal. Finally, as noted above, when we consider forms of special group recognition that are scarce goods, whose provision imposes costs upon other members of society and may profoundly reshape social and political institutions, we require criteria by which to distinguish groups who have a strong claim to recognition from those whose claim is weaker. The theme of 'memory' captures the notion that the claims of those groups are strongest who can show a connection between contemporary patterns of inequality and past patterns of legal and social discrimination on the part of the dominant group or majority against the group in question. That is, where such a history of discrimination has resulted in patterns of structural inequality which cannot be corrected through adherence in the present to principles of non-discrimination, there are strong grounds for forms of special political recognition that aim at reconstructing social institutions so that they no longer reproduce group inequality from one generation to the next.

Now, it seems reasonable to believe that there is a sort of hierarchy of claims that attaches to these different warrants for special group recognition. Thus, differences of 'voice' would seem to require practices and policies that reflect a willingness to listen and respond to a group's distinctive perspective. These first forms of special recognition would likely be the least demanding on the majority and would seem to include a willingness to change practices which, even unintentionally, tend to discriminate against the group in question. A failure of trust between a minority and the majority signifies that the minority group lacks confidence in the majority's capacity or willingness to be responsive to their concerns. In cases where such a lack of trust exists, the minority would seem to have a strong claim to more formal or institutionalized varieties of group recognition. A group whose lack of trust has some foundation in its treatment at the hands of the majority might be assured of equal membership of its members only if policy-making bodies make a practice of consulting with its leaders over issues of particular concern to the minority community. Finally, for groups with a strong 'memory' of disadvantage, whose inequality is deeply entrenched in social structures, only long-term direct participation in political processes is likely to establish the group on a footing of equality. Such groups would seem to have a powerful claim for the strongest forms of special group recognition, including enhanced political representation in legislative bodies and, in some cases, rights of self-government.

How does the position of Muslim immigrant communities measure up against these criteria for group recognition? Certainly, their distinct cultural and religious identity, particularly when combined with the fact that they have been marginalized (to varying degrees) by majority cultures of liberal democracies, would seem to ensure that Muslims do, in fact, have a significantly different experience of social and political institutions and practices from that of the majority. Thus, practices which have been formed without the input of Muslim perspectives might well impose burdens on them that are invisible to the majority. To take an example that has recently been in the news: some public housing in Britain has been constructed such that the toilets happen to face Mecca. While this might seem unimportant to non-Muslims, '[u]sing a toilet while facing Mecca breaches the Islamic code of personal conduct taught at the mosque from childhood'.[43] A concern to treat Muslims with equal concern and respect would certainly seem to translate into a willingness to design housing guidelines to ensure that this problem does not recur, as in fact

---

[43] See Tom Sharatt, 'Muslims Turn to Council to Realign Toilets', *Manchester Guardian Weekly*, 3 April 1994. At one forum where we presented this paper, we were accused angrily of attempting to make the concerns of Muslims appear ridiculous by using this example. One critic said that he was an expert on the Muslim world and had never encountered this norm. To avoid any ambiguity, let us state clearly that it is not our intent to ridicule Muslim concerns. The example cited in the text was drawn from newspaper reports. Moreover, Aldeeb Abu-Salieh in 'The Islamic Conception of Migration', *International Migration Review* 30, 1 (1996), describes a guide for Muslims in foreign countries published by a Lebanese Shia Muslim as including the following among Islamic norms: 'Not to have the face or the back to Mecca while in the toilet, as in the West toilets are not built according to Islamic norms.' This suggests that the case we described was not anomalous. More generally, we would note both that many cultures (including Western ones) have powerful norms and prescriptions associated with the processes of the elimination of bodily wastes and that part of the process of group recognition that we are calling for here involves taking seriously the concerns of others even when they do not match our own notions of what is important.

British housing authorities have done.[44] In short, a commitment to equality would seem to require that the distinctive concerns and practices of Muslims be accommodated in the design of public policy, at least in those cases where doing so does not impose a substantial burden on other members of society. Refusing to do so would be gratuitous and could only be interpreted as an expression of disdain for Muslims. The requirements of equality, in such cases, would not seem to be affected in the least by the fact that Islam is an immigrant culture.

How strong are the foundations of trust between Muslims and non-Muslim political leaders? In Britain, at least prior to the Rushdie affair, there appear to have been some foundations of trust between Muslims and non-Muslims. Although they do not always find them responsive, Muslim community members regularly approach MPs and local council members with requests and for advice.[45] Muslim leaders have been active in seeking accommodations to Islam from local government bodies, particularly in the field of education, and have met with significant, if not total, success. This willingness to pursue political change through normal political channels and established institutions suggests that although claims of Muslims have often not been satisfied, they have not felt that they could not trust officials to attend to their requests with seriousness and some degree of responsiveness. The Rushdie affair, however, appears to have significantly changed this, particularly in so far as Muslims felt that members of the majority were not willing even to listen open-mindedly to the reasons for their outrage, let alone respond to it. The language of Muslim grievance shifted from one of requests to one of demands, and some Muslim leaders were actually grateful for the affair because it mobilized a formerly quite passive Muslim populace. As one Muslim put it

The furore has... helped concentrate the minds of Birmingham's Muslims and helped bring greater attention to the needs of the local community. Religious leaders there have had a long-running battle with the Labour-

[44] In the present case, the issue is whether the housing authority should turn toilets around in housing that was built prior to consultations with Muslims, although it is not clear whether the costs would be borne by the housing council or by the tenants themselves.

[45] Daniele Joly, 'Making a Place for Islam in British Society: Muslims in Birmingham' in Tomas Gerholm and Yngve Georg Lithman (eds), *The New Islamic Presence in Western Europe* (Marshall Publishing: London, 1988), pp 32–52.

run council to have some of their demands recognized, especially with regard to education. Despite their campaigns, *halal* food is still not available in schools, and no single-sex education is provided.[46]

In the wake of the anti-Rushdie demonstrations, Muslims were particularly infuriated by responses such as that of Home Secretary Douglas Hurd, which consisted of a lecture to the effect that they should learn to be integrated further into British life, to become more 'British'.[47] As Bhikhu Parekh, who has been supportive of the Muslim reaction against *The Satanic Verses*, has argued: 'Liberal opinion came down on Muslims like a ton of bricks, ridiculing them, and asking if such barbarians deserved to be citizens of a "civilized" society. Liberals rightly remembered the principle of liberty, but forgot the equally important principles of fairness, compassion and humanity.'[48]

In the wake of the anti-Muslim sentiment that surfaced during the Rushdie affair, the capacity of Muslims to trust non-Muslims to take their concerns seriously and to address them equitably has certainly been damaged. The question of course remains whether the liberal response was itself unreasonable, whether they were right not to entertain much discussion of the reasons behind the demands of Muslims that the book be banned. That is, a loss of trust which results from a group having placed itself outside the boundaries of any possible shared public culture might not impose any obligations of the majority to reach out to them in the name of equality, in contrast to the case of groups excluded by the actions of the majority itself. The question of who is to blame for the heightened alienation of Muslims from non-Muslims is doubtlessly unresolvable to either group's satisfaction, but that does not make it irrelevant to reflections on the extent and form of special recognition that the majority might owe to Muslims.

At the same time, one need not assign blame for the loss of trust in order to reach the conclusion that there is a need for healing relationships between Muslims and non-Muslims if the groups are to be capable of cooperating in the public sphere in the future. There would seem, then, to be a mutual obligation to locate modes

---

[46] See Appignanesi and Maitland (1989), p. 129. (See fn. 39.)

[47] Ibid., pp 134–5.

[48] See Bhikhu Parekh, 'Between Holy Text and Moral Void', *New Statesman and Society*, 23 March 1989, pp 29–33.

of discourse that leave open the possibility of intercultural understanding. As Tariq Modood puts it,

Multiculturalism…is not simply a matter of accepting minorities; newcomers too need to be able to open up and welcome change. This is a point worth making when present conflicts and policies are threatening to make Islam in [Britain] a religion of the ghetto. The current temper of Asian Muslims…is not to seek the common ground,…but to emphasize difference…[Muslims'] self-confidence is returning but currently is at the stage of assertive independence rather than of a dialogue amongst equals.[49]

Finally, on the theme of 'memory', the historical condition of Muslims in Western liberal democracies would not seem to warrant the strongest forms of special group recognition, such as enhanced representation in legislative bodies. Although there certainly has been a clear pattern of discrimination against Muslims, most of it is not sanctioned by law. Moreover, given that Muslims have been a significant presence in Western liberal democracies for less than two generations, it would be extremely difficult to show that the contemporary material and social inequalities that characterize Muslim immigrant communities are a product of that discrimination rather than a vestige of the fact that most Muslims were quite poor when they arrived. The standard of living of many immigrants remains low for the first generation or so after immigration, a phenomenon that cannot be ascribed solely or even primarily to discrimination against them. Indeed, the persistent intergenerational poverty of African-Americans is often contrasted with the rise out of poverty of immigrant groups as a way of demonstrating that poverty itself is not the only force at work in the marginalization of the former.

In sum, then, the claims of Muslim immigrant communities to group recognition are perhaps not as strong as that of some other groups, but are powerful in their own right. At the least, they have a strong claim that non-Muslims should be attentive to the ways in which majority practices may effectively disadvantage them or impose burdens on them which are not borne by members of the majority culture. In addition, because the level of trust between

[49] See Tariq Modood, 'Muslims, Incitement to Hatred and the Law', in John Horton (ed.), *Liberalism, Multiculturalism and Toleration* (Macmillan: London, 1993), p. 152.

Muslims and non-Muslims is currently quite low, a strong argument can be made that Muslim community leaders should be regularly consulted by policy-making bodies on issues that are particularly important to Muslims. Although Muslims would not seem to have a compelling claim to the strongest forms of group recognition, their status as an immigrant community does not altogether vitiate their claims to some forms of group recognition.

## Conclusion

As we hope is clear from the foregoing, our principal purpose here has been quite modest. We do not offer any settled or determinate view of the mutual obligations between liberal democracies and the Muslim immigrant communities within them. Rather, we have written as non-Muslim political theorists, concerned about the need to reconcile the principle of equality with the fact of social difference and about the full citizenship of immigrants within liberal democracies. We have been struck by the vehemence of anti-Muslim sentiment not only in Western societies generally, but particularly within academia; and this was one of our principal sources of motivation to write this piece. We have not intended either to defend or to criticize Islam as such, but rather have hoped to unsettle some of the assumptions that critics of Islam often make. Certainly, we have only scratched the surface of this rich and challenging subject, and are especially aware that any complete account of the appropriate relationship between Muslim immigrants and their liberal-democratic host counties must consult the voices of Muslims themselves.

# III

# Secularism in India:
# The Early Debate

# 6

# India as a Secular State<sup>*</sup>

*D.E. Smith*

## I

## The Concept of the Secular State

The term 'secular state' is commonly used in present-day India to describe the relationship that exists, or which ought to exist, between the state and religion. This in itself is sufficient reason for using the term in these extracts. In addition, the closest equivalent in Anglo-American usage, 'separation of church and state', would be singularly inappropriate and misleading in discussing a country in which the majority religion is Hinduism.

The ideas that have contributed to the conception of the secular state were not produced in a vacuum, as will be shown in the historical survey later in this section. However, it may be well at the outset to indicate in general terms the historical orientation of the conception being expounded. Three brief points will suffice to accomplish this.

First, my conception of the secular state is derived from the liberal-democratic tradition of the West. It is thus to be distinguished from the secularism of the Marxian communist tradition, which is motivated by an active hostility to religion as such. Second, while many aspects of our conception of the secular state are common to all the countries within the liberal-democratic tradition, certain aspects constitute the particular contribution of the US. Third, the conception here expounded is essentially that which can be derived from the Indian Constitution itself.

* This article is excerpted from D.E. Smith, *India as a Secular State* (Princeton University Press, 1963). Dates, names, and statistics are true to the 1963 edition.

The working definition which I would suggest is as follows: The secular state is a state that guarantees individual and corporate freedom of religion, deals with the individual as a citizen irrespective of his religion, is not constitutionally connected to a particular religion, nor seeks either to promote or interfere with religion. Upon closer examination it will be seen that the conception of a secular state involves three distinct but interrelated sets of relationships concerning the state, religion, and the individual. The three sets of relations are:

1. religion and the individual (freedom of religion);
2. the state and the individual (citizenship);
3. the state and religion (separation of state and religion).

It may help to visualize a triangle in which the two angles at the base represent religion and the state; the apex represents the individual. The sides and base of the triangle represent the three sets of relationships mentioned above. I shall now proceed to examine these in some detail.

## Freedom of Religion

This is the relationship between religion and the individual, a relationship from which the third factor (the state) is ideally excluded. Religion, as the word is used here, refers to organized religious groups and also to religious beliefs and practices that may or may not be associated with such groups. Freedom of religion means that the individual is free to consider and to discuss with others the relative claims of differing religions, and to come to a decision without any interference from the state. He is free to reject them all. If he decides to embrace one religion, he has freedom to follow its teachings, participate in its worship and other activities, propagate its doctrines, and hold office in its organizations. If the individual later decides to renounce his religion or to embrace another, he is at liberty to do so.

As noted above, the state is excluded from this relationship. The state cannot dictate religious beliefs to the individual or compel him to profess a particular religion or any religion. It cannot force him to contribute financially toward the support of a religion by taxation. However, there is a limited area in which the secular state can legitimately regulate the manifestation of religion, in the interest of public health, safety, or morals. Thus, the prohibition of human sacrifices, to use an extreme example, would be upheld even though a religion might require such sacrifices.

I have thus far dealt with freedom of religion from the point of view of the individual. The collective aspect of this right is the freedom of two or more individuals to associate for religious purposes and to form permanent organizations to carry out these purposes. In the secular state, freedom of association for religious purposes is safeguarded as carefully as the individual's freedom of conscience. All religious groups have the right to organize, to manage their own affairs in religious matters, to own and acquire property, and to establish and administer educational and charitable institutions.

There are, of course, many other aspects of freedom of religion that could be considered, but the above paragraphs will serve our present purposes as a step toward the definition of the secular state.

## Citizenship

This is the relationship between the state and the individual, and here again the exclusion of the third factor is essential. The secular state views the individual as a citizen, and not as a member of a particular religious group. Religion becomes entirely irrelevant in defining the terms of citizenship; its rights and duties are not affected by the individual's religious beliefs.

Many historical examples could be adduced to show how this principle has often been violated. In some cases citizenship itself and the right to vote have depended on adherence to the state religion. Dissenters were at best regarded as second-class citizens. In some cases, discriminatory taxation penalized religious nonconformists. The holding of public office and employment in government service has sometimes been legally dependent on religious affiliation. All such discrimination by the state on the basis of religion runs directly counter to the conception of the secular state. We have now examined briefly two of the three component parts of the secular state. The first, freedom of religion, relates the individual to religion; the state is excluded from this relationship. The second, citizenship, relates the individual to the state; religion is excluded from this relationship. Thus the integrity of both of these relationships in which the individual is involved depends upon the possibility of excluding the third factor in each case, and this can only be achieved by maintaining a third relationship, separation of state and religion. The closer the connection between the state and a particular religion, the greater the danger that (1) religious qualifications will distort the principle of democratic citizenship, and that (2) the state will interfere with freedom of religion, both individual and corporate. If we return to our graphic representation of the problem this becomes immediately clear. The two sides of the triangle maintain their integrity only by virtue of the third that separates them.

## Separation of State and Religion

The underlying assumption of this concept is simply that religion and the state function in two basically different areas of human activity, each with its own objectives and methods. It is not the function of the state to promote, regulate, direct, or otherwise interfere in religion. Similarly, political power is outside the scope of religion's legitimate aims. The democratic state derives its authority from a secular source ('the consent of the governed') and is not subordinate to ecclesiastical power.

Separation of state and religion is the constitutional arrangement that attempts to give effect to these convictions. Separation involves the rejection of the historical pattern of state churches. Some of the characteristics of the state church system are: an ecclesiastical department within the government, the requirement that the head of state be an adherent of the official religion, the appointment of bishops by the government, the use of public funds to pay the salaries of the clergy, etc. Aspects of the system that characterized earlier periods were the legal enforcement of religious conformity and the distortion of the rights of citizenship by religious tests.

A state religion may be merely a branch of the government and completely dominated by the state; a useful instrument of state policy. In other cases, the state religion may wield the dominant power, and the state may be reduced to the position of being the executive arm of the church. In still other cases a fairly equal partnership may link the two. In any of these three forms the relationship is opposed to the principle of the secular state.

In a secular state all religions are, in one limited respect, subordinate to as well as separate from the state. As voluntary associations of individual citizens, religious groups are under the general laws of the state and responsible for the proper discharge of civil responsibilities (payment of taxes, maintenance of public order, etc.). In this respect religions are viewed by the state in much the same way as it views other voluntary associations based on common social, cultural, or economic interests. However, this minor qualification does not affect the essential principle of separation of state and religion.

Under the principle of separation, both religion and the state have freedom to develop without interfering with one another. Religious groups can organize, frame their own creeds and regulations, choose their own ecclesiastical officers, found their own educational institutions, and finance their own activities, all without interference from the state. Such organized religious groups function as autonomous entities, subject only to the general regulations mentioned in the preceding paragraph.

The state, on the other hand, is free from the financial responsibility of supporting an official religion, from the troublesome problem of deciding religious questions, and from the political meddling of vested ecclesiastical interests. The state is free to devote itself to the temporal concerns that fall within its proper sphere of activity with which it is equipped to deal. Separation of state and religion thus seeks to fulfil the ideal formulated by Cavour, 'a free church in a free state'.

The definition of the secular state in terms of three interrelated components—freedom of religion, citizenship, and separation of state and religion—makes explicit the essential elements that are only implied in other definitions. The problem is usually approached simply in terms of 'church and state', with little clear recognition of the other relationships involved. But the secular state in the liberal-democratic tradition surely means far more than the legal separation of state and religion.

The conception of the secular state outlined above is an ideal that is perfectly achieved in no country. The US comes close, but there are still obvious anomalies as well as important issues yet to be decided. Any modern state within the liberal-democratic tradition will have many of the characteristics of a secular state. The UK, for example, can be regarded as a secular state in many respects, although the existence of a state church goes contrary to one important part of our definition. Basically, what has happened is that the pressure of religious minorities and the growth of liberal and democratic ideas have combined to overthrow the more illiberal aspects of the state–church system. In the UK, there is today a very vital religious liberty and democratic conception of citizenship. The state–church and the monarchy itself have continued to be venerated as forms that link modern England with the past, even though these forms are at variance with the liberal democratic ideas on which the modern state is built.

In stressing the total pattern of relationships as necessary to an understanding of the secular state, there is no desire to minimize the importance of separation of state and religion. It is definitely not a matter of indifference. The history of the past hundred years has clearly indicated a trend in the direction of church–state separation, and with reason. Separation of state and religion is especially important in the newly independent states of Asia, for while liberal-democratic traditions have saved modern western states from the more dangerous historical implications of the state–church system, these traditions have been but recently transplanted into Asia and in general have not yet taken firm root. The Asian state which adopts an official religion may thus be more easily lured into these dangerous implications.[1]

From the above survey it is obvious that, while the principle of separation has made impressive gains, there are still many countries where the state–church system prevails. We must remember that the secular state, as we have defined it, is not to be equated with church–state separation. For the secular state, it will be recalled, is a complex of three vital relationships, of which church–state separation is but one.

Church–state separation can exist simultaneously with flagrant denials of freedom of religion, as in Soviet Russia; this is *not* a secular state. On the other hand, a state–church system can exist simultaneously with broad freedom of religion and a democratic conception of citizenship, as in England; this is in many respects a secular state. This is not to suggest that separation of church and

---

[1] This point is well illustrated by the 1953 agitation against the Ahmedias, a dissident Muslim sect in Pakistan. The Ahmedias were hunted down as heretics by other Muslims. The inability of the government to deal effectively with the disturbances was in part attributable to a basic confusion over what it meant for Pakistan to be an Islamic Republic. See *Report of the Court of Inquiry Constituted under Punjab Act II of 1954 to Inquire into the Punjab Disturbances of 1953* (Superintendent, Government Printing: Lahore, 1954).

state is unimportant. Church–state separation in the context of a liberal-democratic state is the arrangement that most clearly, logically, and effectively preserves the values of individual and corporate freedom of religion and equal citizenship. It is 'the last consequence of the principle of religious liberty and of the neutrality of the state in religious matters'.[2]

As we have seen, the secular state in the West has evolved out of many different kinds of historical situations; many different and even conflicting motives lie behind its development. In France the secular state emerged from centuries of struggle between church and state and was a victory for the tradition of anti-clericalism. In the US, on the other hand, the secular state was achieved with no hostility toward religion as such, and it has continued to evolve on a basis of mutual good feeling between church and state.[3] As we turn now to the problem in the Asian setting, we will find similar differences. The Turkish Republic secularized the state in a manner not unlike that employed by France; the secular state in India, on the other hand, is more reminiscent of the American experience.

# II

# The Problem in the Asian Setting

The secular state is, in origin, a western and not an Asian conception. This is not to deny the obvious fact that certain elements of the secular state, as we have defined it, have a long tradition in Asia. Individual freedom of religion, for example has strong roots in the Hindu and Buddhist countries, but other elements of the conception have been totally lacking. For example, the idea that government should not extend financial aid and other forms of patronage to religion finds no support in Hindu, Buddhist, or Islamic traditions. Village self-government has a long history throughout South and South-East Asia, but this is certainly insufficient to refute the assertion that the parliamentary democracy that is now being experimented within the countries of this

2 Adolph Keller, *Church and State on the Continent* (Epsworth Press: London, 1936), pp 260–3.
3 Jacques.Maritain, *Man and the State* (University of Chicago Press: Chicago, 1951) pp 182–3.

region is based on Western conceptions and practices. Similarly, individual elements of the secular state can be found in South and South-East Asian traditions, but the development of the whole integrated conception has been a Western phenomenon.

The traditional pattern of relationship between religion and political authority in the countries of this area was one of interdependence. It was the duty of the king to promote religion—to build places of worship, to contribute to the maintenance of the clerical class, to use his power to enforce religious regulations relating to doctrine, ritual, of social observances. Religious functionaries were expected to advise, support, and help the king. Through coronation ceremonies and other religious rites in the royal court, the divine legitimation of his temporal power was effected, which provided the essential basis for the willing obedience of his subjects.

There were, of course, important differences in the religion–state relationship, depending upon whether a particular kingdom was Hindu, Buddhist, or Muslim. There were indeed significant differences between one Hindu (or Buddhist, or Muslim) state and another, but the general pattern described above was common to the entire area. In some cases Western imperial rule completely obliterated the traditional religion–state relationship. In other cases, the absence of Western domination (Thailand, Nepal) or the imperial device of indirect rule (the Hindu and Muslim princely states in India, the Malay states, and the Buddhist kingdoms of Laos and Cambodia) permitted the ancient system to continue relatively undisturbed.

The Hindu ruler built temples and endowed them with vast wealth in the form of money, jewels, and lands. The management of the financial affairs of the temples was a normal part of the administration of the state, and in some cases the raja controlled the form of the ceremonies performed in temple worship. The king was the 'protector of cows and Brahmans', imposing severe penalties on those who would dare kill a cow and according Brahmans reverence and preferential treatment in every respect. He was the final arbiter in all matters concerning caste regulations, carrying out the sanctions prescribed by the ancient texts where violations occurred. A Brahman royal chaplain advised the king and performed the sacred ceremonies deemed essential for the success of his rule.

The Buddhist king built and endowed pagodas and shrines, and was the chief patron of the monastic order. The protection of the purity of the Teaching was one of the important functions of the monarch, and the suppression of heresy was sometimes found necessary. When the monastic order became corrupt, it was the function of the king to discipline and reform it. In some cases new sects resulted from the monastic reforms implemented by the royal power. The Buddhist monastic order generally supported the authority of the king and instructed the people to obey him. In Burma, royal patronage of Buddhism was the most important basis for the loyalty of the diverse ethnic groups to the king.

Muslim rulers in South and South-East Asia recognized their obligation to promote Islam by building and administering mosques, giving grants to individuals and institutions devoted to the study of theology and Islamic law, suppressing heretical teaching, and at times directing campaigns of proselytization. A special tax was sometimes imposed on non-Muslims, and Muslims were compelled by the state to fulfill certain religious obligations such as the giving of alms and attendance at the mosque. Doctors of Islamic law (in some cases headed by a Chief Theologian) had an established place in the court as advisers to the king, and during certain periods they exercised great influence over him.

The conception of the secular state, then, is Western in origin and contains important elements that are opposed to traditional Asian conceptions and practices. The question that concerns us here is: What factors are involved in determining the relevance of this Western conception to the countries of South and South-East Asia? Can this conception be successfully transplanted to the countries of this region? We shall seek to identify the religious, historical, political, and social factors that help to explain why the people of a given Asian country are likely to accept, modify, or reject the principle of the secular state. Placing the question in this broader perspective will illuminate the problems of India's experiment with the secular state.

## The Nature of the Major Religions

Hinduism, Buddhism, and Islam are the major religions of this region. There are five aspects of religion that are particularly relevant to our inquiry: the first two concern doctrine, the other three relate to organization.

First, the view of history taken by a religion, that is, whether human history is regarded as real and important, is a vital point. A religion that views history as unreal, or if real, ultimately unimportant, may be assumed to be unconcerned with securing or maintaining temporal power. This should be favourable to the secular state. On the other hand, a religion that views the proper course of history as crucial and central to its task in the world, is more likely to rely upon political power in order to influence history. The challenge to the secular state would be correspondingly greater.

Second, we must consider the attitude of a religion toward other religions. Since the peaceful coexistence of diverse faiths is basic to the secular state, the degree of tolerance shown by the majority religion to other religions will obviously be important. Widespread intolerance would make the secular principle practically impossible to realize.

Third, it will be important to note what capacity a given religion has demonstrated for effective ecclesiastical organization. A highly organized religious institution, like the Roman Catholic Church in the West, is in a position to confront the state and to make demands upon it. In general, the more highly organized the majority religion, the greater the difficulties that will be encountered in making or keeping the state secular.

Fourth, we must consider the historical traditions of separation or fusion of political and religious functions. It is obvious that if the traditional conceptions and practices of a religion support the idea of separation, there will be some basis for the building of a secular state.

Fifth, the extent to which a religion has tended to regulate social life will be significant. All religions prescribe rituals, ceremonies, and festivals that are important to the social life of their peoples, but some go far beyond this to regulate virtually every aspect of society, as in the caste system or Muslim law. The greater the degree of such social regulation by a religion, the more difficult it will be to implement the principles of secularism.

On examining each of the major religions, we arrive at broad generalizations which, for the sake of brevity, are indicated in the chart below. The plus signs indicate factors that are favourable to the secular state; the minus signs indicate factors which militate against it.

## ASIAN RELIGIONS AND THE SECULAR STATE

| | HINDUISM | BUDDHISM | ISLAM |
|---|---|---|---|
| 1. *Theory of history.* Indifference to history would make political arrangements like the secular state more acceptable. | History is metaphysically at a lower level of reality, and is ultimately not significant. + | Metaphysically, similar to Hinduism. In practice, history is taken more seriously. + | History is decisive. A certain pattern of life must be established on earth. − |
| 2. *Attitude toward other religions.* An attitude of tolerance is important in developing a secular state. | Extremely tolerant philosophically, and generally so in practice. + | Missionary religion, but tolerant. + | Theologically intolerant, and often so in practice. − |
| 3. *Capacity for ecclesiastical organization.* The more highly organized a religion, the more difficult to establish a secular state. | Practically no ecclesiastical organization. + | Relatively well organized monastic order, the Sangha. − | *Ulama* (doctors of the law) not effectively organized. + |
| 4. *Political and religious functions.* Tradition of separation of these two functions supports the secular state. | Two functions performed by separate castes. + | Principle of renunciation of world—monks cannot rule. + | Tradition of Prophet Mohammed and Caliphs—fusion of temporal and spiritual authority. − |
| 5. *Tendency to regulate society.* The stronger this tendency, the more difficult to establish a secular state. | Caste system, Hindu law. − | No attempt to regulate society. + | Islamic law—detailed regulation of society. − |

+ = favourable to secular state    − = unfavourable to secular state

## The Role of Religious Minorities

Almost as important as the question of the major religion of a country is the question of what religious minorities exist and their relative strength. We know that religious minorities in the West have played a creative role in the development of the secular state. Until the Reformation, the church–state problem was largely a power struggle between the Roman pontiff and the national monarch (or Holy Roman Emperor, in the earlier period). The Protestant Reformation introduced the phenomenon of religious diversity, and the possibility of religious minorities within a state. While the Catholic minority in seventeenth-century England sought to secure religious *toleration*, the Baptist minority in New England insisted that the real solution had to go beyond this. Only by separation of church and state could differing religious persuasions coexist on a basis of equality, in a state built upon a secular concept of citizenship. Minorities have thus acted as catalytic agents in the process of separating the respective jurisdictions of religion and the state.

The question of minorities is important in considering the prospects for the secular state in South and South-East Asia. The presence of sizable religious minorities, sufficiently well organized and articulate, ought to make a difference. Self-preservation will require that they resist pressures emanating from the majority to give the dominant religion a special place in the structure and administration of the state.

The Muslim minority in India is of impressive size—45 million, or roughly ten per cent of the total population. Psychologically, the Indian Muslim community has had to make many adjustments in the decade since Partition. Despite traditional theology with its conception of the Islamic state, Indian Muslims have quickly realized that their future welfare depends squarely on the secularity of the state. Furthermore, there are Muslim organizations seeking to interpret and reinforce the secular state in India.

Christians are small but important minorities everywhere in South Asia. Christian minorities can potentially play an especially significant role for two reasons. First, as a result of greater familiarity with Western thought on the problems of church and state, Christian nationals may well have a better grasp of the meaning of secularism in state and politics than their Hindu,

Buddhist, or Muslim neighbours. Secondly, the Asian Christian churches are in general sufficiently well organized and skilled in the techniques of communication that they can make their influence felt. The great handicap under which the Christian communities labour is their former identification, in the minds of many, with Western colonial rule.[4]

To sum up, the presence of fairly large religious minorities of the same ethnic stock as the majority, effectively organized and articulate, will be an important factor in the development of the secular state. We may note in passing that India, with her numerous and sizeable minorities (Muslims, Christians, Sikhs, Jains, etc.), compares favourably with other countries of the region in this regard.

## British Religious Neutrality in India

The basic policy that the British evolved in the eighteenth and nineteenth centuries was that of 'religious neutrality'. However, there were various kinds of involvements in religious affairs that produced a somewhat confused interpretation of this simple phrase.

During certain periods in the eighteenth and nineteenth centuries, grants of money were given by the British government for the support of Hindu temples and Muslim mosques, and Christian missionaries were actively discouraged. Under other officials, missionary work was vigorously promoted, and in 1813 Parliament established a legal connection between the government of India and the Church of England. The administration was in general fair, impartial, and secular. By the end of the nineteenth century most educated Indians would have been willing to concede that, despite its partial denial in outward forms, the vital aspect of the principle of religious neutrality was being faithfully adhered to.

## The Pattern of Nationalism

In order to evaluate the prospects for secularism in South and South-East Asia, we must consider not only the legacy of colonial

---

4 'Christian Minorities', in Virginia Thompson and Richard Adloff, *Minority Problems in Southeast Asia* (Stanford University Press: Stanford, 1955).

policies but also the patterns of nationalism that evolved in opposition to Western imperialism. What was the role of religion in the development of the various nationalist movements? A nationalism imbued with the spirit of militant religious revivalism is not likely to lead to a secular independent state.

The Indian National Congress, founded in 1885, reflected principally the values of Victorian liberalism, but for a few years early in this century it came under the control of the Extremists with their Hindu revivalist emphasis. In 1920 leadership of the nationalist movement was assumed by Gandhi. While his personal philosophy and techniques of political action were unmistakably Hindu, he strove unceasingly to promote Hindu–Muslim unity. Jawaharlal Nehru and others influenced by socialist ideology, gave powerful support to the ideal of secular nationalism. Despite occasional lapses in practice, this ideal was the dominant one in the Congress movement, and it continues to be an important foundation stone of the secular state in India.

There are thus four key factors that have a bearing upon the future of secularism in politics in South and South-East Asia: the nature of the major religion, the role of religious minorities, the colonial background, and the pattern of nationalism. India's prospects for maintaining and strengthening her position as a secular state would appear to be relatively good, on the basis of this analysis. As we have seen, the majority religion, Hinduism, has characteristics that are in general conducive to the secular state. The large Muslim minority, the much smaller but well-organized and articulate Christian minority, and others may well be powerful deterrents to any departure from the principle of secularism. The British colonial policy of religious neutrality, although not without ambiguities, provided an essentially secular foundation for government. The last years of the Indian nationalist movement, which culminated in independence, saw the emergence of strong secularist leadership in the person of Jawaharlal Nehru, although Gandhi's non-exclusivist Hindu philosophy also played a major role.

But a discussion of the problems of applying the idea of secularism in Asia would be very incomplete without at least a brief treatment of the first conscious endeavour of a free Asian country to become a secular state. For, a full twenty-five years before the secular Indian Constitution was adopted, the Turkish Republic made such an attempt, and largely succeeded.

## Turkey as a Secular State

The emergence of Turkey in the 1920s as a secular state was remarkable in every respect. Three of the four factors relating to the applicability of secularism, in the analysis above, were unfavourable in the case of Turkey. The last factor, however, was of such tremendous power that it swept the field. The major religion was and is Islam, the most difficult faith to adjust to a secular state. The non-Muslim minorities were composed of ethnically distinct Jews, Armenians, and Greeks, many of whom supported the European enemies of the Turkish Republic and had no part in the movement to secularize the state. Turkey never came under Western colonial rule, and hence did not receive whatever benefits could have been derived from British or French tutelage in religious neutrality.

The pattern of nationalism was, however, clearly one that looked to the West. Turkey's geographical proximity to Europe, and, indeed, the European dominions of the Ottoman Empire, facilitated the Western impact. Western-trained military and naval officers, exiled Turks living in Paris, London, and Geneva, as well as European cultural influences within Turkey, were all part of the background. Turkey's disastrous defeat in the First World War, and the break-up of her once-glorious empire, set the scene for a resentful rejection of the decadent institutions that had allowed all this to happen. Bitter dissatisfaction with Islamic heritage was heightened by the revolts of Arab co-religionists during the war, but climaxed by Caliph Vahid-ud-Din's collusion with Allied invaders in 1919.[5]

At this critical juncture Mustafa Kemal was able to mobilize the Turkish people in a mighty effort to drive out the invaders. His

---

5 Henry E. Allen, *The Turkish Transformation: A Study in Social and Religious Development* (University of Chicago Press: Chicago, 1935), pp 10–43. See also Niyazi Berkes, 'Historical Background of Turkish Secularism', in Richard N. Frye (ed.), *Islam and the West* (Mouton and Company: The Hague, 1957), pp 41–68.

military successes led to final victory in 1922, and he became the heroic idol of Turkey. Mustafa Kemal's desire was to transform Turkey into a modern, Westernized, secular state, and the task could be accomplished only by sweeping reforms. The intelligentsia, as we have noted, were fairly well prepared for moves in this direction. Mustafa Kemal's executive ability and, above all, his immense popularity were utilized to make these steps acceptable to the more conservative peasantry.

It is not possible here to do more than sketch an outline of the steps by which the state was secularized. In 1924 the Grand National Assembly at Ankara abolished the caliphate and banished members of the imperial family from the country. The following year was marked by an Act abolishing all Muslim religious orders. In 1926 a momentous step was taken when the *shari'ah* (Islamic law) was replaced by Western legal codes—a civil code from Switzerland, a penal code from Italy, and a commercial code from Germany.

The 1924 Constitution of the Republic of Turkey had provided that 'the religion of the Turkish state is Islam', but this clause was deleted by an amendment of 1928. The original Constitution provided that the deputies of the Assembly and the president take an oath of office swearing on the Koran; this was changed to an oath on their word of honour. A constitutional amendment also established *laicism* as one of the six cardinal principles of the Turkish Republic. The reforms were effected largely in a spirit of hostility toward the religious authorities. But many Turks interpret these steps also as a much-needed reformation of Islam as a religion. As Professor Smith explained their position, even if the reforms were originally motivated by political considerations, Turkey 'had at the same time liberated and rediscovered true Islam'.[6]

Turkey's experiment in secularism is of particular relevance in view of its influence upon Indian nationalist leaders. Jawaharlal Nehru's first mention of the secular state in his writings (1933) was in connection with the Turkish Republic.[7] In a later work, Nehru mentioned that Mustafa Kemal's building up of a secular state

6 Wilfred Cantwell Smith, *Islam in Modern History* (Princeton University Press: Princeton, 1957), p. 176.
7 Jawaharlal Nehru, *Glimpses of World History* (John Day Company: New York, 1946), p. 706.

gradually produced a silent resentment among the more orthodox of the Indian Muslims. 'This very policy, however, made him more popular among the younger generation of both Hindus and Muslims.'[8]

# III

# The Constitutional Framework

This section examines the basic constitutional provisions that give shape to the concept of the secular state, and their interpretation by the Indian High Courts and Supreme Court. The term 'secular state', it should be noted, does not appear in the Constitution itself. The late Professor K.T. Shah, a member of the Constituent Assembly, attempted on two occasions to secure the inclusion of the word 'secular' in the fundamental law, but without success. His second attempt took the form of a proposed new article that read in part: 'The state in India being secular shall have no concern with any religion, creed or profession of faith.'[9] Shah argued that in view of the tragic results of communalism in India, it would be well to emphasize the secularity of the state in the most explicit terms. His amendment did not receive the support of the law minister, however, and was rejected by the Assembly. The inclusion of such an article in the Constitution, however laudable the intention behind it, would certainly have produced a conflict with Art. 25 which, we shall see, permits extensive state intervention in matters connected with religion in the interest of social reform.

As was pointed out in Section I of this article, it is helpful to think of the secular state as an interconnected set of relationships involving the individual, religion, and the state. We shall now examine the Indian Constitution in terms of the three components of this conception—freedom of religion, citizenship, and separation of state and religion.

## Freedom of Religion

The Indian Constitution provides for the religious liberty of both the individual and associations of individuals united by common

[8] Jawaharlal Nehru, *The Discovery of India* (John Day Company: New York, 1946), p. 352.
[9] *Constituent Assembly Debates*, vol. 7, p. 815.

beliefs, practices, and disciplines. The individual and collective aspects of religious liberty shall be discussed in this order.

## Individual Freedom of Religion

The basic guarantee of this right is found in Art. 25(1):

Subject to public order, *morality* and health and to the other provisions of this Part, all persons are equally entitled to freedom of conscience and the right freely to profess, practice and propagate religion.

In discussions of the origin of this article, attention is frequently drawn to its similarity to the following provision of the 1937 Constitution of Eire: 'Freedom of conscience and the free profession and practice of religion are, subject to public order and morality, guaranteed to every citizen.'[10] There were, however, other sources nearer at hand. The language of the Indian Constitution is very similar to that of the resolution on fundamental rights adopted at the Karachi Congress in 1931: 'Every citizen shall enjoy freedom of conscience and the right freely to profess and practice his religion subject to public order and morality.'[11]

The original draft of the article presented to the Constituent Assembly was even closer to the wording of the Karachi resolution than the final form, for it contained no mention of the right to propagate religion. Some members of the Assembly asserted that the right to propagate was contained in the right to practise religion and that it was therefore unnecessary to specify it. Other members, however, were clearly motivated by the Hindu objection to the kind of propagation that leads to conversions from one religion to another. In this connection it is interesting to note the relevant provision (Art. 5) in the 1959 Constitution of the Kingdom of Nepal. In this Hindu kingdom (the monarch must be an 'adherent of Aryan Culture and Hindu Religion'), freedom of religion is guaranteed as follows: 'Every citizen, subject to the current traditions, shall practice and profess his own religion as handed down from ancient times. Provided that no person shall be entitled to convert another person to his religion.' In the Constituent Assembly of India, however, the demand of the small Christian

10 Art. 44(2).
11 Sadiq Ali (ed.), *Congress and the Problem of Minorities* (Law Journal Press: Allahabad, 1947), pp 119, 129.

minority for an explicit recognition of the right to propagate religion was agreed to.

The freedom of religion guaranteed by the Indian Constitution is not confined to citizens but extends to 'all persons', including aliens. This point, underlined by the Supreme Court in *Ratilal Panchand* v. *State of Bombay*, is of special interest because of the substantial number of foreign Christian missionaries in India, some of whom are exclusively engaged in propagating their faith among the adherents of other religions.[12]

The Constitution thus declares that every person has a fundamental right not only to hold whatever religious beliefs commend themselves to his judgement (freedom of conscience), but also to manifest his beliefs in such overt acts as are prescribed by his religion and to propagate its tenets among others (right to profess, practise, and propagate religion). The exercise of this right is, however, 'subject to public order, morality and health'. Here the Constitution succinctly expresses the limitations on religious liberty that have been evolved by judicial pronouncements in the US and Australia. In a long series of cases the US courts have held that: (1) polygamy may be prohibited by legislation although it is sanctioned by a religious body, (2) a person claiming supernatural healing powers may not use the postal services in order to procure money, (3) religious propaganda on the streets is subject to regulation, etc. Strictly speaking, the language of the Indian Constitution makes freedom of conscience as well as the right freely to profess, practise, and propagate religion subject to state control in the interest of public order, morality, and health. This is, however, simply a case of inaccurate drafting, and the courts have made it clear that the state can have no power over the conscience of the individual—this right is absolute.

The necessity of the state's power to preserve public order was pointedly enunciated when the US Supreme Court asked: 'Suppose that one believed that human sacrifices were a necessary part of religious worship, would it be seriously contended that the civil government under which he lived could not interfere to prevent a sacrifice?'[13] The Indian Penal Code (Sections 295–8) makes it a crime to injure or defile a place of worship or to disturb a religious assembly, etc., even though these actions might be sanctioned by

12 1954 Supreme Court Appeals, p. 546.
13 *Reynolds* v. *United States*, 1878, 98 US, p. 145.

the offender's own religion. Practices like sati, or devadasi dedication that frequently led to temple prostitution, may have some basis in Hindu religion, but the state still has constitutional power to ban them.

The right to freedom of religion is subject not only to public order, morality, and health but to the other provisions of Part III. Therefore, the practice of untouchability (forbidden in Art. 17) could not be protected under Art. 25. Land can be compulsorily acquired by the state with compensation under Art. 31, despite the fact that it is part of a religious endowment.

The Indian courts have sketched out other areas in which freedom of religion is not absolute. It was held that Art. 25(1) did not give a Hindu student the right to perform the ceremonies of his religion in the compound of a Christian college.[14] In another case the Supreme Court held that an optional religious practice need not be protected by the constitutional guarantee of freedom of religion. Thus a Muslim accustomed to sacrificing a cow at Bakr-Id would be compelled to obey a law prohibiting cow slaughter for Islam recognizes as equally valid the sacrifice of a goat.[15]

## Who Defines Religion?

It is obvious that the definition of 'religion' becomes the crucial point in the application of Art. 25(1) to particular cases. And who is to give the authoritative definition: the individual, the religious body, or the state? The US Supreme Court found it difficult to decide in an interesting case involving a compulsory salute to the American flag by schoolchildren. Children whose parents belonged to the religious group called Jehovah's Witnesses disobeyed the state law, refusing to salute the flag on the ground that, according to their religion, this act constituted idolatry, which was a sin. In a case in 1940 the Court upheld the requirement of the flag salute; in effect it said that the state will determine what is religion, and that the state had rightly decided that the compulsory flag salute did not violate religious liberty. Three years later the Court reversed itself and struck down the legislation requiring the flag salute. The Court now said that if a religious body and the individual adherent seriously

[14] *Sanjib Kumar* v. *St. Paul's College*, All India Reporter 1957, Calcutta, p. 524.
[15] *M.H. Quareshi* v. *State of Bihar*, A.I.R. 1958, Supreme Court, p. 731.

regarded this particular requirement as a violation of religious liberty, the state would respect such conscientious objections.[16]

It would obviously be impossible to accept the approach embodied in the latter decision in India, unless one were prepared to abandon all plans of social progress and modernization. As Dr B.R. Ambedkar remarked concerning the relationship of personal laws (Hindu, Muslim, Parsi, etc.) to religion:

The religious conceptions in this country are so vast that they cover every aspect of life from birth to death. There is nothing which is not religion and if personal law is to be saved I am sure about it that in social matters we will come to a standstill.... There is nothing extraordinary in saying that we ought to strive hereafter to limit the definition of religion in such a manner that we shall not extend it beyond beliefs and such rituals as may be connected with ceremonials which are essentially religious. It is not necessary that the sort of laws, for instance, laws relating to tenancy or laws relating to succession, should be governed by religion.... I personally do not understand why religion should be given this vast expansive jurisdiction so as to cover the whole of life and to prevent the legislature from encroaching upon that field.[17]

The Bombay High Court has in several decisions given a very narrow interpretation of religion and the freedom of religion guaranteed by Art. 25(1). In *Ratilal* v. *State of Bombay*, the definition of religion did not even include the rituals and ceremonials referred to by Dr Ambedkar, but was restricted to ethical and moral precepts:

Therefore, whatever binds a man to his own conscience and whatever moral and ethical principles regulate the lives of men, that alone can constitute religion as understood in the Constitution. A religion may have many secular activities, it may have secular aspects, but these secular activities and aspects do not constitute religion as understood by the constitution.[18]

Similarly, in another case religion was interpreted solely in terms of faith and belief, and the authority of a religious body in relation to its members was held to have nothing to do with religion.[19]

The Supreme Court has, however, been unwilling to accept this extraordinarily narrow definition of religion. While unable to go

---

[16] *Minersville School District* v. *Gobitis*, 1940, 310 US, p. 586, and *West Virginia State Board of Education* v. *Barnette*, 1943, 319 US, p. 624.

[17] *Constituent Assembly Debates*, vol. 7, p. 781.

[18] A.I.R. 1953, Bombay, p. 242.

[19] *Taher Saifuddin* v. *Tyebbhai Moosaji*, A.I.R. 1953, Bombay, p. 183.

as far as the US Supreme Court in granting recognition to what are claimed to be religious beliefs and practices, there is nonetheless a vast difference between its interpretation and that cited above.

A religion may not only lay down a code of ethical rules for its followers to accept, it might prescribe rituals and observances, ceremonies and modes of worship which are regarded as integral parts of religion, and these forms and observance might extend even to matters of food and dress.

(This interpretation, incidentally, is strengthened by the rather curious Explanation to Art. 25, which states that the wearing and carrying of *kirpan* shall be included in the profession of the Sikh religion. The *kirpan* is a sword, one of the five emblems which an orthodox Sikh must wear.) In this same Supreme Court judgment, the definition of religion was broadened to include still more.

What constitutes the essential part of a religion is primarily to be ascertained with reference to the doctrines of that religion itself. If the tenets of any religious sect of the Hindus prescribe that offerings of food should be given to the idol at particular hours of the day, that periodical ceremonies should be performed in a certain way at certain periods of the year or that there should be daily recital of sacred texts or oblations to the sacred fire, all these would be regarded as parts of religion and the mere fact that they involve expenditure of money, or employment of priests and servants, or the use of marketable commodities would not make them secular activities partaking of a commercial or economic character.[20]

The Supreme Court's statement that 'what constitutes the essential part of a religion is primarily to be ascertained with reference to the doctrines of that religion itself' should not however be taken too seriously. Much textual and historical evidence could be adduced to show that the caste system constitutes an essential part of Hinduism. But caste practices will certainly not be protected by the Constitution; as a matter of fact, they are indirectly and directly attacked by the Constitution itself. Art. 25(2) grants to the state broad, sweeping powers of interference in religious matters.

## Limitation Imposed by Indian Conditions

The restrictions on freedom of religion based on considerations of public order, morality, and health are obvious ones and have many

20 *Commissioner, Hindu Religious Endowments* v. *Lakshmindra*, 1954, Supreme Court Appeals, pp 431–2.

parallels in the constitutional law of the West. Art. 25(2), however, imposes drastic limitations on the rights just guaranteed in Art. 25(1) and reflects the peculiar needs of Indian society:

Nothing in this article shall affect the operation of any existing law or prevent the state from making any law—

(a) regulating or restricting any economic, financial, political or other secular activity which may be associated with religious practice;
(b) providing for social welfare and reform or the throwing open of Hindu religious institutions of a public character to all classes and sections of Hindus.

Laws providing for the very extensive supervision by the state of temple administration (Hindu religious endowment Acts) have been enacted by virtue of this provision.

The extensive modification of Hindu personal law (marriage, divorce, adoption, succession, etc.) has been effected by legislation based on the provision permitting measures of social welfare and reform. In an interesting case the validity of the Bombay Prevention of Hindu Bigamous Marriages Act of 1946 was upheld by the Bombay High Court. Chief Justice Chagla (a Muslim, later appointed as the Indian ambassador to the US) delivered the judgment of the court and of necessity dealt with the religious question raised by the case:

It is only with very considerable hesitation that I would like to speak about Hindu religion, but it is rather difficult to accept the proposition that polygamy is an integral part of Hindu religion. It is perfectly true that Hindu religion recognizes the necessity of a son for religious efficacy and spiritual salvation. That same religion also recognizes the institution of adoption. Therefore, the Hindu religion provides for the continuation of the line of a Hindu male within the framework of monogamy.

The learned judge went on to argue that, even assuming that polygamy is a recognized institution according to Hindu religious practice, the right of the state to enact this legislation could not be disputed. The enforcement of monogamy among Hindus is a measure of social reform which the state is empowered to legislate by Art. 25(2)(b) 'notwithstanding the fact that it may interfere with the right of a citizen freely to profess, practice, and propagate religion'.[21]

---

[21] *State of Bombay* v. *Narasu Appa*, A.I.R. 1952, Bombay, p. 84.

The same constitutional provision permits legislation opening Hindu religious institutions of a public character to all classes and sections of India. Harijan temple entry laws have been enacted by many of the state legislatures. The central Untouchability (Offences) Act of 1955 provides *inter alia* that any attempt to prevent Harijans from exercising their right of temple entry is punishable with imprisonment, fine, or both.

Art. 25(2) thus authorizes the state to regulate any secular activity associated with religion, to legislate social reforms, and force open the doors of Hindu temples to Harijans. C.H. Alexandrowicz wrote: 'The above clause constitutes in itself a revolution in the traditional conception of religion in India.' The revolution in the state is engaged in 'an extensive programme of disentanglement of religious and secular activities'.[22] This is indeed one aspect of the revolution, best illustrated by the standardization of Hindu personal law as one big step toward a uniform civil code. A secular civil law, equally applicable to all Indian citizens, will be a notable achievement in this process of disentanglement by the secular state.

Another aspect of the revolution envisaged by this clause is, however, the assumption by the state of vast powers of control over the financial administration of Hindu religious institutions. In many respects this development moves in the opposite direction from the process of disentanglement of the religious and the secular. This development is revolutionary in that it constitutes a marked departure from the policies of the last seventy five years of British rule. Essentially however, it represents a return to the pattern of extensive state control of religious institutions found in the ancient and medieval Hindu states and continued by some of the Indian states (Mysore, Travancore, and others) right up to 1947 and after.

Individual freedom of religion, basically guaranteed in Art. 25, is further strengthened by Art. 27, which declares that no person shall be compelled to pay taxes for the support of any particular religion. The interpretation of this provision is considered in another section, 'Taxation and Religious Education'. The protection of the individual's freedom of conscience is also the object of

22 C.H. Alexandrowicz, 'The Secular State in India and in the United States', *Journal of the Indian Law Institute*, 2 (1960), pp 284–5.

Art. 28(3), which forbids compulsory religious instruction or worship in educational institutions recognized or aided by the state.

## Collective Freedom of Religion

Religious denominations as well as individuals have certain important rights; collective freedom of religion is spelled out in Art. 26:

Subject to public order, morality, and health, every religious denomination or any section thereof shall have the right—

(a) to establish and maintain institutions for religious and charitable purposes;
(b) to manage its own affairs in matters of religion;
(c) to own and acquire movable and immovable property; and
(d) to administer such property in accordance with law.

In the West, it is possible to speak of collective freedom of religion with greater precision than in India. The Christian churches are generally well organized, each with its own creedal statements, hierarchy of clergy, canon law or constitution, organs of church government, etc. To a large extent, the conception of separation of church and state presupposes this kind of ecclesiastical organization which is fully capable of internal autonomy. Hinduism and Islam do not fit into this pattern.[23] Western analogies cannot be discarded if India is to continue to progress towards the ideal of the secular state, yet at the same time their limitations must be noted.

The conflict between the internal autonomy of a religious denomination and the role of the state in social reform was most

---

[23] This point is forcibly made in Ved Prakash Luthera's 'The Concept of the Secular State in India', Ph. D. dissertation, University of Delhi, 1958, pp 18–20. Because of the organizational deficiencies of religion in India, the state is called upon to perform many of the regulatory functions which are exercised internally in well-organized religions. Luthera concluded that India is not and cannot be a secular state. I disagree with this conclusion (1) because it proceeds from too narrow a definition of the secular state (Luthera equates it with separation of state and religion, which is only one of the three components in my definition) and (2) because it takes too static a view of Hindu religion which has the potentiality for much greater organizational development.

dramatically manifested in the case of *Taher Saifuddin* v. *Tyebbhai Moosaji*.[24] The Bombay Prevention of Excommunication Act of 1949 prohibits the expulsion of a person from any community of which he is a member; thus depriving him of his rights and privileges. The rights and privileges referred to are those that are legally enforceable by a civil suit and include the right to office or property or to worship in any religious place, and the right of burial or cremation. The head priest of the Dawoodi Bohra community passed two orders of excommunication against a member of the community which were later declared to be void, illegal, and of no effect by virtue of the Prevention of Excommunication Act. The Bombay High Court in this case upheld the constitutionality of the Act which, according to the head priest, deprived his religious denomination of the right 'to manage its own affairs in matters of religion'.

The court reiterated its narrow definition of religion: religion is a matter of a man's faith and belief, and is to be sharply distinguished from *religious practice*. 'Further, it does not seem to us that where a religious denomination claims a right to expel or excommunicate a member, it is managing its own affairs in matters of religion. Religion has nothing whatever to do with the right of excommunication or expulsion.' Excommunication deprives a member of his legal rights and privileges, and a religious denomination which exercises this power is doing much more than managing its own affairs: it is interfering with the rights of its members, and such acts cannot be protected by Art. 26 of the Constitution.

Undoubtedly this decision is diametrically opposed to the basic idea of the freedom of the church in the West. There, the power of spiritual discipline, even to the extent of excommunication, has always been recognized as a prerogative of ecclesiastical authority, whether vested in the clerical hierarchy or in the collective membership of the church. In India, interference by the state in the internal affairs of religious groups, such as the Bombay legislation provides for, is definitely undesirable. At the same time, it should be noted that membership of a 'community' in India is not strictly comparable to membership of a church in the West. The definition of community in the Prevention of Excommunication Act is very broad; a community is a group of people who

[24] A.I.R. 1953, Bombay, p. 183.

by birth, conversion, or the performance of any religious rite are regarded as belonging to the same religion or religious creed, *and it includes a caste or subcaste*. While excommunication in the West is mainly a religious matter, in India the social aspects of the Act are likely to be more significant than the religious. The Bombay legislature, desirous of protecting the rights and privileges of the individual, prohibited excommunication as a measure of social reform.

It is not in the interest of the secular state to strengthen the social role of 'communities' as such. Far from it. Indeed, the present proliferation of highly organized caste associations is a trend which to some degree undermines the secular state. To the extent that the Bombay Act discourages the arbitrary power of such organizations over its members it will serve a useful function. But how to achieve this without interfering with the spiritual discipline which an individual accepts as a condition of member-ship of a religious denomination? Will the Bombay Prevention of Excommunication Act shield the Anglican or the Roman Catholic from the discipline of his ecclesiastical authorities in the same way that this law has operated in relation to the Dawoodi Bohra community?

Another important case that involved the right of a religious denomination to manage its own affairs in matters of religion was *Venkataramana Deveru* v. *State of Mysore*.[25] Briefly, the case concerned the Venkataramana temple belonging to the Gowda Sarswath Brahman community. The Madras Temple Entry Autho-rization Act, supported by Art. 25(2)(b) of the Constitution, threw open all Hindu public temples in the state to Harijans. The trustees of this denominational temple refused admission to Harijans on the grounds that the caste of the prospective worshipper was a relevant matter of religion according to scriptural authority, and that under Art. 26(b) of the Constitution they had the right to manage their own affairs in matters of religion. The Supreme Court admitted that this was a matter of religion, but, faced with the conflict between Art. 25(2)(b) and Art. 26(b) of the Constitution, it approved a compromise arrangement heavily weighted in favour of the rights of Harijans and with but token concessions to the right of a religious denomination to exercise internal autonomy.

[25] A.I.R. 1958, SC, p. 255. See pp 242–3.

It is in the interest of the secular state to strengthen the internal autonomy of religious denominations, although this is little realized by the various legislatures. The demand for social reform and *religious reform* is so pressing that little attention is paid to the principle of separation of state and religion. At the same time, it must again be emphasized that the Gowda Saraswath Brahman community only partly resembles a 'religious denomination' in the Western usage of the word. Probably a *math* (Hindu monastic institution) comes closer to the meaning of this term. A *math* propagates a particular set of doctrines, has a definite number of disciples, and is presided over by a single *guru* or *swami* in whom are vested complete powers over both the spiritual and the temporal affairs of the institution.[26]

Art. 26(c) and (d) recognize the right of a religious denomination to own, acquire, and administer movable and immovable property in accordance with law. It was held, however, that this guarantee did not imply that such property was not liable to compulsory acquisition under the Utter Pradesh Abolition of Zamindari Act. In a case in Orissa, land reforms resulted in the expropriation of a village and surrounding agricultural land dedicated to the maintenance of a Hindu deity. Since compensation was paid, the High Court held that there was only a change in the form of the property.[27]

It should be emphasized that the right of a religious denomination is to administer its property 'in accordance with law'. In Bombay, Madras, and Orissa, religious endowments legislation granted to state officials vast powers of control over the financial affairs of Hindu temples and *math*s. This legislation presupposed a sharp distinction between the 'administration of property' and 'matters of religion' which is simply untenable. The Madras High Court found it difficult to separate the two, since the temporal affairs are managed in order to promote the religious affairs for which the institution exists; they are 'inextricably mixed up'.[28]

---

[26] Some of the modern reformist Hindu movements, of course, are organized very much like religious groups in the West. The Ramakrishna Mission is a standing example of this highly developed kind of ecclesiastical organization.

[27] *Suryapal Singh* v. *State of U.P.*, A.I.R. 1951, Allahabad, p. 674, and *Chintamoni* v. *State of Orissa*, A.I.R. 1958, Orissa, p. 18.

[28] *Lakshmindra Theertha Swamiar* v. *Commissioner of Hindu Religious Endowments*, A.I.R. 1952, Madras, p. 613.

The Supreme Court, however, drew the distinction in clear-cut terms:

Under article 26(b), therefore, a religious denomination or organization enjoys complete autonomy in the matter of deciding as to what rites and ceremonies are essential according to the tenets of the religion they hold and no outside authority has any jurisdiction to interfere with their decision in such matters.

So much for the management of religious affairs; the Court then immediately turned to the financial question:

Of course, the scale of expenses to be incurred in connection with these religious observances would be a matter of administration of property belonging to the religious denomination and can be controlled by secular authorities in accordance with any law laid down by a competent legislature; for it could not be the injunction of any religion to destroy the institution and its endowments by incurring wasteful expenditure on rites and ceremonies.[29]

This crushing blow to the concept of internal autonomy was mitigated only by the Court's observation that a law which would take the right of administration from the hands of a religious denomination altogether and vest it formally and legally in any other authority would constitute a violation of Art. 26(d).

Thus, the right of collective freedom of religion guaranteed by Art. 26 does not provide the kind of protection from state interference which is found in a secular state in the West, the US for example. Art. 30 deals with another aspect of collective freedom of religion:

(1) All minorities, whether based on religion or language, shall have the right to establish and administer educational institutions of their choice.
(2) The state shall not, in granting aid to educational institutions, discriminate against any educational institution on the ground that it is under the management of a minority, whether based on religion or language.

In its advisory opinion on the Kerala Education Bill of 1957, the Supreme Court considered the scope of this special fundamental

---

29 *Commissioner, Hindu Religious Endowments* v. *Lakshmindra Theertha Swamiar*, A.I.R. 1954, SC, p. 291.

right guaranteed to linguistic and religious minorities. Out of the total population of 14.2 million in Kerala there were 3.4 million Christians and 2.5 million Muslims. The Roman Catholics especially felt their educational institutions threatened by the provisions of this legislation drafted by the Communist government of the state.

The Supreme Court made it clear that, with the exception of certain Anglo-Indian institutions provided for under Art. 337, private educational institutions had no constitutional right to receive any grant from the state. Nevertheless, the situation was such that without state aid practically none of these institutions could operate (for example, every Christian school in the state was heavily dependent on government grants). The court declared: 'No educational institution can in actual practice be carried on without aid from the state and if they will not get it unless they surrender their rights they will, by compulsion of financial necessities, be compelled to give up their rights under Art. 30(1).'[30]

Clauses 14 and 15 of the Kerala Education Bill enabled the government under certain circumstances to take over the entire management of aided institutions, and the institutions were made subject to this possibility as a condition for the grant of aid. The Supreme Court declared these clauses unconstitutional. However, it upheld drastic regulations providing for rigid state control over the appointment of teachers, the collection of fees, and the payment of teachers' salaries by the government, etc. The Court observed only that there were 'serious inroads on the right of administration and appear perilously near violating that right'.

## Citizenship

The second component of the secular state, the concept of citizenship, is based on the idea that the individual, not the group, is the basic unit. The individual is confronted by the state which imposes duties and responsibilities upon him; in return the state guarantees rights and grants privileges to the individual. The sum total of these individual–state relationships constitutes the meaning of citizenship.

[30] *In re Kerala Education Bill*, 1957, A.I.R. 1958, SC, p. 983.

## No State Discrimination on Grounds of Religion

In the Indian Constitution there are many provisions dealing with the citizen's relations with the state. Here we shall concern ourselves only with those articles which specifically rule out any religious considerations in defining the rights and duties of the citizen. After guaranteeing in Art. 14 the right to equality before the law and the equal protection of the laws, the Constitution goes on in Art. 15(1) to provide: 'The state shall not discriminate against any citizen on grounds only of religion, race, caste, sex, place of birth or any of them.'

We have already discussed the effect on freedom of religion of legislation prohibiting Hindu polygamy, since it was contended by some that the practice of polygamy was a part of Hindu religion. Also involved, however, is the question whether such legislation does not discriminate against Hindus contrary to Art. 15(1). This was raised in the case referred to previously, *State of Bombay* v. *Narasu Appa.*[31] It was alleged that the Bombay Prevention of Hindu Bigamous Marriages Act discriminated between Hindus and Muslims on the ground of religion and applied a measure of social reform to Hindus, restricting them to monogamy while allowing Muslims to continue the practice of polygamy. Furthermore, Hindus were discriminated against also in relation to Christians and Parsis, since severer penalties were provided in the impugned Act than in the Penal Code applicable to the other two communities for whom monogamy was also the law.

The Bombay High Court upheld the severer penalties on the ground that they were necessary to make the law socially effective. Laying emphasis on the word *only* in Art. 15(1), it held that the legislation did not single out the Hindus on the ground of religion *only.* The legislature had to take into account the social customs and beliefs of the Hindus and other relevant considerations before deciding whether it was necessary to provide special legislation making bigamous marriages illegal. The state was entitled to consider, for example, the relative educational development of the Hindus and the Muslims. 'One community might be prepared to accept and work social reform; another may not yet be prepared for it.... The state may rightly decide to bring about social reform

31 *State of Bombay* v. *Narasu Appa,* A.I.R. 1952, Bombay, p. 84.

by stages, and the stages may be territorial or they may be community-wise.'

In a similar case arising under the Madras Hindu Bigamy Prevention and Divorce Act of 1949, it was held that the Act did not discriminate between Hindus and Muslims on the ground of religion.[32] While only Hindus were affected by the legislation, 'the essence of that classification is not their religion but that they have all along been preserving their personal law peculiar to themselves which was derived from the *Smriti*, commentaries, custom and usage'. According to this interpretation, the Act did not discriminate on the ground of religion since it applied not to those who professed Hindu religion, but to those who were governed by Hindu law! The Madras High Court here indulged in a bit of pure sophistry.

The strained interpretations of the courts notwithstanding, there is absolutely no doubt that such legislation is discriminatory and contrary to Art. 15(1). This is not to suggest that the courts should have declared these laws unconstitutional. During this transitional period when India is struggling to become a modern state, it is precisely the function of the courts to concoct such ingenious interpretations in order to harmonize the permanently valid principle, Art. 15(1) in this case, with the dynamic urge for social reform which has yet to find expression within the antiquated framework of religious civil laws. Not only the Hindu Bigamous Marriages Act, but the whole system of Hindu and Muslim personal law is contrary to Art. 15(1)! It is only when there is a uniform civil code that the courts will be able to afford the luxury of a natural and straightforward interpretation of this fundamental constitutional principle of the secular state.

While the existence of different personal laws contradicts the principle of non-discrimination by the state contained in Art. 15(1), the Constitution itself contradicts this principle in dealing with the problems connected with the caste system. In its special provisions for the Scheduled Castes, Scheduled Tribes, and other backward classes, the Constitution 'introduced what may be called *protective discrimination* in favour of those sections of the community which require urgent support, for, if the principle of equality were applied without any exception, the reorganization of Indian society and

---

[32] *Srinivasa Aiyar* v. *Saraswati Ammal*, A.I.R. 1952, Madras, p. 193.

the uplift of its hitherto neglected strata would be difficult if not impossible'.[33]

One of the problems was the constitutional one, namely of reconciling the principles of protective discrimination and non-discrimination by the state. In certain specific areas this adjustment had already been made in the Constitution as adopted in 1950, but there was no qualification of the non-discrimination principle contained in Art. 15(1). Adverse court decisions necessitated the First Amendment Act, 1951, which *inter alia* inserted Art. 15(4): 'Nothing in this article or in clause (2) of article 29 shall prevent the state from making any special provisions for the advancement of any socially and educationally backward classes of citizens or for the Scheduled Castes and the Scheduled Tribes'. The state is thus permitted to discriminate among citizens on grounds of religion, caste, etc. when providing for the advancement of certain sections of the population.

## Applying the Principle of Non-discrimination

It seems clear that the fundamental conception of citizenship as a relationship between the individual and the state is being seriously undermined by the attempt to deal with the problem of the under-privileged on the basis of the group, especially the caste. Art. 15(1) lays down the basic democratic principle that the state shall not discriminate against any citizen on grounds only of religion, caste, etc. This general principle is then applied to three specific areas: (1) public employment or office, (2) admission to state educational institutions, and (3) voting and representation in legislatures. However, just as Art. 15(1) is qualified by a major exception, there are similar exceptions to the principle of non-discrimination in each of these specific areas.

In regard to public employment the guarantee is stated both positively and negatively. Art. 16(1) asserts the principle of equality of opportunity for all citizens in matters relating to employment or appointment to any office under the state. Negatively, according to Art. 16(2): 'No citizen shall, on grounds only of religion, race, caste, sex, descent, place of birth, residence or any of them, be

---

[33] Alexandrowicz, op. cit., p. 289.

ineligible for, or discriminated against in respect of, any employment or office under the state.'[34]

The Constitution provides for one exception to the principle
of no *religious* qualifications for public office. Art. 16(5) permits
laws requiring that the incumbent of an office connected with
the affairs of a religious institution be an adherent of that
religion. Thus the commissioner and all of his subordinates in
the Madras Hindu Religious Endowments Department must be
Hindus. Although these are all officers of the secular state, the
religious qualification is allowed by this clause.

Another exception to the general principle of non-discrimination is found in Art. 16(4):

Nothing in this article shall prevent the state from making any provision
for the reservation of appointments or posts in favour of any backward
class of citizens which, in the opinion of the state, is not adequately
represented in the services under the state.

Art. 335 of the Constitution states that the claims of the members
of the Scheduled Castes and Scheduled Tribes shall be taken into
consideration in the making of appointments to government posts
and services. Such special consideration must be made 'consistently
with the maintenance of efficiency of administration'. Art. 16(4)
refers to 'any backward class of citizens', which includes the
Scheduled Castes and Tribes as well as others. Furthermore, it goes
beyond the vague provisions of Art. 335 by permitting the state
to reserve certain posts and appointments for these sections of the
population.

## Non-discrimination in Political Functions

The third application of the principle of non-discrimination among
citizens is in the area of voting and representation in the legislatures. Art. 325 states:

There shall be one general electoral roll for every territorial constituency
for election to either House of Parliament or to the House or either House
of the Legislature of a state and no person shall be ineligible for inclusion

[34] Similarly, the Government of India Act, 1935, provided that 'no subject
of His Majesty domiciled in India,shall on grounds of religion, place of birth,
descent, colour or any of them be ineligible for office under the Crown in
India'.

in any such roll or claim to be included in any special electoral roll for any such constituency on grounds only of religion, race, sex or any of them.

The first important provision to be noted here is that there can be no religious or caste requirements for voting. Art. 326 states the principle positively and simply by declaring that elections 'shall be on the basis of adult suffrage'.

The second aspect to be noted is that the system of separate communal electorates, first established in 1909, was abolished. 'There shall be one general electoral roll for every territorial constituency....' Under the old system each of the larger minority communities (Muslims, Christians, Sikhs, etc.) had its electoral roll and a number of reserved seats in the legislatures. Thus, only Muslim voters could vote for Muslim candidates standing for election to seats specifically reserved for Muslims in the legislatures.

While the system of separate electorates was abolished, the Constitution does provide for the reservation of seats for the Scheduled Castes and Scheduled Tribes[35] in the central and state legislatures (Art. 330 and Art. 332). According to the original Art. 334, the reservation of seats was to cease after a period of ten years from the commencement of the Constitution, or in 1960. The eighth amendment, however, extended this reservation for another ten years.

Difficult constitutional problems have arisen over this arrangement, especially under the system of double-member constituencies (one reserved and one general seat). In *V.V. Giri* v. *D.S. Dora* the Supreme Court upheld the election of Scheduled Tribe candidates to both the reserved and the general seats.[36] In 1961

---

[35] As has been noted above, the Constitutional (Scheduled Castes) Order provides that no person who professes a religion different from the Hindu or Sikh religion shall be deemed a member of a Scheduled Caste. In *S. Michael* v. *S. Venkateswaran*, the Madras High Court upheld this order under which a Christian convert from a Scheduled Caste was denied the right to stand for election to a reserved seat in the legislature (A.I.R. 1952, Madras, p. 474). The Constitution also makes provision for the special representation of the Anglo-Indian community in the central and state legislatures by nomination (Art. 331 and Art. 333).

[36] A.I.R. 1959, SC, p. 1318. See S.S. Nigam, 'Equity and the Representation of the Scheduled Classes in Parliament', *Journal of the Indian Law Institute*, 2 (1960), pp 297–320.

Parliament enacted legislation providing for the division of two-member constituencies. While this will eliminate certain problems, it will undoubtedly create others. Thus a non-Scheduled Class person residing in a constituency for which there is a reserved seat will be unable to stand for election to that seat. If he is a person of limited financial resources it will be very difficult for him to conduct an effective election campaign in another constituency where he is less well known.

The provision for joint electorates in Art. 325 refers specifically to elections to the central and state legislatures only. The question arose whether a state law could provide for separate electorates for the members of the various religious communities in elections to local legislative bodies. The Supreme Court in *Nainsukh Das* v. *State of UP* held that such a law went counter to the non-discrimination principle of Art. 15(1). The court observed: 'Now it cannot be seriously disputed that any law providing for elections on the basis of separate electorates for members of different religious communities offends against article 15(1).... The constitutional mandate to the state not to discriminate on the ground, *inter alia*, of religion extends to political as well as to other rights.'[37]

In concluding this section on the constitutional basis for the concept of citizenship in the Indian secular state, a few generalizations may be made. It is obvious that the fundamental principle of equality and non-discrimination in the state's relationships with the individual citizen is seriously compromised in several areas. Almost all of the difficulties have their roots in the state's commendable recognition of its special responsibilities toward those sections of the population which in the past have been the victims of exploitation. However, the approach to the problem has too often identified special need with a caste designation, and there is no doubt that caste-consciousness has thereby been strengthened.

## Separation of State and Religion

We now come to the third component of the secular state. Separation of state and religion is the principle that preserves the integrity of the other two relationships, freedom of religion and

[37] A.I.R. 1953, SC, p. 385.

citizenship. Once the principle of separation of state and religion is abandoned, the way is open for state interference in the individual's religious liberty, and for state discrimination against him if he happens to dissent from the official creed. Even today in some of the democratic states of western Europe, the state–church system retains vestiges of these consequences. The individual may be compelled by taxation to support the official religion, or may be disqualified from the highest office in the state by virtue of his profession of another religion.

In 1947 the US Supreme Court defined separation of church and state as follows:

Neither a state nor the federal government can set up a church. Neither can pass laws which aid one religion, aid all religions, or prefer one religion over another.... No tax in any amount, large or small, can be levied to support any religious activities or institutions, whatever they may be called, or whatever form they may adopt to teach or practice religion. Neither a state nor the federal government can, openly or secretly, participate in the affairs of any religious organizations or groups and vice versa. In the words of Jefferson, the clause against establishment of religion by law was intended to erect 'a wall of separation between church and state'.[38]

In actual practice the separation is not absolute, as is shown by the fact that each house of Congress has a chaplain who daily invokes divine guidance for the proceedings of the legislature. But the statement helps to clarify the meaning of separation of church and state. It is a conception of two separate and mutually non-interfering organizations, each operating within its own sphere of activity.

It is clear that such a thoroughgoing separation of state and religion does not exist in India. We have already discussed the important areas in which state interference in religious matters is permitted by the Constitution: the financial administration of temples and *maths*, the admission of Harijans into Hindu temples, the practice of excommunication from religious communities, the modification of religious personal laws, etc. The chief reason for such state interference is that Hinduism lacks the kind of ecclesiastical organization necessary to set its own house in order; the tremendous urge for effective social and religious reform that

---

[38] *Everson v. Board of Education*, 330 US 1 (1947).

characterizes present-day India can only be satisfied by state action.[39] The organizational deficiency of Hinduism is indeed a serious problem. How can there be separation of church and state where there is no church?

The firmly established principle in the US that the courts will not decide controversies over matters of religious doctrine or ritual has a pale reflection in Indian judicial decisions of some years ago. In 1935 the Bombay High Court held that a civil court is competent to decide whether a particular cult is within Vedic religion or not. In a 1939 case in Madras, it was held that the question whether a particular *namam* or mark should be placed on an idol's forehead was one pertaining to religious ritual and as such was excluded from the cognizance of a civil court.[40] Since 1950, however, the courts have frequently had to deal with doctrinal questions in defining the scope of freedom of religion guaranteed in Art. 25 and Art. 26. For example, the courts have had to determine the correct interpretation of scriptures that forbid the entry of Untouchables into temples, the doctrinal basis for the practice of polygamy in Hinduism, and similar matters. These cases have of course not involved religious controversies between individuals, but between individuals and the legislating state.

There are, however, other aspects of the principle of separation of state and religion that are supported by the Indian Constitution: (1) there is no provision regarding an official state religion, (2) there can be no religious instruction in state schools, and (3) there can be no taxes to support any particular religion.

What the Constitution does not say is just as significant as what it does say. There is no mention made of any official state religion. There is no explicit prohibition of the adoption of a state religion, as in the American Constitution, but it is inconceivable that such a radical step would be attempted without a constitutional amendment. Not only is there no state religion in India but no official recognition is given to the religion of the majority. By way of contrast, the Constitution of Burma before 1961 declared: 'The

---

[39] Earlier it has been argued that Hinduism's lack of organization is a factor which is favourable to the development of a secular state. While this is basically true, the greater opportunity for state intervention in religious affairs constitutes the negative aspect of the situation.

[40] *Devchand Totaram* v. *Ghanasham*, A.I.R. 1935, Bombay, p. 361; *Aiyanchariar Sadagopachariar*, A.I.R. 1939, Madras, p. 757.

state recognizes the special position of Buddhism as the faith professed by the great majority of the citizens of the Union.'[41] Similarly, the Constitution of Eire, which considerably influenced the framers of the Indian Constitution in other matters, recognizes the special position of the Roman Catholic Church. The 1959 Constitution of the Kingdom of Nepal links the state with Hinduism through its description of the monarch as an 'adherent of Aryan Culture and Hindu Religion' (preamble and Art. 1).

The sharpest contrast with the Indian Constitution is, however, the 1956 Constitution of 'the Islamic Republic of Pakistan'. The preamble begins: 'In the name of Allah, the Beneficent, the Merciful; whereas sovereignty over the entire universe belongs to Allah Almighty alone, and the authority to be exercised by the people of Pakistan within the limits prescribed by Him is a sacred trust....'[42] Art. 25, one of the Directive Principles of State Policy, is as follows:

(1) Steps shall be taken to enable the Muslims of Pakistan individually and collectively to order their lives in accordance with the Holy Koran and Sunnah.
(2) The state shall endeavor, as respects the Muslims of Pakistan—
  (a) to provide facilities whereby they may be enabled to understand the meaning of life according to the Holy Koran and Sunnah;
  (b) to make the teaching of the Holy Koran compulsory;
  (c) to promote unity and the observance of Islamic moral standards; and
  (d) to secure the proper organization of zakat, wakfs and mosques.

Art. 32(2) makes an exception to the provisions for equality and non-discrimination among citizens by stating that a person shall not be qualified for election as president unless he is a Muslim. Art. 198(1) asserts: 'No law shall be enacted which is repugnant to the Injunctions of Islam as laid down in the Holy Koran and

41 Constitution of Burma, Art. 21(1). In August 1961 this was amended to read as follows: 'Buddhism being the religion professed by the great majority of the citizens of the Union shall be the State Religion.'
42 The Indian Constitution makes no reference to God except in the forms of oaths or affirmations contained in the Third Schedule. Ministers of the Union, members of Parliament, judges, etc. may either 'swear in the name of God' or 'solemnly affirm' that they will faithfully perform the duties of their respective offices.

Sunnah...and existing law shall be brought into conformity with such Injunctions.'[43] The Constitution of 1956 was abrogated two years later, however, when a military regime headed by General Iskander Mirza was established by a bloodless *coup*.

India has no state religion, nor does it give any constitutional recognition to Hinduism as the religion of the majority of citizens. It is also important to note that there is no Ecclesiastical Department in the central government, such as existed during the British period. Before 1927 the bishops of the established Church of England in India were appointed by the Crown. Right up to 1948, however, the Ecclesiastical Department continued to pay a large number of Christian chaplains and maintain Christian churches out of the public revenues of the country. The unstated principle embodied in the Indian Constitution is that found in the 1931 Karachi resolution of the Indian National Congress: 'The state shall observe neutrality in regard to all religions.'

## Taxation and Religious Education

Art. 27 of the Constitution states: 'No person shall be compelled to pay any taxes, the proceeds of which are specifically appropriated in payment of expenses for the promotion or maintenance of any particular religion or religious denomination.'[44] Several writers have very erroneously equated this provision with the principle laid down in such rigid terms by the US Supreme Court in the Everson case: 'No tax in any amount, large or small, can be levied to support any religious activities or institutions, whatever they may be called, or whatever form they may adopt to teach or practice religion.' The differences of constitutional position on this point between the US and India are considerable.

[43] The draft Constitution of 1952 contained a provision by which legislation suspected of being un-Islamic would be referred to a board of canon lawyers. If the board unanimously found this to be the case, the legislation could be sent back to the legislature with suggested amendments which could only be rejected by the majority of the Muslim members. The Constitution as adopted, however, left the question of repugnancy to the Injunctions of Islam to be determined by Parliament.

[44] Art. 21 of the 1956 Constitution of Pakistan presents an interesting contrast: 'No person shall be compelled to pay any special tax the proceeds of which are to be spent on the propagation or maintenance of any religion *other than his own*' (emphasis added).

First, the Indian Constitution forbids only taxation for the benefit of any *particular* religion. Non-discriminatory taxes for the benefit of *all* religions would be perfectly constitutional. Such an arrangement would in fact be in accord with the general traditions of the Hindu state. It would, however, seriously undermine the fundamental principle of separation of state and religion as it has here been defined. Separation means that it is not the function of the state to aid one religion or to aid all religions.[45] The secular state will not coerce any individual (by taxation or any other means) to support any religion.

Second, Indian and American law vary greatly in their treatment of educational institutions managed by religious bodies. While in the US public funds may be used to support parochial schools only in very limited ways (bus transportation, free lunches, textbooks for the pupils), in India the system of government grants to privately managed schools has over a century of history behind it and is still very important.

Third, in the US no government grants of money may be made to religious institutions.[46] The Indian Constitution explicitly provides for state contributions to Hindu temples and shrines. This surprising provision is found in Art. 290A:

A sum of forty-six lakhs and fifty thousand rupees (4,650,000 rupees) shall be charged on, and paid out of, the Consolidated Fund of the state of Kerala every year to the Travancore Devaswom Fund; and a sum of thirteen lakhs and fifty thousand rupees (1,350,000 rupees) shall be charged on, and paid out of, the Consolidated Fund of the state of Madras every year to the Devaswom Fund established in that state for the maintenance of Hindu temples and shrines in the territories transferred to that state on the first day of November, 1956, from the state of Travancore–Cochin.

[45] This sentence, and my general approach throughout represent the 'wall of separation' approach to the problem. American constitutional law is by no means settled on this fundamental question, and court decisions fluctuate between this and the 'no-preference' doctrine, which envisages limited state aid to all religions on an equal basis.
[46] Protestant, Catholic, and Jewish chaplains, however, serve in the armed forces of the US as commissioned officers. Similarly, in the larger defence service establishments in India, qualified 'Religious Teachers' of the Hindu, Muslim, Sikh, and Christian (Protestant and Catholic) faiths are either engaged as civilians or hold a rank corresponding to that of junior commissioned officers. They conduct religious services and rites and assist at attestation parades when the oath of obedience and discipline is administered to trained recruits.

Briefly, the background of this article is as follows. Before 1949 Travancore and Cochin were contiguous Indian states ruled by Hindu maharajas. The rulers had sanctioned large annual grants of money to the Hindu temples and shrines in their respective states and the management of these institutions was directly controlled by them. The two states were merged in 1949. As the grants made to the temples had been sanctioned in perpetuity, these obligations passed over to the united state of Travancore–Cochin and were detailed in the covenant signed by the two rulers and the government of India.[47] The states' reorganization of 1956 created the state of Kerala to which most of their financial obligations were passed on, although part of it also went to Madras.

There are other examples of this continuation of the old system of state patronage of religious institutions. The Mysore government budget for the year 1960–1 contains some interesting illustrations of this. Under 'Endowments and Charitable Allowance' there are budget estimates for the following: temples (160,000 rupees), *maths* (78,000 rupees), Mohammedan institutions (33,300 rupees).[48] Recurring grants sanctioned in perpetuity were made years ago by the government of the maharaja of Mysore to most of the temples, *maths*, and mosques which now receive these annual allowances. However, some such grants from state revenues have been made in recent years, and it was not until 1958 that a Mysore government order stated: 'No recurring grants either in perpetuity or for a specified period will be sanctioned to religious institutions such as temples, *maths*, etc., in future, merely to augment their income.'[49]

[47] See 'The Covenant Entered into by the Rulers of Travancore and Cochin for the Formation of the United State of Travancore and Cochin', *White Paper of Indian States* (Government of India Press: Delhi, 1950), p. 288.

[48] *Budget Estimates for the Year 1960–1: Expenditures* (Mysore Government Press: Bangalore, 1960), p. 396.

[49] Government order No. RDC to DHR 57, dated 9 July 1958. One of the last fresh cash grants was made by government order No. RD to DHR 57, dated 21 May 1957, in which government 'were pleased to sanction a cash grant of 300 rupees per annum to Sri Degila Math at Kanakapura, the cost being met from 47 Miscellaneous Departments' (a budget subheading under 'Expenditure met from Revenue'). See *Administration Report of the Muzrai Department for the Year 1956–7* (Government Branch Press: Mysore, 1959), p. 21.

There are other items of expenditures for religious institutions provided for in the 1960–1 budget which are clearly *not* in fulfilment of obligations assumed by previous governments of Mysore. One hundred and fifty thousand rupees is the budget estimate for 'Construction and Repairs' of religious institutions and their equipment. In other years similar amounts have been spent for the repair or renovation of temples, temple cars, guest-houses for pilgrims, etc. and for the construction of new temples.[50] It was not until 1958 that the use of public funds for the last-mentioned purpose was stopped. The same government order referred to in the last paragraph also stated: 'No building grants will be sanctioned by government for the construction of new places of worship.'

The use of public funds for sectarian religious purposes is clearly opposed to the principle of separation of state and religion. In India, however, such a practice would stand a very good chance of being held constitutional by the courts. Art. 27 represents a very feeble defence against it. The freedom of a person from compulsion to pay a special religious tax may reinforce the armour of individual rights, but it sidesteps the basic question of public policy. What if there is no special tax, 'the proceeds of which are specifically appropriated in payment of expenses for the promotion or maintenance of any particular religion or religious denomina-tion'? What if, instead, the legislature simply appropriates funds for the promotion of religion out of the general revenue of the state? This is what is happening in Mysore state, and in all probability it is perfectly constitutional.

Art. 28 deals with the question of religious instruction in three different types of educational institutions. The first provision refers to institutions that are of a completely public nature. Clause (1) lays down: 'No religious instruction shall be provided in any educational institution wholly maintained out of state funds.'[51]

---

50 Ibid., pp 17–18.
51 The 1956 Constitution of Pakistan would permit religious instruction in state schools, and such instructions could be made compulsory for those who profess the religion or religions taught. Art. 13(1): 'No person attending any educational institution shall be required to receive religious instruction, or take part in any religious ceremony, or attend religious worship, if such instruction, ceremony or worship relates to a religion *other than his own*' (emphasis added).

The prohibition here is absolute; neither the state nor any private agency may provide religious instruction in state educational institutions.[52] Here we have a stricter adherence to the principle of separation of state and religion than in the previous article examined. Art. 27 would permit taxation for the benefit of all religions but not for 'any particular religion'. The logical counterpart in the field of education would be a provision enabling the state to provide instruction in all religions but not in one particular religion alone. But such is not the case; there is to be 'no religious instruction' in state educational institutions.

Art. 28(2) deals with a second, special type of educational institution in which the state functions in the role of trustee. 'Nothing in clause (1) shall apply to an educational institution which is administered by the state but has been established under any endowment or trust which requires that religious instruction shall be imparted in such institution.' The Banaras Hindu University and the Aligarh Muslim University were established under endowments which require that instruction be imparted in Hinduism and Islam respectively. Although administered by the central government, religious instruction in these universities is permitted by clause (2).

The third type of educational institution is the state-aided denominational school. As we have seen every religious group has the right to establish and administer its own educational institutions. Furthermore, in granting aid to educational institutions, the state may not discriminate against those managed by minority groups. The principle involved in Art. 28(3) is that the state cannot become a party to the active propagation of religion in state-aided institutions by permitting compulsory religious instruction:

No person attending any educational institution recognized by the state or receiving aid out of state funds shall be required to take part in any religious instruction that may be imparted in such institution or to attend any religious worship that may be conducted in such institution or in any premises attached thereto unless such person or, if such person is a minor, his guardian has given his consent thereto.

Any other policy would involve the state in aiding the coercion of its citizens to receive instruction in a particular religion.

[52] *Constituent Assembly Debates*, vol. 7, p. 871.

## An Evaluation of the Constitution

The constitutional framework of the secular state in India has been discussed in terms of its three basic components: freedom of religion, citizenship, and separation of state and religion. There are undoubtedly serious problems in each of these areas. Freedom of religion, especially collective freedom of religion, is compromised by constitutional sanction for extensive state interference in religious affairs. Citizenship based on equality and non-discrimination by the state is weakened by the numerous special provisions made for the underprivileged classes on the basis of caste. Separation of state and religion includes two distinct principles: (1) the non-interference of the state and religious organizations in one another's affairs; and (2) the absence of a legal connection between the state and a particular religion. The Indian Constitution, as already noted, does not subscribe to the first principle; it does, however, uphold the second.

If one evaluates the Constitution solely in terms of abstract legalistic principles, there will indeed be much to criticize. This is especially true if one compares the constitutional basis for secularism in India with that in the US. However, to do this is to ignore the dynamics of the Indian situation. All aspects of contemporary Indian life—political, economic, social, and religious—are in a process of rapid change, and the Indian Constitution is rightly geared to these changes.

Three interrelated developments have a direct bearing on the secular state. First, in order to become a modern state, the state in India is seeking to enlarge its jurisdiction at the expense of religion. The religious regulation of Indian society by caste and Hindu law must give way to regulation by the state. By this process religion is being restricted to an area of life roughly corresponding to its role in the West. Second, the sphere of activity which is left to religion is also the object of extensive reform by the state. This is especially clear in the case of the extremely close supervision of temple administration by the state. The state's role, we have suggested, is closely related to Hinduism's organizational deficiencies. Third, the powerful impulse for social reform demands that the deprived castes, which never enjoyed equality of opportunity, now be given not equality, but privileged treatment by the state, so that their educational, social, and economic status may be rapidly raised.

There is a good chance that twenty years from now, many of India's constitutional anomalies regarding the secular state will have disappeared. It is reasonable to expect that by that time there will be a uniform civil code and that Hindu and Muslim law, as such, will have ceased to exist. Legislation having already dealt with the most serious abuses in Hindu religion, there will be little need for further interference by the state. Bureaucracy being what it is, however, there will likely be more and not less official supervision of temple administration. In twenty years the need for special class privileges which now distort the principle of equal citizenship, should be very much less. In any case, such privileges should be abandoned by that time. Thus, if one is willing to incorporate this dimension of time into this evaluation, the conclusion is that the Constitution of India provides a relatively sound basis for the building of a secular state.

# IV
# The Building of a Secular State

This concluding section attempts to weigh the numerous factors of strength and weakness in the secular state in India. As one surveys the total scene, it is evident that the factors that support secularism are by no means negligible. Those who would dismiss the secular state as a superficial attempt by a handful of Westernized leaders to impose a concept foreign to India's history have not considered all of the facts.

The secular state is built on substantial historical foundations. The Hindu state of ancient, medieval, or modern times was not a narrowly sectarian state in any sense; patronage was frequently extended simultaneously to various sects and religions. The British policy of religious neutrality was the direct antecedent of the secular state, and the legal and administrative institutions introduced by the foreign rulers pointed the way to the development of a common citizenship. India's present system of secular public schools has over a century of history. The mainstream of Indian nationalism, which led to Independence in 1947, had a decidedly secular orientation throughout most of its history.

The religion of the majority in India is Hinduism, a faith which is on the whole favourable to the development of the secular state.

The Hindu view of history is that ultimately it is unreal; a Hindu theocracy, if it should ever be attempted, could claim no support from the ultimate religious and metaphysical values of Hinduism. Hinduism has a strong tradition of freedom of conscience and tolerance of religious diversity. Religious liberty is based not on considerations of political expediency but on the conviction of the ultimate oneness of the religious quest, however numerous the different paths that may be followed. Furthermore, Hinduism lacks the ecclesiastical organization and centralized authority that would be essential for any kind of theocratic challenge to the secular state.

The existence of sizable and influential religious minorities is another factor that strengthens secularism. The minorities are the natural custodians of the secular state. The Muslims and the Sikhs have little in their respective traditions to lend positive support to this concept of the state; they will strengthen Indian secularism chiefly by guarding the rights of their respective communities. Protestant Christians, however, can speak not only as a minority but as a religious group with a significant tradition of church–state separation.

Indo–Pakistan relations have a bearing on the secular state in India in various ways, both negative and positive. Tensions between the two countries may unfortunately produce increased difficulties for the Indian Muslim. But there is another aspect of the situation that impresses itself on thinking people in India. The fact is that India cannot become a Hindu state, either constitution-ally or in practice, without justifying the creation of Pakistan and at the same time imitating that country's policies. While Pakistan has never accepted India's claim that it is a secular state, the adoption of Hinduism as the state religion would confirm the Pakistani interpretation of the history of the last twenty years of the subcontinent. No Indian nationalist would want this to happen.

The Constitution of India is a basic law which, without using the term, clearly erects the structure of a secular state. The Constitution undoubtedly contains certain anomalies in this re-gard, some of them inevitable. However, as long as the provisions relating to religion retain their present form, it is difficult to envisage any fundamental rejection of secularism. In interpreting this Constitution the Supreme Court, through its power of judicial review of legislation, has proved to be another great bulwark against any tendency of the state to restrict freedom of religion.

The political party in power, the Indian National Congress, has behind it a long tradition of non-communal nationalism and has on the whole been faithful to the ideal of the secular state since Independence. It is the party to which the religious minorities (with the exception of the Sikhs) have instinctively looked for the protection of their interests; there is at least a clear ideal that can be appealed to. There are elements of religious revivalism within the Congress, but very weak in comparison to those in the major parties of neighbouring countries (the Sri Lanka Freedom Party in Sri Lanka, the Union Party in Myanmar).

The political parties in India which directly challenge the secular state can claim only a microscopic amount of popular support. The Jana Sangh is the only Hindu party that appears to have the potentiality for an important role on the national political scene. But its total strength at present is represented by 14 seats out of 500 in the Lok Sabha. Outside of the communal parties there has been no movement of any significance to make India a Hindu state.

It is impossible to think of the secular state in India apart from the tremendous influence that Prime Minister Jawaharlal Nehru exercised in implementing this principle. Nehru has indeed been the great champion of Indian secularism, and it is likely that the impact of his convictions will be felt by the body politic long after he has passed from the scene. For India to reject the secular state, it will have to repudiate both Gandhi and Nehru.

The forces of Westernization and modernization at work in India are all on the side of the secular state. Industrialization, urbanization, the break-up of the joint family system, greatly increased literacy, and opportunities for higher education—all tend to promote the general secularization of both private and public life. The indifference to religion that characterizes the contemporary Western outlook has already made a powerful impact on certain sections of Indian society, and the process is a continuing one. Whether good or bad in terms of the individual, this process tends to strengthen the secular state.

There are, to be sure, some very serious problems facing secularism—problems of ill-defined objectives, of faulty policies, of failure in implementation.

# Major Problems for the Secular State

Undoubtedly the most serious problem is that of communalism, using the term now in its broadest sense. It is the tenacious loyalty to caste and community which tends to undermine the secular state at every turn. Communal loyalties easily lead to communal rivalries, and this tendency is greatly accentuated by an underdeveloped economy in which there is never enough of anything to go around. Communal rivalries are endemic in India, and easily erupt into violent conflict.

The most urgent requirement in present-day India is the development at the state and local levels of government of both the *will* and the *means* to put down communal violence quickly and sternly. The fact is that communal agitators and irresponsible communally motivated newspapers are apparently still able to indulge in their anti-social activities with impunity, despite the Preventive Detention Act, the Press Act, and the whole armoury of other state powers. Let it be said plainly: the secular state will be reduced to a hollow mockery if the state cannot protect the life and property of the citizen, be he of a minority or the majority religion, from communal violence.

The prevention of communal violence is the negative function of the state in dealing with the problem of communalism. There is still no state responsibility so fundamental as the preservation of law and order. But the development in India of a truly secular state involves much more, the emotional integration of the nation by which the individual's consciousness of caste or community will be subordinated to his Indian citizenship. In this area also, unfortunately, government policies are not likely to achieve the desired results.

The greatest harm has been done by the attempts of both central and state governments to define economic, social, and educational need in terms of caste groups and to extend aid on that basis. Scholarships, economic aid, reserved posts in government, and reserved seats in colleges are extended not only to the Scheduled Castes and Tribes but to the hundreds of 'other backward classes'. This approach has served only to perpetuate and accentuate caste-consciousness and has resulted in grave injustices in the many cases in which there is no correlation between caste status and economic need.

The second major problem for the secular state is the extensive state interference in Hindu religious institutions. The close supervision or even outright administration of temples and *math*s was one of the traditional functions of the Hindu state. In independent India there is a clear trend for the state to revert to its former role in temple administration. The trend is justified by pointing to the need for reforms in financial administration which the state alone is equipped to bring about. The state has thus become the principal agency of Hindu religious reform. In present-day India there is a strong tendency for the state to do for Hinduism whatever it cannot do for itself because of organizational deficiencies.

In the case of temple administration, there is also a decided tendency for the state to become closely identified with Hinduism through state Hindu religious endowments departments. The distinction between the negative function of regulating temple administration to prevent abuses, which the government is empowered to perform, and the positive promotion of Hindu religion, is either not understood or ignored.

If the state deals with the religion of a minority, there are definite political checks which will tend to limit the extent of the interference. When Hindu legislators and administrators deal with their own religion, that of the majority, there are no such checks. State interference in Hindu temples has been limited somewhat by the judiciary's interpretation of Art. 26 of the Constitution, but it is still very extensive. What is almost totally lacking is the consideration that the concept of the secular state itself imposes certain definite limitations on the functions of government. Not everything that needs to be done should be done by the state.

With the submission of the report of the C.P. Ramaswami Aiyer Commission, it is likely that official involvement in the reform of Hindu religious institutions will increase not only on the state level but possibly through other agencies created by central legislation. This trend constitutes an important problem for the secular state, one of the essential components of which is the separation of state and religion.

The third major problem is the position of religious personal law in the legal structure of present-day India. That a Hindu, a Muslim, and a Christian, all citizens of the same country, should be governed by different inheritance laws is an anachronism indeed in modern India and diametrically opposed to the fundamental principles of secularism. The Constitution declares that the state must strive for a uniform civil code, and important progress has been made by legislation unifying the Hindu law. In enacting this legislation the Indian Parliament took great liberties with the Hindu legal tradition by introducing provisions for divorce, inheritance by daughters, and other revolutionary ideas.

The seemingly innocuous directive principle that 'the state shall endeavour to secure for the citizens a uniform civil code throughout the territory of India' is far-reaching in its implications. Paradoxically, the secular state, in order to establish its sovereignty and confirm its secularity, is required to undertake the most basic possible reform of religion. It is called upon by the Constitution to strip Hinduism and Islam of the socio-legal institutions that have distinguished them as total ways of life; to reduce these two great religious systems to their core of private faith, worship, and practice.

The modification of Hindu law, while painful to the orthodox, has been accepted; after all, the vast majority of the legislators were Hindus. But the next step must inevitably deal with the Shari'ah in one way or another, and the sovereign Parliament must decide what to do with the Holy Law of the Muslim minority. The conception of the secular state both presupposes a uniform civil law, and requires that the religious beliefs of a minority be respected. Probably over ninety per cent of the Indian Muslims feel that their law is of the very essence of Islam. This is the dilemma that must one day be faced.

The fourth and last major problem facing the secular state is one of basic definition. What is the meaning of the term 'secular state' in the Indian context? This might at first appear to be a point of academic significance only, but its practical implications are immediate and profound. The most basic question is simply whether the secular state means (1) a state that aids all religions impartially, or (2) a state that is separate from religion. If the latter, then the ideal will be for the state to aid no religion, to assume no religious functions.

This is an old and familiar problem in the US, and the Supreme Court still vacillates between the 'no-preference' doctrine and that of the 'wall of separation'. The tax exemption granted to all religious institutions illustrates the first doctrine; the absolute prohibition of the appropriation of public funds to support religious institutions illustrates the second. The Constitution of India prohibits only special taxes for the support of 'any particular religion' but would presumably permit a general tax for the support of all religions. This expression of the 'no-preference' doctrine must be contrasted with the 'wall of separation' prohibition of all forms of religious instruction in state schools.

In India there is a strong inclination to support the 'no-preference' doctrine. It is in keeping with some of the traditions of the Hindu state and is closely allied to the neo-Hindu emphasis that all religions are true. There is a real danger that the 'no-preference' doctrine may be used to justify state promotion of a syncretistic 'Universal Religion of Man' which is nevertheless based on Hindu assumptions. This tendency was clearly revealed in the Radhakrishnan report on university education.

There is much at stake in the ultimate decision whether the secular state in India will be a non-sectarian state or a non-religious state. In *McCollum* v. *Board of Education*, the US Supreme Court interpreted separation of church and state as follows: 'Separation is a requirement to abstain from fusing functions of government and of religious sects, not merely to treat them all equally.... Separation means separation, not something less.' This interpretation is still a matter of debate in the US, and other court decisions have taken the contrary view. The acceptance of this position and its application to India is not based on the 'authority' of the American Supreme Court, but after considering all the problems involved, my own conviction is that this interpretation of the secular state provides the clearest and the simplest answers to the questions which India must deal with.

## Is India a Secular State?

We have considered both the strong points and the weaknesses of secularism in India, and must now come to some kind of general conclusion. It is well to remind ourselves that the completely secular state does not exist. Even the classic example, the US, illustrates the reluctance to separate state and religion completely. Presidents and governors issue proclamations urging the citizens to attend their respective places of worship, sessions of federal and state legislatures are opened with prayer, Bible readings and the

Lord's Prayer are still used in many tax-supported schools, and every coin bears the motto 'In God we trust'. While Indian secularism is deficient in several respects when judged by the American standard, in other respects (including all of the points mentioned above) the Indian practice is a closer approximation to the theory of the secular state.

Is India a secular state? My answer is a qualified 'Yes'. It is meaningful to speak of India as a secular state, despite the existence of the problems that have been discussed. India is a secular state in the same sense in which one can say that India is a democracy. Despite various undemocratic features of Indian politics and government, parliamentary democracy is functioning, and with considerable vigour. Similarly, the secular state; the ideal is clearly embodied in the Constitution, and it is being implemented in substantial measure. The question must be answered in terms of a dynamic state which has inherited some difficult problems and is struggling hard to overcome them along generally sound lines.

While there is room for cautious optimism, it would obviously be foolish to think that secularism is so firmly established in India that its future is assured. A war with Pakistan, the flare-up of widespread Hindu–Muslim riots, a more compromising attitude toward communalism on the part of Nehru's successor—any of these possible developments might strengthen the Hindu parties sufficiently to make their challenge to secularism a serious one, if combined with the break-up of the Congress monolith. Nor can we discount a possible upsurge of the latent communal sentiment within certain sections of the Congress itself. The forces of Hindu communalism are biding their time, and it is not unlikely that the future will bring circumstances more congenial to their growth. The secular state is one aspect of India's total democratic experiment, the success of which depends on continued stable leadership, steady progress in economic development, population control, and various other factors. There is obviously much that could go wrong.

The poor showing made by the Hindu communal parties, and the overwhelming success of the Congress in three general elections, can not be interpreted as the deliberate espousal by the huge electorate of the principles of secularism. Many millions are still voting for the Congress as the party of Mahatma Gandhi, and as the late M.N. Roy wrote: 'It is neither a philosopher nor a moralist who has become the idol of the Indian people. The masses pay their homage to a Mahatma—a source of revealed religion and agency of supernatural power.'

It must be recognized that the de-emphasis of religion in public life necessitated by the adoption of a secular constitution has created a real problem; what is required is the development of a sense of loyalty to abstract ideals. The full force of this difficulty has not yet been felt, due to the deep personal devotion which the masses feel toward their prime minister. The Hindu communal parties affirm that 'the misconceived notion of secular democracy cannot inspire the masses'. The argument in these pages is that the notion is well conceived and indeed vital to India's national development; but it cannot be denied that it lacks emotional appeal.

It is far too early to dismiss the possibility of a future Hindu state in India. However, it must be said that, on the basis of the evidence now before us, the possibility does not appear a strong one. The secular state has far more than an even chance of survival in India.

# Appendix to Section III

# Constitutional Provisions Regarding the Secular State

## I. Freedom of Religion

INDIVIDUAL FREEDOM OF RELIGION

Art. 25 (1)   Subject to public order, morality and health and to the other provisions of this Part, all persons are equally entitled to freedom of conscience and the right freely to profess, practice and propagate religion.

(2)   Nothing in this article shall affect the operation of any existing law or prevent the state from making any law—

(a) regulating or restricting any economic, financial, political or other secular activity which may be associated with religious practice;

(b) providing for social welfare and reform or the throwing open of Hindu religious institutions of a public character to all classes and sections of Hindus.

Explanation I—The wearing and carrying of *kirpans* shall be deemed to be included in the profession of the Sikh religion.

Explanation II—In subclause (b) of clause (2), the reference to Hindus shall be construed as including a reference to persons professing the Sikh, Jain or Buddhist religion, and the reference to Hindu religious institutions shall be construed accordingly.

COLLECTIVE FREEDOM OF RELIGION

Art. 26   Subject to public order, morality and health, every religious denomination or any section thereof shall have the right—

(a) to establish and maintain institutions for religious and charitable purposes;

(b) to manage its own affairs in matters of religion;

(c) to own and acquire movable and immovable property; and

(d) to administer such property in accordance with law.

Art. 30 (1)   All minorities, whether based on religion or language, shall have the right to establish and administer educational institutions of their choice.

(2)   The state shall not, in granting aid to educational institutions, discriminate against any educational institution on the ground that it is under the management of a minority, whether based on religion or language.

## II. Citizenship

### NO STATE DISCRIMINATION ON GROUNDS OF RELIGION

Art. 15 (1)  The state shall not discriminate against any citizen on grounds only of religion, race, caste, sex, place of birth or any of them.

(4)  Nothing in this article or in clause (2) of article 29 shall prevent the state from making any special provision for the advancement of any socially and educationally backward classes of citizens or for the Scheduled Castes and the Scheduled Tribes.

### EQUALITY OF OPPORTUNITY IN PUBLIC EMPLOYMENT

Art. 16 (1)  There shall be equality of opportunity for all citizens in matters relating to employment or appointment to any office under the state.

(2)  No citizen shall, on grounds only of religion, race, caste, sex, descent, place of birth, residence or any of them, be ineligible for, or discriminated against in respect of, any employment or office under the state.

(4)  Nothing in this article shall prevent the state from making any provision for the reservation of appointments or posts in favour of any backward class of citizens which, in the opinion of the state, is not adequately represented in the services under the state.

(5)  Nothing in this article shall affect the operation of any law which provides that the incumbent of an office in connection with the affairs of any religious or denominational institution or any members of the governing body thereof shall be a person professing a particular religion or belonging to a particular denomination.

### NO DISCRIMINATION IN EDUCATIONAL INSTITUTIONS

Art. 29 (2)  No citizen shall be denied admission into any educational institution maintained by the state or receiving aid out of state funds on grounds only of religion, race, caste, language or any of them.

### NO COMMUNAL ELECTORATES

Art. 325  There shall be one general electoral roll for every territorial constituency for election to either House of Parliament or to the House or either House of the Legislature of a state and no person shall be ineligible for inclusion in any such roll or claim to be included in any special electoral roll for any such constituency on grounds only of religion, race, caste, sex or any of them.

Art. 330 (1) Seats shall be reserved in the House of the People for—
(a) the Scheduled Castes;
(b) the Scheduled Tribes...

Art. 332(1) Seats shall be reserved for the Scheduled Castes and the Scheduled Tribes...in the Legislative Assembly of every state.

## III. Separation of State and Religion

### NO SPECIAL TAXES FOR PROMOTION OF RELIGION

Art. 27 No person shall be compelled to pay any taxes, the proceeds of which are specifically appropriated in payment of expenses for the promotion or maintenance of any particular religion or religious denomination.

Art. 290A A sum of forty-six lakhs and fifty thousand rupees shall be charged on, and paid out of, the Consolidated Fund of the state of Kerala every year to the Travancore Devaswom Fund; and a sum of thirteen lakhs and fifty thousand rupees shall be charged on, and paid out of, the Consolidated Fund of the state of Madras every year to the Devaswom Fund established in that state for the maintenance of Hindu temples and shrines in the territories transferred to that state on the first day of November, 1956, from the state of Travancore–Cochin.

### NO RELIGIOUS INSTRUCTION IN STATE EDUCATIONAL INSTITUTIONS

Art. 28 (1) No religious instruction shall be provided in any educational institution wholly maintained out of state funds.

(2) Nothing in clause (1) shall apply to an educational institution which is administered by the state but has been established under any endowment or trust which requires that religious instruction shall be imparted in such institution.

(3) No person attending any educational institution recognized by the state or receiving aid out of state funds shall be required to take part in any religious instruction that may be imparted in such institution or to attend any religious worship that may be conducted in such institution or in any premises attached thereto unless such person or, if such person is a minor, his guardian has given his consent thereto.

# 7

# Secularism East and West[*]

*Marc Galanter*

P rofessor Smith has produced a comprehensive survey[1] of the
relations between state and religion in India which will be of
great value to students of modern Indian government and politics
as well as of religion. Moreover, this useful, stimulating, and very
readable study raises questions of compelling interest for all who
are concerned with problems of 'church and state'. India, the seat
of a civilization renowned for elaboration of religious thought and
pervasiveness of religious observance has, even by Professor
Smith's rigorous standards, successfully established a secular state.
In this volume, Professor Smith has undertaken to explain how this
has come about, to analyse the Indian achievement and the
problems that accompany it and, finally to indicate how India may
advance to the full realization of that 'true secularism' which he
so enthusiastically endorses.

Professor Smith discusses Indian aspirations and practices in
terms of their conformity to 'the secular state'. His 'working
definition' of the secular state involves 'three distinct but interrelated, sets of relationships concerning the state, religion, and the
individual'.[2] First, as regards the relation between *religion and the
individual*, '[t]he secular state...guarantees individual and corporate freedom of religion'. Second, as regards the relation between

---

[*] Reprinted from *Comparative Studies in Society and History*, vol. VII, no. 2,
(Jan. 1965).
[1] Donald Eugene Smith, *India as a Secular State* (Princeton University Press:
Princeton, 1963).
[2] I have reproduced this definition in a schematic form which combines two
versions, both found on p. 4.

*the state and the individual*, the secular state 'dealt with the individual as a citizen irrespective of his religion'. Finally, as regards the relation between *the state and religions*, the secular state 'is not constitutionally connected to a particular religion, nor does it seek either to promote or interfere with religion'. It is these three—religious freedom, state indifference to religious affiliation, and separation (that is, neither interference, nor promotion)—that constitute the 'doctrine', 'theory', 'principles', and 'conception' of *the* secular state to which he repeatedly refers and against which he measures Indian practices. This conception is derived from the 'liberal democratic tradition of the West' and it is also said to be 'essentially that which can be derived from the Indian Constitution itself' (pp 3, 4).

In the course of his analysis, Professor Smith treats not only the constitutional prescriptions and their judicial application but also governmental policies and practices, and the opinions and activities of various religious and political groups. This survey is not limited to the more obvious points of intersection between religion and state, but proceeds into the more subtle but not less important aspects of their relationship, such as the government's cultural policy, its handling of communal disturbances, religious aspects of language questions, etc. It is concerned primarily with the period since Independence (major developments are covered through June 1962), but it provides a wealth of historical background, especially from the British period. The chief emphasis is on the development of governmental policy implementing secular principles in various areas of Indian public life. While detailing India's remarkable achievements, Professor Smith points out a number of instances in which the Indian government has failed to implement its secular commitment. His strictures against lapses from impartiality and against the tendency to identify religion with the state are telling. He does not shrink from admonition where he thinks that secular principles have been ignored or misapplied. His critique of Indian practice is generally judicious and thoughtful, based on a broad and sympathetic grasp of Indian problems.

The very thoroughness of his attempt to apply to India 'secular principles' derived from Western (and especially American) experience raises the question of whether and to what extent these conceptions are adequate for describing or evaluating the problems of countries with different religious traditions and political problems. I shall attempt to show that Professor Smith's critique of Indian practice and his prescriptions for Indian progress are unconvincing at crucial points—and that this is due to inadequacies in the theory of the secular state.

Before proceeding to these broader issues, I should like to discuss some of his concrete applications of secular principles to Indian problems. These applications not only display some of the theoretical undergirding of much secular theory in the West, but they lead to certain paradoxes that point to the need for a reformulation of the notion of secularism if it is to serve as a useful descriptive category or as an ideal of more than parochial appeal.

## Separate but Equal

### The Indian Tradition

How is it that unlike her South Asian neighbours, India has resisted the temptation to erect her dominant religion—Hinduism, the religion of 85 per cent of her population and an 'ethnic' rather than a world religion, at that—into an officially supported national religion?[3] The author attributes this to a unique combination of advantages: the nature of Hinduism with its immense doctrinal tolerance and its absence of large-scale organization; the heritage of the British policy of neutrality; the presence of important minorities; and the consistent adherence of the Congress party to non-communal nationalism.

The key factor is the nature of Indian religion itself. Professor Smith mentions Hinduism's tolerance toward other religions, its lack of organization, and the ahistorical character of 'the ultimate philosophical and religious values of Hinduism [which] do not require a Hindu state, or any particular kind of state for that matter' (p. 27). On the other hand, he finds obstacles to secularism in Hinduism's tradition of interdependence between religion and state, in its detailed regulation of social life, and in its incapacity for large-scale organization which makes it dependent upon the state to effect reforms (p. 25).

---

[3] For a pessimistic pre-Independence premonition of intolerant Hindu establishment, see M.S. Bates, *Religious Liberty: An Inquiry* (Harper: London, 1945), pp 57–8

It may, I suspect, be even more difficult to generalize about Hinduism than about other religions. If each of the entities to which the rubric 'religion' is commonly applied is, indeed, a cluster or family of sects and cults rather than a monolithic entity, are the components related in the same way? The vast internal differentiation within Hinduism (and the tolerance of it) may be of as much import for secularism as its tolerance toward outsiders. Hindu cults have for the most part eschewed pretensions to exclusive possession of the truth and have not aspired to embrace all mankind—or even all Hindus. The detailed social regulation associated with Hinduism has not been the enforcement of norms of a supposed universally imperative character, but of regulations whose application was only to a particular class of people. This was in good part self-regulation, with the constituent groups entitled to enforce conformity with their own parochial norms. The king was expected to be the supporter of religion, but his duty was not to enforce some universal Hindu standards upon all, but to lend his support to the self-regulation of a multiplicity of groups with diverse standards.[4]

## Reform

But this favourable endowment is not free of defects. Although it is a tradition of tolerance, Professor Smith reminds us that it is a pattern of interdependence rather than separation. Indian government has customarily been the patron and protector of all religions; a task that was shouldered by the British to a considerable extent. The very lack of organization that makes Hinduism congenial to secularism makes it incapable of instituting large-scale reforms; and its wide tolerance encourages the assumption that such tolerance is shared by all religions and can be promoted as an official doctrine. If the mainstream of the nationalist movement has been

[4] Professor Smith attributes to the British the introduction of 'the revolutionary principle that it was within the province of the state to regulate and *change* society by legislation' (p. 304, author's emphasis). This should be qualified to account for the traditional practice of lending governmental support to efforts for self-reform on the part of groups within the society. The novelty is not so much in the notion of deliberate change as in the relevant unit to be changed and the relevant agency to initiate it.

secular, it has also stimulated Hindu revivalism and a tendency to identify Hinduism with patriotism. The zeal for social and religious reform has combined with the organizational weaknesses of Hinduism to promote a pattern of regulation and reform under state auspices which Professor Smith finds distressingly unsecular.

Professor Smith documents the tendency to state interference in religious matters under the heading of reform: financial administration of temples and monastic institutions, requirement of the admission of untouchables to temples, modification of religious personal law. 'The chief reason for such state interference is that Hinduism lacks the kind of ecclesiastical organization necessary to set its own house in order; the tremendous urge for effective social and religious reform which characterizes present-day India can only be satisfied by state action' (p. 126, cf. p. 231).

How much of this is the proper business of the secular state? Professor Smith has grave misgivings, particularly about the regulation and reform of religious endowments which he finds is in practice tantamount to promoting Hinduism. Indeed 'what has evolved resembles nothing so much as an official ecclesiastical department committed to the advancement of a state religion' (p. 233). He points out that the commissioner of Hindu Religious Endowments in Madras 'today exercises far greater authority over Hindu religion in Madras state than the Archbishop of Canterbury does over the Church of England. The contention that the commissioner is concerned only with financial and administrative affairs and not with religious matters...is based on a sharp distinction between *secular* and *religious* which in this context is simply untenable' (pp 246–7). The Indian Constitution does not recognize the broad 'Western' conception of corporate religious freedom to manage its affairs in all respects—administration of property as well as doctrine and discipline. 'The Western guarantee presupposes the existence of well-organized churches with a tradition of self-government; the Indian provision presupposes largely unorganized religious institutions over which the state had traditionally exercised considerable regulation and control' (p. 247). Not only does state regulation interfere with freedom of religion, but 'the secular state is also compromised by the official promotion of Hinduism which has resulted. The department of Hindu religious endowments has provided a kind of ecclesiastical structure which Hinduism previously lacked' (p. 252, cf. p. 231). Professor

Smith suggests that

The only solution…is that the functions of the state in relation to Hindu religious endowments be cut back to a minimum, with emphasis on financial supervision to prevent misappropriation of funds…. It is only by a drastic reduction in the state's enormous powers of control over religious institutions that full religious freedom and separation of state and religion can be secured in India. [p. 254]

Is the state then forbidden to regulate that vast sector of Indian life which is thought of as religious? According to Professor Smith, 'The basic assumption must be that the secular state will have nothing to do with religious affairs; any departure from this principle must be justified on reasonable secular grounds' (p. 230).

[T]he proper approach of the secular state in matters of religious reform is as follows. Religious reform per se is not a valid function of the secular state; it is not the business of the secular state to concern itself with religious matters. Furthermore, any such interference is likely to violate religious liberty, lead to the state promotion of religion, or both. Religious reform should never be the motive behind state legislation. Valid reforms of religion by the state are the *incidental* results of the state's protection of the public in cases where religious practices clearly tend to injure human beings physically or morally, where religious institutions grossly misuse offerings and endowments made by the public or where social institutions connected with religion violate basic human rights. [p. 233]

Upon examination, this formula turns out to give little guidance.[5] How can we tell if reforms are the basic objective or incidental results of legislation? Surely we are not to take statements of legislative intent at face value; and, apparently, we are not to be guided by the motives of the legislators. Professor Smith regards laws requiring that 'untouchables' be admitted to Hindu temples as unwarranted, in spite of the fact that '[most] Hindu legislators regard temple-entry laws as simply measures of social reform, motivated by humanitarian considerations and concern for social

5 While such a formula might lend itself to judicial application, it is surely no more intellectually satisfying that the 'sharp distinction' between secular and religious which Professor Smith finds 'simply untenable' (see text above at p. 136) or the sophistic 'ingenious interpretations' of the courts, which he approves only as a temporary expedient. (See note 24 below.)

justice. They fail to appreciate the predominant religious aspect in this area of reform' (p. 243). Legislation relieving similar disabilities imposed on 'untouchables' in shops and hotels and other public places is 'properly described' as a matter of social welfare (p. 241). But 'the fact that [temple-entry] involves the practices of religious institutions gives the problem a new dimension, and it becomes primarily a matter of "religious reform"' (p. 242).[6] However, state abolition of the dedication of girls as temple dancers (and of temple dancing as such) 'was completely justified on secular grounds alone; the state could certainly abolish such a practice in the interests of public order, health and morality...' (p. 238). Apparently the fact that temple-dancing involved the 'practices of religious institutions' did not import a 'new dimension' to this problem!

Even if basic and incidental results could be readily distinguished, the question arises whether freedom of religion should be protected against direct minor assaults while open—as we shall see—to the most far-reaching changes as long as they are 'incidental' to some other purpose. Professor Smith would not allow merely any purpose, but only protection from being injured 'physically or morally' or denied 'basic human rights'. But which are the basic human rights on whose behalf the state can interfere? Why do they not include the rights of untouchables?[7] And whose notion of 'morally' is to supervene? If the legislature's, then what is left? Does 'morally' signify the conventional morality of India's ruling groups? Or ordinary Indians? Or ordinary Americans?

## Education

Further problems of separation are encountered in the area of education, where the Indian government has continued the system of paying grants-in-aid to schools conducted by religious bodies. These grants are given on the condition that there is no religious discrimination in admissions and that no student is required to

[6] The objection to the pollution or ritual impurity of the 'untouchable' is, of course, the same in restaurants as in temples. For Professor Smith, these laws 'represent two fundamentally different categories of legislation' (p. 241), apparently because the temple is a 'religious institution'. One wonders whether this includes buildings only or includes, for example, a 'sacred' river.
[7] Cf. note 36 below.

participate in any religious services;[8] similar subsidies are given to non-religious schools. Yet, Professor Smith finds this system 'inconsistent with a strict interpretation of the secular state' since it 'involves the indirect subsidization of religion by the state and thus violates a basic principle of secularism' (p. 361).[9] It is generally conceded that few such religious schools could survive without government grants-in-aid.[10] The Constitution's guarantee to religious minorities that they can have their own schools would have little substance if no financial support was available. But Professor Smith, while recognizing the valuable contributions of these schools, finds that the purity of the secular state weighs more heavily than the making of these rights real for minorities (p. 371).

He notes that there are two broad approaches to the protection of minorities: (1) that which secures 'the equality of the individual citizen', and (2) that which is aimed at the 'protection of the socio-religious group' (p. 405). He says with evident approval that the 'Constitution of India has committed itself to the alternative approach [(1) above] to the protection of minorities...The approach is to secure the equality of the individual citizen' (p. 410). While citing the rejection of the principle of communal representation and of 'political safeguards' for religious minorities as evidence for the adoption of this first approach, he overlooks the extent to which the second approach is also present in the provisions of the Constitution.[11] Art. 30(1) provides that 'All minorities, whether based on religion or language, shall have the right to establish and administer educational institutions of their choice.' Since it is understood that under Indian conditions, this

[8] Constitution of India, 1950, Art. 29(2), Art. 28(3). (All citations to articles are to this Constitution unless otherwise indicated.)
[9] Professor Smith does not indicate why 'indirect' subsidization of religion is unacceptable while indirect (that is, 'incidental') interference with religion is permissible. (See p. 217). Does the valid secular purpose that legitimates incidental interference not do the same for incidental subsidization?
[10] See *In re Kerala Education Bill, 1957*, A.I.R. 1958, SC 956 at 980–1.
[11] Other provisions (besides those quoted in the text below) of the Indian Constitution which embody the second (group protection) approach to minorities are Art. 28(2) which exempts endowed institutions administered by the state from the prohibition of religious instruction in educational institutions maintained out of state funds. For an analogous American ruling, see *Quick Bear* v. *Leupp*, 210 US 50 (1908); Art. 29(1) which provides that any

right would be of little effect without state support, Art. 30(2) provides:

The state shall not, in granting aid to educational institutions, discriminate against any educational institution on the ground that it is under the management of a minority, whether based on religion or language.

His failure to discuss the substantial protections afforded by these provisions (and they are far from being dead letters)[12] is the most serious omission in what is otherwise a remarkably comprehensive account. It is a significant omission, though, for in this accommodation of and cooperation with religious enterprise the Indian pattern of secularism departs quite sharply from the 'true secularism' of Professor Smith. The protection of minorities is not confined to the 'equal citizenship' approach, but includes the 'protection of the socio-religious group'. Professor Smith would allow only the first method since as he tells us, 'my general approach throughout the book represent[s] the "wall of separation approach to the problem"' (p. 129). Although he tells us that 'the conception [of the secular state] here expounded is essentially that which can be derived from the Indian Constitution itself' (p. 4), it appears that the Indian Constitution does not wholly embody the 'wall of separation' notion imputed to it.[13]

---

section of citizens with a distinct language, script, or culture shall have the right to conserve it; the provisions of Part XVI which provide special treatment for the Scheduled Castes and Scheduled Tribes; Art. 350A and Art. 350B which give rights to linguistic minorities.

12 These provisions are mentioned in passing when discussing government interference with the operation of private schools (pp 361–71), but are not discussed in the context of minority rights (p. 405 et seq.). Except for the Kerala *Education Bill* case, A.I.R. 1958, SC 956, the developing judicial protection of these rights is ignored. See *Rev. Sidharajbhai Sabbaj* v. *State of Gujarat*, A.I.R. 1963, SC 540; *State of Bombay* v. *Bombay Education Society*, 17 SCJ 678 (1954); *Dipendra Nath* v. *State of Bihar*, A.I.R. 1962, Patna 101; *Arya Pratinidhi Sabha* v. *State of Bihar*, A.I.R. 1958, Patna 359; Subrota Roy Chaudhury, 'Cultural and Educational Rights of Indian Minorities as Judicially Interpreted', *Public Law* 6 (Autumn 1961), pp 271–88.

13 See Art. 27 which forbids tax monies to be appropriated 'for the promotion or maintenance of *any particular religion*…' (emphasis supplied). Presumably the state is not prohibited from non-discriminatory financial support of religion. Cf. Art. 28(2).

# Cultural Policy

The demand for complete separation raises problems in another field—that of cultural policy. As the country's principle educator, its chief patron of the arts and learning, and the owner of its radio network, the government is charged with the promotion of Indian culture. Difficulties arise because so much of Indian culture is religious; 'although Indian culture is a composite, Hinduism is clearly the most potent factor within that culture' (p. 379). How may the state dispense its subsidies, publishing facilities, academies, and awards so as to promote Indian culture without violating its own secular character? May it support classical religious dancing? May it publish a translation of ancient Hindu scriptures?

It is...necessary to make some distinctions in choosing the elements of Indian culture which a secular state can promote. *Bharata natyam*, one of the schools of south Indian classical dance, was developed in the temples as an integral part of Hindu worship. But the performance of *bharata natyam* today is generally regarded as art, not religion, and is universally appreciated as a valuable form of artistic expression in its own right. There is absolutely no reason why the secular state should not encourage and promote such elements of culture. But the translation of religious scriptures is obviously in a different category. The valuable cultural contributions associated with all the religious traditions of India should be encouraged by the state, provided that these are distinguishable from religion itself. [pp 381–2]

It seems at least doubtful to me that the translation of Hindu scriptures is any more likely to promote or sustain the belief or practice of Hinduism than is a *bharata natyam* performance. This is an empirical question, if one that is not readily answerable.[14] But conceptually, how can one determine that dance is 'distinguishable from religion itself' while scripture is not? Are scriptures the

[14] Perhaps such questions cannot be answered unless some version of Hindu beliefs and practices is considered authoritative or standard. For what promotes one set of beliefs and practices within Hinduism may be detrimental to another set. For example, dissemination of Brahmanic ritual may detract from sects built around heterodox reformers and vice versa. Presumably, most instances of 'promotion' are cases in which some more widespread and prestigious elements within Hinduism are encouraged at the expense of local and unlettered elements. However, it might be difficult to determine whether the *net* effect was to encourage or promote Hinduism.

fundaments of *all* religions?[15] Is it not possible for something to be both a 'valuable form of artistic expression in its own right' and 'religion itself'?

Taking up programmes of devotional songs broadcast over the (government monopoly) All-India Radio, Professor Smith finds it

highly doubtful that such programmes of devotional songs can be justified on any secular ground. The literal message of the songs is of course highly religious, but that is not the most important test. It is rather the general understanding and interpretation of the significance of the music which should be the determining factor. A programme of Negro spirituals or Gregorian chants would be almost totally religious in terms of the words which are sung. Nevertheless, a Western audience will in most cases appreciate the musical form for its own sake *without entering into the religious experience* conveyed by the words. It is quite clear that the Hindu devotional songs are neither sung nor listened to in this spirit. They are means of promoting devotion to the Hindu religion and, however popular they may be with the radio audience, this is not a function of the secular state. [p. 395, italics supplied]

The important criterion then is whether the songs are a means of promoting devotion and this is determined by how the performance is experienced[16]—by the audience, it appears, rather than the performers or the AIR broadcast personnel. Is the religious character of state action to be measured by the perceptions of the state's agents or of the people on the receiving end, or by some independent standard? If by the first, then a group of 'modern-minded' legislators motivated by 'secular' concern for 'morality' and 'basic human rights' would have no bounds in tampering with other people's religion. Also 'modern' irreligious broadcasters might programme endless devotional songs because of their aesthetic qualities. On the other hand, if the 'audience' understanding

15 Unlike Christians, Muslims, and Jews, Hindus share no single authoritative canon of scripture. Nor do particular sacred books necessarily stand in the same relation to their Hindu clientele as the New Testament does to Christians or the Koran to Muslims.

16 Even if a sharp distinction between religious and non-religious experiences were possible, there seems little reason to assume that aesthetic appreciation falls entirely on the non-religious side. One may wonder whether, to the extent that art successfully fuses form and content, appreciation of the 'musical form', of for example Gregorian chants, is so readily distinguishable from religious experience.

is determinative, legislators would be barred from any interference with social forms deemed sacrosanct by large numbers of people, and broadcasters would be required to eschew whatever provoked in their audiences a 'religious experience'. Would this include stirring patriotic appeals? Advocacy of non-violence? Professor Smith does not tell us how he would distinguish 'the religious experience' from others. As the quoted passage indicates, the presence of ostensibly religious content does not invariably signify that something is unsecular.[17] Separation would seem to require some more definite standard for distinguishing the religious from the non-religious.[18]

## Personal Laws

Closely related to these problems of separation of 'church' and state are India's difficulties in creating a common citizenship—that is, in eliminating laws whose incidence depends on religious affiliation. In matters of family law, succession, and religious endowments, Hindus and Muslims are regulated not by general territorial law but by their respective 'personal' laws.[19] To Professor Smith, the existence of these separate personal laws for members of different religious communities is a 'major problem' since it is 'an anachronism indeed in modern India and diametrically opposed to the fundamental principles of secularism' (p. 497, cf. p. 116). The whole 'antiquated' and 'medieval' system of separate personal laws must

[17] Cf. his observation that in the US, 'Christmas has largely become a secularized general festival' and 'virtually no one regards [official Christmas celebrations] as an identification of Christianity with the state' (p. 296). For a dissenting view, see Pfeffer, *Church, State and Freedom* (Boston, 1967), p. 226.
[18] On the difficulties of distinguishing religious phenomena, see W. Cohn, 'Is Religion Universal? Problems of Definition', *Journal for the Scientific Study of Religion* 2 (Oct. 1962), pp 26–33; J. Goody, 'Religion and Ritual: The Definitional Problem', *British Journal of Sociology* 12 (June 1961), pp 142–64; H. Stahmer, 'Defining Religion: Federal Aid and Academic Freedom', in *Religion and the Public Order* (Chicago, 1964), pp 116–46.
[19] Outside these fields, governmental use of religious classifications is forbidden. The 'personal law' is administered in the government courts; the usefulness of analogies with systems like that of Israel (p. 291), where personal law is applied by separate religious courts, is extremely limited.

be replaced by a uniform civil code. 'The conception of the secular state...presupposes a uniform civil law...' (p. 498). The secularization of law which is essential to the emergence of a modern and progressive state means '[t]he complete abolition of Hindu and Muslim law, and their replacement by a uniform civil code...' (p. 232) as promised in the Indian Constitution. Professor Smith is fully aware that this 'will amount to a revolutionary reform of both Hinduism and Islam, for it will strip these two great faiths of the distinctive socio-legal institutions which have made them total ways of life' (p. 234). He observes that '[p]aradoxically, the secular state, in order to...confirm its secularity, is required to undertake the most basic possible reform of religion. It is called upon...to reduce these two great religious systems to their core of private faith, worship, and practice' (p. 498, cf. pp 234, 265–6).

This is indeed paradoxical in the light of Professor Smith's strictures against the tendency of the state to promote religious reforms. Somehow the state, which illegitimately infringes on religious freedom by diversion of surplus funds from richer to poorer temples (p. 252) or opening temples to untouchables, has a mandate to legislate the most 'revolutionary' changes in the nature of religious systems. Firmly convinced of the transcendent value of his secular state, Professor Smith has no hesitation in allowing the state to cut the religions to fit. Such cutting is recommended under the rubric of reducing religious systems to 'their core of private faith, worship and practice'. But while this may be widely accepted as the 'core' of Christianity,[20] with its emphasis on the personal experience of redemptive grace and its projection of religious experience beyond the realm of earthly law, it is not necessarily the 'core' of a religion such as Islam, with its emphasis on the disciplined ordering of social and political life.[21]

Professor Smith approves recent changes in Hindu law which have 'already largely reduced Hinduism to a religion of private faith and worship, finding corporate expression solely though

---

[20] Even so, many find in Christian teachings inspiration for a wide range of restrictions which they feel a proper subject of governmental enforcement.
[21] See Marshall G. S. Hodgson, 'A Comparison of Islam and Christianity as Frameworks for Religious Life', *Diogenes*, no. 32 (Winter 1960), pp 49–74, especially p. 63; K. Callard, *Pakistan: A Political Study* (New York, 1957), ch. VI.

voluntary organizations. Its role as the regulator of society is a thing of the past' (p. 423, cf. p. 331).[22] He believes that a separate Hindu personal law 'will shortly be discarded altogether in favour of a uniform civil code' (p. 330). It is not only desirable but 'inevitable that the same process must take place in Indian Islam, although the initiative cannot come from the state' (p. 423). Professor Smith concedes that '[t]he conception of a social community organized according to the [Islamic] law is in fact part of the essence of historic Islam' (p. 421). Furthermore, 'probably over ninety per cent of the Indian Muslims feel that their law is of the very essence of Islam' (p. 498). Does the secular ideal require that their ability to live by this law be abrogated? Why should their views of the 'essence' of Islam be replaced by the secularist's view of Islam's 'core of private faith, worship, and practice'?

Professor Smith characterizes the system of personal law as outmoded, static, medieval, and anachronistic (p. 422), and its abolition as modern, progressive, dynamic and, indeed, inevitable (p. 291). He speaks of certain provisions of Muslim law as justifying 'medieval social practices' (p. 422)[23] and predicts that so long as they retain their personal law, Indian Muslims will remain 'static' and 'will act as a drag on the progress of the rest of the country' (p. 422). In sum, 'one side represents the static past and the other the dynamic present and future' (p. 265).

What are the virtues of such dynamism? Why is Professor Smith (and many Indian leaders) so certain that a common law of

[22] It should be recalled that the so-called regulation of society by 'Hinduism' was to a very large extent self-regulation on the part of the component groups that made up society. If 'Hinduism' provided widespread and prestigious norms and practices, there was a wide range of choice in each group to adopt so much of these as it felt appropriate, advantageous, and acceptable to its neighbours. Cf. J.D.M. Derrett, 'Law and the Social Order in India before the Muhammadan Conquests', *Journal of Economic and Social History of the Orient*, VII (1964), pp 73–120.

[23] The only 'medieval' practices mentioned are onerous dowries, divorce by repudiation, and polygamy (the last conceded to be declining due to economic pressures). It is obvious that any or all of these might be remedied without abolishing Muslim law. Cf. the Muslim Family Law Ordinance, 1961, in Pakistan. See N.J. Coulson, 'Islamic Family Law: Progress in Pakistan', in J.N.D. Anderson (ed.), *Changing Law in Developing Countries* (London, 1963), pp 240–57.

marriage and inheritance will in fact be so beneficial? Supposedly a common civil law will contain provisions of superior justice and utility, will be more uniform and certain, and finally it will reduce communal divisions and promote the 'emotional integration' of the nation. The first of these arguments does not argue for a civil code any more than for reform of personal law, especially where justice and utility are measured by the feelings of those affected. The second is an argument of convenience, but one wonders if it is weighty enough to violate the deeply held beliefs and abrogate the cherished practices of millions of people who are not interested in this convenience. The real arguments, it seems, are those of national integration and 'the modernization of the state' (pp 265–6). There is reason to doubt that enforced conformity would reduce rather than intensify feelings of difference and communal antagonism—at least in the short run. The Indian legal system is already encumbered with a number of unenforceable laws, embodying reforms that run counter to popular norms. While there are many good reasons for thus using the law as an educational medium and index of national aspirations, there is a cost to be paid in the disrespect for democratic government engendered by widespread evasion—as would inevitably ensue were such a uniform family law to be enacted. Surely there are more profitable ways to promote national unity.

Presumably national integration does not justify or require the obliteration of all differences. But if diversity of beliefs is a good thing, deserving of protection, why not a diversity of marriage laws based on these beliefs? Professor Smith dislikes this because it is 'discrimination'. He characterizes as 'strained interpretations' or worse, the holdings of Indian courts that the existence of separate personal laws is not a violation of Art. 15 of the Constitution, which forbids discrimination by the state on the ground, *inter alia*, of religion (p. 116).[24] Does any classification along religious lines

---

[24] Professor Smith has 'absolutely no doubt that such legislation [abolishing polygamy among Hindus while leaving it undisturbed among Muslims] is discriminatory and contrary to Art. 15(1)' (p. 116); a court that found otherwise (on the ground that the law applied not to Hindus as a religious group but to those governed previously by Hindu law) 'indulged in a bit of pure sophistry' (p. 116). However, Professor Smith does not propose that the courts should have declared reforms of religious law unconstitutional. 'During

amount to discrimination? Is a difference in applicable law corresponding (even roughly) to the varying social practice of different communities inevitably discriminatory? Are these 'communal' groupings more arbitrary than territorial ones? People are equally on notice what to expect and have as great a chance to opt out—not only by conversion, but by registration of a marriage under the Special Marriage Act which makes the 'civil' law applicable to them.[25]

## Caste

In the end, the author's strictures against personal law derive first from his view of what a religion should properly be, that is confined to matters of private belief and worship,[26] and, second, from a rejection of the 'communal' or 'compartmental' nature of present Indian society. He finds that

undoubtedly the most serious problem [of the secular state] is that of communalism…in its broadest sense. It is the tenacious loyalty to caste and community which tends to undermine the secular state at every turn…the development in India of a truly secular state involves…the emotional integration of the nation by which the individual's consciousness of caste or community will be subordinated to his Indian citizenship. [pp 495–6]

The Indian Constitution permits the government to bestow various preferences and benefits on a variety of disadvantaged groups,

---

this transitional period when India is struggling to become a modern state, it is precisely the function of the courts to concoct such ingenious interpretations in order to harmonize the permanently valid principle, Art. 15(1) in this case, with the dynamic urge for social reform which still has to find expression within the antiquated framework of religious "civil laws"' (p. 116).
[25] Under the Special Marriage Act, 1954, it is possible for an individual to give up his personal law without relinquishing his religious identification (p. 278). Expansion of this arrangement into a truly voluntary optional civil law for those who do not wish to be ruled by their personal law is an unexplored and promising alternative to the abolition of separate personal laws. For a discussion of the possibilities and problems of having alternative systems of personal law based on individual choice, see G. Tedeschi, *Studies in Israel Law* (Jerusalem, 1960), pp 257ff.
[26] See below, pp 151ff.

mainly the 'untouchables' (Scheduled Castes), tribal peoples (Scheduled Tribes), and 'socially and educationally' backward classes. The former two are caste and tribal groups designated by the central government; the last are designated at the state level and have comprised a variety of lower caste groups. Professor Smith finds 'the fundamental conception of citizenship as a relationship between the individual and the state is being seriously undermined by the attempt to deal with the problem of the underprivileged on the basis of the group, especially the caste' (p. 119). He finds that the use of caste groups to designate the beneficiaries of preferences 'has served only to perpetuate and accentuate caste consciousness and has resulted in grave injustices in the many cases in which there is no correlation between caste status and economic need' (p. 496). In this, he is in agreement with much enlightened Indian opinion (including some within the government) that prefers abandonment of communal criteria and reliance entirely on economic and educational tests to isolate those deserving of special help.[27]

One cannot but agree that the exclusion from the Scheduled Castes of non-Hindu untouchables, like the disabilities on converts in the Hindu Code Acts, is not only unjustified but runs counter

---

[27] A great deal of criticism has been directed at the abuses of the principle of 'protective discrimination'. It is now clear that the courts will scrutinize carefully both the use of the caste criterion and the extent of the preferences. The case of *Keseva Iyengar* v. *State of Mysore*, A.I.R. 1956, Mysore 20, which allowed runaway application of 'protective discrimination' and which Professor Smith cites as a dark portent (p. 121), is clearly no longer good law and has not been for some years. In *Ramakrishna Singh* v. *State of Mysore*, A.I.R. 1960, Mysore 338, a scheme reserving 45 per cent of seats in professional and technical colleges for members of 145 communities designated as 'backward classes' was struck down. The High Court there found that the selection of these classes was not based on any intelligible principle for isolating the 'socially and educationally backward' to whom preferences may constitutionally be given. In *Balaji* v. *State of Mysore*, A.I.R. 1963, SC 649 (decided after Professor Smith's cut-off date, but referred to by him at p. 320), the Supreme Court held that it was unconstitutional to select backward classes by reference to caste rank or standing. It should be noted, though, that both of these cases allow caste or community to be used as units in selecting the groups that are to be designated as backward, so long as some independent criteria (economic, educational) are used to determine their backwardness. For a detailed discussion of the pre-*Balaji* cases, see 'Equality and "Protective Discrimination" in India', *Rutgers Law Review*, 16 (1961), pp 42–74.

to the constitutional provisions that forbid religious discrimination.[28] But it is not only the needless incorporation of religious qualifications into the schemes for 'protective discrimination' that strikes Professor Smith as unsecular, but the use of caste groups to designate the beneficiaries. It is not merely that caste-consciousness will promote communal (that is religious) consciousness, but that caste groupings are in themselves directly unsecular. (It is, of course, unproven that caste loyalties promote religious communal feeling; it might as plausibly be argued that caste loyalties inhibit wider religious intolerance which might undermine secularism.)[29] Encouragement of caste is condemned not merely as indirectly detrimental to secular principles, but as a direct violation of them. Thus the notion of the 'casteless' society is incorporated into his notion of secular state (p. 316). Not only the nature of religion but of caste must be transformed in order to achieve the secular state. This happy outcome is ordained by history: 'in the long run, education, economic development, and nationalism will push caste into the background and ultimately *eliminate* it. The forces of modernization will prevail in the end, but caste is likely to remain powerful for another generation' (p. 329, italics supplied).

When Professor Smith observes that 'caste practices will certainly not be protected by the Constitution' (p. 107), he overestimates the extent to which the Constitution embodies the concept of the 'casteless' society. Notwithstanding the standard rhetoric about the 'casteless and classless' society, the Constitution is itself quite unclear about the position of the caste group in Indian life. There is a clear commitment to eliminate inequality of status and invidious treatment of lower castes and to have a society in which government takes minimal account of ascriptive ties. But although the caste group, unlike linguistic and religious groups, does not enjoy any constitutional protection as such, it may qualify for some protection as a 'religious denomination' or as a 'cultural group'.[30] In one sense, the autonomy of the caste is enhanced by the constitutional provisions which enshrine as fundamental law

28 'The Problem of Group Membership', *Journal of the Indian Law Institute* 4 (1962), pp 331–57.
29 Cf. Theodore W. Spague, 'The Rivalry of Intolerances in Race Relations', *Social Forces* 28, 1 (1949), p. 68.
30 On the religious denomination point, see note 32 below. It has been argued that caste groups may also merit whatever protection is afforded by Art. 29(1)

that government must regulate individuals directly and not through the medium of the communal group. Regulative and penal measures directed at certain castes are now beyond the power of the government and the caste group enjoys a new freedom from regulation directed to it as a corporate whole.[31]

Paradoxically, the assimilation of caste to religious groupings for purposes of making their recognition a violation of secularism would greatly strengthen the constitutional position of caste groups. For if castes are religious groups, presumably any interference with their corporate autonomy would be a violation of constitutional guarantees to religious groups.[32] This is not entirely hypothetical; some castes have already been recognized by the courts as 'religious denominations' entitled to the protections of Art. 26,[33] and a recent Supreme Court case has held that Art. 26 protects the denomination's right to excommunicate members for the purpose of upholding religious discipline.[34] Since Professor Smith finds a legal ban on excommunication 'definitely undesirable' as state interference with

---

which provides that 'Any section of...citizens...having a distinct language, script or culture of its own shall have a right to conserve the same'. Are castes cultural groups? Apparently, to qualify as a cultural group it is not necessary that the group be a minority nor that its distinctiveness be either religious or linguistic. The scope of the guarantee is not yet clear. Apparently, the right to 'conserve' their culture concerns 'the sphere of intellect and culture'. It appears to include the right to transmit this culture; 'the right to impart instruction in their own institutions to children of their own community in their own language', has been referred to as the 'greater part of the contests of Art. 29', *State of Bombay* v. *Bombay Education Society*, 17 Sup. Ct. J. 678 (1954).

31 See, for example, *State of Rajasthan* v. *Pratap Singh* A.I.R. 1960, SC 1208.
32 Art. 26, Art. 30.
33 *Sri Venkataramana Devaru* v. *State of Mysore* A.I.R. 1958, SC, 255; *State of Kerala* v. *Venkiteswara Prabhu* A.I.R. 1961, Ker. 55; *Commissioner* v. *Sri Lakshmindra Thirtha Swamiar*, 1954, SCR 1005, 1022. Professor Smith commends the decision in the *Devaru* case as significant for taking seriously the limits on state-sponsored reform imposed by guarantees of religious freedom (p. 243). However, the holding there that denominational temples are included within the 'public temples' covered by temple-entry legislation severely circumscribes the rights of denominations.
34 *Saifuddin Saheb* v. *State of Bombay* A.I.R. 1962, SC 854, held unconstitutional a Bombay Act making excommunication a criminal offence. The case

the internal affairs of religious groups (p. 111), his interpretation implies that this, along with other guarantees enjoyed by religious denominations, should be extended to caste groups. The whole realm of practices previously immune from governmental interference[35] under the doctrine of 'caste autonomy' might now qualify for constitutional protection.[36]

## Freedom and the Meaning of 'Religion'

Underlying both Professor Smith's model of the secular state and his critique of Indian practice is the notion that the religious may be readily distinguished from the 'secular' or non-religious; his views throughout depend on a radical distinction between those areas of behaviour and experience which are 'religious' and those that are non-religious or secular. As he says, '[t]he underlying

---

involved a Muslim sect and does not imply a similar protection for caste groups as such; it would presumably protect only those that can qualify as religious denominations. It would probably not protect excommunication that was merely social and was not 'to preserve the essentials of religion'.

[35] It should be noted that the British policy of non-intervention in caste questions cannot be dated definitively from the abolition of the Calcutta Caste Cutcherry (p. 301). A wide variety of caste questions were cognizable in Bombay until 1827 and in Bengal and Madras until 1860. From these dates down to the present a narrower range of caste issues has elicited judicial determination under such rubrics as defamation, rights in temples, and rights to caste property and offices. Caste did appear in the application of Hindu law, but Hindu law was based more on distinctions of *varna* than of caste; it was never the case that intercaste marriages were void, but rather inter-*varna* marriages were (cf. pp 301–2).

[36] Professor Smith would protect certain family and intracaste matters from state interference under the heading of religious freedom (p. 309). Also, collectively, '[c]aste associations will continue to enjoy full freedom to carry on their activities to advance their respective communities. But as soon as an individual or a caste seeks to impose disabilities on other individuals or castes, or prevent them from exercising their lawful rights, state intervention is justified' (p. 309). But one man's 'lawful rights' may be another's disabilities! Do 'rights' include a right of religious fellowship? A right to avoid ritual contamination? Do they include the exclusion of lower-caste Hindus from Jain temples? Of other castes from denominational temples? Are such rights subject to periodic redefinition by government from time to time? Cf. his objections to temple-entry laws above.

assumption of...[the] concept [of separation] is simply that religion and the state function in two basically different areas of human activity, each with its own objectives and methods' (p. 6).[37] However, his understandable reluctance to specify these 'areas', 'objectives', and 'methods', leaves us in some difficulty. Secularism can be measured only when we can identify the religious—no easy task for the inexperienced when we recall that there may be 'predominant religious aspects' in situations in which the actors are mainly unaware of them (p. 243) and, on the other hand, religion may not be present even where there is specifically religious content (Christmas in the US, p. 396, or *bharata natyam* pp 381–2). Is religion to be identified as what the practitioners of a particular variety regard as such? Or is there some independent test beyond self-estimation which the observer may employ? For the most part Professor Smith holds to a descriptive or positive view of religion, in which the estimate of its votaries is determinative. 'If for a thousand years Hindus have regarded a particular social practice as part of their religion it *is* part of their religion' (p. 30, cf. p. 309).

But if religion is to be defined by its practitioners, then its content and proper sphere, that is its 'areas', 'objectives', and 'methods', may differ from one group to another. One group may include diet, another marriage arrangements, a third education, and a fourth civil government as activities falling within the scope of religion. Can religious and secular be distinguished as such or only from the perspective of a particular religious system? Can the proper sphere of religion be determined without some view of the authentic content of religious experience?[38]

---

37 Such a distinction is, of course, more congenial to some religious traditions than others, since it implies a radical dichotomy between profane everyday reality on the one hand, and a sacred and autonomous realm of souls, on the other. It also seems to imply a sacramental church that acts on the institutions of the profane world, but cannot replace them or alter their ultimate character. Such a view may be profoundly unacceptable to other religious traditions which stress the transformation of worldly institutions in accordance with divine precept. See Hodgson, loc. cit. (note 21) at p. 68.

38 If, on the other hand, the distinction is thought to be arbitrary or conventional, either because religion is merely conventional designation or because religious aspects may pervade all activity, then such a distinction is itself a matter of choice or policy and the grounds should be stated.

Professor Smith does not offer us any independent criterion for identifying the religious. He is content with the descriptive or positive view, equating religion with what people claim it is, which predominates in his discussion of the necessity of separating church and state. However, when the discussion turns to freedom of religion, there is a subtle shift. If religion for the latter purpose were to mean the same thing, it would be difficult to uphold the claim that the secular state promotes or permits full freedom of religion. So, although he nowhere else addresses himself to the problem of defining the religious, it is when discussing the Indian constitutional provisions for freedom of religion that he remarks that '[i]t is obvious that the definition of "religion" becomes the crucial point in the application of Art. 25(1)...'. Citing the view of the US Supreme Court that a violation of religious freedom occurs when a state regulation is seriously regarded as such,[39] he observes that '[i]t would obviously be impossible to accept...[this]... approach...in India, unless one were prepared to abandon all plans of social progress and modernization' (p. 105). He then commends to us the view of Dr Ambedkar, chief draftsman of the Indian Constitution, that 'we ought to strive...to limit the definition of religion...[to]...beliefs and such rituals as may be connected with ceremonials which are essentially religious'.[40] Professor Smith never takes us any further than this in defining religion, but it is apparent that when he speaks of the secular state as giving full scope to religious freedom, individual and corporate, it is not religion as understood by its practitioners but is more akin to what Dr Ambedkar calls 'essentially religious'. Dr Ambedkar, as a constitution maker (and an outspoken foe of traditional Hinduism), did not claim to be interested in determining the most adequate criterion of religious phenomena; he was quite forthright

39 Although such a view may be implicit in *West Virginia Board of Education* v. *Barnett* 319 US 624 (1943), which Professor Smith cites as exemplifying this proposition, it does not represent the prevailing American position. While American courts have shown a recent inclination to accept as 'religion' whatever is claimed to be such, this does not imply that whatever is claimed to be within the protected area of religious freedom is protected. (See note 43 below.)

40 *Constituent Assembly Debates*, vol. 7, p. 781, cited at p. 105. But see the author's reaction to the 'untenable' distinction between secular and religious used in Madras' control of Hindu endowments (p. 247) quoted above.

in his desire to curtail existing religious practices and to replace existing religious authority with state power. For Dr Ambedkar, this was frankly a normative rather than a descriptive view of religion. Professor Smith makes a similar but unacknowledged leap from a descriptive to a normative view of religion;[41] from the broad descriptive view in discussing separation as a desideratum to the narrower normative view when discussing freedom of religion as a desideratum. For example, in his treatment of caste, the range of practices that he treats as religious in the descriptive sense for purposes of separation is much broader than those he would admit to be protected as freedom of religion.

What matters are protected from government interference under the heading of freedom of religion?[42] The Indian Supreme Court has rejected the American notion that these protections apply primarily to matters of faith, belief and worship, leaving matters of practice subject to state regulation.[43] Instead, the Indian position is that the guarantees of religious freedom extend to whatever conduct is essential or integral to a particular religion.[44]

---

[41] For example, 'Political power is outside the scope of religion's *legitimate* aims' (p. 6, italics supplied); 'Traditional Hinduism and Islam were far more than "religions" in the usual meaning of the word' (p. 265).

[42] The relevant constitutional provisions are Art. 25 and Art. 26. The most comprehensive and useful account of their judicial interpretation is in N.A. Subramanian, 'Freedom of Religion', *Journal of the Indian Law Institute*, 3 (1961), pp 323–50; see also C.H. Alexandrowicz, 'The Secular State in India and in the United States', *Journal of the Indian Law Institute*, 2 (1960), pp 273–96; Harry E. Groves, 'Religious Freedom', *Journal of the Indian Law Institute*, 4 (1962), pp 190–203.

[43] The American position, roughly, is that religious activities are free to the same extent as identical behaviour proceeding from non-religious motives. Religious activities enjoy no special dispensation from general regulation, even where this impinges heavily on certain religious activities. (See note 60 below.) However, there seems to be a recent shift away from this view to one that confers what John Roché calls 'bonus points' on religiously motivated behaviour. See *Sherbert* v. *Verner*, 374 US 398 (1963); *in Re Jenison*, 375 US 14 (1963), vacating 265 Minn. 96.

[44] Harry E. Groves, loc. cit. (note 42) argues that the provisions of the Indian Constitution allow such wide state regulation of religious practice under the heads of public order, morality, health, etc. that the constitutional position comes to much the same as the American distinction between belief (protected) and practice (subject to regulation).

How is that which is essential to a religion to be determined? According to the Supreme Court, 'what constitutes the essential part of a religion is primarily to be ascertained with reference to the doctrines of that religion itself'.[45] Professor Smith advises us that this statement 'should not be taken too seriously' (p. 107).[46] To the extent that the judiciary substitutes its own estimation of the religious for that of the community involved,[47] the freedom of religion to be enjoyed under secularism is of religion in some normative sense rather than in the broad descriptive one. Unless it is recognized that it is religion in the narrower sense that is meant, the author's claim that his proposed secularism promotes religious freedom falls to the ground. But to the extent that his narrow sense is meant, the claim seems somewhat disingenuous.[48]

[45] From the leading case of *Commissioner, Hindu Religious Endowments* v. *Sri Lakshmindra Thirtha Swamiar*, loc. cit. (note 33), quoted at p. 107. This case marked the definitive rejection of the narrower 'Bombay view' of freedom of religion, derived from the American cases dealing with Mormon polygamy.
[46] He adduces the example of the caste system which is 'an essential part of Hinduism' and implies that since the Supreme Court does not intend to protect caste from all inroads by government it will not feel more inhibited in intruding on other practices regarded as 'religious' by their practitioners. The example of caste is well taken but not conclusive since among the whole array of socio-religious institutions certain phases of caste are especially singled out for reform by the Constitution. See 'Law and Caste in Modern India', *Asian Survey*, 3, 2 (Nov. 1963).
[47] The propensity of the judiciary to credit community estimations of what is religious has vacillated. See Subramanian, loc. cit., note 42. Cf. J.D.M. Derrett's criticism of the tendency to decide such questions by reference to orthodox and literary sources and without reference to the custom and actual beliefs of the community involved. 'The Definition of Religion in India Law', *Bombay Law Reporter*, 61, pp 17ff., and Postscript at p. 38. The most recent swing of the Supreme Court confirms Professor Smith's prediction. In *Durgah Committee* v. *Hussain Ali*, A.I.R. 1961, SC, 1402, 1415 the Court suggests a distinction between religion itself and practices that 'have sprung from merely superstitious beliefs'. In *Shri Govindlalji* v. *State of Rajasthan*, A.I.R. 1963 SC, 1638, 1661, the Court undertakes to disengage the religious from 'obviously secular' matters thought to be religious. For an assessment of these decisions, see B. Parameswara Rao, 'Matters of Religion', *Journal of the Indian Law Institute*, 5 (Oct.–Dec. 1963), pp 509–13.
[48] A more sanguine view of the freedom of religion in Indian secularism is taken by N.A. Subramanian 'Freedom of Religion', *Journal of the Indian Law*

The freedom that is a principle of the secular state is not freedom for religion as it is (in India) but freedom for religion as it ought to be. Professor Smith himself recognizes the paradox that in order to permit separation (presumably for the purpose of promoting religious freedom), the government must undertake to transform India's religions by stripping them of their socio-legal side and reducing them to systems of private faith and worship. But this clearly circumscribes the meaning of freedom of religion that can be promoted by this secularism. It is freedom of conscience and belief and freedom of association to communicate and commemorate such beliefs, but it does not include freedom to live life according to the pattern presently believed to be best or divinely prescribed;[49] instead there is a desire to eliminate from public life such archaic and superstitious attitudes and practices as are incompatible with 'progress', 'morality', and 'basic human rights'. The ultimate argument for the secular state then is not to maximize the presently desired freedoms but to substitute a new and more appropriate or valuable kind of freedom; it is the argument for education or enlightenment—for a fundamental change in their view of the world based upon the premise that we know better— that ours is a superior view of the world.

According to Professor Smith, '[t]he secular state does not operate from any theological position; it has no creed and no religious preferences...' (p. 214, cf. p. 154). This does not prevent Professor Smith from having no doubts about the relative merits

---

*Institute*, 3 (1961), pp 323–50. He notes that 'Among the Fundamental Rights dealt with by the Constitution, those relating to freedom of religion stand in a special category. The importance of Art. 25 and Art. 26 lies not so much in the grant of religious liberty but in its *restriction*....For the first time in Indian legal history, the regulation of religious freedom is envisaged and sanctioned by the organic law...the sphere of law will inevitably tend to encroach on the hitherto preserves of religion...' (p. 350).

49 Where freedom of conscience is identified as the valued core of religious freedom, state regulation of actions based on conscientious beliefs may not appear as an important diminution of religious freedom. Cf. Derrett, loc. cit. (note 47) at p. 19. But to the extent that religious freedom consists of freedom of conscience rather than deeds, no state could possibly abrogate it (except perhaps by coercing opposing actions) by forbidding any action. For a recent attempt to avoid the implications of equating religious liberty with conscience rather than deeds, see A.F. Carillo de Albornoz, *The Basis of Religious Liberty* (London, 1963).

of a creative 'reformulated Hinduism' against 'the stranglehold of static Hindu orthodoxy' (p. 331), and of a 'new individualistic Islam over the present variety' (p. 423). Professor Smith rejects as a suitable basis of secularism the 'proposition that all religions are equally true and ultimately the same', for 'the theory is itself an unverifiable religious dogma and any attempt on the part of the state to propagate it would come into sharp conflict with the basic principles of the secular state' (p. 150). He points out the irony that this universalistic Hinduism, which sees all religions as equally valid and ultimately identical manifestations of a single truth, while itself favourable to a secular state, may tend in itself to become a state-supported dogma unacceptable to those who believe their faiths are uniquely true (p. 150). But just as this universalistic Hinduism is unacceptable to adherents of religions that claim some exclusive patent on cosmic truth, so the notion of religion as essentially private and separate from public life is an equally indefensible dogma to those who hold religion to encompass more than doctrine, worship, and private conduct, but to provide obligatory principles for the ordering of public life. Secularism cannot be entirely neutral among religions when it undertakes to confine them to their proper sphere.[50] For in doing so it must deny notions about the jurisdiction of religious precepts and preceptors which are an integral part of some (perhaps most) religious traditions. Secularism presents a view of the nature of human institutions and ultimately of the structure of the universe different from that found in some or most religious traditions. It proceeds from a competing system of ultimate convictions.[51] These convictions may well be true—or in any case may be insusceptible of verification or refutation since such statements about the nature of religion are as prophetic as descriptive, and we have little reason

[50] Some of the 'religious presuppositions' of strict 'wall of separation' secularism in the American context have been pointed out by John Courtney Murray, 'Law or Prepossessions', *Law and Contemporary Problems* 14 (1949), pp 28ff. Cf. Stahler, loc. cit. (note 18). One need not subscribe to the glib assertion that 'secularism is a religion' in order to affirm that particular 'secular' precepts may be incompatible with particular religious principles.
[51] Presumably a secular position like that proposed in this book might find support from either Christian or humanist convictions depending on whether the kind of religion it entails is preferred because it is more true or merely less mischievous—that is, whether the underlying aim is to encourage personal devotion or personal secularism.

to assume that what prevails is thereby proved the better. But even one who is in general agreement about the desirability and probable direction of change in the nature of Indian society and Indian religion cannot suppress surprise that Professor Smith does not see that his prescriptions for India raise not only practical problems but problems for the notion of the secular state.

## The Prospects for Secularism

If we take the three principles that comprise Professor Smith's 'working definition' of the secular state—Freedom of Religion (individual and corporate), Equality (that is state indifference) among religions, and Separation (that is neither promotion nor interference)—we find that they are not a harmonious set of mutually reinforcing principles by which we can determine the extent to which given political arrangements are in fact secular. Instead, they are a set of potentially incompatible principles which may conflict in concrete situations. Is a degree of separation to be sacrificed to permit greater freedom of religion, for example by support of sectarian schools? Is some individual freedom to be sacrificed to enhance corporate freedom, for example by permitting excommunication? Is some corporate freedom to be sacrificed to secure equal treatment, for example by abolishing personal law? Or should equal treatment in law be sacrificed in order to promote equality in fact, for example by preferences for the lowest castes? Is freedom to be sacrificed to secure separation, for example by banning religious appeals in elections? Is freedom of propagation and criticism to be sacrificed to secure absence of communal tensions, for example by penalizing the 'wounding of religious feelings'.[52] In all these instances the principles do not answer questions but merely ask them. The problems of secularism in India are problems of choice among them.[53]

[52] The criminal law in India is extraordinarily solicitous of religious sentiments. Sec. 298 of the Indian Penal Code provides up to one year imprisonment for deliberately 'wounding the religious feelings of any person' by word, sound, or gesture. And Sec. 295–A provides up to two years imprisonment for maliciously and deliberately insulting 'the religion or religious beliefs' of any class of citizens.

[53] Needless to say, such problems are not absent or unrecognized in the US. A parallel list of conflicts engendered by secular principles could easily be drawn up, involving, for example aid to church-related schools, draft-exemptions for conscientious objections, etc. They reappear, for example in

Professor Smith seems to suggest that at some future time the three principles will converge rather than conflict—when religion is purged of dross, and error, and schooled involuntary organization so that the freedom claimed in its name will be those compatible with equality (indifference) and separation. It is this vision of progress from religion as it is to religion as it ought to be that provides the ground for the reconciliation of the three principles of secularism. In this process the state too may move from its present imperfections to complete secularism.[54]

Progress toward secularism of this kind is found predictable and not without precedent. Regarding the secularization of law, Professor Smith finds 'India is a few paces behind theWestern world in the evolution of its law, but it is on the same path which the West itself has trodden' (p. 269). There is hope too that Indian religions will be remade to fit in with this new order of things. 'The role of Hinduism is being reduced approximately to that of religion in Western society; private faith and worship, and corporate religious life expressed through voluntary organizations' (p. 331). So, in spite of his unhappiness with some present practices, Professor Smith finds that the prospects for Indian secularism are favourable: '[t]here is a good chance that twenty years from now, many of India's constitutional anomalies regarding the secular state will have disappeared' (p. 134).[55]

It appears that American Protestantism—or perhaps most American religions—with its renunciation of political power and governmental support provides a model for what religion is to be

---

the form of what Mr Justice Brennan recently referred to as '…an increasingly troublesome First Amendment paradox: that the logical interrelationship between the establishment and free exercise clauses may produce situations where an injunction against an apparent establishment must be withheld in order to avoid infringement of rights of free exercise', *Abington School District v. Schempp*, 374 US 203 at 247, 296ff (1963).

54 'It is not the function of the state to promote, regulate, direct or otherwise interfere with religion' (p. 6). It is obvious that such utopian detachment is possible if at all, only when religions have confined themselves to areas of activity far removed from public life.

55 Even now '[w]hile Indian secularism is deficient in several respects when judged by the American standard, in other respects…the Indian practice is a closer approximation to the theory of the secular state' (p. 499).

and the US (hopefully to be purged of its remaining anomalies)[56] provides a model of the secular state. The US is 'the classic example' (p. 499). '[W]ith relatively few exceptions the basic principles of religious freedom and church–state separation have been faithfully adhered to throughout 170 years of American history' (p. 17). Even the US has its shortcomings:

Presidents and governors issue proclamations urging the citizens to attend their respective places of worship, sessions of federal and state legislatures are opened with prayer, Bible readings and the Lord's Prayer are still used in many tax-supported schools, and every coin bears the motto 'In God we trust' [p. 499].

All of the deficiencies in the American model seem to be departures from strict separation. The very limited conception of religious freedom does not seem to strike him as any limitation at all. In the US freedom of religion does not include the right to make claims on government for provision of opportunities and resources to implement religious values[57] and it does not include opportunity to enlist state cooperation in regulation of social and ritual life; it is primarily freedom from governmental restriction. But even this freedom stops short of practices (apart from speech) that violate the prevailing consensus on family and sex, education, medicine and health, safety, and (to some extent) scientific rationality.[58] In brief, the American conception of religious liberty is of liberty of conscience and belief but it does not extend to conduct that the overwhelming majority feel to be seriously harmful or offensive

---

56 It remains to be seen whether any secular state can avoid being flavoured by impurities from prevailing religious tradition. In his discussion of the Indian Supreme Court's rather reluctant and tortuous upholding of state laws preventing the slaughter of cows (*M.H. Qureshi* v. *State of Bihar*, A.I.R. 1958 SC 731), he notes that these laws 'must be viewed primarily as attempts to impose the taboos of one religion upon all citizens' (p. 439) and notes that the Court was forced into a 'curious bit of reasoning' in order to reach this result (p. 488). Cf. the reasoning of the US Supreme Court upholding Sunday closing laws in *Gallagher* v. *Crown Kosher Super Market*, 366 US 617 (1961).

57 See Mark De Wolfe Howe, 'Problems of Religious Liberty', in C.J. Friedrich (ed.), *Liberty* (=*Nomos*, IV) (1962), pp 262, 269.

58 Perhaps war and aggression should be included in this list. See *in re Summers*, 325 US 561 (1945); *Hamiltion* v. *Regents*, 293 US 245 (1934).

for example polygamy,[59] non-attendance at school, faith-healing, fortune-telling, snake-handling, use of drugs.[60]

Professor Smith's ideal is a completely secular state which is a projection from the American pattern with an extra dose of separation. Assuming that the peculiar settlements and compromises among the three principles reached in the US are the only reasonable ones, he overlooks the fact that they are compromises and balances rather than mere deficiencies dictated largely by the nature of American religion and society, and that they are not necessarily appropriate to India where there are different kinds of religion and less agreement on what is the proper realm of religious experience.

Professor Smith appears to regard all secularist positions that depart from a strict 'wall of separation' view as espousing merely the 'no preference doctrine' which would not restrict aid to religion, so long as it was non-preferential between religions.[61] However, these two views by no means exhaust the alternatives in the US.[62] And although Professor Smith detects Indian inclina-

---

59 *Reynods* v. *United States*, 89 US 145 (1879); *Davis* v. *Beason*, 133 US 133 (1890); *Late Corporation of the Church* v. *United States*, 136 USD 1 (1890); *Cleveland* v. *US*, 329 US 14 (1946); *Musser* v. *Utah*, 333 US 95 (1948). Among Professor Smith's references to American cases there is only one passing mention of any of the cases suppressing Mormon polygamy; he cites the *Reynolds* case as 'pointedly' enunciating the necessity of the state's power of preserving public order (p. 104).

60 See generally David Fellman, *The Limits of Freedom* (New Brunswick, 1959), pp 24–31; Pfeffer, op. cit. (note 17), pp 572ff; I.H. Rubinstein *Contemporary Religious Jurisprudence* (Chicago, 1948). Since these outrageous practices stand in somewhat the same relation to religious freedom as 'hard-core pornography' stands to freedom of the press, they may conveniently be labelled 'hard-core heresy'. In pointing out these various limitations of the American conception of religious liberty, it is not meant to imply any blanket condemnation of such restrictions. The point is that our easy acceptance of them may make it difficult to appreciate how restricted a sense of religion they imply, thus concealing some of the basic problems for a general formulation of secularism.

61 See pp 498–9, 381, 129n.

62 For attempts to demarcate an interpretation of the American provisions more complex than either strict separation or mere impartiality among religions, see Mark de Wolfe Howe, 'The Constitutional Question', in Miller, et al., *Religion and the Free Society* (Fund for the Republic, 1958), pp 49–63; Wilbur G. Katz, 'The Case for Religious Liberty', in J. Cogley (ed.), *Religion in America* (New York, 1958); Paul Kauper, *Civil Liberties and the Constitution* (Ann Arbor, 1962), ch. 1; Philip Kurland, *Religion and the Law* (Chicago, 1962).

tions toward the 'no preference' view,[63] it is clear that Indian secularism does not conform to either of these patterns. India's Constitution-makers, legislators, and judges have, from whatever mixture of idealism and expediency, fashioned an ingenious set of balances and adjustments that combines their commitment to progress with their respect for freedom. But it is these very balances and accommodations that Professor Smith sees as unfortunate and hopefully temporary. As we have seen, the three principles which comprise secularism are not readily reconcilable and we may expect that compromises and accommodations will have to be made and remade. Are the Indian compromises to be measured against the idealized American pattern?[64] Ultimately we must have some standard for judging whether the embodiment or implementation of these principles is sound, and this must be a standard beyond these three principles themselves—is it liberty, democracy, progress, modernity?

Professor Smith's view is not of alternative patterns of balancing and combining these principles, but of a single scale in which there is more or less secularism. His point of view is 'that of one deeply committed to the principle of the secular state...this principle is so vital a part of modern liberal democracy that it is preferable by far to err on the side of a strict interpretation than to grow careless about it' (p. ix). A strict interpretation means a complete 'wall of separation' approach ruling out governmental cooperation with and accommodation of religion. But is this fully relevant to India where the basic task of secularism is not to banish religion from the political order but to transform and curtail it in the social order.

According to Professor Smith, the secular state 'stands or falls as a basic and inseparable component of the modern liberal

[63] Professor Smith complains of 'the persistent tendency in present-day India to define secularism simply in terms of non-discrimination in the promotion of religion. To most Indians, *secular* means non-communal or non-sectarian, but it does not mean non-religious. For most, the basis of the secular state is not a 'wall of separation' between state and religion, but rather the 'no-preference doctrine' which requires only that no special privileges be granted to any one religion. As defined in this book, the secular state includes the principle that the functions of the state must be non-religious' (p. 381).
[64] The interpretation of the secular state in *McCollum* v. *Board of Education*, 333 US 203 (1948) is said to provide 'the clearest and simplest answers to the questions which India must deal with' (p. 499).

democratic state' (p. viii). There is though little evidence that constitutional separation of church and state has much to do with the effective functioning of modern liberal democracy. There is some correlation of religious freedom (in the narrow sense) and equal citizenship with effective liberal democracy. But virtually all the countries with the best claim to enjoy this form of government lack the 'wall of separation', and many have state churches today.[65] Liberal democracy thrives in an atmosphere of low intensity of religious beliefs and minimal political involvement by religious bodies, but there is no evidence that it requires 'strict separation' to produce these. And if this is the case in the West, where secularism had to face the problem of intolerant and well-organized creeds with political aspirations, how much relevance does the wall of separation have for India where the predominant cluster of religions see themselves as alternative rather than exclusive embodiments of cosmic truth, are not intensely organized, and have so far revealed few political pretensions?[66]

Professor Smith concedes that separation is not historically a pre-condition of religious freedom, but he feels that 'separation of state and religion is especially important in the newly independent states of Asia, [f]or while liberal democratic traditions have saved modern Western states from the more dangerous implications of the state church system, these traditions have been but recently transplanted in Asia and in general have not yet taken firm root' (p. 8). No doubt the implications of a certain amount of state cooperation with religious bodies are less dire than those of 'the state church system'. The observation that the conception of the

[65] For example the UK, Norway, Sweden, and Denmark have (and Switzerland contains) established churches. Holland and Belgium provide extensive financial assistance to sectarian institutions. See Pfeffer, op. cit. (note 17), ch. II.
[66] The very modernization of religion that Professor Smith calls for may be more dangerous to secularism in India than some of the anomalies that he criticizes. With the weakening of communal boundaries, the growth of stronger ecclesiastical organization, increasing use of mass media, greater concern with creed and doctrine rather than local practice, and emphasis on universalistic rather than particularistic appeals, there is the danger that a more widely held, less differentiated, and more standardized Hinduism might emerge to menace the secular state. Perhaps it is a race between the modernization of religion, on the one hand, and the decline of religious zeal, on the other.

secular state is 'Western in origin and contains important elements which are opposed to traditional Asian conceptions and practices' (p. 24) should not obscure the fact that the secular state—and liberal-democratic government, for that matter—are almost as much an innovation in the West as in Asia. Western tradition too contains elements inimical to the secular state. If the concept of secularism was first formulated in the West, the concept of the religious state was most intensely practised there. India can be said to have as long or a longer a tradition of secular government in many respects than most of Western Europe or North America.

Ultimately, this completely secular state is recommended to us as the arrangement most conducive to and most compatible with a complex of conditions that include modernity, progress, nationhood, democracy, individualism, pluralism, and freedom of conscience and conviction. But if these assertions convince us that some kind of secular state is preferable, does it follow that this particular model is required? Apparently we can enjoy at least some, perhaps all, of these things without this particular brand of secularism. One may be convinced that some form of secularism is conducive to and even requisite for these other desirable things. But even if we grant that the brand of secularism Professor Smith prefers is the most truly secular of them all, it does not follow that it thereby contributes the most to the production of the other desiderata. Indeed, the very 'impurities' of a particular secular system may be functional for the production of these values. (For example, state support of denominational schools in India, p. 371.) Like secularism, each of these values covers a whole range of possibilities. Selection of the most appropriate brand of secularism depends in turn upon choices about the most desirable kind of polity, society, and personality. The concrete results of particular patterns of secularism must be evaluated in terms of other values achieved or impeded. And for such a purpose we need to be able to speak in more dimensions than 'more' and 'less' secular. Professor Smith is aware of these conflicts and he does more of this in practice than his conceptual scheme allows. However, for all its virtues, his book might be stronger if it were not encumbered by a single notion of secularism that attempts to serve both as a descriptive category and as a transcultural ideal. To use secularism as a descriptive category requires that there be greater specificity and differentiation so that we have ways of talking about the varieties as well as degrees of freedom, of equality (indifference), of separation. And to serve as an ideal for countries of varying religious experience, secularism must be reformulated from a Western to a universal ideal. For this it requires greater generality to free it from parochial notions of the scope and 'core' of religious experience. For either purpose we require sufficient openness and flexibility to permit consideration of a wide variety of conditions, so that the inevitable judgments regarding the best 'fit' or 'mix' under particular conditions need not be seen as deviations from a single and unvarying model of true secularism. We are informed that 'the present book is the first instalment of the broader study of the relationships between religion and the state in this part of the world' (pp x–xi). It is to be hoped that the author will not only continue his very impressive work of documentation and interpretation but will proceed to clarify and refine the conceptual scheme so that he can make secularism more useful as a descriptive category and more relevant as a transcultural ideal.[67]

67 I would like to thank Stanley Bernstein, Harold Levy, Yosal Rogat, and Phyllis Rolnick for their valuable comments and suggestions. They are not, of course, responsible for the views expressed here.

# 8

# Hinduism, Secularism, and the Indian Judiciary*

*Marc Galanter*

One of the most striking developments in independent India is the successful emergence of an avowedly secular state encompassing the bulk of the world's Hindus.[1] There is disagreement about what this secular state implies—whether it implies a severe aloofness from religion, a benign impartiality toward religion, a corrective oversight of it, or a fond and equal indulgence of all religions. There appears however to be a general agreement that public life is not to be guided by religious doctrines or institutions. There is a widespread commitment to a larger secular order of public life within which religions enjoy freedom, respect, and perhaps support but do not command obedience or provide goals for policy. At the same time, Hinduism is undergoing a vast reformulation and transformation. Indeed, these processes are closely interlinked. The nature of the emerging secular order is dependent upon prevalent conceptions of religion, and the reformulation of religion is powerfully affected by secular institutions and ideas.

This article discusses some aspects of India's legal system as a link or hinge between the secular public order and religion. The modern legal system has transformed the way in which the

* Reprinted from *Philosophy East & West*, 21, 4 (Oct. 1971).
[1] Among the literature on the legal and theoretical aspects of secularism in India are: D. Smith (1963): D. Smith, ed. (1966): Luthera (1964); Galanter (1965); Sharma, ed. (1966); Subrahmanian (1966); *Seminar* (1965); Derrett (1968); Sinha, ed. (1968).

interests and concerns of the component groups within Indian society are accommodated and find expression.[2] In traditional India, many groups (castes, guilds, villages, sects) enjoyed a broad sphere of legal autonomy, and where disputes involving them came before public authorities, the latter were obliged to apply the rules of that group. That is groups generated and carried their own law and enjoyed some assurance that it would be applied to them. In modern India, we find a new dispensation: the component groups within society have lost their former autonomy and isolation. Now groups find expression by influence on the making of general rules formulated at centres of power—by representation and influence in the political sphere, by putting forth claims in terms of general rules applicable to the whole society. The legal system, then, provides a forum in which the aspirations of India's governing modernized Western-educated élite confront the ambitions and concerns of the component groups in Indian society. In this forum the law, as a living tradition of normative learning, encounters and monitors other traditions of prescriptive learning and normative practice. We shall be concerned with India's secularism both as a programme for the relation of law to religion and, as an instance of the general problem of the relation of law to religion, between law and other traditions of normative learning.

## Temple Entry and the Boundaries of Hinduism

I shall approach these general matters by considering in some detail the 1966 case of *Sastri Yagnapurushdasji* v. *Muldas Bhundardas Vaishya*,[3] in which the Supreme Court of India attempted to define the nature and boundaries of Hinduism. In it we find the interplay of these various themes—secularism and Hinduism, traditional groupings and Westernized élite, parochial concerns and national aspirations, legal doctrine and religious learning—presented dramatically and not without a measure of ironic reversal and comic byplay.

[2] Galanter (1966b); Galanter (ch. 2).
[3] A.I.R. 1966, SC at 1119. (Decided on 14 Jan. 1966 by a bench of five, consisting of P.B. Gajendragadkar, C.J.; K.N. Wanchoo; M. Hidayatulla; V. Ramaswami; and P. Satyanarayana Raju. JJ.) The high court judgment from which appeal was taken appeared in I.L.R. 1960, Bom. 467 =LXI Bom. L. Rep. 700 (1968).

Whatever the tenor of its encounter with religion, the law cannot entirely avoid questions of religious identity. Even in a secular state, civil authorities, including the courts, find themselves faced with the necessity of ascertaining what is religious. For example, courts in the US find themselves having to decide what is religious for the purpose of avoiding forbidden 'establishments', for the purpose of determining the scope of religious freedom, and for the purpose of administering statutory dispensations like tax exemptions and conscientious objection to military service. A second kind of problem of religious identity may also arise: whether a particular person or organization in fact belongs to a particular religion. This arises more rarely in the US, but it does appear in church-property disputes, in adoption cases, and in carrying out testamentary requirements.

In India, the courts face quite as many problems in ascertaining religion in general and a great deal more in the way of fixing particular religious identities. This is because the Indian Constitution and legal system embody a different relation of law to religion. Indian law permits application of different bodies of family law on religious lines, permits public laws, like those of religious trusts, to be differentiated according to religion, and permits protective or compensatory discrimination in favour of disadvantaged groups, which may sometimes be determined in part by religion. The penal law in India is extraordinarily solicitous of religious sensibilities and undertakes to protect them from offence. The electoral law attempts to abolish religious appeals in campaigning. In all these areas courts must determine the nature and boundaries of a particular religion. But beyond this, the state is empowered generally to use its broad regulative powers to bring about reforms in religious institutions and practices, and this power is wider with regard to Hinduism than it is in relation to other religions. The state is empowered to assure that Untouchables have full access to Hindu religious institutions.[4]

The issue of temple entry historically came to symbolize the question of the inclusion of Untouchables within the Hindu community.[5] The vexed question of whether Untouchables were

[4] See the qualifications in Art. 25 and Art. 26 of the Constitution of India, especially Art. 25(2)(b).

[5] Galanter (1964b). For a sampling of the broad opposition to temple entry, see Sorabji (1933); Aiyar (1965), p. 107ff; Durkal (1941), pp 2, 99; Iyengar

within the Hindu fold was generally settled in the course of the independence movement and the whole solution is crystallized in the Constitution itself which permits the state to enforce public religious acceptance of Untouchables upon other Hindus. At one time it was widely assumed that religious acceptance was the key to dissolving all the disabilities of the Untouchables. In recent years, however, attention has shifted to provision of more tangible advancements; the matter is generally one of low priority for Untouchables and reformers. Nevertheless, temple-entry measures are of continuing symbolic importance, and conceptually they have remained troublesome to commentators on Indian secularism. Some critics have found in the assertion of public control over temples a flaw in the pattern of Indian secularism either because it violates the integrity of religious premises or interferes in the internal affairs of religious bodies.[6] Other commentators have found in temple entry reason to reject as inappropriate for India this 'separation-of-powers' model of secularism, with its underlying distinction between the intrinsically religious and secular, and profane, church and state.[7]

---

(1935); Krishnamacharya (1930). Restrictions on temple entry are critically analysed in Pillai (1933). Legislation against these restrictions is reviewed in Venkataraman (1946). The changing (and eventually pro-temple-entry laws) views of Gandhi can be traced in Gandhi (1954).

6 D. Smith (1966), pp 241–3. See Luthera (1964) p. 108, where he argues that the eradication of untouchability 'by the state as far as religious institutions are concerned is not consistent with the concept of the secular state....In a secular state the nature of the relations between the Church and its believers is to be settled between themselves'.

7 Blackshield (1966) p. 54, observes that 'the very fact that temple-entry authorization is inconsistent with the "separation of powers" model of secularism ought to suggest that the "separation of powers" model must be wrong'. He concludes that secularism in India must include active state determination of the boundaries of religion. Derrett (1968) p. 510ff, suggests that such state regulation of religious expression and caste religions in the public sphere is a role fully supported by Hindu tradition. Unlike separationists who subsume Hindu religious premises under the private sphere of 'church' as opposed to state, he sees these premises impressed with a public quality and subject to public regulation. Thus he finds that temple-entry laws 'may interfere with the continuance of ancient customs of a religious character, but no human beings are deprived of their religion, for they can decamp and set

Our case involves a group called the Swaminarayana Sampradaya, that is followers of Swami Narayana (1780–1830).[8] I will refer to them simply as Satsangis. They are a puritanical Vaishnavite sect, with several hundred thousand followers, mainly in Gujarat, founded in the 1820s. The sect, it appears, has been conventional and conservative in its views and practices regarding caste distinctions. In Manilal C. Parekh's sympathetic account of the Swaminarayana movement we learn that: 'Even the Untouchables were not excluded from the Satsang. It is true that these were not admitted to the inner part of the temples, but they were made disciples and in one or two places they built temples of their own.'[9] Parekh concludes that in regard to caste distinctions:

Swami Narayana acted as one who was in no sense a social revolutionary. In spite of the fact that he, in common with all the great teachers of the Bhagwat Dharma, opened the way of salvation to all people including the Untouchables and the non-Hindus, he would do nothing which would even distantly suggest that he was out to subvert the Hindu social order.[10]

In 1947, the province of Bombay passed a temple-entry Act, which provided that 'every temple shall be open to Harijans [that is, Untouchables] for worship in the same manner and to the same extent as to any member of the Hindu community or any section thereof...'. Early in 1948 some followers of the sect, anticipating an attempt by local Harijans to enter their temples, filed a suit alleging that their temples were not covered by the 1947 Act. During the pendency of the suit, the Constitution came into force in 1950 and the plaint was amended to urge that the Act was violative of the constitutional guarantee of freedom of religion, which gave every denomination the power to manage its own affairs in matters of religion.[11] Furthermore, the Satsangis

---

up private institutions where they can worship in their own way.... Those whose religious scruples include a belief in Untouchability have been prohibited from practising this: their remedy, if they continue in this belief, is to stay at home and to use only private facilities from which they can still exclude Untouchables'.

[8] On this movement, see Parekh (1936); Monier-Williams (1891).

[9] Parekh (1936), p. 126.

[10] Ibid., p. 292.

[11] Art. 26. (See App.)

contended, their temples were not within the ambit of the Act since they were a distinct and separate religious sect unconnected with the Hindu religion. They asserted that although they were socially and culturally Hindus, religiously they were distinct.

There is no single accepted legal test of who is a Hindu.[12] 'Hinduism', as used officially, is an equivocal term with shifting denotation. Sometimes it is used in an inclusive sense that embraces all the heterodox communions—Jainism, Buddhism, Sikhism, etc.[13] At other times it is used in a varying, narrower sense, meaning followers of more or less Vedic and Brahmanical communitions.[14] The draftsmen of temple-entry laws have aimed at inclusiveness.[15]

The trial court concluded that the Satsangis formed a section of the Hindu community, 'but found that it was not established that their temples were used by non-Satsangis and granted them an

[12] The most prevalent legal test of a Hindu is that developed for the purpose of applying the appropriate personal law, that is deciding who is to have Hindu law applied to him. Historically, this definition was neither a measure of religious belief nor a description of social behaviour; rather, it was a civil status describing everyone subjected to Hindu law in the areas reserved for personal law. Heterodox practice, lack of belief, active support of non-Hindu religious groups, expulsion from a group within Hinduism—none of these removed one from the Hindu category. The individual could venture as far as he wished over any doctrinal or behavioural borders; the gates would not shut behind him so long as he did not explicitly adhere to another religion. This negative definition prevails today. A few years ago the Supreme Court had to decide on the validity of consent to an adoption by one who disavowed belief in the religious efficacy of adoption, in Hindu rituals and scriptures, in *ātman* and salvation. The court found that 'the fact that he does not believe in such things does not make him any less a Hindu....He was born a Hindu and continues to be one until he takes to another religion...whatever may be his personal predilections or views on Hindu religion and its rituals'. *Chandrasekhara Mudaliar* v. *Kulandaivelu Mudaliar*, A.I.R. 1963, SC, 185, 200. See ch. 6.
[13] See, for example, the explanation of Sec. 3 of the Untouchability (Offences) Act (see App.); Hindu Marriage Act, Sec. 2.
[14] See, for example, the use of Hindu in the narrower sense (excluding Jains, Buddhists, etc.) in the President's Order defining Scheduled Castes, *Punjabrao* v. *Meshram*, A.I.R. 1965, SC, 1179. The ambiguity is analogous to that of the term 'Protestant' in contemporary American usage.
[15] See, for example, the Central and Bombay laws in the Appendix. On the shortcomings of these attempts, see ch. 6.

injunction.[16] This was in 1951. Because of appeals on interlocutory order the state's appeal on the merits did not reach the high court until 1957. In the meantime the Bombay Act had been supplanted by the Central Untouchability (Offences) Act of 1955.[17] The Untouchability (Offences) Act had proved to have an unexpected flaw. As the judges read it, it seemed to preserve certain denominational prerogatives so that Untouchables only gained rights of entry if they were members of the Hindu denomination or sect that managed the temple in question.[18] To obviate this difficulty, the state of Bombay in 1956 passed supplementary legislation which provided that every temple open to any class of Hindus should be open to all Hindus.[19] The high court, now reviewing the case on the merits in 1958, found that the new Act was constitutional and that it applied to the Satsangi temples.

When the case reached the Indian Supreme Court in 1966, the principal argument put forward by the Satsangis was that they are 'a religion distinct and separate from the Hindu religion' and consequently outside the scope of the Bombay Act.[20] The immediate question for decision then was whether the Satsangis were Hindus for purposes of the application of the Bombay Act. Rather than undertaking a narrow and technical inquiry into the scope of the temple-entry power and its exercise, the Supreme Court opted to address a much broader question: 'We must inevitably enquire what are the distinctive features of the Hindu religion.'[21] The Court set off to ascertain the nature of Hinduism.

In the course of this inquiry, the Court propounded three different views of Hinduism; or, more accurately, it considered Hinduism from three quite different standpoints. Without

16 That is, on the ground that the Bombay Temple Entry Act only extended rights to Untouchables who were members of the same denomination, an interpretation vindicated by *Bhaichand Tarachand* v. *Bombay*, A.I.R. 1952, Bom. 233.

17 Act XXII of 1955. This Act was passed in exercise of exclusive central competence in penal measures against untouchability. On the extent to which this field was pre-empted from state action, see Galanter (1961a).

18 *State* v. *Puranchand*, A.I.R. 1958, MP, 352. See Galanter (1964b).

19 Bombay Hindu Places of Public Worship (Entry Authorization) Act, 1956 (Act 31 of 1956). Similar legislation has been passed in several other states.

20 A.I.R. 1966, SC at 1127.

21 Ibid., p. 1127.

acknowledgement it shifted from one to the other in the course of its opinion.

The first standpoint is a descriptive one, which sees Hinduism as a complex, indefinable, inclusive aggregation of ways of life.

We find it difficult, if not impossible, to define Hindu religion or even adequately describe it. Unlike other religions in the world, the Hindu religion does not claim any one prophet; it does not worship any one God; it does not subscribe to any one dogma; it does not believe in any one philosophic concept; it does not follow any one set of religious rites or performances; in fact, it does not appear to satisfy the narrow traditional [for traditional, read Western] features of any religion or creed. It may broadly be described as a way of life and nothing more.[22]

There is much more of the same: '...under Hindu philosophy, there is no scope of excommunicating any notion or principle as heretical and rejecting it as such'.[23] Unlike other religions and religious creeds, Hindu religion is not tied to any definite set of philosophic concepts as such.[24]

How then, if no boundaries can be established, can it be ascertained whether a group is within Hinduism or not? In order to do so the Court takes a second standpoint, which we might call the analytic. Beneath the diversity of Hindu philosophy, it finds, 'lie certain broad concepts which can be treated as basic'.[25] These include 'the acceptance of the Veda as the highest authority in religious and philosophical matters', the 'great world rhythm', and 'rebirth and pre-existence'.[26] Having discerned the glimmerings of unity, the Court goes on to ask: 'What, according to this religion, is the ultimate goal of humanity?'[27] And it has little difficulty in answering: 'It is release and freedom from the unceasing cycle of births and rebirths...which is the ultimate aim of Hindu religion and philosophy....'[28] On the means to attain this end 'there is great divergence of views...'[29] but '...all are agreed about the ultimate goal. Therefore it would be inappropriate to apply the traditional [again, read Western] tests in determining the extent of the jurisdiction of the Hindu religion. It can safely be described

22 Ibid., p. 1128.   23 Ibid., p. 1129.
24 Ibid., p. 1130.   25 Ibid., p. 1130.
26 Ibid. The Court adapts this formulation from Radhakrishnan (1923), pp 26, 27.
27 A.I.R. 1966, SC at 1130.
28 Ibid.   29 Ibid.

as a way of life based on certain basic concepts to which we have already referred'.[30] The Court adds yet another 'working formula' borrowed from B.G. Tilak which it says 'brings out succinctly the broad distinctive features of Hindu religion':[31] 'the acceptance of the Vedas with reverence, recognition of the fact that the means or ways of salvation are diverse; realization of the truth that the number of gods to be worshipped is large'.[32]

Having thus defined the undefinable, the Court then proceeds to see whether or not the Satsangis are within the 'Hindu brotherhood'.[33] It finds their claim to be 'a distinct and separate religion different from the Hindu religion [is] entirely misconceived'.[34] First, the sect's founder was a Hindu saint. 'Acceptance of the Vedas with reverence, recognition of the fact that the path of Bhakti or devotion leads to Moksha, and insistence on devotion to Lord Krishna unambiguously and unequivocally proclaim that Swaminarayan was a Hindu saint…who wanted to restore the Hindu religion to its original glory and purity.'[35] The Satsangis had put forth a catalogue of traits that purportedly distinguished them from Hindus—membership by initiation rather than birth, openness to members of all religions, and the worship of Swaminarayan himself. The Court, unimpressed by this catalogue, finds the sect is like others that grew out of the activities of reforming saints who 'basically subscribed to the fundamental notions of the Hindu religion and the Hindu philosophy'.[36]

If the Satsangis are, then, Hindus and within the ambit of the temple-entry Acts, a further question arises: namely whether their constitutional freedom as a denomination to manage their own

---

[30] Ibid., p. 1131.   [31] Ibid.

[32] Ibid. This is attributed to Tilak's *Gitarahasaya*, but I have not been able to locate it.

[33] Ibid., p. 1131.   [34] Ibid., p. 1134.

[35] Ibid.

[36] Ibid., p. 1134. The thinness of these contentions is apparent. The Satsangis could muster little evidence of departure from the mainstream of Hindu beliefs, symbols, and practices. A perusal of the *Sikṣā Patri* (Epistle of Precepts), which Monier-Williams refers to as 'their code of instruction', reveals no such departures. Rather, it points to their acceptance of the *varṇa* order, the special spiritual functions of Brahmins, the Vedas and Purāṇas, the Hindu pantheon, sundry philosophic concepts, and the Hindu legal tradition. Thus:

103. Dharma is the good practice which is enjoined both by the Shrutis

affairs in matters of religion [Art. 26(b)] is violated by the temple-entry laws. Is admission to temples 'a matter of religion'? A few years earlier, another bench of the Supreme Court was faced with a similar conflict between temple-entry powers of the state and a denomination's rights to control admission to its premises.[37] On that occasion, control over participation in temple service was indeed a matter of religion and therefore deserving of some constitutional protection. 'Under the ceremonial law pertaining to temples, who are entitled to enter them for worship and where they are entitled to stand and worship and how the worship is to be conducted are all matters of religion....'[38] While upholding the primacy of the state's temple-entry power, the earlier decision affirmed that what were matters of religion depended on the historically grounded self-estimate of the group in question.

The Court in the present case does not treat this issue explicitly; rather, it extends it disquisition on Hinduism to get around it and to undermine the earlier view. The apprehension of the Satsangis about the pollution of their temple, says the Court, 'is founded on superstition, ignorance and complete misunderstanding of the true teachings of the Hindu religion and of the real significance of the tenets and philosophy taught by Swaminarayan himself'.[39] The Court is no longer speaking analytically of 'basic tenets' but of 'true teaching', as opposed to superstition, and of 'real significant' as opposed to misunderstanding. This is a far cry from the earlier notion that Hinduism is so all-embracing that no principle is heretical. Having moved from the descriptive to the analytical, the court has now shifted its stance once again, this time to a normative perspective from which the different strands within Hinduism can be evaluated and judged. The Court does not attempt explicitly to reconcile its divergent standpoints. How can Hinduism be at one

---

(the Vedas) and by the Smritis (the body of Law as delivered originally by Manu and other inspired legislators)....

97. When a question in regard to usage, practice and penance is to be determined, my followers should refer to the Yagnavalkya Smriti with its commentary called the Mitakshara. [Reprinted in Parekh (1936), pp 336–7.]

37 *Sri Venkataramana Devaru* v. *State of Mysore*, A.I.R. 1958, SC, 255.

38 Ibid., p. 265.

39 A.I.R. 1996 at 1135.

moment so diffuse and inclusive as to defy description and at the next readily analysable into fundamentals? And what do the fundamentals have to do with the Court's evaluation? It is nowhere suggested that the caste views of the Satsangis violate the 'basic concepts' regarding the Vedas, rebirth, multiplicity of means to salvation, etc. Rather than apply its basic concepts, the Court propounds a view of Hinduism, its unity and continuity, that enables it to discern what is authentic and essential and what is not. Underneath the divergent teachings of saints and reformers, 'there is a kind of subtle indescribable unity which keeps them within the sweep of the broad and progressive Hindu religion'.[40] These saints and reformers have 'by their teachings...contributed to make Hindu religion ever alive, youthful and vigorous'.[41] Indeed, 'as a result of the teachings of Ramakrishna and Vivekananda, Hindu religion flowered into its most attractive, progressive and dynamic form'.[42]

In the eyes of the Court, the true teachings of Hinduism are those that make it attractive, progressive, dynamic, alive, youthful, and vigorous. But how is the living stream of progressive and dynamic Hinduism to be separated from the dross of superstition and ignorance? It is clear that not all Hindus agree on which is which. In describing Satsangi beliefs, the Court notes that their scriptures forbid ceremonial intercourse with low-caste people.[43] Apparently at least some present-day Satsangis place a different value on this part of their tradition than does the Court. The Court does not explain the source of its mandate to overrule them on this question

---

[40] Ibid., p. 1130.  [41] Ibid., p. 1134.
[42] Ibid., p. 1130.
[43] The *Siksa Patri* upholds caste distinctions at a number of places. Participation is graded by *varṇa* and special provision is made for 'Untouchables', for example:

    19. Nor shall anyone eat or drink except in Jagannathpuri from a person of a caste lower than one's own....

    24. None shall give up the performance of the duties that are imposed upon the class or the religious order to which he belongs, nor shall he adopt the duties that are enjoined on others....

    41. Those twice-born persons that have received initiation into the worship of Krishna from a proper spiritual preceptor shall always wear on their neck a double-necklace...and they shall make an upright mark on their forehead....

and to substitute its own views of the true teachings of Hinduism. It may seem somewhat uncharitable to chastise people for their complete misunderstanding of the true teachings of Hinduism after rejecting their contention that they are not Hindu.

What exactly is the Court saying about Hinduism? It seems to imply that regulation of temple worship is not a 'matter of religion' within the constitutional protection, and furthermore that invidious caste distinctions are not a part of Hinduism deserving legal recognition. These implications are at variance with the general tenor of the Supreme Court's earlier encounters with caste and Hinduism. Although generally unfriendly to manifestations of caste in public life,[44] the Court has been rather sanguine in its estimation of the caste system and its place within Hinduism.[45] As recently as fifteen months before the Satsangi decision, another bench of the Court observed that the term 'Hindu' (in the narrower sense) referred to 'the orthodox Hindu religion which recognizes castes and contains injunctions based on caste distinctions'.[46] Is the Court now saying that invidious caste distinctions are not a part of Hinduism? Presumably these distinctions, at least in relation to temple attendance, are based upon notions of differential purity and ritual pollution. The Court indicates in its opinion that it is willing to countenance these notions in at least some contexts.[47] How can it determine where distinctions based on ritual purity (for example that between worshipper and officiating priest) are

---

44. Those pure Shudras, who are devotees of Krishna, while practising their own peculiar duties, shall, like the twice-born wear the double necklace and make the vertical mark on the forehead.

45. The Shudras who are lower still have always to wear a double necklace like the others and shall make the round mark on their forehead while eschewing the upright mark.

91. The twice-born should perform at the proper seasons and according to their means, the twelve sacraments, the six daily duties, and the Shradha offerings to the spirits of departed ancestors.

96. All my twice-born disciples who wish good to themselves should read and hear these noble Scriptures. [Reprinted in Parekh (1936), p. 327ff].

44 See, for example, *Bhau Ram* v. *Baij Nath*, A.I.R. 1962, SC, 1476, and ch. 7.

45 For example, *D. Sura Dora* v. *V.V. Giri*, A.I.R. 1959, SC, 1318, and ch. 6.

46 *Punjarao* v. *Meshram*, A.I.R. 1965, SC, 1179 at 1184.

47 A.I.R. 1966 at 1127.

legitimately religious—and thus entitled to governmental protection—and where they are merely superstition and subject to governmental overruling?[48] The Court does not address this as a question of fact; it does not appeal to usage, to popular understanding, or to Hindu learning. Instead, it acts as if it enjoyed a mandate to make such determinations on its own authority.

Was this the only way that the Court could reach a desirable result? It is submitted that the Court might have found a more direct and more craftsmanlike route to the same result.[49] The result itself is by no means a strained or contrived one. In crucial respects the Constitution *is* a charter for the reform of Hinduism. The wording of Art. 25 and Art. 26 establishes the primacy of public interests over religious claims and provides a wide scope for governmentally sponsored reforms. Art. 15 and Art. 17 forbid a whole cluster of usages that are intimately connected with popular Hinduism and have some sanction in Hindu learning. While denominational differences within other religions lie outside state power, the Constitution embodies the notion that divisions within Hinduism need not be accorded the same respect. Art. 25(2)(b) establishes that the state may act to overcome caste

[48] The Court here is cutting into a whole complex of learning about the dynamics of temples, idols, purity, etc. For many Hindus, temples are 'divine powerhouses, no mere prayer halls' [Krishnamacharya (1936) p. 8]—nucleations of divine energy from which radiate spiritual energies which would be dissipated by contact with unfavourable emanations. In order to conserve the efficacy of these repositories of spiritual energy, there are detailed rules regarding the location and construction of temples, installation and consecration of idols, maintenance of requisite states of purity, and avoidance of contamination of various sorts through specific rites and observances. While not all Hindus take concern for contamination so literally or unbendingly, the Court does not indicate the basis in Hindu doctrine for its selectivity. (Of course its basis in public policy is evident.)

[49] Any other disposition of this claim would have permitted appellants' lawyers to elicit a determination of the status of the entire group that violated previous understandings, without any evidence that this new characterization was widely shared by members of the group or that the plaintiffs had a mandate to represent all Satsangis in this matter. Some Satsangi witnesses had contested this contention. See LXI Bom. L.R. at 705. The high court noted that there had been no previous claim of this kind and there was evidence of long-standing acquiescence in census enumeration as Hindus.

and denominational barriers within Hinduism. The law may be used to create an integrated Hindu community by conferring common rights of entry in religious premises. To authorize state use of this power in the case of Satsangi temples, it was necessary only to construe the scope of this power. It was not necessary to consider the nature of Hinduism *per se*. On the verbal level, it would have been sufficient to confirm that this power extends to all who are 'socially' and 'culturally' Hindus, as the Satsangis conceded themselves to be.[50] Or, going deeper, the ambit of the temple-entry power could have been determined in the light of its purpose. Was this the evil that the Constitution-makers were providing against? Was this a case of invidious caste distinctions operating to restrict religious participation? It was an established doctrine that rights conferred under the temple-entry power prevail over denominational claims to exclude outsiders as part of their freedom of religion.[51] Thus it would not have been necessary to determine whether the exclusionary rules of the Satsangis were properly part of their religion or not.

Why then did the Court choose the more circuitous and thorny path? In part, there is a personal explanation. The judgment is the work of the then chief justice, P.B. Gajendragadkar, a man of strong reformist views within Hinduism and with an intensely activist judicial posture on the bench.[52] The chief justice was faced with compulsory retirement two months later. As a militant advocate of a reformist brand of secularism, he was displeased by an earlier series of decisions in which the Supreme Court had declared that what is religion is a matter to be determined by the doctrines of each religious community itself.[53] He felt strongly that this 'auto-determination' of religious rights was a pernicious doctrine which would give great scope to obscurantist religionists and would place beyond state power practices that were inimical

50 LXI Bom L.R. at 703–4.
51 *Sri Venkataramana Devaru* v. *State of Mysore*, A.I.R. 1958, SC, 255.
52 Gajendragadkar (1951); Gajendragadkar (1965). For an assessment of his judicial work, see *Journal of the Indian Law Institute* (1966). For a premonition of the views on Hinduism set forth in the Satsangi case, see the chief justice's inaugural address to the seminar on secularism just a few months before the judgment was delivered [in Sharma (1966), p. 1].
53 For example, *Saiffudin Saheb* v. *State of Bombay*, A.I.R. 1962, SC, 853.

to progress.[54] In several earlier cases, he had taken the opportunity to supply dicta which tended to undermine this view by asserting that matters which were 'obviously secular' or 'based on superstition' would not be deemed religious even if their adherents regarded them as such.[55] In other words, he strongly asserted the right of the courts to an independent power of decision as to what was the 'religion' protected by Art. 25 and Art. 26. He may have hoped that before his retirement, there would be an opportunity to overrule the 'auto-determination' view. The Satsangi case was as close to such an opportunity as he could have hoped to find. The temptation to make the most of it may have been particularly strong because the case concerned untouchability, a subject in relation to which the chief justice was an outspoken and militant reformer. This was one subject on which he might have felt little hesitation in confidently asserting the non-religious character of the claimed practice because he was confident of his grasp of the 'true teachings' of Hinduism.[56]

But the personal predilections of the judgment writer are hardly a sufficient explanation. The other sitting four judges concurred without being moved to dissociate themselves from the opinion in any way. We must then take this as more than an idiosyncratic view. It represents in a pronounced form one tendency which is to be found among the judiciary and more generally among the Westernized, educated ruling élite—a tendency to active reformulation of Hinduism under government auspices in the name of secularism and progress.

[54] Cf. the criticism of Tripathi in Sharma (1966). Blackshield (1966), p. 61, finds 'the Indian Supreme Court's experiments with "auto-determination" by religious institutions of what matters are "religious" *do* seem inconsistent with secularism'. Smith (1963), p. 105 had earlier observed that such an approach could not be accepted in India 'unless one were prepared to abandon all plans of social progress and modernization'. For an opposing view, see Ghouse (1965).

[55] *Durgah Committee* v. *Hussain Ali*, A.I.R. 1961, SC, 1402, 1415; *Shri Govindlalji* v. *State of Rajasthan*, A.I.R. 1963, SC, 1638, 1660–1.

[56] The point is one he has made in innumerable public addresses. In asserting it, the chief justice stands well within a continuing reformist/Gandhian tradition of interpreting Hinduism so as to expunge it of 'untouchability'. For example, see Gandhi (1954) and Sundarananda (1946).

# Alternative Modes of Secularism

The question brought into focus by the Satsangi judgment is the mode in which the secularism embodied in Indian law is to contribute to the transformation of religion in India. In assessing the thrust of India's secularism it is important that we avoid equating secularism with a formal standard of religious neutrality or impartiality on the part of the state. No secular state is or can be merely neutral or impartial among religions, for the state defines the boundaries within which neutrality must operate. For example, the First Amendment of the US Constitution is often said to enjoin state neutrality in religious matters. But it is clear that in the larger sense, American law is not neutral among religions except in a purely formal sense. In defining the boundaries within which neutrality must operate, the First Amendment is a charter for religion as well as for government. It is the basis of a regime which is congenial to those religions that favour private and voluntary observance rather than to those that favour official support of observance. It favours those religions that prefer social and spiritual sanctions over those which would employ official force to support their social and ritual prescriptions. It favours groups which are not exclusive in their claims and are willing to tolerate the presence of alternative and hostile views. It is not so congenial to religions that purport to supply obligatory principles for governance of society or which believe that it is necessary to extirpate error.

A secular state, then, propounds a charter for its religions; it involves a normative view of religion. Certain aspects of what is claimed to be religion are given recognition, support, and encouragement; others are the subject of indifference; finally, some are curtailed and proscribed. Religion, then, is not merely a datum for constitutional law, unaffected by it, and independent of it. It is, in part, the product of that law. The American legal setting, for example, has made and presumably will continue to make a profound contribution toward shaping religion in the US.

The Indian constitutional stance toward religion is more explicit and more complex. The Constitution attempts a delicate combination of religious freedom in the present with a mandate for active governmental promotion of a transformation of India's religions. For example, religions are to be divested of their character as sources of legal regulation of family life.[57] The Constitution also propounds equality among religions, but as we have seen, the state's reforming power with regard to Hinduism is more extensive. The law may be used to abolish caste distinctions by *inter alia* conferring rights of religious participation.

The broad constitutional mandate disposes of the notion that the law might confine itself to ascertaining and respecting a preordained religious sphere as implied by the 'separation of powers' model of secularism. There is a clear commitment to what Anthony Blackshield calls the 'overall arbitral role' in which the law exercises 'the function of regulative oversight and adjustment of the working and of the interlocking of particular social controls...'.[58] But how is this 'arbitral control' to be exercised? Here we may distinguish two alternative modes for the exercise of the law's 'regulative oversight' of religious controls. We might call them the mode of limitation and the mode of intervention. By limitation I refer to the shaping of religion by promulgating public standards and by defining the field in which these secular public standards shall prevail, overruling conflicting assertions of religious authority. By intervention I refer to something beyond this: to an attempt to grasp the levers of religious authority and to reformulate the religious tradition from within, as it were.[59]

---

[57] Art. 44.

[58] Blackshield (1966), p. 60.

[59] For a temple-entry position delicately poised on the border between limitation and intervention, see Gandhi's (1965), p. 140, 1931 depiction of his dream of independent India: 'There will be no untouchability. The "untouchables" will have the same rights as any other. But a Brahmin will not be *made* to touch anybody. He will be free to make himself untouchable and have his own well, his own temple, his own school, and whatever else he can afford, so long as he uses these things without being a nuisance to his neighbours. But he will not be able as some now do to punish untouchables for daring to walk on public streets or using public wells. There will be under Swaraj no such scandal as that of the use of public temples being denied to untouchables when it is allowed to all other Hindus. The authority of the *Vedas* and the other *Shastras* will not be denied, but their interpretation will not rest with individuals but will depend upon the courts of law, in so far as these religious books will be used to regulate public conduct. Conscientious scruples will be respected, but not at the expense of public morals or the rights of others. Those who will have extraordinary scruples will themselves have

At the risk of ignoring elements of overlap and mixture, we might visualize these alternative modes as related on two dimensions: first, the superior or overriding character attributed to the legal norms in cases of overlap, conflict, and characterization; second, the asserted competence and mastery of the legal specialists in authoritative exposition of the religious norms. The relationship between our three modes of secular control may then be depicted in tabular form. The division of the Table into four distinct boxes for purposes of emphasis should not obscure the point that the dimensions in question are continuous rather than dichotomous distinctions. The Table portrays only a part of the range along each dimension. Presumably, by extending it we could encompass various forms of 'religious state'.

Table: Alternative modes of secular control

| External superiority of legal norms | Internal competence of legal specialists | |
|---|---|---|
| | Low | High |
| High | Mode of limitation | Mode of intervention |
| Low | 'Separation of powers' mode | * |

* The situation of high internal competence of legal specialists in religious norms combined with low external superiority of legal over religious norms is not another form of secularism, but defines a condition that would be called a religious state.

Clearly, the Constitution gives government power to promulgate certain reforms, irrespective of Hindu usage. There is a deliberate abandonment of part of Hindu tradition to state regulation. It is clearly the task of the courts to delimit that abandoned part and to interpret the secular public principles that are to apply in its stead. But does the Constitution give the court a mandate to go beyond this, to participate actively in the internal

---

to suffer inconvenience and pay for the luxury. The law will not tolerate any arrogation of superiority by any person or class in the name of custom or religion. All this is my dream.' [Cf. Derrett (1968), p. 510ff.]

reinterpretation of Hinduism, to interpret Hinduism so as to accommodate these governmentally sponsored changes, and to legitimize them in terms of Hindu doctrine? Religious notables, publicists, and scholars are presently engaged in reinterpreting Hindu tradition. Does the Constitution empower the courts to participate actively in this reformulation? Is the Supreme Court a forum for promulgating official interpretations of Hinduism? Is it a Supreme Court of Hinduism?[60]

A number of factors in the Indian religious and political setting may impel judges to take this active interventionist role: the desire to reconcile, to avoid explicit disregard of religious authority, to make reforms palatable, to propagate strongly held views or religion, to teach the unenlightened, and to entertain pleasant images of one's past. There are other factors too that make such judicial activism acceptable and appealing to the educated reformist élite. Members of this élite are distressed by much of popular and traditional Hinduism which they feel lacks the dynamism, the concern for welfare and development, that they feel is necessary for India's progress. They are also distressed by its diffused and fragmented character which in their eyes obstructs national unity, and by its lack of coherence and organization that make the masses unavailable to mobilization for reform and development. These very shortcomings lend legitimacy to judicial activism. The sprawling, disjointed, unorganized character of Hinduism and the parochialism of its spokesmen disqualifies it from a right to self-definition. Since it is so organizationally fragmented and diffused, there are no religious leaders who have a mandate to define it for the entire religious community. To permit each religious dignitary to define it for himself would subvert any attempt at integration. Thus, in the absence of credible spokesmen, only the judges can speak to and for Hinduism as a whole. It is assumed that judicial intervention will have a salutary unifying as well as a reforming influence. Indeed, it is only when the state intervenes to promote

60 It might be argued that the area of untouchability/temple entry called for distinctive and interventionist treatment, because this area is carved out of Hinduism by the Constitution—that is that in effect an ecclesiastical jurisdiction is conferred on the court to interpret untouchability out of Hinduism. Such assertiveness is not evident in other judicial encounters with untouchability [see Galanter (1969)]. Nor is the interventionist stance taken in the Satsangi case explicitly limited to matters concerning untouchability.

unity and infuse modernity that it can create in Hinduism a capacity for self-definition.

There are, I submit, grounds for serious doubts whether such judicial intervention could actually be productive of the values to which the élite subscribe. First, there is a tendency to underrate the strain of such a role on the capacities, energies, and persuasiveness of the judiciary. What, it may be asked, equips judges to prescribe the nature and content of Hinduism? It could be and is argued that the higher judiciary, many of whom are accomplished in Hindu learning or at least steeped in a Hindu atmosphere, are well equipped to filter and refine Hindu tradition and to arrive at assessments of Hinduism that combine fidelity to essentials with a progressive, modern outlook that recognizes the need for reform and growth.

But how is a common-law judge to do this? Is he to confine himself to making an assessment solely on the basis of the record before him? Or may he draw upon his own experience and prepossessions? How about the judge—and there are many—only meagrely acquainted with Hinduism or holding an idiosyncratic view of it? How about the non-Hindu judge? Is he to disqualify himself? Or ought he to sit, but to defer to the opinion of his Hindu colleagues? Or is he equally entitled, as an Indian, to voice the true meaning of Hinduism?

Once qualified to sit, how is the judge to proceed? An exponent of a tradition of textual exegesis, the common-law judge employs certain techniques of selecting authorities, interpreting and reconciling texts, and introducing innovations. Is it open to him to apply these techniques to the Hindu textual tradition? Should not the judge enter into that tradition to ascertain its own internal rules and techniques, its methods of assessing the relative importance of its various elements, and the admissibility of innovations?[61] In the Satsangi case, the court did not consult contemporary Hindu learning. It draws a picture of Hinduism based on Western or Western-inspired scholarly sources[62] and elicits principles from

61 Cf. the impact on Hindu law of its administration by common-law courts which could not satisfactorily exercise the discretionary techniques that give it its flexibility. See ch. 2; Derrett (1968), chs 8, 9.

62 The opinion is remarkable for the extent to which (though written by a judge himself learned in Sanskrit and a descendant of a family of eminent

Hindu tradition by common-law techniques. But if the court cannot enter into Hindu tradition and work within it, how persuasive can it be to the living exponents of that tradition and to their followers?

This is not to suggest that what the courts say is of no effect. Whatever the courts do cannot help but have some impact on Hinduism. The kind of religion that the government and the élite favour may gain some acceptance as a result of judicial promulgation. Like many an earlier reform movement it may succeed in being accepted as a sect alongside all the other movements in Hinduism. But is it likely to have the kind of influence that the élite desire and sway the whole Hindu community? One of the distinctive features of modern India is that there are, for the first time, levers to bring about changes bearing 'across the board' for the entire Hindu community, among them legislation and the courts, and it is the Westernized élite who grasp these levers. The question is: Will it get more thrust from them by using them under the banner of true Hinduism than under that of secular modernism?

It might be argued that the courts should not be shy of prescriptive assessments of Hinduism since their statements will inevitably carry normative overtones. If, in dealing with religious questions, the courts scrupulously avoid prescriptions based on reform views they will in effect give powerful support to existing forms and ossify present practice.

But if the courts deliver 'reformist' decisions, does the addition of religious justifications enhance their effect? Here we need empirical information and we have none. From what little is known about the influence of the decisions of higher courts upon behaviour in other settings, we may surmise that when court decisions are influential it is not through their doctrinal pronouncements but by rechannelling major institutional opportunities and controls and by their liberating effect. The court may provide dissident and progressive elements with institutional support and with rationalization for their non-traditional behaviour or beliefs.

---

*dharmasastrins*) it approached Hinduism through Western and Western-inspired scholarly sources. Apart from the brief quotation from Tilak and another from the *Bhagavad Gita*, the principal authors referred to are Monier-Williams, Max Müller, and S. Radhakrishnan.

But these effects may be relatively independent of whether the justifications provided are secular or religious. Those with serious traditional commitments are unlikely, in any event, to be persuaded by judicial exegesis. Indeed, it might be argued that the masses will do better at reconciling reforms with their religious understandings if the courts disclaim any competence in religious matters and reiterate instead their claim to overriding authority in whatever touches public life.

Quite apart from these problems of effectuating an interventionist approach, there is the question of the cost that might be entailed by its 'success'. The paradoxical character of the interventionist stance is revealed if we inspect the common argument in favour of the Hindu unity. If judicial intervention did assist in making Hinduism unified and organized, would the modern reformist élite be as influential as they are at present? Their anxiety to see Hinduism organized is not to have a spokesman for it as it is, but so that it might be more readily mobilized to be what they think it ought to be. Indeed, government measures may succeed in precipitating a unified structure out of Hinduism. But the lack of unity and organization of traditional society is not only an obstacle to the greater influence of the élite, it is a condition of their present influence. Again, it is assumed that the unification and organization of Hinduism will somehow contribute to national integration. But this is not a self-evident proposition. Perhaps the disunity of Hinduism contributes to national unity. The successful breaking down of Hinduism's capacity to generate and tolerate internal differences may well lessen India's capacity to sustain pluralistic democracy.

The 'success' of interventionism is of course unlikely to be more than partial and localized. In reading the Satsangi judgment one gets the impression that the public being addressed is not the unenlightened mass but the élite itself. The opinion is an occasion for intra-élite debate, using the Satsangis as an object lesson. The concern of the court's judgment is to reduce the dissonance of the élite—a dissonance that derives from their own ambivalence about Hinduism and about secularism. But however successful this approach may be in assuaging the feelings of the educated and resolving their ambivalence, the use of religious justifications is not without danger, for it projects certain illusions about Indian society that increase the capacity of the élite to be seduced by their own tendency to concentrate on illusory verbal reforms. The lawyer's fallacy that behaviour corresponds to legal rules offers powerful reinforcement of the élite's fallacy that the masses are following them—a coincidence of illusions that can lead to dangerous miscalculation about popular sentiment and about the efficacy of legally enacted reforms.

## Conclusion

Lawyers have tended to view the relationship of 'law' and 'morals' as a problem of the sources of legal norms and the scope of legal regulation, a problem, that is, whether law should express or enforce 'morals' (usually taken to mean some generally accepted normative rules). As our example of secularism indicates, there is another side to the relationship—the problem of the autonomy and authority of the various other traditions of normative learning with which the law coexists in society. The law must face the question of the mode in which it should recognize and/or supervise them. The alternatives emerge vividly in the law–religion relationship because religions are systems of control with complex learned traditions, expounded by their own specialists and even with their own doctrines concerning their relationship to law. But the same general problems of relative authoritativeness and competence are present in the relation of law to various simpler and unlettered traditions (for example, the custom of a trade, the usage of a caste) as well as to complex and learned traditions like Hinduism. The 'law and morals' problem reappears in the relation of law to every body of normative learning.

Our analysis of Indian secularism as presenting alternative possibilities for managing the relationship of law to Hindu tradition suggests the possibility of a more generally applicable typology of the relations between law and other bodies of normative learning. We may reformulate our alternative modes of secularism as possible modes in which law can relate to various 'lesser' traditions, for example: (1) delegative recognition of an autonomously defined realm of authority, corresponding to the 'separation of powers' mode of secularism; (2) regulative management of boundaries, conflicts, and characterization of the 'lesser' tradition, corresponding to the 'limitation' mode of secularism; and (3) internal management (for example, interpretation and

innovation) of the 'lesser' tradition by legal specialists, corresponding to the 'intervention' mode of secularism.

This crude typology not only invites refinement, but points to
a range of questions for empirical investigation; questions whose
exploration might illuminate the 'law and morals' debate (which
has been heavily analytic and prescriptive) by adding a descriptive
and comparative dimension. For example, it suggests that we ought
to ask:

1. Do particular legal systems have predominant characteristic
modes in which they relate to other normative traditions?

2. What conditions—demographic, economic, cultural, structural, political—are associated with such differences in style?

3. Do particular areas (religion, economic activity, etc.) inspire
similar treatment by diverse legal systems?

4. What are the implications of different modes of doctrinal
justification for different modes of practice? This gives us another
way of looking at the relation of law as authoritative doctrine and
law as patterns of institutional practice. Does the relation of the
'law of the books' and the 'law in action' vary with the predominant mode of dealing with other normative traditions?

5. Is there a tendency for modes to change over time? Is there
a prevailing direction of change?

6. What are the potentialities and problems of various modes
in deliberately using law as an instrument of social change?

In the view put forth here, both 'church and state' and 'law and
morals' are instances of a wider class, the relation of law to the
whole array of normative traditions with which it coexists in
society. Descriptive and comparative study of the forms of that
coexistence would provide a focus of interest to social, scientific,
and philosophical inquiry into those tensions that lie at the heart
of legal reality—tensions between unity and plurality, stability and
change, and norm and practice.

# Appendix

*Relevant Constitutional and Statutory Provisions*
*Constitution of India (1950)*

Art. 17    *Abolition of Untouchability.*—'Untouchability' is abolished and its practice in any form is forbidden. The enforcement of any disability arising out of 'Untouchability' shall be an offence punishable in accordance with law.

Art. 25    *Freedom of conscience and free profession, practice and propagation of religion.* —(1) Subject to public order, morality and health and to the other provisions of this Part, all persons are equally entitled to freedom of conscience and the right freely to profess, practice and propagate religion. (2) Nothing in this article shall affect the operation of any existing law or prevent the State from making any law—

(a)    regulating or restricting any economic, financial, political or other secular activity which may be associated with religious practice;

(b)    providing for social welfare and reform or the throwing open of Hindu religious institutions of a public character to all classes and sections of Hindus.

Explanation I.—The wearing and carrying of *kirpans* shall be deemed to be included in the profession of the Sikh religion.

Explanation II.—In subclause (b) of clause (2), the reference to Hindus shall be construed as including a reference to persons professing the Sikh, Jaina, or Buddhist religion, and the reference to Hindu religious institutions shall be construed accordingly.

Art. 26    *Freedom to manage religious affairs.* —Subject to public order, morality and health, every religious denomination or any section thereof shall have the right—

(a)    to establish and maintain institutions for religious and charitable purposes;

(b)    to manage its own affairs in matters of religion;

(c)    to own and acquire movable and immovable property; and

(d)    to administer such property in accordance with law.

## *The [Central] Untouchability (Offences) Act,* *(1955 No. 22 of 1955)*

Section 3    *Punishment for enforcing religious disabilities.*—Whoever on the ground of 'untouchability' prevents any person—

(a)    from catering to any place of public worship which is open to other persons professing the religion or belonging to the same religious denomination or any section thereof as such person; or

(b)  from worshipping or offering prayers or performing any religious service in any place of public worship, or bathing in, or using the waters of any sacred tank, well, spring or watercourse, in the same manner and to the same extent as is permissible to other persons professing the same religious denomination or any section thereof, of such person:

shall be punishable with imprisonment which may extend to six months, or with fine which may extend to five hundred rupees, or with both.

Explanation—For the purposes of this section…persons professing the Buddhist, Sikh, or Jaina religion or persons professing the Hindu religion in any of its forms or developments including Virashaivas, Lingayats, Adivasis, followers of Brahma, Prarthana, Arya Samaj and the Swaminarayan Sampradaya shall be deemed to be Hindu.

## The Bombay Hindu Places of Public Worship (Entry Authorization) Act, 1956 (No. 31 of 1956)

Section 2 *Definition*—In this Act, unless the context otherwise requires,

(a)  'place of public worship' whether a temple or by any other name called, to whomsoever belonging, which is dedicated to, or for the benefit of, or is used generally by, Hindus, Jains, Sikhs or Buddhists or any section or class thereof, for the performance of any religious service or for offering prayers therein; and includes all lands and subsidiary shrines appurtenance attached to any such place, and also any sacred tanks, wells, springs and watercourses, the waters of which are worshipped, or are used for bathing or for worship;

(b)  'section' or 'class' of Hindus includes any division, subdivision caste, subcaste, sect or denomination whatsoever of Hindus.

Section 3 *Throwing open of Hindu temples to all classes and sections of Hindus*—Notwithstanding any custom, usage or law for the time being in force, or the decree or order of a court, or anything contained in any instrument, to the contrary, every place of public worship which is open to Hindus generally, or to any section or class thereof, shall be open to all sections and classes of Hindus: and no Hindu of whatsoever section or class shall in any manner be prevented, obstructed or· discouraged from entering such place of public worship, or from worshipping or offering prayers thereat or performing any religious service therein in the like manner and to like extent as any other Hindus of whatsoever section or class may so enter, worship, pray or perform.

# IV

# Secularism in India:
# The Recent Debate

# 9

# Secularism in Its Place

*T.N. Madan**

We live in a world which we call modern or which we wish to be modern. Modernity is generally regarded as both a practical necessity and a moral imperative, a fact and a value. When I say this I am not using the word 'modern' in one of those many trivial senses which I trust we have by now left behind us. Thus, by modernity I do not mean a complete break with tradition. Being modern means larger and deeper things: for example the enlargement of human freedom and the enhancement of the range of choices open to a people in respect to things that matter including their present and future lifestyles. This means being in charge of oneself and this, you will recognize, is one of the connotations of the process of secularization.

The word 'secularization' was first used in 1648, at the end of the Thirty Years' War in Europe, to refer to the transfer of church properties to the exclusive control of the princes. What was a matter-of-fact statement then became later, after the French Revolution, a value statement as well: on 2 November 1789, Talleyrand announced to the French National Assembly that all ecclesiastical goods were at the disposal of the nation, as indeed they should have been. Still later, when George Jacob Holyoake coined the term

* I would like to express my gratitude to the Board of Foreign Scholarships and the US Information Agency for selecting me as a Fulbright Fortieth Anniversary Distinguished Fellow, and to the Association of Asian Studies, particularly its president, Susanne Hoeber Rudolph, for inviting me to address them. Further, I wish to thank Ainslee Embree, Susan Pharr, and Stanley Tambiah for their responses to my presentation. To Alan Babb, Ashis Nandy, and Lloyd and Susanne Rudolph, who helped me clarify several unclear points, I acknowledge my indebtedness with much pleasure.

'secularism' in 1851 and led a rationalist movement of protest in England, secularization was built into the ideology of progress. Secularization, though nowhere more than a fragmentary and incomplete process, has ever since retained a positive connotation.

'Secularization' is nowadays generally employed to refer to, in the words of Peter Berger, 'the process by which sectors of society and culture are removed from the domination of religious institutions and symbols'.[1] While the inner logic of the economic sector perhaps makes it the most convenient arena for secularization, other sectors, notably the political, have been found to be less amenable to it. It is in relation to the latter that the ideology of secularism acquires the most salience.

I believe that in the prevailing circumstances secularism in South Asia as a generally shared credo of life is impossible, as a basis for state action impracticable, and as a blueprint for the foreseeable future impotent. It is impossible as a credo of life because the great majority of the people of South Asia are in their own eyes active adherents of some religious faith. It is impracticable as a basis for state action either because Buddhism and Islam have been declared state or state-protected religions or because the stance of religious neutrality or equidistance is difficult to maintain since religious minorities do not share the majority's view of what this entails for the state. And it is impotent as a blueprint for the future because, by its very nature, it is incapable of countering religious fundamentalism and fanaticism.

Secularism is the dream of a minority that wishes to shape the majority in its own image, that wishes to impose its will upon history but lacks the power to do so under a democratically organized polity. In an open society the state will reflect the character of the society. Secularism is therefore a social myth that draws a cover over the failure of this minority to separate politics from religion in the society in which its members live. From the point of view of the majority, 'secularism' is a vacuous word, a phantom concept, for such people do not know whether it is desirable to privatize religion, and if it is, how this may be done, unless they be Protestant Christians but not if they are Buddhists, Hindus, Muslims, or Sikhs. For the secularist minority to stigmatize the majority as primordially oriented and to preach secularism

---

[1] Peter L. Berger, *The Social Reality of Religion* (Allen Lane: London, 1973), p. 113.

to the latter as the law of human existence is moral arrogance and worse—I say 'worse' since in our time politics takes precedence over ethics—political folly. It is both these—moral arrogance and political folly—because it fails to recognize the immense importance of religion in the lives of the peoples of South Asia. I will not raise here the issue of the definition of religion: suffice it to say that for these peoples their religion establishes their place in society and bestows meaning on their life, more than any other social or cultural factor.

Unable to raise the veil of its illusions, the modernist minority in India today is beset with deep anxieties about the future of secularism in the country and in South Asia generally. Appeals are made day in and day out to foster a modern scientific temper, of which Jawaharlal Nehru is invoked as the principal exponent. Books are written and an unending round of seminars held on the true nature and significance of communalism and how to combat it. Indeed, there is much talk these days in the highest political quarters about the need for stern legislative and executive measures to check the rising and menacing tide of majority and minority fundamentalism and revivalism, and this even as the so-called Hindu society continues splintering.

An astonishing (or should one say impressive?) consensus among Indian Muslims about preserving the Shari`a, or 'holy law', against what they consider the legislative onslaught of a godless state but others call the indispensability of a common civil law as a foundation of the modern state, was witnessed in 1986 in connection with the rights of Muslim divorced women (the Shah Bano case). This has now been followed by the biggest-ever public protest by Muslims since Independence forty years ago, held at New Delhi on 30 March 1987, to demand full possession of a sixteenth-century mosque in the city of Ayodhya in north India, which was built after Babar's invasion at what Hindus believe to have been the birthplace of god-incarnate Rāma. The whole country held its breath, fearful of a counter-demonstration of strength by the Hindus; it took place but luckily there was no major communal flare-up.[2] Meanwhile, Sikh and Hindu fundamentalists continue to face one another in Punjab, and innocent people are killed every day by Sikh terrorists. Social analysts draw

---

2 The Babri Masjid was demolished on 6 Dec. 1992 followed by communal pogroms against Muslims and retaliatory serial bomb-blasts in Bombay.

attention to the contradiction between the undoubted, though slow, spread of secularization in everyday life, on the one hand, and the unmistakable rise of fundamentalism, on the other. But surely these phenomena are only apparently contradictory, for in truth it is the marginalization of religious faith, which is what secularization is, that permits the perversion of religion. There are no fundamentalists or revivalists in traditional society.

The point to stress, then, is that, despite ongoing processes of secularization and deliberate efforts to promote it, secularism as a widely shared world-view has failed to make headway in India. Obviously what exists empirically but not also ideologically exists only weakly. The hopes about the prospects of secularism raised by social scientists in the years soon after Independence—recall the well-known books by Donald Eugene Smith[3] and Rajni Kothari[4]—have been belied, notwithstanding the general acceptability of their view of 'Hinduism' as a broadly tolerant religion. Acute observers of the socio-cultural and political scenes contend that signs of a weakening secularism are in evidence, particularly among the Hindus. Religious books, a recent newspaper report said, continue to outsell all the others in India and, one can be sure, in all the other South Asian countries. Religious pilgrimages attract larger and larger congregations counted in millions. Buildings of religious worship or prayer dot the urban landscape. New Delhi has many new Hindu temples and Sikh gurudwaras, and its most recent modern structure is the Bahai temple facing the old Kalkaji (Hindu) temple, thrown open to worshippers of all faiths late last year. God-men and gurus sit in seminars and roam the streets, and American 'Hare Krishnas' take the initiative in organizing an annual *ratha yātrā* (chariot festival).

While society seethes with these and other expressions of a vibrant religiosity, the feeble character of the Indian policy of state secularism is exposed. At best, Indian secularism has been an inadequately defined 'attitude' (it cannot be called a philosophy of life except when one is discussing the thought of someone like Mahatma Gandhi or Maulana Azad) of 'goodwill towards all religions', *sarvadharma sambhāva*; in a narrower formulation it has

---

3 Donald Eugene Smith, *India as a Secular State* (Oxford University Press: Bombay, 1963).

4 Rajni Kothari, *Politics in India* (Orient Longman: New Delhi, 1970).

been a negative or defensive policy of religious neutrality (*dharma nirpekshtā*) on the part of the state. In either formulation, Indian secularism achieves the opposite of its stated intentions. It trivializes religious difference as well as the notion of the unity of religions, and really fails to provide guidance for viable political action, for it is not a rooted, full-blooded, and well-thought-out *Weltanschauung*, only a strategem. It has been so self-confessedly for fundamentalist organizations such as the Muslim Jamā'at-i-Islāmī.[5] I would like to suggest that it was also so for Jawaharlal Nehru, but let me not anticipate: I will have more to say about Nehru's secularism in a short while. Now, let me dwell a little longer on the infirmity of secularism.

Now, what exactly does the failure of secularism mean? For one thing, it underscores the failure of society and the state to bring under control the divisive forces that resulted in the partition of the subcontinent in 1947. Though forty years have passed and the Midnight's Children are at the threshold of middle age, tempers continue to rage, and occasionally (perhaps too frequently) blood even flows in some places, as a result of the mutual hostility between the followers of different religions.

What produces this hostility? Surely not religious faith itself, for even religious traditions which take an uncompromising view of 'nonbelievers' (that is the followers of other religions) speak with multiple tongues and pregnant ambiguity. The Qur'an, for example, proclaims that there should be no coercion in the matter of faith (2:256). Even an agnostic such as Nehru acknowledged this before the burden of running a secular state fell on his ageing shoulders. As long ago as 1936 he said, 'The communal problem is not a religious problem, it has nothing to do with religion.'[6] It was not religious difference as such but its exploitation by calculating politicians for the achievement of secular ends that produced the communal divide.

It is perhaps one of the tragedies of the twentieth century that a man who had at the beginning of his political career wanted above all to bridge religious differences should have in the end

5  Mushirul-Haq, *Islam in Secular India* (Indian Institute of Advanced Study: Simla, 1972), pp 11–12.
6  Jawaharlal Nehru, *Selected Works of Jawaharlal Nehru* (Orient Longman: New Delhi, 1972–82), p. 82.

contributed to widening them. As is well known the young Muhammad Ali Jinnah was a non-practising Muslim in private life and a secularist in public, but later he (like many others, Hindus and Sikhs as well as Muslims) played with the fire of communal frenzy. Inevitably, perhaps, he became a victim of his own political success, of, as Ayesha Jalal puts it, 'an unthinking mob, fired by blood lust, fear and greed'.[7] I should think he too realized this, for, without any loss of time four days before the formal inauguration of Pakistan, he called upon his people to 'bury the hatchet' and make common citizenship, not communal identity, the basis of the new state.[8] And within a month he reiterated: 'You may belong to any religion, or caste or creed—that has nothing to do with the business of the state.'[9] How close to Nehru he was, and, though he pulled himself far apart for the achievement of his political goals, he obviously remained a secularist.

Tolerance is indeed a value enshrined in all the great religions of mankind, but let me not underplay the historical roots of communal antagonism in South Asia. I am not wholly convinced when our Marxist colleagues argue that communalism is a result of the distortions in the economic base of our societies produced by the colonial mode of production and that the 'communal question was a petty bourgeois question par excellence'.[10] The importance of these distortions may not be minimized, but these analysts should know that South Asia's major religious traditions—Buddhism, Hinduism, Islam, and Sikhism—are totalizing in character, claiming all of a follower's life, so that religion is constitutive of society. In the given pluralist situation, both tolerance and intolerance are expressions of exclusivism. When I say that South Asia's religious traditions are 'totalizing', I am not trying to argue that they do not recognize the distinction between the terms 'religious' and 'secular'. We know that in their distinctive ways all four traditions

[7] Ayesha Jalal, *The Sole Spokesman: Jinnah, Muslim League, and the Demand for Pakistan* (Cambridge University Press: Cambridge, 1985), p. 216.

[8] Sharif ul Mujahid, *Quad-i-Azam Jinnah* (Quad-i-Azam Academy: Karachi, 1981), p. 247.

[9] M.A. Jinnah, *Speeches as Governor-General of Pakistan* (Pakistan Publications: Karachi, 1947–8), p. 48.

[10] Bipan Chandra, *Communalism in Modern India* (Vikas: New Delhi, 1984), p. 40.

make this distinction. I wish I had the time to elaborate on this theme, but then there is perhaps no need to do so here. What needs to be stressed, however, is that these religions have the same view of the relationship between the categories of the 'religious' and the 'secular'.

My studies convince me that in Buddhism, Hinduism, Islam, and Sikhism this relationship is hierarchical (in the sense in which Louis Dumont uses this term). Thus, though Buddhism may well be considered as the one South Asian religious tradition which, by denying supernatural beings any significant role in human life, has the most secularist potential, yet this would be an oversimplified view of it. What is important is not only what Emile Durkheim so clearly perceived, namely the central importance of the category of the 'sacred' in Buddhism, but also (and more significantly in the present context) the fact, so well documented for us by Stanley Tambiah, that the *bhikkhu*, or the world renouncer, is superior to the *chakkavatti*, or the world conqueror, and that neither exists by himself.[11] Similarly, in every Sikh gurudwara the sacred sword is placed for veneration at a lower level than the holy book, the *Granth Sāhab*, which is the repository of the Word (*shabad*), despite the fact that, for the Sikhs, the sword too symbolizes the divinity or, more accurately, the inseparability of the spiritual and the religious functions.

I would like to expand a little more on Hinduism and Islam. I would have preferred not to go all the way back to the *Rig Veda* of three thousand years ago, were it not for the fact that it presents explicitly, employing a fascinating simile, the hierarchical relationship between spiritual authority and temporal power. It would seem that originally the two functions were differentiated, but they were later deliberately brought together, for the regnum (*kshatra*) could not subsist on its own without the sacerdotium (*brahma*) that provided its principle of legitimacy. Says the king to the priest: 'Turn thou unto me so that we may unite...I assign to you the precedence; quickened by thee I shall perform deeds.'[12] The very word used for the priest, *purohita*, points to precedence. What is

11 S.J. Tambiah, *World Conqueror and World Renouncer* (Cambridge University Press: Cambridge, 1976).

12 Ananda Coomaraswamy, *Spiritual Authority and Temporal Power in the Indian Theory of Government* (Munshiram Manoharlal: New Delhi, 1978), p. 8.

more, the priest and the king are united, as husband is to wife, and they must speak with one voice. This is what Dumont would call hierarchical dyarchy or complementarity. Even if one were to look upon the king and the *purohita* as dissociated (rather than united) and thus contend that kingship had become secularized,[13] the hierarchical relation between the two functions survives and is even emphasized. The discrete realms of interest and power (*artha*) are opposed to and yet encompassed by *dharma*.

Let me move on to the *Kautilya Arthashāstra* (? fourth century BC/AD), which has been often enough said to present an amoral theory of political power. Such a reading is, however, contestable. What I find more acceptable is the view that the *Arthashāstra* teaches that the rational pursuit of economic and political ends (*artha*) must be carried out in fulfilment and not violation of *dharma*. More broadly 'artha must be pursued in the framework of *kama*, *dharma* and *moksa*...the principle remains that *artha* to be truly *artha* must be part of a larger totality, individual and social'.[14]

I might add here parenthetically that in traditional Brahmanical political thought, cultural pluralism within the state was accepted and the king was the protector of everybody's *dharma*: being *that* was *his dharma*. Only in very exceptional circumstances, apprehending disorder, might the king have used his authority to abrogate certain customs or usages.[15] Hence the idea of a state religion was not entertained.

I will say no more about the ancient period but only observe that some of these traditional ideas have reverberated in the practice of Hindu kings and their subjects all the way down the corridors of time into the twentieth century.[16] Even today, these ideas are relevant in the context of the only surviving Hindu monarchy of the world, Nepal, where the king is considered an

[13] Louis Dumont, *Homo Hierarchicus: The Caste System and Its Implications* (University of Chicago Press: Chicago, 1980), p. 293.

[14] K.J. Shah, 'Of Artha and the *Arthasāstra*', *Contributions to Indian Sociology*, n. s. 15: 55–73 (1982), p. 72.

[15] Robert Lingat, *The Classical Law of India* (University of California Press: Los Angeles, 1973), p. 226.

[16] A.C. Mayer, 'Perceptions of Princely Rule: Perspectives from a Biography, *Contributions to Indian Sociology*, n. s. 15, 127–54 (1982), pp 127–54.

incarnation of God and yet has to be consecrated by the Brahman royal priest.

In our own times it was, of course, Mahatma Gandhi who restated the traditional point of view in the changed context of the twentieth century, emphasizing the inseparability of religion and politics and the superiority of the former over the latter. 'For me', he said, 'every, the tiniest, activity is governed by what I consider to be my religion.'[17] And, more specifically, there is the well-known early statement that 'those who say that religion has nothing to do with politics do not know what religion means'.[18] For Gandhi religion was the source of absolute value and hence constitutive of social life; politics was the arena of public interest; without the former the latter would become debased. While it was the obligation of the state to ensure that every religion was free to develop according to its own genius, no religion that depended upon state support deserved to survive. In other words, the inseparability of religion and politics in the Indian context, and generally, was for Gandhi fundamentally a distinct issue from the separation of the state from the church in Christendom. When he did advocate that 'religion and state should be separate', he clarified that this was to limit the role of the state to 'secular welfare', and to allow it no admittance into the religious life of the people.[19] Clearly, the hierarchical relationship is irreversible.

Let me now turn briefly to Islam. Traditionally, Islam postulates a single chain of command in the political domain: God–Prophet–caliph–king. God Almighty is the ever-active sovereign of His universe, which is governed by His will. In his own life Prophet Muhammad symbolized the unity of faith (*dīn*) and the material world (*dawle*). His successors (*khalīfa*) were the guardians on whose authority the kings ruled. They (the kings) were but the shadow of God on earth, holding power as a trust and answerable to their maker on the Day of Judgment like everybody else. In India, Ziya-ud-Din Barni, an outstanding medieval (mid-fourteenth century)

---

[17] See Raghavan Iyer (ed.), *The Moral and Political Writings of Mahatma Gandhi*, vol. 1: *Civilization, Politics, and Religion* (Clarendon Press: Oxford, 1986), p. 391.

[18] See M.K. Gandhi, *An Autobiography or The Story of My Experiments with Truth* (Navjivan: Ahmedabad, 1940), p. 383.

[19] See Iyer (1986), p. 395, fn. 17.

theologian and political commentator, wrote of religion and
temporal government, of prophets and kings, as twin brothers, but
without leaving the reader in any doubt about whom he placed
first.[20]

In the twentieth century, Muhammad Iqbal occupies a very
special place as an interpreter of Islam in South Asia. Rejecting the
secularist programme of Turkish nationalists, he wrote: 'In Islam
the spiritual and the temporal are not two distinct domains, and
the nature of an act, however secular in its import, is determined
by the attitude of mind with which the agent does it....In Islam
it is the same reality, which appears as Church looked at from one
point of view and State from another.'[21] Iqbal further explains:
'The ultimate Reality, according to the Quran, is spiritual, and its
life consists in its temporal activity. The spirit finds its opportunities in the natural, the material, the secular. All that is secular
is therefore sacred in the roots of its being.... There is no such
thing as a profane world.... All is holy ground.'[22] In short, to use
the idiom adopted by me, the secular is encompassed by the sacred.

An autonomous ideology of secularism is ruled out. This is how
Fazlur Rahman (a most distinguished South Asian scholar writing
on such subjects today) puts it: 'Secularism destroys the sanctity
and universality (transcendence) of all moral values.'[23] If secularism
is to be eschewed, so .is neo-revivalism to be avoided for its
'intellectual bankruptcy'.[24] Rahman argues that a modern life need
not be detached from religious faith and should indeed be informed
by it, or else Muslims may well lose their very humanity.

This excursus into South Asia's major religious traditions was
important for me to make the point that the search for secular
elements in the cultural traditions of this region is a futile exercise,
for it is not these but an ideology of secularism that is absent and
is resisted. What is important, therefore, is the relationship
between the categories, and this is unmistakably hierarchical, the

---

20 See Theodore de Bary (ed.), *The Sources of Indian Tradition*, vol. 1
(Columbia University Press: New York, 1970), pp 459–60.
21 Iqbal Muhammad, *The Reconstruction of Religious Thought in Islam* (New Taj
Office: Delhi, 1980, p. 154.
22 Ibid., p. 155.
23 Fazlur Rahman, *Islam and Modernity* (University of Chicago Press:
Chicago, 1982), p. 15.
24 Ibid., p. 137.

religious encompassing the secular. Louis Dumont recently reminded us that the doctrine of the subordination of the power of the kings to the authority of the priests, enunciated by Pope Gelasius around the end of the fifth century, perhaps represents 'simply the logical formula for the relation between the two functions'.[25] Indeed, the world's great religious traditions do seem to speak on this vital issue with one voice, or did until the Reformation made a major departure in this regard within the Christian tradition.

Scholars from Max Weber and Ernst Troeltsch to Peter Berger and Louis Dumont have in their different ways pointed to the essential linkages among Protestantism, individualism, and secularization. You all know well Max Weber's poignant statement that 'the fate of our times is characterized by rationalization and intellectualization and, above all, by the "disenchantment of the world". Precisely the ultimate and most sublime values have retreated from public life either into the transcendental realm of mystic life or into the brotherliness of direct and personal relations'.[26] Or, to put it in Peter Berger's succinct summing up, 'Protestantism cut the umbilical cord between heaven and earth.'[27]

This is not the occasion to go into the details of the well-grounded idea that secularization is a gift of Christianity to mankind, but it is important for my present concern to note that the privatization of religion, through the assumption by the individual of the responsibility for his or her own salvation without the intervention of the Church, is very much a late Christian idea. The general secularization of life in the West after the Reformation is significantly, though only partly, an unintended consequence of this religious idea. Luther was indeed a man of his times, a tragic medieval figure, who ushered in a modern age that he would hardly approve of.

But let us not stray too far. How does all this bear upon my present theme, namely the prospects of secularism in India? I put

25 Louis Dumont, *Homo Hierarchicus: The Caste System and Its Implications* (University of Chicago Press: Chicago, 1983), p.15.
26 H.H. Gerth and C.W. Mills (eds), *From Max Weber: Essays in Sociology* (Routledge & Kegan Paul: London, 1948), p. 155.
27 Peter L. Bergers, *The Social Reality of Religion* (Allen Lane: London, 1973), p. 118.

it to you that the idea of secularism, a gift of Christianity, has been built into Western social theorists' paradigms of modernization, and since these paradigms are believed to have universal applicability, the elements that converged historically—that is in a unique manner—to constitute modern life in Europe in the sixteenth and the following three centuries have come to be presented as the requirements of modernization elsewhere, and this must be questioned. Paradoxically, the uniqueness of the history of modern Europe lies, we are asked to believe, in its generalizability.

In other words, secularism as an ideology has emerged from the dialectic of modern science and Protestantism, not from a simple repudiation of religion and the rise of rationalism. Even the Enlightenment—its English and German versions in particular—was not against religion as such but against revealed religion or a transcendental justification for religion. Voltaire's 'dying' declaration was of faith in God and detestation of 'superstition'. Models of modernization, however, prescribe the transfer of secularism to non-Western societies without regard for the character of their religious traditions or for the gifts that these might have to offer. Such transfers are themselves phenomena of the modern secularized world: in traditional or tradition-haunted societies they can only mean conversion and the loss of one's culture, and, if you like, the loss of one's soul. Even in already modern or modernizing societies, unless cultural transfers are made meaningful for the people, they appear as stray behaviouristic traits and attitudinal postures. This means that what is called for is translation; mere transfer will not do.

But translations are not easily achieved. As Bankim Chandra Chatterji (that towering late nineteenth-century Indian intellectual) put it, 'You can translate a word by a word, but behind the word is an idea, the thing which the word denotes, and this idea you cannot translate, if it does not exist among the people in whose language you are translating.'[28] It is imperative, then, that a people must themselves render their historical experience meaningful: others may not do this for them. Borrowed ideas, unless internalized, do not have the power to bestow on us the gift and grace of living.

[28] Partha Chatterjee, *Nationalist Thought and the Colonial World* (Oxford University Press: Delhi, 1986), p. 61.

In this regard, I should like to point out that once a cultural definition of a phenomenon or of a relationship (say, between religion and politics, or society and the state) has crystallized, it follows that subsequent formulations of it, whether endogenous or exogenous, can only be *re*-definitions. Traditions posit memory. Given the face of the unequal social distribution of knowledge and the unequal impress of social change, it is not at all surprising that some elements of tradition should survive better and longer among the ordinary people, who may not think about it but live it, and others among the intelligentsia.

In short, the transferability of the idea of secularism to the countries of South Asia is beset with many difficulties and should not be taken for granted. Secularism must be put in its place: which is not a question of rejecting it but of finding the proper means for its expression. In multi-religious societies, such as those of South Asia, it should be realized that secularism may not be restricted to rationalism, that it is compatible with faith, and that rationalism (as understood in the West) is not the sole motive force of a modern state. What the institutional implications of such a position are is an important question and needs to be worked out.

I am afraid I have already dwelt long enough on the subject to invite the charge of being some kind of a cultural determinist, which I am not. I am aware of the part that creative individuals and dominant minorities play in changing and shaping the course of history. As a student of cultural anthropology I know that even in the simplest of settings cultures, ways of life, are not merely reproduced but are also resisted and changed, more in some places and times and less in others, more successfully by some individuals or groups than by others. In this connection, I must now return to Jawaharlal Nehru as the typical modern Indian intellectual.

It has been argued well by many scholars that while Gandhi put his faith in the reformed, ethically refined individual in creating a better if not ideal society, Nehru considered the shaping of suitable institutions as the best means of achieving the same goal. Of all the modern institutions, it was the state which he believed would be the principal engine of social change. Hegel said that the Hindus were a people and did not constitute a state: this judgment (and similar others) have informed Western social science thinking about India, expressed recently, for instance, in the contrast between primordial bonds and civic ties made by Edward Shils and Clifford Geertz, and others.

Nehru, like many other modern Indians, imbibed the same point of view and obviously wanted to remove the deficiency. The Nehruvian state was first and foremost democratic, but in an economically poor and culturally diverse country it could hardly be truly democratic without being socialist and secularist. I am not here concerned with the course of democracy and socialism in India, but I must make some observations about the difficulties encountered by the secular state established under the Constitution.

I will not enter into the controversy whether the Indian state is at all secular in the sense in which, say, the American state is. But that is only jurisdictionalist.[29] We do not, of course, have a wall of separation in India, for there is no church to wall off, but only the notion of neutrality or equidistance between the state and the religious identity of the people. What makes this idea important is that not only Nehru but all Indians who consider themselves patriotic and modern, nationalist and rationalist, subscribe to it. What makes it impotent is that it is a purely negative strategy and, in the history of mankind, nothing positive has ever been built on denials or negations alone.

An examination of Nehru's writings and speeches brings out very clearly his conviction that religion is a hindrance to 'the tendency to change and progress inherent in human society' and that 'the belief in supernatural agency which ordains everything has led to a certain irresponsibility on the social plane, and emotion and sentimentality have taken the place of reasoned thought and inquiry'.[30] Religion, he confessed candidly, did not 'attract' him for 'behind it lay a method of approach to life's problems which was certainly not that of science'.[31] But, then, he did not worry too much about religion or its political expression, namely communalism, because he passionately believed that these epiphenomena would 'vanish at the touch of reality'.[32] Hence his

[29] V.P. Luthera, *The Concept of the Secular State and India* (Oxford University Press: Calcutta, 1964).
[30] See Jawaharlal Nehru, *The Discovery of India* (Asia: Bombay, 1961), p. 543.
[31] Ibid., p. 26.
[32] See Jawaharlal Nehru, *An Autobiography* (Oxford University Press: Delhi, 1980), p. 469.

insistence that, quoting from a 1931 speech, 'the real thing to my mind is the economic factor. If we lay stress on this and divert public attention to it we shall find automatically that religious differences recede into the background and a common bond unites different groups. The economic bond is stronger than the national one'.[33]

Nehru insisted that his conclusions were not speculative but based on practical experience. Many years later, after mature reflection, he wrote that once the national state came into being it would be economic problems that would acquire salience; there might be 'class conflicts' but not 'religious conflicts, except in so far as religion itself expressed some vested interest'.[34] It is not, therefore, at all surprising that until the very end Nehru was puzzled and pained by Muslim separatism and was deeply distrustful of politicians who exploited religion for political purposes; and yet he was contemptuous of those who took the religious question seriously. Not for him Iqbal's insistence that the cultural question was as important as the economic.[35] The irony of it is that Iqbal too considered himself a socialist!

In the end, that is in 1947, Nehru knew that the battle at hand, though not perhaps the war, had been lost, that the peoples of the subcontinent were not yet advanced enough to share his view of secular politics and the secular state. A retreat was inescapable, but it was not a defeat. Sorrowfully he wrote in 1961, just three years before his death: 'We talk about a secular state in India. It is perhaps not very easy even to find a good word in Hindi for "secular". Some people think it means something opposed to religion. That obviously is not correct.... It is a state which honours all faiths equally and gives them equal opportunities.'[36]

Having thus described Indian secularism, he proceeded in line with his own earlier thinking on the subject: 'Our constitution lays down that we are a secular state, but it must be admitted that this is not wholly reflected in our mass living and thinking. In a country

33 Jawaharlal Nehru, *Selected Works of Jawaharlal Nehru* (Orient Longman: New Delhi, 1972–82), p. 203.
34 See Jawaharlal Nehru, (1961). (See fn. 30).
35 H. Malik, *Moslem Nationalism in India and Pakistan* (Public Affairs Press: Washington, D.C., 1963), p. 253.
36 See S. Gopal (ed.), *Jawaharlal Nehru: An Anthology* (Oxford University Press: Delhi, 1980), p. 330.

like England, the state is...allied to one particular religion.... Nevertheless, the state and the people there function in a largely secular way. Society, therefore, in England is more advanced in this respect than in India, even though our constitution may be, in this matter more advanced.'[37] It is obvious that Nehru had not given up his trust of the secularization process; that his view of religion remained unchanged.

What is noteworthy, therefore, is Nehru's refusal (or failure) to use the coercive powers of the state in hastening this process. In this regard he invites comparison with Lenin and Ataturk, and, if you allow dictatorship, suffers by it. I do not have the time to discuss in any detail this instructively fascinating comparison or pose the question as to the conditions under which a part (state) may dictate to the whole (society), but let me take it up very briefly.

Take Lenin's position. Continuing the Feuerbach–Marx line he asserted that the religious question must not be advanced to 'the first place where it does not belong at all'.[38] To match this by action, he played an active and direct part in the formulation of the 1918 decree on 'the separation of the church from the state and of the school from the church'. While every citizen was in principle free to profess any religion, or none at all, he could not actively propagate it; what is more, the educational function of the Communist party ensured that 'senseless ideas' arising from a false consciousness would be countered.

Similarly, Ataturk proceeded by one deliberate step after another, beginning with the abolition of the Caliphate in 1924, of the religious orders in 1925, of Shari`a courts in 1926, and of Islam as the state religion in 1928. The process of secularization was continued thereafter, and the changes effected were strictly enforced, with Kemal himself often setting the example in even minor points of detail.[39]

Contrast the internal coherence and sense of urgency of these two experiments with the uncertainties of the 1949 Indian Constitution, which sought to establish a secular state (Art. 15) in a society which it allowed and even encouraged to be communally

[37] Ibid., pp 330–1.

[38] See S.C. Dube and V.N. Basilov (eds), *Secularisation in Multi-Religious Societies* (Concept: New Delhi, 1983), p. 173.

[39] Bernard Lewis, *The Emergence of Modern Turkey* (Oxford University Press: London, 1968), pp 239–93.

divided (Art. 25–30). Under the rubric of 'freedom for religion', it allowed citizens not only the profession and practice of their respective religions but also their propagation. Besides, it allowed the establishment of educational institutions along communal lines. A direct reference to secularism had to wait until 1976, when it was introduced into the preamble of the Constitution by the Forty-fourth Amendment.

It must be admitted here that the pluralistic situation that Nehru and the other framers of the Constitution faced was immensely more complex than anything that Lenin, and far less Ataturk, faced; yet the fact remains that Nehru did not use his undoubted hold over the people as a leader of the freedom movement and his vast authority as the head of government to bring communal tendencies under strict control. It is often said that he was too much of a liberal and a cultured aristocrat to think of strong-arm methods; I think he was also too optimistic about the decline of the hold of religion on the minds of people. He did not seem to take into consideration the fact that the ideology of secularism enhances the power of the state by making it a protector of all religious communities and an arbiter in their conflicts.

No wonder, then, that secularism as an alien cultural ideology which, lacks the strong support of the state, has failed to make the desired headway in India. What have done so, apparently and by general agreement, are Hindu revivalism and Muslim and Sikh fundamentalism. This brings me to a last brief observation.

Contrary to what may be presumed, it is not religious zealots alone who contribute to fundamentalism or fanaticism, which are a misunderstanding of religion, reducing it to mere political bickering, but also the secularists who deny the very legitimacy of religion in human life and society and provide a reaction. This latter realization has been slow in coming to Indian intellectuals, but there are some signs of change in this regard. It is thus that old, familiar questions begin to be reformulated. The principal question here could be considered to be not whether Indian society will eventually become secularized as Nehru believed it would but rather in what sense it should become so and by what means. The limitations of secular humanism (so-called) and the falsity of the hope of secularists—namely that all will be well with us if only scientific temper becomes generalized—need to be recognized.

Secularized man can confront fundamentalism and revivalism no more than he may empathize with religion.

Maybe religion is not a fake as Marx asserted; maybe there is something eternal about it as Durkheim maintained. Perhaps men of religion such as Mahatma Gandhi would be our best teachers on the proper relation between religion and politics, values and interest, underlining not only the possibilities of interreligious understanding, which is not the same as an emaciated notion of mutual tolerance or respect, but also opening up avenues of a spiritually justified limitation of the role of religious institutions and symbols in certain areas of contemporary life. The creeping process of secularization, however, slowly erodes the ground on which such men might stand. As Ashis Nandy puts it, 'There is now a peculiar double-bind in Indian politics: the ills of religion have found political expression but the strengths of it have not been available for checking corruption and violence in public life.'[40] My question is: Is everything lost irretrievably?

I must conclude; but I really have no conclusions to offer, no solutions to suggest. Let me hasten to say, however, that I am not advocating the establishment of a Hindu state in India—not at all. It simply will not work. Should you think that I have been sceptical about the claims that are made for secularism, scientific temper, etc., and that I have suggested a contextualized rethinking of these fuzzy ideas, you would be quite right. You would also be right in concluding that I have suggested that the only way secularism in South Asia, understood as interreligious understanding, may succeed would be for us to take both religion and secularism seriously and not reject the former as superstition and reduce the latter to a mask for communalism or mere expediency. Secularism would have to imply that those who profess no religion have a place in society equal to that of others, not higher or lower.

Should you think further that the scepticism to which I have given expression has been easy to come by, cultivate, and accept, you would not be, I am afraid, quite right. Secularism has been the fond hope of many people of my generation in South Asia. But, then, that is my personal problem, and therefore let me say no more about it. I will end simply by recalling the following words of the young Karl Marx, spoken, of course, in a very

[40] Ashis Nandy, 'An Anti-Secularist Manifesto', *Seminar* 314 (1985), p. 17.

different context: 'Ideas which have conquered our minds...to which reason has welded our conscience, are chains from which we cannot break away without breaking our hearts; they are demons which man can vanquish only by submitting to them.'[41]

[41] Karl Lowith, *Max Weber and Karl Marx*, (trans) H. Fantel (Allen & Unwin: London, 1982), p. 23.

# Postscript, 1996

'Secularism in Its Place'[1] was written ten years ago at a time when
most secularists seemed complacently confident that 'scientific
temper', the mantra voiced by Jawaharlal Nehru, would, if vigorously propagated, fulfil its promise of establishing secularism in
India. There were not many intellectuals then who either showed
an awareness of the limitations of secularism as a world-view or
expressed any great unease about the recrudescence of religious
fanaticism in the form of communalized politics or fundamentalist
movements. Although Punjab was already in violent turmoil and
the Shah Bano case had attracted wide attention, the future of the
nation, judged by the prevailing discourse on secularism, did not
seem to be in greater jeopardy than before. In any case, secularism
was considered the sole and adequate remedy. To the best of my
knowledge only a few intellectuals had dissented with this dominant discourse, Ashis Nandy being the most notable among them.[2]

I myself had begun to feel apprehensive that the secularist
discourse tended to underestimate the staying power of religion in
society, and also ignored the fact that religion itself could be a
powerful resource in the struggle against religious extremism. I did
not believe then, and do not do so now, that what needs explaining
is religious tolerance rather than its opposite. The invitation to
address a special session at the annual meetings of the American
Association of Asian Studies, at which Asianists from many parts
of the world were expected to be present, afforded me an excellent
opportunity to present my views on the prospects of secularism
in India. I did so in a deliberately provocative but carefully worded
text, and it did make an impact, although not everybody agreed
with me.

I expressed doubt about the success of secularism as a world-
view, as a political ideology, and as a societal blueprint. Several
critics have quoted the statement in question in a truncated form.[3]

1   T.N. Madan, 'Secularism in Its Place', *The Journal of Asian Studies*, 46, 4,
1987, pp 747–59.
2   Ashis Nandy, 'A Counter-Statement on Humanistic Temper', *Mainstream*,
10 Oct. 1981, and 'An Anti-Secularist Manifesto', *Seminar* 314, (1985), pp 1–11.
3   See F.G. Bailey, 'Religion and Religiosity: Ideas and Their Use', *Contributions to Indian Sociology*, n. s., 25, 2 (1991), p. 226; see U. Baxi, 'Secularism:
Real and Pseudo', in M.M. Sankhdher (ed.), *Secularism in India* (Deep & Deep:

The omission of the reasons I gave for my conclusion is grievous. Let me therefore put the record straight and quote the part of the argument that has been left out by my critics.

It (secularism) is impossible as a credo of life because the great majority of the people of South Asia are in their own eyes active adherents of some religious faith. It is impracticable as a basis for state action either because Buddhism or Islam have been declared state or state-protected religions, or because the stance of religious neutrality or equidistance is difficult to maintain since religious minorities do not share the majority's view of what this entails for the state. And it is impotent as a blueprint for the future because, by its very nature, it is incapable of countering religious fundamentalism and fanaticism.[4]

It will be seen that what occurs in my text primarily as a statement of the facts on the ground and only secondarily as my interpretation of them, appears, because of partial quotation, as an acerbic ideological attack on secularism. Now, I do have my reservations about this Enlightenment ideology, more so about the received wisdom regarding it, and so have many other scholars.[5] The statement in question was intended to state some of them and to draw attention to their implications for the Indian political experiment. Some critics (not the ones mentioned above) have, however, jumped to the conclusion that, since I have reservations about secularism as presented in the prevailing discourse, I must therefore be a supporter of communalism. This is patently absurd.

To return to the original text itself. I had cautioned dogmatic secularists that in a democracy it is not easy for a minority to impose its will upon the majority. There is, however, a double misunderstanding here. First, I did not say that the secularist minority was trying to impose secularization upon the majority: what I mentioned specifically was the ideology of secularism. It is imperative that we distinguish between secularization (in Béteille's words, 'a social process that unfolds itself on its own, as it were') and secularism ('an ideology that some members of society strive

New Delhi, 1992), p. 89; A. Béteille, 'Secularism and the Intellectuals', *Economic and Political Weekly*, 29, 10 (1994), p. 560.
4 T.N. Madan (1987), p. 748 (See fn. 1).
5 S. Toulmin, *Cosmopolis: The Hidden Agenda of Modernity* (The Free Press: New York, 1990).

consciously to espouse and promote'). I myself have made this very distinction several times over in my writings. For instance, I distinguished between secularization as a 'process' and as a 'thesis'. I maintain, however, that those intellectuals who proclaim that religion is not only a 'fake', but also necessarily an evil, and therefore present secularism as a morally superior soteriology, are seeking to impose their will on the people.

To draw attention to the limitations of the original ideology of secularism and its Indian version does not necessarily imply that one rejects the ideologies totally or the institutions that embody them. Critiques may well result in strengthening the institutions concerned if the necessary corrective or reinforcing measures are carefully put in place. I am sceptical about the easy confidence of secularists regarding unproblematic adaptation.

Apropos my stress on the positive significance of religion, Béteille observes: 'What causes the most anxiety to secular intellectuals is a conception of religion which demands that every aspect of every individual's life be brought under religious scrutiny and control.'[6] He refers to it as the 'totalizing aims' of religion, more demanding in some cases than in others. The crucial question is, he writes, 'how much space will be allowed within society by doctrinaire religion for the growth of secular ideas and institutions'.[7] I agree that this is a key question and, as Béteille acknowledges, it applies, *mutatis mutandis*, to all doctrinaire ideologies, religious as well as secular.

Looking back, it seems that I did perhaps overemphasize the holistic character of traditional religions, particularly Hinduism, in the 1987 essay. Both Béteille and Bailey assert this in their critiques. Quoting from my essay 'Religion in India',[8] Bailey points out that when I write that 'religion is constitutive of society, and the traditional vision of life is holistic', I can be understood as saying that 'society is religion, an ideology'.[9] An almost identical sentence exists in 'Secularism in Its Place': 'For Gandhi religion was the source of absolute value and hence constitutive of social life.'[10]

---

[6] A. Béteille, (1994), p. 562. (See fn. 2).
[7] Ibid., p. 564.
[8] T.N. Madan, 'Religion in India', *Daedalus*, 118, 4 (1989), pp 747–59.
[9] See F.G. Bailey (1991), p. 223. (See fn. 2).

It appears that in the passage from the concrete case (Gandhi's position) to the general thesis (holistic character of Hinduism), I may have overstated my argument. It would obviously be a throwback to an untenable Durkheimian sociological extremism to envisage a society in which the secular is non-existent, and I did not mean to propose such a monistic thesis. In 'Religion in India' itself I wrote: 'The point is not that the religious domain is not distinguished from the secular, but rather that the secular is regarded as encompassed by the religious.'[11]

I would like to emphasize that I do not read the Hindu tradition (so-called) as a denial of the existence of what may be called secular elements, but rather as a statement of a particular kind of relation between the religious and the secular, namely the hierarchical (encompassing the contrary). Although I use the language made familiar to us by Louis Dumont, the idea of encompassment itself may be derived from the key concept of *purushartha*, or the triple goals of human endeavour (*dharma, artha, kama*) as presented in, say, the *Arthashāstra* or the *Manusmriti*.

Moreover, my reference to the traditional view of the hierarchical relationship of the sacerdotal and the royal functions is relevant to the extent that the Hindu tradition does not provide us with a dualistic view of the kind that Christianity does, although it admits of a diversity of religious traditions within its broad framework and outside it. The Christian distinction between the sacred and secular domains is widely held to have contributed to the success of the modern ideology of secularism in the West. As I pointed out in 'Secularism in Its Place', a Hindu or a Sikh, or a Muslim for that matter, would find it more difficult to make sense of the notion of 'privatization of religion' than, perhaps, a Christian does.

This does not mean that Indians have first to be converted to Christianity before they may be expected to appreciate the virtues of secularism in the sense of its being the ideology of secularization. It only draws attention to the need for greater efforts on the part of Indian intellectuals to clarify the notion of secularism in a context-sensitive manner, drawing upon India's pluralist traditions. There is sufficient historical and ethnographical evidence that it is

10 T.N. Madan (1987), p. 752. (See fn. 1).
11 T.N. Madan (1989), p. 116. (See fn. 7).

the masses of this country, Hindus and Muslims alike, who are comfortable with religious pluralism, and indeed practise it in one form or another. The traditional élite, from whom the great majority of today's intellectuals are descended, generally disapprove of such pluralism as the superstitious ways of the masses.

Not only have Indian intellectuals to make greater efforts to clarify the notion of secularism but also have to devise the most effective ways of communication, carrying the people with them, although not in the manner of the politicians. Unless they do this, the intellectuals will succeed only in convincing one another. Secularism has to be rescued from the prevailing semantic conflation, but this should not mean the imposition of one particular meaning on it, and it has to be made into a national ethos. This will take doing and it will take time.

# 10

# The Politics of Secularism and the Recovery of Religious Tolerance

*Ashis Nandy*

## I

## Faith, Ideology, and the Self

A significant aspect of the post-colonial structures of knowledge in the third world is a peculiar form of imperialism of categories. Under such imperialism, a conceptual domain is sometimes hegemonized by a concept produced and honed in the West, hegemonized so effectively that the original domain vanishes from our awareness. Intellect and intelligence become IQ, the oral cultures become the cultures of the non-literate or the uneducated, the oppressed become the proletariat, social change becomes development. After a while, people begin to forget that IQ is only a crude measure of intelligence and some day someone else may think up another kind of index to assess the same thing: that social change did not begin with development nor will it stop once the idea of development dies a natural or unnatural death.

In the following pages, I seek to provide a political preface to the recovery of a well-known domain of public concern in South Asia, ethnic and especially religious tolerance from the hegemonic language of secularism popularized by the Westernized intellectuals and middle classes in this part of the world. This language, whatever may have been its positive contributions to humane governance and to religious tolerance earlier, has increasingly become a cover for the complicity of the modern intellectuals and the modernizing middle classes of South Asia in the new forms of religious violence that have entered the Asian scene. These are the forms in which the state, the media, and the ideologies of national security, development, and modernity propagated by the modern intelligentsia and the middle classes play crucial roles.

To provide the political preface I have promised, I shall first have to describe four trends that have become clearly visible in South Asia during this century but particularly after the Second World War.

The first and the most important of these trends is that each religion in our part of the world has been split into two: faith and ideology. Both are inappropriate terms but I give them, in this article, specific private meanings to serve my purpose. By faith I mean religion as a way of life, a tradition that is definitionally non-monolithic and operationally plural. I say 'definitionally' because, unless a religion is geographically and culturally confined to a small area, religion as a way of life has to in effect turn into a confederation of a number of ways of life, linked by a common faith having some theological space for heterogeneity.

By ideology I mean religion as a subnational, national, or cross-national identifier of populations contesting for or protecting non-religious, usually political or socio-economic, interests. Such religions-as-ideologies usually get identified with one or more texts which, rather than the ways of life of the believers, then become the final identifiers of the pure forms of the religions. The tests help anchor the ideologies in something seemingly concrete and delimited and in effect provide a set of manageable operational definitions.

The two categories are not mutually exclusive; they are like two axes on which could be plotted the state of contemporary religions. One way of explaining the difference between the two is to conceive of ideology as something that, for individuals and people who believe in it, needs to be constantly protected and faith as something that the faithful usually expect to protect them. For a faith always includes a theory of transcendence and usually sanctions the experience of transcendence, whereas an ideology tends to bypass or fear theories and experiences of transcendence, except when they could be used for secular purposes.

The modern state always prefers to deal with religious ideologies rather than with faiths. It is wary of both forms of religion but it finds the ways of life more inchoate and, hence, unmanageable, even though it is faith rather than ideology that has traditionally shown more pliability and catholicity. It is religion-as-faith that prompted 200,000 Indians to declare themselves to be Mohammedan Hindus in the census of 1911; and it was the catholicity of faith that prompted Mole-Salam Girasia Rajputs to traditionally have two names for every member of the community, one Hindu and one Muslim.[1] It is religion-as-ideology, on the other hand, that prompted a significant proportion of the Punjabi-speaking Hindus to declare Hindi as their mother tongue, thus underlining the differences between Sikhism and Hinduism and sowing the seeds for the creation of a new minority. Likewise, it is religion-as-ideology that has provided a potent tool to the Jama'at-e-Islami to disown the traditional, plural forms of Islam in the Indian subcontinent and disjunct official religion from everyday life, to produce a pre-packaged Islam for Muslims uprooted and decultured by the processes of engineered social change in the region.

Second, during the last two centuries or so, there has grown a tendency to view the older faiths of the region through the eyes of post-medieval European Christianity and its various offshoots—such as the masculine Christianity associated with nineteenth-century missionaries like Joshua Marshman and William Carey in South Asia or its mirror image in the orthodox modernism vended by the likes of Frederich Engels and Thomas Huxley. Because this particular Eurocentric way of looking at faiths gradually came to be associated with the dominant culture of the colonial states in the region, it subsumes under it a set of clear polarities: centre versus periphery, true faith versus its distortions, civil versus primordial, and great traditions versus local cultures.

It is a part of the same story that in each of the dyads, the second category is set up to lose. It is also a part of the same story that, once the colonial concept of state was internalized by the societies of the region through the nationalist ideology, in turn heavily influenced by the Western theories of state and statecraft,[2] the

---

1 Shamoon T. Lokhandwala, 'Indian Islam: Composite Culture and Integration', *New Quest* 50 (March–April 1985), pp 87–101.
2 For instance, Partha Chatterjee, *Nationalist Thought and the Colonial World: A Derivative Discourse?* (Oxford University Press: New Delhi, 1986).

nascent nation-states of the region took upon themselves the same
civilizing mission that the colonial states had once taken upon
themselves vis-à-vis the ancient faiths of the subcontinent.

Third, the idea of secularism, an import from nineteenth-
century Europe into South Asia, has acquired immense potency
in the middle-class cultures and state sectors of South Asia, thanks
to its connection with and response to religion-as-ideology. Secularism has little to say about cultures—it is definitionally ethnophobic
and frequently ethnocidal, unless of course cultures and those
living by cultures are willing to show total subservience to the
modern nation-state and become ornaments or adjuncts to modern
living—and the orthodox secularists have no clue to the way a
religion can link up different faiths or ways of life according to its
own configurative principles.

To such secularists, religion is an ideology in opposition to the
ideology of modern statecraft and, therefore, needs to be contained.
They feel even more uncomfortable with religion-as-faith claiming
to have its own principles of tolerance and intolerance, for that
claim denies the state and the middle-class ideologues of the state
the right to be the ultimate reservoir of sanity and the ultimate
arbiter among different religions and communities.[3] This denial is
particularly galling to those who see the clash between two faiths
merely as a clash of socio-economic interests, not as a simultaneous
clash between conflicting interests and a philosophical encounter
between two metaphysics. The Westernized middle classes and
literati of South Asia love to see all such differences as liabilities
and as sources of ethnic violence.

Fourth, the imported idea of secularism has become increasingly
incompatible and, as it were, uncomfortable with the somewhat
fluid definitions of the self with which many South Asian cultures

---

[3] Jyoti Ananthu has drawn my attention to the inadequacy of the term
'tolerance', used more than once in this article because it itself is a product
of the secular world-view. She gives the example of Kakasaheb Kalelkar
distinguished freedom fighter and Gandhian, who used to talk of *samanvaya*
(crudely synthetism), which cannot be based only on tolerance. Trilokinath
Madan ('Secularism in Its Place', *The Journal of Asian Studies* 46, 4 (1987),
pp 747–59) has used the term 'understanding' which seems less demanding than
Kalelkar's term. I reluctantly retain the expression 'tolerance' because it
presumes the least from the ordinary citizen by way of knowledge and
empathy.

live.[4] Such a self, which can be conceptually viewed as a configuration of selves, simultaneously shapes, invokes, and reflects the configurative principles of religions-as-faiths. It also happens to be a negation of the modern concept of selfhood acquired partly from the Enlightenment West and partly from a rediscovery of previously recessive elements in Indian traditions. Religion-as-ideology, working with the concept of well-bounded, mutually exclusive religious identities, on the other hand, is more compatible with and analogous to the definition of the self as a well-bounded, individuated entity clearly separable from the non-self. Such individuation is rapidly taking place in South Asian societies and, to that extent, more exclusive definitions of the self, too, are emerging in these societies as a byproduct of secularization.[5]

A more fluid definition of the self is not merely more compatible with religion-as-faith, it also has—and depends more upon—a distinctive set of the non-selves and anti-selves (to coin a neologism analogous to anti-heroes). At one plane, these anti-selves are similar to what Carl Rogers used to call, infelicitously, the 'not-me'—and some others call rejected selves. At another plane, they, the anti-selves, are counterpoints without which the self just cannot be defined in the major cultures of this part of the world. It is the self in conjunction with its anti-selves and its distinctive concept of the non-self which define the domain of the self. Religion-as-faith is more compatible with such a complex self-definition; secularism has no inkling of this distinct, though certainly not unique, form of self-definition in South Asia. This is because secularism is, as T.N. Madan puts it, a gift of Christianity, by which he presumably means a gift of post-medieval European Christianity.

It is in the context of these four processes that I shall now discuss the scope and limits of the ideology of secularism in India and its

---

[4] Though I am speaking here of cultural selfhood, this description is perfectly compatible with psychoanalytic studies of self and separation, particularly ego boundaries, in India. For a recent example, see Alan Roland, 'Psychoanalysis in India and Japan: Toward a Comparative Psychoanalysis', *The American Journal of Psychoanalysis* (1991), 51, 1, pp 1–10.

[5] Cf. Donald F. Miller, 'Five Theses on the Question of Religion in India Today: A Response to Ashis Nandy's "An Anti-Secularist Manifesto"', Paper presented at the Conference on 'What's Happening to India?', Melbourne, 4–7 Dec. 1986.

326 Secularism and Its Critics

relationship with the new forms of ethnic violence we have been witnessing.

# II

# The Fate of Secularism

I must admit at this point that I am not a secularist. Infact I can be called an anti-secularist. I say this with some trepidation because in the company in which I move, this is not a fashionable position to take. Fortunately, such is the pull of the ideology of secularism in India today that recently, when I wrote an anti-secularist manifesto, many interpreted the article to be a hidden homage to secularism.

I call myself an anti-secularist because I feel that the ideology and politics of secularism have more or less exhausted their possibilities. And we may now have to work with a different conceptual frame which is already vaguely visible at the borders of Indian political culture. When I say that the ideology and politics of secularism have exhausted themselves, I have in mind the standard English meaning of the word 'secularism'. As we know, there are two meanings of the word current in modern and semi-modern India and, for that matter, in the whole of this subcontinent. One of the two meanings you can easily find out if you consult any standard dictionary. But you will have difficulty finding the other, for it is a non-standard local meaning which, many like to believe, is typically and distinctively Indian or South Asian (as we shall see below, it also has a Western tail, but that tail is now increasingly vestigial).

The first meaning becomes clear when people talk of secular trends in history or economics, or when they speak of secularizing the state. The word 'secularism' has been used in this sense in the West for over three hundred years. This secularism chalks out an area in public life where religion is not admitted. One can have religion in one's private life; one can be a good Hindu or a good Muslim within one's home or at one's place of worship. But when one enters public life, one is expected to leave one's faith behind. This ideology of secularism is associated with slogans like 'we are Indians first, Hindus second' or 'we are Indians first, then Sikhs'. Implicit in the ideology is the belief that managing the public realm is a science that is essentially universal, that religion, to the extent it is opposed to the Baconian world-image of science, is an open or potential threat to any modern polity.

In contrast, the non-Western meaning of secularism revolves around equal respect for all religions. This is the way it is usually put by public figures. Less crudely stated, it implies that while the public life may or may not be kept free of religion, it must have space for a continuous dialogue among religious traditions and between the religious and the secular—that, in the ultimate analysis, each major faith in the region includes *within* it an in-house version of the other faiths both as an internal criticism and as a reminder of the diversity of the theory of transcendence.

Recently, Ali Akhtar Khan has drawn attention to the fact that George Jacob Holyoake, who coined the word secularism in 1850, advocated a secularism accommodative of religion, a secularism that would moreover emphasize diversities and coexistence in the matter of faith. His contemporary, Joseph Bradlaugh, on the other hand, believed in a secularism that rejected religion and made science its deity.[6] Most non-modern Indians (that is Indians who would have reduced the late Professor Max Weber to tears), pushed around by the political and cultural forces unleashed by colonialism still operating in Indian society, have unwittingly opted for the accommodative and pluralist meaning while India's Westernized intellectuals have consciously opted for the abolition of religion from the public sphere.

In other words, the accommodative meaning is more compatible with the meaning the majority of Indians, independently of Bradlaugh, have given to the word 'secularism'. This meaning has always disconcerted the country's Westernized intellectuals. They have seen such people's secularism·as an adulterated one and as compromising true secularism. This despite the fact that the ultimate symbol of religious tolerance for modern India, Gandhi, obviously had this adulterated meaning in mind on the few occasions when he seemed to plead for secularism. This is clear from his notorious claim that those who thought that religion and politics could be kept separate, understood neither religion nor politics.

The saving grace in all this is that, while the scientific, rational meaning of secularism has dominated India's middle-class public

6 Imtiaz Ahmed, 'Muslims and Boycott Call: Political Realities Ignored', *The Times of India*, 14 Jan. 1987.

consciousness, the Indian people and, till recently most practising
Indian politicians, have depended on the accommodative meaning.
The danger is that the first meaning is supported by the accelerating
process of modernization in India. As a consequence now, there
is a clearer fit between the declared ideology of the modern Indian
nation-state and the secularism that fears religions and ethnicities.
Sociologist Imtiaz Ahmed euphemistically calls this fearful, ner-
vous secularism the new liberalism of the Indian élites.

Associated with this—what, then, the South Asians perceive as
the more scientific Western meaning of secularism—is a hidden
political hierarchy. I have spelt out this hierarchy previously
elsewhere but I shall nevertheless have to restate it to make the
rest of my argument. This hierarchy makes a fourfold classification
of the political actors in the subcontinent.

At the top of the hierarchy are those who are believers neither
in public nor in private. They are supposed to be scientific and
rational, and they are expected to ultimately not only rule this
society but also dominate its political culture. An obvious example
is Jawaharlal Nehru. Though we are now told, with a great deal
of embarrassment, that he believed in astrology and tantra, Nehru
rightfully belongs to this rung because he always made the modern
Indian a little ashamed of their religious beliefs and ethnic origins,
and convinced them that he himself had the courage and the
rationality to neither believe in private nor in public. By common
consent of the Indian middle classes, Nehru provided a perfect role
model for the twentieth-century citizens of the flawed cultural
reality called India. It is the Nehruvian model that informs the
following charming letter, written last year by a distinguished
former ambassador, to the editor of India's best-known national
daily:

M.V. Kamath asks in his article 'Where do we find the India?' My dear
friend and colleague, the late Ambassdor M.R.A. Beg, often used to say:
'Don't you think, old boy, that the only Indians are we wogs [Westernized
Oriental Gentlemen]?' However quaint it may have sounded 30 years ago,
the validity of this statement has increasingly become apparent over the
years.[7]

On the second rung of the ladder are those who choose not to
appear as believers in public despite being devout believers in

7 Gurbachan Singh, 'Where's the Indian?', *The Times of India*, 21 Sept. 1986.

private. I can think of no better example of the type than Indira Gandhi. She was a genuine non-believer in her public life (she after all died in the hands of her own Sikh guards, rather than accept the advice of her security officers to change the guards) but in private she was a devout Hindu who had to make her seventy-one—or was it sixty-nine?—pilgrimages. Both the selves of Indira Gandhi were genuine and together they represented a sizeable portion of the Indian middle classes. (A number of rulers in this part of the world fit this category—from Ayub Khan to Lal Bahadur Shastri to Sheikh Mujibur Rahman. Though the Westernized literati in the South Asian societies have never cared much for this model of religious and ethnic tolerance, they have been usually willing to accept the model as a reasonable compromise with the 'underdeveloped' cultures of South Asia.)

On the third rung are those who are believers in public but do not believe in private. This may at first seem an odd category, but one or two examples will make clear its meaning and also partially explain why this category includes problematic men and women. To me the two illustrious examples of the genre from our part of the world are Mohammad Ali Jinnah who was an agnostic in private life but took up the cause of Islam successfully in public, and V.D. Savarkar who was an atheist in private life but declared Hinduism as his political ideology. More recently, when Bhimrao Ambedkar converted to Buddhism, he probably entered this category from the first.

Such persons can sometimes be dangerous because to them religion is a political tool and a means of fighting one's own and one's community's sense of cultural inadequacy. Religion to them is not a matter of piety. Their private denial of belief only puts the secularist off guard who cannot fathom the seriousness with which the Jinnahs and the Savarkars take religion as a political instrument. On the other hand, their public faith puts the faithful off guard because the latter never discerns the contempt in which the heroes hold the common run of the faithful. Often these heroes invoke the classical versions of their faiths to underplay, marginalize, or even delegitimize the existing ways of life associated with their faiths. The goal of those holding such an instrumental view of religion has always been to homogenize their co-believers into proper political formations and, for that reason, to eliminate those parts of religion that smack of folkways and threaten to legitimize diversities, interfaith dialogue, and theological poly-centrism.

At the bottom of the hierarchy are those who are believers in private as well as in public. The best and most notorious example is that of Gandhi who openly believed both in private and in public, and gave his belief spectacular play in politics. This category has its strengths and weaknesses. One may say that exactly as the category manifests its strength in someone like Gandhi, Khan Abdul Gaffar Khan, and Maulana Bhasani, it shows its weakness in others like Ayatollah Khomeini in Iran or Jarnail Singh Bhindranwale in the Punjab. The category can even throw up grand eccentrics. Chaudhuri Rehmat Ali, fifty years, ago used to stand on Fridays outside the King's College gate at Cambridge and chant like a street hawker, 'Come and buy Pakistan—my earth-shaking pamphlet.'[8]

The four categories are not neat and in real life they rarely come in their pure forms. Often the same person can move from one to the other. Thus, Rahi Masoom Raza, being a scriptwriter for commercial Hindi films and being at home with spectacular changes of heart, comfortably oscillates between the first two categories.

This Babri Masjid and Ram Janambhoomi temple should be demolished...we as Indians are not interested in Babri Masjid, Rama Janambhoomi...as secular people we must crush the religious fanatics.[9]

Only ten months earlier Raza had, with as much passion, said:

I, Rahi Masoom Raza son of the late Mr Syed Bashir Hasan Abidi, a Muslim and one of the direct descendants of the Prophet of Islam, hereby condemn Mr Z.A. Ansari for his un-Islamic and anti-Muslim speeches in Parliament. The Quran nowhere says that a Muslim should have four wives.[10]

For the moment I shall not go into such issues. All I shall add is that in India, we have been always slightly embarrassed about this modern classification or ordering in our political life, for we know

8 Mulk Raj Anand, 'New Light on Iqbal', *Indian Express*, Sept. 1985.
9 Rahi Masoom Raza, in 'How to Resolve the Babri Masjid–Ram Janmabhoomi Dispute', *Sunday Observer*, 18 Jan. 1987.
10 Rahi Masoom Raza, 'In Favour of Change' (letter to the editor), *The Illustrated Weekly of India*, 16 March 1986.

that the Father of the Nation does not fare very well when the classification is applied to him.

Fortunately for some modern Indians, the embarrassment has been resolved by the fact that this classification is not working well today. It is not working well because it has led neither to the elimination of religion and ethnicity from politics nor to greater religious and ethnic tolerance. This is not the case only with us; this is the case with every society which has been put to the Indians, at some time or other, as an ideal secular society.

Thus, problems of ethnicity and secularization haunt today not merely some of the capitals of the world, Washington, Bonn, Paris, and Moscow, they even haunt the country which the older South Asians have been trained to view as remarkably free from the divisiveness of ethnicity and religion. For instance, for some hundred and fifty years Indians have been told that one of the reasons Britain dominated India and one of the reasons why Indians were colonized was that they were not secular, whereas Britain was. That was why the Indians did not know how to live together, whereas Britain was a world power, perfectly integrated and fired by the true spirit of secular nationalism. Now we find that after nearly three hundred years of secularism, the Irish, the Scots, and the Welsh together are creating as many problems for Britain as some of the religions or regions are creating for Indians.

Why is the old ideology of secularism not working in India? There are many reasons for this; I shall mention only a few, confining myself specifically to the problem of religion as it has got intertwined with the political process in the country.

First, in the early years of Independence, when the national élite was small and a large section of it had face-to-face contacts, we could screen people entering public life, specially the upper levels of the public services and high politics, for their commitment to secularism. Thanks to the growth of democratic participation in politics—India has gone through ten general elections and innumerable local and state elections—such screening is no longer possible. We can no longer ensure that those who reach the highest levels of the army, police, bureaucracy, or politics believe in old-style secular politics.

To give one example, at the time of writing, two ministers of the central cabinet in India and a number of individuals in the higher echelons of the ruling party have been accused of not only encouraging, organizing, and running a communal riot, but also of protecting the guilty and publicly threatening civil rights workers engaged in relief works. One chief minister was recently accused of importing rioters from another state on payment of professional fees to precipitate a communal riot as an antidote to violent intercaste conflicts. Another organized a riot three years ago so that he could impose a curfew in the state capital to stop his political opponents from demonstrating their strength in the legislature.

Such instances would have been unthinkable only ten years ago. They have become thinkable today because India's ultra-élites can no longer informally screen decision-makers the way they once used to; political participation in the country is growing, and the country's political institutions, particularly the main parties that increasingly look like electoral machines, are under too much of a strain to allow such screening. Religion *has* entered public life but through the back door.

Second, it has become more and more obvious to a large number of people that modernity is now no longer the ideology of a small minority; it is now the organizing principle of the dominant culture of politics. The idea that religions dominate India, that there is a handful of modern Indians fighting a rearguard action against that domination, is no longer convincing to many modernizing Indians. These Indians see the society around them—and often their own children—leaving no scope for a compromise between the old and new, and opting for a way of life that fundamentally negates the traditional concepts of a good life and a desirable society. These Indians now sense the 'irreversibility' of secularization and they know that, even in this subcontinent, religion-as-faith is being pushed to the corner. Much of the fanaticism and violence associated with religion comes today from the sense of defeat of the believers, from their feelings of impotency, and from their free-floating anger and self-hatred while facing a world which is increasingly secular and desacralized.

Also, when the state makes a plea to a minority community to secularize or to confine itself to only secular politics, it in effect tells the community to 'soften' its faith so that it can be more truly integrated in the nation-state. Usually it also simultaneously offers the community a gesture in the form of a tacit promise that it would force the majority also to ultimately dilute its faith. What the state implicitly says to a religious community, the intelligentsia often explicitly tells the individual, 'give up your faith, at least in public; others will do so too and together everyone will live in freedom from religious intolerance'. As it happens, however reasonable the solution may look to the already secularized, it is hardly appealing to the faithful, to whom religion is an overall theory of life, including public life, and life does not seem worth living without a theory, however imperfect, of transcendence.

Third, while appealing to the believers to keep the public sphere free of religion, the modern nation-state has no means of ensuring that the ideologies of secularism, development, and nationalism themselves do not begin to act as faiths intolerant of others. That is while the modern state builds up pressures on citizens to give up their faith in public, it guarantees no protection to them against the sufferings inflicted by the state itself in the name of its ideology. On the contrary, with the help of modern communications and the secular coercive power at its command, the state frequently uses its ideology to silence its non-conforming citizens. The role of such secular ideology in many societies today is no different from the crusading and inquisitorial role of religious ideologies, and in such societies, the citizens are often less protected against the ideology of the state than against religious ideologies or theocratic forces. Certainly in India, the ideas of nation-building, scientific growth, security, modernization, and development have become parts of a left-handed, quasi-religious practice—a new demonology, a *tantra* with a built-in code of violence.

In other words, to many Indians today, secularism comes as a part of a larger package consisting of a set of standardized ideological products and social processes—development, mega-science, and national security being some of the most prominent among them. This package often plays the same role vis-à-vis the people of the society—sanctioning or justifying violence against the weak and the dissenting—that the church, the *ulema*, the *sangha*, or the Brahmans played in earlier times.

Finally, the proposition that the values derived from the secular ideology of the state would be a better guide to political action and to a less violent and richer political life (in comparison to the values derived from the religious faith) has become even more unconvincing to large parts of Indian society than it was a few decades ago. It has become increasingly clear that, as far as public morality goes, the culture of the Indian state has very little moral authority left; nor have the ideologies that tend to conceptualize the state as the pivot to guide a devout Hindu, Muslim, or Sikh in his or her day-to-day public behaviour lies splintered around us. The deification of the state may go well with those Indians who have access to the state or thrive on its patronage, but palls on most decent citizens outside the charmed circle of the state sector. Obviously, we are at a point of time when old-style secularism can no longer pretend to guide moral or political action. All that the ideology of secularism can do now is to sanction the imposition of an imported language of politics on a traditional society that has an open polity. Let me spell this out.

In most post-colonial societies, when religion, politics, or religion-and-politics are discussed, there is an invisible reference point. This reference point is the Western Man. Not the Western Man in reality or the Western Man of history, but the Western Man as the defeated civilizations of our times have construed him. This Western Man rules the world, it seems to the defeated, because of his superior understanding of the relationship between religion and politics. To cope with this success, every major religious community in the region has produced three responses—I should say two responses and one non-response. These responses have clear-cut relationships with the splitting of religions described at the beginning of this article; actually, they derive from the split.

The first response—the spirit of which is difficult to capture—is to model oneself on the Western Man. Here something more than mimicry or 'imitation' is involved. The response consists in a desperate attempt to capture, within one's own self and culture, traits seen as the reasons for the West's success on the world stage. Seemingly it is a liberal, synthesizing response, and it is often justified as a universal response. For long it has been part of the political and cultural repertoire of modern India. A neat example is my friend, mathematician–philosopher, Raojibhai C. Patel's lament on the decline of the secular state in India, in which the analysis is almost entirely in terms of the Western experience with religion and politics, and the conclusions are all about India.[11]

---

[11] Raojibhai C. Patel, 'Building Secular State, Need to Subordinate Religion', *The Times of India*, 17 Sept. 1986.

The second response to the Western Man is that of the zealot. The zealot's sole goal is to somehow defeat the Western Man at his own game, the way Japan, for instance, has done in economic affairs. This is a crude way of describing a complex response but it does convey that what passes as fundamentalism, fanaticism, or revivalism is often only another form of Westernization becoming popular among the psychologically uprooted middle classes in South Asia. (A recent newspaper interview of nuclear physicist A.Q. Khan of Pakistan is a copy-book instance of such a response.)[12] In India at least the heart of the response is the faith that what Japan has done in economy, one can do in the case of religion and politics. One can, for example, decontaminate Hinduism of its folk elements, turn it into a classical Vedantic faith, and then give it additional teeth with the aid of Western technology and secular statecraft, so that the Hindus can take on and ultimately defeat all their external and internal enemies, if necessary by liquidating all forms of ethnic plurality within Hinduism and India, to equal the Western Man as a new *Übermenschen*. The zealot judges the success or failure of a religion only by this criterion.

Historian Giri Deshinkar gives the example of a book on *Mantrasastra*, written by one of the Śankarācāryas known for his zealotry, which justifies the sacred book by claiming that its conclusions are supported by modern science, as if that made the text more sacred. The title page of the book—a commentary on an ancient text by a guru of the world, a *jagadguru*—also says that its author is a BA, LLB. If this is the state of the Indian élite's cultural self-confidence, it is not surprising that newspapers carry every other month full-page advertisements by Maharishi Mahesh Yogi suggesting that Vedanta is true because quantum physics says so.

Such responses of the zealot are the ultimate admission of defeat. They constitute the cultural bed on which grows the revivalism of the defeated, the so-called fundamental movements in South Asia, based on the zealot's instrumental concept of religion as an ideological principle for political mobilization and state formation. Modern scholarship sees zealotry as a retrogression into primitivism and as a pathology of traditions. At closer sight it proves to be a by-product and a pathology of modernity. For instance, whatever the revivalist Hindu may seek to revive, it is not

12 'Pak a Few Steps from Bomb', *The Times of India*, 29 Jan. 1987.

Hinduism. The pathetically comic, martial uniform of khaki shorts, which the RSS cadres have to wear, tell it all. Modelled on the uniform of the colonial police, the khaki shorts not only identify the RSS as an illegitimate child of Western colonialism but as a direct progeny of the semiticizing Hindu reform movements under colonialism, Orientalist concepts of 'proper' religion, and upon the modern Western concepts of the nation-state, nationality, and nationalism. Once such concepts of religion and state are imported into Hinduism, the inevitable happens. One begins to judge the everyday lifestyle of the Hindus, their diversity and heterogeneity negatively, usually with a clear touch of hostility and contempt. Likewise, there is nothing fundamentally Islamic about the fundamentalist Muslims who have to constantly try to disenfranchise the ordinary Muslims as peripheral and delegitimize the religious practices of a huge majority of Muslims the world over as un-Islamic. The same forces are operating within Sikhism and Sri Lankan Buddhism, too.

There is however a third response that comes usually from the non-modern majority of a society, though to the globalized middle-class intellectuals it may look like the response of a minority. This response does not keep religion separate from politics, but it does say that the traditional ways of life have, over the centuries, developed internal principles of tolerance, and these principles must have a play in contemporary politics. This response affirms that religious communities in traditional societies *have* known how to live with one another. It is not modern Indian which has tolerated Judaism in India for nearly two thousand years, Christianity from before the time it went to Europe, and Zoroastrianism for over twelve hundred years; it is traditional India which has shown such tolerance. That is why today, as India gets modernized, religious violence is increasing. In earlier centuries, according to available records, interreligious riots were rare and localized; even after Independence we used to have only one event of religious strife a week; now we have more than an incident a day. Over ninety per cent of these riots begin in urban India within and around the industrial areas. Even now, Indian villages and small towns can take credit for largely having avoided communal riots. (Thus we find that after ten years of bitterness since the mid-1980s, the Punjab villages are still free of riots; they have only seen assassinations by small gangs of terrorists and riot-like situations in the cities.) Obviously, somewhere and somehow, religious violence has something to do with the urban–industrial vision of life and with the political processes the vision lets loose.

It is the awareness of this political process that has convinced a small but growing number of Indian political analysts that it is from non-modern India, from the traditions and principles of religious tolerance encoded in the everyday life associated with the different faiths of India, that one will have to seek clues to the renewal of Indian political culture. This is a less difficult task than it at first seems. Let us not forget that the great symbols of religious tolerance in India over the last two thousand years have not been modern, though the moderns have managed to hijack some of these symbols.

For example, when the modern Indians project the ideology of secularism into the past, to say that Emperor Ashoka was 'secular', they ignore that Ashoka was not exactly a secular ruler; he was a practising Buddhist even in his public life. He based his tolerance on Buddhism, not on secularism. Likewise, the other symbol of interreligious amity in modern India, Emperor Akbar, derived his tolerance not from secularism but from Islam; he believed that tolerance was the message of Islam. And in this century, Gandhi derived his religious tolerance from Hinduism, not from secular politics.

Modern India has much to answer for. So have the cosmopolitan intellectuals in South Asia who have been insensitive to the traditions of interreligious understanding in their societies. These traditions may have become creaky but so is, it is now pretty obvious, the ideology of secularism itself. As we are finding out the hard way, the new forms of religious violence in this part of the world are becoming paradoxically, increasingly secular. The anti-Sikh riots that took place in Delhi in November 1984, the anti-Muslim riots in Ahmedabad in 1985 during the anti-reservation stir, and the 'anti-Hindu' riots in Bangalore in 1986 were all associated not so much with religious hatred as with political cost calculations and/or economic greed.[13] The same can be said about the riots at Moradabad, Bhiwandi, and Hyderabad earlier. Zealotry has produced many riots, but secular politics, too, has now begun to produce its own version of 'religious riots'. As for the victims

---

13 A comparable example from outside India will be Sunil Bastian, 'Political Economy of Ethnic Violence in Sri Lanka: The July 1983 Riots', in Veena Das (ed.), *Mirrors of Violence: Communities, Riots and Survivors* (Oxford University Press: New Delhi, 1991), pp 286–304.

of a riot, the fact that the riot might have been organized and led by persons motivated by political cost calculations and not by religious bigotry can hardly be a solace.

The moral of the story is this: it is time to recognize that, instead of trying to build religious tolerance on the good faith or conscience of a small group of de-ethnicized, middle-class politicians, bureaucrats, and intellectuals, a far more serious venture would be to explore the philosophy, the symbolism, and the theology of tolerance in the faiths of the citizens and hope that the state systems in South Asia may learn something about religious tolerance from everyday Hinduism, Islam, Buddhism, or Sikhism rather than wish that ordinary Hindus, Muslims, Buddhists, and Sikhs will learn tolerance from the various fashionable secular theories of statecraft.

## III

## The Heart of Darkness

The last point needs to be further clarified, and I shall try to provide this clarification by putting my arguments in a larger psychological and cultural frame. The accompanying Table provides an outline of the frame, (though the Table also shows the dangers of clarifying a live issue by casting one's argument in the language of the social sciences, for the argument, as it is summarized in the Table, has already become, I can see, somewhat reified and opaque).

The Table admits that the Western concept of secularism *has* played a crucial role in South Asian societies, *has* worked as a check against some forms of ethnic intolerance and violence, and *has* contributed to humane governance at certain times and places.

By the same token, however, the Table also suggests that secularism cannot cope with many of the new fears and intolerance of religions and ethnicities, nor provide any protection against the new forms of violence that have come to be associated with such intolerance. Nor can secularism contain those who provide the major justifications for calculated pogroms and ethnocides in terms of the dominant ideology of the state.

These new forms of intolerance and violence are sustained by a different configuration of social and psychological forces. The

| Sectors involved | Typical violence | Model of violence | Locus of ideology | Nature of motives | Effective counter-ideology |
|---|---|---|---|---|---|
| Non-modern, peripheralized believers | Religious wars | Traditional sacrifice (of self or other) | Faith | Passion | Critiques of faith/agnosticism |
| Semi-modern zealots | Riots | Exorcism/search for parity | State | Passion and interest | Secularism |
| Modern rationalists | Manufactured riots or 'assembly-line' violence | Experimental science (vivisection) or industrial management | Bismarckian concept of state | Interest | Critiques of objectification and desacralization |

rubrics in the Table allude both to these forces as well as to the growing irrelevance of the broad models proposed by a number of important empirical social and psychological studies undertaken in the 1950s and 1960s by those studying social distance in the manner of E. Bogardus, by Erich Fromm in his early writings, by Theodor Adorno and his associates working on the authoritarian personality, by Milton Rokeach and his followers exploring dogmatism, and by Bruno Bettelheim.[14] The stereotyping, authoritarian submission, sadomasochism, and the heavy use of the ego defences of projection, displacement, and rationalization that, according to some of those studies, went with authoritarianism and dogmatism have not become irrelevant, as Sudhir Kakar shows once again in a recent paper.[15] There are resolute demonologies that divide religious communities and endorse ethnic violence, but these have begun to play a less and less central role in such violence. They have become increasingly one of the psychological markers of those participating in the mobs involved in rioting or in pogroms, not of those planning, initiating, or legitimizing mob-action.

This is another way of saying that the planners, instigators, and legitimizers of religious and ethnic violence can now be identified as secular users of non-secular forces or impulses in the society. There is very little continuity between their motivational structures and that of the street mobs which act out the wishes of the organizers of a riot. Only the mobs now represent, and that too partially, the violence produced by the predisposing factors described in the social science literature of earlier decades. In the place of these factors have come a new set of personality traits and defence mechanisms, the most important of which are the more 'primitive' defences such as isolation and denial. These defences ensure, paradoxically, the primacy of cognitive factors in violence over the affective and the conative.

The involvement of these newly important ego defences in human violence were also first noticed in the 1950s and 1960s, but

[14] Erich Fromm, *Escape from Freedom* (Farrar and Rinehart: New York, 1941); Bruno Bettelheim, *Surviving and Other Essays* (Thames and Hudson: London, 1979); T.W. Adorno *et al.*, *The Authoritarian Personality* (Norton: New York, 1950); Milton Rokeach, *The Open and Closed Mind* (Basic Books: New York, 1960).

[15] Sudhir Kakar, 'Some Unconscious Aspects of Ethnic Violence in India', in Das, *Mirrors of Violence*, pp 135–45.

those who drew attention to them did so in passing (for instance, Erich Fromm in one of his incarnations and Bruno Bettelheim) or from outside the ambit of empirical social sciences (for instance, Joseph Conrad and Hannah Arendt).[16] Moreover, these early analyses of the 'new violence' were primarily concerned with 'extreme situations', to use Bettelheim's term, and not with the less technologized and less extreme violence of religious feuds or riots. Even when the violence these analyses dealt with did not directly involve genocide and mass murders, they involved memories of genocide and mass murders, as in the well-known book by Alexander and Margarete Mitscherlich.[17]

Only now have we become fully aware of the destructive potentials of the once-low-grade but now-persistent violence flowing from objectification, scientization, and bureaucratic rationality. The reasons for this heightened awareness are obvious enough. As the modern nation-state system and the modern thought machine enter the interstices of even the most traditional societies, those in power or those who hope to be in power in these societies begin to view statecraft in fully secular, scientific, amoral, and dispassionate terms.[18] The modernist élites in such societies then begin to fear the divisiveness of minorities and the diversity that religious and ethnic plurality introduces into a nation-state. These élites then begin to see all religions and all forms of ethnicity as a hurdle to nation-building and state formation, and as a danger to the technology of statecraft and political management. The new nation-states in many societies tend to look at religion and

---

16 Erich Fromm, *Anatomy of Human Destructiveness* (Holt, Rinehart & Winston, New York, 1973); Hannah Arendt, *Eichmann in Jerusalem* (Viking: New York, 1963) and *On Violence*, (Allen & Unwin: London, 1969); Joseph Conrad, *The Heart of Darkness* (Penguin: Harmondsworth, 1973).

17 Alexander and Margarete Mitscherlich, *The Inability to Mourn: Principles of Collective Behaviour* (Grove: New York, 1984).

18 That is, in terms of what Tarique Banuri calls the impersonality postulate in his 'Modernization and its Discontents: A Culture Perspective on the Theories of Development', in Frederique Apffei Marglin and Stephen Marglin (eds), *Dominating Knowledge: Development, Culture and Resistance* (Clarendon Press: Oxford, 1990), pp 73–101. See also Ashis Nandy, 'Science, Authoritarianism and Culture: On the Scope and Limits of Isolation Outside the Clinic', in Nandy, *Traditions, Tyranny and Utopias: Essays in the Politics of Awareness.* (Oxford University Press: New Delhi, 1987), pp 95–126.

ethnicity in the way the nineteenth-century colonial powers looked at distant cultures that came under their domination—at best as 'things' to be studied, 'engineered', ghettoized, museumized, or preserved in reservations; at worst, as inferior cultures opposed to the principles of modern living and inconsistent with the game of modern politics, science, and development, and therefore deservedly facing extinction. No wonder that the political cultures of South Asia began to produce a plethora of official social scientists who are the perfect analogues of the colonial anthropologists who once studied the 'Hindoos' and the 'Mohammedans' on behalf of their king and country.

This state of mind is the basic format of the internal colonialism that is at work today. The economic exploitation to which the epithet 'internal colonialism' is mechanically applied by radical economists is no more than a by-product of the internal colonialism I am speaking about. This colonialism validates the proposal, which can be teased out of the works of a number of philosophers, such as Hannah Arendt and Herbert Marcuse, that the most extreme forms of violence in our times come not from faulty passions or human irrationality but from faulty ideologies and unrestrained instrumental rationality. Demonology is now for the mobs; secular rationality for those who organize, instigate, or lead the mobs. Unless of course one conceptualizes modern statecraft itself as a left-handed, magical technology and as a new demonology. (Thanks to a few secretly taken photographs of some of the participants in the violence, one image that has persisted in my mind from the days of the anti-Sikh pogrom at Delhi in 1984 is that of a scion of a prominent family that owns one of Delhi's most exclusive boutiques directing with his golf club a gang of ill-clad arsonists. I suspect that the image has the potential to serve as the metaphor for the new forms of social violence in modern India.)

As I have already said, this state-linked internal colonialism uses legitimating core concepts like national security, development, modern science, and technology. Any society, for that matter any aggregate, that gives unrestrained play or support to these concepts gets automatically linked to the colonial structure of the present-day world and is doomed to promote violence and expropriation, particularly of the kind directed against the smaller minorities such as the tribals and the less numerous sects who can neither hit back against the state nor any longer live isolated from the modern market.

Secularism has become a handy adjunct to this set of legitimating core concepts. It helps those swarming around the nation-state, either as élites or as counter-élites, to legitimize themselves as the sole arbiters among traditional communities, to claim for themselves monopoly on religious and ethnic tolerance and on political rationality. To accept the ideology of secularism is to accept the ideologies of progress and modernity as the new justifications of domination and the use of violence to sustain these ideologies as the new opiates of the masses.

Gandhi, an arch anti-secularist if we use the proper scientific meaning of the word 'secularist', claimed that his religion was his politics and his politics was his religion. He was not a cultural relativist and his rejection of the first principle of secularism—the separation of religion and politics—was not a political strategy meant to ensure his political survival in a uniquely multi-ethnic society like India. Indeed, I have been told by sociologist Bhupinder Singh that Gandhi may have borrowed this anti-secular formulation from William Blake. Whatever be its source, in some version or the other this formulation is becoming the common response of those who have sensed the new forms of man-made violence unleashed by post-seventeenth-century Europe in the name of the Enlightenment values. These forms of violence, which have already taken a toll of about a hundred million human lives in this century, have come under closer critical scrutiny in recent decades principally because they have come home to roost in the heart of Europe and North America, thanks to the Third Reich, the Gulag, the two World Wars, and the threat of nuclear annihilation.

Many modern Indians who try to sell Gandhi as a secularist find his attitude to the separation of religion and politics highly embarrassing, if not positively painful. They like to see Gandhi as a hidden modernist who merely used a traditional religious idiom to mobilize his unorganized society to fight colonialism. Nothing can be more disingenuous. Gandhi's religious tolerance came from his anti-secularism, which in turn came from his unconditional rejection of modernity, and he never wavered in his stand. Note the following exchange between him and a correspondent of the *Chicago Tribune* in 1931.

'Sir, twenty three years ago you wrote a book *Hind Swaraj*, which stunned India and rest of the world with its terrible onslaught on modern western civilization. Have you changed mind about any of the things you have said in it?'

'Not a bit. My ideas about the evils of western civilization still stand. If I republish the book tomorrow, I would scarcely change a word.'[19]

Religious tolerance outside the bounds of secularism is exactly what it says it is. It not only means tolerance of religions but also tolerance that is religious. It therefore squarely locates itself in traditions outside the ideological grid of modernity. Gandhi used to say that he was a *sanatani*, an orthodox Hindu. It was as a *sanatani* Hindu that he claimed to be simultaneously a Muslim, a Sikh, and a Christian, and he granted the same plural identity to those belonging to other faiths. Traditional Hinduism, or rather *sanatan dharma*, was the source of his religious tolerance. It is instructive that the Hindu nationalists who killed him—that too after three unsuccessful attempts to kill him over the previous twenty years—did so in the name of secular statecraft. That secular statecraft now seeks to dominate Indian political culture, sometimes in the name of Gandhi himself. Urban, Westernized, middle-class, Brahmanic, Hindu nationalists and Hindu modernists often flaunt Gandhi's tolerance as an indicator of Hindu catholicity but contemptuously reject that part of his ideology which insisted that religious tolerance, to be tolerance, must impute to other faiths the same spirit of tolerance. Whether a large enough proportion of those belonging to the other religious traditions show *in practice* and *at a particular point of time and place* the same tolerance or not is a secondary matter. Because it is the imputation of presumption of tolerance in others, not its existence, that defines one's own tolerance in the Gandhian world-view and praxis. That presumption must become the major source of tolerance for those who want to fight the new violence of our times, whether they are believers or not.

---

[19] Quoted in T.S. Ananthu, 'Going Beyond the Intellect: A Gandhian Approach to Scientific Education' (Gandhi Peace Foundation: New Delhi, 1981), mimeo., p. 1.

# 11

# Secularism and Tolerance*

*Partha Chatterjee*

There is little doubt that in the last two or three years we have seen a genuine renewal of both thinking and activism among left-democratic forces in India on the question of the fight for secularism. An important element of the new thinking is the re-examination of the theoretical and historical foundations of the liberal-democratic state in India, and of its relation to the history and theory of the modern state in Europe and the Americas.

An interesting point of entry into the problem is provided by the parallels recently drawn between the rise of fascism in Europe in the 1920s and 1930s, and that of the Hindu Right in India in the last few years. Sumit Sarkar, among others, has noted some of the chilling similarities.[1] But a more careful look at precisely this comparison will, I think, lead us to ask a basic and somewhat unsettling question: Is secularism an adequate, or even appropriate, ground on which to meet the political challenge of Hindu majoritarianism?

The Nazi campaigns against Jews and other minority groups did not call for an abandonment of the secular principles of the state in Germany. If anything, Nazi rule was accompanied by an attempt to de-Christianize public life and to undermine the influence of the Catholic as well as the various Protestant churches. Fascist ideology did not seek the union of state and religion in Italy, where the presence of a large peasant population and the hold of Catholicism

* This is a revised version of the article that appeared in the *Economic and Political Weekly* 29, 28 (9 July 1994), pp 1768–77.
[1] Sumit Sarkar, 'The Fascism of the Sangh Parivar', *Economic and Political Weekly* (30 January 1993), pp 163–7; Jan Brenman, 'The Hindu Right: Comparisons with Nazi Germany', *The Times of India*, 15 March 1993.

might be supposed to have provided an opportune condition for such a demand—and this despite the virtually open collaboration of the Roman Church with Mussolini's regime. Nazi Germany and fascist Italy are, of course, only two examples of a feature that has been noticed many times in the career of the modern state in many countries of the world: namely that state policies of religious intolerance, or of discrimination against religious and other ethnic minorities, do not necessarily require the collapsing of state and religion, nor do they presuppose the existence of theocratic institutions.

The point is relevant in the context of the current politics of the Hindu right in India. It is necessary to ask why the political leadership of that movement chooses so meticulously to describe its adversaries as 'pseudo-secularists', conceding thereby its approval of the ideal as such of the secular state. None of the serious political statements made by that leadership contains any advocacy of theocratic institutions; and, notwithstanding the exuberance of a few sadhus celebrating their sudden rise to political prominence, it is unlikely that a conception of the 'Hindu Rashtra' will be seriously propagated which will include, for instance, a principle that the laws of the state be in conformity with this or that *samhitā* or even with the general spirit of the *Dharmasāstra*. In this sense, the leading element in the current movement of the Hindu Right can be said to have undergone a considerable shift in position from, let us say, that of the Hindu Mahasabha at the time of the debate over the Hindu Code Bill some forty years ago. Its position is also quite unlike that of most contemporary Islamic fundamentalist movements, which explicitly reject the theoretical separation of state and religion as 'Western' and un-Islamic. It is similarly unlike the fundamentalist strand within the Sikh movements in recent years. The majoritarianism of the Hindu Right, it seems to me, is perfectly at peace with the institutional procedures of the 'Western' or 'modern' state.

Indeed, the mature and most formidable statement of the new political conception of 'Hindutva' is unlikely to pit itself at all against the idea of the secular state. The persuasive power, and even the emotional charge, that the Hindutva campaign appears to have gained in recent years does not depend on its demanding legislative enforcement of ritual or scriptural injunctions, a role for religious institutions in legislative or judicial processes, compulsory religious instruction, state support for religious bodies, censorship of science, literature, and art in order to safeguard religious dogma, or any other similar demand undermining the secular character of the existing Indian state. This is not to say that in the frenzied mêlée produced by the Hindutva brigade such noises would not be made; the point is that anti-secular demands of this type are not crucial to the political thrust, or even the public appeal, of the campaign.

Indeed, in its most sophisticated forms, the campaign of the Hindu Right often seeks to mobilize on its behalf the will of an interventionist modernizing state, in order to erase the presence of religious or ethnic particularism from the domains of law or public life, and to supply, in the name of 'national culture', a homogenized content to the notion of citizenship. In this role, the Hindu Right in fact seeks to project itself as a principled modernist critic of Islamic or Sikh fundamentalism, and to accuse the 'pseudo-secularists' of preaching tolerance for religious obscurantism and bigotry. The most recent example of this is the Allahabad High Court pronouncement on divorce practices among Muslims by a judge well known for his views on the constitutional sanctity of Lord Rama.

Thus, the comparison with fascism in Europe points to the very real possibility of a Hindu Right locating itself quite firmly within the domain of the modernizing state, and using all of the ideological resources of that state to lead the charge against people who do not conform to its version of the 'national culture'. From this position, the Hindu Right can not only deflect accusations of being anti-secular, but can even use the arguments for interventionist secularization to promote intolerance and violence against minorities.

As a matter of fact, the comparison with Nazi Germany also extends to the exact point that provides the Hindutva campaign with its venomous charge: as Sarkar notes, '...the Muslim here becomes the near exact equivalent of the Jew'. The very fact of belonging to this minority religious community is sufficient to put a question mark against the status of a Muslim as a citizen of India. The term 'communal', in this twisted language, is reserved for the Muslim, whereas the 'pseudo-secular' is the Hindu who defends the right of the Muslim citizen. (Note once more that the term 'secular' itself is not made a target of attack). Similarly, on the vexed question of migrants from Bangladesh, the Hindu immigrant is by

definition a 'refugee' while the Muslim is an 'infiltrator'. A whole
series of stereotypical features, now sickeningly familiar in their
repetitiveness, are then adduced in order to declare as dubious the
historical, civil, and political status of the Muslim within the Indian
state. In short, the current campaign of the Hindu Right is directed
not against the principle of the secular state, but rather towards
mobilizing the legal powers of that state in order to systematically
persecute and terrorize a specific religious minority within its
population.

The question then is as follows: Is the defence of secularism an
appropriate ground for meeting the challenge of the Hindu Right?
Or should it be fought where the attack is being made, that is
should the response be a defence of the duty of the democratic state
to ensure policies of religious toleration? The question is important
because it reminds us that not all aggressive majoritarianisms pose
the same sort of problem in the context of the democratic state:
Islamic fundamentalism in Pakistan or Bangladesh or Sinhala
chauvinism in Sri Lanka do not necessarily have available to them
the same political strategies as the majoritarian politics of the
Hindu right in India. It also warns us of the very real theoretical
possibility that secularization and religious toleration may sometimes work at cross-purposes.[2] It is necessary therefore to be clear
about what is implied by these concepts.

---

[2] Ashis Nandy makes a distinction between religion-as-faith, by which he
means a way of life that is operationally plural and tolerant, and religion-
as-ideology, which identifies and enumerates populations of followers fighting
for non-religious, usually political and economic, interests. He then suggests,
quite correctly, that the politics of secularism is part of the same process of
formation of modern state practices which promotes religion-as-ideology.
Nandy's conclusion is that rather than relying on secularism of a modernized
élite we should 'explore the philosophy, the symbolism and the theology of
tolerance in the various faiths of the citizens and hope that the state systems
in South Asia may learn something about religious tolerance from everyday
Hinduism, Islam, Buddhism, and/or Sikhism...'. 'The Politics of Secularism
and the Recovery of Religious Tolerance', in Veena Das (ed.), *Mirrors of
Violence: Communities, Riots and Survivors in South Asia* (Oxford University
Press: New Delhi, 1990), pp 69–93. I am raising the same doubt about whether
secularism necessarily ensures toleration, but, unlike Nandy, I am here looking
for political possibilities *within* the domain of the modern state institutions
as they now exist in India.

# Meaning of Secularism

At the very outset, let us face up to a point that will invariably be made in any discussion on 'secularism' in India, namely that in the Indian context the word has very different meanings from its standard use in the English language. This fact is sometimes cited as confirmation of the 'inevitable' difference in the meanings of a concept in two dissimilar cultures ('India is not Europe: secularism in India cannot mean the same thing as it does in Europe'). At other times, it is used to underline the 'inevitable' shortcomings of the modern state in India ('There cannot be a secular state in India because Indians have an incorrect concept of secularism').

Of course, it could also be argued that this comparison with European conceptions is irrelevant if our purpose is to intervene in the Indian debate on the subject. What does it matter if secularism means something else in European and American political discourse? As long as there are reasonably clear and commonly agreed referents for the word in the Indian context, we should go ahead and address ourselves to the specifically Indian meaning of secularism.

Unfortunately, the matter cannot be settled that easily. The Indian meanings of 'secularism' did not emerge in ignorance of the European or American meanings of the word. I also think that in its current usage in India, with apparently well-defined 'Indian' referents, the loud and often acrimonious Indian debate on secularism is never entirely innocent of its Western genealogies. To pretend that the Indian meaning of secularism has marked out a conceptual world all of its own, untroubled by its differences with Western secularism, is to take an ideological position which refuses either to recognize or to justify its own grounds.

In fact, I wish to make an even stronger argument. Commenting upon Raymond William's justly famous *Keywords*, Quentin Skinner has pointed out that a concept takes on a new meaning not (as one would usually suppose) when arguments that it should be applied to a new circumstance succeed, but rather when such arguments fail.[3] Thus, if one is to consider the 'new' meaning

[3] Quentin Skinner, 'Language and Political Change', in Terence Ball, James Farr, and Russell L. Hanson (eds), *Political Innovation and Conceptual Change* (Cambridge University Press: Cambridge, 1989), pp 6–23.

acquired by the word 'secularism' in India, it is not as though the plea of the advocates of secularism that the concept bears application to modern Indian state and society has won general acceptance, and that the concept has thereby taken on a new meaning. If that had been the case, the 'original' meaning of the word as understood in its standard sense in the West would have remained unmutilated; it would only have widened its range of referents by including within it the specific circumstances of the Indian situation. The reason why arguments have to be made about 'secularism' having a new *meaning* in India is because there are serious difficulties in applying the standard meaning of the word to the Indian circumstances. The 'original' concept, in other words, will not easily admit the Indian case within its range of referents.

This, of course, could be a good pretext for insisting that Indians have their own concept of secularism which is different from the Western concept bearing the same name; that, it could be argued, is exactly why the Western concept cannot be applied to the Indian case. The argument then would be about a difference in concepts: if the concept is different, the question of referential equivalence cannot be a very crucial issue. At most, it would be a matter of family resemblances, but conceptually Western secularism and Indian secularism would inhabit entirely autonomous discursive domains.

That, it is needless to say, is hardly the case. We could begin by asking why, in all recent discussions in India on the relation between religion and the state, the central concept is named by the English words 'secular' and 'secularism' or, in the Indian languages, by neologisms such as *dharma-nirapekshata* which are translations of those English words and are clearly meant to refer to the range of meanings indicated by the English terms. As far as I know, there does not exist in any Indian language a term for 'secular' or 'secularism' which is standardly used in talking about the role of religion in the modern state and society and whose meaning can be immediately explicated without having recourse to the English terms.

What this implies is that although the use of dharma in *dharma-nirapekshata* or mazhab in *ghair-mazhabi* might open up conceptual or referential possibilities in Indian discourse which was unavailable to the concept of secularism in the West, the continued use of an awkward neologism, besides of course the continued use of the English term itself, indicates that the more stable and well-defined reference for the concept lies in the Western political discourse about the modern state.[4] In fact, it is clear from the discussions among the Indian political and intellectual élites at least from the 1920s that the proponents of the secular state in India never had any doubt at all about the meaning of the concept of secularism; all the doubts were about whether that concept would find a congenial field of application in the Indian social and political context. The continued use of the term 'secularism' is, it seems to me, an expression of the desire of the modernizing élite to see the 'original' meaning of the concept actualized in India. The resort to 'new meanings' is, to invoke Skinner's point once more, a mark of the failure of this attempt.

It might prove instructive to do a 'history of ideas' exercise for the use of the word 'secularism' in Indian political discourse in the last hundred years, but this is not the place for it. What is important for our purposes is a discussion of how the nationalist project of putting an end to colonial rule and inaugurating an independent nation-state became implicated, from its very birth, in a contradictory movement with regard to the modernist mission of secularization.

## British Rule, Nationalism, and the Separation of State and Religion

Ignoring the details of a complicated history, it would not be widely off the mark to say that by the latter half of the nineteenth century, the British power in India had arrived at a reasonably firm policy of not involving the state in matters of religion. It tried to keep neutral on disputes over religion, and was particularly careful not to be seen as promoting Christianity. Immediately after the

---

[4] Even in the mid-1960s, Ziya-ul Hasan Faruqi was complaining about the use of *ghair mazhabi* and *la-dini*. '*Ghayr mazhabi* means something contrary to religious commandments and *la-dini* is irreligious or atheistic.... The common man was very easily led to conclude that the Indian state was against religion. It is, however, gratifying to see that the Urdu papers have started to transliterate the word 'secular'. 'Indian Muslims and the Ideology of the Secular State', in Donald Eugene Smith (ed.), *South Asian Politics and Religion* (Princeton University Press: Princeton, 1966), pp 138–49.

assumption of power by the Crown in 1858, the most significant step was taken in instituting equality before the law by enacting uniform codes of civil and criminal law. The area left out, however, was that of personal law which continued to be governed by the respective religious laws as recognized and interpreted by the courts. The reason why personal law was not brought within the scope of a uniform civil code was, precisely, the reluctance of the colonial state to intervene in matters close to the very heart of religious doctrine and practice. In the matter of religious endowments, while the British power in its early years took over many of the functions of patronage and administration previously carried out by Indian rulers, by the middle of the nineteenth century it largely renounced those responsibilities and handed them over to local trusts and committees.

As far as the modernizing efforts of the Indian élite are concerned, the nineteenth-century attempts at 'social reform' by soliciting the legal intervention of the colonial state are well known. In the second half of the nineteenth century, however, the rise of nationalism led to a refusal on the part of the Indian élite to let the colonial state enter into areas that were regarded as crucial to the cultural identity of the nation. This did not mean a halt to the project of 'reform': all it meant was a shift in the agency of reform—from the legal authority of the colonial state to the moral authority of the national community.[5] This shift is crucial: not so much because of its apparent coincidence with the policy of non-intervention of the colonial state in matters of religion in the late nineteenth century, but because of the underlying assumption in nationalist thinking about the role of state legislation in religion— legal intervention in the cause of religious reform was not undesirable *per se*, but it was undesirable when the state was colonial. As it happened, there was considerable change in the social beliefs and practices of the sections that came to constitute the new middle class in the period leading up to independence in 1947. Not only was there change in the actual practices surrounding family and personal relations, and even in many religious practices, without there being any significant change in the laws of the state, but,

5 I have discussed the point more elaborately in *The Nation and Its Fragments: Colonial and Post-colonial Histories* (Princeton University Press: Princeton, 1993).

perhaps more important, there was an overwhelming tide in the dominant attitudes among these sections in favour of the legitimacy of 'social reform'. These reformist opinions affected the educated sections in virtually all parts of the country, and found a voice in most religious and caste communities.

One of the dramatic results of this cumulation of reformist desire within the nationalist middle class was the sudden spate of new legislation on religious and social matters immediately after Independence. This is actually an extremely significant episode in the development of the nation-state in India, and its deeply problematic nature has been seldom noticed in the current debates over secularism. It needs to be described in some detail.

## Religious Reform and the Nation-State

Even as the provisions of the new Constitution of India were being discussed in the Constituent Assembly, some of the provincial legislatures had begun to enact laws for the reform of religious institutions and practices. One of the most significant of these was the Madras Devadasis (Prevention of Dedication) Act, 1947, which outlawed the institution of dedicating young girls to temple deities, and prohibited 'dancing by a woman...in the precincts of any temple or other religious institution, or in any procession of a Hindu deity, idol or object of worship...'.[6] Equally important was the Madras Temple Entry Authorization Act, 1947, which made it a punishable offence to prevent any person on the ground of untouchability from entering or worshipping in a Hindu temple. This Act was immediately followed by similar legislation in the Central Provinces, Bihar, Bombay, and other provinces, and finally by the temple-entry provisions in the Constitution of India.

Although in the course of the debates over these enactments, views were often expressed about the need to 'remove a blot on the Hindu religion', it was clearly possible to justify some of the laws on purely secular grounds. Thus, the *devadasi* system could be declared unlawful on the ground that it was a form of bondage or of enforced prostitution. Similarly, 'temple entry' was sometimes defended by extending the argument that the denial of access

[6] Cited in Donald Eugene Smith, *India as a Secular State* (Princeton University Press: Princeton, 1963), p. 239.

to public places on the ground of untouchability was unlawful. However, a contradiction appeared in this 'civil rights' argument since all places of worship were not necessarily thrown open to all citizens; only Hindu temples were declared open for all Hindus, and non-Hindus could be, and actually still are, denied entry. But even more problematically, the right of worship 'of all classes and sections of Hindus' at 'Hindu religious institutions of public character', as Article 25(2) of the Constitution has it, necessarily implies that the state has to take up the onus of interpreting even doctrinal and ritual injunctions in order to assert the *religious* legitimacy of forms of worship that would not be discriminatory in terms of caste.[7]

Still more difficult to justify on non-religious grounds was a reformist law like the Madras Animal and Bird Sacrifices Abolition Act, 1950. The view that animal sacrifices were repugnant and represented a primitive form of worship was clearly the product of a very specific religious interpretation of *religious* ritual, and could be described as a sectional opinion even among Hindus. (It might even be described as a view that was biased against the religious practices of the lower castes, especially in southern India.) Yet in bringing about this 'purification' of the Hindu religion, the legislative wing of the state was seen as the appropriate instrument.

The period after Independence also saw, apart from reformist legislation of this kind, an enormous increase in the involvement of the state administration in the management of the affairs of Hindu temples. The most significant enabling legislation in this regard was the Madras Hindu Religious and Charitable Endowments Act, 1951, which created an entire department of government devoted to the administration of Hindu religious

---

[7] In fact, the courts, recognizing that the right of a religious denomination 'to manage its own affairs in matters of religion' [Article 26(b)] could come into conflict with the right of the state to throw open Hindu temples to all classes of Hindus [Article 25(2)(b)], have had to come up with ingenious, and often extremely arbitrary, arrangements in order to strike a compromise between the two provisions. Some of these judgments are referred to in Smith, *India as a Secular State*, pp 242–3. For a detailed account of a case illustrating the extent of judicial involvement in the interpretation of religious doctrine and ritual, see Arjun Appadurai, *Worship and Conflict Under Colonial Rule: A South India Case* (Cambridge University Press: Cambridge, 1981), pp 36–50.

endowments.[8] The legal argument here is, of course, that the religious denomination concerned still retains the right to manage its own affairs in matters of religion, while the secular matters concerned with the management of the property of the endowment is taken over by the state. But this is a separation of functions that is impossible to maintain in practice. Thus, if the administrators choose to spend the endowment funds on opening hospitals or universities rather than on more elaborate ceremonies or on religious instruction, then the choice will affect the way in which the religious affairs of the endowment are managed. The issue has given rise to several disputes in court about the specific demarcation between the religious and the secular functions, and to further legislation, in Madras as well as in other parts of India. The resulting situation led one commentator in the early 1960s to remark that 'the commissioner for Hindu religious endowments, a public servant of the secular state, today exercises far greater authority over Hindu religion in Madras state than the Archbishop of Canterbury does over the Church of England'.[9]

Once again, it is possible to provide a non-religious ground for state intervention in the administration of religious establishments, namely prevention of misappropriation of endowment funds and ensuring the proper supervision of what is after all a public property. But what has been envisaged and actually practised since

8 Actually, the increased role of the government in controlling the administration of Hindu temples in Madras began with the Religious Endowments Acts of 1925 and 1927. It is interesting to note that there was nationalist opposition to the move at the time. S. Satyamurthi said during the debates in the provincial legislature in 1923 that 'the blighting hand of this Government will also fall tight on our temples and *maths*, with the result that they will also become part of the great machinery which the Hon'ble Minister and his colleagues are blackening every day'. During the debates preceding the 1951 Act, on the other hand, T.S.S. Rajan, the Law Minister, said, '...the fear of interfering with religious institutions has always been there with an alien Government but with us it is very different. Ours may be called a secular Government, and so it is. But it does not absolve us from protecting the funds of the institutions which are meant for the service of the people'. For an account of these changes in law, see Chandra Y. Mudaliar, *The Secular State and Religious Institutions in India: A Study of the Administration of Hindu Public Religious Trusts in Madras* (Fritz Steiner Verlag: Wiesbaden, 1974).
9 Smith, *India as a Secular State*, p. 246.

Independence goes well beyond this strictly negative role of the state. Clearly, the prevailing views about the reform of Hindu religion saw it as entirely fitting that the representative and administrative wings of the state should take up the responsibility of managing Hindu temples in, as it were, the 'public interest' of the general body of Hindus.

The reformist agenda was, of course, carried out most comprehensively during the making of the Constitution and subsequently in the enactment in 1955 of what is known as the Hindu Code Bill.[10] During the discussions, objections were raised that in seeking to change personal law, the state was encroaching upon an area protected by the right to religious freedom. B.R. Ambedkar's reply to these objections summed up the general attitude of the reformist leadership:

The religious conceptions in this country are so vast that they cover every aspect of life from birth to death. There is nothing which is not religion and if personal law is to be saved I am sure about it that in social matters we will come to a standstill....There is nothing extraordinary in saying that we ought to strive hereafter to limit the definition of religion in such a manner that we shall not extend it beyond beliefs and such rituals as may be connected with ceremonials which are essentially religious. It is not necessary that the sort of laws, for instance, laws relating to tenancy or laws relating to succession, should be governed by religion....I personally do not understand why religion should be given this vast expansive jurisdiction so as to cover the whole of life and to prevent the legislature from encroaching upon that field.[11]

Impelled by this reformist urge, the Indian Parliament proceeded to cut through the immensely complicated web of local and sectarian variations that enveloped the corpus known as 'Hindu law' as it had emerged through the colonial courts, and to lay down a single code of personal law for all Hindu citizens. Many of the new provisions were far-reaching in their departure from traditional Brahmanical principles. Thus, the new code legalized inter-caste marriage; it legalized divorce and prohibited polygamy; it

10 Actually, a series of laws called the Hindu Marriage Bill, the Hindu Succession Bill, the Hindu Minority and Guardianship Bill, and the Hindu Adoptions and Maintenance Bill.

11 *Constituent Assembly Debates* (Government of India: New Delhi, 1946–50), vol. 7, p. 781.

gave to the daughter the same rights of inheritance as the son, and permitted the adoption of daughters as well as of sons. In justifying these changes, the proponents of reform not only made the argument that 'tradition' could not remain stagnant and needed to be reinterpreted in the light of changing conditions, but they also had to engage in the exercise of deciding what was or was not essential to 'Hindu religion'. Once again, the anomaly has provoked comments from critical observers: 'An official of the secular state [the law minister] became an interpreter of Hindu religion, quoting and expounding the ancient Sanskrit scriptures in defence of his bill.'[12]

Clearly, it is necessary here to understand the force and internal consistency of the nationalist–modernist project which sought, in one and the same move, to rationalize the domain of religious discourse and to secularize the public domain of personal law. It would be little more than reactionary to rail against the 'Western-educated Hindu' who is scandalized by the profusion of avaricious and corrupt priests at Hindu temples, and who, influenced by Christian ideas of service and piety, rides roughshod over the 'traditional Hindu notions' that a religious gift was never made for any specific purpose; that the priest entrusted with the management of a temple could for all practical purposes treat the property and its proceeds as matters within his personal jurisdiction; and that, unlike the Christian church, a temple was a place 'in which the idol condescends to receive visitors, who are expected to bring offerings with them, like subjects presenting themselves before a maharaja'.[13] More serious, of course, is the criticism that by using the state as the agency of what was very often only religious reform, the political leadership of the new nation-state flagrantly violated the principle of separation of state and religion.[14] This is

12 Smith, *India as a Secular State*, pp 281–2.
13 See, for instance, J. Duncan M. Derrett, 'The Reform of Hindu Religious Endowments', in Smith (ed.), *South Asian Politics and Religion*, pp 311–36.
14 The two most comprehensive studies on the subject of the secular state in India make this point. V.P. Luthera in *The Concept of the Secular State and India* (Oxford University Press: Calcutta, 1964) concludes that India should not properly be regarded as a secular state. D.E. Smith in *India as a Secular State* disagrees, arguing that Luthera bases his conclusion on too narrow a definition of the secular state, but nevertheless points out the numerous anomalies in the current situation.

a matter we will now consider in detail, but it is nevertheless necessary to point out that the violation of this principle of the secular state was justified precisely by the desire to secularize.

## Anomalies of the Secular State

What are the characteristics of the secular state? Three principles are usually mentioned in the liberal-democratic doctrine on this subject.[15] The first is the principle of *liberty* which requires that the state permit the practice of any religion, within the limits set by certain other basic rights which the state is also required to protect. The second is the principle of *equality* which requires that the state not give preference to one religion over another. The third is the principle of *neutrality* which is best described as the requirement that the state not give preference to the religious over the non-religious and which leads, in combination with the liberty and equality principles, to what is known in the US constitutional law as the 'wall-of-separation' doctrine: namely that the state not involve itself with religious affairs or organizations.[16]

Looking now at the doctrine of the secular state as it has evolved in practice in India, it is clear that whereas all three principles have been invoked to justify the secular state, their application has been contradictory and has led to major anomalies. The principle of liberty, which implies a right of freedom of religion, has been incorporated in the Constitution which gives to every citizen— subject to public order, morality, and health—not only the equal

[15] For a recent exchange on this matter, see Robert Audi, 'The Separation of Church and State and the Obligations of Citizenship', *Philosophy and Public Affairs* 18, 3 (Summer 1989), pp 259–96; Paul J. Weithman, 'Separation of Church and State: Some Questions for Professor Audi', *Philosophy and Public Affairs* 20, 1 (Winter 1991), pp 52–65; Robert Audi, 'Religious Commitment and Secular Reason: A Reply to Professor Weithman', *Philosophy and Public Affairs* 20, 1 (Winter 1991), pp 66–76.

[16] The US Supreme Court defined the doctrine as follows: 'Neither a state nor the federal government can set up a church. Neither can pass laws which aid one religion, aid all religions, or prefer one religion over another.... Neither a state nor the federal government can, openly or secretly, participate in the affairs of any religious organization or groups and vice versa.' *Everson v. Board of Education*, 330 US 1 (1947), cited in Smith, *India as a Secular State*, pp 125–6.

right to freedom of conscience but also, quite specifically, 'the right freely to profess, practise and propagate religion'. It also gives 'to every religious denomination or any section thereof certain collective rights of religion'. Besides, it specifically mentions the right of 'all minorities, whether based on religion or language', to establish and administer their own educational institutions. Limiting these rights of freedom of religion, however, is the right of the state to regulate 'any economic, financial, political or other secular activity which may be associated with religious practice', to provide for social welfare and reform, and to throw open Hindu religious institutions to all sections of Hindus. This limit to the liberty principle is what enabled the extensive reform under state auspices of Hindu personal law, and of the administration of Hindu temples.

The liberal-democratic doctrine of freedom of religion does recognize, of course, that this right will be limited by other basic human rights. Thus, for instance, it would be perfectly justified for the state to deny that, let us say, human sacrifice or causing injury to human beings, or as we have already noted in the case of *devadasis*, enforced servitude to a deity or temple, constitutes permissible religious practice. However, it is also recognized that there are many grey areas where it is difficult to lay down the limit. A case very often cited in this connection is the legal prohibition of polygamy even when it may be sanctioned by a particular religion: the argument that polygamy necessarily violates other basic human rights is often thought of as problematical.

But no matter where this limit is drawn, it is surely required by the idea of the secular state that the liberty principle be limited only by the need to protect some other universal basic right, and not by appeal to a particular interpretation of religious doctrine. This, as we have mentioned before, has not been possible in India. The urge to undertake by legislation the reform of Hindu personal law and Hindu religious institutions made it difficult for the state not to transgress into the area of religious reform itself. Both the legislature and the courts were led into the exercise of interpreting religious doctrine on religious grounds. Thus, in deciding the legally permissible limits of state regulation of religious institutions, it became necessary to identify those practices that were *essentially* of a religious character; but, in accordance with the judicial procedures of a modern state, this decision could not be

360 *Secularism and Its Critics*

left to the religious denomination itself but had to be determined 'as an objective question' by the courts.[17] It can be easily seen that this could lead to the entanglement of the state in a series of disputes that are mainly religious in character.

It could, of course, be argued that given the dual character of personal law—inherited from the colonial period as religious law that had been recognized and codified as the laws of the state—and in the absence of appropriate institutions of the Hindu religion through which religious reform could be organized and carried out outside the arena of the state, there was no alternative to state intervention in this matter. Which other agency was there with the requisite power and legitimacy to undertake the reform of religious practices? The force and persuasiveness of this argument for the modernist leadership of independent India can hardly be overstated. The desire was in fact to initiate a process of rational interpretation of religious doctrine, and to find a representative and credible institutional process for the reform of religious practice. That the use of state legislation to achieve this modernist purpose must come into conflict with another modernist principle, of the freedom of religion, is one of the anomalies of the secular state in India.

The second principle—that of equality—is also explicitly recognized in the Indian Constitution which prohibits the state from discriminating against any citizen on the basis only of religion or caste, except when it makes special provisions for the advancement of socially and educationally backward classes or for Scheduled Castes and Scheduled Tribes. Such special provisions in the form of reserved quotas in employment and education, or of reserved seats in representative bodies, have of course led to much controversy in India in the last few decades. But these disputes about the validity or positive discrimination in favour of underprivileged castes or tribes have almost never taken the form of a dispute about equality on the ground of religion. Indeed, although the institution of caste itself is supposed to derive its basis from the doctrines of the Brahmanical religion, the recent debates in the political arena about caste discrimination usually do not make any appeals at all to religious doctrines. There is only one significant way in wh.

---

[17] *Durgah Committee* v. *A. Hussain*, 1961, SC 1402 (1415), cited in Durga D. Basu, *Constitutional Law of India* (Prentice-Hall of India: New Delhi, 1977), p. 84.

the question of positive discrimination in favour of Scheduled
Castes is circumscribed by religion: in order to qualify as a member
of a Scheduled Caste, a person must profess to be either Hindu or
Sikh; a public declaration of the adoption of any other religion
would lead to disqualification. However, in some recent provisions
relating to 'other backward classes', especially in the much-
disputed recommendations of the Mandal Commission, attempts
have been made to go beyond this limitation.

The problem with the equality principle which concerns us
more directly is the way in which it has been affected by the project
of reforming Hindu religion by state legislation. All the legislative
and administrative measures we have mentioned before concern
the institutions and practices of the Hindus, including the reform
of personal laws and of religious endowments. That this was
discriminatory was argued in the 1950s by the socially conservative
sections of Hindu opinion, and by political parties like the Hindu
Mahasabha which were opposed to the idea of reform itself. But
the fact that the use of state legislation to bring about reforms in
only the religion of the majority was creating a serious anomaly
in the very notion of equal citizenship was pointed out by only
a few lone voices within the progressive sections. One such
belonged to J.B. Kripalani, the socialist leader, who argued: 'If we
are a democratic state, I submit we must make laws not for one
community alone....It is not the Mahasabhites who alone are
communal: it is the government also that is communal, whatever
it may say.' Elaborating, he said,

If they [the Members of Parliament] single out the Hindu community for
their reforming zeal, they cannot escape the charge of being communalists
in the sense that they favour the Hindu community and are indifferent
to the good of the Muslim community or the Catholic
community....Whether the marriage bill favours the Hindu community
or places it at a disadvantage, both ways, it becomes a communal
measure.[18]

The basic problem here was obvious. If it was accepted that the
state could intervene in religious institutions or practices in order
to protect other social and economic rights, then what was the
ground for intervening only in the affairs of one religious community and not of others? Clearly, the first principle—that of freedom

18 Cited in Smith, *India as a Secular State*, pp 286, 288.

of religion—could not be invoked here only for the minority communities when it had been set aside in the case of the majority community.

The problem has been got around by resorting to what is essentially a pragmatic argument. It is suggested that for historical reasons, there is a certain lag in the readiness of the different communities to accept reforms intended to rationalize the domain of personal law. In any case, if equality of citizenship is what is desired, it already stands compromised by the very system of religion-based personal laws inherited from colonial times. What should be done, therefore, is to first declare the desirability of replacing the separate personal laws by a uniform civil code, but to proceed towards this objective in a pragmatic way, respecting the sensitivity of the religious communities about their freedom of religion, and going ahead with state-sponsored reforms only when the communities themselves are ready to accept them. Accordingly, there is an item in the non-justiciable Directive Principles of the Constitution which declares that the state should endeavour to provide a uniform civil code for all citizens. On the other hand, those claiming to speak on behalf of the minority communities tend to take a firm stand in the freedom of religion principle, and to deny that the state should have any right at all to interfere in their religious affairs. The anomaly has, in the last few years, provided some of the most potent ammunition to the Hindu right in its campaign against what it describes as the 'appeasement' of minorities.

It would not be irrelevant to mention here that there have also occurred, among the minority religious communities in India, not entirely dissimilar movements for the reform of religious laws and institutions. In the earlier decades of this century, there were organized attempts, for instance, to put an end to local customary practices among Muslim communities in various parts of India and replace them with a uniform Muslim personal law. This campaign, led in particular by the Jamat al-ulama-i—Hind of Deoband—well known for its closeness to the Indian National Congress, was directed against the recognition by the courts of special marriage and inheritance practices among communities such as the Mapilla of southern India, the Memon of western India, and various groups in Rajasthan and Punjab. The argument given was not only that such practices were 'un-Islamic'; specific criticisms were also made of how these customs were backward and iniquitous, especially in the matter of the treatment of women. The preamble to a bill to change the customary succession law of the Mapilla, for instance, said, using a rhetoric not unlike what would be used later for the reform of Hindu law, 'The Muhammadan community now feels the incongruity of the usage and looks upon the prevailing custom as a discredit to their religion and to their community.'[19]

The reform campaigns led to a series of new laws in various provinces and in the central legislature, such as the Mapilla Succession Act, 1918, the Cutchi Memons Act, 1920 and 1938, and the NWFP Muslim Personal Law (Shari`at) Application Act, 1935 (which was the first time that the terms 'Muslim personal law' and 'Shari'at were used interchangeably in law). The culmination of these campaigns for a uniform set of personal laws for all Muslims in India was reached with the passing of the so-called Shari'at Act by the central legislature in 1937. Interestingly, it was because of the persistent efforts of Muhammad Ali Jinnah, whose political standing was in this case exceeded by his prestige as a legal luminary, that only certain sections of this Act were required to be applied compulsorily to all Muslims; on other matters its provisions were optional.

The logic of completing the process of uniform application of Muslim personal law has continued in independent India. The optional clauses in the 1937 Act have been removed. The Act has been applied to areas that were earlier excluded: especially the princely states that merged with India after 1947, the latest in that series being Cooch Behar where the local customary law for Muslims was superseded by the Shari`at laws through legislation by the Left Front government of West Bengal in 1980.

Thus, even while resisting the idea of a uniform civil code on the ground that this would be a fundamental encroachment on the freedom of religion and destructive of the cultural identity of religious minorities, the Muslim leadership in India has not shunned state intervention altogether. One notices, in fact, the same attempt to seek rationalization and uniformity as one sees in the case of Hindu personal law or Hindu religious institutions. The crucial difference after 1947 is, of course, that unlike the majority

---

19 Cited in Tahir Mahmood, *Muslim Personal Law: Role of the State in the Indian Subcontinent* (All India Reporter: Nagpur, 1983), p. 21.

community, the minorities are unwilling to grant to a legislature elected by universal suffrage the power to legislate the reform of their religions. On the other hand, there do not exist any other institutions which have the representative legitimacy to supervise such a process of reform. That, to put it in a nutshell, is the present impasse on the equality principle.

The third principle we have mentioned of the secular state—that of the separation of state and religion—has also been recognized in the Constitution, which declares that there shall be no official state religion, no religious instruction in state schools, and no taxes to support any particular religion. But, as we have seen, the state has become entangled in the affairs of religion in numerous ways. This was the case even in colonial times, but the degree and extent of the entanglement, paradoxically, has increased since Independence. Nor is this involvement limited only to the sorts of cases we have mentioned before, which were the results of state-sponsored religious reform. Many of the older systems of state patronage of religious institutions, carried out by the colonial government or by the princely states, still continue under the present regime. Thus, Article 290A of the Constitution makes a specific provision of money to be paid every year by the governments of Kerala and Tamil Nadu to the Travancore Devaswom Fund. Article 28(2) says that although there will be no religious instruction in educational institutions wholly maintained out of state funds, this would not apply to those institutions where the original endowment or trust requires that religious instruction be given. Under this provision, Banaras Hindu University and Aligarh Muslim University, both central universities, do impart religious instruction. Besides, there are numerous educational institutions all over the country run by religious denominations which receive state financial aid.

The conclusion is inescapable that the 'wall of separation' doctrine of the US constitutional law can hardly be applied to the present Indian situation (as indeed it cannot in the case of many European democracies, but there at least it could be argued that the entanglements are politically insignificant and often obsolete remnants of older legal conventions). This is precisely the ground on which the argument is sometimes made that 'Indian secularism' has to have a different meaning from 'Western secularism'. What is suggested in fact is that the cultural and historical realities of the

Indian situation call for a *different* relationship between state and civil society than what is regarded as normative in Western political discourse, at least in the matter of religion. Sometimes it is said that in Indian conditions, the neutrality principle cannot apply; the state will necessarily have to involve itself in the affairs of religion. What must be regarded as normative here is an extension of the equality principle, that is that the state should favour all religions equally. This argument, however, cannot offer a defence for the selective intervention of the state in reforming the personal laws only of the majority community. On the other hand, arguments are also made about secularism having 'many meanings',[20] suggesting thereby that a democratic state must be expected to protect cultural diversity and the right of people to follow their own culture. The difficulty is that this demand cannot be easily squared with the homogenizing secular desire for, let us say, a uniform civil code.

Where we end up then is in a quandary. The desire for a secular state must concede defeat even as it claims to have discovered new meanings of secularism. On the other hand, the respect for cultural diversity and different ways of life finds it impossible to articulate itself in the unitary rationalism of the language of rights. It seems to me that there is no viable way out of this problem within the given contours of liberal-democratic theory, which must define the relation between the relatively autonomous domains of state and civil society always in terms of individual rights. As has been noticed for many other aspects of the emerging forms of non-Western modernity, this is one more instance where the supposedly universal forms of the modern state turn out to be inadequate for the post-colonial world.

To reconfigure the problem posed by the career of the secular state in India, we will need to locate it on a somewhat different conceptual ground. In the remainder of this paper, I will suggest the outlines of an alternative theoretical argument which holds the promise of taking us outside the dilemmas of the secular modernist discourse. In this, I will not take the easy route of appealing to an 'Indian exception'. In other words, I will not trot out yet another version of the 'new meaning of secularism' argument. But to avoid that route, I must locate my problem on a ground which will

20 Sumit Sarkar, 'The Fascism of the Sangh Parivar'.

include, at one and the same time, the history of the rise of the modern state in both its Western and non-Western forms. I will attempt to do this by invoking Michel Foucault.

## The Liberal-Democratic Conundrum

But before I do that, let me briefly refer to the current state of the debate over minority rights in liberal political theory, and why I think the problem posed by the Indian situation will not find any satisfactory answers within the terms of that debate. A reference to this theoretical corpus is necessary because, first, left democratic thinking in India on secularism and minority rights shares many of its premises with liberal-democratic thought, and second, the legally instituted processes of the state and the public domain in India have clearly avowed affiliations to the conceptual world of liberal political theory. Pointing out the limits of liberal thought will also allow me, then, to make the suggestion that political practice in India must seek to develop new institutional sites that cut across the divide between state sovereignty on the one hand and people's rights on the other.

To begin with, liberal political theory in its strict sense cannot recognize the validity of any collective rights of cultural groups. Liberalism must hold as a fundamental principle the idea that the state, and indeed all public institutions, will treat all citizens equally, regardless of race, sex, religion, or other cultural particularities. It is only when everyone is treated equally, liberals will argue, that the basic needs of people, shared universally by all, can be adequately and fairly satisfied. These universal needs will include not only 'material' goods such as livelihood, health care, and education, but also 'cultural' goods such as religious freedom, free speech, free association, etc. But in order to guarantee freedom and equality at the same time, the locus of rights must be the individual citizen, the bearer of universal needs; to recognize rights that belong only to particular cultural groups within the body of citizens is to destroy both equality and freedom.

Needless to say, this purist version of the liberal doctrine is regarded as unduly rigid and narrow by many who otherwise identify with the values of liberal-democratic politics. But the attempts to make room, within the doctrines of liberalism, for some recognition of collective cultural identities have not yielded solutions that enjoy wide acceptance. I cannot enter here into the details of this controversy which, spurred on by the challenge of 'multiculturalism' in many Western countries, has emerged as perhaps the liveliest area of debate in contemporary liberal philosophy. A mention only of the principal modes of argument insofar as they are relevant to the problems posed by the Indian situation will have to suffice.

One response to the problem of fundamental moral disagreements caused by a plurality of conflicting—and sometimes incommensurable—cultural values is to seek an extension of the principle of neutrality in order to preclude such conflicts from the political arena. The argument here is that, just as in the case of religion, the existence of fundamentally divergent moral values in society would imply that there is no rational way in which reasonable people might resolve the dispute; and since the state should not arbitrarily favour one set of beliefs over another, it must not be asked to intervene in such conflicts. John Rawls and Thomas Nagel, among others, have made arguments of this kind, seeking thereby to extend the notions of state impartiality and religious toleration to other areas of moral disagreement.[21]

Not all liberals, however, like the deep scepticism and 'epistemic abstinence' implied in this view.[22] More relevant for us, however, is the criticism made from within liberal theory that these attempts to cope with diversity by taking the disputes off the political agenda are 'increasingly evasive. They offer a false impartiality in place of social recognition of the persistence of fundamental conflicts of value in our society'.[23] If this is a judgement that can be made for societies where the 'wall of separation' doctrine is solidly established, the remoteness of these arguments from the realities of the Indian situation hardly needs to be emphasized.

21 John Rawls, 'Justice as Fairness: Political not Metaphysical', *Philosophy and Public Affairs* 14 (1985), pp 248–51; John Rawls, 'The Priority of the Right and Ideas of the Good', *Philosophy and Public Affairs* 17 (1988), pp 260–4; Thomas Nagel, 'Moral Conflict and Political Legitimacy', *Philosophy and Public Affairs* 16 (1987), pp 218–40.

22 For instance, Joseph Raz, 'Facing Diversity: The Case of Epistemic Abstinence', *Philosophy and Public Affairs* 19 (1990), pp 3–46.

23 Amy Gutmann and Dennis Thompson, 'Moral Conflict and Political Consensus', *Ethics* 101 (October 1990), pp 64–88.

However, rather than evade the question of cultural diversity, some theorists have attempted to take up the 'justice as fairness' idea developed by liberals such as John Rawls and Ronald Dworkin, and extend it to cultural groups. Justice, according to this argument, requires that undeserved or 'morally arbitrary' disadvantages should be removed or compensated for. If such disadvantages attach to persons because they were born into particular minority cultural groups, then liberal equality itself must demand that individual rights be differentially allocated on the basis of culture. Will Kymlicka has made such a case for the recognition of the rights of cultural minorities whose very survival as distinct groups is in question.[24]

We should note, of course, that the examples usually given in this liberal literature to illustrate the need for minority cultural rights are those of the indigenous peoples of North America and Australia. But in principle there is no reason why the argument about 'being disadvantaged' should be restricted only to such indubitable cases of endangered cultural groups; it should apply to any group that can be reasonably defined as a cultural minority within a given political entity. And this is where its problems as a liberal theory become insuperable. Could a collective cultural right be used as an instrument to perpetuate thoroughly illiberal practices within the group? Would individual members of such groups have the right to leave the group? If an individual right of exit is granted, would that not in effect undermine the right of the group to preserve its identity? On the other hand, if a right of exit is denied, would we still have a liberal society?[25]

Clearly, it is extremely hard to justify the granting of substantively different collective rights to cultural groups on the basis of liberalism's commitment to procedural equality and universal citizenship. Several recent attempts to make a case for special rights for cultural minorities and oppressed groups, have consequently gone on to question the idea of universal citizenship itself: in doing

[24] Will Kymlicka, *Liberalism, Community and Culture* (Oxford University Press: Oxford, 1989).
[25] See, for example the following exchange: Chandran Kukathas, 'Are there any Cultural Rights?' and Will Kymlicka, 'The Rights of Minority Cultures', *Political Theory* 20, 1 (February 1992), pp 105–46; Kukathas, 'Cultural Rights Again', *Political Theory* 20, 4 (November 1992), pp 674–80.

this, the arguments come fairly close to upholding some sort of cultural relativism. The charge that is made against universal citizenship is not merely that it forces everyone into a single homogeneous cultural mould, thus threatening the distinct identities of minority groups, but that the homogeneous mould itself is by no means a neutral one, being invariably the culture of the dominant group, so that it is not everybody but only the minorities and the disadvantaged who are forced to forego their cultural identities. That being the case, neither universalism nor neutrality can have any moral priority over the rights of cultural groups to protect their autonomous existence.

Once again, arguments such as this go well beyond the recognized limits of the liberal doctrine; and even those who are sympathetic to the demands for the protection of plural cultural identities feel compelled to assert that the recognition of difference cannot mean the abandonment of all commitment to a universalist framework of reason.[26] Usually, therefore, the 'challenge of multiculturalism' is sought to be met by asserting the value of diversity itself for the flowering of culture, and making room for divergent ways of life *within* a fundamentally agreed set of universalist values. Even when one expects recognition of one's 'right to culture', therefore, one must always be prepared to act within a culture of rights and thus give reasons for insisting on being different.[27]

None of these liberal arguments seem to have enough strength to come to grips with the problems posed by the Indian situation. Apart from resorting to platitudes about the value of diversity, respect for other ways of life, and the need for furthering understanding between different cultures, they do not provide any means for relocating the institutions of rights or refashioning the practices of identity in order to get out of what often appears to be a political impasse.

[26] See, for example, Charles Taylor, *Multiculturalism and the Politics of Recognition* (Princeton University Press: Princeton, 1992); Amy Gutmann, 'The Challenge of Multiculturalism in Political Ethics', *Philosophy and Public Affairs* 22 (1993), pp 73–206.

[27] Rajeev Bhargava has sought to make the case for the rights of minorities in India in these terms. See 'The Right to Culture', in K.N. Panikkar (ed.), *Communalism in India: History, Politics and Culture* (Manohar: New Delhi, 1991), pp 165–72.

## Governmentality

I make use of Foucault's idea of governmentality not because I think it is conceptually neat or free of difficulties. Nor is the way in which I will use the idea here one that, as far as I know, Foucault has advanced himself. I could have, therefore, gone on from the preceding paragraph to set out my own scheme for re-problematizing the issue of secularism in India, without making this gesture towards Foucault. The reason I think the reference is necessary, however, is that by invoking Foucault I will be better able to emphasize the need to shift our focus from the rigid framework laid out by the concepts of sovereignty and right, to the constantly shifting *strategic* locations of the politics of identity and difference.

Foucault's idea of governmentality[28] reminds us, first, that cutting across the liberal divide between state and civil society there is a very specific form of power that entrenches itself in modern society, having as its goal the well-being of a population, its mode of reasoning a certain instrumental notion of economy, and its apparatus an elaborate network of surveillance. True, there have been other attempts at conceptualizing this ubiquitous form of modern power: most notably in Max Weber's theory of rationalization and bureaucracy, or more recently in the writings of the Frankfurt School, and in our own time in those of Jürgen Habermas. However, unlike Weberian sociology, Foucault's idea of governmentality does not lend itself to appropriation by a liberal doctrine characterizing the state as a domain of coercion ('monopoly of legitimate violence') and civil society as the zone of freedom. The idea of governmentality—and this is its second important feature—insists that by exercising itself through forms of representation, and hence by offering itself as an aspect of the self-disciplining of the very population over which it is exercised, the modern form of power, whether inside or outside the domain of the state, is capable of allowing for an immensely flexible braiding of coercion and consent.

[28] See, in particular, Michel Foucault, 'Governmentality', in Garham Burchell, Colin Gordon and Peter Miller (eds), *The Foucault Effect: Studies in Governmentality* (University of Chicago Press: Chicago, 1991), pp 87–104; and 'Politics and Reason', in Foucault, *Politics, Philosophy, Culture: Interviews and Other Writings 1977–84* (Routledge: New York, 1988), pp 57–85.

If we bear in mind these features of the modern regime of power, it will be easier for us to grasp what is at stake in the politics of secularization. It is naive to think of secularization as simply the onward march of rationality, devoid of coercion and power struggles. Even if secularization as a process of the decreasing significance of religion in public life is connected with such 'objective' social process as mechanization or the segmentation of social relationships (as sociologists such as Bryan Wilson have argued),[29] it does not necessarily evoke a uniform set of responses from all groups. Indeed, contrary phenomena such as religious revivalism, fundamentalism, and the rise of new cults have sometimes also been explained as the consequence of the same processes of mechanization or segmentation. Similarly, arguments about the need to hold on to a universalist framework of reason even as one acknowledges the fact of difference ('deliberative universalism' or 'discourse ethics') tend to sound like pious homilies because they ignore the strategic context of power in which identity or difference is often asserted.

The limit of liberal-rationalist theory is reached when one is forced to acknowledge that, within the specific strategic configuration of a power contestation, what is asserted in a collective cultural right is in fact *the right not to offer a reason for being different*. Thus when a minority group demands a cultural right, it in fact says, 'We have our own reasons for doing things the way we do, but since you don't share the fundamentals of our worldview, you will never come to understand or appreciate those reasons. Therefore, leave us alone and let us mind our own business'. If this demand is admitted, it amounts in effect to a concession to cultural relativism.

But the matter does not necessarily end there. Foucault's notion of governmentality leads us to examine the other aspect of this strategic contestation. Why is the demand made in the language of rights? Why are the ideas of autonomy and freedom invoked? Even as one asserts a basic incommensurability in frameworks of reason, why does one nevertheless say, 'We have our own reasons'?

29 Bryan Wilson, *Religion in Secular Society* (Watts: London, 1966); Wilson, *Religion in Sociological Perspective* (Oxford University Press: Oxford, 1982). Also, David Martin, *A General Theory of Secularization* (Basil Blackwell: Oxford, 1978).

Consider then the two aspects of the process that Foucault describes as the 'governmentalization of the state': juridical sovereignty on the one hand, governmental technology on the other. In his account of this process in Western Europe since the eighteenth century, Foucault tends to suggest that the second aspect completely envelops and contains the first.[30] That is to say, in distributing itself throughout the social body by means of the technologies of governmental power, the modern regime no longer retains a distinct aspect of sovereignty. I do not think, however, that this is a necessary implication of Foucault's argument. On the contrary, I find it more useful—especially of course in situations where the sway of governmental power is far from general—to look for a disjuncture between the two aspects, and thus to identify the sites of application of power where governmentality is unable to successfully encompass sovereignty.

The assertion of minority cultural rights occurs on precisely such a site. It is because of a contestation on the ground of sovereignty that the right is asserted *against governmentality*. To say 'We will not give reasons for not being like you' is to resist entering that deliberative or discursive space where the technologies of governmentality operate. But then, in a situation like this, the only way to resist submitting to the powers of sovereignty is literally to declare oneself unreasonable.

## Toleration and Democracy

It is necessary for me to clarify here that in the remainder of this paper, I will be concerned exclusively with finding a defensible argument for minority cultural rights in the given legal–political situation prevailing in India. I am not therefore proposing an

---

30 'Maybe what is really important for our modernity—that is, for our present—is not so much the *étatisation* of society, as the "governmentalization" of the state.... This governmentalization of the state is a singularly paradoxical phenomenon, since if in fact the problems of governmentality and the techniques of government have become the only political issue, the only real space for political struggle and contestation, this is because the governmentalization of the state is at the same time what has permitted the state to survive, and it is possible to suppose that if the state is what it is today, this is so precisely thanks to this governmentality, which is at once internal and external to the state....' (Foucault, 'Governmentality', p. 103).

abstract institutional scheme for the protection of minority rights in general. Nor will I be concerned with hypothetical questions such as: 'If your proposal is put into practice, what will happen to national unity?' I am not arguing from the position of the state; consequently, the problem as I see it, is not what the state, or those who think and act on behalf of the state, can grant to the minorities. My problem is to find a defensible ground for a strategic politics, both within and outside the field defined by the institutions of the state, in which a minority group, or one who is prepared to think from the position of a minority group, can engage in India today.

When a group asserts a right against governmentality, that is a right not to offer reasons for being different, can it expect others to respect its autonomy and be tolerant of its 'unreasonable' ways? The liberal understanding of toleration will have serious problems with such a request. If toleration is the willing acceptance of something of which one disapproves, then it is usually justified on one of three grounds: a contractualist argument (persons entering into the social contract cannot know beforehand which religion they will end up having and hence, will agree to mutual toleration),[31] a consequentialist argument (the consequences of acting tolerantly are better than those of acting intolerantly),[32] or an argument about respect for persons.[33] We have already pointed out the inappropriateness of a contractualist solution to the problems posed by the Indian situation. The consequentialist argument is precisely what is used when it is said that one must go slow on the universal civil code. But this is only a pragmatic argument for toleration, based on a tactical consideration about the costs of imposing what is otherwise the right thing to do. As such, it always remains vulnerable to righteous moral attack.

The principle of respect for persons does provide a moral argument for toleration. It acknowledges the right of the tolerated,

31 The most well-known such argument is in John Rawls, *A Theory of Justice* (Oxford University Press: London, 1971), pp 205–21.
32 See for instance Preston King, *Toleration* (George, Allen and Unwin: London, 1976); D.D. Raphael, 'The Intolerable', in Susan Mendus (ed.), *Justifying Toleration: Conceptual and Historical Perspectives* (Cambridge University Press: Cambridge, 1988), pp 137–53.
33 For instance, Joseph Raz, 'Autonomy, Toleration and the Harm Principle', in Mendus (ed.), *Justifying Toleration*, pp 155–75.

and construes toleration as something that can be claimed as an entitlement. It also sets limits to toleration and thereby resolves the problem of justifying something of which one disapproves: toleration is required by the principle of respect for persons, but practices which fail to show respect for persons need not be tolerated. Applying this principle to the case of minority cultural rights, one can easily see where the difficulty will arise. If a group is intolerant towards its own members and shows inadequate respect for persons, how can it claim tolerance from others? If indeed the group chooses not to enter into a reasonable dialogue with others on the validity of its practices, how can it claim respect for its ways?

Once again, I think that the strategic location of the contestation over cultural rights is crucial. The assertion of a right to be different does not exhaust all of the points where the contestation is grounded. Equally important is the other half of the assertion: 'We have our own reasons for doing things the way we do'. This implies the existence of a field of reasons, of processes through which reasons can be exchanged and validated, even if such processes are open only to those who share the viewpoint of the group. The existence of this autonomous discursive field may only be implied and not activated, but the implication is a necessary part of the assertion of cultural autonomy as a matter of *right*.[34]

The liberal doctrine tends to treat the question of collective rights of cultural minorities from a position of externality. Thus, its usual stand on tolerating cultural groups with illiberal practices is to advocate some sort of right of exit for individual dissident members. (One is reminded of the insistence of the liberal Jinnah that not all sections of the Shari`at Bill should apply compulsorily to all Muslims.) The argument I am advancing would, however,

---

[34] In some ways, this is the obverse of the implication which Ashis Nandy derives from his Gandhian conception of tolerance. His 'religious' conception of tolerance 'must impute to other faiths the same spirit of tolerance. Whether a large enough proportion of those belonging to the other religious traditions show in practice and at a particular point of time and place the same tolerance or not is a secondary matter.' Because it is the imputation or presumption of tolerance in others, not its existence, which defines one's own tolerance…'. Nandy, 'The Politics of Secularism'. My search is in the other direction. I am looking for a 'political' conception of tolerance which will set out the practical conditions I must meet in order to demand and expect tolerance from others.

give a very different construction to the concept of toleration. Toleration here would require one to accept that there will be political contexts where a group could insist on its right not to give reasons for doing things differently, provided it explains itself adequately in its own chosen forum. In other words, toleration here would be premised on autonomy and respect for persons, but it would be sensitive to the varying political salience of the institutional contexts in which reasons are debated.

To return to the specificities of the Indian situation, then, my approach would not call for any axiomatic approval to a uniform civil code for all citizens. Rather, it would start from the historically given reality of separate religion-based personal laws and the intricate involvement of state agencies in the affairs of religious institutions. Here, equal citizenship already stands qualified by the legal recognition of religious differences; the 'wall of separation' doctrine cannot be strictly applied either. Given the inapplicability of the neutrality principle, therefore, it becomes necessary to find a criterion by which state involvement, when it occurs in the domain of religion, can appear to the members of a religious group as both legitimate and fair. It seems to me that toleration, as described above, can supply us with this criterion.

Let us construct an argument for someone who is prepared to defend the cultural rights of minority religious groups in India. The 'minority group', she will say, is not the invention of some perverse sectarian imagination: it is an actually existing category of Indian citizenship—constitutionally defined, legally administered, and politically invoked at every opportunity. Some people in India happen to be born into minority groups; a few others choose to enter them by conversion. In either case, many aspects of the status of such people as legal and political subjects are defined by the fact that they belong to minority groups. If there is any perversity in this, our advocate will point out, it lies in the specific compulsion of the history of the Indian state and its nationalist politics. That being so, one could not fairly be asked to simply forget one's status as belonging to a minority. What must be conceded instead is one's right to negotiate that status in the public arena.

Addressing the general body of citizens from her position within the minority group, then, our advocate will demand toleration for the beliefs of the group. On the other hand, addressing other members of her group, she will demand that the group publicly seek and obtain from its members consent for its practices, in so far as those practices have regulative power over the members. She will point out that if the group was to demand and expect toleration from others, it would have to satisfy the condition of representativeness. Our advocate will therefore demand more open and democratic debate within her community. Even if it is true, she will say, that the validity of the practices of the religious group can be discussed and judged only in its own forums, those institutions must satisfy the same criteria of publicity and representativeness that members of the group demand of all public institutions having regulatory functions. That, she will insist, is the necessary implication of engaging in the politics of collective rights.

She will not of course claim to have a blueprint of the form of representative institutions which her community might develop, and she will certainly resist any attempt by the state to legislate into existence representative bodies for minority groups as prerequisites for the protection of minority rights. The appropriate representative bodies, she will know, could only achieve their actual form through a political process carried out primarily within each minority group. But by resisting, on the one hand, the normalizing attempt of the national state to define, classify, and fix the identity of minorities on their behalf (the minorities, while constituting a legally distinct category of citizens, can only be acted upon by the general body of citizens; they cannot represent themselves), and demanding, on the other, that regulative powers within the community be established on a more democratic and internally representative basis, our protagonist will try to engage in a strategic politics that is neither integrationist nor separatist. She will in fact locate herself precisely at the cusp where she can face, on the one side, the assimilationist powers of governmental technology and resist, on the grounds of autonomy and self-representation, its universalist idea of citizenship; and, on the other side, struggle, once again on the grounds of autonomy and self-representation, for the emergence of more representative public institutions and practices within her community.

Needless to say, there will be many objections to her politics, even from her own comrades. Would not her disavowal of the idea of universal citizenship mean a splitting up of national society into mutually exclusive and rigidly separated ethnic groups? To this question, our protagonist could give the abstract answer that universal citizenship is merely the form offered by the bourgeois-liberal state to ensure the legal–political conditions for the deployment and exploitation of differences in civil society; universal citizenship normalizes the reproduction of differences by pretending that everyone is the same. More concretely, she could point out that nowhere has the sway of universal citizenship meant the end of either ethnic difference or discrimination on cultural grounds. The lines of difference and discrimination dissolve at some points, only to reappear at others. What is problematic here is not so much the existence of bounded categories of population, which the classificatory devices of modern governmental technologies will inevitably impose, but rather the inability of people to negotiate, through a continuous and democratic process of self-representation, the actual content of those categories. That is the new politics that one must try to initiate within the old forms of the modern state.

She will also be asked whether, by discounting universal citizenship, she is not throwing away the possibility of using the emancipatory potential of the ideas of liberty and equality. After all, does not the liberal–secular idea of equal rights still hold out the most powerful ideological means to fight against unjust and often tyrannical practices within many religious communities, especially regarding the treatment of women? To this, the answer will be that it is not a choice of one or the other. To pursue a strategic politics of demanding toleration, one would not need to oppose the liberal–secular principles of the modern state. One would, however, need to rearrange one's strategic priorities. One would be rather more sceptical of the promise that an interventionist secular state would, by legislation or judicial decisions, bring about progressive reform within minority religious groups. Instead, one would tend to favour the harder option, which rests on the belief that if the struggle is for progressive change in social practices sanctioned by religion, then that struggle must be launched and won within the religious communities themselves. There are no historical shortcuts here.

A strategic politics of demanding toleration does not require one to regurgitate the tired slogans about the universality of discursive reason. Instead, it takes seriously the possibility that at particular conjunctures and on specific issues, there could occur an honest refusal to engage in reasonable discourse. But it does not, for that reason, need to fully subscribe to a theory of cultural relativism. Indeed, it could claim to be agnostic in this matter. All it needs to do is to locate itself at those specific points where universal discourse is resisted (remembering that those points could not exhaust the whole field of politics: for example those who will refuse to discuss their rules of marriage or inheritance in a general legislative body might be perfectly willing to debate in that forum the rates of income tax or the policy of public health), and then engage in a twofold struggle—resist homogenization from the outside, and push for democratization inside. That, in brief, would be a strategic politics of toleration.

Contrary to the apprehensions of many who think of minority religious groups as inherently authoritarian and opposed to the democratization of their religious institutions, it is unlikely, I think, that the principal impediment to the opening of such processes within the religious communities will come from the minority groups themselves. There is considerable historical evidence to suggest that when collective cultural rights have been asserted on behalf of minority religious groups in India, they have often been backed by the claim of popular consent through democratic processes. Thus, the campaign in the 1920s for reform in the management of Sikh gurudwaras was accompanied by the Akali demand that Sikh shrines and religious establishments be handed over to elected bodies. Indeed, the campaign was successful in forcing a reluctant colonial government to provide, in the Sikh Gurudwaras and Shrines Bill, 1925, for a committee elected by all adult Sikhs, men and women, to take over the management of Sikh religious places.[35] The Shiromani Gurudwara Prabandhak Committee was perhaps the first legally constituted public body in colonial India for which the principle of universal suffrage was recognized. It is also important to note that the so-called 'traditional' *ulema* in India, when campaigning in the 1920s for the reform of Muslim religious institutions demanded from the colonial government that officially appointed bodies such as Wakf committees be replaced by representative bodies elected by local Muslims.[36] The persuasive

[35] For this history, see Mohinder Singh, *The Akali Movement* (Macmillan: Delhi, 1978).
[36] Tahir Mahmood, *Muslim Personal Law*, pp 66–7.

force of the claim for representativeness is often irresistible in the politics of collective rights.

The more serious opposition to this proposal is likely to come from those who will see in the representative public institutions of the religious communities, a threat to the sovereign powers of the state. If such institutions are to be given any role in the regulation of the lives and activities of its members, then their very stature as elected bodies representative of their constituents will be construed as diminishing the sovereignty of the state. I can hear the murmurs already: 'Remember how the SGPC was used to provide legitimacy to Sikh separatism? Imagine what will happen if Muslims get their own parliament!' The deadweight of juridical sovereignty cannot be easily pushed aside even by those who otherwise subscribe to ideas of autonomy and self-regulating civil social institutions.

I do not, therefore, make these proposals for a reconfiguration of the problem of secularism in India and a redefinition of the concept of toleration with any degree of optimism. All I can hope for is that, faced with a potentially disastrous political impasse, some at least will prefer to err on the side of democracy.

# 12

# Secularism, Nationalism, and Modernity*

*Akeel Bilgrami*

## I

The deployment of the term 'modernity' in the rhetoric of contemporary culture is various, and variously nuanced. The source of this variety lies partly in its being what J.L. Austin once called a 'boo/hurrah', word; that is in its deployment both as a term of commendation and opprobrium. In this article I will look at the present tendency of certain sections of the Indian intelligentsia to see modernity as the source of our present communal troubles. I will be opposing this tendency, but not so much to praise 'modernity' as to bury it as a category of analysis. I will argue that there should be a moratorium on terms such as 'modernity' and the disputes surrounding them, for they are not categories that enhance explanation and understanding of political and cultural developments in contemporary Indian politics and history.

The specific target of the recent attack on 'modernity' is the conception of a modern and secular state that emerged during the ideological articulations of the nationalist movement, and flowered as a fully-fledged vision in the years of independence under Nehru's leadership, mostly due to his own explicit articulations and efforts

* I am grateful for comments and advice to Sumit Sarkar, Rajeev Bhargava, Aijaz Ahmad, Sugata Bose, Amartya Sen, and to questions and comments from members of various audiences present when I delivered this paper, of which this is an edited transcript, at Delhi University, JNU, Harvard University, Yale University, and Columbia University.

at construction of a modern nation-state. I don't particularly wish to defend Nehru (though a glance at the deterioration of politics since his time suggests that there is much in him to be defended), so much as to say that the whole dispute is ill-configured.

The present anti-modernist and anti-nationalist mood is very widespread and may be found in a variety of scholarly and journalistic writing on a range of different subjects, but I will, for the sake of precision and detail, focus on the writings of Ashis Nandy, which grapple specifically with the subject of communalism and secularism in Indian politics.

His work has been widely influential not only in academic circles but also amongst intelligentsia at large because we have all been so struck by the extremity of the recent communalist tendency, that we yearn for that extremity to be matched in an exaggeratedly radical explanation of it, which is offered by the unambiguous anti-modernist historical analysis that Nandy's writings provide.

Let us then begin with a question that is perhaps on all our minds. For seventeen initial years the leadership of independent India fell into the hands of Nehru and the Congress Party. Nehru's vision of a modern, secular India is generally conceded even by his most vocal critics as being a genuine and honourable commitment. A comparison with the long stretches of either anti-secular or undemocratic regimes in Pakistan after the untimely death of Jinnah (who after leading a communal nationalist movement adopted much the same vision as Nehru's for the newly created Muslim nation), and also a comparison with what might have happened if some other leaders had been at the helm in India instead of Nehru, must allow the conclusion that to a considerable degree Nehru did succeed. But if we look around us today in the period before and after the destruction of the mosque at Ayodhya, we can only judge the secular success of his long rule as, at best, a holding process. To describe Nehru's success in terms of a holding process is of course to describe it as a success of a very limited sort. The question then is: Why is it that the Nehruvian vision of a secular India failed to take hold?

Nandy's answer and the general sense of the intelligentsia is that there was something deeply flawed in the vision itself. On this there is a mounting consensus, and indeed I think it would be accurate to say that in the past few years there has been widespread and accumulated deflation of Nehru's stature to be found in the intellectual and political mood of the country.[1] I want to briefly assess this mood because I believe there is much that is mistaken in its principal claims. I also think that there is a strand of criticism that can be made against the general trajectory of Nehruvian secular thought that does not emerge at all in Nandy's anti-modernist polemic, but one that is worth airing because it provides a different answer from that given by Nandy to the question posed above; and it may also provide an instructive basis for rethinking the methodological and philosophical bases for secularism in India. However, I will not be able to substantially develop any positive suggestions in this brief discussion.[2]

The contemporary critique of Nehru usually begins by laying down a fundamental distinction in the very idea of religion, a distinction between religions as faiths and ways of life, on the one hand, and as constructed ideologies, on the other. This is intended as a contrast between a more accommodating, non-monolithic, and pluralist religious folk tradition of Hinduism and Islam, on the one hand, and the Brahmanical RSS and Muslim League versions of them on the other. The latter are said to amount to constructed religious ideologies that were intolerant of heterodoxy within themselves as well as intolerant of one another. The critique's target is by implication modernity itself, for its claim is that it is the polity in its modern framework of *nationhood and its statecraft* which is the source of such ideological constructions, distorting those more 'innocent' aspects of religion that amount to 'ways of life' rather than systems of thought geared to political advancement. The critique then suggests that once one accepts the inevitability of the ideological framework of modernity, then there is nothing left to do in combating sectarian and communal sentiment and action than to formulate a secular vision which *itself* amounts to an oppressive nationalist and statist ideology. Thus Nehru's vision would be described as one of a modernist tyranny

---

[1] This is not just on the issue of secularism of course, but equally so on issues of political economy.

[2] I do develop in more positive detail the alternative conception of the secular ideal, only passingly hinted at the end of this article, in my forthcoming *Politics and the Moral Psychology of Cultural Identity* (Harvard University Press, also to be published by Oxford University Press in India).

that just as surely (as the narrow communalisms) stands against the pluralist and tolerant traditions that existed in the uncontaminated traditions of religions as faiths and ways of life prior to modernity's distortions. That was Nehru's primary contribution then: a perversely modernist and rationalist imposition of a vision that was foreign to the natural tendencies of Hinduism and Islam in their traditional pre-modern spiritual and societal formations, a vision accompanied by all the destructive modern institutional commitment to centralized government, parliamentary democracy, not to mention heavy industry as well as metropolitan consumption and displacement of traditional ways of life. The echoes of Gandhi here are vivid, and Ashis Nandy is explicit in describing this alternative secular vision in Gandhian terms.

This critique of Nehru is careful (though perhaps not always careful enough) to be critical also of contemporary Hindu nationalism in India, as was Gandhi himself, despite his Hinduism and his traditionalism. Nandy makes great dialectical use of the fact that Gandhi was assassinated by a Hindu nationalist, arguing that Gandhi's politics and pluralist version of Hinduism posed a threat to the élitist pseudo-unification of Hinduism that flowered in the ideology of upper-caste Hindus and in orthodox Brahmanical culture, as represented paradigmatically in the Chitpavans, the caste to which Nathuram Godse (his assassin) belonged.

Now it should be emphasized that what is novel and interesting about this critique of Hindu nationalism is that it is intended to be *part of a larger critique* in two different ways.

First, it is intended as part of a *general* diagnosis in which Hindu Nationalism is to be seen as a special instance of the more general wrong that is identified in nationalism itself, which is a modern state of mind in which the very ideal of 'nation' has built into it as a form of necessity the ideal of a nation-state, with its commitment to such things as development, national security, rigidly codified forms of an increasingly centralized polity, and above all the habit of exclusion of some other people or nation in its very self-definition and self-understanding. There is apparently no separating these more general wrongs of nationalism from what is wrong with Hindu nationalism, for otherwise we would have missed the more hidden explanatory conceptual sources of this particular movement.

Second, the critique of Hindu nationalism is intended to be *of*

384 Secularism and Its Critics

*a piece* with the critique of Nehruvian secularism. That is, such a communal nationalism, itself a product of modernity, owes its very existence to the oppositional but at the same time *internal* dialectical relation it bears to that other product of modernity, Nehruvian secularism. The claim is that the latter is an alien imposition upon a people who have never wished to separate religion from politics in their everyday life and thinking, and therefore leaves that people no choice but to turn to the only religious politics allowed by modernity's stranglehold, that is Hindu nationalism. Thus secular tyranny breeds Hindu nationalist resistance, which threatens with the promise of its own form of tyranny. Such are the travails that modernity has visited upon us.

Both these underlying features of the argument are of the utmost importance to it, and they are what make it genuinely interesting: but the arugment's effort at explaining the failure of Nehruvian secularism is greatly marred by its narrowing and uncritical anti-nationalism, its skewed historiography, and its traditionalist nostalgia. In consequence it mislocates the real fault-line in the secular doctrines of the nationalist movement, which have nothing much to do with 'modernity'. But before I get to that, let me say something by way of secpticism about some of its central diagnostic claims.

First of all, though there is no gainsaying the humanism inherent in Gandhi's politics, it is also foolish and sentimental to deny the Brahmanical elements in it. There is the plain and well-known fact that Gandhi, no less than the Chitpavan nationalist Tilak (however different their nationalist sensibilities were in other respects), encouraged the communal Hindu elements in the national movement by using Hindu symbolism to mobilize mass nationalist feeling. As is also well known, his support of the reactionary Muslim Khilafat movement had exactly the same motives and the same communalist effect on the Muslim population. I won't say a word more about this since this point is very well understood by many who have studied the national movement, even cursorily. More importantly, there is some strenuous simplification in the critique's insistence that nationalism was the bad seed that turned a more pristine Hinduism and Islam into communal ideologies in India.

As I said, Nandy has a deep dislike of Hindu nationalists and it is quite unfair and missing the point to simply criticize him, as many have done, for holding a view convergent with Hindutvà ideology just because he is critical of Nehru and secularism. However, despite his differences with and abhorrence for them, on a quite different and much more theoretical plane, there is an assumption of some importance shared by Nandy and the Hindu nationalists he is criticizing. This is the assumption that nationalism is a single element that may be transparently grasped. How do they both share it?

The Hindu nationalists subscribe to this assumption in their conviction that there is no genuinely nationalist position other than theirs. This egregiously overlooks the fact that at present, with all the obsessive globalization and surrender to the demands of international capital and the credit agencies of the West, it is *nationalism* that is and must be a central plank in any genuinely Left programme that resists this tendency.

Equally, on the other hand, Nandy subscribes to the assumption for the quite different reason that he believes that nationalism is the single and common explanatory category that underlies the wrongs of the seemingly diverse and opposed standpoints of both secularism and Hindu nationalism. However, as Lenin convincingly pointed out, it is not a single category and is in fact far more omnibus and frustrating to analyse than Nandy allows and for that reason it is unlikely that it can be an explanatory concept at all. The variety of nationalisms, indeed the variety of ingredients that go into particular nationalisms at different stages and sometimes even at the same stage, make this inevitable. Some obvious examples: (1) it is plain for all to see that it would serve no purpose, for instance, to lump together, say, Palestinian nationalism with Zionist nationalism; (2) nor serve any explanatory purpose to lump together German nationalism in the following four periods: before 1848, after 1918, under Bismarck, and under Nazism; (3) closer to our specific area of interest, it would be pointless to integrate in any explanation, on the one hand, Jinnah's and the Muslim League's nationalism in its first two decades with, on the other hand, his nationalism after several frustrated dealings with the Congress party in the 1920s and his return to India after his failures in England. Just these three examples respectively show, (1) that nationalism can displace a people from their homeland or strive to find a state for a displaced people; (2) it can have an intrinsic tie to social democracy, liberal democracy, autocracy, or fascism;

(3) it can work harmoniously with other communities and its representatives in an anti-imperialist struggle or it can be as divisive of a people in its anti-imperialist struggle as the imperialism it struggles against is in the policies by which it rules over the same people. All these ingredients of nationalism are themselves often explained by underlying economic and social forces and interests in different periods, or sometimes warring with one another in the same period. The Indian National Congress, almost throughout its long history, has provided a home for most of these ingredients of nationalism and has, not surprisingly, represented a variety of the underlying social and economic interests. We cannot therefore assume that the failures of Nehru's secularism are going to be usefully and illuminatingly diagnosed in any terms that give a central and clear place to some transparently grasped notion of 'nationalism'.

There is a sort of desperate, last-ditch retort of those who resist the point I am making here against Nandy's generalized anti-nationalism. The point, remember, is not merely that not all nationalisms are bad, but that 'nationalism' is not transparently characterizeable. The retort is that for all this lack of transparency, there is an undeniable defining exclusivity that unites all the many kinds of nationalism that I am insisting on.

The significance of this claim is highly questionable. One of the frustrating features that go into making 'nationalism' the compendious and opaque notion it is, is that some of its most narrowing and tyrannical aspects are a product of it being neurotically *inclusivist* (as, to take just one example, in the 'national' image of Pakistan during Zia's regime). To say, in these contexts, that nationalism is defined upon exclusivity rings false because the fact that it excludes some people or other is innocuous and academic, when compared to the fact that what is most salient about it is that it lends a deaf ear to the demands of regional autonomy because of its *inclusivism* (in the name of Islam, in our example). In these contexts, that inclusivism is its defining feature and the exclusivism peripheral.

Now it is possible to respond in defence of Nandy, and in a sense respond correctly, that in most cases of such inclusivism there is an *underlying* exclusivity having to do with the fact that a set of dominant economic interests at the centre find it necessary to *exclude* regional interests, particularly the interests of the regional masses, even as they insistently *include* them *superficially* into the ideal of the nation (in Pakistan's case, via an appeal to Islamist ideology). That is to say the inclusivist, unifying nationalist image of an Islamist Pakistan is an ideological perpetration in order for an underlying exclusivist agenda for a dominant, centrist, Punjabi ruling-élite to maintain their hold over the bureaucracy (and the military) and, thereby, eventually over the investible resources of the economy and the various elements which concentrate it in their hands. In the erstwhile Soviet Union (to take another example) the rampant inclusivism that gave no quarter to regional demands for autonomy was also based on an exclusivism of dominant Russian interests at the centre that kept a Russian élite in control of a massive state–capitalist apparatus.

I do not wish to quarrel with this interpretation of the inclusivity in nationalism that I was pointing to, as harbouring a deeper and underlying exclusivity in the agenda of ruling élites (in our examples, a Punjabi-dominated or a Russian-dominated ruling élite). But notice that if we grant its essential correctness, we are granting something that takes the burden of the exclusivism away from *nationalism* to one or other set of economic interests, that is to say from nationalism to an élite-dominated capitalism in its less and more statist forms. This shift in emphasis is however a concession to my overall criticism that the real work here is not being done by nationalism in the way Nandy requires, but by the quite different categories by which exclusivism is now being explicated. If that is what is doing the real work, it makes no *distinctive* point to say that it is nationalism that is the bad seed that accounts for the failure of Nehru's secularism. With such exclusivism, we have come such a distance from Nandy's critique that we cannot recognize it as his position any longer. Now, I do not doubt that Nandy has it in mind to *integrate capitalism too* with statism, nationalism, modernity, and secularism in a single apocalyptic diagnosis, but that does not mean that this interpretation of an exclusivist element in nationalism can be assimilated into his critique. Even if it is undeniable that the regional élite's economic interests surrounding capital that gave rise to the exclusivism in my examples are distinctly interests of the modern period, and even if they are often accompanied by secular postures, the weight of analysis in Nandy's integrated diagnosis is not on these interests but on very different elements. As a result, this interpretation, which stresses these interests, need not in any way be implicated at all in his overall critique of modernity and secularism. I will therefore return to his position proper rather than this defence of his position, which is no defence at all, but its abandonment.

These remarks about the bootlessness of using 'nationalism' to explain anything only begin to uncover the misidentifications in Nandy's diagnosis of the failure of Nehruvian secularism. Lying behind the uncritical anti-nationalism is a specific sort of naiveté in the critique's historiography. As I said, Nandy makes much of the idea that religions as tolerant ways of life, in the sense that Gandhi embraced and promoted them, were undermined by the ideological religious constructions and institutions of modernity. In the case of Hinduism, it is the Brahmanical ideological constructions that distracted from the pluralist and quotidian religious habits of ordinary people. But such a historiography, with its crude periodization in such categories as 'modernity', hides the fact that all the basic elements in the construction of Brahmanism (especially in north India) were in place well before the deliverances of modernity. This should give us a general pause about the somewhat glib tendency to say that communalism like nationalism is a purely 'modern' phenomenon.

The idea of a monolithic, majoritarian, pseudo-unifying Hinduism is, as we tend to say today, a 'construct'. This is indeed what Nandy says about it. But as construction often will, the process goes back a long way into the recesses of Indian history and has helped to perpetuate the most remarkably resilient inegalitarian social formation in the world. It is the product of a sustained effort over centuries on the part of the upper castes to sustain their hold not only on the bases of political power but also on the Hindu psyche. Brahmanical ascendancy had its ancient origins in a priesthood that shaped its alliances with kings and their officials as well as with the landed gentry. Through the control of religious ritual and the language of ritual—Sanskrit—and with the force of the Kshatriyas (the predominantly military caste) behind them, it gradually created a nationwide hegemony for the upper castes. Under both the feudal rulers during the period of Muslim rule and later in the colonial state, upper-caste Hindus flourished in the state apparatus. In the colonial period this abiding hold over the centres of power, aided by the codifications of language and custom in the Orientalist discursive space, allowed this Brahmanical ideological tradition to co-opt all efforts at the reform of Hinduism, from the

Arya Samaj movement in the north to the Brahmo Samaj movement in Bengal; even intellectual and social movements that began with the avowed intention of raising the status and the political consciousness of the lower castes deteriorated into either élitist or anti-Muslim organizations.

I say all this to stress that the construction began to take snape much before the onset of modernity. Also it does no favours to historical understanding to let the periodization inherent in the very category of 'modernity' and its opposites (however we describe them, whether as 'pre-Enlightenment' or 'post-modern') shape *from the outside* how we must diagnose and explain particular social phenomena. When any such political or social phenomenon (such as Brahmanism, which is central to Nandy's identification of the modern source of communalism) has a deep and long-standing antecedent strain, it is better to adopt a historiography that places upon it particular and different historical explanations as to why the phenomenon, with some abiding core characteristics, shifts its saliencies or takes on new complexions, or why it increases its levels and thresholds of urgency in different historical periods. To take an example of the latter: despite the long history of the Brahmanical construction, the particularly frenzied communal passion of the Hindu nationalists that has been unleashed over the past few years can partly be explained as a violent, and in many respects fascistically modelled, effort to arrest the quickly accumulated ideological effects of recent efforts to *undermine* Brahmanical hegemony, and to expose the dissimulations of a unified, majoritarian Hindu society by adopting the policy of affirmative action in favour of the backward castes. I make this point with a very specific theoretical end in view, which is to show that local historical explanations can be given for the changes and the rise and fall of intensity in what is a *long-standing* social phenomenon. Nandy's own appeal to various aspects of the modern and colonial period in the understanding of Hindu nationalism should, I believe, be read as local in precisely this way rather than in the way he presents them (though obviously it is a good deal less local than the particular explanation I have just rehearsed of the *most recent* communal outbursts). This reading lowers the high profile given to periodization in Nandy's implicit historiography, and hence allows us to say something very different from his main claim. It allows us to say that to the extent that categories such as 'modernity' have explanatory force at all, it is only because this or that aspect of modern life and polity offers *local* explanations of *local* changes in *non*-local phenomena (such as Brahmanism) that often pre-date modernity. This last point has devastating implications for Nandy's own positive alternative to the Nehruvian secular ideal.

If the construction of a unified, Brahmanical version of Hinduism, which (on Nandy's own account) is the basis of Hindu nationalism, pre-dates modernity, a question arises as to what new complexion it acquired in colonial and post-colonial India. The answer is that what electoral politics in the provinces under the many decades of British rule, as well as certain forces in the national movement, brought into this construction is a growing mass element. To this, industrialization introduced a more variegated caste complexion through a co-option of the commercial castes into the constructed hegemony of a monolithic Hinduism. This answer is by no means complete, but the instructive underlying moral I want to stress is that once we give up the primacy of periodization and accept the reality of the accumulation and consolidation of long-present tendencies in our understanding of Hindu nationalism, we are less likely to think of these modern consolidations of it as effaceable for a return to a more traditional Hindu mentality that Nandy favours.

The current idiom, which has it that such social phenomena as Brahmanical Hinduism are *constructed*, and to which I have succumbed, must now have its bluff called. We have to be carefully specific in calling the bluff. Most critical responses to the idea of 'construction' in social theory seek to defuse the idea by pointing out that everything is constructed, so no particular gain is made in calling something a 'construction'. Though there is a point to these responses, the point by itself is not necessarily as effective as those who make it think, since clearly there may be grades of constructiveness. Here is an analogy: just as in scientific theory, despite Kuhn's point that everything scientists observe is theory-laden, there are grades of theory-ladenness (electrons are more theory-laden than tables and chairs, greater theoretical knowledge underlies the observation that something is an electron than the observation that something is a table). But the analogy breaks down. It might be the difference between constructiveness in social theory and theory-ladenness in scientific theory. It might be said that the former has been introduced by social theorists to mark our own inventiveness—'invented traditions', 'imagined communities'—in order to contrast with the greater reality of objective, non-constructed phenomena. Thus, the difference between Brahmanism and my left arm. (In the case of scientific theory there is no sensible claim to the effect that tables and chairs have greater objective reality than electrons. They are simply constituted by less background knowledge.) Even if true, however, this makes no difference to the point I want to make with the analogy. What the point about *grades* of constructiveness does is to force us to look to *particular* constructions to see *how* entrenched they are as constructions, and therefore *how* effaceable they are as constructions. That is why I have been stressing the very deep-seated and long-standing layers of construction over centuries in the phenomenon of Brahmanical Hinduism, which plays such a central role in Nandy's claim that Hindu nationalism is a construct of modernity. This slowly developing consolidation of it over centuries, which takes on a new local form in this century's Hindu nationalism, is therefore a construct that is not easy to dislodge or efface. Its grade of constructiveness shows it to be very securely lodged and so it is a fantasy to think that there can be an easy return to a pre-Brahmanical golden period of pluralist tolerance. In the particular case of Brahmanism, the breezy tendency of those who produce the rhetoric of 'construction' to believe that the very notion of 'constructions' (unlike the notion of more objective and independent reality) implies that they are effaceable human inventions and imaginations, is completely misplaced. When they are consolidated over long periods of accumulated construction, constructs are less and less like invented figments that the anti-objectivist philosophical tendency inherent in constructivist rhetoric suggests. They cannot then be thought of as effaceable, not even easily malleable, simply by virtue of having been diagnosed as 'constructions'. They are as real and often as entrenched as anything that any more traditional idiom and objectivist philosophical tendency described. Therefore, the more subdued and low-profile understanding of historical periodization I have suggested above against Nandy should instruct us that we would do better to recognize constructs not as figments, but as fused into the polity, and into the sensibility of citizens, and increasingly consolidated by modern developments; and therefore instruct us in turn to look instead for a dialectic by which they may be superseded within the constraints we have available among our other modern constructions rather than to think in terms of their eradication or effacement in order to return to some earlier period of pre-modernity (which might of course, in turn, be the construction of our own imaginations, now that we have opened up this Pandora's box of 'constructions').

The separatist electoral politics that was first introduced by the British and whose vote-bank mentality now seems fairly entrenched (and constantly revivable) in a functioning formal democracy, as well as the other institutions of modern statecraft and an increasingly modern economy, are not exactly disposable features of the Indian political sensibility. It goes without saying that there may and should be fruitful and sensible discussion about matters relating to the deliverances of modernity such as: Should there be so much stress on capital-intensive technologies? Should there be such a centralized government? etc. But even if we laid a great deal more stress on labour-intensive technologies, even if we stressed decentralized local government and autonomy much more than we have so far done, this would not coincide with Nandy's conception of a pre-modern political psyche where there will be no potential for the exploitation of one's communal identity in the political spheres of election and government. These spheres are by now entrenched in Indian society, and precisely for that reason the sense in which religion is relevant to politics today cannot any longer be purely spiritual or quotidian and ritualistic, as Nandy's somewhat selective Gandhian politics envisages. It is, in turn, just for this reason again that Nehruvian secularism thought it best to separate religion from politics, because given the existence of these spheres it believed that the linkage of politics with religion could only be exploited for divisive and majoritarian ends. It seems to me quite one-sided then to place the blame for Hindu nationalism on its internal dialectical oppositional link to Nehru's secularism, for it seems quite wrong under these circumstances of electoral democracy that are here to stay, to see a yearning to bring religion back into politics as something that is an 'innocent' protest against the tyrannies of Nehru's secularism. It misdescribes matters to say that the yearning *itself* is innocent but modernity disallows the yearning to be fulfilled by anything but a divisive communalism. The right thing to say is that in these circumstances of an ineradicable modernity, particularly if one views modernity as a fallen and sinful condition, the yearning of a religious people to bring their religion into politics cannot, simply cannot, any longer be seen as obviously innocent. Its entry into politics is fraught with precisely the dangers that Nehru and his followers saw, dangers that have been realized in scarcely credible proportions of menace over the past three years.

Though the underlying flaw in the prevalent anti-Nehru intellectual climate is to misdescribe the sense in which religion may enter politics in India, given the realities of a slowly consolidating democracy and modern state, this is not in itself to suggest that the particular form of the Nehruvian insistence on a separation of religion from politics is feasible either. To a large extent the rhetoric of the theory and practice of secularism in Nehru's way of conceiving of the separation takes the form of an unwillingness to acknowledge that there are religious communitarian voices in politics. The unwillingness to some degree comes from a prima facie understandable fear that to acknowledge them would be to encourage and entrench them. This fear dominated Nehru's thinking about secularism and was central to his theoretical formulations of secular liberalism, and also to a number of practical steps and strategies adopted by the Congress party before and after Independence. But the evidence suggests, as I will argue, that not acknowledging them has had its even more serious pitfalls; and that it has prevented any effort to formulate alternative frameworks for secularism than the traditional framework of the standard liberal tradition which in India—as I said earlier—has not amounted to more than a holding process. I will hint at one such alternative framework in the next two sections of this article, an alternative which is based not on an acknowledgement of communitarian commitments in politics that amounts to seeing them as a normative good, but rather one that sees them as a descriptive fact. One can acknowledge something without commending it, *but rather* as a fact that has to be transcended *via a dialectical process in which its acknowledgement necessarily plays a central role*. An acknowledgement in this minimal descriptive form is necessary because, in the context of a country with India's colonial and post-colonial history, separation of religion from politics has to be *earned, not assumed* at the outset. Such a critique of Nehru will share none of Nandy's hostility towards modernity; in fact, it will not particularly connect with the debate about modernity and enlightenment and its various goods and evils. Its trajectory is quite different.

# II

What I see as the fault-line in Nehru's thinking about secularism is roughly this. It was indeed an imposition but, as I have been saying, the sense in which it is an imposition is not that it was a modern intrusion into an essentially traditionalist religious population. It is not that because, as I also said, the population under an evolving electoral democracy throughout this century willy-nilly has come to see religion entering politics in non-traditionalist, modern political modes. It is an imposition rather in the sense that it assumed that *secularism stood outside the substantive arena of political commitments*. It was not in there with Hinduism and Islam as one among *substantive* contested political commitments to be *negotiated* as any other contested commitment must be negotiated, one with the other.

I should immediately warn against a facile conflation. It may be thought that what I am doing is objecting to an imposition by *the state* of a doctrine of secularism upon a people who have never been secular in this sense. Also, in turn it may be thought that this is not all that different from Nandy's (and others') charge of an imposition made against Nehru, since states that impose entire ways of life upon a people are wholly a project of modernity.[3] Let me leave aside for the present, in any case dubious, the idea that only modern states impose ways of life upon people, dubious because it seems to me a wholly unjustified extrapolation to go from the fact that the *scale* of imposition that modern states are capable of implementing is larger to the idea that it is a *novelty* of the modern state to impose ways of life. That is not the conflation I had in mind. The conflation is the failure to see that in charging Nehru with imposing a non-negotiated secularism, I am saying something quite orthogonal to the charge that his was a statist imposition. Perhaps it *was* a statist imposition but that is not what my charge is claiming. Rather it is claiming that what the state imposed was not a doctrine that was an outcome of a negotiation

[3] This charge of statist imposition against Nehru's vision is made very explicitly by Nandy, Madan, and the others cited in fn. 1 and reprinted in this volume.

between different communities. This critique cannot be equated with a critique of statism, leave alone modern statism, because it may be quite inevitable in our times that, at least at the centre, and probably also in the regions, even a highly negotiated secularism may have to be adopted and implemented by the state (no doubt ideally after an inflow of negotiation from the grass-roots). There is no reason to think that a scepticism about Nehru's secularism along these lines should amount in itself to a critique of the very idea of statehood, because there is nothing inherent in the concept of state which makes it logically impossible that it should adopt such a substantive, negotiated policy outcome, difficult though it may be to fashion such a state in the face of decades of its imposition of a non-negotiated secularism.

Proof of the fact that my criticism of Nehru does not coincide with a critique of statehood lies in the fact that the criticism applies to a period before Independence, that is before statehood was acquired. It is very important to point out that Nehru's failure to provide for a creative dialogue between communities is not just a failure of the immediate post-Independence period of policy formulation by the state. There are very crucial historical antecedents to it; antecedents which may have made inevitable the post-Independence secularist policies whose non-substantive theoretical status and non-negotiated origins I am criticizing. For two or three decades prior to Independence the Congress under Nehru refused to let a secular policy emerge through negotiation between different communitarian voices, by denying at every step in the various conferrings with the British, Jinnah's demand that the Muslim League represent the Muslims, a Sikh leader represent the Sikhs, and a Harijan leader represent the untouchable community. The ground for this denial was simply that as a secular party they could not accept that they did *not* represent *all* these communities.[4] Secularism thus never got the chance to *emerge* out of a creative dialogue between these different communities. It was *sui generis*. This Archimedean[5] existence gave secularism procedural priority, but in doing so it gave it no abiding substantive authority. As a

---

4 I do not intend this remark to be in the spirit of recent works written in defence of Jinnah against Congress caricature, useful as that project might be. See fn. 6 for the reason why.

5 The use of the term 'Archimedean' as a description of Nehruvian secularism is meant to echo Archimedes' boast that he could move the universe if he were only given some position outside it. Thus my point that the Nehruvian secular

result, it could be nothing more than a holding process, already under strain in the time of its charismatic architect, and increasingly ineffective after his death. It is this Archimedeanism of doctrine, and not its statist imposition, that I think is the deepest flaw in Nehru's vision and has nothing essentially to do with modernity and its various Nandian cognates: Rationality, Science, Technology, Industry....

Though I believe it with conviction, given the brevity with which I have had to make this criticism of Nehru, I should add several cautionary remarks in order to be fair to Nehru's position. For one thing, I do not mean to suggest that Jinnah and the Muslim League represented the mass of the Muslim people at these stages of the anti-colonial movement; Jinnah only represented the urban middle class and was not in an ideal position to play a role in bringing about the sort of negotiated ideal of secularism that I am gesturing at. Nor am I suggesting that these various élitist fora at which Jinnah demanded communal representation could be the loci for the kind of creative dialogue between communities that would have been necessary. However, neither of these cautionary remarks undermine the general point of my criticism of Nehru's position. That general point was to call attention to the horizon of the Congress high command's thinking about secularism in the pre-Independence period; a horizon on which *any* conception of a *negotiated* ideal of secularism was not so much as visible. Putting Jinnah and the élitist parleys aside, the truth is that even *Congress* Muslim leaders such as Azad were never given a prominent negotiating voice in a communal dialogue with their Hindu counterparts in conferrings within the supposedly *mass* party of which they were members. The question of the need for such a dialogue within the party in order to eventually find a substantive secularism in the future never even arose. The transcendent ideal of secularism that Nehru assumed made such a question irrelevant.

However, the last and most important of the cautionary remarks I wish to make might be seen as attempting to provide

---

ideal stood outside or *external* to the arena of substantive political commitments and did not emerge from a process of genuine negotiation and dialogue between these commitments. For this latter kind of secularism, that emerges from an *internal* dialectic between communities, I use the labels 'emergent' or 'substantive' secularism in the text that follows.

an answer to this line of criticism of Nehru. It is possible that Nehru and the Congress leadership assumed something which to some extent was true: that the Congress party was a large and relatively accommodating and (communally speaking) quite comprehensively subscribed nationalist party in a way that the Muslim League had ceased to be. And on the basis of that premise, they could draw the conclusion that an *implicitly and tacitly* conducted negotiation between the component elements in the subscription was already inherent in the party's claims to being secular. In other words, the secularism of a party, premised on the assumption of such a comprehensive communal subscription, had *built into it* by its very nature (that is what I mean by 'tacitly' or implicitly) the negotiated origins I am denying to it. This is a subtle and interesting argument which I think had always been at the back of Nehru's mind in his rather primitively presented writings and speeches on secularism. This argument I feel deserves scrutiny rather than dismissal.[6]

I say that this argument was at the back of Nehru's mind partly because it was often pushed into the background by the rhetoric of quite a different argument that Nehru voiced, which was roughly the argument of the Left programme, namely that a proper focus on the issue of class and the implementation of a Leftist programme of economic equality would allow the nation to bypass the difficulties that issued from religious and communal differences. Speaking generally, this argument is very attractive. However, apart from a few years in the 1930s, even Nehru did not voice

[6] One of the things that the longer project mentioned in fn. 2, of which this article is a part, does is look much harder and longer at this argument, particularly on the claims of the Congress that its Muslim leaders were representatives of the Muslim community in a sense that amounted to the community having negotiating status. This is a very controversial and troublesome claim and needs a careful historical examination of the role of Azad and others in Congress politics. It is one of the fundamental inadequacies of (the otherwise very useful) recent defences of Jinnah against Congress caricature that they do not look at this issue thoroughly enough, nor demonstrate why the position of Congress Muslim leaders on the shape and direction of the nationalist movement was not superior to his. To demonstrate it would require a precise assessment of this argument relying on this problematic idea of 'implicit negotiation' within the 'composite' Congress party.

this argument with genuine conviction; and in any case, if he were thinking honestly, he should have known that it would have been empty rhetoric to do so since he must have been well aware that the right wing of the party was in growing ascendancy in Congress politics despite his dominant presence, and there was no realistic chance of the programme being implemented. Given that fact, the negotiative ideal of secularism became all the more pressing, and it can to some extent be argued that it should have been pressing anyway.

To return to what I call Nehru's argument from 'implicit' negotiation for his secularism. I strongly suspect that scrutiny of the argument will show, not so much that its premise (about the Congress party's comprehensive communal subscription) is false, but that the very idea of 'implicit' or 'tacit' negotiation, which is derived simply from the fact of compositeness, is not an idea that can in the end be cashed out theoretically by any confirmational and evidential procedure. As a term of art or theory, such a notion of 'implicit negotiation' yields no obvious or even not-so-obvious inferences that can be observed to confirm or undermine its explanatory theoretical status. Hence the argument is not convincing because there is no bridge that takes one from the idea that an anti-colonial movement and a post-colonial party is 'composite' (a favourite word of the Congress to describe its wide spectrum of communal representation) to the idea that it stands for a substantive secularism.[7] My point is that to claim that the *mere fact of 'compositeness'* amounts to an *'implicit'* negotiation among the compositional communal elements that would yield such a secularism is a sophistical move that does nothing to bridge that gap in the argument. It is a mere fraudulent *labelling* of a non-existing bridging link between 'compositeness' and what I term a 'substantive' secularism. The label 'implicit' just serves to hide the fact that something rather substantive needed to build the necessary bridge from the party's compositeness to a substantive secularism was manifestly avoided by the Congress party.[8]

[7] This point is generalizable to a number of anti-colonial national movements and post-colonial parties in other parts of the world with multicommunal and multitribal societies, as the African National Congress is discovering.
[8] There is scope for misunderstanding here. I have no *general* scepticism against the qualifier 'tacit' or 'implicit' attaching to some theoretical and explanatory notion. I have no doubt that in history and social theory, as elsewhere, such

In reaction to this failure it would be a mistake to formulate an alternative vision of secularism that harked back nostalgically to the idea of a pre-modern India. Since, as I have argued, the sense in which it is a failure is not so much to do with it being a modernist imposition on a traditional people, but rather with its rarefied, non-negotiable status, the correct reaction to it should be to acknowledge that secularism can only *emerge* as a value by negotiation between the substantive commitments of particular religious communities. It must emerge from the bottom up with the moderate political voices and assumptions of different communities being brought into negotiating both procedure and substance, primarily relating to codification of law.

A civil code, had it emerged in this way, would very likely have pre-empted the present controversy surrounding the idea of a 'uniform' civil code. By climbing down from its position of *starting* with secularism with the proclamation that 'we do not acknowledge community voices in politics and as secularists we stand for everybody', and instead giving a participatory negotiating voice to the moderate elements in different communities, it would have pre-empted Muslim fears about the idea of a 'uniform' civil code and Hindu resentment at Nehru's failure to endorse that idea. Also, it could thereby have *ended* with secularism by earning it rather than assuming it as an Archimedean posture. It is thus because of the Archimedean rather than emergent character of India's adopted secularism that Nehru and other leaders refused to give genuine voice to Muslim leaders within or outside the Congress, thereby generating deep resentment in a shrill minority of Muslim voices, that gradually began to take centrestage in the 1940s; and this led inevitably to the Congress having to pay attention to these voices in ways that were manifestly unsecular, most crucially by providing special status to Muslim law. It was the *internal logic* of the

---

qualifiers have an important role to play in our understanding of various theoretical phenomena. To take one example somewhat far afield from our present concerns, Chomsky's notion of 'tacit syntactic knowledge' has a very powerful explanatory role in generative grammar. That role is so secure only because the idea of tacit syntactic knowledge, as Chomsky demonstrates, explains so much of the observable linguistic performance of individual speakers. That sort of demonstration is precisely what is not forthcoming for the idea of 'tacit' negotiation invoked by the argument I am criticizing.

development of the non-negotiated methodological character it began with, that it would later inevitably find itself in a situation in which this special status seemed the only fair treatment of India's most substantial minority—thus giving rise to aggressive resentment among the Hindus, which in turn bred reactionary fear amongst Muslims of relinquishing their special status. In short, I am arguing that it is precisely the refusal to acknowledge the existence of communities and communitarian commitments in the first place that leads first to the failure of *democratizing* the communal voices in a way that propels the moderate element forward as the most representative and vocal opinion within the communities; and this refusal as a result forces the state to have to continually capitulate to the demands of the loudest, most unrepresentative, reactionary communal elements within the communities on visible public issues, such as to the demands of communal Hindus on the Ayodhya issue or the demands of communal Muslims on the Muslim Women's Bill; and capitulate much before that, for instance to the Hindu Right on the question of Urdu, and the communal Muslim element on a separate personal code.

An alternative substantive secularism, emergent rather than assumed, sees itself as one amongst other doctrines such as Islam and Hinduism; a doctrine that its proponents must persuade all others (including Muslims and Hindus, whose voices it acknowledges) to agree to as an outcome of negotiation. Thus, secularists must start *in* the political arena with its *substantive* commitments to its secular principles, facing up to other substantive doctrinal and political commitments of the communities, and working towards the adoption of their secular principles—by democratizing these communities and thereby giving them the confidence to embrace, from elements within their own evaluative framework and point of view, arguments in favour of these principles. In this picture we can describe the difference between secularism and communitarian commitments in a way quite different from Nehru's dominant rhetoric. In my conception, what makes secularism different from these specific politico-religious commitments is not any longer that it has an Archimedean and non-substantive status, but rather that it is an outcome of a negotiation among these specific commitments. This gives secularism quite a different place and function in the polity, and in the minds of citizens, than Islam or Hinduism could possibly have. Yet this difference does not amount to wholesale transcendence from these substantive communitarian commitments in politics. If secularism transcends religious politics in the way I am suggesting, it does so *from within*, not because it has from the outset a shimmering philosophical existence separate from religious political commitments. It does so rather because, *after* climbing up the ladder of dialectical engagement with religious politics (via a dialogue with acknowledged substantive religious commitments in politics), this emergent secularism might be in a position to kick that ladder of religious politics away. There is no paradox here of a doctrine emerging from its opposite, no more so than in any movement of synthesis, for the point is essentially Hegelian. Unlike the pure liberal fantasy of a secularism established by an ahistorical, philosophical ('transcendental', to use Kant's term) argument, the argument being proposed is essentially dialectical, where secularism emerges from a creative playing out (no historical inevitability is essential to *this* Hegelian proposal) of a substantive communitarian politics that is prevalent at a certain historical juncture.

When it is hard won in these ways, secularism is much more likely to amount to something more than a holding process. This is so not merely because (unlike Nehru's secularism) it acknowledges as its very starting point the reality of the inseparability of religion from politics, but also because, at the same time, it does not shun a realistic appreciation of the entrenched facts of modern political life, which Nehru (unlike his contemporary critics) was right to embrace wholeheartedly. This way of looking at things gives a philosophical basis to the widespread but somewhat vague anti-Nehru feeling (shared by a variety of different political positions today) that in a country like India we cannot any longer embrace a secularism that separates religion from politics. It does so without in any way ceding ground to those who draw quite the wrong conclusions from this vague feeling: it cedes nothing to the Hindu nationalist, nor to the Muslim communalist, nor even to Ashis Nandy's nostalgia for a bygone pre-modernism. The crucial importance of seeing things in this way lies precisely in the fact that it counters what is a dangerously easy and uncritical tendency today: the tendency to move from this vague but understandable feeling of the inseparability of religion from politics to one or other of these conclusions. It counters this tendency by a very specific philosophical consolidation of this feeling, so that these conclusions that are often derived from it now no longer seem compulsory. Or, to put it more strongly (and more correctly), such philosophical consolidation of this understandable feeling allows us to see these conclusions derived from the feeling as, simply, *non-sequiturs*.

I have sought in this article to distinguish between two notions of secularism by criticizing the Nehruvian vision from a perspective quite different to Ashis Nandy's. Unlike Nandy, I did not argue that the failure of Nehru's secularism flowed from its being an Enlightenment-laden ideological imposition of modernity. Rather, I argued that it was characterized more by a deep methodological flaw, which made it an imposition in a far more abstract sense. It was a failure in the quite different sense that it pretended, both before and after Independence, to stand outside substantive and contested value commitments, and was thus not able to withstand the assault of the reactionary and authoritarian elements in the value commitments that never pretended to be anything *but* substantive and contested, the commitments, that is of the nationalist Hindu, the communalist Muslim, and the nationalist Sikh.

# III

# Postscript

The last two sections have been excerpted from a much longer article of mine entitled 'Two Concepts of Secularism: Reason, Modernity and the Secular Ideal'.[9] When that first appeared in print, it seems to have given rise to a great deal of misunderstanding, some of it based on rank and elementary confusion, but some of it perhaps stemming from the very compressed nature of a few passages in which the central ideas were expressed and partly perhaps from the difficulty presented by what must seem an odd disciplinary combination of abstract argument in an unfamiliar philosophical rhetoric of analytic philosophy with more straightforward and familiar political and historical analysis. Let me take this opportunity, therefore, of making things clearer and more explicit, and to do so partly by situating these ideas in the context of other writings of mine.

[9] *Economic and Political Weekly*, 29, 28 (9 July 1994), pp 1749–61.

In some earlier articles written in the immediate aftermath of the remarkable events that followed the publication of Salman Rushdie's *The Satanic Verses*, I had argued that the Western media's and editorialists' defence of Rushdie in the name of free speech was perfectly acceptable for its conclusion, but thoroughly misguided in the way it came to that conclusion. What it failed to do was to present the claims of free speech as a conclusion of an argument that appealed to values to which the Muslim critics of Rushdie also subscribed. Instead, it appealed to standard liberal slogans based on long-standing liberal philosophies, assuming throughout that there are long-standing and familiar arguments for these fundamental rights, and claiming that any denial of them is familiarly mistaken, and especially so when denials come from those who live in the West (say, the Muslims in the north of England) where people should know better, that is where the arguments of the liberal tradition are well understood and well consolidated by political experience. My point was that even if there was an unambiguous record of commitment to free speech in the West (a doubtful empirical claim in the first place, which I put aside because my criticism was intended as more conceptual and basic), the fact of immigration (a phenomenon well understood by the author they were defending, and a fact often resulting from the policies of Western countries in need of cheap labour in the wake of the devastations caused by the Second World War) was a fact that gave the lie to the claim that the West could claim the primacy of free speech among other values on the grounds of arguments long familiar in the Western tradition of politics and political thought. Immigration had made Islam a *world* religion, spreading in less dramatic forms its sphere to the West, that had already been spread by conquest in earlier centuries. Islam was a religion in *their own* midst; a religion of the *West* as a result of immigration, and so there was no point describing the situation as one of 'if you live *here*, you must be like *us*, and accept the primacy of free speech on grounds familiar to us, even in the face of blasphemy against your religion'. No point because the 'you' was now one of the 'us' that comprises the West: that immigration ensured so. There was therefore no choice but to drop the pretensions of standard and familiar liberal theory and engage with Muslims *in an internal argument*, finding reasons within *their* other value commitments to give them an argument in favour of embracing freedom of expression. This meant undertaking a serious study of the conflictual nature of populations embracing this world religion, and seeking to provide arguments that stressed the values of the side of the conflict over the other. *This* undertaking could not, by its very nature, be carried out with the rhetoric of 'There should be *progress* toward Enlightenment values' or 'If you live here, you must be more like us in the political values you embrace'.

In short, I myself had defended Rushdie, but by a process of internal reasoning with his Muslim critics and not by expounding liberal conclusions on the basis of standard political and philosophical arguments of the standard liberal tradition. I had described this as an 'internal' argument against the censorious Muslim response to his book and in favour of Rushdie.

In a subsequent article entitled 'What is a Muslim?' I took up in detail the doctrinal, methodological, as well as political and historical issues involved in providing Muslims with such an internal argument. This meant observing conflicts amongst Muslims and their values, studying their moral psychology of defensiveness toward the West in the context of colonial history and the neocolonial present, and it meant a study of differential aspects of the Quran and its historical context of origin. All these ingredients went into the construction of an argument in that article with the ultimate goal of saying something in favour of reform that would appeal to values held by Muslims themselves.

In all these papers I made a sustained philosophical and methodological claim, which was that when you disagree politically or ideologically, there must be *internal* argument with one another if the outcomes are going to be stable, for if that does not happen, the outcome of the argument could always be perceived as being an alien imposition upon those whom it went against. Thus, for example in the Rushdie case, the outcome that would not relent on free speech would be perceived as an alien imposition to accept, which would be to have surrendered to *another's* values in the face of impending but hostile modernity. I actually think that matters are worse than that, and cannot really even make *theoretically coherent* the notion of any other kind of argument or reason than an internal one. Thus, the governing assumption of all these articles was that all argument should be of an internal nature, where one party in a disagreement gave reasons in favour of its own position against another's by showing that the other could also embrace it via his own commitments since there was tension or conflict within his commitments. In other words, the Muslim populations of the world were themselves in conflict between values that implied censorship and values that implied anti-absolutism, and it was possible to appeal to the latter values held by an overwhelming majority of Muslims (even in Iran) to forge an argument in favour of free speech. That was exactly my strategy for Muslim reform in general, in the second of the earlier articles just referred to, and my line of defence of Rushdie in particular, in the first. I did not think that the strategy would be either easily or immediately effective, but had argued that it was, both practically and theoretically, the only cogent line of argument available for either of these conclusions.

In the article from which the present paper is excerpted I sought to sketch very briefly the conception of secularism that would emerge via such internal reasoning and argumentation, and a conception of the liberal state that would make such an emergence possible. I called it a 'negotiated' and 'emergent' secularism, and contrasted this with what I called 'Archimedean' secularism which had no place for internal arguments but presumed the *externally* established truth of liberal doctrine, that is a secularism established by the notion of external reason that is the hallmark of the standard liberal tradition from Mill to Rawls. Now, it is this position of mine, couched as it is in the rhetoric of 'internal' versus 'external' reasons or arguments, which is poised for the spectacular misin-terpretation I spoke of at the beginning of this Postscript. (I am being a little coy when I say 'poised' since I actually spent three months recently attempting to correct this misinterpretation among some of my closest friends in Delhi.) Let me explain why it is a misinterpretation by briefly considering a certain Foucauldian position which is adapted by Partha Chatterjee in his recent article on secularism.[10]

Chatterjee argues that in a multicommunal society like India, which has granted minority rights to minority religious commu-nities in its Constitution, secular liberalism is powerless to cope with the need for personal law reform. He is however of the view that this need not be devastating for those who find the personal law of one or other community unacceptably illiberal. He boldly proposes that the answer to this impasse is that we should extend the notion of democracy and its representative institutions

---

10 Partha Chatterjee, 'Secularism and Toleration', *Economic and Political Weekly* (9 July 1994), reproduced in Ch. 11 above.

to intracommunity sites, opening up thereby the possibility of internal reform of personal law. A wayward browser of my article, seeing the word 'internal' in my use of the notion of 'internal reasons' for Islamic reform, and seeing it again in Chatterjee's account of 'internal reform', may conclude that we have convergent views, even though I have made no commitment to or even mentioned intracommunity democratic institutions, and insisted throughout on the necessity for statist reform. My point here is not just to say that this is dumbfounding conflation, but to quickly explore how Chatterjee's Foucauldian position and mine differ, for the difference is essential to this article's promised task of sketching an alternative framework for conceiving a secular state.

It is not so much that I think that any internal reform on intracommunity sites is a bad thing or ought to be discouraged. No secularist could find any objection to it as a general point, but Chatterjee's specific proposal of democratic and representative institutions within communities amounts to an acknowledging of communities in an institutionalized and *normative* way that I was eschewing at the end of Section 1. My own strategy was to arrive at a secularism by a far more minimal and *descriptive* acknowledgement of communities. Nehruvian secularist fears of entrenching communities by acknowledging them are far more justified against Chatterjee's version of acknowledgement of communities than mine, and for that reason alone one should be wary of his proposal as a basis for a secular polity struggling to achieve secular outcomes like the reform of anti-secular personal law.[11]

---

11 There is in any case a somewhat inconsistent disregard on Chatterjee's part for the coercive possibilities of intracommunitarian statism that would be created by his own proposal. After all, if individuals within the community dissent from majoritarian outcomes in the deliberations of a community's representative institutions, why should this not amount to those individuals being coerced just as much as communities claim to be coerced by secular majoritarianism at the extra-community or national level. The only reason I can think of for Chatterjee's blindness to this possibility is that his communitarianism conceives communities as the ultimate repository of social good, not the individual or the state. That would allow him to disregard concern about the intracommunal statism being coercive of individuals within the community. Such a strong conception of the social constitution of the individual by the community amounts to a rather dangerous theoretical consolidation of traditionalism and social conservatism.

Chatterjee is driven to his conclusion of intracommunity democracy in India as a result of the crucial use he makes of an idea in Foucault, the idea of governmentality.[12] The critique of sovereignty inherent in Foucault's idea is put to use by Chatterjee to rule out the possibility that there can be any statist reform that provides reasons and is non-coercive. Essential to the strategy is the appeal to a relativism about the very notion of reasons. As he says:

> To say 'we will not give reasons for not being like you' is to resist entering that deliberative or discursive spaces where the technologies of governmentality operate. But then in a situation like this, the only way to resist submitting to the powers of sovereignty is to literally declare oneself unreasonable.

The general trajectory of his article, and that sentence in particular, reveals something extremely startling and interesting. That is that Chatterjee, for all his manifestly communitarian sympathies, shares an assumption with his most bitter dialectical foe, the classical liberal tradition. It is the assumption that if, in the face of identity-constituting fundamental commitments, one cannot make coherent the classical liberal picture of reason or justification (what I above called external reason or justification or argument) for the liberal and secular state, then reasons must fall out of the picture and the liberal state must necessarily be coercive because some communities may find it incommensurate. That is the crux of his use of the notion of 'governmentality'. But it is also the crucial assumption of the standard Archimedean liberal tradition that sees no scope for liberal argument over and above its externalist, Archimedean position. Here too it is taken for granted that if there were no Archimedean reason given for the justification of these secular, liberal principles, then there would be nothing to stop the slide into communitarian mayhem. Chatterjee would find the description 'mayhem' tendentious, but he would be wholly in agreement with what was being described. For both classical liberalism and for Foucault, it is external reasons or bust. Despite their deep differences of attitude toward the liberal state, for both of them, the liberal state is necessarily Archimedean. If

---

12 Michel Foucault, 'Governmentality' in Garham Burchell, Colin Gordon, and Peter Miller (eds), *The Foucault Effect: Studies in Governmentality* (University of Chicago Press: Chicago, 1991).

Archimedeanism is not able to deal with the moral psychology of communal identity, then for both of them, the liberal state must necessarily pass into something else, something more coercive, or it must remain non-coercive by giving in to communitarianism in the hope that there will be intracommunity efforts at reform.

I find in this assumption they share, a quite impoverished conception of the options. Both Chatterjee and the traditional liberals believe that there is no other choice between Archimedean liberalism and communitarianism. Since I do not believe that Archimedean liberalism is either theoretically coherent or practically stable in contexts of certain kinds of historically situated multi-communal societies, I reject the first option for the reasons I have been advancing. As for the second option, I feel no sentimental glow about communities and tradition that Chatterjee, Nandy, and others feel, and I have spent the first part of the essay giving reasons for finding their anti-modernism besides the point for any interesting and substantial point to emerge about secularism in India today.

What I now want to argue against is a very specific consequence of their seeing the options in this restricted way. Because the traditional liberal and the communitarian see no other options to their own and to one another's doctrines, they both agree that in the context of the specific issue of Muslim Personal Law in India today, the entire debate must be governed by a certain disjunction, a certain either/or. If there is to be a change in Muslim Personal Law, it must *either* be statist reform by a secular liberal state imposing its Archimedean secularism *or* it must be internal reform within the formalized institutions or the civil society of the communities. The theoretical space I want to clear is this. I want to plead that Archimedean liberalism and communitarianism are not the only options, and there is the notion of an emergent and negotiated secularism. In this connection I want to say that the disjunction between statist reform and internal reform is not really a disjunction at all. It is only if we work with an impoverished view of the options that we will think that statist reform and internal reform are disjointed.

The framework I have been setting up in these papers of giving internal reasons to one another in a political disagreement offers a way of clearing such a space. This framework allows us to refuse to see why it is that theorizing about the secular state should have it that *internal* reform cannot take place on a *statist* site. This may seem initially startling, a contradiction in terms, but the suggestion is that it will seem so only within the standardly impoverished framework; one which, as I said, is shared both by Chatterjee and his dialectical enemy, the classical liberal. My proposal for an alternative seeks a way of refusing to allow that the liberal secular state should necessarily be seen as coercive in the Foucauldian way against the values of a religious community just because one recognizes the limitations of liberalism's Archimedean aspirations. Since, for Chatterjee, internal reform is *ex hypothesi* non-coercive, a liberal secular state in the present proposal may be seen by all parties to the dispute as non-coercive. After all it still is in the range of reasons. It is just that the rejection of Archimedeanism, of external reasons, still leaves it open that the state can be the site of internal reasoning, whereby the substantive values of communitarian commitments can be addressed and, if necessary, *different* substantive internal reasons be given to each of them for a common secular outcome. This ought to be a genuinely liberating perspective, and it is a perspective clearly in sight so long as space is kept available for the notion of internal reasons. Chatterjee raises the spectre of governmentality only because he sees no scope for internal reasons. Exclusively non-statist *internal reform*, then, is the last resort of relativists, who can find no role for *internal reasons*. But a proper understanding of the moral psychology in my framework should demonstrate that relativism poses no such drastic threat. Why not?

The giving of internal reasons to another necessarily seeks to find the other's moral–psychological economy inconsistent in the values it espouses. And the giving of internal reasons is the process of convincing the other that one of the inconsistent sets of values should trump the other. The possibility of such reason-giving is a permanent one. This is because agents and communities—unlike perhaps rational automating—are not monsters of consistency, their desires and values are often in conflict, and certainly they are permanently in *potential* conflict since agents and communities live in an environment that is changing and often such changes will inject conflict into their values. This is just what Hegel called History and the dialectic it engenders. What Foucault bizarrely fails to see, despite some extraordinarily acute specific historical analyses of some social institutions, is that the success of his historical analyses yields him his general conclusions in political philosophy only because he is blind to this Hegelian insight about History. It is true that there is no a priori argument against relativism once we see the deep practical and theoretical limitations of Archimedean strategies in politics. Even so, I am claiming that the full picture of a historically sensitive moral and political psychology with its scope for internal reasons should cause a sea of governmentality and relativistic anxiety to subside.

I have therefore argued that we can dismount the seesaw of statist versus internal reform by clearing space for the liberating idea that internal reform can happen on a statist site. By this, I mean that the state can bring about reform in a way that speaks to the value commitments of communities whom it is seeking to reform, and thus speaks to them internally in a way that they themselves might have done on intracommunity sites in Chatterjee's conception. The general point is that internal reasons can be given to a community by another, by the secular state, and so the idea of internal reform can be transformed from something that necessarily happens on intracommunity sites (as in Chatterjee's picture of things) to one that can happen on a statist site. A state that arrives at secular outcomes in this way need not be seen as any more coercive than the procedures by which these outcomes are delivered on intracommunity sites. Only the relativist who dogmatically denies any scope for *one* giving internal reasons to *another* would deny this; but the circumstances under which relativism actually holds any threat are ones in which there is a sort of permanent impasse between perfectly and unchangingly internally consistent political viewpoints that disagree with one another. Such circumstances are likely to be so rare, if they are conceivable at all, that it is theoretically quite unsound to formulate a framework for secularism, as Chatterjee does, which elevates them to the normal circumstances that secular doctrine must address. Relativism may not be refutable on logical or conceptual a priori grounds, as Archimedean conceptions of reason might imply, but equally relativism cannot be thought to describe the normal conditions for which theories and political frameworks and institutions must be constructed. What I am suggesting by contrast is that a clear conception of the scope for internal reasoning in politics captures far better than either Archimedeanism or relativism the normal conditions in which multicommunal societies find themselves.

To see things this way is to see the liberal state as being able
to provide a field of force of internal reasons addressing different
communitarian perspectives from within their own internal substantive commitments and unsettling them into awareness of their
own internal inconsistencies so as to eventually provide for a
common secular outcome, each on different internal grounds. Such
a theoretical view of the liberal state is of course dramatically
different from the way in which the liberal stage appears in
Archimedean conceptions. I want however to stress that it is also
measurably different from the face-saving retreat of recent political
theorists in the face of communitarian attack. Thus take for
instance Laclau in a recent paper entitled the 'The Question of
Identity'.[13] After considering in detail the difficulty that ethnic
identity raises for the universalities of secular liberalism of the
classical picture, he explicitly rejects all 'secular eschatologies', as
he calls them, and is prepared to see universality in politics retreat
to the sparest minimum that makes democracy possible in the first
place. Pointing out that even the particularists talk in the idiom
of rights when they demand rights for minorities, he finds in this
a universalist discourse that enables democracy, even if not the full
prestige of secular liberalism. He frankly admits that universality
so conceived has no body and content; it is, as he puts it, a whole
vocabulary of empty signifiers that surface precisely in such
paradoxical phenomena as communitarians necessarily succumbing
to the rhetoric of minority rights. But why should we allow the
difficulties raised by identity to abandon full secular outcomes for
such manifestly skimpy universals in liberal politics? To see the
state as a possible field of force for internal reasons is precisely not
to adopt the strategy of retreating to thinner and thinner neutral
ground that all communities and particular identities must minimally share. It is rather precisely to give up on seeking neutral
common agreement which may be necessarily thin gruel in a
multicommunal society and instead for the state to seek for the
thicker brew of a fully secular outcome via a signing up to
a common secular outcome for *different (therefore non-neutral)
reasons* from *within* their own very different substantive value
economies.

13 In Edwin Wilmsen and Patrick Mcallister (eds), *The Politics of Difference*
(University of Chicago Press: Chicago, 1996).

It is for this idea of internal-directed changes sought by the state within the value commitments of communities that I introduced the theoretical term 'negotiations'. I call it a theoretical term because it is a term of art, a placeholder for anything that brings to effect a certain kind of value outcome via internal reasoning. A secularism which is the outcome of changes so achieved would then be, what I have called, a 'negotiated' secularism, and if the changes were brought about on statist sites, it would be the achievement of a non-Archimedean secular state; one to which, without doubt, both the classical liberal and Foucault would take grave objection—the classical liberal because she is blind to any other but an Archimedean liberalism, and Foucault because his exaggerated anxieties about relativism have generated his peculiarly influential kind of anti-statist neurosis.

I am keen to stress the highly theoretical nature of what is intended here by the term 'negotiation' because I want to warn against an unthinkingly vulgar interpretation of the idea that might result by confusing it with what the term connotes in more common usage. In particular, I want to warn against what is intended as either certain limited forms of alliances or certain cynical concessions by the state to communities for manifestly unsecular outcomes.

Thus, for instance, it stands apart from something like the Leninist concept of class alliances, where the agreement concerns only circumstantial matters, but the identity of the most supported desires, the values, remains uncontaminated by the negotiation. It stands distinct from this concept since what negotiation is intended to achieve is a *revision* in communitarian commitments; revision instead *toward secularism* (the very thing that Archimedeanism aspires to via its externalist philosophical argumentation) via internally directed reasoning.

So also, it is distinct from the sort of thing that Sumit Sarkar attributed to me in a recent paper before criticizing my idea of a negotiated secularism.[14] He says:

Through a detailed critique of Partha Chatterjee and Ashis Nandy, Akeel Bilgrami, I think, rightly rejects as unsustainable any vision of secularism which harked back nostalgically to the idea of a pre-modern India. His

14 Sumit Sarkar, 'The Anti-Secularist Critique of Hindutva: Problems of a Shared Discursive Space', *Germinal*, 1 (1994).

alternative, however, is to acknowledge that secularism is a value through negotiation.... Partha Chatterjee, interestingly, comes to a rather similar conclusion.... At the practical or pragmatic level the curious thing about Bilgrami and Chatterjee is their lack of originality. This, after all, is what the much-abused Indian secular state policy at its worst has often amounted to: efforts at placating conservative or communal Hindu and Muslim community leaders simultaneously. The classic recent example would be Rajiv Gandhi in 1986, opening the locks of Ayodhya and surrendering to Muslim fundamentalist pressure on the Shah Bano case....

Well, I have said something earlier about the point-missing conflation of my position with Chatterjee's, and I don't know what to say about originality, since I was not in any case trying to be original, seeking only to say what I thought was true. It did surprise me though to be told that what I did say was anticipated by Rajiv Gandhi since it was part of the point of the entire paper that Sumit Sarkar was criticizing that we need a diagnosis of why an avowedly secular state seemed so often to appeal to the most shrill and communal among the voices in a community, when it did appeal to the community. Why, for instance, did Rajiv Gandhi take it for granted that he should not listen instead to the voices of the impressive mass of Muslim women who demonstrated outside the Parliament during the episode of the Muslim Women's Bill? Or, to put it more generally and diagnostically, how is it that an avowedly secular state finds itself repeatedly failing to be in a position to confidently assume that the moderate voices which, even if less shrill, are surely the more numerous and more representative of public opinion on such things as the status of a mosque or of personal laws, or in an earlier period, the status of Urdu and soon. How is it that when it does repeatedly appeal to or address an issue that is necessarily located in community it tends to appeal to the far smaller but more vocal reactionary element. In short, how is it that the state has over decades failed to democratize the vast mass of ordinary people in a community, so that the reactionary element is seen to be exactly what it is, a small and unrepresentative minority within the community? I had suggested that part of the longer diagnosis of this phenomenon might be that even before statehood was acquired, secularism was the Archimedean rhetoric of a party that for six decades was nevertheless marked by the making of concessions to the

Mahasabhite and then subsequently other forces of the Hindu Right within the Congress party and the communal Muslim forces outside the party. I had speculated that the pursuit of a less Archimedean rhetoric, and instead the sturdy engagement of contestation by internal reasoning with the communities, may have pre-empted the need for constantly having to make concessions to the most communal elements in order to keep them subdued.

The ideal here is necessarily a delicate one to bring into practice, but as an ideal it strives to do at the site of a state what Chatterjee thinks can only be done at intracommunal sites. Chatterjee's argument is a simple one and it has its logic. If you grant rights to minority communities, then there is a danger that a small sub-minority of shrill reactionary voices within it will dominate the communitarian space you will create, so you must introduce intra-communal democratic and representative institutions to stay their influence. But the logic need not get going in the first place, if the state were to be the site where this democratization occurs. It cannot be such a site if its commitments to secularism were entirely Archimedean in the first place at the time that it made concessions to the reactionary communitarian elements, but perhaps it could be by a serious engagement through internal argument with the substantial values of communities.

What a secular state, trying to cope with communitarian political voices on specific issues of the kind mentioned above, can do to give those voices the confidence to attend to the conflicts within their own thinking and values, and then internally reason them toward progressive and secular commitments is not an easy question. However, no Hegelian question is easy. What gives confidence and what overcomes defensiveness in a community is various, and it is impossible to list, codify or generalize it independently in a very local context. That is why the conditions that make possible a negotiated secularism should not be pinned down more specifically than the concept in its generality allows. This is the reason why I have insisted on defining the term in a 'whatever-it-takes' formula, and then tried negatively to say what it is definitely not. It is possible that ignoring direct attention to the communitarian issues and focusing on class—a familiar, long-standing, and extremely attractive strategy—would be effective, but it is in the first place not at all obvious that very specific ongoing issues such as the personal laws of Muslims will go away so simply, and in any case it is not obvious at all that the sort of Left programme that would have to be effective for that to happen is one which we can expect to be implemented in our immediate times. Speaking historically, I think it is not at all obvious that even its most vigorous proponent in the mainstream national movement—Nehru himself—seriously believed that it could be implemented except for about two and a half years in the 1930s. None of this suggests that the Left programme should be abandoned, only that other secular strategies should *not* be abandoned in the interim.

This is why I have been attempting to study a possibly illuminating prototype of a more realistic ideal, or at any rate an illuminating approximation of it, in our recent history (though one that did not abide even for three full years), the case perhaps of Bengal at the time of the C.R. Das Pact. Consider the following very specific case. A close look at the details that surrounded the woman suffrage bill which was passed in 1925 in the provincial legislative council, after having been defeated four years earlier, very strongly suggests that the Pact was central to this progressive and secular legislative reversal. Muslim members of the legislative assembly had voted predominantly against the bill in 1921, but by 1925 it was the Muslim members, specially the Swarajist Muslims, but non-Swarajists and other unaffiliated Muslims too, who had been emboldened to vote for it in large enough numbers to make the difference and get the bill passed. This was done despite the fact that the party made an explicit decision not to put pressure on them to do so. The Pact gave them the confidence to allow the secular nationalist arguments that were pressed by their nationalist colleagues to internally trump their own earlier argument for the opposite conclusion that stricter observance of purdah among their women would inhibit them from voting and put the community to a disadvantage. I think we can see in the dialectic of this legislative turnaround and in this moment of the Bengal Pact, which was in other ways too a very dynamic period in Bengali history, a sense of what I had in mind by a field of force of internal reasons being carried out on a statist site by which a progressive and secular outcome can be achieved.

I think that there were other revealing moments (revealing of the acknowledgement of the need for a less Archimedean stand) during the national movement—such as the Muslim Mass Contact Programme, which was even more quickly aborted than the Bengal Pact. What the programme revealed was a somewhat panicky acknowledgement on the part of the Congress party that their rhetoric of compositeness was quite ineffective and had done nothing very much to democratize the Muslim voices in the country so that the progressive among them could emerge as the representative voice. The very fact that it was a Muslim mass contact programme was an acknowledgement—at least implicitly—that their Archimedean secular stance had been quite blind to the need to democratize *Muslims*, so that they did not get hijacked into the narrow and élitist communal direction that Jinnah's politics was aiming to direct them. It is only such a democratization of a *community* that could have the effect of giving its moderate leadership a position of centrestage necessary for an eventual secular outcome. It would not be idle, indeed quite interesting, to speculate whether the Muslim Mass Contact Programme, had it not been prematurely and abruptly arrested by the party's own leadership, would have had the sort of democratizing effect within the community whose name the movement took, and therefore had the confidence-inducing effect within the community, which I am claiming is a necessary condition for the sort of negotiated alternative to Archimedeanism, on the one hand, and internal intracommunitarian reform on the other. Admittedly it would not exactly have been on a secular statist site since an independent state had not been achieved, but it would have been a genuine proxy for, after all, it would have been at the site of a secular party gearing itself to *acquire statehood*.

These are all details. I hope, however, that they convey something at a concrete level of the theoretical space I have been trying to clear. That was the space which lay under a thoroughly misleading and conceptually impoverishing disjunction that I began with. It is a space sensitive to the moral psychology of identity which is missing in the classical liberal formulations of secular doctrine, at the same time it does not permit any scope for this sensitivity to degenerate into a relativistic and anti-statist communitarianism. Foucault's disciples have a right to be despairing of the state in the face of its many failures, though one wishes they would also remember its many successes. Despair however is one thing to which anyone has a right, depending on how they perceive and interpret the facts around them. It is quite another thing to erect their despair into a philosophical doctrine that entails a sort of virtually a priori pessimism about the state. The space that Chatterjee and the general disjunction—of which his position is one disjunct—fails to find is one that gives us an equal right to take a different attitude than despair in the face of the state's failures since it allows us a question, which for him is necessarily bogus: 'Why can't we struggle to improve the state?' This article has tried to develop a very abstract and perhaps needlessly complicated argument to make that space and that simple question possible. Political theory generally, and liberal doctrine in particular, desperately need rigorous formulations to fill such a space.

# 13

# The Crisis of Secularism in India

*Stanley J. Tambiah*

## Introduction

I n India today, it is widely said in academic and journalistic writings, and even more significantly in the speeches of politicians inside and outside Parliament, that the country is experiencing a 'crisis of the nation-state' and together with it a 'crisis of secularism', by which is meant a challenge to the Indian state's responsibility and mandate to preserve its 'secular character'. The secularism in question concerns the relation between the state and the multiple religious communities of India with their different practices. The challenge to this 'secular nation-state' reached a crisis point when crowds in the name of Hindutva, espousing the cause of 'liberating God Ram', demolished the Babri mosque in Ayodhya on 6 December 1992, in defiance of a Supreme Court order, and justified that action by asserting that the *vox populi* had the right to supersede the 'rule of law'. This claim is forcefully illustrated by these words spoken by Murli Manohar Joshi, the BJP leader: 'The birthplace of Rama is a matter of faith and it cannot be determined in a court of law.'

Both sides, those who profess some version of Nehruvian liberal democracy, the official charter of the Indian National Congress, and those who are advocates of Hindu nationalism, explicitly refer to the crisis of secular politics, the former upholding secularism as a necessary norm and the latter denigrating it as 'pseudo-secularism', out of touch with the people's religious, cultural, and social traditions.

This is an extraordinary 'discourse', especially when one realizes that the word 'secularism' connotes many meanings in the West where it was coined, because issues of the connection between religion and politics are a matter of current debate and discussion there too, including societies like the US where the relation between 'church and state' has become a debated and contested issue. From a comparative standpoint, what is the understanding of 'secular politics', especially the relation between the Indian state and India's multiple religious communities, among those who debate this issue today? There are some distinctive features to the Indian discourse that have to be fleshed out.

## The Connotations of 'Secularism' in the West

The concept of 'secularism' as understood in the West has many connotations and associations. Historically, secularism as an orientation to the world is linked to two major interrelated processes in Europe. There were certain theological developments within Protestantism that stimulated and legitimated scientific investigations as a search for laws of nature that God had instituted and the discovery of which will attest to the glory of God; in time, however, the search for laws of nature made God himself otiose or distant to scientific activity which tended to gain its own internal autonomy and legitimacy among practitioners committed to the rules of the game. The second stream that fed into secularism was the dominance achieved in European thought from the seventeenth century onwards by Enlightenment rationalism, a well-known exemplification being Cartesian mechanistic philosophy. Historically speaking, 'secularization' has also been used to label the process by which an ecclesiastical state or sovereignty is converted to a lay one.

Thus one principal characterization of secularism in the contemporary West is that it seeks the understanding of the workings of the world and the cosmos in terms of natural causation or natural laws, thereby rejecting metaphysical and theological explanations and objectives.[1] Another understanding is that secularism is the process by which sectors of society and culture are removed or

1 *The Shorter Oxford English Dictionary* has something like this in view when it defines secularism as 'the doctrine that morality should be based on regard to the well-being of mankind in the present life, to the exclusion of all considerations drawn from belief in God or in a future state'.

separated out from religious symbols and institutions so as to constitute their own domains.

In narrower and more focused theories regarding the charter of the 'state' as a political entity, and the characterization of 'politics' as a separate domain, secularism has been linked to certain substantive issues, generally labelled as those pertaining to the 'separation of state and church'. One such is that national education should be purely secular, and in this sense a 'secularist' is an advocate of restructuring education to 'secular' subjects. A less absolute view is one which holds that educational institutions totally supported by the state should not impart religious instruction or sponsor religious rituals at their official functions. In the US, the debated and divisive issues such as the admissibility of school prayer in public schools, the teaching of 'creationist' dogmas, the provision of state aid to private denominational educational institutions, are seen as germane to the interpretation and implementation of 'the establishment of religion' clause in Art. 1 of the US Constitution, which declares that government shall neither prescribe nor proscribe religion.[2]

## The Gandhi–Nehru View on the Relation Between Religion and State

It is common knowledge that Nehru had no firm or marked belief in or commitment to religion, while in strong contrast, Gandhi's personal life was imbued with his attachment to religion. This did not mean that Nehru had no sense of the part the various religious traditions of India played in the lives of many Indians; nor did it mean that Gandhi did not think it imperative to draw a boundary where the provenance of religion stopped in relation to the affairs of the Indian state.

As is well known, Gandhi's writings were prolific and he pronounced views on many matters. Here we are primarily interested in how he saw the relation between religion and state

[2] The First Amendment to the Constitution (Art. 1) has this opening sentence: 'Congress shall make no law respecting an establishment of religion, or prohibiting the free exercise thereof.' This declaration concerns a certain specification of what Congress may or may not do as lawmaker in regard to religion.

in an independent India. *Hind Swaraj*, written in Gujarati in 1909 and published in English translation in 1910, is usually considered a good statement of the basic elements of Gandhi's politics. This text is famous for Gandhi's rejection of the objectives of modernity, progress, and industrialism, for the India he desired to see come into its own, and his assertion that khadi was the only true economic basis for Indian society constituted of millions of villagers. His utopian concept of *Ramarajya* did imagine a return to a perfect system of division of labour practising reciprocity and not competition, and he did express earlier an idealistic rejection of complex legal and political institutions as the basis of a civil society and a state system that would distance the rulers from the ruled. But he also realized that in practical terms Congressmen would have to have seek election to legislatures, and that state machinery would have to be instituted to run the government.

Gandhi at the same time was an ardent advocate of an Indian nationalist movement as a basis for political mobilization for the task of freeing India from the yoke of imperialism and subjection to the Westerners; whatever his differences with the socialist, progress-minded, and atheistic Nehru, both stood together in regard to the realization that India was pluralistic in religion, language, and customs, and that it was necessary for the Indian state of the future to be accommodating of religious diversity, while observing an even-handed neutrality. As early as 1909, Gandhi had written in *Hind Swaraj:* 'India cannot cease to be one nation, because people belonging to different religions live in it....In no part of the world are one nationality and one religion synonymous terms; nor has it ever been so in India.'[3]

Gandhi had as his unswerving purpose the winning of independence for India and the constitution of a united nation, and in a society where multiple religions were observed, this nation-making project entailed a separation of religion and state. He thus proclaimed: 'I swear by my religion, I will die for it. But it is my personal affair. The State has nothing to do with it. The State will look after your secular welfare, health, communication, foreign

---

[3] Quoted by Justice Ahmadi on p. 46 in *S.R. Bommai* v. *Union of India.* Constitution of India, Art. 356. Judgment of the Supreme Court of India by a Special Bench of nine judges along with written submissions of Counsels, SCA 1994 (2), Scale vol. II, no. 1, 14–20 March.

relations, currency and so on, but not my religion. That is everybody's personal concern.'[4]

It was in affirmation of this separation, though lacking Gandhi's intense personal religiosity that Nehru wrote in 1945: 'I am convinced that the future government of free India must be secular in the sense that government will not associate itself with any religious faith but will give freedom to all religious functions.'[5] During the Constitutional Assembly debates, Nehru held that the establishment of a secular state in this sense was an act of faith; an act of faith above all for the majority community because they will have to demonstrate that they can behave towards other (religious) minorities in a generous, fair, and just manner. Nehru, Gandhi, and some other Congress leaders maintained that the essential features of their position were that there shall be no state discrimination on the grounds of religion or religious affiliation against any person professing any particular form of religious faith, and that there should not be any state patronage of any religion or extension of patronage to any one religion to the exclusion of, or in preference to, others.

In current Indian political circles the Nehruvian conception of secular policies, espoused by many Indian supporters of liberal democracy, does not mean the rejection of the transcendental values of religion or that society should be irreligious; on the contrary, there is acceptance that all religions are meaningful and that they should have a valid place in the life of the nation. However, religion is not a component in defining nationality or citizenship. The state should be neutral as between the country's many religions and tolerant of all.[6]

The Indian philosopher and sometime President of the Union of India, Sarvepalli Radhakrishnan has given this exegesis which might qualify as one 'official' Indian specification[7] of secular politics:

[4] Ibid., p. 46.  [5] Ibid., p. 46.

[6] I take this explication from Ainslie Embree, 'The Function of the Rashtriya Swayamsevak: To Define the Hindu Nation', in Martin E. Marty and R. Scott Appleby (eds), *Accounting for Fundamentalism. The Dynamic Character of Movements*, The Fundamentalism Project, vol. 4. (University of Chicago Press: Chicago, 1994), ch. 22.

[7] I call it one specification because it expresses ideas about religion that Nehru himself might have avoided. It is consonant with Gandhi's faith in the Supreme and the reality of the unseen spirit.

When India is said to be a secular state, it does not mean we reject the reality of an unseen spirit or the relevance of religion to life or that we exalt-irreligion. It does not mean that Secularism itself becomes a positive religion or that the State assumes divine prerogatives. Though faith in the Supreme is the basic principle of the Indian tradition, the Indian State will not identify itself with or be controlled by any particular religion. We hold that no one religion should be accorded special privileges in national life or international relations for that would be a violation of the basic principles of democracy and contrary to the best interests of religion and government....No person should suffer any form of disability or discrimination because of his religion but all alike should be free to share to the fullest degree in the common life. This is the basic principle involved in the separation of Church and State.[8]

Now, while Nehru and the so-called Nehruvian conception of secularism has been excoriated and denigrated by certain opponents (principally on the grounds of Nehru's alleged personal atheism and his commitment to post-Enlightenment European liberal humanism), it has nevertheless to be appreciated that Nehru's (and Gandhi's) advocacy of the Indian state's 'secular' posture was necessitated by two overriding circumstances, particular to India. The first was that, precisely because Indian society at large was constituted of a diversity of cultures, languages, religions, and customs, it was necessary, if India was to become one nation in unity, to cultivate the public morality of tolerance and accommodation. Thus the secular state was a requirement of the project of nationhood. Second, the very trauma of Partition, which nevertheless left within the boundaries of India a very considerable majority of Muslims, made it imperative, as Nehru and Gandhi both eloquently held, for the Hindus as the majority population to be generous towards and accommodative of Muslim ways (even if this implied imposing on Hindus in the short run more rigorous state-imposed standards). It has to be underscored that whatever of Gandhi's advocacy of *Ramarajya* derived from deeply held revisionary Hindu values, on this matter of imperative tolerance towards Muslims and their incorporation in the Indian polity, there is a gaping difference between Gandhi's political philosophy and that of present-day Hindu nationalism of the BJP variety.

[8] Sarvepalli Radhakrishnan, *Recovery of Faith* (Harper Brothers: New York, 1955), p. 202.

# Problems of Nehruvian Secularism

Mahatma Gandhi was assassinated in 1948, and it was Jawaharlal Nehru who dominated the Indian political scene into the 1960s. In Indian political discourses, it is Nehru who is identified as the chief architect and articulator of the relation between the state and religion. The Nehruvian view of the state's neutrality towards all religions, while accepting the significance of the religious life to Indians, and while being tolerant, does not give clear directives as to how this pragmatic and diplomatic view is to be implemented when disputes regarding differential claims on state support were advanced by different religious groups or when religious groups collided over religious practices that allegedly infringed their respective rights and their autonomies. In this respect, the Nehruvian orientation might have unwittingly sheltered a time bomb, that did explode in the form of the Shah Bano case which I address shortly.

The wording of the second section of Art. 25 lends weight to the supposition that liberals like Nehru and others in the Congress, avoided the establishment clause similar to that in the US Constitution because they did not want to prohibit the state from legislating against some of the 'non-egalitarian' and 'caste-ridden' prejudices legitimated by Hindu practices—such as denial of temple entry to *harijans*, early marriage of female children, pollution rules impinging on low castes and women in certain physiological states (menstruation, childbirth), etc. One comment is however appropriate here. There was something large-hearted and genuinely accommodative in Nehru's attitude to Muslims in India as a significant minority that tends to be forgotten by those sections in India that currently denounce his version of secularism. While Nehru was keen on reforming or mitigating certain abuses in Hindu society, he at the same time maintained that Congress should be generous towards the Muslims and desist from intrusively disturbing Muslim sensibilities by advocating reforms in those of their practices that appeared 'undemocratic' or 'inegalitarian'.

Be that as it may, Art. 25, which recognizes religious freedom, subject to public order, morality and health, and other fundamental rights and subject to the states' authority to regulate or restrict any economic, financial, political, or other secular activity associated with religious practice, provides no unambiguous criteria for evaluating a demand for legislative intervention in the name of welfare and justice by a Hindu majority that may be detrimental to the distinctive practices and norms of a minority like the Muslims. Also, it tells us nothing as to how one can realistically separate financial or political and other so-called 'secular' dimensions from the 'religious' dimensions in an institutionalized religious movement propagating its faith and seeking a voice in the public life of the country. In this respect, this article contains the greatest possibilities for generating disputes about the demarcation of the boundaries that separate the 'sacred' or 'religious' from the 'secular'. For example, the question of demarcation integrally raises the issue whether the Constitution (and legislation deriving from its influence) urges and requires that party politics and democratic elections, being associated with the state, are secular matters and should not therefore invoke religious advocacy. This critical issue penetrates to the heart of 'Hindu nationalism' and has an awesome grip on contemporary Indian politics. Likewise it is not clear on the conditions under which a general conception of fundamental rights applicable to all citizens supersedes those religious practices that are deemed discordant with those rights.[9]

Some of the articles harbour problematic implications for the relation between state and religion in India that are not fully evident at first sight. For example, might Art. 30, in so far as it gives educational institutions run by religious bodies the right to receive grants and aid from the state, unduly favour these religious bodies, and furthermore signify mandatory state support for them? In so far as Art. 44 enjoins the state to strive to secure a uniform civil code, will it, if necessary, declare void the religious practices that it finds an obstruction to its uniform provisions, and if so how does the state separate 'civil' matters from 'religious' matters? This last issue will tax us when we later consider the celebrated Shah Bano case.

[9] One may well ask whether Art. 25 goes so far as to imply the following reading by Justice Sawant in the recent Supreme Court decision: 'One thing which prominently emerges from [the doctrine of] secularism under the Constitution is that…the encroachment of religion into secular activities is strictly prohibited….When the State allows citizens to practice and profess their religions, it does not whether explicitly or implicitly allow them to introduce religion into non-religious and secular activities of the State.' *S.R. Bommai* v. *Union of India*, op. cit., p. 105.

Despite the wounds of Partition and the hostile communal tensions and collective violence it engendered, many of India's leaders had doggedly marched on a path away from 'communalism' and towards their conception of a secular nation-state,[10] and were committed to the preservation of the integrity of the legal system in the judiciary. Jawaharlal Nehru, above all, was the politician and statesman who sought to preserve the Congress party as a non-communal and pluralistic organization committed to representative politics. In Nehru's eyes, 'communalism' was 'anti-national'; he declared that a committee member of the Congress could not simultaneously be a member of the committee of a communal organization such as the Hindu Mahasabha or the RSS.

In Nehru's eyes the quintessential form of 'communalism' was a political party or organization formed on a religious basis and devoted to promoting a religious cause. (Indeed, in the British colonial era, the term 'communalism' was used to describe political activities and causes directed by religious affiliation and interests.) Politics advocating religious aim was necessarily divisive in a society that was religiously plural. Nehru in *The Discovery of India* had written that once a national state was realized in India, there might occur 'class conflicts' but 'not religious conflicts, except in so far as religion itself expresses some vested interest'.[11] He would live to see his idealistic hopes betrayed not long after Independence.

Nehru was personally an 'agnostic' and felt that organized religion promoted above all the monster of communalism.[12] He however, maintained that religious affiliation was a private matter; the point being that in India no one's civic rights should be infringed because of his or her religious allegiance.

---

[10] The Constituent Assembly had implied but not actually inscribed in the Constitution of 1950 that India shall be a secular state. (The word 'secular' was consciously inserted into the preamble of the Constitution later in 1976.)
[11] J. Nehru, *Selected Works*, vol. 5, p. 203.
[12] In his *Toward Freedom: The Autobiography of Jawaharlal Nehru* (John Day Company: New York, 1941), p. 240. He wrote in uncompromising terms: 'The spectacle of what is called religion, or at any rate organized religion in India and elsewhere, has filled me with horror, and I have frequently condemned it, and wished to make a clean sweep of it. Almost always it seems to stand for blind belief and reaction, dogma and bigotry, superstition and exploitation and the preservation of vested interests.'

The truth of the matter is that the various sections of the Indian Congress, even at the height of Nehru's magisterial and lofty view of a secular Indian nationalism, had no consistent or uniform understanding of the relation between politics and religion. For example, the Congress already had Hindu traditionalists who were sympathetic to the views of the Hindu Mahasabha[13] and were determined to keep close watch on the sincerity of Indian Muslims whose loyalty was considered suspect. The closing months of 1947 had already revealed a tension in the orientations of, and relationships between, Nehru, the Prime Minister, and Patel, the Home Minister. Patel, who had his following in the Congress, 'while upholding the principles of rule of law and a fair treatment of all communities, was prepared to question the sincerity of Pakistan and to challenge Indian Muslims to prove their loyalty to the country'.[14] And the Kashmir issue helped to sustain this wariness on the part of Hindu nationalists. At a later time, perhaps more realistic and wiser about the relevance of religion to Indian communities, Nehru said in 1961 that secularism of the state does not mean opposition to religion; it implies rather 'a state which honours all faiths equally and gives them equal opportunities'. At the same time, the only pragmatic basis for conducting politics is that religion play no part in it (that is, secularism in politics implied a separation of state and religion).

## Issues Raised by the Shah Bano Case (1985)

The Shah Bano case in a profound sense bears on two issues for India as a polity made up of plural religious and cultural communities:

1. Should there be, and is there a necessity for, a uniform civil law code applicable to all citizens of India or should the customary 'personal laws' of different religio-cultural communities

13 Dr Shyama Prasad Mookerjee, a former president of the Hindu Mahasabha, and presumably with links to its moderate elements, was the Minister for Industries and Supplies in the council of ministers at the centre. Another notable activist who worked to implement Hindi as the national language was P. Tandon who was elected as President of the Congress for a brief period.
14 Bruce Graham, *Hindu Nationalism and Indian Politics* (Cambridge University Press: Cambridge, 1993), p. 9. Patel however cautioned both the Hindu Mahasabha and the RSS not to offend the Muslims living in India.

be permitted to be observed even though they manifest substantive differences in matters such as gender roles and rights, marriage, divorce, inheritance, property rights, etc.?

2. If different systems of personal laws are recognized as legitimate, how is the issue to be faced if there is a conflict or contradiction between the personal laws of different religio-cultural communities and provisions that are considered 'Fundamental Rights' applicable to all citizens? Indeed, Art. 13(1) of the Indian Constitution does state that all laws in force, in so far as they are inconsistent with the Fundamental Rights shall be void; the Fundamental Rights include the tenet of equal protection of the laws for all citizens, non-discrimination of persons on the basis of race, caste, sex, religious affiliation, place of birth, etc.

To consider the Shah Bano case in full context we have to first go back to the time of the British Raj,[15] and subsequently to the deliberations that led to the framing of the Indian Constitution after Independence.

When the British annexed and became rulers of Bengal, Orissa, and Bihar in the latter part of the eighteenth century, they instituted a system of courts and, in a list drawn up in 1772, recognized matters such as marriage, adoption, maintenance payments, endowments, and the like as relating to the domain of 'personal laws', a category which they demarcated partly 'arbitrarily' but which they understood to be designating customary civil practices of different regional peoples and communities on the basis of advice given by certain Hindu and Muslim experts and interpreters. This system and tradition was continued until 1947, the time of transfer of power. Over the colonial period, judgments and precedents accumulated in the form of case law and gave a reality to phenomena such as Islamic Law applicable to Muslims and variable codes ultimately 'deriving' from the *Dharmashastras* and the more specific codes (such as Mitakshara and Dayabhaga, etc.) as having provenance over 'Hindus' of various regions claiming collective identities.[16] Thus there were

---

[15] I am indebted to Professor John Mansfield for the details of this discussion, and for the conceptualization of the relevant issues. See especially Mansfield, 'The Personal Laws of a Uniform Civil Code', in Robert Baird (ed.), *Religion and Law in Independent India* (in press).

[16] Simultaneously in Sri Lanka, the British codified different systems such as Thesavalamai for the Jaffna Tamils, Roman–Dutch law for the low country Sinhalese, Muslim law, etc.

listed topics under personal laws, with unlisted topics being progressively excluded from this category. Occasionally, judgment by the British rulers that a practice was 'in plain conflict with...the achievements of a more advanced and civilized society' motivated them to interpolate modifications and revisions.[17] 'Justice, equity, and good conscience might provide the rule of decision on a listed topic if personal law gave no clear answer, or if the parties were of different religions and there was a conflict of personal laws.'[18]

The Constituent Assembly debate, at the time the Constitution was being drafted, on the desirability of a uniform civil code is interesting for the arguments for and against that were presented. While Congress leaders of Nehruvian persuasion tended to think that a uniform civil code was an essential part of India's identity as a secular state, certain Muslim opponents made the case that their personal law was part of their religion and therefore the state should not legislate on such a matter. Some Muslims considered that their personal law dealing with divorce, marriage, and inheritance derived from the Koran and was therefore unalterable, while others, while acknowledging the need for a uniform code in the long run, said the time for it had not yet come and that the consent of the Muslims had to be gradually obtained. In the end, the objective of a uniform civil code for India was left in the status of a 'directive principle' included in the Indian Constitution, which said that 'the state shall endeavour to secure for the citizens a uniform civil code throughout the territory of India' (Art. 35 in the Draft Constitution; Art. 44 in the present Constitution).

We may thus say that since Independence and after the adoption of the Indian Constitution, the matter of continuation of 'personal laws' has not been fully clarified. While it was generally recognized that all extant laws in force should continue, whether this under-standing extended to personal laws has been contested. At the time of the framing of the Constitution, some Muslim members of the Constituent Assembly explicitly advocated that Muslim law be given special protection but this concession was not written into the Constitution. While Indian courts in certain instances have not recognized 'personal laws' as being protected, in practice

[17] Quoted by Mansfield, op. cit., p. 148.
[18] Ibid., p. 148.

in other instances personal laws have continued to be operative to the present time.[19]

Now, let us turn to the Shah Bano case itself and briefly review it in the light of this background, and the realization that one of the things that Nehru and the Congress party failed to do at the height of their prestige and power in the 1950s was to frame a common civil code for India. It is debatable whether they could have achieved this result given India's religious and cultural pluralism. The Shah Bano case erupted in 1985 in the context of ambiguous precedents. Shah Bano, a divorced Muslim wife, sued for maintenance. The Bench Chief Justice ruled that Muslims were subject to the maintenance provisions (as stated in the Indian Code of Criminal Procedure), and also went on to pronounce gratuitously that this ruling was in accord with Islamic law. (He appears to have based this interpretation on the basis of the Islamic concept of *mehr*.)

This judicial ruling that invoked a reading of Islamic law angered a number of Muslim mullahs who favoured a different interpretation, and feared that such a unifying and homogenizing step would lead to the erosion of Muslim identity, and in any case objected to a judge's competence to interpret Muslim law at all. The Muslim Personal Law Board intervened on behalf of Shah Bano's husband and having been unsuccessful in their appeal to the Supreme Court, took their case to Parliament. The Congress (I) had already suffered reverses in the by-elections in Uttar Pradesh, Assam, and Gujarat. It is alleged that Rajiv Gandhi, who had electoral considerations in mind, persuaded the Indian Parliament to pass a statute, entitled Muslim Women (Protection of Rights on

---

[19] As Mansfield, op. cit., p. 140, explains: 'Article 44 of the Directive Principles of State Policy in the Indian Constitution gives expression to the goal of a uniform civil code. It proclaims: "The state shall endeavour to secure for the citizens a uniform civil code throughout the territory of India." Like the other Directive Principles, this one "shall not be enforceable by any court, but...[is] nevertheless fundamental in the governance of the country and it shall be the duty of the State to apply...[it] in making laws". The Constitution thus did not abolish the system of personal laws or require that there be a uniform civil code; a uniform civil code was held up as an ideal towards which the state should strive.'

Divorce) Act, 1986, which undid the Shah Bano case decision. According to this new codification of Muslim personal law,

the divorced woman's husband is obliged only to return the *mehr* (dower or marriage settlement) and pay her maintenance during the period of *iddat* (the period of three months following the divorce). If the divorced woman is not able to maintain herself after the *iddat* period her maintenance will be the responsibility of her children, or parents, or those relatives who would be entitled to inherit her property upon her death; if she has no relatives or if they have no means to pay her maintenance the magistrate may direct the State Wakf Boards (administrators of Muslim trust funds) to pay the maintenance determined by him.[20]

Shah Bano herself, under pressure from the mullahs, withdrew her claim.[21] However, the earlier court decision is still on record, and there is a powerful drive among some court judges not to treat Muslims as a category excluded from provisions that are viewed as national in scope and applicable to all citizens.

The government's decision (the government in question here being that of Rajiv Gandhi associated with the Indian National Congress as the ruling party) to allow Muslim personal law to prevail in reversal of the court decision is one of the conspicuous grievances voiced by the leaders of the various component units of the Hindu nationalist movement (*sangh parivar*). It is constantly held forth by them as a case of the Congress's favouritism towards the Muslim minority at the expense of the sentiments and interests of the Hindu majority.[22] It was also vigorously protested by

20 Zakia Pathak and Rajeswari Sunder Rajan, 'Shahbano', in Judith Butler and Joan W. Scott, *Feminists Theorize the Political* (Routledge: New York, 1992), pp 257–79.

21 In an open letter, Shah Bano rejected the Supreme Court judgment saying, 'Since this judgment is contrary to the Quran and the *hadith* and is an open interference in Muslim personal law, I, Shahbano, being Muslim, reject it and dissociate myself from every judgment which is contrary to the Islamic Shariat. I am aware of the agony and distress to which this judgment has subjected the Muslims of India today.' See 'Open Letter to Muslims', *Inquilab*, 13 Nov. 1985, rpt. in Asghar Ali Engineer (ed.), *The Shah Bano Controversy* (Orient Longman: Hyderabad, 1987), p. 211.

22 It seems that L.K. Advani, the BJP leader, had stated his willingness to accept a national uniform civil code applicable to all communities and groups.

activist women's organizations as regressive with regard to women's rights.[23]

We may conclude by noting that in India today there are multiple views on the question of the desirability and necessity for a uniform civil code. Let me list three, which are not exhaustive.

First, there are those who advocate a single civil code for all citizens, and what is somewhat curious and unexpected is that this view is held by Hindu nationalists of the BJP, RSS, VHP varieties, Hindu and Muslim and other liberals and 'secularists', and by many feminists of Hindu and Muslim and other origins, and signifies a

---

[23] For a fuller enumeration of these demonstrations, see Pathak and Rajan, op. cit. Here are some examples. Five organizations presented a joint memorandum to the Prime Minister which contained these statements:

> Given the fact that the dismally low status of women is a reality for all sections of women regardless of caste or community, the necessity for affording minimum legal protection to all women is self-evident....The unseemly controversy over Section 125 aims at excluding a large section of women from minimum legal protection in the name of religion.

The organizations were the All India Democratic Women's Association, the National Federation of Indian Women, the All India Lawyers' Association, the Young Women's Christian Association, and the Mahila Dakshata Samiti.

'On January 30, 1986, the women's wing of the Rashtriya Ekjoot held a *dharna* (demonstration) in Bombay to demand a common civil code.'

Between September 1985 and May 1986 Muslim women organized similar *dharna*s in all parts of the country from Darbhanga in Bihar to Pune in Maharashtra; hundreds of Muslim divorcees supported by various organizations agitated against the bill.

'Thirty-five women's organizations joined together for a rally organized by the Women's Liberation Movement in Bombay on March 21, 1986, to demand a secular code.'

'On May 5, 1985, while the bill was being passed, women's organizations in the capital protested outside Parliament, chaining themselves to the iron gates of the building to symbolize their plight. Over a hundred women courted arrest.'

'Muslim women in Delhi, including university teachers and other professionals, formed the Committee for the Protection of Rights of Muslim Women and held a convention on April 26, 1986, in New Delhi.'

These are examples of how 'the feminist collectivity, by embracing the individual woman's [Shah Bano's] cause, converted her resistance into a significant operation within a [collective] feminist politics.'

convergence of position among groups that do not share similar interests and views.

Second, there are the pragmatists, who shy away from imposing a general principle, and prefer that there be case-by-case adjudication and a cumulative challenge to the status quo. This position implies an open-ended gradualism.

Finally, there are those who allow the Muslims to continue with their previous adjudication procedures, including their *khadi* courts, and the possibility of multiple or flexible interpretations of Koranic principles by their religious authorities differentiated by sect, place, and juridical traditions. A number of Muslims would fall within this group, and some non-Muslims would also favour this attitude of laissez-faire and tolerance.

## The Hindu Nationalist Critique of Nehruvian Secularism

Historically, the focal organization connected with the project of Hindu nationalism was the RSS which was founded in Nagpur in 1925. In succeeding years, around it were formed the family (*parivar*) of front organizations, namely the VHP (formed in 1965 as a quasi-militant body) and the BJP (which was constituted as a political party around 1980, its predecessor being the Bharatiya Jana Sangh).

The first leader of the RSS, Dr Keshav Baliram Hedgewar, was influenced by the writings of Vinayak Damodar Savarkar who proposed that India's indigenous cultures and peoples manifested sufficiently similar elements that together constituted a larger encompassing Hindu nation.[24] Interestingly, Savarkar was an atheist and a rationalist, who distinguished between religion and culture, and his programme was, from his point of view, one of national rejuvenation and not religious revival. Significantly, Savarkar excluded Islam from his notion of Hindutva, because he considered that Islam carried cultural components that did not fit into the Hindu way of life as a collectivity.

Early leaders of the RSS developed the following kernel ideas. The formal constitutional aims of the RSS were stated in general

24 See *Hindutva: Who is a Hindu* (1969) and *Hindu Rashtra Darshan* (1984).

socio-cultural terms as follows: 'To eradicate differences among Hindus; to make them realize the greatness of their past; to inculcate in them a spirit of self-sacrifice and selfless devotion to Hindu society as a whole; to build up an organized and well-disciplined corporate life; and to bring about the regeneration of Hindu society.'[25]

The stress on the centrality of Hindu culture as the defining element of both religion and nation was given wide currency by Madhav Sadashiv Golwalkar, Hedgewar's successor, in a little pamphlet, *We or Our Nation Defined*, first published in 1939. 'The nation', he said, 'is a compound of the famous five units: geography, race, religion, culture and language.'[26] Such formulations obviously and immediately have vital implications for the identity and status of India's immense Muslim population of nearly 100 million, and other groups such as Sikhs, Buddhists, and Christians. (The RSS claims that Sikhs and Buddhists are Hindus, which is at odds with the former's own sense of commitment to their distinctive religion.)

The formulations of some RSS spokesmen do not care to cite canonical authority from scriptures, or refer to any holy foundation texts in Hinduism, or to any defined dogmas. Hinduism is not predicated on the historicity of an individual founder or on the authority of a book or canon. Hedgewar pointed to the overarching concept of dharma as forming the heart of Hinduism: on the one hand it relates to the proper 'rehabilitation of the mind' and, on the other, to the 'adjustment of individuals towards a harmonious corporate existence'. Hindu coincides with *rashtra* or 'nationality' and therefore Hindus are automatically true nationals. 'Members of other religions, if they denied they were Hindus were also denying that they were Indians.'[27]

Most commentators appear to agree that the full-time volunteer workers, the *pracharaks*, who took vows of continence and

[25] Ainslie Embree's translation of the Hindi original text by Goyal entitled *Rashtriya Swayamsevak Sangh*. See Ainslie T. Embree, 'The Function of the Rashtriya Swayamsevak Sangh: To Define the Hindu Nation', in Martin E. Marty and T. Scott Appleby (eds), *Accounting for Fundamentalism: The Dynamic Character of Movements* (University of Chicago Press: Chicago, 1944), p. 619.

[26] Ibid., p. 631.

[27] Ibid., p. 623.

austerity, 'tend to belong to the upper castes and to the urban middle class, which means that they are college educated, although seldom it would appear at one of the prestigious colleges'.[28] The ordinary RSS volunteers or *swayamsevaks* recruited were encouraged to think of themselves as a brotherhood dedicated to the improvement of Hindu society and to the eventual creation of a Hindu *rashtra* or Hindu nation. It is relevant to note that the movement was especially active in the Punjab and in northern India during the period of high communal tension during Partition. The RSS leaders have never reconciled themselves to the partition of India, which they view as an inconsolable tragedy perpetuated by Muslims.

The RSS ideology harps on the degradation and decline of Indian society by virtue of its disunity and the seduction of its élites by Western culture and values. There is a need, it said, for a regeneration in order to recapture the glories of the past and for a change in the life of contemporary Indians. The youthful neophytes, the *shakhas* (subordinate workers in local branches), after initiation in a public ceremony experienced an expanded identity as members of a collectivity devoted to the task of regeneration of Mother India—an identity larger than the parochial ones of caste and village.

In general, RSS literature berates sections of the 'de-Hinduized intelligentsia' who are influenced by Western education and culture, who think that the Indian nation is a modern construct, and that Hinduism was not a definable religion, only a conglomeration of superstitious practices. Golwalkar charged the Indian National Congress with the fabrication of a new sense of nationality on the basis of these British-hatched misconceptions. The Indian National Congress's, especially Nehru's, commitment to a special definition of 'secularism' as a solution to governing India and managing its religious diversity is rejected as concealing the reality of Indian life deeply grounded in Hindu culture. In terms of the RSS definition of the Hindu nation, four categories of people are enemies of India: Indian followers of foreign religions such as Islam and Christianity; Communists and their sympathizers; Westernized members of the Indian intelligentsia; and foreign powers. The powerful and explosive charge the RSS leaders

---

[28] Ibid., p. 626.

(followed by the VHP and the BJP) made against the Congress is that after Independence, Nehru and the Congress party failed to build a new society because of their allegiance to the false dogma of secularism which was used to win the electoral support of minorities, especially the Muslims and Christians.

The success of the RSS and its allies is a reaction to a sense of personal failure or frustration experienced by many people, especially young men of the middle class, who feel that they have not shared in the benefits of the sweeping changes that have taken place in India since 1947 and that they have been marginalized by the urban élites in terms of opportunities for advancement and influence. The educated unemployed youth in India is a vast constituency of discontented and volatile persons ready to be mobilized for populist politics of the kind promoted by the Hindu nationalists.

There are several reasons for the success of the Hindutva movement and its dynamic electoral performance in recent years (especially 1991–3):

1. The Congress party has over the years manifested an increasing disarray and has been riddled by both corruption and factionalism. Its long periods in power, its unwieldiness and internal divisiveness, and its loss of collective purpose have created the space for a challenger who could mobilize many urban-based middle and lower classes in terms of a collective Hindu identity and populist cultural rhetoric.

2. The insurgency mounted by radicalized Sikhs and the Khalistan secessionist movement together with the disastrous worsening civil war in Kashmir, which led to the flight of many Kashmiri Hindus, seriously put in jeopardy the continuing unity of India, and there has been much anxiety, especially among India's burgeoning middle classes, concerning the threat of the country's political fragmentation and attendant economic losses.

3. On 7 August 1990, the then Prime Minister V.P. Singh, who was leader of the Janata Dal party, took the fateful step of announcing the implementation of the Mandal Commission Report which had been produced in 1980[29] and shelved for some time. This report advocated affirmative action on behalf of what have been

---

[29] Report of the Backward Classes Commission, 1980, part I, vols 1 & 2, Government of India.

called 'other backward classes' (OBCs), who are distinguished from the Scheduled Castes and Scheduled Tribes. The latter, on account of their constituency, about 22.5 per cent of the country's population, had already been allotted 22.5 per cent of jobs in all services and public sector undertakings of the central government. The Mandal Report, calculating the OBCs to amount to around 52 per cent of India's population, recommended for them a reservation of 27 per cent of certain levels of central government employment.[30]

V.P. Singh's announcement was ill-timed, and had the explosive result of nationwide student protests, including some much publicized immolations, especially from the ranks of the upper and middle 'clean castes' who feared the diminution of their own employment opportunities. The high rate of unemployment among educated youth is a perennial problem, and their fears were well grounded. Most critically, the announcement triggering an escalation of intercaste tensions and a disruption of the educational system, and provoking the intervention of the army, allowed the BJP to exploit the ferment and to dramatically revive and escalate the Babri Masjid–Ram Janmabhumi dispute and precipitate a national crisis. BJP President Advani announced that he would lead a *rath yatra* (chariot tour) from Gujarat to Ayodhya. V.P. Singh's national coalition government, of which the BJP was a component, fell apart. Violence erupted. Advani was arrested on 7 November 1990, and the BJP withdrew from the coalition. V.P. Singh resigned and the stage was set for the BJP to emerge as a major contender for power in the following years.

## The Anti-secularist Critique in India: Two Essays by Madan and Nandy

In recent times, not only the ardent advocates of Hindu Nationalism but many Indian intellectuals, academicians, politicians, and journalists have agonized over and debated the issue of the desirability and viability of the Indian state's commitment to

---

30 Thus the backward classes as a whole (that is SCs, STs, and OBCs) would together be eligible for 49.5 per cent of the central government employment in question.

secular politics. In particular, Professors T.N. Madan and Ashish Nandy, in two influential essays, have questioned the meaningfulness and relevance of 'secularism' as a charter and guiding light of the policies of the Indian state. Let me comment on each essay in turn. It is relevant to note that both essays were written well *before* the demolition of the Ayodhya mosque by Hindu nationalists in December 1992, and both have roundly condemned this action and other excesses committed by the nationalists.

Madan, quoting Peter Berger, specifies 'secularization' as 'the process by which sectors of society and culture are removed from the domination of religious institutions and symbols'.[31] Madan's trenchant submission is that

at present secularism in South Asia as a generally shared credo of life is *impossible*, as a basis for state action impracticable, and as a blueprint for the foreseeable future *impotent*. It is impossible as a credo of life because the great majority of the people of South Asia are in their own eyes active adherents of some religious faith; it is impracticable as a basis for state action either because Buddhism and Islam have been declared state religions,[32] or because the stance of religious neutrality or equidistance is difficult to maintain since religious minorities do not share the majority's view of what this entails for the state; and it is impotent as a blueprint for the future because, by its very nature it is incapable of countering religious fundamentalism and fanaticism.

Madan characterizes all of South Asia's major religions—Buddhism, Hinduism, Islam, and Sikhism—as being both 'totalizing' and 'hierarchical' in character. He says they are totalizing in the sense that they all claim 'all of a follower's life' so that religion is constitutive of society; hierarchical in the sense that the 'religious', the sacred or spiritual moral domain or category, encompasses the secular or temporal power in a hierarchical as well as a complementary relation.[33]

---

[31] T.N. Madan, 'Secularism in Its Place', *Journal of Asian Studies* 46, 4 (1987), pp 747–59 and Ch. 10 above. The quotation is from Peter Berger, *The Social Reality of Religion* (London, 1973), p. 113.

[32] Madan has in mind here I suppose the status of Buddhism in Sri Lanka, where it is now accorded 'the foremost place' in the Constitution, and of Islam in Pakistan.

[33] The indices of this are: the valuation of the *bhikkhu* as superior to the ruler in Buddhism, the holy book (*Granth Saheb*) being accorded higher place than

Reminding us that secularism as an ideology emerged 'from the dialectic of modern science and Protestantism' in Europe, Madan observes: 'Models of modernization...prescribe the transfer of secularism to other societies without regard for the character of their religious traditions.' 'The transferability of the idea of secularism to the countries of South Asia is beset with many difficulties and should not be taken for granted.' Furthermore, keeping in view the rise of many potent religio-nationalist movements in recent times, Madan issues the telling caution: if secularism cannot empathize with religion, it cannot cope with religious fundamentalism and revivalism either. Indeed, '*it is the marginalization of religious faith, which is what secularization is, that permits the perversion of religion* in *the form* of religious fundamentalism' (emphasis added).

Madan contrasts the Nehruvian 'defensive policy of religious neutrality on the part of the state', which is only embraced by a 'modernist minority' in India, with the Gandhian perspective, which is more in accord with the grain of Indian values. 'For Gandhi religion was the source of value and hence constitutive of social life; politics was the arena of public interest; without the former the latter would become debased.' From Gandhi's point of view, it was the obligation of the state to ensure that every religion was free to develop according to its own goals; but while Gandhi held that religion and politics were inseparable in the Indian context, he also held that: 'A society or group which depends partly or wholly on state aid for the existence of religion, does not deserve or, better still, does not have any religion worth the name.' Gandhi thus concurred with the need to separate the state from the patronage or support of temple, church, and other institutions of worship.[34]

Now, the question arises as to how the Gandhian perspective on religion and politics actually translates into political practice in an arena of multiple religious affiliations. It may well be that secularists who deny the legitimacy of religion may by their lack of sensitivity 'contribute to fundamentalism or revivalism', but like Nehru seem to think that fundamentalist movements, qua

---

the sacred sword in the Sikh *gurudwara*, and in Hinduism, *dharma* being valued as superior to and encompassing *artha*.

[34] See *Harijan*, 27 March 1947. I owe this reference to T.N. Madan.

'politicization' of religion, are 'perversions of religion...'.[35] Madan
confesses that 'I really have no conclusions to offer, no solutions
to suggest', and cites Nandy's own perplexity in the face of the
excesses of Hindu nationalism: 'There is now a peculiar double-
bind in Indian politics; the ills of religion have found political
expression but the strengths of it have not been available for
checking corruption and violence in public life.'[36] Let us now turn
to the Nandy essay and pursue its logic.

Ashis Nandy, in a characteristically challenging essay declares
as his manifesto: 'I am not a secularist. In fact, I can be called an
anti-secularist.'[37] The aim of his essay, Nandy declares, is 'the
recovery of a well-known domain of public concern in South Asia,
ethnic and, especially religious tolerance, from the hegemonic
language of secularism popularized by Westernized intellectuals
and middle classes exposed to the globally dominant language of
the nation-state in this part of the world'. Nandy identifies and
develops two trends that became 'clearly visible in South Asia
during this century, particularly after the Second World War': The
first is that each religion has 'split into two: faith and ideology'.
He admits that he gives these terms his own 'specific private
meanings'. 'By faith I mean religion as a way of life, a tradition
which is definitionally non-monolithic and operationally plural....
By ideology I mean religion as a sub-national or cross-national
identifier of populations contesting for or protecting non-religious,
usually political or socio-economic interests.' By religion-as-faith,
Nandy seems to identify traditional religion which recognized
pluralism *within* religious complexes like Hinduism and Islam as
well as between them. Religion-as-faith is indexed to religious
practices that comprise a way of life rather than by text-oriented
fundamentalism or revivalism.

35 Madan cites Nehru as stating in 1936 that 'communal problems' have
'nothing to do with religion', and adds this comment as expressing his own
view: 'It was not religious difference as such but *its exploitation by calculating
politicians* for the achievement of secular ends—let me repeat, secular ends—
which produced the communal divide.'
36 Madan, op. cit., cites from Ashis Nandy, 'An Anti-secularist Manifesto',
*Seminar* 314 (1980), p. 4.
37 Ashis Nandy, 'The Politics of Secularism and the Recovery of Religious
Tolerance', in Veena Das (ed.), *Mirrors of Violence: Communities, Riots and
Survivors in South Asia* (Oxford University Press: New Delhi, 1990), p. 73 and
Ch. 10 above.

Nandy sees Gandhi's ideas and actions as exemplifying religious tolerance in this traditional mode, which is integrally linked to Gandhi's anti-secularism and his rejection of modernity. For Gandhi, religion infused his politics and vice versa. An essential component of this perspective is the attribution of an attitude of tolerance to other persons and in others' religions. It is clear that Nandy pins the label 'religion-as-ideology' onto moderns who practise 'politicized' religion, that is modern forms of militant religious fundamentalism, revivalism, and militancy, examples of which being the Jama'at-e-Islami, Bhindranwale's movement, and Hindu nationalism. Nandy refers to these as cases of 'politics entering religion through the back door'.[38]

The idea of secularism, an import from nineteenth-century Europe, especially through evangelical Christianity, has 'acquired immense potency in the middle-class cultures and state sectors of South Asia, thanks to its connection with and response to religion-as-ideology'.[39] The nascent nation-states of South Asia, and their ruling agents, took upon themselves the same civilizing mission that the colonial states had once taken upon themselves vis-à-vis the ancient faiths of the subcontinent. 'Religion has entered public life through the back door.'[40]

Nandy indicts the modern state as the purveyor of a new type of intolerance, which is the mirror image of the intolerance of fundamentalist and politicized religion. 'While appealing to believers to keep the public sphere free of religion, the modern nation-state has no means of ensuring that the ideologies of secularism, development and nationalism themselves do not begin to act as faiths intolerant of other faiths.' Sufferings are inflicted on people by the state itself in the name of ideology. 'In fact, with the help of modern communications and the secular coercive power at its command, the state can use its ideology to silence its non-conforming citizens....Certainly in India, the ideas of nation-building, scientific growth, security, modernization and development have become parts of a left-handed demonology, a tantra with a built-

---

[38] Nandy's scathing remarks on RSS volunteers dressed in their khaki shorts makes clear his antipathy towards them as violators of religion-as-faith.

[39] Nandy imputes notions of bounded self, and of exclusive religious identity, as compatible with religion-as-ideology and with the views of secularists. This notion of self and identity is a gift of Christianity (ibid., pp 72–3).

[40] Ibid., p. 79.

in code of violence.'[41] Secularism powerfully impacts on many Indians 'as part of a larger package; development, mega science, and national security, sanctioning or justifying violence against the weak and the dissenting'.[42]

Nandy recognizes that many Indians 'have now come to sense that it is modernity which rules the world and, even in this subcontinent, religion-as-faith is being pushed to the corner. *Much of the fanaticism and violence associated with religion comes today from the sense of defeat of the believers, from their free floating anger and self-hatred while facing a world which is increasingly secular and desacralized*' (emphasis added). In an extraordinary associational move, Nandy links up the 'instrumental' exploitative rationality of the Hindu and other fundamentalist planners and instigators of ethnic and religious violence with the bureaucratic rationality of the ruling modernist élites who 'see all religions and all forms of ethnicity as a hurdle to nation-building and state formation and as a danger to the technology of statecraft and political management'.[43] This latter state of mind which 'ghettoed and museumized religion and ethnicity—has also infected *today's official social scientists* who are analogues of the colonial anthropologist and are practising a form of internal colonialism'. 'To accept the ideology of secularism is to accept the ideologies of progress and modernity as the new justifications of domination, and the use of violence to sustain these ideologies as the new opiates of the masses.'[44]

How plausible is Nandy's separation of the planners and instigators of collective political violence from the rank-and-file participants in that violence, and attributing primarily to the former an instrumental rationality (which manipulates and exploits ethnic and religious prejudice)? And how plausible is the submission that the instrumental rationality of the planners and instigators of violence accords with the instrumental rationality of the ruling bureaucratic élites whose Western-style secularism excludes the relevance of religion for politics? Are the Hedgewars and Golwalkars of the past, who were early leaders of the RSS, and the modern advocates of Hindutva—like Advani, Vajpayee, and Joshi of the BJP, Singhal of the VHP, Thackeray of the Shiv Sena—and their associates, who are involved in the promotion of militant

---

[41] Ibid., p. 80.   [42] Ibid., p. 81.
[43] Ibid., p. 88.   [44] Ibid., p. 90.

Hindu ethnonationalism, arch representatives of a bureaucratic-type instrumental rationality that is similar to that espoused by the ruling élites of the nation-state who are devoted to secularizing politics? Did Bhindranwale and his lieutenants involved in violence for the sake of Khalistan fit this profile? The answer seems to be no if one examines the writings, speeches, and exhortations of Savarkar, Golwalkar, and Bhindranwale, though the current leaders of the BJP, RSS, and VHP may fit better with Nandy's characterization. Moreover, the Hindu nationalist (and other ethnonationalist) ideologues, whom I have cited before, have relentlessly and vociferously criticized the 'Westernized' middle classes and administrative élites as imitators of Western ideals and distanced from their Hindu cultural roots. For me, one of the weaknesses of Nandy's essay is that he fails to give a coherent account of the experiential and motivational bases of these leaders' forceful commitment to revivalism and religio-cultural renovation and how this programme of action emerged both from their background of 'traditional' religion and their exposure to modern global processes.

A second difficulty stems from Nandy's distinction between 'religion-as-faith', which was (and is) practised by 'most non-modern Indians' and 'religion-as-ideology', which is the perspective of the Westernized middle classes and élite bureaucrats who use religion to pursue secular ends. The vital issue for me is how does the mass of most non-modern Indians, allegedly practising religion as faith, become drawn and swept into the massive Hindu nationalist campaigns, rallies, processions, and mass actions? How do large numbers of ordinary folk, Muslims, Hindus, Sikhs, Tamils, Maharashtrians, etc. who allegedly lived in peaceful coexistence and shared reciprocities for long periods of everyday life suddenly and quickly become engulfed in the cause of 'religion-as-ideology' and erupt in violence, hate, and intolerance. For the masses, Nandy has offered a sketchy answer in terms of 'the sense of defeat of the believers' and their 'feelings of impotence...and free floating anger and self-hatred while facing a world which is increasingly secular and desacralized'. This answer may be insufficient.

In terms of the modern context of mass democratic politics and the wide use of mass communication, media, and technology for mass mobilization, it is not the postulation of a stark *divide* (as here) between religion-as-faith and religion-as-ideology that is illuminating as a point of departure; rather, it is the non-problematic ease of transition from everyday coexistence to mobilized violence, through the stimulation *provided* by mass media propagandist messages, appealing to collective identity and simultaneously to expectations of hope and identity formation and anxieties or fear about an uncertain future, that we have to map and delineate. The power and performative efficacy of Hindu nationalism for those engaged and energized and possessed by it has to be sketched in fuller motivational and experiential terms, and be related to the circumstances and technologies of competitive mass participatory electoral politics and the pursuit of preferential collective entitlements, in order to gain a better understanding of today's ethnonationalist politics.

Amartya Sen has recently observed in reaction to the Ayodhya episode and the upsurge of Hindu nationalism that secularism, understood as the tolerance of different religions and also of people who believe in none,

is in fact, a part of a more comprehensive idea—that of India as an integrally pluralist country, made up of different religious beliefs, distinct language groups, divergent social practices. Secularism is one aspect—a very important one—of the recognition of that larger idea of heterogeneous identity...sectarian forces that seek to demolish Indian secularism will have to deal with the presence and rights of the many Muslims in India [100 or more million of them, the third largest Muslim population in any country], but also with India's regional, social and cultural diversity. Toleration of differences is not easily divisible....Given the diversity and contrasts within India, there is not, in the comprehensive politics of the country, much alternative to secularism as an essential part of overall pluralism.[45]

This voice of reason is difficult to resist. However, it does not sufficiently tell us why the plural complexity in India periodically generates certain divisive issues, conundrums, and particularized, even incommensurable motivations, and in what manner we can subjectively comprehend why the nation-state of India and its troubled version of secularist politics are in crisis, and why these crises are not easily resolved.

It is worth remarking in conclusion that there are two agreements of opinion among Indian intellectuals, whether they are

[45] Amartya Sen, 'The Threats to Secular India', *The New York Times Review of Books* 50, 7 (8 April 1993), pp 26–7.

sympathizers of the Nehruvian stance of secular democracy, namely 'not opposition to religion but the removal of religion from public affairs, the separation of state from all faiths', as for example defended by Sarvepalli Gopal,[46] or of the singular posture of being 'anti-secularists', like Ashis Nandy's, which recognizes that in India religion cannot be cordoned off from politics because it informs all sides of an Indian's life. Both strands agree that Hinduism as traditionally practised in India is for the most part accommodative of the coexistence of plural religions, and second, Hindu nationalism of the current sort (as promoted by the RSS, BJP, VHP, the Shiv Sena, and Bajrang Dal) is a distortion and perversion of Hinduism because it has *politicized religion*, mobilizing and exploiting religion instrumentally for political ends, thereby making it a divisive force providing no meeting ground for followers of different faiths.

## Prospects of Secularism: Hindutva Versus the Secular State

On 6 December 1992, the Babri Masjid was demolished in defiance of the stay order of the Supreme Court, and on that same day the Uttar Pradesh government voluntarily resigned, duly followed by the proclamation issued by the President of the Union dissolving the Legislative Assembly of the state. In the wake of the ensuing riots and arson in a string of cities stretching from Calcutta to Bombay, the Union Government also issued a ban on the RSS, VHP, and Bajrang Dal, which, along with the BJP, had mobilized the *kar sevaks* to assemble in Ayodhya in the days preceding the demolition. The order for this ban was issued on 10 December under the Unlawful Activities (Prevention) Act of 1967. Five days later, on the charge that their state governments supported these banned 'communal' organizations and were unable or unwilling to stem the violence and destruction of property the President again issued proclamations dismissing the state governments and the state legislative assemblies in Madhya Pradesh, Rajasthan, and Himachal Pradesh.

---

46 S. Gopal (ed.), *Anatomy of Confrontation: The Babri Masjid–Ram Janmabhumi Issue* (Penguin India: New Delhi, 1991), see Gopal's 'Introduction', p. 13.

The validity of these proclamations was challenged by writ petitions submitted in the high courts of the three aforementioned states (because the government of Uttar Pradesh had voluntarily resigned, there was no challenge from the state). The petition challenging the proclamation in regard to Madhya Pradesh was allowed by its high court, and the appeal against the decision of that court was preferred in the Supreme Court by the Union of India. At the same time the writ petitions that were pending in the high courts of Rajasthan and Himachal Pradesh were transferred to the Supreme Court, and it is with the collective judgment of a Special Bench of nine judges of the Supreme Court on the validity of the proclamations in the three states that we are concerned in this section.[47]

The nine judges of the Supreme Court unequivocally accepted the contentions of the Union of India that the President's proclamations against the states were justified because they 'could not be trusted to adhere to secularism when they had admittedly come to power on the political plank of constructing Shri Ram Mandir on the site of the mosque by relocating the mosque elsewhere which meant by destroying it and then reconstructing it at another place'.[48] From a judicial point of view, the Supreme Court judges used one piece of legislation as a decisive consideration that nailed the case on behalf of the Union of India. That was the Representation of People Act 1951, Section 29A. This Act holds that a political party, or a group of individual citizens of India calling itself a political party, has the right to make an application to the Election Commission for registration as a political party. The applicant undertakes to bear true faith and allegiance to the Constitution of India. (The Constitution, we might remark, calls for a commitment to 'democracy', 'socialism', and 'secularism' of the state, and the pledge to uphold 'the sovereignty and integrity

---

[47] The judgment of the Supreme Court also covers the validity of proclamations of dissolutions previously made by the President of the Union against the governments of Karnataka on 4 April 1989 and Meghalaya on 11 Oct. 1991. In fact, the title of the judgment, *S.R. Bommai* v. *Union of India*, refers to the petition submitted by Mr Bommai against the dissolution of the Karnataka State Legislature. It is interesting that the court held that the proclamation against Meghalaya was invalid (but not necessary to enforce because of subsequent developments there after fresh elections had been held).

[48] *Bommai* v. *U.O.I.*, op. cit., p. 102.

of the nation'.) Now the critical subsection 3A of Section 123 of the aforementioned Act says, explains Judge Ramaswamy, that 'the promotion of, or attempt to promote feelings of enmity or hatred between different classes of Indian citizens, on grounds of religion or caste, etc. by a candidate, his election agent, or any person with his consent, to further the election prospects of that candidate or for prejudicially affecting the election of any candidate [is] declared a corrupt practice. A political party, therefore, should not ignore the fundamental features of the Constitution and the laws'.[49]

The manifestos issued by the BJP, the reports of governors recommending presidential proclamations, as well as the sustained campaigns of the BJP (and its allied organizations), as characterized by the Union counsel and the Union's 'White Paper' were accepted by the judges as proof of contravention of the Representation of People Act of 1951. Justice Ramaswamy underscored this verdict with the crushing [ungrammatical] assertion: 'Rise of fundamentalism and communalization of politics are anti-secularism. They encourage separatist and divisive forces and become breeding grounds for national disintegration and fail the parliamentary democratic system and the Constitution.'[50] The unanimous conclusion of the nine judges of the Supreme Court was that the proclamations dated 15 December 1992 and the actions taken by the President dismissing the ministries and dissolving the legislative assemblies in the states of Madhya Pradesh, Rajasthan, and Himachal Pradesh were not unconstitutional. At the same time the court laid down that 'the validity of Proclamation issued by the President under Art. 356(1) is judicially reviewable to the extent of examining whether it was issued on the basis of any material at all or whether the material was relevant or whether the proclamation was issued in the *mala fide* exercise of the power'. When a prima facie case is made in the challenge to the Proclamation, the burden is on the Union Government to prove that the material did in fact exist, and such material may be either the report of the governor or something other than the report. Since the provisions contained in clause (3) of Art. 356 are intended to be a check on the powers of the President under clause (10), it will not be permissible for the President to exercise powers and to take irreversible actions

[49] Ibid., p. 126.
[50] Ibid., p. 128.

until at least both houses of Parliament have approved of the proclamation.

This landmark judgment in laying down that the President's proclamation under Art. 356(1) was judicially reviewable ensured that India's Union Government could not in future arbitrarily and without due cause dissolve state governments and impose Presidential rule. It is a notable curb on the centre, ensuring the continuance of democracy in India and, in federal terms, strengthening the rights of states to withstand authoritarian moves from the centre. On the other hand, the judgment also stipulated that if state governments violate the principles of 'secularism' as enshrined in the Constitution, they can indeed be dismissed. Justice Sawant declared in memorable words:

Secularism is a part of the basic structure of the Constitution. The acts of a State Government which are calculated to subvert or sabotage secularism as enshrined in our Constitution, can lawfully be deemed to give rise to a situation in which the Government of the State cannot be carried on in accordance with the provisions of the Constitution.[51]

Indeed, it might perhaps even be said that the central agenda of the court was to attempt to spell out what secularism ought to and might mean as a compass for orienting Indian politics, and to this theme I turn again in conclusion.

One of the insistently and repetitively asserted features of the entire lengthy Supreme Court judgment was the space taken by all six separately written verdicts in explicating how the Indian Constitution linked 'democracy', 'secularism', and the 'state' as an integral triad. The judges leisurely and at length cite various 'authorities' whose views buttress their interpretations,[52] in which 'secularism of the state', as asserted in the Constitution and its provisions, appears as a critical theme. Thus, what 'secularism', whatever its shape and entailments elsewhere (in the West), means

[51] Ibid., p. 107. Kuldip Singh co-signed Justice Sawant's verdict.
[52] Aside from a sprinkling of European commentators (for example Jeremy Bentham, Charles Broadlaugh) and excerpts from Gandhi and Nehru, there was resort to the much-favoured philosopher Sarvepalli Radhakrishnan. Dr Ambedkar also figures as a framer of the Constitution. Also of interest is that the lectures of some previous eminent Indian jurists devoted to this topic are cited: examples are Justice Chinappa Reddy's Ambedkar Memorial Lecture on 'Indian Constitution and Secularism' (n.d.), and Shri M.C. Setalvad's 1965 Patel Memorial Lecture on 'Secularism'.

in the *Indian context*, especially as it relates to the 'secular perspective of the Indian state', surfaces as a major preoccupation of the judges. It raised for them a host of questions and discussions relating to the relation between the Indian state and the diverse religions of India, the scope of the state's 'neutrality' and equidistance towards religions, the significance and importance of religion in the life of the people (civil society), the demarcation between the secular activities of the state and the religious practices and institutions of the people, the ways in which the state in an even-handed manner may enable the religious life of Indians and also intervene in that life to ensure Fundamental Rights, and the like.

Let me cite some excerpts from the judgment, which supports the point that a litigation that was ostensibly about the relation between the powers vested in the Federal Union of India and those vested in its constituent states became an occasion for the Supreme Court to expound, not necessarily with perfect clarity, on matters that are of vital concern to contemporary India: democracy, secularism, religious pluralism, 'nationhood', and the relation between religion and politics.

1. It was with the weapons of secularism and non-violence that Mahatma Gandhi fought the battle for independence against the mighty colonial rules. (Justice Ahmadi)
2. Secularism is one of the basic features of the Constitution. While freedom of religion is guaranteed to all persons in India, from the point of view of the State, the religion, faith or belief of a person is immaterial. To the State, all are equal and are entitled to be treated equally. In matters of State, religion has no place. No political party can simultaneously be a religious party. Politics and religion cannot be mixed. Any state government which pursues unsecular policies or unsecular course of action acts contrary to the Constitutional mandate and renders itself amenable to action under Art. 356. (Justice S.C. Agarwal and Justice B.P. Jeevan Reddy).
3. Democracy stands for freedom of conscience and belief, tolerance and mutual respect. India being a plural society with multireligious faiths, diverse creeds, castes and cultures, secularism is the bastion to build fraternity, and amity with dignity of person as its constitutional policy.... The state guarantees individual and corporate religious freedom and deals with an individual as citizen irrespective of his faith and religious belief and does not promote any particular religion nor profess one against another. *The concept of the secular State is, therefore, essential for successful working of the democratic form of Government.* (Justice Ramaswamy)

4. The coming of the partition emphasized the great importance of secularism. Notwithstanding the partition, a large Muslim minority consisting of a tenth of the population continued to be citizens of independent India. There are other important minority groups of citizens. In the circumstances, a secular Constitution for independent India under which all religions could enjoy equal freedom and all citizens equal rights and which could weld together in one nation, the different religious communities became inevitable. (Justice Sawant and Justice Kuldip Singh)

What might be the impact of the Supreme Court's judgment on India's future politics is difficult to gauge.

N. Ram, editor of *Frontline*, assessed the significance of the judgment as follows:

The apex court has done the country and the political system proud. Its judgement is a tremendous blow to the BJP, to the cause of Hindutva and Hindu Rashtra and to every other brand of communalism. In the battle against the adversaries of secularism, the corner has been turned, constitutionally speaking. The path has been cleared to introduce intelligently targeted and tough legislation against the mixing of religion and politics.[53]

But there are however two questions to which the answers are by no means clear. First, can the Supreme Court judgment reviewed above effectively and unambiguously in many contexts separate religion from politics and can it effectively deter or prevent political parties in India from 'mixing religion with politics' now and in the future? Second, is there a wide discrepancy today between the tenor of the Supreme Court's judgment affirming secularism, and the mood of the public in many states showing electoral support for the BJP and a lack of trust in the Congress (I)?[54]

[53] N. Ram 'Securing Secularism and Federation in India—A Landmark Judgement', *Tamil Times*, 15 Aug. 1994, p. 27.
[54] The BJP had its first notable electoral success in 1991 when it won 22 per cent of the national vote, secured 119 seats, and became the country's largest opposition party. It also took control of the governments of four states comprising the Hindi-speaking heartland of north India, namely Uttar Pradesh, Madhya Pradesh, Himachal Pradesh, and Rajasthan. In the 1993 elections, forced by the dissolution of BJP governments in the aftermath of the demolition, the BJP managed to win in Delhi and regain the state of

The truth of the matter in mid-1995 (when this article was being written) is that the BJP as a political party championing Hindutva is not only active in politics, but has in the most recent state assembly elections in March 1995 in Gujarat gained a governing majority, and also been able to form a government in alliance with the Shiv Sena in Maharashtra.[55] It is also the principal opposition in the assemblies of the states of Karnataka and Bihar. The BJP's (and the *sangh parivar's*) continuing capacity to mobilize and energize crowds by the potent use of sacred symbols and rituals, including pilgrimage and *kar seva*, cannot be underestimated. The volatility of Indian politics is such that the BJP seemed to be in an electoral slump in November 1993 when it lost power in the three northern states of Uttar Pradesh, Madhya Pradesh, and Himachal Pradesh. But after riding to power in Maharashtra and Gujarat, and emerging as the principal opposition party in Bihar in the recent assembly elections, coupled with its impressive performance in Karnataka, L.K. Advani confidently pronounced in April 1995 that 'the BJP is growing rapidly, while the Congress (I) is collapsing at an even faster pace'.[56] The comment in *India Today* was that 'Advani may not be exaggerating. In four states which account for 107 of the 545 Lok Sabha seats, the BJP is in power, while it is the main opposition party in five other state legislatures including those of Uttar Pradesh, Madhya Pradesh, Bihar, and Karnataka, which between them account for half the country's population. Against this, the Congress (I) can count as its strong-holds states that together account for less than a fifth of the country's population.'[57] Moreover, at that time the BJP was the only party wanting early elections.

---

Rajasthan, but it lost power in the states of UP, HP, and MP. This was a blow to the BJP but it must be borne in mind that it had managed to increase its percentage of votes in all four states, winning 36.11 per cent votes with the Congress trailing behind with 26.14 per cent. Moreover, the 1995 state assembly elections produced results that put the BJP in a stronger position in the state than in 1993, thereby enabling it to make a strong bid for national power in the following national elections.

[55] By 1996, the BJP had once again lost power in Gujarat to a coalition led by rebels within the party.

[56] 'Bracing for the Bigger Battles', *India Today*, 30 April 1995, p. 14.

[57] Ibid.

However, the BJP's recent comeback may be partly due to the lesson it learned over the Ayodhya issue, that Hindutva alone cannot be the clarion call to power, that it must broaden its policies and devote attention to other issues of efficient government, social reform, and economic expansion, and play down and distance itself from the VHP cause of 'liberating' the Hindu shrines in Mathura and Varanasi. It is beginning to realize that it has to woo the Scheduled Castes and Scheduled Tribes (Backward Classes) and even make overtures to the minorities, especially the Muslims, and tone down the vitriolic propaganda of the Shiv Sena. But how far can it go in this direction without losing its upper and middle caste base for whom Hindutva is a promise of their dominance in a country which at present cannot distribute benefits to all persons. The BJP is at the moment benefiting from the disenchantment with the Congress establishment, but its future depends on how it can widen its electoral base and at the same time make sense of a non-sectarian restoration of Hindu cultural identity. Some commentators have remarked that if the BJP is ever to form a national government is has to move ideologically towards the 'centre' in order to broaden its all-India constituency, shed its ideological radicalism, and enlarge its Hindu nationalist embrace. There are 'self-correcting mechanisms' in Indian democracy,[58] and constraints in India's vast polity and varied society at large that might push the BJP to a less divisive amalgam of religion and politics.

Finally, it is relevant to note that the Supreme Court has in one instance made a clarification as to how 'secular' matters are to be distinguished from 'religious' matters even in the case of religious institutions that have material interests. In October 1994 the Supreme Court asserted that where Ram was born or whether a temple stood previously on the site of Babri Masjid were not judicially reviewable questions; but it was entitled to inquire into the property issue, such as who in fact owns the land on which the mosque stood until December 1992. In this instance, the Court ruled that religious beliefs and mythological claims cannot negate its legal oversight over 'secular' questions such as the rights

58 As claimed by Ashutosh Varshney in 'The Self-corrective Mechanisms of Indian Democracy' in *Seminar India, 1994*, Annual Number (January 1995), Delhi.

of ownership of property.[59] Is the line between the religious and the secular equally decidable in other circumstances, such as raised by the Shah Bano case or by women's rights to abortion? And what kind of accommodations and concessions might the Indian state make towards requests by religious communities and what might it deny; for example school prayer and religious instruction in state (public) schools? As I have suggested before, Art. 25 of the Constitution may continue to pose problems for a government which wishes to impose a set of general laws on its citizens in respect to welfare, health, Fundamental Rights, protection of women and children, social discrimination, and so on, which may collide with religious and socio-religious institutions and practices in places.

---

[59] In this respect the Supreme Court had numerous precedents established during the British Raj when by means of administrative arrangements and laws regarding the management of temporalities and temple properties, endowments, and trusts, the colonial authorities adjudicated property revenue, income, and ritual service claims, and certain other disputes between the priests themselves and between priests and the laity. The British performed the same role in Sri Lanka with regard to Buddhist and Hindu and other temporalities. On this matter, for India, see, for example, Arjun Appadurai, *Worship and Conflict under Colonial Rule* (Cambridge University Press: Cambridge, 1981); C.J. Fuller, *Servants of the Goddess: The Priest of a South Indian Temple* (Cambridge University Press: Cambridge, 1984); Harjot Oberoi, *The Construction of Religious Boundaries, Culture Identity and Diversity in Sikh Tradition* (Oxford University Press: New Delhi, 1994).

# 14

# Secularism and Its Discontents[*]

*Amartya Sen*

## Introduction

When India became independent nearly half a century ago, much emphasis was placed on its secularism, and there were few voices dissenting from that priority. In contrast, there are now persistent pronouncements deeply critical of Indian secularism, and attacks have come from quite different quarters. In this article, I want to examine these discontents.

Before proceeding further, I should say a few words on the audience to which this analysis is addressed. Issues of national, social, and communal identities and their political correlates have received, in recent years, extensive analyses from scholars with much expertise in the field. The subject is, however, also of interest to many others, within India and outside. It would be a pity if an insistence on extensive prior knowledge about details of Indian history or contemporary state were to shut out potential readers from joining in this discussion. This heterogeneity of readership calls, I believe, for a style of presentation that might well be irritating to the knowledgeable expert.[1] I must, therefore, ask for

[*] For helpful discussion I am grateful to Sabyasachi Bhattacharya, Sugata Bose, Joshua Greene, Emma Rothschild, and the editor of this volume.
[1] In a somewhat comparable context, in presenting his essays on 'Africa in the Philosophy of Culture', Kwame Anthony Appiah notes that a work of this kind 'is bound to spend some of its time telling each of its readers something that he or she already knows, and he anticipates that some readers will ask why the author has explained what does not need explaining'. *In My Father's House* (Oxford University Press: New York, 1992), p. xi. This reader is grateful to Appiah for not assuming knowledge of things that any 'Africanist' would know very well. The present essay, similarly, is not for the 'Indianist' only.

tolerance from the bored, but given the assertive nature of this article, I am well aware that boredom is not the thing that would most irritate *some* readers.

Many of the barbed attacks on secularism in India tend to come from activists engaged in practical politics, many of them associated with the BJP (Bharatiya Janata Pary), which has been described as 'the principal political party representing the ideosense, logy of Hindu nationalism in the electoral arena'.[2] Sometimes the attacks have come from the Shiv Sena, the locally powerful militant Hindu party based in Maharashtra and its capital, Mumbai. Persistent critiques of secularism are also associated with the RSS (Rashtriya Sevak Sangh), which does not participate in elections, but which has been the moving force behind a good deal of Hindu activist politics, including providing leadership and direction to the BJP and other parts of the so-called *Sangh parivar* (the 'family' of like-minded organizations oriented towards a Hinduism-based Indian politics).

However, intellectual scepticism about secularism is not confined to those actively engaged in politics. Indeed, eloquent expressions of this scepticism can be found also in the high theory of Indian culture and society.[3] Many of the attacks are quite removed from the BJP and other official organs of Hindu nationalism. In addressing the issue of Indian secularism it is important to take note of the range as well as the vigour of these critiques, and also the fact that they come from varying quarters and use quite distinct arguments. If today 'secularism, the ideological mainstay of multireligious India, looks pale and exhausted',[4] the nature of that predicament would be misidentified—and somewhat minimized—if it were to be seen simply in terms of the politics of Hindu sectarianism. While the attacks on secularism have often

2 Ashutosh Varshney, 'Contested Meanings: Indian National Unity, Hindu Nationalism, and the Politics of Anxiety', *Daedalus* 122 (1993), p. 231.

3 See particularly T.N. Madan, 'Coping with Ethnic Diversity: A South Asian Perspective', in Stuart Plattner (ed.), *Prospects for Plural Societies* (American Ethnological Society, Washington, D.C., 1984), and 'Secularism in Its Place', *Journal of Asian Studies* 46 (1987); and Ashis Nandy, 'An Anti-Secular Manifesto', *Seminar* 314 (1985), and 'The Politics of Secularism and the Recovery of Religious Tolerance', *Alternatives* 13 (1988).

4 Varshney, 'Contested Meanings: Indian National Unity, Hindu Nationalism, and the Politics of Anxiety', p. 227.

come from exactly that quarter, there are other elements too, and the subject calls for a wider analysis and response.

Despite this broad and forceful challenge, secularist intellectuals in India tend to be somewhat reluctant to debate this rather unattractive subject. Reliance is placed instead, usually implicitly, on the well-established and unquestioning tradition of seeing secularism as a good and solid political virtue for a pluralist democracy. As an unreformed secularist myself, I understand, and to some extent share, this reluctance, but also believe that addressing these criticisms is important. This is so not only because the condemnations have implications for political and intellectual life in contemporary India, but also because it is useful for secularists to face these issues explicitly—to scrutinize and re-examine the habitually accepted priorities, as well as the reasoning underlying them. There is much need for self-examination of beliefs—nowhere more so than in practical reason and political philosophy.[5] Hence this attempt at discussing some of the critical questions about secularism that have been forcefully raised.

## Incompleteness of Secularism and the Need to Go Beyond

The nature of secularism as a *principle* requires some clarification as well as scrutiny. Some of the choices considered under the heading of secularism lie, I would argue, beyond its immediate scope. Secularism in the political—as opposed to ecclesiastical—sense requires the separation of the state from any particular religious order. It goes against giving any religion a privileged position in the activities of the state. It is important to be clear as to what the denial of such a privileged position would or would not imply. The requirement is not that the state must steer clear of any association with any religious matter whatsoever. Rather, what is needed is to ensure that in so far as the state has to deal with different religions and members of different religious communities, there must be a basic symmetry of treatment.

5 In this context, see also Charles Taylor et al., *Multiculturalism and the Politics of Recognition* (Princeton University Press: Princeton, 1993).

Therefore, to be secular in the political sense, the state does not have to withdraw from dealing with religions and religious communities altogether. For example, it is no violation of secularism for a state to protect everyone's right to worship as he or she chooses, even though in doing this the state has to work *with*— and *for*—religious communities. In the absence of asymmetric solicitude (such as protecting the rights of worship for one religious community, but not others), the preservation of religious freedom does not breach the principle of secularism.

The important point to note here is that the requirement of symmetric treatment still leaves open the question as to what *form* that symmetry should take. To illustrate with an example, the state may decide that it must not offer financial—or other—support to any hospital with any religious connection whatever or, alternatively, it can provide support to *all* hospitals, without in any way discriminating between the respective religious connections (or no connection at all). While the former may appear to be, superficially, 'more secular' (as it certainly is in the 'associative' sense, since it shuns religious connections altogether), the latter is also *politically* quite secular in the sense that the state, in this case, supports hospitals *irrespective* of whether or not there are any religious connections (and if so, what), and in this way, keeps the state and the religions quite separate.

Since the two forms are both politically secular, a 'secularist' has to face the choice between them (and other options with secular symmetry). Secularism closes some alternatives, but still allows several distinct options. There is, thus, a need—in dealing with religions and religious communities—to take up questions that lie 'beyond' secularism. While this article is concerned with scrutinizing attacks on secularism as a political requirement, the organizational issues that lie beyond secularism must also be characterized.[6] In analysing the role of secularism in India, note must be taken of its intrinsic 'incompleteness', including the problems that this incompleteness leads to, as well as the opportunities it offers.

[6] Some of the arguments presented here draw on an earlier paper (my Nehru Lecture at Trinity College, Cambridge, on 5 February 1993), published under the title 'Threats to Indian Secularism', in *The New York Review of Books* (7 April 1993).

# Critical Arguments

Scepticism about Indian secularism takes many different forms. I shall consider, in particular, six distinct lines of argument. This may be sufficient for a single article, but I do not claim that all anti-secularist attacks are covered by the arguments considered here.

## The 'Non-existence' Critique

Perhaps the simplest version of scepticism about Indian secularism comes from those who see nothing much there; at least nothing of real significance. For example, the typical Western journalists often regard Indian secularism as essentially non-existent, and their language tends to contrast 'Hindu India' (or 'mainly Hindu India') with 'Muslim Pakistan' (or 'mainly Muslim Pakistan'). Certainly, Indian secularism has never been a gripping thought in broad Western perceptions, and recent pictures of politically militant Hindus demolishing an old mosque in Ayodhya have not helped to change these perceptions. Indian protestations about secularism are often seen in the West as sanctimonious nonsense—hard to take seriously in weighty discourses on international affairs and in the making of foreign policy by powerful and responsible Western states that dominate the world of contemporary international politics.

## The 'Favouritism' Critique

A second line of attack argues that in the guise of secularism, the Indian Constitution and political and legal traditions really favour the minority community of Muslims, giving them a privileged status not enjoyed by the majority community of Hindus. This 'favouritism' critique is popular with many of the leaders and supporters of the Hindu activist parties. The rhetoric of this attack can vary from wanting to 'reject' secularism to arguing for what is called 'true secularism' ('shorn of favouring the Muslims').

## The 'Prior Identity' Critique

A third line of critique is more intellectual than the first two. It sees the identity of being a Hindu, or a Muslim, or a Sikh to be politically 'prior' to being an Indian. The Indian identity is 'built up' from the *constitutive* elements of separate identities. In one version of the identity argument, it is asserted that given the preponderance of Hindus in the country, any Indian national identity cannot but be a function of some form or other of a largely Hindu identity. Another version would go further and aim at a homogeneous identity as a necessary basis of nationhood (in line with the picturesque analogy that 'a salad bowl does not produce cohesion; a melting pot does',[7] and move on from that proposition to the claim that only a shared cultural outlook, which in India can only be a largely Hindu view, can produce such a cohesion. Even the unity of India derives, it is argued, from the 'cementing force' of Hinduism.

## The 'Muslim Sectarianism' Critique

In another line of critique, the proposed dominance of Hindu identity in 'Indianness' turns not on the logic of numbers, but is 'forced on the Hindus' it is argued, by the 'failure' of the Muslims to see themselves as Indians first. This form of argument draws heavily on what is seen as the historical failure of Muslim rulers in India to identify themselves with others in the country, always seeing Muslims as a separate and preferred group. It is also claimed that Muslim kings systematically destroyed Hindu temples and religious sites whenever they had the chance to do so.

Jinnah's 'two-nation theory', formulated before Independence (and historically important in the partition of India), is seen as a continuation of the evident Muslim refusal to identify with other Indians. It is argued that while the partition of India has found a 'homeland' for the Muslims of the subcontinent, the Muslims left in India are unintegrated and are basically not 'loyal' to India. The 'evidential' part of this line of critique is, thus, supposed to include suspicions of Muslim disloyalty in contemporary India as well as particular readings of Indian history.

## The 'Anti-modernist' Critique

Contemporary intellectual trends, primarily in the West but also (somewhat derivatively) in India, give much room for assailing

7 See Varshney's helpful characterizations of different claims associated with 'Hindu nationalism', in his 'Contested Meanings', pp 230–1; see also Ashis Nandy, 'The Ramjanmabhumi Movement and the Fear of Self', mimeographed paper, presented at the Harvard Centre for International Affairs, April 1992.

what is called 'modernism'. The fifth line of critique joins force with this rejection of 'modernism' by attacking secularism as a part of the folly of 'modernism'. While post-modernist criticisms of secularism can take many different forms, the more effective assaults on 'secularism as modernism' in India, at this time, combine general anti-modernism with some specific yearning for India's past when things are supposed to have been less problematic in this respect (particularly in terms of peaceful coexistence of different religions). Elements of such understanding tend to form integral parts of the intellectual critiques of some contemporary social analysts.

Ashis Nandy notes that 'as India gets modernized, religious violence is increasing', and he expresses admiration for 'traditional ways of life [which] have, over the centuries, developed internal principles of tolerance'.[8] The denunciation of secularism that follows from this line of reasoning is well captured in Nandy's sharp conclusion: 'To accept the ideology of secularism is to accept the ideologies of progress and modernity as the new justification of domination, and the use of violence to achieve and sustain ideologies as the new opiates of the masses' (p. 192).

## The 'Cultural' Critique

The sixth—and last—critique I shall consider takes the ambitiously 'foundational' view that India is, in essence, a 'Hindu country', and that as a result it would be culturally quite wrong to treat Hinduism as simply one of the various religions of India. It is Hinduism, in this view, that makes India what it is, and to require secularism, with its insistence on treating different religions symmetrically, must turn an epistemic error into a political blunder.

This line of criticism often draws on analogies with formally Christian regimes such as Britain, where the particular history of the country and the special role of its 'own religion' are 'fully acknowledged'. For example, the Archbishop of Canterbury conducts political ceremonies of state at the highest level ('no nonsense about secularism there'). Similarly, the British laws of blasphemy are specifically protective of Christianity and of no

[8] Nandy, 'The Politics of Secularism and the Recovery of Religious Tolerance', p. 188. See also Madan, 'Secularism in Its Place'.

other religion (just as in Pakistan the domain of blasphemy laws penalize 'insults' only to Islam). India, it is complained, denies its indigenous cultural commitment in not providing anything like a similarly privileged status to its 'own' tradition, to wit, the predominantly Hindu heritage.

I shall consider these half a dozen critiques in turn. As was stated before, other grounds for rejection of secularism have also been offered. Some of these critiques involve elaborate conceptual compositions and estimable intricacy of language, and are not breathtakingly easy to penetrate (even armed with a dictionary of neologisms, on the one hand, and courage, on the other). I shall confine myself only to the six lines of criticism of secularism identified earlier, without pretending to be dealing with all the arguments against secularism that have actually been proposed.

## On the 'Non-existence' Critique

Is the 'non-existence' critique to be taken seriously? Many Indian intellectuals tend to view this kind of opinion with some contempt, and are rather reluctant to respond to what they see as obduracy (or worse) of Western observers. This is sometimes combined with a general theory that it does not really matter what 'others' think about India (at most, this is something for the Indian embassies to worry about). This studied non-response is not only insular (ignoring the importance of international understanding in the contemporary world), but also overlooks how crucial the outside perceptions have historically been to the identity of Indians themselves.[9] Even the composite conception of Hinduism as one religion includes the impact of the outsiders' view of the classificatory unity of the religious beliefs and practices in the country.

There is also the recent phenomenon of the support provided by opulent expatriates from the subcontinent to community-based political movements—of Sikhs, Muslims, *and* Hindus—back at 'home'. Because of the relevance of what they read and react to, we can scarcely take foreign reporting on India as 'inconsequential'—even for immediate issues of internal politics in India.

[9] I have touched on this question in my paper 'India and the West', *The New Republic*, 7 June 1993.

The 'non-existence' critique has certainly to be addressed (even if the more informed reader would decide to switch off while that addressing takes place). Is India really the Hindu counterpart of Pakistan? When British India was partitioned, Pakistan chose to be an Islamic Republic, whereas India chose a secular Constitution.[10] Is that distinction significant? It is true that in standard Western journalism, little significance is attached to the contrast, and those in India who would like the country to abandon its secularism often cite this 'forced parity' in Western vision as proof enough that there is something rather hopeless in India's attempt at secularism when the new masters of global politics cannot even tell what on earth is being attempted in India.

Yet the distinction between a secular republic and a religion-based state is really rather important from the legal point of view, and its political implications are also quite extensive. This applies to different levels of social arrangements, including the operations of the courts, going all the way up to the headship of the state. For example, unlike Pakistan, whose Constitution requires that the head of the state be a Muslim, India imposes no comparable requirement, and the country has had non-Hindus (including Muslims and Sikhs) as Presidents and as holders of other prominent and influential offices in government and in the judiciary (including the Supreme Court).

Similarly, to take another example, it is not possible, because of the secularist Constitution of India, to have asymmetric laws of blasphemy applied to one religion only, as it is in Pakistan. There *is* a difference between the legal status that Pakistan gives to Islam (as it must in an 'Islamic Republic') and the lack of a comparable legal status of Hinduism in India. Not surprisingly, the 'non-existence' critique is aired much more frequently abroad than at home, and often takes the form of an implicit presumption—colouring Western analyses of the subcontinent—rather than being aired as an explicit assertion. That hardened belief turns on overlooking extensive and important features of the Indian Constitution and polity.

10 The emergence of Pakistan as a 'Muslim state', under the leadership of Mohammad Ali Jinnah, has a complex—and circumstantially quite contingent—history, on which see particularly Ayesha Jalal, *The Sole Spokesman: Jinnah, the Muslim League and the Demand for Pakistan* (Cambridge University Press: Cambridge, 1985).

Two qualifications should, however, be introduced here. First, the 'non-existence' critique must not be confused with the claim—not infrequently made (often by staunch secularists)—that despite the elements of legal symmetry, Hindus still have a substantive advantage over Muslims in many spheres. This would be, typically, an argument for practising secularism 'more fully' in India, rather than for 'rubbishing' the secularism that already exists. Second, the rejection of the 'non-existence' critique does not identify the exact *form* of secularism that exists in India (nor of course assert anything like the 'superiority' of that specific form of secularism). Indeed, as was discussed earlier, the acceptance of secularism still leaves many questions unanswered about the attitude of the state to different religions. Even when the basic need for symmetry in the political and legal treatment of different religious communities is accepted, we still have to decide on the shape that this symmetry should take, and what the exact domain and reach of that symmetry might be.

To illustrate, symmetry regarding blasphemy laws can be achieved with different formulae—varying from applying it to *all* religions to applying it to *none*. While the former option fits in immediately with a secularist withdrawal of the state from religious affairs, the latter option pursues symmetry between religions in a way that favours no religion in particular. Just as a secular state can protect the liberty of *all* citizens to worship as they please (or not to worship), irrespective of their religious beliefs (and this could not be seen, as was analysed earlier, as a violation of secularism), secularism can, in principle, take the form of 'shielding' every religious community against whatever that community seriously deems as blasphemy. I am not, of course, recommending such 'universal anti-blasphemy laws'; indeed, I would argue very firmly against anti-blasphemy laws in general. My rejection of 'universal anti-blasphemy laws' is not based on seeing them as anti-secular, but on other grounds that go beyond secularism: in particular, the need to prevent religious intolerance and persecution, and the practical infeasibility of making anti-blasphemy laws really 'universal', covering *all* religions in India (including those of the variety of tribal communities that constitute an underprivileged minority in India). The need to choose between different secular forms remains, but this is a very different contention from

saying that the requirement of Indian secularism makes no difference—that it is 'immaterial'.

## On the 'Favouritism' Critique

The 'favouritism' critique turns on interpreting and highlighting
some legal differences between the various communities. They
have been much discussed recently in the activist Hindu political
literature. The differences in 'personal laws' have been particularly
in focus.

It is pointed out, for example, that while a Hindu can be
prosecuted for polygamy, a Muslim man can have up to four wives,
in line with what is taken to be the Islamic legal position (although,
in practice, this provision is extremely rarely invoked by Indian
Muslims). Attention is drawn also to other differences, for example
between the provision for wives in the event of a divorce, where
Muslim women (in line with a certain reading of Islamic law) have
less generous guarantees than that which other Indian women
have—a subject that came to some prominence in the context of
the Supreme Court's judgment on the famous 'Shah Bano case'
(involving the right of support of a divorced Muslim woman from
her estranged and more opulent husband). The existence of these
differences has been cited repeatedly by Hindu political activists
to claim that Hindus, as the majority community, are discriminated against in India, whereas Muslims are allowed to have their
own 'personal laws' and 'special privileges'.

This line of reasoning has many problems. First, if these
examples indicate any 'favouritism', in giving 'special privileges',
in the treatment of the different communities, this can hardly be
a favouritism for Muslims in general. Any unfairness that is there
is surely one against *Muslim women*, rather than against *Hindu men*.
A narrowly 'male'—indeed sexist—point of view is rather conspicuous in the form that these political complaints often take.

Second, it is not the case that the personal laws of the Hindus
have been somehow overridden in post-Independence India by
some uniform civil code. The separate status of Hindu personal
laws has *in general* survived. The issue of a uniform civil code has
to be distinguished from the fact that the Hindu laws were
reformed after Independence, particularly during 1955 and 1956
(with little opposition—indeed they resulted from political move-

ments *within* the Hindu communities). The possibility of polygamy was explicitly ruled out by the reforms of the Hindu laws.
It did not follow from some 'uniform' civil codes being imposed
on the Hindus but not the Muslims. Nor did it make the Hindu
personal laws inoperative—quite the contrary. Several other provisions were introduced *within* the Hindu laws themselves,    but
the domain of Hindu personal laws continues to be quite substantial.

The makers of the Indian Constitution did express some
preference for 'uniformity of fundamental laws, civil and criminal',
which was seen by Dr Ambedkar (the leader of the team that
framed the Constitution of India) as important for maintaining the
unity of the country.[11] In the event, however, such uniformity was
not incorporated in the Constitution that emerged, and the
preference for uniformity was only included as a 'Directive
Principle of State Policy'—*without* enforceability. The principle
that was adopted demanded that 'the State shall endeavour to
secure for the citizens a uniform civil code throughout the territory
of India'. Like all the 'Directive Principles' enunciated in the Indian
Constitution, this was seen as 'fundamental in the governance of
the country' and it was specified that 'it shall be the duty of the
State to apply' this principle, but at the same time this principle
(like the other 'directive' ones) 'shall not be enforceable by any
court'.[12]

It is, of course, up to the courts to see how far to go in line
with this Directive Principle. In the much-debated case of the 'Shah
Bano judgment', involving a Muslim woman's right to a better
financial deal at the time of divorce, the Indian Supreme Court did
indeed make a move in the direction of uniformity.[13] The Court

11 On the history of this aspect of Indian laws, see John H. Mansfield, 'The
Personal Laws or a Uniform Civil Code?', in Robert Baird (ed.), *Religion and
Law in Independent India* (Manohar: Delhi, 1993), which also provides a
balanced review of the pros and cons of the case for submerging different
personal laws in India in a 'uniform civil code'. See also Tahir Mahmood,
*Muslim Personal Law: Role of the State in the Indian Subcontinent* (Nagpur,
second edn, 1983).

12 Constitution of India, Art. 37.

13 This was done by the Supreme Court by giving priority—over the
provisions of Islamic law for divorce settlements—to section 125 of the Code
of Criminal Procedure, which requires a person of adequate means to protect

also revealed some disappointment at the government's failure to move in the direction of a uniform civil code in line with the 'constitutional ideal' (and noted that this constitutional provision had 'remained a dead letter'). Indeed, as one observer has noted, 'the intensity of Muslim reaction to the Supreme Court's judgment in that case was partly explained by the inclusion of this utterance and the suggestion that what the government had failed to do, the Court itself might undertake'.[14] The 'Muslim reaction' was not, however, by any means uniform, and there was support as well as criticism for the Supreme Court's judgment, from different sections of that community.[15] It was Rajiv Gandhi's Congress government that ultimately 'caved in', and enacted fresh legislation that further supported the 'separatist' view, rather than following the Supreme Court's push in the direction of greater uniformity.

The general issue of asymmetric treatment is indeed an important one, and there would, of course, be nothing non-secular in pursuing the possibility of making the provisions of a set of uniform civil laws that apply even-handedly to individuals of *all* the communities. On the other hand, as was argued earlier in this article the principles of secularism will also permit an arrangement by which separate personal laws continue well into the future (so long as the different religious communities are treated with symmetry). In arguing against the latter option, considerations of justice may well be raised that demand some symmetry not only in the way the different religious communities are treated, but also in the way fairness is applied across other classificatory distinctions

---

from destitution and vagrancy one's relations (including one's spouse, minor children, handicapped adult children, and aged parents). For critical analyses of the rather complex considerations involved in the Shah Bano case, see Asghar Ali Engineer, *The Shah Bano Controversy* (Ajanta Publishers: Delhi, 1987), and Veena Das, *Critical Events* (Oxford University Press: New Delhi, 1992, ch. IV). Also see Mansfield, 'Personal Laws or a Uniform Civil Code?'.
14 Mansfield, 'Personal Laws or a Uniform Civil Code', p. 140.
15 The Supreme Court had also taken this opportunity of commenting on the disadvantaged position of women in India (not just amongst Muslims, but also amongst Hindus), and had called for greater justice in this field. The Shah Bano case did indeed also receive much attention from the women's political groups.

(for example between the different classes, between women and men, between the poor and the rich, between the 'élite' and the 'subalterns', and so on).

The choice between these two options—and intermediate ones—remains open, and certainly cannot be closed in one direction or the other by the requirements of secularism alone. To note this is not a concession of the failure of secularism, but rather an acknowledgement of its circumscribed domain and the affirmation of the need to go beyond secularism—with other principles of fairness and justice—to identify specific legal and social forms. While there is not much substance in the charge of 'favouritism' benefiting Muslims, and certainly no general case against secularism can be constructed on that line of reasoning, it is useful to integrate the discussion on secularism with the principles—such as those of justice—that lie beyond it. We have to distinguish, in particular, between (1) the need for symmetry among different religious communities (a secularist consideration) and (2) the question of what form that symmetry should take (a concern that has to be consolidated with other principles of justice which take us well beyond secularism into, on the one hand, the importance that may be attached to group autonomy of religious communities and, on the other, the inescapable issue of equity for different groups of Indians, classified in non-religious categories: class, gender, etc.).

## On the 'Prior-identity' Critique

The question of political and religious identities raises issues of a rather different kind. There can be little doubt that many Indians—indeed most Indians—have religious beliefs of one kind or another, and regard these beliefs to be important in their personal lives. The issue that is raised by the claimed priority of this identity in the political context is not the general importance of religious beliefs in *personal* or even *social* behaviour, but the specific relevance of that identity in *political* matters (with and without the involvement of the state).

It is useful in this context to recollect the contrast between the religiosity of political leaders in pre-Independence India and their respective beliefs in a secular identity. Jinnah, the great advocate of the 'two-nation theory' and the founding father of the Islamic Republic of Pakistan, was scarcely a devout Muslim, whereas Maulana

Abul Kalam Azad, the President of the Indian National Congress and a major leader of the Indian Union, was a deeply religious Muslim.[16] Similarly, Shyama Prasad Mukhopadhyay, the leader of the Hindu Mahasabha, had very few Hindu practices compared with, say, Mahatma Gandhi, who was both actively religious in personal life and in social practice (for example he held regular prayer meetings that were open to the public) and also staunchly secularist in politics (insisting on symmetric political treatment of different religions and on an effective separation of the state and religions). When Mahatma Gandhi was murdered by an extremist Hindu politician, the complaint against him was not that he did not follow Hindusim in his personal life or in his social activities, but that he was, allegedly, very 'soft' on Muslims in political matters, and did not give priority to Hindu interests in politics.

The importance of religious identity has to be separated from the relevance of that identity in the political context. It is, thus, odd to require that an Indian must 'go through' her religious identity first, *before* asserting her Indianness, and even less plausible to insist that the Indian identity *must* be 'built up' on the constitutive basis of the different religious identities. That assertion of priority comes not only from religious sectarians (particularly, in recent years, the so-called 'Hindu nationalists'), but also from those who have been especially worried about the usurping role of the state (as opposed to community) and about the violences committed by the state. In this context, the issue of a national identity is often identified, misleadingly I believe, with the philosophy of a 'nation-state', thus giving an inescapably 'statist' orientation to the very conception of any political unity *across* religious communities and other social divisions. It is certainly

16 Indeed, Azad was among the 'traditional' Muslims, as opposed to the 'reformers' (for example from the Aligarh school). On the intricacies of Azad's religious and political attitudes, see Ayesha Jalal, 'Exploding Communalism: The Politics of Muslim Identity in South Asia', in Sugata Bose and Ayesha Jalal (eds), *Nationalism, Democracy and Development: State and Politics in India* (Oxford University Press: New Delhi, 1997, Ch. 5). Jalal also discusses the much broader question of a general misfit between (1) the reformism–traditionalism division among Muslims in pre-partition India, and (2) the division between Muslims who favoured an undivided India and those who wanted Pakistan. In particular, quite often the Muslim traditionalists opted to stay on in India (as Azad himself did), especially after the Khilafat movement.

true that in the emergence or consolidation of that unity, the nation-state may well have an important instrumental role, but the state need not be central to the conceptual foundation of this unity, nor provide its constructive genesis. It is, for example, not a 'category mistake' to think of the Indian nation prior to 1947 as encompassing the residents of the so-called 'native states' (such as Travancore), and also of the non-British colonial territories (such as Goa), even though they did not 'belong to' the same *state* at all. It is a mistake to think that the idea of a nation requires the prior presence of a national state.

A second problem in this line of reasoning concerns the use of this route to arrive at the proposed Hindu view of India. Even if the religious identities were somehow 'prior' to the political identity of being an Indian, one could scarcely derive the view of a Hindu India based on that argument alone. The non-Hindu communities—Muslims in particular, but also Christians, Sikhs, Jains, Parsis, and others—are scarcely 'marginal' in the country even in numerical terms.

India has well over a hundred million Muslims, not much less than Pakistan, and rather more than Bangladesh. Indeed, in terms of the number of Muslim citizens, India is the third largest Muslim country in the world. To see India just as a Hindu country is a fairly bizarre idea in the face of that fact alone, not to mention the intermingling of Hindus and Muslims in the social and cultural life of India (in literature, music, painting, and the like). Also, Indian religious plurality extends far beyond the Hindu–Muslim division. There is a large and prominent Sikh population, and a substantial number of Christians, whose settlements go back at least to the fourth century AD (considerably earlier than the time-period when Britain had any Christians at all). There have also been Jewish settlements in India from just after the fall of Jerusalem. Parsis moved to India many hundreds of years ago to escape less tolerant Iran. To this we have to add the millions of Jains and practitioners of Buddhism, which had been, for a long period, the official religion of many of the Indian emperors (including the great Ashoka, in the third century BC, who had ruled over the largest empire in the history of the subcontinent).

Furthermore, large also is the number of Indians who are atheist or agnostic (as Jawaharlal Nehru himself was), and that tradition in India goes well back to the ancient times (to Carvaka and the Lokayata, among other agnostic schools). The classificatory conventions of the Indian statistics tend to disestablish the recognition of such heterodox beliefs, since the categories used represent what in India has come to be called 'community', without recording actual religious beliefs (for example, an atheist born in a Hindu family is classified as Hindu, reflecting the so-called 'community background').

Those who framed the Indian Constitution wanted to give appropriate recognition to the extensive religious pluralism of the Indian people, and did not want to derive the notion of Indianness from any specific religious identity in particular. As Dr Ambedkar, the leader of the Indian Constituent Assembly, put it, 'if the Muslims in India are a separate nation, then, of course, India is not a nation'.[17] Given the heterogeneity of India and of the Indians, there is no real political alternative to ensuring some basic symmetry and an effective separation of the state from each particular religion.[18]

The programme of deriving an Indian identity via a Hindu identity, thus, encounters problems from two different directions. First, it suffers from insufficient discrimination between (1) *personal and social* religious involvement and (2) giving *political* priority to that involvement (against symmetric treatment of different religions). Second, it fails to recognize the implications of India's immense religious diversity.

Indeed, the issue of religious plurality does not relate only to the relationship between Hindus and followers of other faiths (or none). It also concerns the divergences *within* Hinduism itself. The divisions do, of course, include those of caste, and the nature of contemporary Indian politics reflects this at different levels with inescapable force. But the diversities that characterize Hinduism are not just of caste. They also encompass divergent beliefs, distinct customs, and different schools of religious thought.

---

[17] In his insightful paper 'Hindu/Muslim/Indian', in *Public Culture* 5, 1 (Fall 1992), Faisal Devji begins with this (and another) quotation from Ambedkar, and goes on to critically scrutinize the relation between different identities (raising issues that are much broader than those addressed here).

[18] See also Nur Yalman, 'On Secularism and Its Critics: Notes on Turkey, India and Iran', *Contributions to Indian Sociology* 25 (1991). See also Gary Jeffrey Jacobson, 'Three Models of the Secular Constitution', mimeo., Williams College, 1995, and the literature cited there.

Even the ancient classification of 'six systems of philosophy' in India acknowledged deeply diverse beliefs and reasoning. More recently, when the authoritative Hindu scholar Madhava Acharya of the fourteenth century (head of the religious order in Sringeri in Mysore) wrote his famous Sanskrit treatise *Sarvadarsana Samgraha* ('collection of all philosophies'), he devoted sixteen chapters to as many different schools of Hindu religious thought (beginning, in fact, with the atheism of the Carvaka school, which is the subject of the first chapter). He examined in some detail how each religious school differed from the others, and what their own arguments were in favour of their respective beliefs and what counter-arguments could be raised against them (even though he did not flinch from coming out, ultimately, in support of his own Vaishnavite beliefs in the last chapter).

Indeed, seeing Hinduism as a unified religion is a comparatively recent development. The term 'Hindu' was traditionally used mainly as a signifier of location and country, rather than of any homogeneous religious belief. The word derives from the river Indus or 'Sindhu' (the cradle of the Indus valley civilization that flourished from around 3000 BC), and the name of that river is also the source of the word 'India' itself. The Persians and the Greeks saw India as the land around and beyond the Indus, and Hindus were the native people of that land. Muslims from India were at one stage called 'Hindavi' Muslims, in Persian as well as Arabic, and there are plenty of references in early British documents to 'Hindoo Muslims' and 'Hindoo Christians', to distinguish them respectively from Muslims and Christians from outside India.

A pervasive plurality of religious beliefs and traditions characterizes Hinduism as a religion. The point can be illustrated with the attitude to Rama, in whose name so much of the current Hindu political activism is being invoked (including demolition of the Babri mosque in Ayodhya, 'the birthplace of Rama'). The identification of Rama with divinity is common in the north and west of India, but elsewhere (for example in my native Bengal), Rama is largely the heroic king of the epic *Ramayana*, rather than God incarnate. The *Ramayana* itself is, of course, widely popular, as an epic, everywhere in India, and has been so outside India too—in Thailand and Indonesia for example (even Ayutthaya, the historical capital of Thailand, is a cognate of Ayodhya). But the power and

influence of the epic *Ramayana*—a wonderful literary achievement—has to be distinguished from the particular issue of Rama's
divinity.

Indeed, in *Ramayana* itself, the epic hero Rama is treated very
much as a good and self-sacrificing king rather than as God, and
there is even an interesting occasion on which he is lectured by
a sceptical pundit called Javali: 'O Rama, be wise, there exists no
world but this, that is certain! Enjoy that which is present and cast
behind thee that which is unpleasant.'[19] Even though the *Ramayana*
records that Rama chose to spurn that fearless advice, he emerges
principally as a good and pious king, not as divinity incarnate.

Indeed, Rabindranath Tagore, in his *Vision of India's History*,
showers Rama with special praise precisely because Rama, as
Tagore put it, 'appeared as divine to the primitive tribes, some of
whom had the totem of monkey, some that of bear'.[20] Tagore's
remark, which might appear to be rather irreverent to a Rama
disciple, only serves to illustrate the extent to which the attitude
to Rama varies across the country. Another great Bengali poet,
Madhusudhan Dutt, chooses Rama's adversary, Meghnad, as the
hero of his dramatic poetry, and Rama and his brothers do not
emerge as particularly admirable in that classic—and highly popular—book.

The same can be said about the claims to pre-eminent divinity
of the other putatively divine characters in one part of India or
another. If we must use the analogy of the 'melting pot' and the
'salad bowl', to which a reference was made earlier, the Hindu
traditions do not constitute a melting pot in any sense whatever.
This need not, of course, prevent Hindus from living together in
great harmony and mutual tolerance, but then the same goes for
a community of Hindus, Muslims, Christians, Sikhs, Jains, Buddhists, Parsis, Jews, and people without any religion. Not only is
there, in general, no necessity to build up an Indian identity from
any 'prior' assertion of individual religious identities, it is hard to
get to a unified Indian identity from the rich diversity of Hindu
traditions across the country.

[19] English translation from H.P. Shastri, *The Ramayana of Valmiki* (London,
1952), p. 389.
[20] Rabindranath Tagore, *A Vision of India's History* (Visva-Bharati: Calcutta,
1951, rpt. 1962), p. 32.

# On the 'Muslim Sectarianism' Critique

I turn now to the issue of the alleged Muslim disloyalty to India. Spirited anecdotes abound on this subject, varying from the alleged frequency of Indian Muslims spying for Pakistan to their tendency, we are told, of cheering the Pakistan cricket team in test matches (whether or not Indian Muslims do this in any significant number—I don't know of any evidence in that direction—I ought to confess that this non-Muslim author often does just that, when the Pakistan team plays as well as it frequently does).

There is, in fact, no serious evidence for the hypothesis of the political disloyalty of the Indian Muslims. In fact, a great many Muslims stayed on in post-Partition India (instead of going to Pakistan) as a deliberate decision to remain where they felt they belonged. In the Indian armed forces, diplomatic services, and administration, Muslims have no different a record on loyalty to India than Hindus and other Indians have. (Even on the momentous subject of cricket, India has, in fact, been led for many years by its Muslim captain, Mohammad Azharuddin.) There is no significant empirical evidence to substantiate the critique, and the unfairness of this specious line of reasoning is quite hard to beat.[21]

Allegations of Muslim sectarianism are sometimes linked up with a certain reading of Indian history (though 'reading' may well be the wrong word to use here). Muslim kings were, it is claimed, consistently alienated from their Hindu subjects. They destroyed, allegedly, as many Hindu temples as they could and asserted their alienation in other noticeable ways.

Was that, in fact, the case? Muslim invaders in north India did indeed destroy many Hindu temples and, certainly between the 11th and the 13th century, the early Muslim invaders and

---

21 The case of Kashmir is, of course, different in several respects, including its separate history and the peculiar politics of its accession to India and its aftermath. The evident disaffection of a substantial part of the Kashmiri Muslim population relates to the very special political circumstances obtaining there and the treatment they have received respectively from both India and Pakistan. The Kashmir issue certainly demands political attention on its own (I am not taking up that thorny question here), but the special circumstances influencing the viewpoints of three million Kashmiri Muslims can scarcely be used to question the strong record of national loyalty and solidarity of the 110 million Muslims in general in India.

raiders demolished or mutilated a remarkably large number of temples, along with causing general devastation. For example, Sultan Mahmud, coming from Ghazni (in what is now Afghanistan), repeatedly invaded north and west India in the eleventh century, and devastated cities as well as temples, including famous ones in Mathura, Kanauj, and what is now Kathiawar (where the plundered and devastated Somnath temple had been widely renowned for its treasures). The destructive record gradually receded with the Indianization of Islamic rulers, but it would still be foolish to claim that no demolition of Hindu sites ever occurred under the Indian Muslim kings (no matter how infrequent such demolitions might have become). The real question is what to conclude from these facts.

In the context of defending the importance of secularism in contemporary India, it is not in any way essential to make any claim whatsoever about how Muslim emperors of the past behaved—whether they were sectarian or assimilative, oppressive or tolerant. There is no intrinsic reason why a defence of India's secularism must take a position on what, say, the Mughals did or did not do. The 'guilt' of Muslim kings, if any, need not be 'transferred' to the 110 million Muslims who live in India today. Also, we can scarcely form a view of the political commitments of Muslims in contemporary India, or of their political loyalties, by checking what Muslim kings might or might not have done many centuries ago.

However, in the political discussions that accompanied the activist incursions of Hindu communal politics (for example the demolition of the Babri mosque), a certain characterization of the Mughal rule—not just of Aurangzeb, but more sweepingly of the Mughals in general—was constantly invoked. No view of Muslims in contemporary India can really be formed on the basis of the conduct of Muslim kings in the past (this general point must be firmly asserted first). Nevertheless, we cannot escape addressing this contingent historical issue, since the two questions are strongly linked in the minds of many political activists, and a non-response would appear to them (and to those influenced by that line of reasoning) to be unsatisfactory—or worse.[22]

22 This relates to a methodological point I have tried to discuss elsewhere that the historical arguments in which we have to engage, given their *supposed*

It is, in fact, not possible to find any kind of uniformity in the attitude of Muslim kings to the Hindu population. They varied greatly in terms of sympathy for their subjects, as had the Hindu and Buddhist kings before them. Some were friendly to their subjects, others were not. Some were keen' on converting the Hindus, others were not. It is hard to construct a picture of persistent persecution of Hindus by Muslim kings—tempting though that hypothesis clearly is to some Hindu politicians.[23]

The anti-Hindu bias of Emperor Aurangzeb is often cited and made much of. He clearly did have considerable intolerance of Hinduism, and there is indeed evidence of his destroying some temples, imposing special taxes on Hindus, and so on. But to see Aurangzeb as the representative Muslim monarch of India—or for that matter as the typical Mughal emperor—would be a serious falsification of history.

None of the other Mughals, in fact, showed anything like the intolerance of Aurangzeb, and some had made great efforts to treat the different religious communities in an even-handed way. The great emperor Akbar, who reigned between 1556 and 1605, was of course deeply interested in Hindu philosophy and culture, and attempted to establish something of a synthetic religion (the

---

political importance, may not be the ones we ourselves would accept as particularly significant. To leave unaddressed the charge of a generally 'anti-Hindu attitude' of the Mughal kings would be politically unconvincing to those with whom we argue, even though we may not ourselves think that the behaviour of the Mughals would matter one way or the other in assessing the claims of Muslims in contemporary India. On this, see my 'Interpreting India's Past', mimeo.

23 The present political attempt to portray the Muslim rulers in general, and the Mughals in particular, as intolerant of Hindus contrasts sharply from the assessments of earlier Hindu religious leaders. For example, Sri Aurobindo who established the famous ashram in Pondicherry saw the history of Muslim rule in India in a very different light. *The Spirit and Form of Indian Polity* (Arya Publishing House: Calcutta, 1947), pp 86–9:

[T]he Mussulman domination ceased very rapidly to be a foreign rule....The Mugal empire was a great and magnificent construction and an immense amount of political genius and talent was employed in its creation and maintenance. It was as splendid, powerful and beneficent and, it may be added, in spite of Aurangzeb's fanatical zeal, infinitely more liberal and tolerant in religion than any medieval or contemporary European kingdom or empire.

Din-i-Ilahi) drawing on the different faiths in India. His court was filled with Hindu as well as Muslim intellectuals, artists, and musicians, and he tried in every way to be non-sectarian and symmetric in the treatment of his subjects. But Akbar was not by any means unique among the Mughal emperors in seeing Hindus differently from the way Aurangzeb preferred to view them.

It is actually interesting to consider Aurangzeb in his familial setting (in the context of others with whom he was associated), not in isolation. None of his immediate family seemed to have shared Aurangzeb's intense sectarianism. His elder brother, Dara Shikoh, was greatly interested in Hindu philosophy and had himself, with the help of some scholars, prepared a Persian translation of some of the Upanishads. Dara Shikoh had somewhat stronger claims to the Mughal throne than Aurangzeb had, since he was the eldest and the favourite son of his father, Emperor Shah Jahan. Aurangzeb grabbed the throne after fighting and defeating Dara, who was tortured and beheaded by the former who also imprisoned their father Shah Jahan for the rest of his life (leaving him, the builder of the Taj Mahal, to gaze at his creation, in captivity, from some distance). Aurangzeb's anti-Hindu position contrasted sharply—and may even have been dialectically influenced by—the electric and somewhat Hinduized brother whom he hated so much.

But Dara was not the only relation Aurangzeb had to encounter; he was, in fact, surrounded by people who differed from him in their attitude towards Hindus. Even his own son, also called Akbar, who had rebelled against his father in 1681, joined the Hindu Rajput kings to fight his father. After the Rajputs were pushed back by Aurangzeb's army, Akbar continued his battle against the Mughal empire by joining Raja Sambhaji, the son of Shivaji who fought the Mughals and who is much revered by contemporary Hindu activists. Even the name of the Hindu activist party 'Shiv Sena', referred to earlier, invokes Shivaji who has become such a cult figure among militant Hindus.[24] Also, among

---

[24] Shivaji himself was, it appears, quite respectful of other religions. Some historians (such as Sir Jadunath Sarkar, the author of *Shivaji and His Times*, published in 1919) attribute to him a forceful letter sent to Aurangzeb on religious tolerance. The letter contrasts Aurangzeb's intolerance with the policies of earlier Mughals (Akbar, Jahangir, Shah Jahan), and then says this:

> If Your Majesty places any faith in those books by distinction called divine, you will there be instructed that God is the God of all mankind, not the God of Muslims alone. The Pagan and the Muslim are equally

the proposals that the Shiv Sena made immediately after its victory in the state elections in Maharashtra was the motion to rename the city of Aurangabad after Raja Sambhaji himself. Akbar also had fairly acrimonious correspondence with his father, defending the excellence of his Hindu allies against his father's vilification of such people. Aurangzeb had to encounter his son's theorizing, in addition to his elder brother's philosophy, on the subject of respect for Hindus.

No general picture of consistent hostility of the Muslim kings to their Hindu subject emerges from Indian history. No matter what the relevance of this line of inquiry is in judging Muslim integration today (as already stated, I believe that relevance to be rather slight), this line of reasoning breaks down even in terms of the basic facts on which the thesis is meant to draw. The overwhelming fact that remains is the loyalty of the large Muslim population in India, and the clear recognition that their record is not in any way different from those of the other religious communities, including Hindus.

## On the 'Anti-modernist' Critique

Turning now to the anti-modernist critique of secularism, is it really the case that 'as India gets modernized, religious violence is increasing' (as Ashis Nandy says)? There are certainly periods in history in which this is exactly what has happened. For example,

---

in His presence....In fine, the tribute you demand from the Hindus is repugnant to justice. [Vincent Smith in Percival Spear (ed.) *The Oxford History of India*, 4th edn (Oxford University Press: London, 1974), pp 417–18]

This letter may or may not have been actually authored by Shivaji (an alternative hypothesis attributes the authorship to Rana Raj Singh of Mewar/ Udaipur), but it would be consistent with his attitude to the religions of others. Indeed, the Mughal historian Khafi Khan, who was no admirer of Shivaji in other respects, nevertheless had the following to say about his treatment of Muslims:

[Shivaji] made it a rule that wherever his followers were plundering, they should do no harm to the mosques, the book of God, or the women of anyone. Whenever a copy of the sacred Quran came into his hands, he treated it with respect, and gave it to some of his Musalman followers. [Vincent Smith, *The Oxford History of India*, p. 412]

the communal riots immediately preceding the partition of the country in 1947 almost certainly took many more lives than any violence between the different communities earlier on in Indian history. As the country has moved on from there (presumably not decreasing in 'modernity'), the general level of violence has fallen from its peak in the 1940s—indeed the number of incidents have been quite tiny *in comparison* with what happened half a century ago.

We must not, however, interpret Ashis Nandy's statement too literally. The thesis presented deals with a presumed shift in the *long run*, away from a pre-modern situation in which 'traditional ways of life' had 'over the centuries, developed internal principles of tolerance'. There is undoubtedly some plausibility in such a diagnosis—there is some evidence that the level of communal violence did indeed increase with colonial rule. On the other hand, even in India's pre-colonial past there have been periods (for example between the eleventh and the thirteenth centuries, as discussed earlier) in which violence, especially by sectarian armed forces, escalated sharply, and then ebbed. But Nandy is right to assert that, in general, 'principles of tolerance' have tended to develop eventually, as people of different backgrounds have settled down to live next to one another. It is not, I believe, central to Nandy's thesis to check whether the time trend of communal violence has been consistently upwards, nor particularly interesting to compare the numbers killed in recent years vis-à-vis those in the past (the massive increase in the absolute size of the population would bias those numbers anyway). The point rather is the thesis that principles of tolerance do develop in multi-community societies, unless they are disrupted by contrary moves, and Nandy sees the development of 'modernism' as just such a move.

But what exactly *is* modernism that could so disrupt the process of tolerance? The concept of modernity is not an easy one to identify, even though many post-modernists seem to share the modernists' comfortable belief in the easily characterized nature of modernism. We might resist being sent off on an errand of finding the 'true meaning of modernism', and concentrate instead on the specific depiction of 'secularism as modernism', which is central to Nandy's concern. The point of departure would then be the argument forcefully presented by Nandy (as was quoted earlier):

'to accept the ideology of secularism is to accept the ideologies of progress and modernity as the new justification of domination, and the use of violence to achieve and sustain ideologies as the new opiates of the masses'. This is quite a grand vision, but would seem to be, nevertheless, based on an odd characterization of secularism. The principle of secularism basically demands (as was discussed earlier) symmetric treatment of different religious communities in politics and in the affairs of the state. It is not obvious why such symmetric treatment must somehow involve 'the use of violence to achieve and sustain ideologies as the new opiates of the masses'.

I am aware that the nation-state is under great suspicion these days as a constant perpetrator of violence, and indeed the state does manage to do many violent things. What is not clear is why taking a symmetric attitude to different communities would encourage, or add to, such state violence. To invoke some concepts much favoured in contemporary theory, it is not, of course, difficult to conceive that a state might 'homogenize' to 'hegemonize', but it seems, at best, intensely abstract to see this happening whenever the state stops favouring one religious community over another (as secularism requires). If the experience of British colonial rule is meant to be taken as a guide on how secularism can be used to accentuate communal violence, surely we ought to see more clearly how 'divide and rule' is used for this purpose, rather than a programme of 'unite and homogenize'. Indeed, a non-sectarian and symmetric approach to governance and statecraft may do a lot to reduce tension and violence. Also, since the concept of secularism applies to politics in general (not just to state policy), it is also worth asserting that secular politics may well reduce, rather than add to, the violence that many societies standardly have (when political attitudes are non-symmetric, sectarian, and suspicious across the boundaries of the respective communities).

It is, thus, hard to escape the suspicion that something has gone oddly wrong in the cited diagnostics. Nor is it obvious why secular symmetry should be characteristic only of 'modernity'. Indeed, even ancient states run by, say, an Ashoka or an Akbar did some things to achieve just such symmetric treatments, and there is no evidence that these historical attempts at secular symmetry *increased*, rather than lessening, communal violence.

I would argue that it is not really helpful to see secularism and modernism in these oddly formulaic terms. Indeed, 'the principles of tolerance', on which Nandy relies, is not really that remote from taking a symmetric view of other communities, and it is less than fair to political secularism to be depicted in the way it is in these indictments. The development of secular attitudes and politics can surely be a *part* of that mechanism of tolerance, rather than running against it, unless we choose to define secularism in some very special way.

The idea of 'modernity' is also deeply problematic—in general and also in the postulated relation with secularism. Was Ashoka or Akbar more or less 'modern' than Aurangzeb? Perhaps the question being raised here can be illustrated with another historical example, involving differences between contemporaries. Consider the contrast between the sectarian destruction caused by Sultan Mahmud of Ghazni in the eleventh century (to which reference was made earlier) and the reactions of Alberuni, the Arab-Iranian traveller (and distinguished mathematician), who accompanied Mahmud to India and felt revolted by the violence he saw:

Mahmud utterly ruined the prosperity of the country, and performed there wonderful exploits, by which Hindus became like atoms of dust scattered in all directions.[25]

He went on to suggest—perhaps overgeneralizing a little—that the Hindus, as a result, 'cherish, of course, the most inveterate aversion towards all Muslims'. That 'aversion' was, happily, not enough to prevent Alberuni from having a large number of Hindu friends and collaborators, with whose help he mastered Sanskrit and studied the contemporary Indian treatises on mathematics, astronomy, sculpture, philosophy, and religion.[26]

However, Alberuni did not stop there, but proceeded to provide an analysis of why people of one background tend to be suspicious of those from other backgrounds, and identified the need for a balanced understanding of these problems—a good starting point for the symmetry that is essential for secularism:

[25] Ainslie T. Embree (ed.), *Alberuni's India*, trans. Edward C. Sachau(Norton: New York, 1971), Ch. I, p. 22.
[26] In fact, Alberuni's work and his translations of Indian mathematical and astronomical treatises had great influence in continuing the Arabic studies (well established by the eighth century) of Indian science and mathematics, which reached Europe through the Arabs.

...in all manners and usages, [the Hindus] differ from us to such a degree as to frighten their children with us, with our dress, and our ways and customs, and as to declare us to be devil's breed, and our doings as the very opposite of all that is good and proper. By the by, we must confess, in order to be just, that a similar depreciation of foreigners not only prevails among us and the Hindus, but is common to all nations towards each other.[27]

Those who like 'modernism' would probably prefer to see Alberuni as a 'modern' intellectual of some kind (albeit from the eleventh century), but that would be a rather far-fetched reaction.

In fact, modernism is not really the issue at all. The substantive views of Alberuni, with their emphasis on an unbiased understanding and a symmetric tolerance of different communities, are a positive force in the direction of reducing violence and mindless destruction, and that approach cannot be torn away from the pursuit of secularism, no matter whether we call it 'modern', 'pre-modern', or 'post-modern'. I conclude this section by noting that the characterization of secularism as modernism is not particularly cogent, nor does it provide an especially persuasive basis for rejecting secularism. (There is also the 'bigger' issue, not unrelated to the preceding discussion, as to whether the 'anti-modernists' are not too respectful of 'modernism', seeing the idea of modernity as cogent and coherent—but that subject I have to postpone for a later occasion.)

## On the 'Cultural' Critique

I turn, finally, to the 'cultural' critique, and to the suggestion that India should really be seen as a 'Hindu country' in cultural terms. This, it is argued, militates against secularism in India, since secularism denies that basic recognition.

There are two questions to be raised here. First, even if it were right to see Indian culture as basically Hindu culture, it would be very odd to alienate, on that ground, the right to equal political and legal treatment of minorities (including the political standing and rights of the 110 million Indian Muslims). Why should the cultural dominance of one tradition, even if true, reduce the political entitlements and rights of those from other traditions?

[27] Ainslie T. Embree (ed.), *Alberuni's India*, pt I, ch. 1, p. 20.

What have they done to lose their rights, as citizens, to fair and equal treatment?

Incidentally, the analogy—often invoked—with religious asymmetry in Britain is quite misleading in this context, despite the considerable role that the Archbishop of Canterbury plays in state functions. The domain of symmetric treatment can, of course, be fruitfully extended in Britain, for example, through more even-handed financing of different community-oriented schools (not favouring only Christian schools), or, for that matter, through removing the disparity in blasphemy laws (perhaps by removing these laws altogether). Nevertheless, in most matters of legal or political rights, or of protective and supportive state action, the treatment of citizens from different communities in Britain is fairly symmetric already, and the limits of asymmetry are well defined and stationary.[28] The stationarity is quite important, since a self-conscious rejection of secularism in India today would almost certainly usher in fresh and serious asymmetry of treatment.

The second problem with the thesis under examination is that its reading of Indian culture is extremely narrow. The cultural inheritance of contemporary India from its past combines Islamic influences with Hindu and other traditions, and the results of their interaction can be seen plentifully in literature, music, painting, architecture, and many other fields. The point is not only that so many of the major contributions in these various fields of Indian culture have come from Islamic writers, musicians, painters, and so on, but also that their works are thoroughly integrated with those of others.

Indeed, even the nature of Hindu religious beliefs and practices has been substantially influenced by contact with Islamic ideas and values.[29] The impact of Islamic Sufi thought is readily recognizable in parts of contemporary Hindu literature. Further, religious poets like Kabir and Dadu were born Muslim but transcended sectional boundaries (one of Kabir's verses declared: 'Kabir is the child of

[28] The treatment of immigrants, or of suspected immigrants, in Britain is, however, a different matter altogether—not a subject of much glory for Britain. The remark in the text refers to citizens.

[29] On this, see Kshiti Mohan Sen, *Hinduism* (Penguin Books: Harmondsworth, 1960). He discusses the interrelations in greater detail in his Bengali book *Bharate Hindu–Mushalmaner Jukto Sadhana* (Visva-Bharati: Calcutta, 1949).

Allah and of Ram: He is my Guru, He is my Pir').[30] They were strongly affected by Hindu devotional poetry and, in turn, profoundly influenced it. There is, in fact, no communal line to be drawn through Indian literature and arts, setting Hindus and Muslims on separate sides.[31]

Another serious problem with the narrow reading of 'Indian culture as Hindu culture' is the entailed neglect of many major achievements of Indian civilization that have nothing much to do with religious thinking at all. The focus on the distinctly Hindu religious tradition effectively leaves out of the accounting the rationalist traditions of India. This would be a serious neglect for a country in which some of the decisive steps in algebra, geometry, and astronomy were taken, where the decimal system emerged, where classical philosophy dealt extensively with epistemology and logic along with secular ethics, where people invented games like chess, pioneered sex education, and initiated systematic political economy and formal linguistics. It would be absurd to overlook, in characterizing the culture of India, the works of mathematicians such as Aryabhata or Brahmagupta, or poets and dramatists such as Kalidasa or Sudraka, or logicians such as Nagarjuna, or linguists such as Panini, or sex educationists such as Vatsayana, or political economists such as Kautilya.

To be sure, in his famous *History of British India*, published in 1817, James Mill did elaborate just such a view of India; an India that is intellectually bankrupt but full of religious ideas (not to mention Mill's pointer to barbarous social customs). Mill's 'history', written without visiting India or learning any Indian language, may have, in some ways, well served the purpose of training young British officers getting ready to cross the seas and

---

[30] See *One Hundred Poems of Kabir*, trans. Rabindranath Tagore (Macmillan: London, 1915), verse LXIX. See also Kshiti Mohan Sen, *Hinduism*, chs 18 and 19, and his collection of Kabir's poems and his Bengali commentary on *Kabir* (Visva-Bharati: Calcutta, 1910, 1911), reissued with an Introduction by Sabyasachi Bhattacharya (Ananda Publishers: Calcutta, 1995).

[31] The tradition of integrated work has continued straight through to modern art forms, such as the cinema, where Muslims and Hindus thoroughly intermingle. Even the films on Hindu themes frequently rely on Muslim writers or actors (for example Rahi Masoom Raza wrote the script for the film version of the hugely successful Hindu epic *Mahabharata*, made for Indian television).

484 Secularism and Its Critics

rule a subject nation, but it would scarcely suffice as a basis of understanding the nature of Indian culture. The identification of Indian culture specifically with Hinduism not only demotes the role of Muslim and other non-Hindu contributors, but also the major creations outside the fields of religious thought in general. The cultural bigotry that ignores the contributions of Muslims also demolishes much else.

The 'cultural' critique of secularism, based on identifying India in distinctly Hindu terms, thus suffers from both (1) a spurious cultural diagnosis, and (2) a political non-sequitur on making rights conditional on historical cultural contribution.

## A Concluding Remark

The discontent with secularism in India has produced many distinct and interesting lines of argument, which are certainly worth scrutinizing, but—as has been argued here—they do not do much to undermine the basic case for secularism in this country. It is hard to escape the need to see India as an integrally pluralist society, and to accept the necessity of symmetric treatment and secular politics as crucial parts of that recognition.

Secularism is basically a demand for symmetric political treatment of different religious communities, and its acceptance still leaves open many other questions, particularly dealing with the choice between the forms that symmetry can legitimately take. Balanced political treatment can be achieved, as I have discussed, in rather disparate ways, and it does make a difference as to which of the ways is chosen. These issues must remain central to the political debates and arguments that India must have.

It is not being claimed here that the secular approach is trouble-free. Among the many forms that secularism can take, there are some that are clearly less just or fair than others. The communal lines are not the only contrasts that divide the country—there is class, gender, language, location, and many other lines of separation. There are also difficult issues of balancing group autonomy and individual freedom.

There is, furthermore, a real difference between achieving symmetry through the sum-total of the collective intolerances of the different communities rather than through the union of their respective tolerances. Anything that causes the wrath of any of the major communities in India is presently taken to be a potential candidate for proscription. We have to ask whether that is the form that symmetric treatment should take.

There remain many uncomfortable questions of this kind. However, the case for re-examining those issues does not contradict the overarching argument for secularism and the overwhelming need for symmetric treatment of different communities and religions in India. There are good reasons to resist the contrary enticements that have been so plentifully offered recently. The winter of our discontent might not be giving way, right now, to a 'glorious summer', but the abandonment of secularism would make things far more wintry than they currently are. There is work to be done, but not through moving in the constricted and constraining direction that is being so forcefully proposed at this time. There is more force in the proposal than reason.

# 15

# What is Secularism For?[*]

*Rajeev Bhargava*

## I

## Giving Secularism Its Due

The demolished Babri Masjid not only brought into sharper focus the estranged relations between Hindus and Muslims in India today but also the larger issue of whether or not people belonging and deeply committed to different faiths can live together. Moreover, the demolition was widely believed by non-religious people to be a frontal attack on the secular Constitution of India. The ferocity with which militant Hindus attacked. and challenged the Constitution left many people wondering whether believers and non-believers could live together at all. It was earlier thought that the ideology of secularism enabled people with different faiths as well as believers and non-believers not merely to coexist but to live together well. The demolition certainly put to rest any complacency in the possibility of secularism automatically solving the vexed problem of diverse people living together.

The attack on secularism, the strongest yet in post-Independence India, was not, however, entirely new. The BJP in many earlier

---

[*] This contribution combines two articles, 'Giving Secularism its Due', published in the *Economic and Political Weekly* (9 July 1994), and 'Is There Place for Secularism in India?', presented at East-West Centre, Hawaii as part of a conference organized by the Centre for Transcultural Studies, Chicago and the Centre for Cultural Studies, Hawaii, in Dec. 1994. The two articles would not have been possible without discussions with Charles Taylor, Javeed Alam, Akeel Bilgrami, Neeladri Bhattacharya, Tani Sandhu, Alok Rai, Rustam Bharucha, Achin Vanaik, Partha Chatterjee, Sumit Sarkar, and Jerry Cohen.

incarnations had challenged it persistently. Grievances against it have been frequently expressed by many other groups and intellectuals. Briefly, there are three objections to the doctrine and to the state guided by it. First, and most generally, that it is unsuited to Indian conditions by virtue of its profoundly Christian and therefore, Western character. Secularism, it is argued, is a contentious creed with its own dogmas that is incompatible or at least sits uneasily with homespun, indigenous world-views. Second, that it is deeply insensitive to religious people. By forcing people to think of their religion as a matter of private preference, it uncouples the link between religion and community, and deprives people of their sense of identity. Third, that a secular state pretends to be neutral but is partial either to the unbeliever or to the minority community. These critics of secularism claim that with the aid of a series of legislative Acts, the state has attempted to neutralize the communal identity of Hindus. While Hindus have been compelled, so the argument goes, to view themselves primarily as non-religious individuals, Muslims are sometimes permitted and often encouraged to frame their identity purely in terms of their religion. In sum, the secular state in India is far from neutral. While its official doctrine professes neutrality, it is both anti-religious and pro-Muslim. A vociferous section allegedly representing the entire Hindu community claims that a Hindu society is saddled with an anti-Hindu state.

I do not believe any of these claims to be true. But then in human affairs, sifting truth from falsehood, as we know all too well, is a delicate and complicated matter. Social facts are not exhausted by whatever people currently believe to be the case but nor do they stand completely apart from it. It is enough reason to take them seriously if these claims are not obviously false. But this admits that at least something can be said in their favour, that some arguments to substantiate these claims exist. Is this so? Are these arguments available? And if available, are they sound? I do not think that such arguments are to be readily found but I shall presume that they can be devised. As for how good they are, it is the burden of this contribution to demonstrate that they are not. Unlike many other secularists, I do not dismiss these claims—a luxurious option that I fear no longer remains—but I hope to show that they are not as sound as is widely believed. This is my primary intent: to save secularism from its critics and give what is due to it.

My secondary purpose, as a political theorist, is to try to construct a theory of secularism, to develop arguments in favour of secularism that any secularist may use wherever the need arises. In the first part, therefore, I try to develop the outlines of such a theory. I claim that a proper theory of secularism must not only justify the separation of religion from politics but also offer a sketch of how the two must relate after separation. This I claim depends on the kind of separation we envisage. In developing such a theory, I distinguish its two principal forms, one which I call political (or politico-moral) secularism, and the other, ethical secularism. In the second part, I examine in detail the doctrine of political secularism. Political secularism, I claim, has two versions, one that excludes religion from politics and the other that advocates a principle of political neutrality. I examine and try to meet the objections to both these versions. Finally, in the third part, I briefly discuss one version of ethical secularism and claim that under conditions of diversity, it remains a defensible ideal. Since overwhelming reasons in favour of political and ethical secularism exist, the case for secularism, I believe, is overdetermined.

## Outline of a Theory of Secularism

What is secularism? It is widely accepted that secularism advocates the separation of politics from religion. It follows that an adequate theory of secularism must answer at least three questions: First, is it possible to separate religion and politics? Second, why must religion be separated from politics? What justifies the separation of religion and politics? Third, how, after separation, must the two relate to one another? What kind of separation must it be? The conceptual structure of the theory is built around an answer to these questions and therefore stands or falls with it.

The first question can be quickly disposed of. I agree that in subcontinental cultures, it is difficult to disentangle the religious from the non-religious and, therefore, practically impossible to strictly separate every religious from every non-religious practice. If secularism meant the general separation of religious and non-religious practices, then, at least in India, it would be a political non-starter. But rather than espouse the untenable thesis of the separation of all religious and non-religious practices, it is possible to argue instead for the separation of some religious and non-religious institutions. For example, the demand that electoral constituencies not be classified along religious grounds does not entail that every single religious belief be expunged from political practices.

The secularism I envisage does not deny the difficulty of disentangling religious and non-religious practices. What distinguishes it is its advocacy of the value of separating *some* of these actions in their institutionalized forms, largely because it finds the alternative option less satisfactory. It follows that secularism is compatible with the view that the complete secularization of society is neither possible nor desirable.

## Why Separate?

Why is the alternative to secularism less valuable? Why must religion be separated from politics? Several arguments can be proffered to justify separation. Consider first the argument from the value of autonomy. Religious and political institutions must on this view be separated from one another because both are very powerful institutions that command people's unqualified allegiance.[1] Both have the potential to undermine our capacity to think ourselves. If the two are identical or strongly overlap, then the resulting intermix is likely to thwart autonomy more than when they are separate. The second is an argument from equality. No person by virtue of being a member of one institution should be guaranteed membership in another institution. Separation is required in order to ensure a subtle and complex egalitarian system.[2] Third, democracy requires that there be no concentration of power in any one institution or in any one group. If people with authority in religious affairs begin to exercise power in political matters then this inevitably undermines democratic values. For the sake of democracy, therefore, religious and political institutions must be separated. Separation is required to curb political and religious absolutism. Finally, consider the argument from the value of a fully transparent life. It might be argued that it is worthwhile to lead a life free of all illusions. Religion is a storehouse of superstition

[1] The best advocates of this view are undoubtedly Mill and Kant.
[2] On this, see, for example, M. Walzer, 'Liberalism and the Art of Separation', *Political Theory* 12, 3 (Aug. 1984), pp 315–30.

and falsehood. A life free of illusion then is a life without religion. If this is generally true, then it must be true of our political life. Our polity must be governed by true and self-evident principles, not by false and obscure dogmas. It follows that religion and politics must be separated.

Two other arguments, different in kind from the first three, are also available. The first of these is an argument from instrumental rationality.[3] Instrumental rationality requires that we use the best means to achieve the professed objective. The coercive nature of the state renders it utterly dysfunctional in religious contexts. Therefore, to pin any hopes on it is irrational. On this view, religion is a matter of deep conviction. Matters that lie at this level of depth cannot be altered by force.[4] Religious disputes cannot be settled and religious beliefs cannot be transformed by coercive methods. It is irrational, therefore, to mix religion with politics because the very point of religion is lost by such intermingling. Religion must be separated from politics not because of the inherent deficiencies of religion but because of the coercive character of the state.

Finally, we can take recourse to, what I call, an argument from ordinary life.[5] In this view, ultimate ideals involve qualitative distinctions of worth, necessitating a contrast between what is valuable and what is demeaning, or lowly.[6] Competing ultimate ideals, it follows, will have incompatible ideals of what is worthy and unworthy. Moreover, what is of ultimate worth for one is demeaning for the other and vice versa. A clash of such ideals has

[3] On this, the classic statement is that of John Locke, *An Essay Concerning Toleration* (Routledge: London, 1991). See also S. Mendus, *Toleration and the Limits of Liberalism* (Macmillan: London, 1989), ch. 2.

[4] I am not here interested in the validity of this argument. There is good reason to believe that over a long enough period of time, coercion can generate genuine conviction. On this point, see Brian Barry, *Liberty and Justice* (Clarendon Press: Oxford, 1991), pp 27–8.

[5] On the notion of ordinary life, see Charles Taylor, *Sources of the Self: The Making of Modern Identity* (CUP: Cambridge, 1989), pt III. By ordinary life is meant life spent in the production and reproduction of life as distinct from life spent in the pursuit of some ultimate ideal.

[6] On high ideals, see Charles Taylor, ibid. For a related though different distinction between want-regarding and ideal-regarding principles, see Brian Barry, *Political Argument* (Harvester: Wheatsheaf, 1990), pp 38–41.

the potential of depriving people of leading even a minimally decent existence, an ordinary life.[7] To secure an ordinary life, to protect basic this-worldly goods, all ultimate ideals must be expunged from the affairs of the state whose sole business is to procure for everyone minimum standards of decent living. On any account, ultimate ideals are definitionally constitutive of religious world-views. It follows that religion too must be separated from the affairs of the state. The separation of religion from politics is required in order to avert unbearable suffering and degradation of life. In particular, loss of life and liberty is evil and must not be taken away from anyone, no matter to which religious community he belongs.

To sum up, ordinary life requires that an acceptable minimum standard of human interaction exist and that it is barbaric to fall below it. Some procedures of interpersonal conduct are required simply to prevent the social system from falling apart. But a conflict of comprehensive conceptions of worthy existence, of the high ideals of different kinds of believers and unbelievers can have precisely such an effect. That is why high religious ideals must be separated from politics, the principle end of which must be to maintain some procedures of interpersonal conduct so that everyone is able to live at least an ordinary existence.

All these arguments supply the point of separation. It follows that if circumstances obtain in which the point of separation is lost, then religion and politics need not be separated from each other. For example, if separating religion from politics itself deprives

---

[7] The argument from ordinary life takes two forms, depending upon whether ordinary life is placed within the framework of self-interest or within a perspective that places high premium on minimal concern for the other. The first argument leads to the fortuitous efficacy of a minimally decent existence. The second not only realizes the importance of the social conditions of ordinary life but sees an important role for small moral ideals in its production and reproduction. It brings about decent living on a more secure footing, not least because a clash of brute interests generates as much cruelty as a conflict of ultimate ideas. Although I do not always appear to distinguish the two arguments, it is the second one that I intend; and I speak of politico-moral secularism. The most notable contemporary version, though not exactly in the form presented here, is available in John Rawls, 'The Idea of Overlapping Consensus', *Oxford Journal of Legal Studies* 7, 1, pp 1–25, and in Charles Larmore, 'Political Liberalism', *Political Theory*, 18, 3 (Aug. 1990), pp 339–60.

people of decent ordinary living then there is little point left in secularism. If the point of a secular state is to secure this-worldly goods to every citizen, then a deprivation or an unfair distribution of such goods generates a crisis in the legitimacy of such a state. On the argument from ordinary life, the secular state fails to meet its professed objective when it fails to provide its citizens basic, secular goods.

We also need to note that the first three arguments for secularism are grounded in perfectionism.[8] In each of these arguments the separation of religion from politics is required for the sake of a better life, where better is what serves an ultimate ideal. For example secularism is required for autonomy or equality or democracy because an autonomous life is infinitely better than a heteronomous existence, an egalitarian society better in every respect than a hierarchical order, and a democratic polity of greater overall worth than, say, autocracy. The last two arguments, however, do not depend on, indeed they appear to shun, perfectionist justifications. An appeal to any ultimate ideal cannot form part of any set of reasons offered in favour of the actions of such secular states. Anti-perfectionist justifications need not deny the existence or validity of such ideals, but seek from the state a policy of restraint and tolerance. If the distinction between perfectionism and anti-perfectionism is valid then we have two broad categories of secularism, one perfectionist and the other anti-perfectionist. I shall call the first kind 'ethical secularism' because it seeks the separation of religion from politics by virtue of the contribution it makes to the realization of some ultimate ideal. The second type of secularism I shall call 'political secularism' because, rather than contribute to the realization of some external, comprehensive set of ultimate ideals, the separation of religion from politics, on this view, merely makes for a more livable polity.

## What is Separation?

I have been talking up to now about the reasons for secularism. It is time to dwell a little more on its nature. We must ask what

[8] They are perfectionist not because they invoke ideals in contrast to mere desire or interest but because the ideals to which they appeal implicate ultimate standards which judge the overall quality of human life. It follows from

kind of separation is being sought by advocates of secularism. Broadly, there are two kinds. The first identifies separation with exclusion. For the second, to separate is to mark distance or boundaries.[9] Let me elaborate.

Clearly, the demand for separation comes in the wake of some undesirable pre-existing unity, in this case, a complete intermesh of religion and politics. Against the view that religion and politics have an identical overall agenda, a common, indistinguishable project, the separationists argue for a parting of ways. This much is uncontroversial. But from here, a bifurcation occurs. One avenue leads to total exclusion; separation here means the meticulous refusal of any contact whatsoever between religion and politics. Politics must keep off religion. This stand-offishness may be robust or mild. When robust, it generates mutual hostility. For example on this view, the secular state must be anti-religious. This anti-religiosity may be interventionist or non-interventionist. In its interventionist form the state actively discourages religion. In its non-interventionist incarnation it typifies a hysterical Brahmanical attitude. Religion is untouchable, so any contact with it contaminates secularist purity. Secularism here becomes a doctrine of political taboo; it prohibits contact with certain kinds of activities. The milder variety of exclusion of religion from politics proposes that religious and political institutions live as indifferent strangers to one another. At best, this mutual incomprehension leads to some perplexity. But no further curiosity is possible.

The second view on separation does not demand total exclusion. Some contact is possible but some distance too. Indeed, the relation between religion and politics requires neither fusion nor complete disengagement, but what can be called principled distance. Principled distance itself takes two forms. I believe the first entails a commitment to some version of political neutrality. Only when religion has been distanced from politics can the state do its best to help or to hinder different sorts of believers and unbelievers to

---

what is stated here that room for smaller ideals, irreducible to desires, exists within non-perfectionist doctrines.

[9] The distinction between exclusion and neutrality is borrowed from Joseph Raz, *The Morality of Freedom* (Clarendon Press: Oxford, 1986), p. 10. However, by subsuming neutrality under principled distance, I alter and broaden its scope.

an equal degree.[10] The second form of principled distance requires that the boundaries between religion and politics be respected. Religion and politics form distinct spheres with their own respective areas of jurisdiction.[11] Each is valuable in its own right. Religion and politics respect one another as well as their own limits. The world of worship and congregation of prayer and conscience must not be intruded upon by politicians and bureaucrats. Likewise, deeply religious people, in particular, leaders of religious communities, must not tread on the toes of politicians.

This completes the theoretical outline of secularism which allows us to distinguish four versions of secularism: (a) ethical secularism that excludes all religions from the affairs of the state, (b) ethical secularism that requires that the state maintain a principled distance from all religions, (c) political secularism that excludes all ultimate ideals including religions from the affairs of the state, and finally, (d) political secularism that demands that the state be principally distanced from all religious and non-religious ultimate ideals. Generally, ethical secularism is found cohabiting with exclusionary separation. Those who espouse the cause of secularism in order to secure full-blooded autonomy or full participatory democracy or perfect equality wish to exclude religion altogether from political affairs. In other words, (a) and (b) are not distinguished at all. But there are only sociological and no philosophical reasons why this need be so. At least one version of ethical secularism does not identify separation with exclusion. Similarly, (c) and (d) are not always distinguished and political secularism is almost always identified with (d). But forms of political secularism exist that depend upon total exclusion of religion from politics.

## Political Secularism

Let me now address myself to the charge that secularism is insensitive to religion, that a society embodying secular principles is bound to alienate the believer.[12] Recall that ethical secularism

10 Alan Montefiore (ed.), *Neutrality and Impartiality* (CUP, 1975), p. 5.
11 On this, see Walzer, *Liberalism and the Art of Separation*, as well as J. Raz, *The Morality of Freedom*, ch. 14.
12 For a discussion of these issues, see W. Galston, *Liberal Purposes* (CUP, 1991).

justifies the separation of religion from politics by appealing to ultimate ideals. It follows that ethical secularism can be effectively criticized if it is shown that the cause of equality or democracy can be better advanced by mixing, not separating, religion from politics. I know of no such argument but if it exists or can be furnished I shall be only too happy to meet its challenge. Suppose it is accepted that a commitment to democracy, equality, and autonomy entails a corresponding commitment to ethical secularism, but then the fact that the protection of other equally significant values that lend to the life of the believer all its point requires that secularism be abandoned. The question, therefore, is: Can people who value personal autonomy and equality live together with those religious people who have different, deeper values? Or, will the believer remain forever estranged from a secular society?

I believe it must be conceded that ethical secularism frontally assaults all those who see their identity primarily with reference to their own religion and who wish not to dilute its character. Those who wish religion to occupy and dominate public space or offer only those religious reasons in public, no matter how incomprehensible to others, cannot but see wholesale aggression in ethical secularism. There is a deep, quite irreconcilable conflict between ethical secularism and religion.[13] This conflict gets further exacerbated when ethical secularism seeks, by state intervention or intellectual fiat, to totally exclude from politics all religious beliefs. If secularism were to be identified only with the first version of ethical secularism, with (a), then believers and secularists could hardly ever live together. People with a pronounced religious identity will not accept secularism but, as we have seen above, secularism is not just (a). If so, we must persist with the question: can believers and secularists live together? Can they accept secularism?

I believe that believers of different faiths can live with one another and with atheists in a society guided by political secularism. Recall that political secularism justifies the separation of religion from politics either by excluding from politics all ultimate ideals or by an appeal to the principle of political neutrality. A particular religion is excluded from politics on the same ground as other religions and the ultimate ideals of the unbeliever, and if the government resolves to help or to hinder the activities of one

---

13 A version of ethical secularism exists, however, which is not deeply at odds with religion. See below at p. 508.

religious community, then it helps or hinders the activities of other religious communities as well as of the community of unbelievers. Because it seeks independence from or is neutral towards all ultimate ideals, political secularism stands a good chance of gaining the allegiance of believers. This is possible because excessive demands are not made on any group, and such modifications as are required do not threaten its identity or existence. Ethical secularism requires that the believer give up everything of significance. Political secularism demands only that everyone—believer, non-believer—gives up a little bit of what is of exclusive importance in order to sustain that which is generally valuable. If everyone is assured that politics will not be invaded by any one particular ultimate ideal then all are likely to restrict the scope of their respective ideals.

Let me take an example. It is a commonplace that believers deeply value the fact of belonging to a community and reinforce their identity through collective rituals. Proponents personal of autonomy, however, see little point in such a life. Clearly, some religious ways of being are incompatible with ethical secularism. But secularism can be delinked from ethical conceptions and be given a purely political character. If the state does not take upon itself the task of improving the quality of autonomous living or of making people less and less dependent on what is widely believed to be cognitively false or illusory, then it is not unlikely that believers will easily put up with it. The philosophy of secularism that grounds such a state accommodates religious orthodoxy, heteronomous interdependence, and tradition because it does not presuppose a high degree of autonomy, full-blooded egalitarianism, or mandatory and intense political participation.[14] Thus, even

---

14 My position is not an advocacy of a reconciliatory stance towards inequality or political apathy (which, anyway, must not be confused with hierarchical social relations such as slavery and serfdom or with political dictatorship). I am all for the abolition of caste inequalities and for the deepening of democratic values, but insist that secularism being made an integral component of a minimalist agenda of decent human existence. At times, the fight for it should be kept distinct from a struggle for equality and for greater political participation. In other words, part of the problem of secularism is that it is unduly overburdened, asked to do too much on behalf of other important values. I cannot, therefore, agree with the insistence upon the presence of the voice of every oppressed group whenever secularism is espoused.

believers can accept the separation of religion from politics; even they can be secular.[15]

It can hardly be forgotten that this is how secularism developed initially, in response to situations of interreligious conflict. In conditions of religious warfare and more generally in the face of irresolvable conflicts, the only way of excluding the blind pursuit of ultimate ideals, of expelling from public life the frenzy and hysteria that they usually generate, and of protecting ordinary life, is to embrace political secularism. Indeed, this is exactly how the Indian version of secularism was consolidated in the aftermath of Partition where Hindu–Muslim sectarian violence killed off over half a million people.

This last point is important. It is widely believed that secularism entails the separation of church and state, that this separation was a result of protracted struggles between the authority of the church and the power of the state, that this process is peculiar to the history of Western civilization, in particular to developments within Christianity where a distinction between this-worldly and other-worldly values is of pivotal significance. If all this is accepted, then it is not difficult to show that secularism is an exclusively Western idea and, therefore, in all other cultures, its place, deep down, can never be secure. However, the historical narrative of secularism cannot be properly understood when viewed exclusively in the light of the struggle between the church and the state. Equally, if not more, important for secularism is the struggle to make the state relatively independent of deeply conflicting religious groups. In the West, the warring religious groups from whom the state needed independence continued to view themselves as Christians and did not eventually become totally independent of one another. In other cultures contesting religious groups sharing the same metaphysical matrix not only fought for the dominance of their own particular formulation of ultimate ideals, but also succeeded in carving out for themselves a separate religious identity. However, whenever conflicts became uncontainable and insufferable, something resembling a politically secular state simply had to emerge.

What I am trying to say is simple enough. At no point of time in the history of humankind has any society existed with one and

[15] This is a development of the principal point made by Larmore in *Political Liberalism*.

only one set of ultimate ideals. Moreover, many of these ultimate ideals or particular formulations of these have conflicted with one another. In such times, humanity has either got caught in an escalating spiral of violence and cruelty or come to the realization that even ultimate ideals need to be delimited. In short, it has recurrently stumbled upon something resembling political secularism. Political secularism, must then be seen as part of the family of views that arises in response to a fundamental human predicament. It is neither purely Christian nor peculiarly Western. It grows wherever there is a persistent clash of ultimate ideals perceived to be incompatible.

## The Exclusion of Religion from Politics

Political secularism is not, however, without its own problems. Critics argue that despite its anti-perfectionist stance, it carries a disguised perfectionist bias of its own. Indeed, even the believer might argue that the claim of political secularism that it is totally free of all ultimate ideals is mere pretence. An alternative formulation of the same point is this: It is widely believed that for political secularism, the right is prior to the good.[16] This is unsustainable; either it is impossible to draw a distinction between the right and the good, or the right presupposes its own constitutive good, so that the good, despite claims to the contrary, is prior to the right. It follows that political secularism is grounded in its own conception of the good life; its own comprehensive set of ultimate ideals.

Can political secularism meet this objection? I believe it can. To begin with, we need to distinguish between strong and weak varieties of exclusion. Strong exclusion requires that every single ideal be debarred from politics. The scope of exclusion extends to all ideal-regarding principles. The only public policies that matter are grounded in the desires of people. Weak exclusion is satisfied with banishing from public life only ultimate ideals and has ample room for ideals that lie at the intersection of incompatible ultimate ideals. Recall that political secularism requires the exclusion of ultimate ideals for the protection of ordinary life, for our need to

16 On the priority of the right over the good, see John Rawls, 'The Priority of Right and Ideas of the Good', *Philosophy and Public Affairs* 17, 4 (1988), pp 251–76. Also see Will Kymlicka, *Liberalism, Community and Culture* (Clarendon Press: Oxford, 1989), pp 21–40.

live, eat, talk, and relate to one another. These are the small ideals of political secularism. They are small but they rule out big evils in the name of which death, unnecessary suffering, illegitimate censorship, and social isolation are justified. Political secularism is incompatible with all kinds of barbarisms. It depends on simple moral injunctions like: Don't kill! Don't use force! Don't exploit or humiliate the other!, injunctions without which living together is impossible.

But are ultimate ideals totally out of place in a secular world? Is not detachment from our ultimate ideals too heavy a price to pay for a secular polity? Will life not be severely impoverished without our highest ideals? Let me clarify. First, political secularism need not be hostile to ultimate ideals. It proposes that we lodge them in their proper place, not that we forsake them altogether. Second, though it seeks their exclusion, it need not do so indiscriminately. All ultimate ideals need not even be excluded from politics. Third, within the public world, it distinguishes the coercive from the non-coercive. All it demands is the exclusion of some ultimate ideals from the coercive public sphere, namely the state. Which ones must be so excluded? Only those that have begun to generate heat, that are excessively controversial. And what does a political secularist mean by a controversial ultimate ideal? Let us probe a bit more. We must allow competing high ideals to enter the public sphere, which implies not only that they come into a common space but that they be freely scrutinized by publicly deployed reason. Sometimes on assessment, there is common agreement as to their worth. At other times, however, a profound disagreement may emerge. What is valuable from one point of view may be utterly useless from another. This is not threatening so long as people understand one another's reasons for holding contending positions. But when mutual understanding breaks down and, far from making sense of each other, people become deaf to one another, when, in other words, there is a clear signal that, rather than talk, people are inclined to use force instead, the conclusion must be drawn that ultimate ideals have become notoriously controversial, and therefore must be taken off the public agenda. Political secularism seeks the exclusion of such controversial ultimate ideals.

The reintroduction of ideals into secularism also clarifies the relationship between the right and the good. Critics of the priority of the right over the good, such as Charles Taylor, claim that 'the good is what, in its articulation, gives the point of the rules which define the right'.[17] This is partly true. I agree that the right derives its point from the good. But from this it does not follow that any particular good has priority over the right or that the good has priority over the right no matter what the context.

I believe in a functional conception of the right. The right is required in order to realize the good. So far Taylor is correct. The problem, however, is that there exist many goods, and mostly in a competitive relationship. The right is required because the pursuit of good life is unstable, perhaps even impossible without it. One can model the relationship between the right and the good on an analogy with the Marxist conception of the relationship between base and superstructure.[18] Imagine four struts dug into the ground but dangerously moving about with the force of wind. Now put a roof on the struts. Obviously, the roof is supported by the struts, but the struts in turn are stabilized by the roof. The struts need the support of the roof but the roof exists only to stabilize them. Both can claim priority and both can be correct, depending on the context and the problem they address. Likewise with the right and the good. By providing a framework of rules, the right both limits the good and makes a stable quest for it possible. There is nothing incompatible in the claim that the pursuit of good life is impossible without the right, but that it exists only for its sake.

Let me relate this point to the earlier talk of ultimate ideals. Whenever ultimate ideals clash, right has a priority. But this does not mean that the right is prior to every ideal. The whole point of a right is to serve small, perhaps even some uncontroversial, high ideals. Right is not prior to these ideals. The order of priority is therefore as follows: uncontroversial, mostly small ideals-right-controversial ultimate ideals.[19] This is the lexical order of political secularism.

17 For example, see Charles Taylor, op. cit., p. 89.
18 Cohen uses this illuminating example when discussing the relationship between base and superstructure, See G.A. Cohen, *Karl Marx's Theory of History* (Clarendon Press: Oxford, 1978), p. 231. I find it useful for understanding the relationship between the right and the good.
19 It goes without saying that some ultimate ideals are so controversial in the sense specified above that it is difficult to see how they can survive within a liberal-democratic public sphere for long. An ideal that not merely

# Political Neutrality

A second objection rejects the claim that a politically secular state is neutral. It is frequently claimed that the Indian state is 'pseudo-secular', that its secular character is a convenient stance to obscure the fact that it favours ideals of the unbeliever and the religious minorities and specifically hinders Hindu objectives. Occasionally this appears as a purely empirical claim that the Indian state happens not to be neutral; but I suspect lurking underneath is the more serious objection on conceptual grounds that political neutrality is in principle impossible, that secularism as a doctrine of neutrality is implausible. Therefore, if no state can be neutral, then a state that discriminates in favour of unbelievers and the Muslim minority must be replaced by one that is unabashedly pro-Hindu.[20]

Exactly what kind of neutrality are we discussing here? I take the doctrine of state-neutrality to mean the view that a state must to an equal degree help or hinder all relevant individuals and groups. However, in public fora and perhaps even among some political theorists, an interpretation of neutrality found particularly when charges of partiality are levelled against specific state policies is as follows: the principle of neutrality states that always, in the beginning or at the end, in intention and in outcome, and no matter what the context, an agent purporting to be neutral must help or hinder the good of everyone to an equal degree.[21] This is strict objectivist

---

contingently but constitutively espouses hatred of entire groups must, from the standpoint of political secularism, be excluded from the public sphere.
20 An attack on the neutrality of the state is different though related to the critique that political secularism cannot exclude all ultimate ideals. Different because the scope of neutrality is broader than that of exclusion and related because, at least as I see it, exclusion is a limit (special) case of neutrality. While the requirement that all high ideals be excluded from politics entails neutrality, political neutrality does not necessarily mean that high ideals too be excluded from politics. All that political neutrality necessitates is that the state help or hinder (or do neither) actual or possible ideals to an equal degree, not that they be altogether excluded from politics. Therefore, arguments that apply to neutrality apply equally to politics of exclusion but arguments for or against exclusion may not apply to neutrality. This is why neutrality requires separate consideration.
21 For a helpful discussion of the distinction between outcome-neutrality and neutrality of aim or what I call intention-neutrality, see Richard J. Arneson,

neutrality, a view of impartiality from a place that does not exist anywhere in this world, a God's-eye view of neutrality.[22]

I have no doubt that this neutrality is possible for God and therefore this notion is not entirely incoherent. Consider Ravi, a member of team X at the football field playing team Y. A goal has just been scored against his team. He can rightly seek God's help on the plea that since God is known to have equal concern for all, His support for team Y is reason enough for Him to now show concern for the good of team X. Lo and behold! Ravi scores a goal and now that outcome matches intention, the neutrality of God is fully confirmed. Now Ravi, an accomplished footballer, also fancies himself as a great scholar, and applies for the job of a professor that attracts other candidates too. He can with equal justification demand even in this different context, that he be given the job—no matter what his ability or suitability in comparison to others—and that if he fails to get this particular job, neutrality requires that he get, early enough, an equally cushy job.

Now, if the state is the march of God on earth (with apologies to Hegel), then it is reasonable for us to expect from it precisely this kind of neutrality. So suppose that by refusing to grant alimony to Shah Bano, the state supports the Shariat, then orthodox Hindus, like our fictitious Ravi, can justifiably seek the help of the state to, say, bar the entry of Dalits into temples; and if the doors of the Masjid are unlocked, then Muslims can demand that the next time an orthodox north Indian Brahman objects to cow-slaughter, the state should not heed him. After all, the state must not only maintain intention-neutrality but also outcome-neutrality with regard to the good of both religious communities, and because the reach of the state, like God's, is everywhere, it may be justifiably expected that it maintain neutrality in all contexts.

Unfortunately for this conception, however, what is coherent for God may be incoherent when seen from the human point of view. Since democracy cannot but help encourage the belief that the state is a palpable human institution—who can fail to see a

---

'Neutrality and Utility', *Canadian Journal of Philosophy* 20, 2 (June 1990), pp 215–40. Also see J. Raz, *The Morality of Freedom* (Clarendon Press: Oxford, 1986).

[22] I see, of course, the irony involved in saying this in the context of a possible dispute between believers and unbelievers.

human hand in the making of a democratic state?—the irrelevance of a God's-eye view of neutrality becomes blindingly obvious. Take once again the example mentioned above. In helping the cause of orthodox Hindus and Muslims, the state has undermined the good of those seeking the exclusion of religion from politics (which include secular Hindus, secular Muslims, as well as unbelievers). The state fails to be totally neutral; it cannot meet the requirements of divine neutrality.

Shall we forget then about state neutrality or is another, more plausible conception of neutrality available? Consider a teacher marking answer scripts. Now, neutrality certainly requires that she begin marking with equal concern for all, with an impartial attitude, but not that she grade everyone identically. The outcome is expected and bound to be good for some and bad for others, or at least not good to the same degree for all, but surely it must be judged fair if the teacher began with an equal concern for all her students. The teacher may intend identity of outcome but cannot be held guilty of favouritism if she fails to achieve it. Neutrality does not need identity of outcome.

Second, neutrality is context-specific and therefore a notion of what is relevant to the context must be built into a reasonable conception of neutrality. We must always begin by asking: neutrality in which context and for what? To take the same example, neutrality in this context requires that in the assessment of answer sheets, the teacher not award grades on the basis of colour, religion, kinship, or nationality, but judge by appropriate standards the actual performance of the candidate. Neutrality demands that no consideration irrelevant to the issue at hand enter the assessment of the parties affected by it. The whole point of neutrality is to expunge all irrelevant considerations from the context in order to focus solely on the issue at hand and then to bring to bear on that issue only those standards that are relevant.

The idea of appropriate standards implies that some goods must enter and others exit the picture. Some valuable things do not count because in this context other things value more. Neutrality is always with regard to some things (goods) in order that some other things, more significant in this context, be realized. Neutrality fails when there is dependence on some irrelevant good, but it also loses its point the moment it strives to be independent of all goods. My world-view matters; it matters to me deeply, but how is it in any way relevant when I judge the analytical skills of my student? Equally, when grading students, I can hardly ignore the good lying behind it that gives the activity its purpose, namely to ferret out those who have learnt analytical skills from those who have not. God may desire, irrespective of our conception of what is good or bad, that all of us win all the time but we humans can hope only that we bring an appropriate conception of goodness to bear upon our judgment of the winner. Neutrality without any link with appropriate goodness for which it is meant is meaningless and chimerical. Perhaps, some partiality relevant to goodness is inevitable and necessary for impartiality to take off the ground. One cannot therefore eliminate partiality completely; indeed one must not. For, as our example shows, neutrality requires only that partiality be grounded in reasonableness and be relevant to the issue: the teacher respects neutrality even though, indeed precisely because, she awards low grades to those who have performed poorly.

I have argued that neutrality does not imply that a neutral policy be independent of all goods. Neutrality is always for something; it has a point, a purpose. Besides, it is never brought into play with respect to everything and everyone. It is not purposeless and free floating. Although, intentionally or as a byproduct, outcome-neutrality is occasionally possible, it is never guaranteed; hence, in most contexts, it is reasonable to only hope for intention-neutrality. It follows that a defensible conception of political neutrality is this: Always, at the beginning, with regard to some good in a specified context, the state must intend to help or hinder all relevant individuals and groups to an equal degree.

What is the given context of the politically secular state and to what good is it antecedently committed? The secular state functions within a society that is ineradicably diverse, which has individuals and groups with different, often conflicting, conceptions of ultimate ideals. Its commitment to ordinary life overrides its attachment to ultimate ideals. This entails that it guarantees all its citizens a decent life crucial to which is the availability of material goods and self-esteem. The relevant goods which in this context give neutrality its point are distributive justice and self-respect. This much partiality is already a constitutive feature of a politically secular state, indeed necessary if neutrality is to function at all. It follows that a secular state is neutral only to those who display commitment to these small ideals. It is not meant to be neutral to those who bring controversial high ideals into public life, no matter how they affect others, or who wish to impose their external preference on others, no matter what suffering they cause. To my mind, a state is politically neutral, if in a context of deeply conflicting high ideals, and for the sake of a decent life to all individuals and groups, its policies intend to help or hinder to an equal degree all those sensitive to this context and committed to these goods.

It follows that individuals and groups, including of course religious groups, who conform to norms without which a decent life to all is impossible can legitimately expect the state to help their cause, and help it as much as it helps others. When disputes arise between individuals or groups, a state is perfectly neutral even when it favours those who stick by norms to which the state is antecedently committed, and penalizes those who do not. Take the case of Shah Bano. Suppose that it is decided, either on the ground that individual rights are infringed or, upon interpretation, that no essential violation of religious duties follows, that she must be granted maintenance. Abiding by this decision, the state acts against those who refuse to comply with it. I do not think that in this apparent instance of disfavour to a group, the state has abandoned neutrality. Similarly, the state is not guilty of partiality to rule-abiding citizens if it acts to rectify the violation of law on 6 December 1992. In either case, allegations that the state is pseudo-secular are entirely misplaced.

Of course the Indian state has not always been neutral even in this sense. For good or bad, it has deviated from the principle of neutrality on a number of occasions. It did so when it carried out a series of reforms within Hinduism, but left orthodox Islam intact. For example it changed Hindu personal law quite significantly: polygamy made illegal, the right to divorce introduced, child marriage abolished, intercaste marriages legally recognized. Furthermore, it prohibited animal sacrifices within the precincts of a temple, abolished *devadasi* dedication, regulated the activities of criminals masquerading as holy men, introduced temple-entry rights for Harijans and reformed temple administration. Clearly, all this has helped or hindered, depending on the point of view, the cause of Hinduism, and since the state has been non-interventionist with regard to Islam, it has not been neutral.

More recently, however, it has abandoned neutrality in favour of sectarians within the Hindu and Muslim pantheon. As mentioned, the Shah Bano issue is such a case in point. My contention has not, however, been that the Indian state has been neutral, only that political neutrality is not impossible. My dispute with the anti-secularist is not an empirical one. I am not here challenging his claim that the Indian state is 'pseudo-secular', but I believe that even if the Indian state met the requirements of political neutrality, the anti-secularist would continue to call it pseudo-secular because his judgment is grounded in a hard objectivist view of neutrality. From that point of view, upholding the Constitution of India is pseudo-secular, and punishing offenders of the law is tantamount to abandoning neutrality.

The crux of the matter is that if we are forced to choose between a God's-eye view of neutrality and unabashed partiality, then sensible realism dictates that we select the latter. But these are not the only available options. Faced with a choice between the principle of political neutrality outlined here and unmitigated partiality, I fail to see why political neutrality cannot be chosen, particularly under conditions of conflicting diversity. State-neutrality, and, therefore secularism, remains a valuable political idea.

## Procedural Neutrality

Before I end the discussion of neutrality, I would like to talk about another issue. Philosophical discussion on neutrality has not only distinguished outcome-neutrality from intention-neutrality but also intention-neutrality from neutrality of procedure.[23] According to neutrality of procedure, 'state policies should be justified without appealing to the presumed intrinsic superiority of any particular conception of the good life'. Can state policies be neutral in this sense and should they be so neutral? I believe, in some circumstances, they can and they should.

This issue has a direct bearing on some of the debates in India and generally for political legitimacy anywhere in the world. Suppose that the state in its intentions is neutral but that this neutrality is justified in terms that directly invoke one religion, say, Hinduism. This is not unknown in India. It is frequently

---

23 On neutrality of procedure, see R. Arneson, op. cit.

claimed that the state in India is secular because Hinduism is tolerant, that the protection of minorities depends on the goodwill of the majority, and, therefore, that the inherent secularism of Hinduism alone can sustain communal harmony. On these grounds it is claimed that a Hindu state would be a secular state. Let me not deny this. Let us accept that Hinduism has a strong tradition of tolerance towards other religions. A state defended by Hindu-specific reasons meets the requirements of intention-neutrality. But what about procedural neutrality? Is it not violated? It is, and for that reason such a state lacks overall political legitimacy. To gain legitimacy, a politically secular state must either rely on justifications framed without making any reference to Hinduism or also on reasons given by other faiths and atheism.

It may be argued here that to give up Hindu reasons for a secular state is deeply frustrating for Hindus. It might even be said that these Hindu reasons are deeply tied to people's identity and, therefore, the cost of excluding these reasons is too much for them to bear. I believe, however, that the cost of not giving them up would be greater, for an insistence upon Hindu reasons is certain to quicken the drift towards the alienation of non-Hindus in India. Hindus must realize that, in some contexts, to supply only Hindu reasons is unjustified or counter-productive. But why should people who believe in the truth of their claim refrain from making it public? Indeed, their claim may even be objectively true. Why should it remain hidden?

I think the answer here is simple: the whole point of furnishing reasons for a secular state is that despite deep differences we need to live together. Besides, the whole purpose of providing reasons is not just to convince ourselves but also others. If that is so, supplying only Hindu reasons involves us in a kind of performative contradiction: we wish to live together and to convince each other of the need to do so, but our reasons flatly frustrate this objective. Therefore, if we continue to look for Hindu reasons for the state, then either we don't know our minds or else our real intentions are different from what we say. We say something but we mean something different. We talk of living together but we want to live apart.

It might still be said that although procedural neutrality is desirable, it is far too stringent a requirement to expect people, even if temporarily and in some contexts, to forget about their religious identity. This forgetting is easy for people who see religion as a matter of individual preference but almost impossible for those whose primary identity is religious. My response to this objection, first of all, is that it is hardly anyone's claim that religious identity has to be forgotten; only that in some specified contexts it need not be publicly exhibited. Nor is it claimed that justifications for the secular state must be furnished even when they contradict the basic tenets of one's religion. Indeed, they must not only be compatible but be derivable from it. In addition, it is demanded that they be also derivable from other religious world-views and that they, for the sake of overall legitimacy, must be formulated in a language available to all. I do not believe that this is a particularly severe requirement to meet, especially when the alternative facing a people is open and continuous deep discord.

## Ethical Secularism

Another challenge that secularism must meet is this. It might be argued that while it purports to be a way of living together, secularism has no conception of togetherness. This is certainly true of political secularism. A society guided by principles of political secularism cannot in the long run be a viable community.

A number of issues are involved in the problem raised above, many of which have resurfaced in the debate between liberals and communitarians. I shall begin by drawing a distinction between the politics of living together and the politics of living together well. The two politics involve different degrees of community. To live together well one needs a high degree of community, but merely living together is possible with a relatively low level of community.

Political secularism merely provides a way of living together, not a way of living together well. It has an extremely weak conception of community, if at all. This can be seen in the following way. I do not think anyone doubts that the world of my community is smaller than the world of all humans. Therefore, respecting minimal conditions of human interaction—as advocated by political secularism—does not entail that all those who I minimally respect be members of my community. True, I owe to all members of my community minimal respect, but from this it does not follow that all those to whom I owe minimal respect be members of my community. I have for, example, an obligation to be decent to outsiders. Clearly, political secularism fails to furnish a criterion of community, of citizenship. It tells us what, if we decide to live together, we should minimally do in relation to one another but not with who we should live together or how we can live together well.

I do not think that the notion of living together well should be given up. It follows that I do not find political secularism fully satisfactory. It is good enough in circumstances of deep and open discord but in more propitious contexts it is far from adequate.

I have claimed that of the two conceptions of secularism, political secularism has a better chance of acceptance, but we now find that political secularism has no place for the idea of living together well. Do we conclude therefore that for living together well, secularism must be given up? Let me straighten out an issue before providing a brief answer to this question. A fairly well-entrenched stereotype of the liberal portrays her as committed to a conception of low level community. The communitarian, on the other hand, always enjoins a high level of community. The liberal, in other words, is believed to be equipped with the politics of living together and the communitarian with the politics of living together well.

This picture of liberals and communitarians is not entirely inaccurate.[24] No-nonsense liberals believe that living together well is either impossible or undesirable. No-nonsense communications believe that one either lives together well or does not live together at all. For both it is an all-or-nothing matter. Communitarians believe in the constitutive desirability of communities. Many communitarians further believe that such communities must be dense and, finally, that such dense communities must be political in the sense of being distinct from social relationships such as the family. Since liberals believe that such dense political communities are chimerical, and since they share with the communitarians the view that only such communities make possible living together well, they give up altogether the notion of living together well.

It appears then that while secularism and liberalism are bound up with each other, room within secularism for communitarianism does not exist. Exactly the conclusion we had arrived at a moment

---

24 As Dworkin, Raz, and Rawls have shown, liberals have a fairly strong conception of a community.

ago. Fortunately, this view is mistaken. Recall that ethical secularism separates religion from politics for the sake of an ultimate ideal. Recall also that one kind of separation entails that there be separate self-limiting spheres of religion and politics. Raz has shown us precisely how this separation is linked to a distinct conception of toleration as also to a pluralist community.[25] In a pluralist community one tolerates the other not despite one's disagreement but on the understanding that incommensurable values cannot always be realized at the same time in the same sphere, and that, therefore, one has to tolerate the limitations of others. Pluralism, and the idea of toleration that lies at its core, then becomes one of the very high ideals that require the separation of religion from politics. We now obtain a distinct version of ethical secularism that has barely found a mention in the discussion above.

Let me sum up. Political secularism has little or no conception of community. It is non-communitarian. From this, it does not follow that there are no secular communitarians and that to live together well we must prepare a gingerly mix of political secularism and non-secular communitarianism.[26] I believe the pluralist version of ethical secularism, which is both secular and communitarian, is worth exploring and enriching. It is superior to political secularism though the level and quality of motivation that it requires is not always easy to obtain. Ethical secularism is better but difficult, political secularism somewhat less attractive

25 See Raz, *The Morality of Freedom* (Claredon Press: Oxford, 1986).
26 This proposal is frequently made and this mixture takes two forms. One, majoritarian, in which we are required to be politically secular up to a point. For example, some rights (for example, religious and property rights) are granted to everyone. But then, in addition to secularism, we are asked to follow a strong communitarian ethic of the majority. If the majority is religious then we live in, say, a Hindu state that protects liberties of unbelievers as well as of religious minorities but does not necessarily grant full citizenship rights to them. Likewise, if unbelievers happen to constitute the majority, then religious liberty may be granted to believers, though they remain ineffective members within the political community. In the second more palatable form, minorities are granted certain privileges and immunities in order to simply ensure their cultural survival. The logic of numbers makes the second form more desirable than the first, but I do not consider either to be the best possible form of political community. Under circumstances of deep diversity, only ethical secularism, by its more positive defence of different religious and cultural viewpoints, can fulfil the ideal of a political community.

but well within our reach. Both insist upon the separation of religion and politics without undermining either. Both should be invoked to justify a secular state. But in the short run and in some contexts, political secularism may not only be a good fall-back strategy but the only available way to prevent a community from falling apart.

# II

# Postscript: Is There Place for Secularism in India?

'Giving Secularism Its Due' was written in the immediate aftermath of the demolition of Babri Masjid, and reflects its bitter aftertaste. Its principal objective was to defend the view that holds secularism as an integral part of a minimally decent society, the basic condition without which other substantive values cannot be realized. I argued that its content was minimally moral and relatively uncontroversial. I denied that separation means exclusion or entails mutual insulation of religion and state institutions, and claimed, instead, that separation also means principled distance, a strategy which accommodates both intervention and abstention of state institutions in relation to religious practices. This minimalist secularism that keeps a principled distance of the state from religious institutions in order to secure an acceptable minimal standard of living for ordinary citizens and to avert unbearable sufferings and degradation of life, I called political secularism. I contrasted it to ethical secularism that is linked to thicker, substantive, but also controversial, values. Finally, I argued that this minimalist secularism must be understood in the context of deeply conflicting religious groups rather than in terms of the struggle for power between the church and the state. Implicit in the paper was a desire to show that the link between secularism and Protestantism is pointlessly overemphasized, and its connection with conditions of radical religious diversity not given enough importance.

Looking back, it seems obvious to me that I wanted to develop and defend a conception of secularism with the widest possible appeal, acceptable to both the non-religious as well as religious people. I, therefore, felt the need to delink secularism from controversial substantive values, such as autonomy that I personally affirm. In calling it political secularism, I assumed a certain conception of political, namely as an arena of conflict resolution rather than as the domain where people persuade one another why a particular set of substantive values must be followed. In doing so I relied indirectly on a right-based secularism; one that tended to overemphasize the importance of following procedures rather than matters of substance. I had worked out, without fully realizing this, a position sometimes resembling Charles Larmore's constrained modus vivendi, and at other times, Stuart Hampshire's basic procedural justice.[27] A constrained modus vivendi involves practical accommodation constrained by an agreement on general normative premises. According to Larmore, these premises include mutual respect and ground the neutrality of the state in the political sphere. The resemblance with Hampshire is more striking. I quote from him:

A basic level of morality, a bare minimum, which is entirely negative, and without this bare minimum as a foundation no morality directed towards the greater goods can be applicable and can survive in practice. A rock-bottom and preliminary morality of justice and fair dealing is needed to keep a balance between competing moralities and to support respected procedures of arbitration between them. Otherwise any society becomes an unstable clash of fanaticism. Procedural justice is for this reason a necessary support of any morality in which more positive virtues are valued.

Over time I became increasingly sceptical of the watertight distinction between the right and the good, and of the possibility or desirability of a secularism that had strong elements of pure proceduralism. It is true that my conception of political secularism was proposed only as a fall-back strategy and, therefore, of limited, contextual value. I said that it was necessary to fully work out a conception of ethical secularism, particularly because of the weak conception of community and virtually no conception of active citizenship with which political secularism works. Indeed, the idea of citizen implicit in political secularism is of a passive recipient of benefits from the state, not of an active participant. Ironically, what political secularism lacks is a properly political conception. Bearing this in mind, in what follows, I propose a distinction

27 C. Larmore, *Patterns of Moral Complexity* (Cambridge University Press: Cambridge, 1987), pp 70–7; Stuart Hampshire, *Innocence and Experience* (Harvard University Press: Cambridge, Mass., 1989), pp 72–8.

between hyper-substantive and ultra-procedural secularism, both of which I distinguish from what I call contextual secularism.

Though I did not make it explicit in 'Giving Secularism its Due', my principal interlocutors, indeed my adversaries, were Professors T.N. Madan and Ashis Nandy. By claiming that secularism did not necessarily exclude religion from politics, I argued against their view that secularism is necessarily anti-religious. In proposing that the history of secularism cannot be properly understood by an exclusive reference to church–state separation, I challenged Madan's thesis that secularism is a gift of Christianity. In this postscript, I develop these points by directly addressing the Madan–Nandy thesis of the futility and undesirability of secularism. I further argue that both fail to grasp the precise nature of Indian secularism. Throughout, I reiterate my view that the real challenge is to work out an alternative conception of, not to seek an alternative to, secularism. Against those who reject secularism, I offer reasons for its desirability and ineradicability. To those who defend it, I show the valuable elements in the anti-secularist critique and explain why my preferred version of secularism is better than other vulnerable variants. However, before I do so, I amend the theoretical outline of secularism proposed in the earlier paper.

Let me return to the question posed in the paper: Why must religion be separated from state institutions? Recall that several arguments can be offered to justify separation. For example, if autonomy, equality, or democracy are valuable and if religious institutions tend to thwart their realization, and if further, the whole purpose of political institutions is to protect and promote these values, then political and religious institutions must be separated. So suppose that we value the ability of people to step back from their social roles and positions, and distance themselves from the beliefs and values to critically examine, revise, even reject them. Suppose also that some political institutions are designed to sustain this capacity (for example, civic freedoms) and some religious institutions obstruct their free exercise, we might legitimately conclude then that the protection of this capacity requires the separation of religion and politics.

It is obvious that such an argument invokes substantive values (some weighty purpose that gives meaning to our lives) to separate religion and politics. Notice that each of these substantive values can also be turned into an ultimate ideal. Such ultimate ideals can be integrated to form a coherent, well-structured, world-view which may then be called upon to help separate religion and politics. Furthermore, in invoking this world-view, differing substantive values as well as rules and procedures may be wholly disregarded. The entire perspective may so antecedently tilt in favour of this set of ultimate ideals that nothing else stands in its way. When the separation of religion and politics relies on a set of ultimate values, the resultant secularism is hyper-substantive. Hyper-substantive secularism brushes aside rules, procedures, or even values that fall outside its framework. At best, an instrumentalist stance towards them is permissible. More than that it cannot allow. Hyper-substantive secularism is an absolutist version of secularism. Ultra-procedural secularism, the other version, equally absolutist but fundamentally different in another sense, is part of a set of doctrines that are suspicious of all ultimate ideals and do not invoke them in the justification of the separation of religion and politics. This needs explanation.

Ultimate ideals, I maintain, involve qualitative distinctions of worth, necessitating a contrast between the valuable and the demeaning and lowly. Competing ultimate ideals, it follows, will have incompatible ideas of what is worthy and what is not. Moreover, what is of ultimate worth to one is demeaning to the other and vice versa. A clash of such incompatible ideals has the potential of disrupting social life. It might therefore be argued that some procedures need to be evolved to manage such conflicts and sustain social order. One way of doing this is to disengage ourselves from all substantive values in order to arrive at a set of universally acceptable procedures, possessing absolute priority over all substantive values. Such a doctrine is wholly non-substantive, abstracts not just from a set of ultimate ideals but from every possible ideal or substantive value, and is committed more or less to the philosophy of rule for rule's sake. No matter what the issue at stake, which goods under dispute, and even when a genuinely worthwhile good is wilfully, meaninglessly obstructed by vain desires, procedural norms have overriding value. Like hyper-substantive secularism, ultra-procedural secularism is absolutist and seeks an unconditional separation of religion and politics on grounds claimed to be comprehensive, universally applicable, authoritative, and final.

In contrast to hyper-substantive and ultra-procedural variants, I spell out features of a third form of secularism that seeks the separation of religion and politics but from a non-absolutist standpoint. Since it rejects absolutism, it purports to avoid the pitfalls of both hyper-substantivism and ultra-proceduralism. It attempts to combine substantive values and procedures without a priori commitment to the absolute priority of either. This is why it is contextualist. Unlike ultra-procedural secularism, contextualist secularism has room for ultimate ideals and allows them in the public arena. It is neither obsessively opposed to them nor hysterical about their internal conflicts. But when such conflicts introduce a surfeit of passion and frenzy into public life, threatening thereby the structure of ordinary, but dignified, life of all citizens, then it relies on minimal procedures to control and sometimes remove from political life all controversial ultimate ideals. This sensitivity to procedures distinguishes it from hyper-substantive secularism. Since ultimate ideals are constitutive of religious world-views, contextual secularism separates religion or religious ideology from politics whenever ordinary life is threatened. Notice, finally, that it is committed not merely to the preservation of life but to any substantive value consistent with a life of dignity for all. For example, the structure of an ordinary life of dignity for all rules out discrimination on grounds of religion.

I had proposed that separation need not always be seen as demanding total exclusion of religion from state institutions. Some contact is possible but also some distance. The relation between religion and politics requires neither fusion nor complete disengagement but what I call principled distance. It is important that principled distance be distinguished from mere equidistance. In the strategy of principled distance, the state intervenes or refrains from interfering, depending on which of the two better promotes religious liberty and equality of citizenship. If this is so, the state may not be able to relate to every religion in exactly the same way, intervene to the same degree or in the same manner. All it must ensure is that the inclusion of religion into politics or its exclusion from it be guided by non-sectarian principles consistent with a set of values constitutive of a life of equal dignity for all.

This completes the theoretical restatement of secularism that allows us to distinguish three distinct versions of secularism: (a) hyper-substantive secularism that excludes religion from politics; (b) ultra-procedural secularism that also excludes religion from politics. (The terms 'hyper' and 'ultra' are meant to convey that these versions of secularism cannot advocate a policy of principled distance but must, for different reasons, exclude religion from politics); and finally (c) contextual secularism that allows politics to keep a principled distance from religious institutions.

I must not be coy about my own preference: I vote for contextual secularism. The impulse behind contextual secularism is to secure a dignified life for all, prevent discrimination on grounds of religion, check religious bigotry, and manage frenzied internecine conflicts that plunge societies into barbarism and into an escalating spiral of violence and cruelty. The intermingling of religion and politics is permissible as long as it helps meet these objectives but if any form of blending defeats these aims, then their amalgamation must be restricted. The precise form of these restraints cannot be decided a priori but must be worked out by each society. No society can determine for all times, in all contexts, the form of separation best suited to it. Only contextual secularism grasps that *many forms of separation lie between total exclusion and complete fusion.* For some, secularism is identical to the privatization of the religion; for others, it means a wall of separation between religion and politics in the public sphere. But other versions are also possible. Within limits imposed by the general form of secular doctrines, each society must work out its own version. Not taking this into account is part of the difficulty in hyper-substantive and ultra-procedural secularism.

## Indian Secularism

Which of these forms has dominated Indian politics? Which has most influenced the Indian Constitution and effectively guided the Indian state? Naturally, there cannot be a simple answer to this question. The complex network of institutions that forms the Indian state has not been regulated at all times by any one version. At best, one can say that its policies and practices have been guided sometimes by elements of one version and at other times by elements of other versions of secularism. The character of the Indian Constitution, on the other hand, was decisively shaped not only by a diffused social-democratic impulse, but by contextual secularism, predominantly in response to deteriorating

Hindu–Muslim relations. Secularism anywhere in the world is required to check the growth of fanaticism and to manage interreligious conflicts. It must everywhere prohibit the persecution of religious groups and individuals, but in India it has had to take on the additional burden of ensuring that conflicts between religious communities, even when they are not purely religious in character but ensue from the identification of people by religious markers, do not cross a moral threshold. However exploitative and violent modern nation-states may be and whatever the complicity of secularism with the more perverted aspects of nationalism, in countries where religious identifiers are crucial in the individuation of communities, secularism is required to prevent a Bosnia-like inferno.

It was primarily to tackle this problem that the Indian state excluded religion on contextualist (political) grounds, for example by refusing to allow (i) separate electorates, (ii) reserved constituencies for religious communities, (iii) reservations for jobs on the basis of religious classification, and (iv) the organization of states on the basis of religion. This exclusion of religion from politics was guided solely by the need to inhibit religious and communal conflict and to avoid a Partition-like scenario. However, the motive that excluded religion from state institutions also influenced its inclusion in policy matters of cultural import. For example a uniform charter of rights was not considered absolutely essential for national integration. Separate rights were granted to minority religious communities to enable them to live with dignity. Integration was seen not to be identical with complete assimilation or absorption.

Secularism was justified not only to sustain intercommunal solidarity but to protect the structure of ordinary life. The same motive propelled the state to undertake the reform of Hinduism on these contextualist (ethical) grounds. By making polygamy illegal, introducing the right to divorce, abolishing child marriage, legally recognizing intercaste marriages, and introducing temple- entry rights for Dalits, the state intervened in religious matters to protect the ordinary but dignified life of its citizens. What are we to conclude from this about the nature of Indian secularism?

A tendency exists in the literature on secularism in India to first posit a highly idealized version of secularism derived partly from, say the American or the French experience, and then judge the practice of the secular state in India by standards evolved from these models. (Secularists have often done this and then lamented the failure of Indian secularism. Opponents of secularism likewise have used this ploy to first show the inconsistencies of Indian secularism and then concluded that the collapse of secularism in India is imminent.) To illustrate this point let me take the example of Donald Smith's *India as a Secular State* which is still the *locus classicus* on the subject.[28] Smith's conception of the secular state involves three distinct but interrelated relations concerning the state, religion, and the individual. The first relation concerns individuals and their religion from which the state is excluded. Individuals are thereby free to decide the merits of the respective claims of different religions without coercive interference of the state. They are free to revise or reject the religion they were born into or they have chosen. The second relation concerns that between individuals and the state from which religion is excluded. Here, the state views individuals without taking into account their religious affiliation. The rights and duties of citizens are not affected by the religious beliefs held by individuals. For example no discrimination exists in the holding of public office or taxation. Finally, for Smith, the integrity of both these relations is dependent on the third, between the state and different religions. Here, he argues, secularism entails separation of powers, that is the mutual exclusion of state and religion, in order that they operate effectively and equally in their own respective domains. Just as it is not the function of the state to promote, regulate, direct, or interfere in religion, just so political power is outside the scope of the legitimate objectives of religion. For Smith, therefore, secularism means the strict separation of religion and the state for the sake of the religious liberty and equal citizenship of individuals.

Clearly, on this account of secularism any intervention in Hinduism, for example the legal ban on the prohibition of Dalits into the temple, is illegitimate interference in religious affairs and therefore compromises secularism. Similarly, the protection of socio-religious groups is also inconsistent with an individualistically grounded secularism. For example, the right to personal laws

28 D.E. Smith, *India as a Secular State* (Oxford University Press: Bombay and London, 1963), see Ch. 6 above.

entails a departure from secularism simply on the ground that it depends on a classification that is communally suspect. Together, these policies violate the ideal of neutrality or equidistance that plays a pivotal role in Smith's view of secularism. Smith believed that despite these flaws the Indian state, at least in the early 1960s, was secular. However, he also believed that these constituted serious deviations from the model of secularism and unless brought quickly in line, the secular state in India would plummet into crisis. Was he correct?

Marc Galanter thinks that he was not and, in a review of Smith's book claimed that his secularism is derived from the American model with an 'extra dose of separation'.[29] Galanter's assessment is accurate. If we abandon the view that political secularism entails a unique set of state policies valid under all conditions which provide the yardstick by which the secularity of any state is to be judged, then we can better understand why, despite 'deviation' from the ideal, the state in India continues to embody a model of *secularism*. This can be shown even if we stick by Smith's working definition of secularism as consisting of three relations. Smith's first relation embodies the principle of religious liberty construed individualistically, that is pertaining to the religious beliefs of individuals. However it is possible to give a non-individualistic construal of religious liberty. Here we speak not of the beliefs of individuals but of the practices of groups. Religious liberty means distancing the state from the practices of religious groups. The first principle of secularism therefore grants to a religious community a right to its own practices. Smith's second relation embodies the value of equal citizenship. But this entails—and I cannot here substantiate my claim—that we tolerate the attempt of radically differing groups to determine the nature and direction of society as they best see it. On this view then, the public presence of religious practices of groups is guaranteed and entailed by the recognition of group-differentiated citizenship rights. For Smith, secularism entails a charter of uniform rights. But it is clear that the commitment of secularism to equal citizenship can dictate group-specific rights and, therefore, differentiated citizenship. Smith's third principle pertains to non-establishment and, therefore, to a strict separation of religion from state, under which both

[29] See Ch. 7 of this volume.

religion and the state have freedom to develop without interfering with each other. However, separation need not mean strict non-interference, mutual exclusion, or equidistance, but a policy of principled distance that entails a flexible approach on the question of intervention or abstention combining both, depending on the context, nature, or the current state of religions.

To sum up my view, (a) secularism is fully compatible with, indeed even dictates, a defence of differentiated citizenship and the rights of religious groups, and (b) the secularity of the state does not necessitate strict intervention, non-interference, or equidistance, but rather any or all of these, as the case may be. In short, the secular state is one that keeps a principled distance from religion. If this is so, a criticism that the Indian state has not been secular because of its failure to maintain equidistance is mistaken. A secular state need not be equidistant from all religious communities and may interfere in one religion more than in another. All this goes to show that a critique of Indian secularism on the ground that it acknowledges group rights or it fails to be neutral will not wash.

Has the Indian state consistently followed contextualist secularism? Contextual secularism advocates state intervention for the sake of substantive values. So does hyper-substantive secularism. The danger of one slipping into the other is always present. Indeed, occasionally this slippage is neither accidental nor unintended. In India, the courts have frequently interpreted religion from a wholly rationalist standpoint and conducted its reform purely on that basis. They have rationally determined both the essential tenets of Hinduism and the religious identities of people. One such case has been discussed illuminatingly by Galanter.[30] A puritanical Vaishnavite sect called Satsangis reacted to the temple-entry Act of 1947 by filing a suit alleging that its temples were not covered by this Act and that, therefore, it was not obliged to permit Harijan entry into the precincts. In 1950, it even challenged that Act by not only claiming that every denomination had a right to manage its internal affairs as it deemed fit, but also that it was a separate and distinct religious sect unconnected with the religion of Hindus. When the matter was brought to the Supreme Court, it had two clear options: to conduct a narrow and technical inquiry into the scope of temple-entry power or to examine the much broader

[30] See Ch. 8 of this volume.

question concerning the distinctive features of Hinduism. The Court chose the second option. It first determined the essential features of Hinduism, then declared the Satsangis as Hindus, and enjoined them to be good Hindus by not misconstruing the true teachings of Hinduism or be guided by superstition and ignorance. Hinduism, the Court proposed, must be made progressive, attractive, and dynamic. Personally, I believe the Court acted in good faith and with honourable intention but its paternalistic and rationalist bias flowing from a hyper-substantive world-view is unmistakably visible.

The same hyper-substantive motives were probably present in the decision of the Court to grant alimony to Shah Bano, though it could easily have been determined by the more justifiable need to enable all Indian citizens to live a life of dignity. For this reason, the decision was widely seen to undermine the very cultural survival of Muslims in India. As is well known, the government set the decision of the Court aside and enacted a law that effectively made provisions of the Shariat an integral part of secular law. Taking an ultra-procedural stance, it pleaded helplessness in the matter. An unfortunate anomaly was therefore created. Hindu customs were tampered with on hyper-substantive grounds, while the impossibility of change in a Muslim personal law singularly detrimental to the ordinary life of Muslim women was accepted by the state under the cover of ultra-proceduralism. This rather blatant violation of the neutrality principle gave credence to the charge of minorityism.

To the question: 'Is India a secular state?', Donald Eugene Smith provided an affirmative answer in the 1960s. I agree with that assessment but for different reasons. India was never intended to be either a hyper-substantive or an ultra-procedural secular state. It was never meant to exclude every religious practice or institution from the domain of politics. The dominant justification of the policies and practices of the Indian state was done by appealing to contextual secularism of the principled distance variety: exclude religion for some purposes and include it to achieve other objectives, but always out of non-sectarian considerations. What has become of it now when judged by standards of contextual secularism? All in all, a great deal of degeneration; the Indian state has increasingly lost sight of its objectives and acted more and more on a sectarian basis. It has let religion enter politics when it ought to have excluded it, excluded religion when much could have been achieved by inclusion, each time on *sectarian grounds*. The crisis of Indian secularism is undoubtedly real, but not because of conceptual flaws inherent in its theoretical structure.

## The Madan–Nandy Thesis

Let me now take the Madan–Nandy thesis advocating the abandonment of secularism. I begin with Madan's views. Professor Madan's paper put forward three distinct but interrelated claims. First, that if secularism is viewed as a shared credo of life it is impossible in South Asia. Second, that it is impracticable as a basis for state action. Finally, it is impotent as a blueprint for the foreseeable future. The impossibility argument depends on his claim that the distinction between the sacred and the profane, crucial to secularism, is either unavailable or available only when encompassed by the sacred. Under cultural conditions of hierarchy, the domains of the religious and the secular cannot have equal validity in their separate spheres. If so, secularism, born out of a dialectic between Protestant Christianity and the Enlightenment cannot take root in India. Let me call this the cultural inadaptibility thesis. He further argues that the pervasiveness of religion makes secularism impractical by making disestablishment or neutrality (equidistance) extremely difficult. Finally, for Madan, secularism does not possess the requisite resources to fight fundamentalism, because deep down the two possess a similar structure. In fact, secularism produces, or at least encourages, religious fundamentalism as a backlash. It is futile therefore to view it as a blueprint for action.

Madan provides two independent reasons for the mismatch between secularism and Indian culture, making a case of sorts for the overdetermination of its failure. (a) If a secular world-view could take root in India, then it could easily be invoked to remove religion from public life. But this is unlikely ever to happen. Madan could here have meant that religious and secular world-views embody competing sets of ultimate ideals, and then claimed the inappropriateness of the secular world-view in cultures dominated by religions. He, however, clearly believes that the demand for the removal of religion from public life is predicated within the secular framework upon a particular view of mainstream Enlightenment that religion is irrational. This makes scientific management and rationalism secular-friendly. Indeed, secularism can even be delineated as the view that seeks the ejection of religion from public life so that it can be replaced by rational principles.[31] (b) The removal of religion without invoking the secular world-view could well have been possible had Indian religions permitted it. But for reasons mentioned above no Indian religion allows this. Any attempt to forcibly evict religion from the public sphere provokes a strong cultural resistance, to meet which the secular state is strongly tempted to use its coercive apparatus. Madan grudgingly credits Nehru for not exercising the Turkish option. However, it is undeniable that Nehruvian ideologues have been drawn to the use of state institutions for achievement of secular objectives. At least part of the responsibility for the eruption of religious bigotry and communal violence, Madan argues, must be laid at their door.

In contrast to Madan's guarded attack on modernization, Nandy's is flamboyant and sweeping. Nandy begins by drawing a distinction between religion-as-faith and religion-as-ideology; a faith when it is 'a way of life, a tradition which is definitionally non-monolithic and operationally plural', an ideology when it is 'a subnational, national or cross-national identifier of populations contesting for or protecting non-religious, usually political or socio-economic, interests'.[32] Modernization first produces religion-as-ideology and then generates secularism to meet its challenge to the 'ideology of modern statecraft'. It is clear from the context that by modern statecraft Nandy means the scientific management of state institutions. The public realm is a contested arena between religion, on the one hand and science, on the other. By excluding religion from public life, secularism enables its takeover by science. For Nandy, the ties of secularism with scientific politics and the nation-state are obvious.

For Nandy, this modern scientific nationalist secularism is in crisis. Nandy reiterates the thesis of the cultural inappropriateness

[31] See T.N. Madan, 'Secularism in Its Place', in T.N. Madan (ed.), *Religion in India* (Oxford University Press: New Delhi, 1991), p. 398, and Ch. 9 above.
[32] Ashis Nandy, 'The Politics of Secularism and the Recovery of Religious Tolerance', in Veena Das (ed.), *Mirrors of Violence* (Oxford University Press: New Delhi, 1990), pp 69–93.

of secularism on grounds that the public–private distinction lying at the heart of modern secularism makes no sense to the faithful. To ask believers to expunge their faith from the public realm is to compel them to lead meaningless lives. Put differently, religion cannot become merely a matter of private preference. Where religion is of 'immense importance' and the public–private distinction immaterial, religion inevitably enters public life through the back door. This explains the communalization of politics. Furthermore, over time secularism has been transformed into an intolerant ideology with nation-building, scientific growth, modernization, and development as its allies or constituents. Apart from deepening the alienation of believers, this secularism breeds both old and new forms of violence against which there is little succour. Old because the backlash of marginalized believers reinvigorates fanaticism and bigotry; new because it generates communal violence as well as conflicts between the nation-state and religious communities.

What solutions are offered by Madan to counter bigotry and intolerance? Madan gives two incompatible proposals. First, the immediate suspension of the demand that religion be removed from public life so that the resources of toleration present within each religion are utilized to prevent religious fanaticism—a strategy with no place for modern secularism. Second, an alternative remedy that rejects available versions of secularism but admits to the need for some form of modern secularism appropriate to the cultural context of India. The emphasis on the word 'modern' is crucial here and makes all the difference to how we read his proposal. When taken seriously it cannot be equated with the so-called Indian version of secularism that advocates respect for all religions. This version is entirely homespun and consistent with the non-modern. But Madan could not possibly mean this or else he would not espouse in place of mere transfer a translation of secularism. On this second reading, putting 'secularism in its place' must mean finding for modern secularism an appropriate means of expression in its specific Indian setting.

Nandy's solution is less ambivalent than Madan's, although I believe there is space even in his writings for an alternative proposal consistent with modern secularism. The first solution openly demands a rejection of secularism and emphasizes the need to cement notions of tolerance by using the symbolism and theology of the various faiths in India. But Nandy distinguishes between two conceptions of secularism. The first, the standard Western sense discussed above and the second, to which he himself owes allegiance, an alternative, non-Western meaning of secularism, more accommodative and compatible with the meaning the majority of Indians have given to the word 'secularism'. This secularism implies that 'while public life may or may not be kept free of religion, it must have space for a continuous dialogue among religious traditions and between the religious and the secular, so that in the ultimate analysis, each of the major faiths in the region includes within it an in-house version of the other faiths, both as internal criticisms and as a reminder of the diversity of the theories of transcendence'.

Here much depends on what he means by the term secular. Is it deployed in its modern sense or is it the secular of traditional religions? Is he prepared to allow for non-religious, secular theories of transcendence? If yes, then there is room for an alternative, modern secularism. The difficulty is that although he works with two forms of secularism, he possesses only one version of modernity. And since he rejects that modernity, he is left in the end not with an alternative version of modern secularism but with notions of tolerance that rely exclusively on traditional religions.

Before examining how this thesis relates to the three forms of secularism outlined above, let me say something on what I have called the cultural inadaptability thesis. Madan exaggerates the importance of the cultural inadaptability thesis by not properly acknowledging the availability of two distinct models of secularism, only one of which holds out the promise of being a genuinely transcultural ideal. I call the first the church–state model and the second, the religious-strife model. The church–state model, a 'gift of Christianity', is culture specific and has two dimensions. First, it reflects an intraélite struggle for power, and proposes the sharing of power. Second, by fighting religious absolutism, it helps legitimize internal dissent within a single religion. For example in its struggle to enlarge religious freedom, the laity could enlist the support of the state. However, toleration of dissent within one's own religion is entirely compatible with intolerance of the religious other. Similarly, separation of power does not entail sharing it with people with radically different religious beliefs and practices. Secularism derived from the church–state model cannot accommodate deep diversity and, therefore, must be distinguished from the version of secularism that flows from the religious-strife model. This variant develops first by tolerating religious others, then by allowing them full liberty, and later by granting them equal  citizenship rights, by making religious affiliation irrelevant to one's citizenship. The birth of modern secularism—modern because of its commitment to liberty and equality—must therefore be traced back to the religious-strife rather than the church–state model. Because Western practice embodies both these models, the two are rarely disentangled and modern secularism is viewed as emerging directly from the church–state model. This however misrepresents the history of Western secularism. Moreover, if one conflates these two models one is forever doomed to see secularism as a culturally specific gift of Christianity of no great relevance to India. But the religious-strife model has deep roots and is therefore also valid in India. The absence of the church–state model does not affect the development of political secularism so long as conditions exist for the applicability of the religious-strife model. Madan's article fails to grasp this point and is therefore fundamentally flawed.

I must now ask how this critique relates to the three forms of secularism outlined above. The Madan–Nandy critique is effective against hyper-substantive elements in the Indian state and against the entire ideology of hyper-substantive secularism. The terms 'modern' and 'development' function in the lexicon of secular ideologues as symbols for their hyper-substantivism. Such terms are prize targets for the Madan–Nandy critique. But Madan and Nandy (a) do not clearly or sufficiently distinguish hyper-substantive from ultra-procedural secularism, (b) view separation only as exclusion, and, (c) not recognizing contextual secularism in either of its forms, identify secularism only with absolutism. In brief, for both Nandy and Madan, a successful critique of (a) hyper-substantive secularism knocks down the whole edifice of modern secularism. I differ down to my bones with this· approach. If one follows this logic, then resources of tolerance available in religious traditions alone can save humanity from bigotry and sectarian violence. This logic need not be accepted.

Let me quickly reiterate that I am sympathetic to the Madan–Nandy critique of hyper-substantive secularism that excludes religion from the public realm. In its primary objective, to unsettle the hysterical anti-religiosity of hyper-substantive secularism, it is successful. It however fails to see that under the veneer of anti-religiosity lie the deeper motivations of hyper-substantive secularism, rescued for secularism by its contextual forms to prevent the systematic neglect and dismissal of smaller this-worldly goods by invoking the high ideals of religions. This motivation is concealed by the critique's own obsessive need to rehabilitate religious tradition.

More importantly, however, the focus on hyper-substantive secularism obscures the other deep motivations underlying both ultra-procedural secularism that I reject and contextual secularism that I endorse and defend. These motivations depend on the gradual realization that a clash of ultimate ideals (philosophical encounter between rival metaphysics, as Nandy innocently puts it) can occasionally be disastrous and, importantly, a valuable life exists below the summit of ultimate ideals. Some of the modern processes which Nandy calls 'demonic' emerge in direct response to these beleaguered issues. Before I attempt to distance myself from these critics of secularism, it is this forgotten dimension of modern processes that I wish to capture.

Madan and Nandy attack the secularist attempt to privatize religion and to rationalize politics. What motivations lie behind individualization and rationalization? One general answer is this.[33] Traditional religions, we might say, are ethical visions, embodying conceptions of the good life and possessing a core of substantive values meant to move and be followed by all. A robust conception of the good cannot be sustained by an individual; for building and support, it requires entire cultural communities. In other words, it needs enormous social power. When two or more such conceptions coexist peacefully, they add to the richness of human existence. But when they conflict with one another the battle that ensues is not fought in the abstract, merely in the minds of people, but involves powerful communities. A sharp and persistent clash between them leads to endless destruction. Who can forget the intersectarian religious wars in Europe, particularly in France? Such societies made two moves in response to spiralling disorder.

[33] Readers are obviously not expected to read this as an attempt at historical explanation. It is more akin to a thought experiment.

First, to drain communities of their power by disaggregating them, made possible by a simultaneous alteration in people's primary self-identification that ceased now to refer to communities. Second, the transformation of the notion of an objective good valid for everybody into a subjective preference. This conversion of objective good into mere preference entailed a loss of depth, but also implied a gain. By evacuating communities of their power, the sting from intercommunal conflicts was removed. A reduction of depth was accompanied by the elimination of aggressive bite from situations of social conflict. This resulted in the resolution of three distinct problems. First, bigotry was aborted. Second, discrimination on grounds of religion was prevented. Third, the sharper edges of conflicts between religious communities were blunted. The process of secularization can be seen to involve a transformation of social goods into individual preferences and the disempowerment of discordant religious communities. Secularism is the doctrine that upholds the validity of this process, at least in the political arena.

What of the collision between individuals over conflicting preferences? How are matters to be decided now? Here, so the story goes, it is individuals who transfer their power to public institutions. They part with these powers for a predictable and impartial settlement of conflicts to be achieved by a system of rules to be followed by everyone. Under what conditions can procedures that yield this system be devised? When reason has disengaged not only from all particular interests but also from all contexts, practices, and traditions. Such a disengaged reason gives a uniquely determinate framework of rules of conflict resolution. A reliance on individuals to arbitrarily manage conflicting preferences is less efficient than a dependence on a framework of rational, impersonal rules. No matter what the nature of conflict, operating this system yields the most efficient solution.

We can see clearly that the Madan–Nandy critique is successfully aimed not only at hyper-substantive secularism but also against this ultra-procedural (bureaucratic-individualist) variant. To deploy impersonal, purely procedural reason to settle intercommunal conflict over substantive values is grossly mistaken. This approach utterly misunderstands the issue at stake and, when its own inherent deficiencies begin to surface, tends more and more to set reason aside and use force instead. By showing its success against both hyper-substantive and ultra-procedural secularism, I believe I have strengthened the Madan–Nandy thesis. In doing so, however, I have also captured the real motivations underlying ultra-procedural secularism: to prevent the vicious clash of communities irreconcilably opposed to one another and to foil the persecution of the group defeated in the battle.

It is these underlying motivations to which the Madan–Nandy thesis is blind. At any rate, it does not fully see them. This is partly due to its failure to disentangle the two variants of absolutist secularism. Hyper-substantive and ultra-procedural secularism are propelled by different motivations. One, obsessed by its own substantive values, wishes to change the world in accordance with its own idea of the good. The other, indifferent to the conceptions of the good, is concerned solely with order and conflict management. By the two versions and obscuring from its vision the ultra-procedural view, the Madan–Nandy thesis simplifies, indeed misrecognizes, the complex motivations underlying even the vulnerable forms of secularism it justifiably attacks. The source of the rational management of politics does not lie only in the need to defend the secular world-view. It also springs from the necessity to settle conflicts. More significantly, beneath the surface obsession of rules lies the 'accommodative spirit of pluralism'. For the Madan–Nandy thesis, the only motivation propelling secularism is the blind defence of its own ultimate ideals. It cannot see the resources of toleration in any version of secularism because it focuses only on the version that does not possess such a resource. The motivations underlying secularism are too diverse to be easily pigeonholed.

In short, the Madan–Nandy thesis (i) conflates the two versions, (ii) simplifies or fails to notice the complex motivations underlying secularism, and (iii) not finding in secularism the motivation to deal with rival substantive values falls for succour straight into the lap of religious traditions.

Let me put the point differently. The Madan–Nandy view is that secularism is invalidated where and when religion is of immense importance to people. But their attack on secularism obscures that, with all its inadequacies, secularism was invented for precisely those conditions where different religions mattered equally deeply to people. Modern secularism arose because the resources of tolerance within traditional religion had exhausted their possibility. Now that it appears to be faltering, we cannot innocently return to resources with proven inadequacy. True, ultra-procedural secularism cannot do justice to an important set of human motivations, but the slot left vacant by its rejection cannot be filled only by religious tradition. Why do Madan and Nandy believe that it can do so? I believe this is due to a strong whiff of vulgar Gandhianism in their views. I want to say more on this, but for the moment, I want to bring into the fold of my discussion Partha Chatterjee's argument against secularism.

In my discussion of the Madan–Nandy thesis, I claimed that hyper-substantive and ultra-procedural elements enter the bureaucratic-individualist secularism successfully targeted by Madan and Nandy. The same elements also infiltrate democracies and open them out to the anti-secular critique. When Chatterjee claims that the 'majoritarianism of the Hindu right is perfectly at peace with the institutions and procedures of the modern state', I believe he means everything that Nandy means by it and more.[34] What more? Electoral politics and institutions of representative democracy. Even democratic versions of secularism are unable to resolve interreligious or communal conflict and, more importantly, to prevent the persecution of religious minorities.

I am in part agreement with Chatterjee's thesis. Let me reconstruct it to show why. On some views, a modern democracy presupposes antecedently individuated individuals; individuals without fundamental commitments or constitutive attachments to communities, who come into the political arena only with their preferences. They express their preferences and then submit to a procedure of decision-making—and herein resides their ultra-proceduralism—according to which all identical preferences, internal or external, are aggregated, counted and the set that outnumbers all others determines public policy. In theory, preferences are never stable and since minorities and majorities are predicated upon fluctuating preferences, no permanent majorities and minorities exist in societies that follow such decision-making procedures. In practice, however, preferences are congealed. The same set of

---

[34] Partha Chatterjee, 'Secularism and Toleration', *Economic and Political Weekly* (9 July 1994), p. 1768. See Ch. 11 of this volume.

individuals can continue to have the same preferences, and if these preferences are always greater in number than other preferences, then a strict compliance with precisely these procedures can lead to permanent majorities and, therefore, to permanently disadvantaged minorities. Without measures to check this outcome, these democracies can mutate into majoritarian tyrannies.

This is likely to happen particularly where constitutive attachments have not disappeared or still matter to people, despite strong formal injunctions against exhibiting them in public. Since they cannot be wholly bracketed, they enter the public arena as if mediated by individual choice and more or less predetermine the outcome of decision-making. The tyrannical rule of religious majorities and the persecution of minorities is compatible with ultra-proceduralist (democratic) secularism. An obsession with procedures even in its democratic incarnation produces an undesirable result. A religious majority without formally inducting religion into bureaucratic and democratic institutions can take them over and frustrate secular objectives. Like Madan and Nandy, Chatterjee finds no hope of salvaging secularism, and quite like them, he too is mistaken. The flaw in Chatterjee's argument is that his conception is much too close to Smith's and equally insensitive to the theoretical basis of Indian secularism. It fails to accommodate the idea of principled distance to have room for the view that to promote religious liberty and equal citizenship, the state *may have to treat different religious communities differently*. Indian secularism is committed to the notion of equal respect, which does not always entail equal treatment; rather, it means treating individuals or groups as equals. Equal respect, it follows, may entail differential treatment. Because Chatterjee is unable to see this he believes that differential treatment entails a departure from secular principles. Like Smith, Chatterjee also believes that secularism cannot stomach the idea of community rights. This is mistaken too. The plain truth is that Chatterjee and indeed most critics of secularism fail to grasp that under her own conditions of modernity, India had worked out a conception of secularism that is not a replication of the American or the French model. Why has this happened? This needs a long answer. I briefly touch upon it as I discuss vulgar Gandhianism, the Achilles heel of the Madan–Nandy–Chatterjee thesis.

## *Vulgar Gandhianism*

What is vulgar Gandhianism (VG)? By calling it so, I am not suggesting that this position is a perversion of the essential tenets of Gandhi's thought. Nor am I claiming that it has no sophisticated exponents.[35] This vision is vulgar only in the sense that rather than pursue a richer, subtler, more promising Gandhian strategy of developing an alternative modernity, it succumbs to a motivated blindness towards all forms of modernity.[36] It lapses into an ideology in the same sense in which fundamentalist Islam is an ideology: too certain of its own premises and disproportionately agitated in its rejection of modernity. Of the many features of this ideology, I mention only three here. First, its penchant for sentimental communities. Second, its inconsistent pluralism. Third, its tenacious, hemeralopic stupor in the midst of ineradicable modernity.

A lament for Hindu–Muslim brotherhood is often heard both amongst well-meaning secularists and non-secularists. Once, not long ago, kiosks at railway platforms served Hindu tea and Muslim tea but Hindus and Muslims lived like brothers of a family. Now the two are served the same tea but a deep emotional schism exists between them. Divided by separate customs, the two communities were emotionally integrated. Now, they are united by a common way of life but have no feelings for one another.[37] Can we overcome this emotional diremption? A nostalgia for communities, heterogeneous but held together by strong emotions, able to contain particular differences with an overarching fused identity, is a notable characteristic of VG.

This fraternal ambit cannot however include the modern secularist. After all he alone is to blame for the chasm that now

---

35 This needs reiteration. I mean neither to say that Nandy and Madan are vulgar Gandhians nor that their position is unsophisticated. For me VG is an ideal–typical ideological system, traces of which are present in not only Madan and Nandy, indeed in Gandhi himself, but also in the writings of several modernists.

36 Support for this interpretation of Gandhi can be found for example in A. Parel, 'The Doctrine of Swaraj in Gandhi's Philosophy', in Upendra Baxi and Bhikhu Parekh (eds), *Crisis and Change in Contemporary India* (Sage: New Delhi, 1995), p. 62.

37 I heard the sociologist Imtiaz Ahmed narrate this.

exists between believers. This point can be formulated differently: VG is inconsistently pluralist. Let me explain. I consider pluralism to be the view that all possible values constitutive of a reasonable idea of human flourishing cannot be achieved in one tradition or community, but require for their fullest realization several traditions, cultures, and communities. For the pluralist, there exist both conceptual and practical limits to the attainment of all values in one tradition, culture, or community. Conceptual limits show up due to the incompatibility of one set of values with another. Practical limits are revealed because values can neither be realized instantly nor exclusively by individual effort. They need time, commitment, and the power of an entire community. If a people commits itself to one set of values, then others are neglected. Now, the vulgar Gandhian is a pluralist when it comes to traditional civilizations and faiths, ever ready to recognize the limitations of his own faith and forever willing to learn from other religions. By virtue of this pluralist belief, he respects all faiths and hopes that ways of living together can be found by delving deep into the resources of any religious tradition, but he is recalcitrant and unable to extend this privilege to modern civilization. Modernity is an iron cage of intolerance and violence. Unabashedly individualist, it is immoral. Unfailingly rationalist, it is inhuman. Unconditionally atheistic, it is narcissistic and overbearing. It respects no substantive goods and is insensitive to the potential depth of interpersonal relations. In stark contrast, traditional civilizations are humble, harmonious, and tolerant, respectful of persons and substantive goods.

Not that the vulgar Gandhian ignores deficiencies in tradition and faith. Gandhi himself recognized, for example, the evil of untouchability in Hinduism, but this he viewed as a perversion of traditional faith. A distinction is drawn here between the essential teachings of Hinduism and its perversions. VG admits that this distinction applies to other religions. For example, the current practice of Islam violates the teaching of the Quran by disrespecting women. But modern secularism is so perverse and contaminated at birth that no distinction is conceivable between defensible and vitiated versions. Nothing can overcome its original stigma. VG is marked by an inconsistent and fractured pluralism.

So, VG is inconsistently pluralistic because it blindly rejects modernity in its entirety. But not only does it find modernity undesirable, it is insensitive to its inescapability, and unaware of the extent to which his own position is shaped by it. On the irreversibility of modernity I shall speak in broad, very general terms of three features to which VG is particularly insensitive.

First, nationalism and the nation-state. VG lambasts impersonal nation-states and views its replacement by smaller, warmer communities as mandatory. This belief is bolstered today by the panoramic breakdown of large nation-states. However, what we are currently witnessing is a reconfiguration, not the disappearance, of nation-states. Undoubtedly larger nations are desegregating into smaller units, but small nation-states are coming together to form larger units too and nations seceding from one unit are merging with another. Largish imagined communities integrally linked to a vast array of modern practices are here to stay in the foreseeable future.

This has several implications that VG fails to acknowledge. First, integration in largish, impersonal societies cannot be grounded in emotions alone but must rely primarily on some form of rational principles. These principles need not be universal, but nor can they be useful if wholly embedded in lived practices. They must in part be articulated and made explicit. For VG, principles of tolerance are, however, wholly embodied in the lived practices of small local communities and are incapable of being applied to large impersonal societies. Moreover, VG fails to realize that the resources of traditional faith are incapable of knitting together or grounding the politics of modern, multifaith societies. To be sure, such resources play an important role in the internal reform of these faiths, especially in isolating bigots and fundamentalists. Here VG has a point. But the question of internal reform of each religion must be kept distinct from questions of forming a common public space acceptable to all religious groups. Such principles may have limited application and value, but they cannot flow solely from or be restricted to the traditions of each religious group.

Second, there is no going back on democratization. I mean at least two things by democratization. (i) Equalization: no individual or group is willing to subordinate itself to another individual, group, or community. The legitimating principle of subordination has lost its power. This hardly means that subordination has disappeared, but it does imply that to survive its forms must become more devious and opaque. There is here some internal tension in VG. The idea of sentimental community is compatible with inequality and leads VG occasionally into the benevolent big brother syndrome. However, benevolent or not, democratization has no place for big brothers. On the other hand, the acceptance of equality not only undermines the idea of sentimental community, but also generates severe inconsistencies in VG. (ii) The legitimating ideology of force has also declined. Enforced assimilation may have been possible in medieval contexts, but under modern conditions, it is ruled out. Any use of force to bring people into the mainstream is resisted. Now, VG is committed to resisting the use of force but fails to realize that much of the ideological weight of its position stems directly from the resources of modernity.

The third irreversible feature of modernity is the value attached to ordinary life. In pre-modern times, a hierarchy in favour of a life governed by ultimate ideals existed in comparison with the life of the householder. A life of contemplation, political participation, or surrender to God was infinitely superior to a life spent in the pursuit of mere this-worldly happiness. Modernity has shattered this hierarchy. A life of 'superior values' can no longer so easily trump ordinary life. Much of this is linked to the process of equalization mentioned earlier. For example, under conditions of feudalism, it was fairly common not only to draw a distinction between desires and ultimate values, but also to demand the sacrifice of desires for the sake of higher values. In principle, such ideologies were meant to be universally followed. As we know, reality was quite different. An established hierarchy prevailed within desires; the desires of a privileged few were always more important, for the sake of which, all in the name of ultimate ideals, the desires of all others had to be forsaken. Equalization has meant that in principle the desire of one person counts for as much as the desire of another. Modernity has given us the recognition that talk of ultimate values frequently plays an important role in subordinating the desires of many to the desires of a few. I am far from suggesting that modernity has no place for ultimate values; rather, I wish to draw attention to the space it has opened up between the world of ultimate values and the sphere of desires where the links between the two are more openly acknowledged and cemented. It follows that principles of mutual tolerance need no longer rely exclusively on grand moral universals but must also relate to the ordinary desires of people. I believe Gandhi himself was acutely sensitive to this modern space. VG, on the other hand, sways between two options: either (a) reject this modern space, stick to a high moral ground, and face irrelevance, or (b) accept it and admit inconsistency.

I have sought to argue that the anti-modernist rhetoric of VG is accompanied by an implicit commitment to modernist premises and that therefore VG is inconsistent in a way that is non-trivial and damaging. I made much the same point in discussing the Madan–Nandy–Chatterjee thesis. Something from their anti-secular manifestos can be salvaged—their critique of hyper-substantive and ultra-procedural secularism, for example. The resources of VG help in mounting a negative critique of some versions of secularism, but no positive alternative, without admitting glaring inconsistencies, can be constructed from them. This is disastrous from the angle of the simmering conundrum in response to which Indian secularism was first evolved, that is the Hindu–Muslim problem. Unable to go beyond the horizons of available secularism and of VG, we may, like Chatterjee, almost abandon the very idea of Hindus and Muslims living together. Alternatively, we may further explore the resources of modern secularism. In the next section, I try to identify two versions of the non-absolutist, contextualist forms of secularism. There is first the more admirable ethical secularism grounded in the idea of an emergent common good brought to fruition through the processes of participatory democracy. Second, as a fall-back strategy, we have a rights-based (political) secularism. I shall briefly speak of each of these.

## Contextual Secularism

Contextual Secularism is the view that under certain conditions, religious and political institutions must be separated on the basis of non-sectarian principles consistent with some features constitutive of the modern political arena. It takes seriously the claim that separation does not always mean exclusion; principled distance is also one of its forms. This immediately implies that this secularism does not hysterically shun traditional or modern religious institutions. Those who define their identities in terms of traditional practices or modern institutions are not automatically debarred from the public sphere. Indeed, different kinds of believers and unbelievers enter this arena on an equal footing to begin formulating, through a formal structure of dialogue and deliberation, a substantive common good capable of providing a solid basis for their social and political order and can generate new forms of solidarity.[38] They can however hardly begin to do so unless they discover a minimally overlapping good within the framework of participatory democracy. Once they accept this shared vantage point they must expect through a long process of deliberation and negotiation, a transformation of identities with which they first enter the process. In other words, they must prepare to forge new identities that refer to a common good realized in future through a process to which they are committed by their participation. These new identities must in part be shaped by the modern political arena as well as by all participating conceptions of the good and mould in turn the very sphere that helped form them. The participation of people who are constitutively attached to traditional and modern religious practices is consistent with modern secularism. This is so because the idea of separation qua principled distance is built into a commitment to participatory democracy. Any intermingling of religion in whatever form with politics that violates the basis of equal participation in the democratic process is to be abjured. I believe this is a fairly robust conception of modern secularism. Unlike hyper-substantive and ultra-procedural versions, it is not designed to alienate believers. Notice also that by bringing back fairly divergent conceptions of the good into the political process, we retrieve the depth missing from ultra-procedural secularism. A commitment to participatory democracy and an openness to a future common good takes the sting out of conflicts. Indeed, conflicts in these forms are indicators of the health of secular democracy.

However, this kind of 'politics of the common good' is not always possible. The life-cycle of large societies shows that they swing gently or sharply, from unanimity to radical difference. Let me explain. Imagine a continuum with unanimity at one extreme, say N1, and radical difference on the other, say N10. I believe the politics of the common good is possible when large societies are

---

[38] This is how I wish to construe Akeel Bilgrami's suggestive proposal of negotiated secularism in 'Two Conceptions of Secularism', *Economic and Political Weekly* (9 July 1994), pp 1749–61.

at the centre, N5, or towards N1. However, the further we move towards N10, the less possible and more difficult it is to carry out the politics of the common good. Under these conditions, if societies are to stem complete disintegration, they have to resort to the politics of right. In other words, every society must as a fall-back strategy be able to deploy the rights discourse.

What form does a rights-based secularism take? Is it not another form of ultra-procedural secularism? It is widely believed so. If it is, can it be given a different form in which it is detached from it? Critics of the politics of right do not think so. It is crucial to my argument to show that a rights-based secularism is necessary and a form not of ultra-procedural but of contextual secularism. In order to show this, I must first discuss the circumstances under which the politics of rights is needed. In my view, the proper place of rights is within an unmistakably demarcated space adjacent, on one side, to an area occupied by conflicting desires and to an area inhabited by the common good, on the other. I want to emphasize the word 'common' here. In political theory, a sharp distinction is first drawn between the right and the good, and then a relation of priority proposed of one over the other. I believe that this line of pursuing the issue is misleading because an indefensible and false opposition is drawn between the right and the good. Indeed, the notion of right depends on and cannot be made sense of independent of the notion of the good.

To understand this, suppose that, under relative conditions of scarcity, a conflict of preferences exists among individuals, say over high-rise buildings for the rich and modest housing for the poor. How would a society adjudicate in this conflict? It can do so by ranking them arbitrarily or with the aid of lots. Or else it can distinguish between things that it merely desires and those that it values. In other words, it can evaluate desires and isolate worth-while ones from those supported by temporary but intense feelings. A society can then decide whether it values buildings, momentarily tantalizing some, or simple dwellings that perma-nently shelter others. Once values are identified, an adjudication in the conflict between mere desires and values is possible. We can say then that although skyscrapers are not undesirable, it is dwellings for the needy that are truly valued and for this reason people have a right to them. The good life conceived by this society includes satisfying the basic needs of everyone. In the ensuing conflict between mere desire and value, rights line up solidly behind value or the good. It follows that although the right is distinguished from the good, it is integrally tied to and designed to support it against mere preferences. We can demand, for example, that others abstain from interference or be obliged not to intervene in the pursuit of values, even when their realization directly frustrates the satisfaction of whatever a particular society has deemed of little or no worth.

Each group or society needs rights to protect what it values against its own whims and fancies, to pre-commit itself that it will not give things up simply because they are currently out of favour. Importantly, however, it also needs protection against the radically divergent values of other groups in the same society or the good of other societies. The discourse of rights plays a crucial role in conditions where differing conceptions of the good are in potential conflict. A society with its own conceptions of the good needs special protection against particular goods masquerading as common good and guarantees against the enforcement of a non-existent common good. The rights discourse flourishes, therefore, in conditions of fairly radical difference. They are designed to be particularly effective against false proponents of the common good. In brief, the discourse of rights establishes, under conditions of difference, the priority of the good both over desires and the supra-common good.

It is important to sever the links between the discourse of rights and ultra-proceduralism. True, a commitment to rights entails an obligation to comply with procedures. But, procedures have no value independent of the good. We cannot appeal to procedures in a conflict between values and desires. It is true that rights have no substantive content of their own, and when defined independently of any good, are purely formal. They function only after they have absorbed, by osmosis, the entire substantive content of a given good. An analogy may help. Imagine the printed text on a page. Of the many words on it, the more important ones are italicized. When italicized, the substantive content of the letters and the meaning of words is unaltered. The italicized letters simply take on the substantive content of the unitalicized ones. Italicization highlights and bolsters the existing content. The relation between rights and the good is akin to the relation between italicized and non-italicized letters. Rights take over, highlight, and reinforce the good.

Equally important to note is that this discourse works as much with individualist as with non-individualist conceptions.[39] It is not necessarily tied to the notion of an individual individuated antecedently of constitutive attachments and fundamental commitments. My discussion makes it clear that the good protected by the politics of right against the possible onslaught of a supra-common good is socially constituted and sustained. Those who see an ineluctable tie between individual desires and rights cannot comprehend how the idea of community good can be admitted within the discourse of rights. This linkage between rights and the good of small communities is central to the notion of minority rights. The inability to accommodate the notion of minority rights compels some to desperately try to reduce minority rights to individual preference. However, minority rights are irreducible to individual preferences and fully embody the valuable idea that in certain contexts the good of the small community has to be protected not only against the whims of its own members but also against the so-called common good of the larger community and the state.

I have argued that an obsession with procedure, an indifference or opposition to the good, or a commitment to individualism is not the distinguishing mark of the discourse of rights. Rather, its individuation is pivoted on the acknowledgement of differences that resist immediate assimilation into a common good and on the need to hold off the persistent tendency within ourselves to be overcome by our own currently fancied desires. Such safeguards and guarantees are legally enforceable, and state institutions, such as the court, perform an indispensable function. It follows that in conditions of differing and conflicting groups or communities, state institutions have to play a crucial role in protecting group rights, particularly the rights of smaller, endangered communities.

So what does a rights-based secularism look like? Since it acknowledges difference—difference between religious communities and between religious and non-religious communities—it is unmistakably distinguishable from hyper-substantive secularism. Because it abstracts not from every substantive content but only

---

[39] I do not deny that historically the discourse of rights has emerged along with the discourse of desires and with individualism. Over time, however, it has distanced itself from both.

from those that are identifiably controversial or posing to be universal, it is not of the same breed as ultra-procedural secularism either. Nor does it exclude constitutive attachments or religious communities from the political arena. Indeed, it readily brings them in. Under certain conditions, it grants immunity, privileges, and guarantees to these communities, particularly to smaller ones. Surely, it cannot protect the good of small religious communities unless they come into the political arena—there would be no one to be protected and nothing to guarantee if the good was antecedently expelled from the political sphere. But the goods of all communities must also be safeguarded against the whims of their own members as well as the fancies of others. No religious community can hope to bring its internal or external fancies into the political arena. Furthermore, a minimally overlapping good exists, namely the ordinary but dignified life for all that cannot be undermined in the name of any ultimate ideal. When this is threatened, all ultimate ideals including those infused with religious flavour, need to be expelled from the public arena. In this sense, a rights-based secularism requires that political institutions keep a principled distance from religious institutions and practices.

Does a rights-based secularism foreclose the possibility of common deliberation and the option of ever working out a genuinely common good? True, rights do prevent further sharpening of difference but do they not obstruct every possibility of overcoming them? Those who favour the politics of the common good appear to have a legitimate fear that the discourse of rights entrenches divisions.[40] This is a real danger, and to meet this challenge the entire discourse of rights needs modification. One way of doing so is this: Rights enter the political space precisely when different individuals and groups have abandoned deliberation over the common good; currently, differences cannot be overcome. But adherents of rights have not given up hope that whenever propitious circumstances arise they will pick up the threads from where they snapped. In other words, an implicit commitment to conducting a dialogue in future exists within the discourse of rights. The discourse of rights occupies the space where people have

---

[40] On this, see Charles Taylor's illuminating article, 'Alternative Futures', in *Reconciling the Solitudes* (McGill–Queen's University Press: Montreal and Kingston, 1993).

neither entirely given up the hope of living together nor yet arrived at an agreement over crucial substantive issues that could bind them into a reasonable and vibrant unified existence. They abjure the use of force against others, shun action in haste that snap whatever tenuous bond exists between groups and individuals, and in full knowledge that the common good is currently non-existent, remain committed to its existence in the future. A thin commitment to a larger pattern of living together is implicit in the discourse of rights. There is a bigger, imagined community lurking in the horizon of every community that enjoys rights.

Let me return to India. Before a heterogeneous society such as ours, five options exist at any time. By far the best option is to forever and only have the politics of the common good. The next best, when conditions permit, is to have a politics of the common good and deploy, as a fall-back strategy, the politics of right. Next, to make do exclusively with the politics of right. The fourth, to altogether abandon participation and rights. Here, individuals and groups are shut out from participatory democracy and are unable to get courts to enforce their claims. Under such conditions, discrimination, subordination, and exploitation thrive. Finally, a society may plunge into what Hobbes famously called 'the war of all against all'—in other words, a Bosnian suicide. I believe that most societies such as ours are stuck at level-4. India is fortunate however to have a Constitution that envisions and supports a society that has raised itself to level-2. I believe the least we can do is to lift ourselves to level-3, continuing in the meanwhile to refurbish, by a critical reinterpretation of its articles, our faith in the Constitution.

I have claimed that the initial formulation of Indian secularism was spurred by the need to tackle the Hindu–Muslim problem. Grounds for that motivation exist even today. In post-Partition India, relations between the two communities are estranged more than ever before. What form of secularism is best equipped to deal with this schism? What does secularism in India mean today? Primarily, (i) a strong defence of minority rights, to be supplemented, on the one hand, by (ii) deploying the resources of religious tolerance to isolate bigotry and encourage internal reform and, on the other hand, by (iii) consolidating whatever space of the common good already exists.

# Bibliography

Ahmad, Aijaz, 'Azad's Careers: Roads Taken and Not Taken', in Mushiral Hasan (ed.), *Islam and Indian Nationalism: Reflections on Abul Kalam Azad* (Manohar: Delhi, 1992).

Ahmed, Imtiaz (ed.), *Family Kinship and Marriage among Muslims in India* (Manohar: New Delhi, 1976).

————— (ed.), *Caste and Social Stratification among Muslims in India*, 2nd edn (Manohar: New Delhi, 1978).

Ahmed, Rafiuddin, 'Redefining Muslim Identity in South Asia: The Transformation of Jamaat-i-Islami', in Martin E. Marty and R. Scott Appleby (eds), *Accounting for Fundamentalisms* (University of Chicago Press: Chicago, 1994).

Al-Attas, Syed Muhammad Naquib, *Islam, Secularism and the Philosophy of the Future* (Mansell: London, 1985).

Albornox, A.F. Carillo de, *The Basis of Religious Liberty* (London, 1963).

Allen, Henry E., *The Turkish Transformation: A Study in Social and Religious Development* (University of Chicago Press: Chicago, 1935).

Anandhi, S., 'Collective Identity and Secularism: Discourse on the Dravidian Movement in Tamil Nadu', *Social Action* 44, 1 (1994).

Anderson, Benedict, *Imagined Communities: Reflections on the Origin and Spread of Nationalism* (Verso: London, 1983; 2nd edn, 1991).

Appadurai, Arjun, *Worship and Conflict Under Colonial Rule: The South Indian Case* (Cambridge University Press: Cambridge, 1981).

Arapura, J.G., 'India's Philosophical Response to Religious Pluralism', in Howard G. Coward (ed.), *Modern Indian Response to Religious Pluralism* (State University of New York Press: Albany, 1987).

544    *Bibliography*

Audi, Robert, 'The Separation of Church and State and the Obligations of Citizenship', *Philosophy and Public Affairs* 18, 3 (Summer 1989).

—— 'Religious Commitment and Secular Reason: A Reply to Prof Weithman', *Philosophy and Public Affairs* 20, 1 (Winter 1991).

Banerjee, Sumanta, '"Hindutva" Ideology and Social Psychology', *Economic and Political Weekly* (*EPW*) (19 Jan. 1991).

Barry, Brian, *Liberty and Justice* (Clarendon Press: Oxford, 1991).

Basu, Tapan et al., *Khakhi Shorts and Saffron Flags* (Orient Longman: Hyderabad, 1993).

Bates, M.S., *Religious Liberty: An Inquiry* (Harper, 1945).

Baxi, Upendra, 'The Struggle for the Redefinition of Secularism in India: Some Preliminary Reflections', *Social Action* 44, 1 (1994).

—— 'Secularism: Real or Pseudo', in M.M. Sankhader (ed.), *Secularism in India* (Deep and Deep: New Delhi, 1992).

Bayly, C.A., *Local Roots of Indian Politics* (Oxford University Press: London, 1975).

Berger, Peter, *The Social Reality of Religion* (Faber & Faber: London, 1969).

Berkes, Niyaxi, 'Historical Background of Turkish Secularism', in Richard N. Fuye (ed.), *Islam and the West* (Mouton and Company: The Hague, 1957).

Bhargava, Rajeev, 'Giving Secularism its Due', *EPW* (9 July 1994).

—— 'How Not to Defend Secularism', *South Asian Bulletin* 14, 1 (1994).

—— 'The Right to Culture', in K.N. Panikkar (ed.), *Communalism in India: History, Politics and Culture* (Manohar: New Delhi, 1991).

—— 'Religious and Secular Identities', in Upendra Baxi and Bhikhu Parekh (eds), *Crisis and Change in Contemporary India* (Sage: New Delhi, 1995).

Bharucha, Rustam, *The Question of Faith* (Orient Longman: New Delhi, 1993).

Bilgrami, Akeel, 'Two Concepts of Secularism: Reason, Modernity and Archimedean Ideal', *EPW* (9 July 1994).

Binter, Leonard, *Islamic Liberalism: A Critique of Development Ideologies* (University of Chicago Press: Chicago, 1988).

Bose, N.K., *Calcutta: A Social Survey* (Lalvani Publishers: Bombay, 1968).

Chadwick, Owen, *The Secularization of the European Mind in the Nineteenth Century* (Cambridge University Press: Cambridge, 1975).

Chatterjee, Partha, *Nationalist Thought and the Colonial World: A Derivative Discourse?* (Oxford University Press: New Delhi, 1986).

Chawdhury, Subroto Roy, 'Cultural and Educational Rights of Indian Minorities as Judicially Interpreted', *Public Law* 6 (1961).

Cox, Harvey, *The Secular City: Secularization and Urbanization in Theological Perspective* (Macmillan: New York, 1965).

Derrett, J.D.M., *Religion, Law and the State in India* (Faber & Faber: London, 1968).

Dube, S.C. and V.H. Basilov (eds), *Secularization in Multi-Religion Societies* (Concept: New Delhi, 1983).

Dumont, Louis, 'Religion, Politics and History in India: Collected Papers', in *Indian Sociology* (Mouton: Paris, 1970).

Eliade, Mircea, *The Sacred and the Profane* (Harper and Row: New York, 1961).

Galeotti, Anna Elizabetta, 'Citizenship and Equality: The Place for Toleration', *Political Theory* 21(A) (1993).

Ghouse, Mohammad, 'Religious Freedom and the Supreme Court of India', *Aligarh Law Journal* 2 (1965).

Glasner, Peter F., *The Sociology of Secularization* (Routledge & Kegan Paul: London, 1977).

Goody, J., 'Religion and Ritual: The Definitional Problem', *British Journal of Sociology* 12 (June 1961).

Gopal, S. (ed.), *Anatomy of Confrontation: The Babri Masjid–Ram Janmabhumi Issue* (Penguin: New Delhi, 1991).

Greenawalt, Kent, *Religious Convictions and Political Choice*, (Oxford University Press: New York, 1988).

Grewal, O.P. and K.L. Tuteja, 'Communalism and Fundamental-ism: A Dangerous Form of Anti-Democratic Politics', *EPW* 24 (Nov. 1990).

Gupta, Dipankar, 'Secularization and Minoritization: Limits of Heroic Thoughts', *EPW* (2 Sept. 1995).

Gutmann, Amy, 'The Challenge of Multiculturalism in Political Ethics', *Philosophy and Public Affairs* 22, 3 (1993).

Hall, S., 'Notes on Deconstructing the Popular!', in R. Samuel (ed.), *Peoples History and Socialist Theory* (Routledge & Kegan Paul: London, 1981).

Haq, Mushir-ul, *Islam in Secular India* (Indian Institute of Advanced Study: Shimla, 1972).

Hasan, Mushirul, *Nationalism and Communal Politics in India* (Manohar: New Delhi, 1979).

Heredia, Rudolf. C. and Edrranrd Mathias (eds), *Secularism and Liberation: Perspective and Strategies for India Today* (Indian Social Institute: New Delhi, 1995).

Horton, John (ed.), *Liberalism, Multiculturalism and Toleration* (Macmillan: London, 1993).

Howe, Mark de Wolfe, 'Problems of Religious Liberty', in C.J. Friedrich (ed.), *Liberty* (Nomos, IV), 1962.

Huntington, Samuel, 'The Clash of Civilizations?' *Foreign Affairs* 72(B) (Summer 1993).

Iqbal, Muhammad, *The Reconstruction of Religious Thought in Islam* (New Taj Office: Delhi, rpt. 1980).

Iyengar, G. Aravamula, *The Temple Entry by Harijans*, 2nd edn (Sanatan Dharma Printing Agency: Nellore, 1935).

James, William, *The Varieties of Religious Experience* (Harvard University Press: Cambridge, Mass., 1985).

Joshi, P.C., 'Secularism and Religiosity of the Oppressed: Some Reflections', *Man and Development* 9, 4 (1987).

Jurgensmeyer, Mark, *Religion: A Social Vision* (University of California Press: Berkeley, 1982).

————, 'Non-Violence', in Mircea Eliade (ed.), *The Encyclopedia of Religion* (Macmillan: New York, 1987).

Kakar, Sudhir, 'Reflections on Religious Group Identity', *Seminar* 402 (Feb. 1993).

Kaviraj, S., 'Religion, Politics and Modernity', in U. Baxi and B. Parekh (eds), *Crisis and Change in Contemporary India* (Sage: New Delhi, 1995).

Keller, Adolf, *Church and State on the European Continent* (Epirorth Press: London, 1936).

King, Preston, *Toleration* (George, Allen & Unwin: London, 1976).

Kothari, Rajni, 'Cultural Context of Communalism in India', in S. Arokiasamy (ed.), *Responding to Communalism* (Delhi, 1991).

————— 'Pluralism and Secularism: Lessons of Ayodhya', *EPW* (19–26 Dec. 1992).

Krishnamacharya, U.P., *Temple Worship and Temple Entry*, 2nd edn (Nellore, 1936).

Kukathas, Chandran, 'Are there any Cultural Rights', *Political Theory* 20, 1 (Feb. 1992).

———— 'Cultural Rights Again', *Political Theory* 20, 4 (Nov. 1992).

Kumar, Krishna, 'Secularism: Its Politics and Pedagogy', *EPW* (4–11 Nov. 1989).

Kymlicka, Will, 'Individual and Community Rights', in Judith Baker (ed.), *Group Rights* (University of Toronto Press: Toronto).

———— *Multicultural Citizenship: A Liberal Theory of Minority Rights* (Oxford University Press: Clarendon, 1989).

———— *Liberalism, Community and Culture* (Oxford University Press: Oxford, 1989).

———— 'Liberalism and the Politicization of Ethnicity', *Canadian Journal of Law and Jurisprudence* 4 (1991).

———— 'The Rights of Minority Cultures', *Political Theory* 20 (1 Feb. 1992).

Larmore, Charles, 'Political Liberalism', *Political Theory* 18, 3 (August 1990).

Locke, John, *A Letter Concerning Toleration (1689)*, edited by James Tully (Hackett: Indianapolis, 1983).

Lokhandwala, Shamoon T., 'Indian Islam: Composite Culture and Integration', *New Quest* 50 (March–April 1985).

Luthera, V.P., *The Concept of the Secular State and India* (Oxford University Press: Calcutta, 1964).

Madan, T.N., 'Religion in India', *Daedalus* 118 (1989).

———— (ed.), *Religion in India* (Oxford University Press: Delhi, 1991).

———— *Modern Myths, Locked Minds* (Oxford University Press: Delhi, 1996).

Madison, James, 'Memorial and Remonstrance against Religious Assessments' (1785), in Marvin Meyers (ed.), *The Mind of the Founder*, rev. ed. (University Press of Herr England: Hanover, N.H., 1981).

Mahmood, Tahir, *Muslim Personal Law: Role of the State in the Indian Subcontinent* (Nagpur, 2nd edn 1983).

Mansfield, John H., 'The Personal Laws in a Uniform Civil Code?', in Robert Baird (ed.), *Religion and Law in Independent India* (Manohar: Delhi, 1993).

Martin, David, *A General Theory of Secularization* (Basil Blackwell: Oxford, 1978).

Marty, Martin E. and R. Scott Appleby, *Accounting for Fundamentalism: The Dynamic Character of Movements* (University of Chicago Press: Chicago, 1994).

Matsuda, Mary, 'Public Response to Racist Speech: Considering the Victim's Story', *Michigan Law Review* 87 (1989).

Meland, Bernard, *The Secularization of Culture* (Oxford University Press: New York, 1966).

Mendus, S., *Toleration and the Limits of Liberalism* (Macmillan, 1989).

Nandy, Ashis, 'An Anti-Secularist Manifesto', *Seminar* 314 (1985).

———— 'The Politics of Secularism and the Recovery of Religious Tolerance', in Veena Das (ed.), *Mirrors of Violence: Communities, Riots and Survivors in South Asia* (Oxford University Press: New Delhi, 1990).

Nauriya, Anil, 'Relationship between State and Religion', *EPW* 25 (Feb. 1989).

Pandey, Gyanendra, 'Hindus and Others: The Militant Hindu Construction', *EPW* 28 (Dec. 1991).

Parekh, Bhikhu, 'Between Holy Text and Moral Void', *New Statesman and Society*, 23 March 1989.

———— 'The Cultural Particularity of Liberal Democracy', in David Held (ed.), *Prospects for Democracy: North, South, East, West* (Polity Press: Cambridge, 1993).

Pfeffer, Leo, *Church, State and Freedom*, rev. edn (Beacon Press: Boston, 1967).

Rahman, Fazlur, *Islam and Modernity* (University of Chicago Press: Chicago, 1982).

Rai, Alok, 'Addled Only in Parts: Strange Case of Indian Secularism'. *EPW* (16 Dec. 1989).

Raphael, D., 'The Intolerable', in Susan Mendus (ed.), *Justifying Toleration: Conceptual Historical Perspectives* (Cambridge University Press: Cambridge, 1988).

Rapport, David, 'Fear and Trembling: Terrorism in Three Religious Traditions', *American Political Science Review* 78 (1984).

Rawls, John, *Political Liberalism* (Columbia University Press: New York, 1993).

———— 'Justice and Fairness: Political not Metaphysical', *Philosophy and Public Affairs* 14 (Summer 1985).

Sandel, Michael, *Liberalism and the Limits of Justice* (Cambridge University Press: Cambridge, 1982).

Sangari, Kumkum, 'Politics of Diversity: Religious Committees and Multiple Patriarchies', *EPW* (23 Dec. 1995).

Sapir, Edward, 'The Meaning of Religion', in D.G. Mandelbaum (ed.), *Selected Writings of Edward Sapir in Language, Culture and Personality* (University of California Press: Berkeley, 1949).

Saran, A.K., 'Hinduism and Economic Development in India', *Archives de sociologic des religions* 15 (1963).

Sarkar, Sumit, 'The Fascism of the Sangha Parivar', *EPW* (30 Jan. 1993).

Schwarz, Alan, 'No Imposition of Religion: The Establishment Clause Value', *Yale Law Journal* 77 (1968).

*Seminar*, 'Secularism, a Symposium on the Implication of National Policy', 67 (March, 1965).

Sen, Amartya, 'The Threats to Secular India', *The New York Times Review of Books* 40, 7 (8 April 1993).

Sen, Kshiti Mohan, *Hinduism* (Penguin Books: Harmondsworth, 1960).

Sharma, G.S. (ed.), *Secularism: Its Implication for Law and Life in India* (N.M. Tripathy Pvt. Ltd: Bombay, 1966).

Shiner, Larry, 'Towards a Theology of Secularization', *Journal of Religion* 45 (1965).

———— 'The Concept of Secularization in Empirical Research', *Journal for the Scientific Study of Religion* 6, 2 (1967).

Singh, Attar, *Secularism and the Sikh Faith* (Guru Nanak Dev University: Amritsar, 1973).

Sinha, V.K. (ed.), *Secularism in India* (Lalvani Publishing House: Bombay).

Smith, Donald, Eugene, *South Asian Politics and Religion* (Princeton University Press: Princeton, 1963).

———— *South Asian Politics and Religion* (Princeton University Press: Princeton, 1966).

Smith, Wilfrid Cantwell, *The Meaning and End of Religion* (Fortress Press: Minneapolis, 1991, original edn. 1962).

Spaque, Theodore W., 'The Rivalry of Intolerances in Race Relations', *Social Forces* 28, 1 (1949).

Stahmer, H., 'Defining Religion: Federal Aid and Academic Freedom', in *Religion and the Public Order* (Chicago, 1964).

Subrahmanian, N., 'Hinduism and Secularism', *Bulletin of the Institute of Traditional Cultures*, pt I (Madras, 1966).

Swomley, John M., *Religious Liberty and Secular State* (Prometheus Books: New York, 1987).

Tambiah, Stanley J., *Levelling Crowds: Ethnocentric Conflicts and Collective Violence* (UCLA Press: Berkeley, 1961).

———— *Culture, Thought and Social Action: An Anthropological Perspective* (Harvard University Press: Cambridge, MA, 1985).

Taylor, Charles, *Sources of the Self* (Cambridge University Press: Cambridge, 1989).

———— *Multiculturalism and the Politics of Recognition* (Princeton University Press: Princeton, 1992).

Thapar Romila, 'Imagined Religious Communities? Ancient History and the Modern Search for a Hindu Identity', *Modern Asian Studies* 23, 2 (1989).

Tyabji, Naseer, 'Political Economy of Secularism: Rediscovery of India', *EPW* (9 July 1994).

Vanaik, Achin, *Communalism Contested: Religion, Modernity and Secularization* (Vistaar Publications: New Delhi, 1997).

———— 'Reactions on Ayodhya', *EPW* (24 April 1993).

———— 'Situating Threat of Hindu Nationalism: Problems with Fascist Paradigm', *EPW* (9 July 1994).

———— 'Reflections on Communalism and Nationalism in India', *New Left Review* 196 (1991).

Vithal, B.P.R., 'Roots of Hindu Fundamentalism', *EPW* (20–27 Feb. 1993).

Walzer, M., 'Liberalism and the Art of Separation', *Political Theory* 12, 3 (August 1984).

Weber, Max, *The Religion of India: The Sociology of Hinduism and Buddhism*, (trans) H.H. Gerth and Don Martindale (Free Press: Glencoe, Ill., 1958).

Weithman, Paul J., 'Separation of Church and State: Some Questions for Professor Audi', *Philosophy and Public Affairs* 20, 1 (Winter 1991).

Wilson, Bryan, *Religion in Secular Society* (Watts: London, 1966).

———— *Religion in Sociological Perspective* (Oxford University Press: Oxford, 1982).

Wittgenstein, Ludwig, *Culture and Value* (University of Chicago Press: Chicago, 1984).

Young, Iris Marion, 'Polity and Group Difference: A Critique of the Ideal of Universal Citizenship', *Ethics* 99 (1989).